THE ARAB WORLD

ANCHOR BOOKS

DOUBLEDAY

New York   London   Toronto   Sydney   Auckland

For Sherri
with best wishes
Elizabeth Warnock Fernea
Robert A. Fernea

ELIZABETH WARNOCK FERNEA
& ROBERT A. FERNEA

The Arab World

FORTY YEARS OF CHANGE

Photographs by Thomas Hartwell

AN ANCHOR BOOK
PUBLISHED BY DOUBLEDAY
a division of Bantam Doubleday Dell Publishing Group, Inc.
1540 Broadway, New York, New York 10036

ANCHOR BOOKS, DOUBLEDAY, and the portrayal of an anchor are trademarks of
Doubleday, a division of Bantam Doubleday Dell Publishing Group, Inc.

The Arab World: Forty Years of Change was originally published as
The Arab World: Personal Encounters by Anchor Books/Doubleday in 1985.

Permissions acknowledgments appear on page 552.

BOOK DESIGN BY SUSAN YURAN

Library of Congress Cataloging-in-Publication Data

Fernea, Elizabeth Warnock.
    The Arab world : forty years of change / Elizabeth Warnock Fernea and Robert A.
Fernea
      p.   cm.
    Updated and expanded ed. of The Arab world. 1st ed. 1985.
    Includes index.
    1. Arab countries. I. Fernea, Robert A. (Robert Alan), 1932–   . II. Fernea,
Elizabeth Warnock. Arab World. III. Title.
DS36.7.F47   1997
909'.09749270825—DC21   96-49257
                                                                             CIP

ISBN 0-385-48520-4
Anchor Books Editions: 1985, 1987, 1997
10 9 8 7 6 5 4 3 2 1

In Memory of

MALCOLM H. KERR

1931–1984

Beirut

Scholar, Colleague, Friend

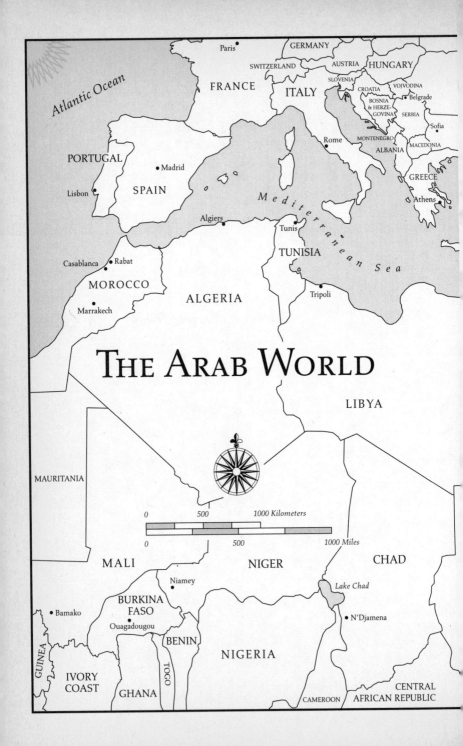

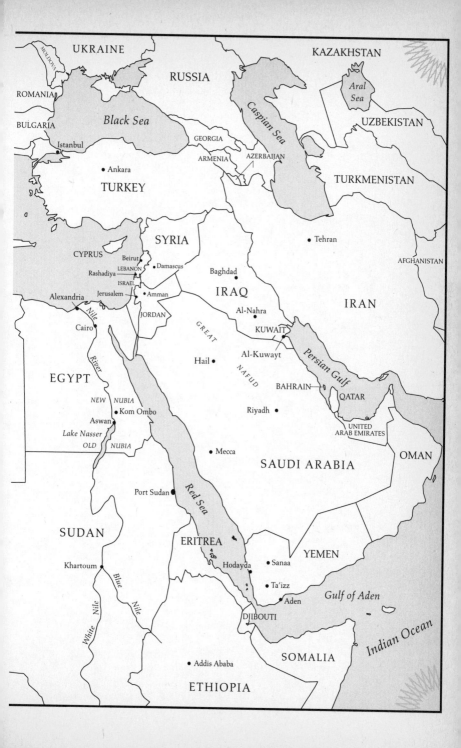

Contents

IV Egypt

V Saudi Arabia

VI Israel and the West Bank

VII Iraq

Preface/Acknowledgments

THE BOOK THAT FOLLOWS IS BASED on forty years of experience in the Middle East, primarily in the Arab world. We lived for two years in Iraq and for eight years in Egypt, where our three children were born. We spent a year and a half in Morocco and have lived in other parts of the region for briefer periods. Bob, a cultural anthropologist, has written books about Iraq and Egyptian Nubia and done research in Afghanistan, Jordan, Morocco, and Saudi Arabia. B.J. (Elizabeth) has written books about Iraq, Egypt, and Morocco and produced documentary films about Arab women. We speak reasonably good colloquial Arabic and French.

Since the first edition of this book appeared in 1985, we have returned to the Middle East several times, to Lebanon, Jordan and Morocco, Egypt, Israel and the West Bank. In the spring of 1996 we were able to return to Iraq, where we began our long sojourn to the Middle East more than forty years ago.

Many institutions and individuals have helped us over the years in our projects of writing and research. We have been the fortunate recipients, both singly and together, of grants from the National Science Foundation, the Oriental Institute of the University of Chicago, the American Research Center in Egypt, the Ford Foundation, the MacArthur Foundation, the Fulbright Commission, and the National Endowment for the Humanities.

Our son, David, and his wife, Kim, made it possible for us to spend the spring of 1991 in Egypt, when they assumed responsibility for Bob's mother's care in Austin, Texas. The American University in Cairo's invitation to Bob to be a Distinguished Visiting Professor in the spring of 1996 helped make the return visit to Iraq financially viable.

The University of Texas at Austin has been our home since 1966. Bob is professor of anthropology, and B.J. is professor of English; we both teach courses in the Center for Middle Eastern Studies, currently directed by Dr. Abraham Marcus. We want to acknowledge its directors and its staff, past and present, for consistent support over the years.

For our research, Deborah Littrell has been helpful, as have been Sharon Doerre, Jennifer O'Connor, Mary Karam, Mark Zeineddin, and Amy Mills. Diane Watts assisted with design and format. Virginia Howell and Geraldine Behrens typed the many drafts of the six new chapters and three new comment-essays, and we are grateful for their cheerfulness as well as their efficiency.

It is impossible to name all our friends and colleagues in the Arab world and in the United States who have contributed to the making of this book. Special thanks, however, for various assistance must be accorded to Basima Bezirgan, Cathy Sullivan and Alain McNamara, Wm. Roger Louis, Dagmar Hamilton, the late Izzat Ghurani, Salah-Dine Hammoud, Safia Mohsen, Abdulaziz Abbassi, Peter Gubser, Amal Nashashibi, Yaron Shemer, Rebecca and Amer Salti, Murad and Fiona al-Essawy, Laila Ahmed, Sidney Monas, Carolyn Osborn, Laila Shoukri al-Hamamsy, Heather Taylor, Donald Cole, Marjorie Payne, Cora Boyett, Marcelle Wahba and Derek Farwagi, Abdulla Hassan, Nina Berman, Martha Diase, Selim Nasser, Humphrey Davies and Kristina Nelson Davies, Bouthaina el-Nasseri, Ferial Ghazoul and Nicholas Hopkins, Lamia al-Gailani, Hoda al-Namani, Adel and Marcelle al-Zein, Anis and Bassam al-Namani, Judy Blanc, Rita Giacoman, Salim Tamari, Susan Ziadeh, Carl Hershiser, Heba Handoussa, and Kamal Mujid, Cynthia Nelson, Nawal Hassan, Hassan Aziz Hassan, Annes McCann-Baker and Ron Baker.

Many thanks to our longtime editor Sally Arteseros, who first liked the idea of this multivoiced book and saw it through its original 1985 incarnation as an Anchor/Doubleday publication. Martha Levin, our present editor at Anchor/Doubleday, encouraged the expanded and updated edition that follows, an edition that has been aided in its development by Rob McQuilkin, also at Anchor/Doubleday. We thank them all for their trust, perception, patience, and thoughtful support. But we do not hold them or anyone else responsible for our opinions, which are our own.

November 1996
Austin, Texas

WE FIRST WENT TO THE ARAB WORLD more than forty years ago and have remained involved in studying, writing, filming, and teaching about the area ever since. It was August 1956 when we docked in the port of Beirut on our way to southern Iraq, where Bob completed two years of research for his doctorate in social anthropology from the University of Chicago. Later we lived in Egypt for six years; our three children were born there, and Bob taught at the American University in Cairo. Although we have called Texas home since 1966, we have continued to return to the Middle East for longer and shorter periods of research and residence in Morocco, Egypt, Saudi Arabia, Jordan, Lebanon, Israel, and the West Bank. In the spring of 1996 we were fortunate to be able to return to Iraq, to Baghdad and to the small town of Al-Nahra, where we began our long sojourn in Arab lands.

Forty years ago we knew very little about the Middle East. The field now known as Middle Eastern studies did not exist then. Some vague images were no doubt lodged in our heads, images gleaned from reading about the pyramids of Egypt, the cradle of civilization in Mesopotamia, and the tales of the Arabian Nights. We had some memory from childhood of North Africa, accounts of the campaign that was crucial in deciding the course of World War II. Carleton Coon had just written *Caravan: The Story of the Middle East*. We read it carefully and we studied colloquial Iraqi Arabic. B.J.'s mother, an enthusiastic high school teacher, assured her the women of the area needed help. Bob searched, but found few anthropological studies to compare with his own proposed work. We were basically ignorant. Gradually, we learned about the region, through research and teaching, and also through friendship. The book that follows is an effort to communicate to the reader some of our own understandings, gained through those personal experiences.

The Middle East has changed dramatically since 1956, as has America's relationship to the area. Today we are told that the Middle East, like Africa, Asia, Europe, and Latin America, is an important part of the new economic world order, that interdependent global community of which America is supposedly the responsible and informed (senior) partner. But received accounts of the Middle East, both in academe and in the general media, leave out the subjects of the picture. The statistical and quantitative analyses of oil production, political alliances, and arms sales are to us background information, signs of the times in terms of which we think of persons and places we know. For, sadly, the people of the Middle East still remain as distant from the general American public as they were nearly half a century ago when we embarked on what we then perceived as a great adventure. Today, on television, on film, Arab peoples are seen running for cover in Beirut or Jerusalem, in Algiers or Basra; they turn away from the lens of the television journalist, shield themselves behind veils, robes, sunglasses, tears; or, masked, brandish weapons at the screen. The very nearness of the television images, presented without explanation or background, accentuates the differences between "us" and "them"; "they" dress differently, look different, seem to worship a different god. Only President Anwar Sadat appeared to cross the barrier from stranger to familiar figure in the American media. But President Sadat is dead.

These images of the Arab peoples regularly seen by millions of Americans are far removed from our own impressions, our own experiences in the Middle East. We are quite aware of both the similarities and the differences between the two regions. But we are also aware that none of these differences and similarities is fixed, and that life in the Arab world, like life everywhere else, is people, people resisting but accommodating themselves to constant change. Out of our concern over the incomplete images, even stereotypes, that Americans have of Arabs, and out of our concern with the ongoing processes of change that are affecting us in America as well as in the Arab world, we have written this book. Our friends and acquaintances there, of course, cannot be representative of the entire Middle East, but they are certainly a part and a product of the area. And the changes in their lives reflect the larger transformations in their societies, changes that are affecting the lives of everyone.

Social change is often discussed in abstract terms, but people do not live according to abstractions, ours or others'. Most of the time we live in terms of the problems of daily life: chores, pleasures, disappointments, meetings, duties, work, failures. To understand the processes of change over forty years, its effects on families and individuals, we must turn to the patterns of people's lives.

This book is written in a multivoiced form. We first offer the reader different kinds of personal encounters over time with people we have known for years, in Egypt, Iraq, Morocco, and Lebanon, and with people we have met more recently, in Jordan, Saudi Arabia, Israel, and Palestine. Encounters are meetings, but they are also forms of exchanges: experiences of daily life, ours and theirs.

These narratives of "personal encounters" are juxtaposed with essays, or comments, in which we have tried to set the human experiences recounted in a larger intellectual context, in an effort to "make sense" of things. Our friend Aisha's personal tragedies in the city of Marrakech are related to an essay on the role and function of the family in the Middle East. The description of the recent rise in religious practice among Egyptian friends can be seen in the context of a more general discussion of the meaning of what has been termed religious fundamentalism. And Bob's account of his sojourn in Saudi Arabia is paired with an essay considering the role of the cultural anthropologist in the field.

Since 1962, when the colonial period officially ended and a group of new independent nations emerged, the Arab world has been forced to absorb in less than two generations the social and technological transformations that took more than two hundred years to become part of Western society. "The sting of change lies not in change itself, but in change that has no meaning," E. H. Frankel has written. For the Arab world the relentless pace of change has understandably left people anxious and uncertain about the possibilities the future holds. The movement from farm to city, the growth of a new middle class, the growth of consumerism have all taken place through the region's diversified participation in the international capitalist system; this has affected every person in the Middle East.

This is true for both rich and poor Arab countries. Those that are rich—Saudi Arabia, Kuwait, Libya, Iraq, the Gulf States—are rapidly expanding their own economies while importing labor from other Arab nations and from other countries in the Third World. In 1956 it was commonly said that Egyptians *never* migrated. In 1996 at least 10 percent of the entire Egyptian labor force was living and working outside Egypt, and the number is probably rising. Moreover, many Egyptians have now left their country for good.

Oil-rich Arabs may remain at home, but they are investing capital gains in economies outside their own countries, including the United States; Saudi Arabia is now sixteenth on the list of America's international trade partners. Thus, Arab oil wealth as well as Arab petroleum is in diverse ways spreading out to people who live far from the refineries and gushers, in America, and also in Europe and Asia.

Money from oil wealth is also currently helping to rebuild Beirut, after the devastating ten-year civil war, as we discovered on a recent visit. All the poorer Arab countries, in fact, look for support from their richer cousins, but most of it comes home in the paychecks of the migrant workers. In the case of Lebanon, it is millionaire President Rafik al-Hariri who has brought his money home from Saudi Arabia to spend rebuilding his own country.

Education, like oil, is a matter of great importance throughout the Arab world, for the new nations promised education to all children, free, children who now constitute half the area's population. However, the rapid growth in the number of children and the limited resources of poorer countries are creating great differences in the ability of the Middle Eastern governments to meet these educational demands. Despite the promises of their governments, educated young people are also often unable to find jobs, as the experiences of our friend Aisha's sons demonstrate, and this has created unrest in the youth whose rising expectations have been frustrated.

Common experiences are now communicated across the Arab world's national boundaries through local media, books, films, videos, and tape cassettes. Eleven daily newspapers are published in Cairo alone; five in Casablanca; nine in Baghdad, despite a recent shortage of paper since the end of the Gulf War.

As was true earlier in the United States, however, the real breakthrough over the last generation has been the widespread dissemination of television broadcasting. Ninety-two percent of all Egyptians now own television sets, and the effects were made clear to us during recent visits to Cairo and to Nubia. Morocco, Iraq, Saudi Arabia, and Lebanon have government-owned and -controlled television corporations, as do Israel and the new Palestinian authority. But satellite dishes, legal and illegal, make information much harder to control than when we first went to the region.

Television in the Arab world, like television everywhere, is proving to be a divertissement as well as a source of discontent. It provides inexpensive entertainment, yet at the same time shows lifestyles and consumer goods (in Western-style commercials) that are beyond the pocketbooks of the average viewer. Consumer expectations are raised without the means of fulfillment, and the result is frustration. This is especially true in Egypt. Television is also being used for public education and for the promulgation of government policy. Kuwait has adapted *Sesame Street* for its children, and Egypt offers daily tutoring sessions in mathematics, for instance. In all Arab countries government-approved religious instruction is daily fare. Often the state not only controls local television programs but also restricts the amount of Western programming, in an effort to encourage indigenous programs and reduce foreign influences. In these contexts television becomes a powerful instrument for the governments to present and discuss their policies.

ALL THE ARAB COUNTRIES were directly or indirectly affected by the Western colonial presence from 1800 to 1962, and many are still recovering from what they view as the humiliation of that presence, as we have tried to indicate in the essay "Colonialism East and West." Among many of our friends, a new sense of common identity as Muslims is evident. In Morocco, in Egypt, in Saudi Arabia, in Jordan and Lebanon, people spoke to us about the need to return to roots, to reaffirm the basics: family ties, parent-child relationships, religious beliefs. They said they wanted the convenience of modern technology, but not the values of the West at the expense of their own ways of life. The rise of movements urging a return to traditional male and female roles of behavior and a restatement of belief in Islam, the religion of 90 percent of the people, should not be too surprising to Americans, who are experiencing some aspects of the same phenomenon in their own country. However, in the Arab world, this "return to roots" is also fueled by a sense of resistance to the West, its old colonial rule now replaced by contemporary forms of political and economic domination.

The fifty-year-old conflict between Israelis and Palestinians has been a constant part of our Middle Eastern experience. Yet, though Western media coverage would suggest to the average American that this conflict is the central focus of life in the Arab world, this is hardly the case. The presence of Israel is still seen as a "foreign" invasion, though one that must be endured. The birth of a Palestinian state, its tentative recognition by Israel, and its uncertain future are of much greater concern in the region. Since the 1993 peace accords, there have been stopgap attempts at joint Israeli-Palestinian economic efforts, as we found during our filmmaking research. And though the twenty-three nations in the area may express support for Palestinian independence, and even provide funds for Palestinian institutions, their principal concerns are with their own peoples.

When we first went to the Arab world forty years ago, Americans in Arab countries were almost a novelty. Of course, America had already become notorious for its support of Israel, but most of the region lacked a tangible American presence. Our foreign aid programs were still limited and our involvement in the local economies slight, restrained by efforts toward self-sufficiency on the part of newly nationalized Arab governments. The American refusal to support the Franco-British attempt to take over the Suez Canal in the fall of 1956 came weeks after our arrival in Iraq, sweetening the waters for us, taking away some of the bitterness developing over the massive American support for Israel. Suddenly, as Americans, we were anticolonialists, popular for a time. That popularity faded rapidly in the years that followed.

News about America was also hard to get in most of the Arab world forty years ago; the BBC was much stronger on our shortwave radio than the Voice of America, and publications like *Time* magazine and the *International Herald Tribune* were only available in luxury hotels. In Iraq the foreign goods for sale came from Great Britain, the former colonial power. The number of British civil servants working for the Iraqi government or in the British Embassy was still large enough to keep a British country club going in Baghdad. There was much to remind us that Iraq had been (and to a degree was still) ruled by the British; America seemed far away, and a few friends in our embassy were all we had to remind us of home.

Today the reverse is true. America is everywhere, even in Lebanon and Iraq, where we are conspicuous by our absence, and where everyone wonders about our next political moves. Attention these days is fixed on America as the world superpower, the power that can make war or peace, can blockade or assist an Arab government. People of all classes in both urban and rural settings are familiar with American events and personalities. America is a constant factor to be taken into account; like the weather, it cannot be avoided. American products are sold almost everywhere, and American companies are a growing presence in Egypt and Jordan, as they long have been in Saudi Arabia. English is the language of commerce and trade and shares with Arabic the labels on many locally produced products. CNN is continually monitored on television sets in offices and in homes. Satellite dishes cover the roofs of buildings in every Arab country, and even in Iraq, where they are illegal, they are often present, if out of sight. Thus, programs and news from our country flood the channels and fill the minds of Arab viewers.

Imagine what it would be like to have a foreign country so much a part of our lives in the United States, another country far more powerful and much richer than ourselves, with another language and another major religion and with styles of life we considered immoral. Imagine hearing about this country night and day and knowing that much of one's well-being depended on that foreign country. The very thought of such an invasion of our public space is abhorrent to us. Yet this is what the American relationship to the Middle East has become. Forty years ago, what our country was doing was a curiosity to our Iraqi friends. In 1996, before the elections, they looked at us and asked, "Will Clinton or will Dole stop the blockade?" "Why does your government want to starve us?" Is it surprising to find that some Middle Easterners feel that "friendship" with Westerners is perfidious, the last thing they need? Even some of our old Arab friends now believe that they know more about our country than we do, and many of them do not like what they know. Perhaps they are right. To Arabs or Israelis, at any rate, we are a constant, unavoidable presence in their lives.

For Americans the rise of Islam as a primary source of identity in the Arab world should be seen in this light. To reinvent themselves again as a modern Muslim community, to search for local solutions to their problems in a Muslim frame of reference, is one way for the Arab world to counter the tremendous impact of America and the West on contemporary Muslim societies. In terms of this new stress on religious identity, our friends in the Middle East these days see their duties as Muslims as part of their responsibilities as teachers, scientists, farmers, tradespeople, or family members. For many people, religious identity supersedes national identity and constitutes the discourse within which all political and social issues should be discussed and in which their national governments can be legitimately criticized. In this sense religion is not the "opium of the masses," a way of obscuring internal conflicts, but rather is a way of articulating these conflicts, of invigorating struggles for greater equity between rich and poor and the powerful and the weak.

But if modern Islam today serves to color Middle Eastern people's view of America in the Middle East, it also affects American views of the Arab world. In the minds of Americans Islam has become objectified; it is a "thing" with which the United States must deal, a monolithic threat to our interests which may strike at us anywhere. In American public usage the term "Muslim" has come close to indicating a race or an ethnicity; certainly, that was the way the term was used in discussions of the Bosnian conflict. Seeing terrorism as a result of the reinvigoration of Islamic belief, however, is not at all useful, for this view obscures the sources of people's discontent in the area: government corruption, class conflict, unemployment, overpopulation. (The total number of people in the area has grown from 160 million to 220 million in the past fifteen years.) If we in America do not look past religious rhetoric for reasons for violence, then religion in the Arab world will become our own opium in the West, the source of our own ignorance. The interdependence of our common well-being is too important to permit such fantasies. Americans share with Arabs common beliefs in monotheistic religion and many ideas about family and community. Our science, our language, even our diet, have been influenced by discoveries made long ago by Arabs. Like friends or cousins who have drifted apart over the years, we are now being brought back together by the force of circumstance: the processes of world capitalism and the common desire for peace.

THE INCIDENTS IN THIS BOOK are all real, as are the people, although in some cases we have changed names and in rare incidences created composite characters so that individuals might not be embarrassed. For over a quarter of a century people in many countries of the Arab world have welcomed us, tolerated us, educated us. How our friends are struggling to come to terms with their new conditions of life in the Middle East is, above all else, what we want to share in the chapters and comments that follow. We hope our efforts may serve to illuminate for our fellow Americans some of the complex human dilemmas the people of the Arab world are facing today.

1 Lebanon

At daybreak we come down to the harbor
Where ships have spread sails for departure.
And we cry, "O beloved sea,
As near as the eyelids of our eyes,
We are eager for the voyage. . . .
Shepherds have told us of those islands
Where people have challenged destiny,
Planted settlements like teeth in the desert
That have grown into cities of light, and of glory
To fill one's eyes with wonder.
Of such magical cities,
Men dream in childhood.

Yusuf al-Khal
THE VOYAGE

IN THE COURTYARD OF THE French Archaeological Institute hostel, where we stayed on first arriving in Lebanon, a fine Alexander Calder mobile turned gently in the sunshine and sea breeze that marked the early Mediterranean fall. Red and black, it was obviously very modern and yet it seemed to fit perfectly with the old Lebanese house, its stone stairway and rooms built around the spacious, sunny, whitewashed courtyard. Within the institute library the high windows were bordered with pointed arches in the Islamic style; the stained glass was arranged within the windows so that the light formed shifting patterns of color upon the floor, upon the modern rush chairs, the dark, carved Druze chest, the shelves of old books and new scholarly publications from Europe and America.

Bob and I sat up on the balcony, reveling in our new adventure in this beautiful setting. We had docked in Alexandria a week before but had not been allowed to land because of rioting there. President Gamal Abdel Nasser, the new president of Egypt, who had ousted King Farouk in 1952, now had the audacity to nationalize the Suez Canal. Stockholders in France and Britain were incredulous and outraged. "The gyppies just can't do this to us" was the general European sentiment. Other authoritative voices were assuring it would only be a matter of days before the canal would stop working; the Egyptians would soon come crawling back to London and Paris, begging for the European pilots to return, for the European engineers to run the locks. Meanwhile, our ship had sailed on to the friendlier shores of Lebanon. And here we sat, watching the scene outside, waiting for Bob Adams to arrive from the University of Chicago before we all set out across the desert to Baghdad. The Jewish school nearby was full of children, their chanting reverberating up and down the narrow lane. To our left the local streetcar went binging along the rails. The passengers sat stiffly in baggy pants and turbans, all-enveloping cloaks, French-made skirts and sweaters, white body-fitting shirts and pants. An occasional embroidered hat, a patterned vest, signaled another representative of Lebanon's many ethnic and religious groups. From the balcony we saw people in turbans, skullcaps, flat pillboxes, fezzes, and veils both black and white climbing onto the streetcars, jumping off. These were exotic signs of a diversity of origins which we still could not decode.

Yet what were we to make of the brass plate affixed to a white wall in the courtyard of the French Archaeological Institute? The plate commemorated the Emir Abd al-Kader, who fought against the first French settlements in Algeria, escaped to Morocco, and was eventually captured by the French. We saw that small square of shining brass each time we climbed the stairs:

EMIR ABD AL-KADER, LEADER OF HIS PEOPLE,
LIVED HERE IN EXILE UNDER FRENCH PROTECTION
FOR SEVEN MONTHS IN THE YEAR 1856.

French protection? Or house arrest? No one would say.

Still, overall, we were enchanted with Beirut. Our ship had sailed into port two days before in bright sunshine, the houses gleaming white on the hills and the mountains rising behind the city, terraced green ridge upon ridge. The sky was blue, the sun warm but not hot. The next day we had climbed onto the streetcar in front of the French Institute and sat on the woven rush seats reminiscent of my childhood, when I had taken my aunt Rose's plump hand and gone with her on the Old State Street car into downtown Chicago.

It seemed incredible to be riding a streetcar in Beirut, ancient Phoenicia, where Greek sailors had caroused two thousand years before, and where today people walked about as though this were just another ordinary city.

"I don't like the ice cream, though," I said.

It was funny, the ice cream, sweet and stringy like taffy—long on sugar and short on milk, Bob said. "But that's just because we're prejudiced Americans," he carefully added.

I agreed, and we happily dined on other great specialties more to our taste: *shawarma* (sliced barbecued lamb), fresh tiny wild strawberries brought in from the mountains, and tabooli, a marvelous salad made from parsley and tomatoes and cracked wheat.

Downtown, we wandered into the Bourse, through the markets, looking at banks of scarlet flowers, yellow asters, and white roses. We looked at wine, at auto parts, at fine French furniture, head scarves, long Arab cloaks, plumbing fixtures, cement, perfumes, tiles. Goods from all over the world seemed to be laid out before our eyes on stands and counters, on small rugs and colorful lengths of cloth spread out on the ground. Occasionally, someone would holler:

"Hey! This main drag. You American?"

"Here, George, good English cloth, see!"

"Brooklyn Bridge, ha ha! Good price!"

BOB ADAMS ARRIVED, our visas were duly stamped, and before we set off in the University of Chicago Jeep across the desert to Baghdad, we were invited to dine at the summer home of M. Henri Seyrig, the director of the institute. "A simple dinner of native dishes," he said. His messenger offered to drive us to the mountain retreat above Aley.

Dusk was coming down over the sea as we climbed, the setting sun staining the rock ridges pink as we wound around them in the Jeep, shading the oleanders, pink and white, muting the red tiled roofs of the stone houses in the mountain villages. We braked and paused for bleating sheep, for a few cows being chased by a boy in a skullcap and an embroidered shirt, for a procession of women in red dresses, with diaphanous colored veils that spread out behind them in the evening breeze, like halos.

M. Seyrig greeted us on the terrace of his summer house, a man in late middle age, small and compact, dark, and with a gracious manner, an inquisitive eye. After aperitifs, dinner was served by a woman servant in bloomers and embroidered blouse, her hair tied up in one of those evanescent veils, this one purple. A simple meal of native foods, yes—delicious *shawarma*, rice, salad.

We sat with M. Seyrig, looking out over the dark valley dotted with rows of tiny flickering lights marking the houses along the terraces we had just climbed. The sea, studded with flecks of foam glimmering white on the black water, seemed scarcely distinguishable from the land. Behind us hung modern canvases by an unfamiliar Parisian painter, great strokes of orange, green, black, and crimson in unexpected combinations, on the walls of the whitewashed summer house. To our right a Maronite cathedral loomed in the dusk, reflecting dim light among shrubs and trees.

The woman in the purple head scarf served dessert: fried bananas in rum. We had thick, strong coffee.

"Yes," murmured M. Seyrig. "This region is ageless in its beauty."

"It is very beautiful," I replied.

What else was there to be said? We were young and impressionable, full of ourselves and our new adventure, our new marriage, our new lives. The vista of hills stretched below us, darkly clotted with fig trees; some aromatic bush vied for sweetness with the fumes of rum from our dessert. The sea washed and foamed far below. The evening posed the possibilities of sensual delights that were almost overwhelming. M. Seyrig seemed part of this setting, so relaxed, so knowledgeable. Perhaps it was the conjunction of ancient splendor, natural beauty, and the modern wall-high swaths of bravura color in the paintings behind us that left us speechless. We were from America, a new world, and all this mixing of old and new seemed unreal, strange, something to experience but hard to feel part of. Yet wonderful. The hills. The fig trees. The cathedral and the modern paintings. The dark-haired woman and the bananas with rum.

BEIRUT, 1960, 1964

DURING THE YEARS TO COME, when we lived in Iraq and Egypt, Beirut continued to be the closest thing to a visit home. In some ways, we felt a bit ashamed of the fact that we should enjoy American pleasures in

Beirut when we were supposed to be involved in the patterns of Arab culture. We admitted to each other that Uncle Sam's hamburger restaurant and its American-style ice cream seemed awfully good—the first time around on each visit, at least.

But it was more than familiar sights and sounds. Beirut seemed to us a hopeful place, a sign of the future, where the church bells could ring on Sundays, the synagogues fill up on Saturdays, and the calls to prayer from the mosques sound throughout the week. Whenever doubt flickered like a shadow across our lantern-slide images of the great peaceful future of the Middle East, we thought about Lebanon and Beirut, Switzerland of the Middle East, ancient Phoenician port, where all races and religions mixed, talked, enjoyed a free press and a constitutional government, and made a great deal of money from banking and trade. We saw some hope in all of this. East and West seemed to combine here without perceptible strain.

We said to ourselves that Lebanon felt like America because it shared many of our much vaunted freedoms. Was that true? There was freedom of speech, it seemed. College texts described the Lebanese constitution as a model of religious and ethnic accord. Political asylum was taken for granted. If we felt a sense of relief from just being in Beirut, so did hundreds of others with much better reasons, political exiles from throughout the region.

Beirut provided free trade and the appropriate political atmosphere for high-rolling international capitalism. The two were not unrelated, of course. Business was booming without hindrance; taxes and duties were low. Everyone seemed to carry on his or her affairs without bothering others. The focus was on living well and accumulating the means to do so. As the major trade center of the Middle East, home of international banking and of most foreign concerns who wanted a Middle East location free of government interference, Beirut was needed by all parties, friendly or otherwise.

And so life in this sea-blown oasis seemed assured through long sunny summers and long sunny winters. Foreign experts, exiles, businessmen, and educators came and went, and the future looked bright and full of promise, at least in downtown Beirut.

> The sun's valleys have no color.
> Children's nails have no color.
> Bracelets of fire have no color.
> Screaming has no color.
> Beirut . . . you are screaming.

Hoda al-Namani
I REMEMBER I WAS A POINT, I WAS A CIRCLE

AFTER AN ABSENCE OF TEN YEARS, Bob and I had come back to live in the Arab world again. We were alone, like the first time: our children, Laura Ann, David, and Laila, were far away in America, studying, we trusted, intellectually stimulating and perhaps even useful subjects in colleges and universities. This time we were supposedly able to look at the region with more experienced eyes. After talking about the Middle East in anthropology courses for fifteen years, Bob was setting out to revisit some of the countries of earlier research, to update his firsthand experience. I had a National Endowment for the Humanities grant to make an educational film about social change from a woman's perspective. A new experience for me.

We did not feel self-assured. We felt nervous, for we knew the Arab world had changed radically. But we also felt fortunate, for we had been given the opportunity to come back and see that change for ourselves.

As we peered out the window of our Middle East Airlines plane, now settling into Beirut, once a brightly lighted San Francisco in the Middle East, there was nothing visible but the winking reflectors along the runway—and darkness.

The airport was nearly empty, and Bob's voice inquiring about taxis sounded very loud. No one was there to meet us, although we had sent telexes and cables. Obviously, the machinery was not working. We knew why, but we did not want to remind each other. Civil disorder. In beautiful Lebanon. Civil war.

The customs official in a crumpled khaki uniform looked vaguely at our luggage. We were waiting for him to stamp it, chalk it, pass it, but he did nothing. Finally, realizing we were waiting for him, or perhaps deciding to take notice of us, he gestured us past. He was the last representative of state authority we would meet during our stay in Lebanon. The family in front of us, the only other passengers to deplane in Beirut, got into a waiting car outside the airport and drove off. We were left with a row of shouting drivers, all of them after our business. The only business.

"Here, George, over here!"

George? Echoes of the past. (Bob had once wondered if they knew that was his father's first name.)

Bob was already bargaining with a quieter, middle-aged man, and our bags were stowed into an old American Chevrolet, fifties style, fins and all. But the cab, after a roaring, revving start, stopped again. Out of gas already? The light inside the cab flashed on, and we found ourselves blinking into the faces of two young men, wearing baseball caps and uniforms, not of the New York Yankees but of some military group. Pants, shirt, hat, all of camouflage cloth. The young men flicked their flashlights over us, in the way policemen do to suspects in B movies. We could see their faces. And then the flashlights moved upward, as a signal to go on, and we rolled slowly past the checkpoint. I looked back at it curiously, nervously, as the taxi picked up speed. It was a lean-to with a tin roof, banked by piles of sandbags. One of the men had already disappeared into the hut, but the other, his rifle slung casually over one shoulder (was it a machine gun?), was staring after us. For a panicky moment I wondered if he would run after us, *shoot* at us. Maybe we were guilty of something we didn't even know about?

But no, the taxi had moved straight out the airport road. I relaxed a bit. But—*whoosh*, the taxi came to a sudden halt again. Checkpoint two. Another lean-to, surrounded by sandbags. The cab light was flicked on again, and another man came to look us over. This one wore a red beret and army fatigues, but he had the same kind of gun. A cigarette was burning between his lips; the smoke came through the open window and filled the damp air of the cab.

Checkpoint-two man shifted his rifle, removed his cigarette, and waved us on. Off went the overhead light. The taxi was roomy, as big American cars are, but its springs must have been recently installed— badly, for when the car moved, we moved back and forth with those springs, over the slippery, plastic-covered seats.

"Four more to go!" cried the driver cheerfully in excellent English.

"Four what?"

"Four more checks like that," he replied curtly, and speeded ahead on the empty, silent route to town. In the darkness little could be seen but dark blotches beside the road, marking hollows and holes where buildings had presumably once stood. The yellow glare of the headlights glinted off jagged trees and broken bricks, illuminated shadows that might or might not have been people, occasionally picked out piles of rubbish, twisted piping, car parts, chunks of cement that had been imperfectly swept so the road could remain open. Could this be Beirut?

Another jolt. Another stop. Another set of guards. These men sported green rather than red berets and they looked younger than our own children, now in their early twenties. One stroked a tentative mustache. The gun he carried was not tentative, however, and he seemed to be holding onto it in a way that suggested it could be aimed in our direction rather quickly. I tried to sit up straighter in the slippery taxi seat so as not to appear intimidated. Although we had been in Beirut for less than an hour, I found I was already thinking in clichés, about smelling fear everywhere, terror lurking in the streets. But I did smell fear. Bob sat up straight next to me and stared silently at our observers. Was I smelling our own fear?

"Yallah!" The wave of the arm. The taxi light clicking off. We lurched forward into the dark again.

A brand-new sign ahead on the left proclaimed in shocking-pink and white neon, "Supermarché." The Supermarché was not open, however, so late at night: around it lay more piles of rubble, these more neatly stacked than the ones we had seen before. We speeded around an empty traffic circle where half an acacia tree still stood, the partially severed branches flapping about like incongruous tattered flags.

Beirut. Meeting place of East and West.

Checkpoint four. The men at this one were sleepy. They sat in their sandbagged bivouac, listening to the radio from which an old recording blared forth. It was Um Kulthum, Egypt's great beloved chanteuse, singing still in that rich full voice, though she had been dead nearly a decade. The men preferred her music to us, obviously, for they waved us past with hardly a glance.

A jumbled group of buildings. We seemed to be heading away from Beirut to the sea.

"This is the only way. Can't go the other way," the driver said cryptically. "Blocked by a raid. We change the route depending on what's going on, what's been blown up recently, who's in charge," explained the driver.

"I understand. Just remembered from the last time we were here."

"When was that?"

"Nineteen sixty-four."

The driver snorted. Twice.

We drove in silence. Checkpoint five looked larger, more substantial. One of the three guards was reading a book by the light of a kerosene lantern. The old oil barrels edging the sandbags were smeared with slogans which had run in the rain. Paint? Blood? Martial music blared from the radio inside. We slowed to a stop, and an old man with a heavyset face peered at us for a second and gestured us on. He held in his hand a *stikan* of tea, the little fluted gold-banded glass out of which we had drunk so many gallons of pleasant sweet tea over past years, the tea of traditional Arab hospitality. The first familiar sight.

"Why did you come back?" the driver asked.

"To see friends at the American University."

"American University." He laughed. "Called PLO University these days."

We turned in from the sea near the British Embassy and stopped at a high gate, whose pointed spikes were wound about with barbed wire. Two guards emerged. The cab light flicked on.

"American University," announced the driver. "You're here."

Bob got out and went to the gate.

I watched from the taxi while he gestured, spoke, was given a telephone. The taxi motor continued to run, hiccuping at various speeds. Was our friend Jim not there? Would we be obliged to turn around and drive back to the airport, past the rubble and the six checkpoints, to wait for the next plane out?

"Sure your friend's here?" said the taxi driver.

"Oh yes," I said, more loudly than I intended. "Yes, he's here."

"You English or American?"

"American."

The taxi driver laughed and shook his head. "Americans at the PLO University. Would you believe it? You guys don't even talk to the PLO at home."

Fortunately, I did not have to reply, for something was happening at the gatehouse. Bob leaned into the open taxi window.

"Jim's here but we have to wait for him to come to the gatehouse to vouch for us. Security is pretty tight."

He nodded toward the American University guards. In their neat, dark blue suits, they looked very different from the armed men we had seen along the airport road. Their weapons were not carried carelessly either, and in fact were not even visible, I saw with satisfaction. But a second later I found myself looking wildly for their weapons. Surely they were armed, for the good of the university? Certainly they would be professional enough to be armed. Yet what could the driver mean, this was *PLO* University?

I sat in the taxi. The motor continued to hiccup. The guard looked pointedly at his watch. Bob leaned against the side of the taxi, appearing casual, but I could see his fists clenched in tension.

"Bob!" A familiar figure stepped from the darkness into the gatehouse light. I could barely restrain myself from saying triumphantly to the taxi driver, "See! We *do* have a friend here."

We drove through the gatehouse, toward the faculty apartment building where Jim lived. Even on the campus in the taxi with Jim, an ex-student of Bob's and an old friend, the alien atmosphere of the city seemed to prevail, and we traveled the half mile in silence. There was relief but little joy in our meeting.

We woke in the morning to bright sunshine, but when I looked out across Jim's ground-floor terrace, the Mediterranean glittered through a screen of barbed wire, two feet high, which topped the stone campus wall and had, through time, become entwined with the crimson bougainvillea.

"That's the way it is," said Jim. "The whole campus is under strict security. It has to be. Everyone thinks the American University at Beirut is full of its enemies: Maronites, Shias, Sunnis, Nasserites . . . and Palestinians, of course."

"And the PLO?" asked Bob.

"We don't discriminate on this campus," said Jim.

"What does that mean?" I asked.

"Exactly what I said," he replied.

The city seemed in a suspended state of siege. The American University had a rather special position; it could afford to lay expensive barbed wire, like jagged lengths of dangerous embroidery, along the tops of all the high walls that enclosed the campus: its beautiful old stone buildings and tennis courts had been built in 1866, a time when the colonial foreigners, even those who went to do good, expected to live well. Many of the new, expensive modern apartment buildings did likewise; and one of the buildings leading up from the American University to Rue Hamra, commercial center of West Beirut, had its own antiaircraft gun on the roof, above the penthouse. I saw the black massive front of the emplacement on our second day in Beirut, and pointed it out in amazement to my friend Penny Williams, the artist.

She shrugged. "Of course," she replied. "Things that look amazing to you are now taken as a matter of course by everybody. Here, quick, B.J.," and she shoved me into the open door of a photo shop. High above us an ominous popping sounded, seemed to burst out, stop, then burst out again.

"What's that?"

"The Israeli planes are breaking the sound barrier," said Penny matter-of-factly. "They fly over every so often. Part of the war of nerves."

"But why are we in here? They're not bombing."

"No," the man behind the photo shop counter said, "but you never know."

"And then," went on Penny, in a tone I associated with teachers trying to present difficult information to dull students, "the antiaircraft defense often fires, and bits of shrapnel from those shells fall down long afterward. Somebody was hit yesterday by a stray piece of shrapnel just walking along Rue Hamra."

"Yes," said the shop owner. "Have to be careful these days."

Street smarts. Or, more accurately, war-in-the-street smarts. People went out jogging very early as Jim and Bob had done that morning, and they did their grocery shopping long before noon, for the militia were known to be late sleepers, and thus shelling usually did not seriously get going till afternoon.

The civil war had theoretically ended in 1976, but five years later many sorts of struggles continued. Various religious factions sometimes clashed briefly or shelled each other's positions across the city. An auto accident on a side street became the excuse for a pitched, armed battle. No one knew what the day would bring.

Life had returned more or less to normal, people said, but the scars of the war were all around us. The whole center of the old city was gone, the Bourse, the flower market, Ajami's restaurant, where we had dined with such pleasure twenty years ago. What was left was split in two between Christian sector and Muslim sector. The streetcars we had ridden long ago had disappeared. The slit in the city was marked by what was euphemistically known as the Green Line, but far from being a strip of lawn and garden, the line was a no-man's-land, blasted and broken, over which two sets of militia guarded several sets of checkpoints.

Many people had to cross the line every day from home to work, and on bad days or threatened bad days, absenteeism in offices and businesses was a major problem.

Yet schools remained open most of the time, and banks and stores continued to do business. Vegetable merchants wheeled their carts full of peppers and tomatoes, oranges and grapefruit, across the Green Line into the areas of Beirut that still functioned. Newspapers were published in Arabic and French, restaurants served meals, and the telephones worked occasionally. Nightlife, it was true, had ceased almost completely, for it was not safe to be out on the streets after dark. The old days of nightclubbing along the Corniche till daybreak or gambling in the casinos was over; Beirutis had retreated into their homes, or what was left of them. But the sidewalk cafés did a brisk business in the morning, and lunch was still a time to entertain friends and colleagues.

The media image of Beirut living in the face of constant anxiety and terror was further confused for us by the fact that many people looked so well dressed, so well fed, so well wined and dined, at least in

West Beirut. It was not uncommon to see a bookstore owner setting out the newest French novels while next door, in a collection of rubble, the rubble's owner and proprietor was hawking Cacharel blouses, hung on a length of wire across the jagged stones and chunks of smashed cement.

And Penny, when I asked her about a great hole in the front garden of their seaside apartment house, said no, it wasn't a shell, it was a well.

"A well?"

During the war, water supplies were often cut off, explained Penny, so the tenants had contributed toward the wages of a well driller.

Individual persons were reported to have performed great acts of bravery during the troubles, but since the truce, the country "seemed to go nowhere," one of the professors at the American University (AUB) said. "Everybody's waiting for everyone else to settle down, stop fighting."

And, Bob pointed out, no outside forces had appeared, as in the past, when Greek, Roman, Ottoman, and French occupation forces had come in to "pacify" Lebanon. Even the U.S. Marines, who had appeared in 1958, had not turned up.

"Lebanon is a great trading post," someone said bitterly. "It didn't ask to be a model nation. The West—you—wanted to make us into a showpiece. But we're the ones who are stuck with it."

Frozen in strife. The image seemed contradictory, impossible. Yet it served, somehow, to convey the feeling of the city, where life went on, a kind of life anyway, but the old mechanisms of national government had wound down to a faint murmur, and even the street signs were gone. As we traveled through the city, visiting old friends, we had a confusing sense of déjà vu one minute, which would be rudely dispelled the next. "No," Bob would say. "This isn't right. There was a church here." But no more. From a distance we could see the famous Pigeon Rocks standing in the sea, and the golden beach would begin to unfold as we approached; but before we reached the old scenic point the view disappeared, blocked by rows of makeshift shops that had sprung up, unzoned and unsupervised, along the seafront. The middle-class shopping center of the city had moved to the beach, where, presumably, one could see an enemy coming and take one's most valuable stock to shelter.

"I find it hard to see how people can go on living day after day with such confusion and insecurity," I said to Hind al-Sayed, a Lebanese sculptor who had invited me to tea. We had mutual friends in America.

"Some people have left," she replied, "but many people can't. All they own is here, and their families, or their business, or their health, keep them here. Some of those who left before came back to find everything gone."

"So now they are determined to stay?" I ask.

"Yes, but they don't stay just for these material reasons; you in the West always stress that, see it as the spring of all action. Materialism!"

I bridled. "Not really. There is a lot more to the quality of life in the West than just that. You know that. You yourself studied in Paris, Hind. Don't you miss it?"

"No," she said abruptly. "Oh, don't misunderstand. I learned a great deal, but I find these days I'm not much interested in the West anymore. It seems finished, over with."

"The West? Finished?" I returned. "We *are* still the center of the industrial world," I heard myself proclaiming, maybe a bit too loudly.

She smiled, a gentle softening of the angular features, the broad forehead and deep-set eyes. "There you go again, off on materialism . . ."

"I didn't mean just that," I protested.

"I know," she said. "Let's look at it another way. You asked me how people can bear to stay here. It's often terrible. Of course many can't leave, but still whatever is going on here, it's alive. We are beginning things, changing things our own way. It is painful, this birthing process, but it is alive. The West does seem dead, or at least in decline. Look at your television programs, your drug problems."

I protested, talked about changes in America, movements for women's rights, desegregation, issues that didn't receive much coverage in the Arab world because of stereotypes about the West. "Soaps like *Dallas* are what a lot of you would *like* to think about us," I exclaimed forcefully.

Hind smiled that gentle smile again. "You sound like *we* did ten years ago. We thought the Western way would solve all our problems. *We* know better now. The West is no answer for us."

"Well . . ." I rose to defend my country. Always critical when at home, Bob and I had to admit that we were full of patriotism when abroad. *We* could say those things about ourselves at home, but *they* shouldn't say them over here, went our argument to ourselves. *They* must see the full picture, grasp the subtleties, before jumping to conclusions, we felt rather defensively.

Hind listened politely, partly, I am sure, out of deference to the mutual friends who had brought us together. We drank our tea and sat quietly, but without the ease of friends.

"Goodbye," she said. "Be careful."

Be careful, B.J. Be careful, Bob. Those admonitions, recited like a litany, followed us each time we left Jim's apartment, arrived in another friend's house, left the friend's house. *Be careful.*

We were careful. It didn't take long to learn some basic street smarts. Sheer instinct for survival taught us that if caught on the streets when afternoon shelling began, one ran close to the sides of the buildings and ducked into the nearest open bookstore or hotel lobby or restaurant to stay until the raid, or the "exchange," as some people called it, was over. The sight of the money changers pulling down their iron shutters was a signal that something more serious than a mere "exchange" might be on the way. Hence, one ducked into a place where one could stay for a while. Restaurants were the best.

Once safe inside a restaurant, we felt liberated, freed, safe from oblivion, and, like everyone else in the restaurant, laughed louder than usual, told many jokes, ordered the best wines and the specialties of the house—*shish taouk* at La Pasha, kibbe at Maarouche, and the fish catch of the day at Faysal's. During these times, the waiters always seemed to fly around, giving especially good service, and the music poured out of the stereo: Arabic music with pipes and drums and violins, French love songs, old Beatles hits.

Music of several cultures. Wine from France, wine from Lebanon. Meat. Fruit. Tangible pleasures. Reassuring laughter. With a sense of fin-de-siècle, repressing thoughts of present dangers, we watched it all, strangers, outsiders, caught up and held, like flies in amber, in a kind of suspended life that bore no relation whatsoever to those old halcyon days of the fifties. We were lucky. We could always leave, we said to ourselves. Didn't we have American passports? The people of Beirut, descendants of the quiet, pleasant people we had watched going up and down on the old streetcar years before, dressed in the garments that were signs of their group, their religious belief, their gender—these people were trying to survive in an incomprehensible, totally changed world. They went to school, they shopped, they worked, they ate lunch, they made love, and then fighting broke out and things stopped dead . . . for a moment.

Beginnings and endings. We walked down streets that ended in the middle, like life in Beirut, which seemed periodically to come to a dead stop. Traffic would suddenly be blocked by broken pieces of buildings, and yet after a ten-minute detour around total desolation, traffic would be resumed. Life went on. It seemed as though Beirut was holding on, waiting for a savior. But none came.

What had Hind said? "It is painful." The same could be said of both living and dying. Which was it?

We were invited to lunch by our old friends Hoda and Abdul Kader al-Namani. I would go early in a taxi, we decided, and have some time by myself with Hoda; Bob would come on his own, as he had appointments at the university beforehand. It sounded like a logical program, but of course we had not counted on the realities of trying to get from one part of Beirut to another, especially to an apartment house like the al-Namanis', which was close to the Green Line.

An hour and a half after I had set out from AUB, the taxi deposited me in front of the al-Namanis' house.

As she embraced me, Hoda burst into tears. We had not seen each other for fifteen years, but her tears were not totally nostalgia for past friendship.

"Thank God you arrived safely," she cried, wiping her tears with a lace-edged handkerchief. "You haven't been here for ages, you don't know the problems. Oh, B.J., it's good to see you." She wept again. "I'm sorry to be so emotional—we Arabs are supposed to be overly emotional, I guess—but you never know these days what's going to happen from one minute to the next. I mean, from the time I talked to you this morning on the phone until now, the whole route from AUB to here could have been changed by a shelling, or a shifting of the militia checkpoint. You just never know. And with Abdul Kader ill—"

"Yes, I heard. I am so sorry."

"He is better and will be at lunch," said Hoda firmly. "I'll take you back to see him in a moment, but he is resting now."

"Hoda, I've heard about you over the years." I smiled, blinking my own wet eyes. "Not just the poetry—you're famous enough for that in many parts of the Arab world—no, about your political activities."

"My *political* activities?" Hoda all but whooped.

Hoda's laugh was the same. I remembered that laugh well, a well-bred giggle that had first endeared her to me, long ago in Cairo, when she was the extremely beautiful, extremely fashionable wife of the dean at the American University in Cairo. She had organized a baby shower for me twenty-two years ago, before Laura Ann was born. Abdul Kader, a professor of physics, was Hoda's first cousin and husband, a good twenty years her senior, gentle in his dry humor, respected for his fair judgments, Bob said. But it was Hoda one remembered in the receiving lines we passed down in the old days of formal receptions and cross-cultural dinner parties, when we felt that the American University in Cairo was a living example of the American spirit of liberty and academic freedom, an island in the military regime. Lugubrious occasions, usually, but Hoda lightened them, partly by her beauty, but also because she could not maintain a serious mien. She tried, but she was an ebullient person and she could not help laughing. The laugh was irrepressible in the face of pomposity, pedantry, or even heavy-handed gallantry—whether German, French, Swiss, Egyptian, American, or British. She took each formal remark addressed to her with a grain of salt and a giggle and charmed everyone.

Hoda had been born in Damascus; her great-grandfather was an illustrious Sufi poet, her distant ancestor a renowned historian of Islam. Her generous-spirited amusement was perhaps a product of her background, her knowledge of her own ancestry, her sense of her place in the world. Western pomposity was no different from Egyptian pomposity, after all; over the centuries Damascene sophistication and humor had absorbed such peccadilloes, though not without a certain sense of cultural superiority, it was true. Hoda had none of that arrogance; we thought she must have a secret life; when I asked, she said, "I write poetry, but no one publishes it."

"How are the children?" Hoda interrupted my thoughts.

"They've all grown up!"

"My boys are, too," said Hoda. "Bassam and Anis will be here for lunch; they are *men*." She giggled then. "How old we seem to have become, my friend."

I nodded. "But how little we've changed," I said. We both giggled.

"Hoda." I stopped. "You are a famous poet now. What does that have to do with your political activities?"

"Shhh," said Hoda lightly, but her eyes sparkled. "Not before Mama, please."

"Your mother's here from Damascus?"

"Come in, Mama. You remember B.J. She and Dorothy Shane came to us in Damascus a long time ago."

"In the big house, Hoda dear?" A small woman, somewhat stooped, took hold of the arm of my chair and peered around into my face. Yes, it *was* Hoda's mother, twenty years older, dressed in black, her hair henna-colored and a bit gray at the roots, but her bright eyes clear; and she was wearing the most exotic carpet slippers I had ever seen, all brocade, with tassels fore and aft. That was indeed Hoda's mother, whom I remembered vividly from my 1964 visit to Hoda's house in Damascus, a brief vacation when Laila, our youngest child, had just turned two.

"No, Mama," Hoda corrected her. "B.J. came to see us in the new apartment."

"Ah yes." The old lady sat in a matching rose velvet chair nearby and looked me up and down. "Ah yes, I took you to the souk to buy brocade, didn't I, while Hoda and your other friend were too tired! Yes, yes." She nodded her head and took a cigarette from the Damascene box on the table.

"Mama, you know what the doctor said about smoking."

"I know." She inhaled and a smile of great voluptuous enjoyment came over the wrinkled face with the bright eyes. "Ah yes. I know." The old lady put one hand up to her hair, to adjust it, a coquettish gesture that did not look ridiculous, despite the imperfectly dyed hair, the stooped back. Hoda's mother, Aida, was still a presence.

"You have very nice shoes, B.J.," she said suddenly, and I felt as though I had been given the fashion award of the month, for Mme Aida had worn clothes of great distinction at home in Damascus. She had changed for every meal, and also for tea every afternoon. Tea was the time when her brother had come for his daily call, and Hoda, Dorothy, and I had been banished to the bedroom like immature schoolgirls.

"All these years," Hoda had explained to Dorothy and me, sitting on our beds in the guest room, "and he still comes every day."

"But why?" asked Dorothy.

"To ask her advice," said Hoda. "My uncle is the minister of defense. Who else can he trust to give him advice in these troubled times?"

"Your mother, as his older sister, can manipulate the foreign affairs of the entire country of Syria," I suggested, laughing.

"No, no, of course not," Hoda replied. "But he talks things over with her. Everybody needs a trusted confidant. Mama knows more about what's going on in the government than I ever will."

"As, for instance . . ."

"Well, she told me he was worried about a friend of ours, a young colonel in the army who was getting very ambitious and wanted to launch an attack on the Golan Heights. My uncle felt that was ridiculous, suicidal at the time, but our young friend was stirring up his fellow officers. What is your advice, dear sister? he asked, and Mama pointed out that his wife was not too well, so why not offer the colonel and his wife a nice mission to Paris? That sort of thing."

"Power behind the throne," murmured Dorothy.

"No," said Hoda. "Not that, not that cliché. We are talking about the power of *family ties,* men and women. It takes different forms in response to different needs."

Dorothy and I did not pursue the argument. It was obvious, however, that Mme Aida was a force to be reckoned with, even as she changed her clothes five times a day, wrote a little in her journal, thought about menus, knitted for her grandchildren, and attended to her role as chief daily adviser to the minister of defense.

Now she sat beside me, smoking a forbidden cigarette, past eighty, and still noticing the cut of my shoes. "Appearance," she might have said, as my mother and grandmother used to say, "has a great deal to do with one's effectiveness."

"So how is your husband?" she asked.

"He is fine, thank you. He is coming to lunch and is looking forward to meeting you."

She smiled enigmatically, finished the cigarette, and said to Hoda,

"I will wait in the other room for the little boys to come from the park."

"Okay, Mama," and to me, "She slips in and out of the past these days, but as you can see she was right in the present when she was talking to you."

"Yes," I said. "Iron hand in velvet glove, I see, still."

"What?"

"A cliché, my dear, used to describe strong women."

"Oh yes, I see." Hoda thought about it. "Yes, that is Mama exactly."

"Now, Hoda, tell me, what are you doing these days?"

"Let us greet Abdul Kader first," she said, and smiled. "More polite."

Ah yes. The gentle critic was what we had called her, Dorothy and I, in the years we wrote together, the three of us, in Cairo, Hoda, Dorothy, myself—meeting every other week at each other's home and reading aloud our newest "pearls" of prose and poetry.

"The thing about Americans," she was saying as we moved down the carpeted hall, hung with tapestries and Bokhara embroideries, "is that they are unpredicted."

"The word is really *'unpredictable,'*" I corrected, "but why *not* 'unpredicted'? Why couldn't that be an unpredicted quality, since Americans are unpredictable?"

Hoda clapped her hands with pleasure. "Words! Words! Yes, it's the same. I was afraid you would have changed and gotten dull, B.J."

"Girls!" The stern voice was that of Mme Aida at the door of her bedroom. "Can't you be quiet? Your husband, Hoda, is ill."

The closed door was on our left. Hoda took a deep breath. "He may not know you, B.J. His last stroke was bad; he is recovering very slowly."

The square bedroom was simply furnished. In the large mahogany bed lay Abdul Kader, a long waxen figure covered by starched white sheets and a green plaid afghan with fringes. Hoda came up close beside him.

"Abd, here is B.J. Remember B.J. from Cairo? She had her first baby there."

"It was a girl." The words came slowly but distinctly from the ashen lips of Abdul Kader, and he tried to raise his head from his single pillow and look at me.

I took his hand, long and cool, bony and waxen yellow like his face. "How are you, Abdul Kader?"

He nodded slowly, twice. Then his eyes wandered. "W-where is—"

"Bob? My husband?"

A nod.

"He is coming for lunch."

Another nod. A faint stretching of the ashy lips, the preparation for a smile.

"We will get you some lunch, my dear." Hoda bent over, kissed him, and smoothed the pillow, unnecessarily, since the pillow seemed unwrinkled.

His eyes followed her, in her red-embroidered black dress, her black hair tied back with a narrow red silk ribbon.

"We'll see you in a few minutes, when Bob comes," I said.

In the hall Hoda cried, "He spoke! He spoke! It doesn't happen every day, it has been really bad, trying to regain the speech . . ."

"Do you have a speech therapist?"

Hoda stared. "Speech therapist? Where are we going to find a speech therapist in Beirut today? People like that have all left."

She led me back to the living room, saying, "Other people are coming to lunch to meet you and Bob. It might be fun. Is Bob bringing your friend Jim from AUB?"

"Yes. Can I help?"

"Thank you." We made our way into the kitchen. "We don't have servants anymore, they won't come here, we're too close to the line. You can see the museum from here"—she pointed out the window a few blocks down—"there, see the checkpoint? Those soldiers are just boys, B.J., they sit there all day." She sighed. "Do you wonder they sometimes just shoot off their guns—I mean, they don't read, they don't do anything except just sit there . . ."

"And that," I said firmly as I chopped parsley to go on top of the *tahina*, around the eggplant casserole, "brings us to your political activities. There's no escape. Tell me, famous Hoda al-Namani, what you've been doing. I've heard about you even in faraway America!"

"Your friends exaggerate, I'm sure," demurred Hoda, moving back and forth from the kitchen, while I did as I was told and laid out the heavy silver forks and knives and spoons on the lace-covered mahogany dining room table. Salads, *baba ghanooj, tahina,* cucumbers in yogurt, a great epergne of red apples and oranges; glasses for wine and juice. On the sideboard, below the dark canvas of an academically presented still life, stood bottles of wine (French, Lebanese), a cake with chocolate icing. "Yes, yes," said Hoda. "I will tell you, I promise. Let's just get the food ready; Anis will bring the kibbe and kebab when he comes from the office, the rice and the aubergines will stay warm in the oven, with the meatballs—"

"Hoda, you have enough for twenty people, not twelve. Will Abdul Kader come to the table?"

"No, no," absently. "I will feed him." Then, in a different tone, "You know us, my dear, we cook like mad, have a lot of things, and then we eat it for days afterward, us Arabs—we Arabs, that is . . ." Smiling as she corrected herself.

"I thought the idea was to give the leftovers to the poor," I said mischievously.

She laughed. "You've read too many books about us, B.J. It's about time you came back here to live for a while. The world has changed; *our* world has changed. It's not like it was."

"Well, I can *see* that," and I looked out the window at the militia point near the museum, a point along the scarred line that split the city in two.

"Yes, you can see it, B.J., but you can't *feel* what it means," replied Hoda shortly. "That feeling fills us all days and all nights, the anxiety, the worry when the shells go over whistling, the worry when they don't. While Abdul Kader lay there with his first stroke, they cut off the water, the boys brought it in pails from the bank where Anis works, they came in the car with pails of water on the floor. We felt lucky to have those pails of water. Some people were not so lucky—"

"But—"

She held up her hand. "And that is how my so-called political activities began," she said. "One night someone banged on our door, crying please help me, please help me, my son is very sick, on the other side, and has to go to the hospital, I know you are the poet, they might listen to you and let me cross, please, please . . .

"It was after the curfew, so theoretically no crossing was allowed," went on Hoda, "and I thought what if it were Abdul Kader who was dying, so I got dressed and I went out on the street and I explained to the soldiers at the checkpoint about the woman's son, and they let her across. One of the soldiers said are you really Hoda al-Namani, and I said yes, and he said I've read your poems. Next time it was easier to help somebody across. That's all."

"That's *all?*"

"Well, you know poets are respected here, we're able to do these things because poetry is . . . what it is . . . it has *honor* in the Arab world."

"Weren't you afraid to go out there in the middle of the night, knowing they might just shoot?"

Hoda stared. "Of course. Wouldn't you be? I was scared to death."

"I think your family must be proud. You're fulfilling the Arabic poetic tradition, after all, fighting beside the armies, speaking up in political rallies."

"Proud?" Hoda turned. "No, not proud. Not even Abdul Kader is proud, nor the boys, I think, though they don't talk about it. They don't like me to go out, they're afraid for me, now especially because people are saying that my poetry, my *Sufi mystical* poetry, is becoming political. Look at this." She broke off arranging lettuce leaves artfully around the tabooli salad to get a scrapbook and show me a long interview in Arabic. "This one says I'm with the Palestinians, another one says I'm with the Sunni Muslims. The point is I am a *poet.*" She fairly shouted the word. "Poets are political always, because they are concerned with *life* and what is reality and all that . . . but I have to confess I hate all this nonsense"—she stuck the page in the scrapbook—"and I say so. What is happening to us? Oh God, what has *already* happened to us?

"Guests." She patted her hair in the hall mirror before she opened the door. Mme Aida was behind her, looking expectant. "Here they are, to meet you and Bob and your friend Jim," she called back. "Where *is* Bob?

"Nadia Twainey, my friend the poet; Muhammad Hallaj, you know his work, maybe, he is a Palestinian sculptor; this is B.J., my friend from America . . . her husband will be here soon . . . Where is your husband, Nadia? . . . Oh, I'm sorry, the flu is everywhere this winter . . . Oh yes, Sonia, I believe we did meet in the newspaper office one day, you are with Muhammad, welcome, and this is your sister Jihan, *ahlan wusahlan, enchantée* . . ."

We moved forward into the living room, followed by Hoda's mother, who looked carefully at everyone, out of those bright old eyes, admiring the chic clothes of the women, a black suit, a lilac silk dress, gold glittering at ears and wrists. Anis and Bassam came in from the hall. Bob and Jim followed.

Hoda's mother got up and came to be introduced to Bob and Jim. They were polite but then drifted off, Bob to talk to Anis, the younger son, who worked at the bank, and to Bassam, who had finished his Ph.D. at Columbia and was scheduled to go into the diplomatic service of Lebanon, "if there is any Lebanon left," I heard him say wryly.

"B.J.," hissed Hoda's mother to me in Arabic. "He is handsome still, your husband. You are lucky." She patted my hand. "Poor Abdul Kader. He might as well be dead." She looked strangely calm about the situation.

"It's hard for Hoda," I offered.

"Yes, but she has her *work*, you know," emphasizing the word in a somewhat sarcastic way.

Hoda was laying out the lunch, with Anis's help.

"We must eat," she announced. "*Tfaddalluu. Le dîner est servi.* Please!"

We filed in and circled the table with its tempting, aromatic dishes, picking up the heavy silverware, the thick damask napkins. Suddenly, Abdul Kader appeared, walking very slowly, supported by Bob and Bassam. He wore a dressing gown of old dark green brocade, a color that diminished the ashy quality of his skin. He accepted a glass of tomato juice and sat down near the dining room table.

Hoda put her hand on his arm, then went back to her guests. His eyes followed her. In the black and red gown, the red silk ribbon holding back her lustrous hair, she was explaining to Bob and Jim the sources of the Sufi poetic vocabulary, its meanings for Arab readers with knowledge of this rich literary tradition.

But at the center of one of her better-known poems is a simple, frightening line: "Despair began to spread like darkness, bullets began to make shadows, pointed shadows."

Not even the half-grown boys who guarded the checkpoints along the scarred line that split the city needed to know their Sufi symbolic heritage to understand that. They heard it all around them, every night, as they crouched, machine guns at the ready, in their lean-tos of old oil barrels and sandbags, four blocks from this house where we were dining elegantly on all the fruits of the Lebanese countryside and the refined wines of the West.

"I am tired, Hoda," said Abdul Kader. He rose with difficulty, and Anis and Hoda escorted him down the hallway and back to the mahogany bed.

Mme Aida watched them go, then settled herself in one of the rose velvet chairs, lit another forbidden cigarette, and waited for someone to bring her coffee.

THE TAXI DRIVER'S derisive titling of the American University as PLO University was not a joke people laughed at. The PLO was real, it was controversial, and it was relatively new on the Middle Eastern scene. In 1956 there was no PLO. Instead, we heard about Palestinian refugees living in camps and supported by the United Nations Relief and Works Administration (UNRWA), with contributions from the United States and other well-intentioned countries. We heard about how victimized the refugees felt themselves to be, but then the major step on the road to reconciliation was thought to be some form of compensation from Israel for the land it had seized from the Palestinians. The idea of an independent Palestinian homeland was not often discussed among Westerners in the Middle East; for many Palestinians it was a question not so much of a homeland as of returning to their own lands in Israel, a state that was still regarded as an unpleasant aberration which would soon pass.

In 1958 and 1959, while we were living in the United States, we were inclined to express optimism in saying that the passage of time might help, might heal. Young Arabs and Jews would grow up together in the Middle East and come to share similar outlooks and a desire for peace. Common economic interests would prevail; political differences would diminish in intensity. Such optimism was not uncommon among Western "specialists" at that time; indeed, before the 1967 war, even sophisticated Arabs would be heard expressing much the same sentiment—privately, of course.

What had happened in the past quarter century had completely belied our naïvely optimistic predictions. The "cause," the "desire to return to the homeland," had not disappeared but after the '67 war had taken the form of an ideological commitment superseding the political differences that had preoccupied the educated Palestinians of the fifties and early sixties, and transcending the class differences between the camp refugees and the prosperous Palestinians in other Arab countries. The new generation of Palestinians, whether the children of those driven from their homes or of Arabs still in Israel, became more organized, more determined, and more conscious of their past and their common cultural heritage than were their parents. The Palestine Liberation Organization was born. In 1981 people in Beirut talked about revolution.

Revolution? The word was not mentioned a generation ago except in reference to the still-recent struggle against direct colonial rule, or the current fight against colonial puppets, such as Nuri Sa'id's government in Iraq. Now, among the Palestinians, the *jeel al-nakba* (generation of the disaster) had been replaced by the *jeel al-thawra* (generation of the revolution). But revolution against what? No one could satisfactorily explain to us what this meant.

The issue seemed an interesting one to pursue, for my grant to make an educational film about social change in the Arab world from the women's perspective was to include political change. Since women's participation in the Palestinian movement or revolution was a new development, I thought it might be a good way of documenting both the political activity and the changing roles of women in the Arab world. But when we tried to talk to friends in Beirut about the whole subject, people's attitudes toward the "generation of the revolution" surprised us.

"Why do you want to make a film about the Palestinians?" people would ask. "Why not about us? We have suffered just as much." I replied that I saw the struggle as an example of a people's own desire for self-determination, and perhaps worth recording for the universal human qualities involved, similar to such struggles in other parts of the world and at other times in history.

"But what about us, the Lebanese?" people would insist. Suspicion, amusement, cynicism, disbelief, greeted us. We replied that indeed the Lebanese had suffered a great deal. But they were the victims of whom? The Palestinians, the Israelis, the Americans? Individuals of various sects and political opinions blamed different groups.

Would Lebanese friends be willing to discuss the situation, their doubts and fears, on film? People said no. They said it was becoming too dangerous to speak. "The Palestinians will probably be willing," they said. "They *want* to speak."

But it appeared we could not simply take a taxi to PLO headquarters and ask for permission to film or to visit the refugee camps. We had to be introduced. Thus, Dick Scott, longtime professor of philosophy at AUB, took me to visit Anny Kanafani, Danish-born widow of Ghassan Kanafani. Kanafani had tragically died in 1975 when his car was firebombed. A talented painter and writer, he had been a highly visible and articulate interpreter of the Palestinian cause while alive; dead, he became an immediate martyr.

"I want to do a film about women and the family," I said, "not the politics, but the people, and how they are dealing with constant crises."

Mme Kanafani nodded and promised to make some phone calls.

But in the end, it was two anonymous students at AUB, who had heard Bob lecture, who called and offered to set up a meeting with Majid Abu Sharrar, a member of the PLO Central Committee. We knew the students only as Hassan and Ali; they never gave us their second names because they said they did not want their parents to know they were involved.

The morning of the meeting, Ali and Hassan picked us up in a red VW bug, and as we maneuvered through the hair-raising daytime traffic—no police, no stoplights, no rules—Ali lectured us.

"The PLO are the only true revolutionaries in the Arab world."

"But what are they rebelling against?"

"It is a revolution against injustice, against the past, a revolution for a better future," said Hassan.

"A revolution for a return," said Ali.

Bob explained that we thought of revolution as a struggle against a particular government, a particular set of circumstances.

"Yes," said Ali. "You are right. That is what we are talking about. That set of circumstances is PALESTINE." His voice capitalized the word.

From the sea we had turned in and headed toward the airport, where market stalls, more makeshift than the ones along the beach, lined the road.

"These merchants are the ones most recently bombed out," explained Ali. "They don't need a permit here."

Ahead, where a large overpass arched over the main road, a heterogeneous collection of vehicles had gathered: old American trucks, Mercedeses, Jeeps, Peugeots. "It's the taxi station for the south," said Ali, "where you would go, *monsieur* and *madame*, if you got permission to visit the refugee camps." People with children and chickens and bundles and bags waited on curbs.

"Did we come this way before?" asked Bob.

"Probably not," said Ali. "They just reopened the road yesterday."

Past the taxi station we wound up the hill to the Arab University and turned left into a small street. Beside a store advertising Italian men's shirts at incredible reductions, Ali maneuvered his VW into an unpaved parking lot and we got out.

Ahead of us on the sidewalk, next to the display of Italian shirts, stood a symmetrical arrangement of sandbags and empty gasoline barrels, like those at the checkpoint stations along the airport road. But this checkpoint was set up next to a building, an apartment building. Two young men in those ubiquitous camouflage uniforms and baseball caps lounged beside the building, which was unmarked except for posters bearing names and slogans and photographs of the young men and women who had, said Ali, died for the revolution. The posters of the martyrs. Some were peeling from age and weather, the poster paper torn and shredded so that only an eye or a bit of mustache of the martyr was left affixed to the cement wall, a wall pocked with bullet scars and pitted by the hits of long-range shells. A few of the martyr posters were new, recently slapped on with paste; the ridges where the paste had not smoothed out showed like ripples of the sea across the young faces—startled, smiling, purposeful, scared faces of dead men and women.

"PLO. The Unified Command Headquarters," Ali said to us in low and somewhat reverent tones.

Bob and I looked at each other, then at the pair of young men in camouflage battle dress by the sandbags, who stood up straighter as we approached. They wore their machine guns over their shoulders as casually as backpacks or golf bags, but as we came nearer, their hands moved across their chests toward the weapons, slowly, purposefully.

Ali said hastily, "We have an appointment with Majid Abu Sharrar."

We were signaled in, to the elevator, and rose upward three flights to a bare hallway where other soldiers stood, guarding the door. "We have an appointment with Majid Abu Sharrar," repeated Ali.

"Not here," said the soldier, barring our passage with a rifle. We stood in the elevator uncertainly, the door opening and shutting.

Ali looked surprised and uncomfortable. "But we called," he said. "We were told to come *now.*"

A young girl emerged from a half-opened door that gave onto the hall we faced. She was thin; she wore very tight jeans and a gray sweatshirt. Her hair was cut in a fashionable Afro and she wore long gold earrings and Texas cowboy boots.

"Majid will be here soon," she said, tossing us a quick smile. "Let them wait in the office. Come on, Youssef!"

Tea was brought on a tin tray, tea in those tiny fluted glasses with gold rims, not by the girl, but by a boy in T-shirt and camouflage pants, wearing combat boots too large for him. He could not have been more than fourteen. He smiled engagingly at us.

"Welcome," he said.

Finally, Majid Abu Sharrar appeared, a dark-haired middle-aged man, handsome in dark suit and striped tie. Only the bulge of a weapon on his hip distinguished him from the businessmen lunching in restaurants on Rue Hamra. We shook hands. He looked at us carefully but did not smile. He read through the proposal for a film on Palestinian women, talked briefly with us about how we would do it, agreed it was a good idea, and gave us his personal phone numbers (two). While we sat there, he telephoned the PLO's public relations office to formally announce his agreement to our filming and give his permission for us to visit the refugee camps in the south.

Majid Abu Sharrar was as good as his word. When we returned to Lebanon in the spring, official permission was waiting for us, and we were able to head south to the refugee camps, to begin making final arrangements for filming.

Six months later, after I had taught my morning class at the University of Texas in Austin, a student came up with a recent French newspaper. "Another PLO leader has been assassinated," he said, pointing to a short article on the firebombing of a car in Beirut. A Peugeot 504. The dead man was Majid Abu Sharrar.

BUT THE FILM DID GET MADE. The all-woman crew arrived: Marilyn Gaunt, director; Diane Tammes, camera; Diana Ruston, sound; Lena Jayyusi, assistant. In May 1981, despite dire warnings from American and Lebanese friends and officials, we all headed south to Rashadiyah, one of the oldest Palestinian refugee camps. Since 1948, it has stood six miles from the Lebanese border with Israel. A young "translator" accompanied us, our representative from the Beirut office of the PLO. We were invited to stay in the house of Abu Zhivago, director of youth activities in the camp (soccer, gymnastics) and his wife, Um Zhivago, the only woman on the central committee that governed the camp. We filmed them at home, with their children, and at work. We filmed some of the nine thousand residents in their everyday lives, but focused on how the women were dealing with life under constant threat of attack. *Women Under Siege*, a thirty-minute documentary, premiered on Channel Four Television, London, in the fall of 1981 and was selected for later showing at the Royal Anthropological Institute Film Festival, also in London. But it was not shown on American television.

A year later, in 1982, came the Israeli invasion of Lebanon, followed by the massacre at the camps of Sabra and Shatila. We never heard from our friends in Rashadiyah again, though we were told that many had left, including Um and Abu Zhivago. Some were wounded, killed, or missing. As of 1982, Rashadiyah was still there on the border, smaller, poorer, but still home to Palestinian refugees who had no other place to seek refuge.

LEBANON AS IDEAL COMPROMISE

AMERICAN SOCIAL SCIENTISTS WITH Middle Eastern interests in the 1950s were entranced by Lebanon's apparent success in generating a free, capitalist, and pluralist society in which Muslim and Christian could live and work side by side in prosperity and harmony. The success of this constitutional state in which Muslims and Christians were given equal representation was frequently cited as an example of how religious differences could be mediated through institutionalized relationships, rather than becoming a basis for communal strife. Indeed, compromise and mediation were discovered as a basic form of interpersonal and intergroup relations at all levels of Lebanese society, and studies were devoted to the exploration of this as a model of both rural and urban social processes.

Implicitly, it was recognized that Lebanon was well on its way to becoming a class-organized society, but certainly a "healthy" one in which upward mobility, unhampered by ethnic or religious discrimination, would continue to provide opportunity for self-betterment. The Beirut elite included families from all the major religious groups in the country. The American University in Beirut, most prestigious among the several local institutions of higher education, had a student body with representatives from all the minorities, even though the core of its enrollment was the children of the elite and the near elite of Beirut itself, as well as of the entire Arab world. So, as in America, education provided possibilities for upward mobility available to anyone who could qualify for admission and pay the bills. The need for a college-educated labor force seemed inexhaustible as the banks and businesses multiplied. There was no suppressed minority in Lebanon, it was argued, no underclass of people who did all the dirty work.

Except the Palestinians. Of course, the refugee problem was unfortunate. The poorest and least well educated Palestinians had ended up in the camps around Beirut while the middle class moved to better districts of the city or went to other Arab countries. This was hardly Lebanon's fault. It was up to the United Nations to take care of training and relocating the refugees. Admirers of Lebanon's model constitution certainly didn't feel the need to take the Palestinians into account in contemplating the country's rosy future.

If political scientists waxed enthusiastic over the constitutional mediation of intergroup relations in Lebanon, social anthropologists were no less excited over the way in which kinship ties seemed to bridge class differences and offer a leg up in the world even for country cousins without benefit of formal education. Ties of blood took precedence over all else, obligating the rich to help their poor relatives. It was a question of honor. A wealthy relative in Beirut could be called upon to provide jobs for village kinfolk or help them deal with government officials or educational expenses. Politicians distributed their favors among kin in return for their support (in elections, of course), and kinship extended outward to include hundreds of relatives over great distances. It was ward politics writ large, tying together town and country, rich and poor, and guaranteeing admirable stability while the rest of the Middle East experienced the traumas of revolution and military coups.

The notion that ties of kinship could mesh with constitutional government and result in a modern, progressive nation was very pleasing to liberal American political scientists and anthropologists alike, for it suggested that modern legal institutions and traditional patterns of human relationship could coexist rather than replace each other. As long as Shia and Sunni, Maronite and Orthodox leadership all had a hand in the Lebanese government, and thus had a portion of patronage and influence to share among the less fortunate members of their respective clienteles, how could differences between the haves and the have-nots become a matter of general importance? The only problem was that each group must continue to get its fair share. But since Lebanon was the principal center of East-West trade in the Middle East, there seemed no reason why local prosperity should falter. Self-interest would continue to make the status quo more attractive than any attempt at radical change.

Thus, class differences and kinship networks were seen to be in complementary distribution in Lebanon. The lines of possible conflict were balanced by ties of common interest. Peaceful coexistence between class and ethnic groups seemed assured.

How does one explain the total inadequacy of this 1950s "expert" opinion about Lebanon? How could the seeds of civil conflict, already taking root in the late fifties and early sixties, have been so completely overlooked or underestimated by American specialists? In part to blame, of course, was the nature of research on which such opinion was based. Anthropologists studied villages; political scientists studied "political institutions." In both cases the forest was overlooked and the trees were a focus of myopic attention, though of course everyone was behaving according to the best tradition of his or her discipline. In fact, even all of Lebanon would not have been sufficient as the unit of study if scholars were to have predicted that this country, a defenseless outpost of Western and Middle Eastern capitalism, was soon to be seized by contesting foreign powers and torn apart. Furthermore, Western social science of the fifties was possessed by a quest for social order; even conflict was seen as producing in-group solidarity, never as the basis for further and greater disorder.

Nor was sufficient attention paid by foreign observers to the fact that Beirut, the center of Lebanon, is a commercial, not an industrial, city. Factories, large-scale manufacturers, might have offered opportunities for "free" labor, detached from established sects and kin groups, a chance for a working class to develop which could have included Palestinians along with Lebanese. But a commercial city is full of businesspeople who hire only their own kind. White-collar jobs predominated; a broad-scale working class never developed. Thus, the refugees of 1948 were still refugees when they were joined by thousands more Palestinians in the aftermath of the 1967 war, and it was the children of refugees, facing the same future, who provided the rank and file of the PLO.

So it was the Palestinians, their thirst for their lost homeland unrelieved by their position in Lebanon, who were overlooked and underestimated in the 1950s and 1960s by American social scientists—and American politicians. To have reckoned with this unhappy population full of hatred for the Israelis, and equally resentful toward the Lebanese well-to-do and the Americans with their unfulfilled promises, would have been to admit to ourselves a level of blame and responsibility we still refuse to accept.

> No doubt
> *Peace-making should be easy. But I ask*
> *when did the tigers pull their own claws out?*
>
> Ilyas Farhat
> QUATRAINS

MIDDLE EAST AIRLINES was the last airline to desert Beirut during the ten years of the Lebanese civil war, and the first to return after hostilities ended in 1991. Thus, it seemed appropriate to be on Middle East Airlines for our first trip back to Beirut in fourteen years.

Tom Hartwell had come along to take pictures of the city, which, we were told, was in the throes of enthusiastic reconstruction. While skimming the clouds from Cairo to Beirut, Middle East Airlines served us a lunch of cold roast chicken and salad washed down with French champagne and Evian water. This seemed a good omen for what we might find in newly peaceful Beirut.

We had last seen Beirut under fire in 1981, a traumatic and dangerous time. Then the airline ground facilities had been a shambles. Now here we were landing smoothly at a completely rebuilt airport. The walls, newly painted, bore scenic posters of touristic Lebanon: the Roman pillars of Baalbek; reconstruction in the center of Beirut; the famous cedars photographed in the snowy northern mountains. We proffered our pieces-of-paper visas to the passport control official, who sat at a new desk in a freshly starched uniform. He stamped them and actually smiled.

Our dear friend Hoda al-Namani and her son Anis were waiting for us. In five minutes we were outside the airport, loading our luggage into Anis's new Chevrolet van.

"Welcome! Welcome!" Hoda repeated, smiling as she climbed in front with Anis.

We were stopped momentarily at the guard box outside the airport. The policeman tipped his hat and motioned us on.

"That's a change," said Bob. "Last time, we were stopped every other block by different militias, and they all seemed to be teenage boys with Kalashnikovs."

"And they just didn't stand there," put in Tom. "They were shooting at us, at the plane, everywhere." Tom had actually caught a piece of shrapnel in his flight jacket while running for cover during a 1986 photographic assignment for *Time*.

"Oh," said Hoda firmly, "let's not talk about then. It's over. Come and have supper. We are all happy to be back in a *quiet* Beirut and we're glad to see you back, too."

Neither of us mentioned our last meeting, the day of condolences on the death of Abdul Kader, Hoda's husband. Their apartment stood in a house near the Green Line, the unmarked boundary between the major warring factions, who continued to bombard the house even while the religious sheikh was intoning the *fatiha*, the Koranic prayers for the dead. Anis, the younger, banker son now driving us into the city, and Bassam, the older, now Lebanese consul in London, had moved heavy furniture against the closed velvet drapes to muffle the sounds of the shelling that punctuated, erratically and frighteningly, the rise and fall of the sheikh's deep voice as he recited the prayers. The Namanis had finally left Beirut for London in 1986, as the war continued and the apartment building became the center of fiercer and fiercer battles.

But the family was also one of the first to return when peace broke out. Anis and Bassam had come as advance guards, had urged their mother not to return to the old flat. She was determined, however, to reclaim her home, despite the fact that it had been nearly destroyed.

"Even the faucets were gone from the bathrooms," Hoda told us later, "and the electric wires had been chopped off at the ceiling. But the walls and the floor and ceiling were there, so we could manage."

We sped along in the darkness in Anis's van. Shifting light and shadow from the new streetlights revealed dark humps which could have been houses or ruins, squares that could have been frames for new construction or leftovers from bombed buildings. Who could say?

"We will do some touring in the morning, Bob," said Anis in reply to our unasked questions. "There's a lot going on, but it's hard to see at night. At least the streetlights are working." He sighed. "And don't forget, we're still recovering from a long and horrible siege."

"Horrible," repeated Hoda. "And parts of it are still horrible." She wore black pants and blouse, appropriate dress for artists world-wide. But she also wore a black voile jacket over the blouse, sheer, captivating, and she had fixed big circles of silver in her ears. The fashionable Hoda I remembered. "But our house is the same again, B.J. You will see."

Anis was on his cellular phone, taking the curves along the Mediterranean with one hand. "Start up the generator, Lamshiat," he was saying. "Yes, now. We're nearly there."

"Mother insisted on coming back to this building," he explained, "even though the owners of the building still hadn't done basic repairs. So don't expect too much."

We turned onto a quiet street, and when Anis had parked and doused the car lights, we could see nothing at all. There were no street-lights here.

"Electricity and water are unreliable," went on Anis, "so we bought a generator for Mother. It's on the balcony." He laughed shortly. "A generator of her very own."

Hoda giggled, the first time she had laughed, and I immediately felt better. Her laughter was something I remembered and had savored for years—laughter at pomposity and boredom—polite but cheerful, a good tonic in any social climate.

"You will see, B.J.," she repeated.

The elevator was not working, so we climbed the stairs with the help of flashlights, to find a red candle in an ornate brass candlestick burning outside Hoda's front door, which was now two front doors, one of heavy metal to discourage bullets, one of proper polished wood.

"That looks like it would keep anyone out," said Bob in some awe.

Hoda looked at him. "With machine guns, they shot the hinges off very easily," she said. And to prove her point, as Anis raised the candle, we could see long scars in the metal.

Lamshiat, young, brown, and slim, opened the inner door. She was smiling.

"I did turn on the generator, *madame*, yes," she said in a smooth rush of words, "honoring your guests from the United States."

She ushered us into the apartment, which, after the dark of the street and the stairs, seemed to fairly blaze with electric light. We walked through one room after another, familiar rooms, Hoda turning on lights in French wall sconces, in rosy-shaded lamps, in the crystal chandelier in the dining room, where the table was set for dinner. Here was the furniture I remembered, the silver fruit basket on the heavy mahogany sideboard, the velvet chairs, the balconies open to the dark streets below and to the friendly winking of lights in the occupied flats opposite.

"Hoda, it's as though you never left. It's just like it was," I murmured.

She clapped her hands. "What do you think, Bob?"

"It *is* like it was," he answered. "How did you do it?"

"Well, it wasn't easy," she said, and glanced at Anis, who was pouring himself and Tom and Bob drinks from the sideboard. "Everyone helped. Anis. Bassam. Friends. We moved everything out in 1986, shipped it to London for the five years we were there, shipped it back again."

We dined by the light of the glittering chandelier, a European meal of soups and meats and breads. But for dessert, we had *mugli,* the concoction of walnuts, almonds, cinnamon, and caraway devised specially to be served at Middle Eastern celebrations of births and the naming of children. Why for us?

"It's for Beirut, not for you," Hoda told us a bit shyly, as though afraid we would laugh at her sentimentality. But of course we did not. We felt honored and welcome.

"Beirut," repeated Anis.

"They say it's picking up, at least that's what my journalist friends say," put in Tom.

"Well, it's never going to be like it used to be," said Anis firmly. "It'll never be the center of Middle Eastern economic life like it was before the war."

Tom protested. "Surely the Gulf bankers will come back."

Anis shook his head. "No, it's different now. The old sheikhs have sons who've been to business school in London and the States. They drive Mercedeses and Porsches like their dads, but they can also

handle computerized banking. They don't need Lebanese bankers to
hold their hands anymore.''

"But still," said Bob, "there must be lots of money in Beirut."

"No, Bob, not so much," answered Anis. "My bank is the biggest
in Beirut. It has a capital of sixty million dollars. No comparison with
London, where half the daily worldwide trading of two hundred billion
is done. No," Anis repeated, "in the future when all the Arab states
have signed their peace accords, I suppose money will come through
London and Tel Aviv, not Beirut."

Bob and Tom looked uncomfortable. The idea of the Arab world
doing its international business through Tel Aviv was hard for them to
accept.

"I don't know . . ." ventured Tom.

And the lights went out. We were plunged into civil war darkness. Hoda called to Lamshiat, who could be heard moving toward the
back balcony where the generator had been installed, behind the
kitchen and servants' room. "No, Lamshiat! Don't start it. Let it cool."

Hoda turned to us. "Last week that girl started a fire when the
candle caught the benzine. I lost a good linen sheet smothering the
flames."

Tom was standing up. "Thank you very much," he said. "I
should be moving on to my hotel downtown."

Anis, who had gone to inspect the generator, came back with
flashlights. "I'll take you, Tom, on my way home."

"Good night."

"Good night, Mother. Take care, good night."

We could hear Anis and Tom making their way down the broken
stairs with the aid of flashlights, stumbling and laughing as they went.
Hoda was lighting more candles that stood ready for such emergencies,
in candlesticks of silver, brass, china, copper.

The soft light flickered over the golden bananas and the darkly
shadowed plums heaped in the silver fruit basket, on the sideboard over
the blue wineglasses and the remains of dinner on the table.

Bob and I and Hoda moved into the living room and sat quietly,
sipping the last of the wine. It seemed incredible that we should be
sitting here again after fourteen years, that all the furnishings around
us—the chairs, drapes, tables, sideboard, the chandelier, silver fruit basket, the candelabra, and the wineglasses—had been packed away for five

long years and only recently returned to their proper places in this comfortable and elegant room. A slight breeze moved the flowers on the coffee table, carrying a strong whiff of benzine and burning tallow, bringing us back to reality, to the problems of everyday life, in a city still trying to put itself together.

We stood up in the dark, and the electricity suddenly flared on again. Lamshiat marched in, a slight brown figure wearing a triumphant expression on her oval face. "It came on, *madame*. You see. It came on by itself. Yes!"

"Yes, yes," answered Hoda impatiently, but she laughed again and turned to us. "Let's get to bed before it goes off again!"

THE CIVIL WAR BROUGHT OUT the best and the worst in Lebanese society, people said to us in the shops, at the American University, in the restaurants, in the homes of old and new friends. The constant but unpredictable clashes in the streets made everyone wary, careful, including us as we had walked about the embattled city in 1981. Yet the conflicts came and went, in waves. According to Rosemary Sayigh, our friend the sociologist who stayed in Beirut during most of the conflict, a horrible period of killing and shooting and shelling would be followed by a pause. "And then we'd have a few days of peace," she said. "We'd all shop, jog on the beach, go about our business, teach classes." Rosemary had done so herself at the American University of Beirut.

We had noted the resilience of merchants in 1981, merchants who were bombed out one day and who might set up shop in the ruins the following day, displaying a few choice pieces of merchandise. This phenomenon was admiringly noted by Western journalists, who wrote about "the indomitable Lebanese merchants, who never miss a chance to make a sale." Individualism, they wrote, "is triumphing here." The need to make a living was also, obviously, a consideration.

As the conflict went on and on, the principal merchants and bankers got tired of dealing with the constant insecurity and moved out of the center of Beirut to set up shop in smaller communities along its periphery. By 1995 Antelias and Jounieh, once sleepy villages, were booming commercial suburbs offering some of the best selections of goods, restaurants, and movie houses in the greater Beirut region. The big disadvantage of Antelias and Jounieh, however, is the horrendous traffic, which winds sluggishly along the two-lane coastal highway, still the only access out of the center of the city. Thus none of our Lebanese friends thought central Beirut was in danger of slow decline. On the contrary, the convenience of its location, the excellent port, and institutions like the American University combined to make the area both appealing and profitable.

Individualism is triumphing once more in an ambitious effort to restore Beirut. The principal individual involved is Rafik al-Hariri, president of Lebanon, who made a huge fortune in Saudi Arabia in the construction business and who then came back to apply his financial and organizational acumen to the rebuilding of his native land. Since he did not live in Lebanon during the period of the civil war, his claim to leadership is not blemished by past association with any of the sides in the conflict.

Hariri, a Sunni Muslim, was asked by political and economic leaders to form a government in 1992, after elections that more or less sealed a truce between Lebanon's different warring factions. At the time, he announced his intention to invest his own money in the reconstruction of Lebanon, and it seems obvious that his continued expenditure of personal funds for both commercial and humanitarian purposes has helped ensure his continuing political success.

The main instrument of Hariri's reconstruction plan is an economic consortium whose initials spell out "Solidère." The upbeat name of the group, like a response in a French football rally, is both celebrated and reviled in Beirut. The first criticism heard everywhere was that the consortium, supposedly financed independently through Lebanese and foreign nations, was headed by the president himself. "Too much power in the hands of one man" is the general opinion.

How was the president able to justify this bold act? We met with Ramez Maluf, Solidère's public relations director, in the Solidère office. The answer, he told us, lay in old Lebanese law, which allowed community development committees (CDCs) to be created as independent entities to improve neighborhoods afflicted by war or other disasters. Hariri supposedly said, "Why not do the whole downtown on the same principle?" He had not only the idea but his own money to back it up.

"We've heard some criticism of this approach," Bob said.

"Of course," replied Maluf. He used the entry of a waiter bringing us hospitable cups of Turkish coffee to let a small pause stretch on. He sipped his coffee, looked again at Bob, and smiled cheerily.

"There will always be critics of success. And Solidère is successful. But remember, it's not just Hariri. We have a hundred thousand shareholders. Hariri only owns six percent of the pie. And there's no doubt that this project has already transformed Lebanon."

"Already?" echoed Bob. "I thought the plans specified three years, even ten."

"Yes, yes, to be completely finished. But the marketplace is set to open in 1998," Ramez said. "And you should have seen it here before we started working."

"Well, we spent some time here in 1981. Things were pretty bad then," answered Bob.

Ramez leaned forward and focused on us. "So you saw some of the problems we're having to deal with. And you've been here long enough this time, I hear, to see how the city moved out to Jounieh and Antelias. Why? Because the center had gone to hell."

Bob and I said nothing.

"For years, my friends," he continued, and a certain amount of passion had crept into his voice, "there were open sewers everywhere. Rats would jump into your car if you drove downtown with your windows open. Terrible. Disease. All that. And squatters filled the buildings . . ."

"Yes," said Bob, who now leaned forward himself. "What about the squatters?"

"They have been compensated for moving out," Ramez answered quickly, dropping the subject.

WE MET A CRITIC OF Solidère in a brand-new chrome and glass coffee shop near the Art Museum, one of the few dignified beautiful old Beirut buildings left intact by the ravages of the civil war. A couple sat next to us, holding hands, he in designer jeans and tight-fitting shirt, she in a miniskirt and a low-cut cotton top. They were drinking espresso, as we were, and it was excellent (coffee imported from Italy, the waiter said). The cream puffs were baked this morning, the waiter added.

The young man with whom we had an appointment was late. He is a political analyst in a local think tank which devoted itself to the consideration of the problems facing all of Lebanon in these postwar years.

"I'm sorry. I was delayed on the road. The traffic's awful," he said. "But I'm so glad to meet you. I read your book *The Arab World,* in college."

"We're trying to update *The Arab World,*" explained Bob. "And we're interested in Solidère, its backers and its critics."

The young man smiled. He ordered himself an espresso, "but no cream puff," and said to us, "You must certainly see why we are very critical of Solidère's approach. Can you imagine such a thing being allowed in the United States? The president a major investor in such a consortium?"

Bob nodded and agreed. "But of course it isn't the same situation," he pointed out. "Who else is going to lay out cash to do such mundane things as build new sewage lines?"

The young man looked surprised. Clearly, he expected us to agree with him and lambaste President Hariri for his unbelievable arrogance in gathering so much power, economic as well as political, to himself. He looked down and concentrated on his coffee. Then he raised his head, and his face wore an exasperated look as he tried to deal with these dense foreigners who had spent so much time in the Arab world they had clearly forgotten the ideals of their American heritage: church and state apart, politics and economics proceeding along separate pathways. He smiled bravely and took another tack.

"But the plans are so bourgeois," he said. "Shopping malls à la Dallas or Los Angeles or something similar. What about our Arab heritage? Surely, you can understand our need to continue that heritage?"

Bob smiled. "I do understand that, believe me. But ask yourself, what would a traditional but modern Arab market look like? Small shops close to each other, selling lots of different things. Called boutiques, maybe? All kinds of people walking close together, stopping in cafés, boys checking out the girls—hey, that sounds to me like a mall!"

The young man was polite. "I see what you mean, Professor Fernea. But I guess what I'm saying about Solidère is that we had hoped for a more democratic approach to the rebuilding of Lebanon."

Bob relented. "Yes, of course," he allowed. "But what is the alternative to Solidère?"

"A good question," he answered. He finished his coffee and rose to shake hands. "You might enjoy visiting the museum," he suggested. "And some of the old houses are very beautiful. That's all part of our heritage, too," he added, "as well as the malls!"

We walked to the museum in the clear May air, admiring the fine old stone houses along the way, set in gardens, where bougainvillea spilled scarlet and orange blossoms over the walls. The museum itself occupied one of these old houses.

The young man was right, of course: the venerable old houses and the gleaming coffee shops were the combination of old and new that was the hoped-for model for a modern Lebanon, one that would provide for all citizens and ideally would be achieved by a national consensus.

But consensus has never been easy to achieve in Lebanon, a country that has always honored ethno-religious independence, and where a laissez-faire attitude toward the relation between business and government has been carried to extremes. Some of the academic experts, while praising Lebanese individual enterprise during the long trials of the civil war, have questioned whether this kind of individualism is what is needed in the long run. A stronger sense of national community could have overcome the small, fierce parochial and confessional concerns that helped split Lebanon into warring groups. Such a sense will clearly have to develop if peace is to continue.

No taxis were to be found, so we kept walking, toward Hoda's house on the Green Line, that old battle line that divided East from West, Muslim from Christian, during the civil war. Here devastation was the rule. We walked past parts of buildings, broken trees, deep ditches, some half-full of standing water, past clumps of twisted iron standing up in weedy fields.

"Didn't Naples look something like this after World War II?" Bob asked. "Even in the fifties, when we went through, there were whole blocks of bombed-out buildings, and people living in them."

Here and there, along the streets, apartments still stood, but their outer walls had been blasted away, literally stripped off, so we could see into the ruins of what had once been people's homes: a room totally bare except for a fireplace and one hanging wooden shutter; another where flowered paper still covered the back wall. On the very top floor of a corner building, the sun caught a flash of blue; it was a recliner chair, positioned close to the open side of the once-spacious apartment. An old man was sitting in the blue recliner. Hands folded on his knees, he surveyed us from his perch—we were two of many strangers who walked daily through what was left of his city, the city once called the Paris of the Middle East. Was that a blanket behind the old man? Or was it a tarpaulin, rolled up like a window blind to be unrolled at night to shield part of the old man's room from public sight?

"He must have a great view of the sea," I said sadly.

We walked along, but Bob turned back. The old man still seemed to be watching us.

"I wonder where he'll end up, poor guy," said Bob. "He hasn't left, even if he has been compensated, as the Solidère people say. I hate the term 'squatter,' " he added firmly. "It's demeaning."

"Is it the term or the way such people are treated that's demeaning?" I asked.

There were exceptions, of course, to the general appearance of destruction that pervaded Beirut. Here and there buildings had been refurbished, presumably by their owners. Painted in fresh colors of blue, white, pink, green, they stood out among the ruins like wildflowers in a stony field.

Cars roared along the roads, between the scarred buildings, but no taxis. We kept walking, passing vendors hawking, along the broken streets, items eminently usable in this changing, slowly rebuilding city: large and small flashlights; handheld fans, battery-operated; plastic water bottles. By the time we reached the boulevard that marks the Green Line, the road was divided by a median of crude but effective obstacles. It was a way to recycle worn-out tires. One tire was set flat on the ground, another propped upright inside it, and the perpendicular construction was held in place by a jagged slab of broken stone. No one seemed likely to jump these barriers and risk smashing their clean, bright cars, the new cars that were being imported daily into the reviving economic market of Lebanon.

Finally, we reached the turnoff to Hoda's house, marked by film flyers, pasted on the corner wall, advertising the new American comedy flic *Dumb and Dumber*. And here, though the streets had been partially repaved, covering up the bomb craters, wires were strung around the street, as they were strung everywhere in Beirut, fine thin wires, spliced wires, wires covered with metal cables.

Later that afternoon when Anis drove us all on a tour of old and new Beirut, Bob asked about the skeins of wires everywhere. Anis called it a healthy sign.

"They're telephone wires," he said, "and electric wires that might soon make my mother's balcony generator unnecessary."

But the wires were looped carelessly across streets and wound around houses like giant webs spun of steel, some close enough to the ground to be risky.

"True, true," Anis allowed. "Actually, I've already complained about the phone wires by my mother's house. The phone is her lifeline, and ours too. We *need* the phones. How can we make money otherwise? Isn't that what Lebanese are supposed to do?" He laughed.

Someone is making money, for he told us that a square meter of land in West Beirut costs $3,000. An apartment in one of the newly rising blocks along the seashore, with magnificent views of the blue Mediterranean, goes for $1 million to $3 million.

"Who is buying?" asked Bob.

"Saudis, Gulf Arabs," Anis answered. "A few Lebanese who profited during the war."

"Profited?" I asked incredulously.

"Ever heard of the arms trade, merchants of death, all that business, dear?" Bob asked sweetly.

"Yes," said Hoda. "Life is not like before. The elites in Beirut used to be intellectuals, poets, painters, doctors, professors—well, at least people who were well educated and had good taste. Now it's just money. Money and influence, *wasta*. Who you know. Who can speak for you. Who *will* speak for you."

"But that's always been the case, hasn't it?" Bob said.

Anis laughed. "Of course. Mother knows that. What she means is that the people she knew who used to have *wasta* don't seem to have it anymore. A new set has taken over. And we have to change, too."

CHANGE. Art is also changing. Hoda, who raised her children in Cairo in the sixties and did some modest writing then, had now become a celebrity in Beirut. At least, this was the way it seemed to Bob and me.

Her poetry is now widely published in newspapers and magazines throughout the Arabic-speaking world. Many of her poems about the *intifada*, about the Lebanese camped out in the lobby of her apartment building, about Beirut's wartime ordeal, were first published in *Nahar*, perhaps Beirut's most widely respected daily newspaper. Though deeply personal, her work is also a broader commentary on the human condition, a commentary that has grown out of her pain over the suffering and destruction of her country and her countrymen.

Recently, a prominent Lebanese composer came to tea and took away with him the text of her most recent work, a play in verse set in hell. The characters represent the four principal antagonists in the civil war: the Sunni Muslims, Shia Muslims, Maronite Christians, and Greek Orthodox Christians. In Hoda's play, God is passing judgment on their actions, explaining why they all deserve to burn in hell. This is to be the libretto of an opera the composer has scheduled to premiere in an international arts festival. The festival, to celebrate Lebanon's new peace, is funded by a grant from the Hariri Foundation.

"President Hariri?" Bob asked. "Solidère?"

"Oh yes," said Anis with a smile. "The president's personal foundation has been a great donor to the arts and sciences. That's another of his activities!"

"I wrote that play during the war," explained Hoda. "But of course no one would even publish it then. It was considered too inflammatory," she said.

Hoda actually had become not only a celebrity but a kind of legend, for her poetry, yes, but also because of her steadfast devotion to her city, and her refusal to leave, even after most of her friends and relatives had fled. What had finally prompted her departure? I asked.

"A bomb," she answered.

"A bomb?" I hadn't heard this part of the story.

"Yes. One day a soldier came to my door and told me they were leaving. The battle line was moving back and they'd put a bomb in the foyer so the building would go up if the enemy tried to shell it."

"He *told* you. Why?"

"Well, you know, B.J., they were nice to me, those young soldiers. I told you all that long ago. They'd read my poems and liked them."

I did remember, for when I'd come that last day, fourteen years ago, to pay my respects on the death of Abdul Kader, Hoda's husband, the soldiers were there in the foyer. Young. Weary. Unshaven. Sitting on the marble floor, backs against sandbags, rifles propped against the wall nearby. They had sprung up at my arrival, but when I explained I'd come to see the poet whose husband had just died, they nodded and waved me up the stairs. They knew Hoda, all right. They'd warned her so she, the last resident, wouldn't be blown up with the building.

"So how did you get out?"

"They brought me a ladder before they left and I used it to get down. I was afraid the bomb would go off if I walked on the lobby floor. I mean, I didn't know exactly where the bomb was—and if it was safe, why, then, did the soldier bring me a ladder?"

"So you went down by yourself?"

"Yes. Out on the balcony, down the ladder, and up to that little store at the end of the street, and I called Anis and he came and got me. Yes, they were shooting, but I dodged in and out."

She was wearing black again, with the sheer chiffon overshirt, and gold hoops in her ears. She didn't look much like a grandmother who was friendly with civil war militias on both sides and who also had enough grit to climb down a high ladder onto the street in the middle of a pitched battle. If Hoda had become an example of compassion and determination to her Lebanese fellow citizens, she was a good one.

And lately, Hoda had taken up painting again. She had joined some elementary classes when we all lived in Cairo and she was clearly more talented than most, but Bob and I were quite unprepared for the mature abstractions she was exhibiting regularly—in London during their stay there, and a new show in Beirut, closed just before we came.

"The president wanted one of them," she said, pleased. "But so far he hasn't come over to choose."

"Mother needs to sell some paintings," said Anis. He had come over for tea with his two young daughters while his wife gave a paper at an economic conference in Alexandria. "Don't give them away, sell them!" he added good-naturedly.

Hoda smiled. "Your daughters are talented, too," she said, and Anis's girls jumped up and down, pleased to be praised by their glamorous grandmother.

Anis said, a bit proudly, "Did Mother tell you she's been invited to take part in a show organized by the French ambassador?"

Bob and I looked at her. "Everyone was asked to create something in a traditional Arab genre," she said. "Calligraphy. I was a bit surprised. Some of our famous painters have never done calligraphy in all their lives!"

"So did you agree? Did other Lebanese artists agree?" asked Bob.

"Yes, yes, I agreed," said Hoda. "Most people agreed . . ."

"Why—if that's not the genre they work in?" Bob was curious.

Hoda looked at Anis and they both laughed, a bit embarrassed.

"Well," said Hoda, "the French ambassador, after all . . ." She spread her hands and smiled at our naïveté.

Yes, indeed, I thought, the French ambassador. The Lebanese love affair with the French was long and sustained, and had survived pacification, colonial rule, the imposition of French curricula into the Lebanese schools, missionaries, civil war, and economic relationships. French had in recent years been slowly replaced by English and Arabic as the languages of commerce, but it lived on, with French cuisine, wine, furniture, and fashion, in the homes and hearts of the elite, both Muslim and Christian.

American influence had taken hold early with the nineteenth-century founding of the American University of Beirut, and grown in the 1950s when President Eisenhower stopped the Suez war and sent American troops to keep the peace. But that influence almost disappeared with the dreadful events of the seventies and eighties: the blowing up of the marine barracks (241 dead); the destruction of the American Embassy along the Corniche (50 dead); the kidnapping of American journalists and teachers; and the senseless and as yet unsolved assassination of our old friend Malcolm Kerr, president of the American University and himself the descendant of American educators and clergy with ties to Beirut.

In 1995 the continued American support for the Israeli "buffer zone," the ten-mile swath of Lebanon along the southern border, was seen as counterproductive to Lebanese security and a sore point in American-Lebanese diplomatic relations. The Americans stated that the Israeli presence was necessary to match and to prevent the rocket firing and other incursions into Israel by the Iran-supported Hezbollah, the

Party of God. Lebanon, American policy-makers pronounced, would remain closed to Americans until the Lebanese "dealt with" and "put out of commission" the Shia communities that fought against the Israeli occupation. Another issue was the ubiquitous presence of the Syrians throughout Lebanon. Since attacking the Syrians or the Hezbollah or both was tantamount to asking the fragile coalition of Muslims and Christians that formed the current central government to become immersed in a new civil war, it was not likely to happen soon.

The French, however, had no such qualms. At the end of the civil war in 1991, they had quickly reestablished economic and political ties. We met French businessmen wherever we went, we saw that shops in Ras Beirut and in Antelias stocked clothes from Paris at good prices, and we were told that several French firms were involved in the construction plans of Solidère. The French had also launched a cultural offensive. The Société des Arts Décoratifs, an international trade show of French furniture, painting, design, textiles, and other crafts, had set up shop near the port, a long gleaming snowy white tent, with tricolors flying from its top and sides.

The calligraphy show, to which Hoda had contributed two large abstractions, was a French curtsy toward local art. A concert and poetry reading, to which Hoda had also been invited, was scheduled later in June. For these events the French ambassador was the guiding patron, and had offered as the site for the showings the old ambassadorial residence on the Green Line, closed since a terrible night of bombardment during the war years had killed the then ambassador, his wife, and several aides and embassy guards. The calligraphy show was to include a ceremonial reopening of the nineteenth-century gates, a reaffirmation of the friendship between France and Lebanon. Showing Lebanese art in a French setting on Lebanese soil would recast, in symbolic terms, the old colonial embrace.

The engraved card invited Mme al-Namani and her family to a *vernissage* on May 31, 1995. The French word *vernissage* conveys much more a sense of anticipation, of emotional excitement, than does the prosaic English equivalent, "opening reception." *Vernissage* has as its root *vernis* (greenery) and implies blossoming, rebirth, renaissance.

"We might as well go," said Hoda tentatively.

From her tone I was not certain she wanted us along.

"No, no," Hoda protested. "I want you to come. You don't have to, but if you do, maybe Tom," she added with a giggle, "could take pictures of me, of us."

She paused a moment. "But I don't think there will be food. The French never overdo these things." She hid a smile.

"What about Anis? Isn't he invited, too?"

"Yes, but he needs to pick up his wife, Nahid, from the airport. The conference went well, he says."

"Solved all the economic problems of the area, no doubt," quipped Tom.

Hoda stared at him. "You are joking, I know. But Nahid told Anis over the phone that there were fifteen hundred firms represented there. Even some Israelis."

"Big business," said Bob cryptically, but Hoda did not smile.

So we dressed in our best and walked with Hoda out the door of her shell-shocked apartment building and across the wide boulevard with its tire-and-broken-stone barriers that had only five years ago served as a battle line, a crossing point of prisoners, businessmen, orphans, arms shipments. In the high stone wall that continued half a mile along the east side of the boulevard, a set of heavy metal gates stood ajar. After eight years the old French official residence was open again, for art, for social life, for diplomatic receptions. The sun was bright and the great, unpruned fica trees in front of the residence cast the kind of dappled shade one expects to find in the French countryside. Artists (at least we presumed they were artists) clustered at the entrance, marking who was coming and going. A dignified French gentleman (we presumed he was French) sat at a desk by the front door, dispensing tickets and name tags.

The residence was a shell, a ruin. A huge and magnificent ruin, but still a ruin, the scarred remnants of its walls exhibiting traces of eighteenth- and nineteenth-century French and Lebanese architectural styles. The stone floor was still there, though scarred and pitted by shells, and the marble staircase that wound gracefully round and up to the floors above bore a sign in Arabic and French: "Unsafe: do not go beyond this point."

Easels had been placed in the windowless banquet halls and in small sheltered nooks created by the protective stone buttresses in the walls. Arabic calligraphy was exhibited on long scrolls of parchment, decorated by illuminated borders of leaves. There was calligraphy carved in wood, and in stone, calligraphy inked in tiny exquisite patterns, calligraphy with the name of God hidden in the swirls of a rose, a peacock, a boat. And calligraphy in French as well, a long poem by Comte Kristian Joseph Ostrowski, which began *"O filles du Liban sous les tulipes roisers."* The modern abstractions, in oils and acrylics, paid obeisance in their lines and swaths of color to the forms of the Arabic language.

Hoda's works were there, too, layers of gold overlaid on the canvases, the calligraphic signs, black, abstracted within the gold.

"This is awful, don't you think, Hoda?" A middle-aged man with a ravaged face came up to us. "I refused to have my paintings shown in this charnel house."

Hoda introduced us with a somewhat embarrassed air. "This is Wagih Nakhleh, our most esteemed painter."

"How do you do?" I said politely.

He responded by urging me to come outside, "where my paintings show to best advantage." I followed him meekly.

"Here!" He gestured toward two huge dark canvases, set where the dying sun glinted on the raised textures of thick paint, applied liberally in greens and scarlets with a kind of urgent power from one end of the painting to the other.

"Mmm," I murmured.

He pulled me back. "See, *madame,* from this perspective it is easier to see what I am communicating."

Fortunately before I could reply, he rushed on, "The French! The French! What do they think they're doing, asking us to show among the *ruins,* the ruins!"

"It's very dramatic," offered Bob. He and Tom had joined the three of us. "And quite romantic, really. Rather Gothic."

"Why not a *new* building, a clean well-ordered place, instead of this . . . this travesty!" The painter's wide-flung arm embraced the ruined mansion, its grassy lawns, and the fica trees that were said to be a hundred years old. "Do they show their own French art here? No, they set up a special *new* tent for that. But this *ruin* is good enough for Lebanese art."

"Well, you have a point," agreed Bob, but before he had finished his sentence, the artist was gone, to another group, where we could see the same gesticulations with, presumably, the same complaints.

Hoda said, "He's not the only one who feels that way. But when the French ambassador asks . . ."

"Did you see the memorial plaque in the front, under the trees?" Tom asked. "The names of the eleven French who died when this place was shelled. No plaques around to *American* casualties. It would take a whole wall! And what about Lebanese?"

"Well, this is French ground, so to speak," said Bob. "You're not going to find plaques to Americans on the French ambassador's lawn, even on a ruined lawn." He paused, then added, "But did you read the plaque? The list was alphabetical, so the ambassador's name and rank were near the bottom. The French always surprise me."

Hoda looked back at the shell of the great stone mansion where she and other Lebanese of all religious and political backgrounds had shown their art together. "The French know how to do things very well," she said. "Even if there's no food—or even drink!"

"Isn't it wonderful, Hoda?" said a young woman as we walked out toward the residency gates. A white head scarf framed her face. "What are you and your husband doing here in Beirut?" she asked me as Hoda introduced her friend as a young poet.

"We were in Beirut in 1981 and wrote about the city. Now we're back to update that book."

"How is the city different?" she asked.

"There's no war going on at least," I answered. "But the scars!" I looked back at the blasted marble pillars and the gaping holes in the stone walls.

"Yes," she said, her eyes following mine. "But the scaffolding is up, can't you see? It takes time to rebuild. And this is only *one* art show. We have them every day almost—there's a great cultural renaissance going on in Beirut. Believe me, *madame*, we want to live. But it takes time to heal."

Many more than those eleven French Embassy employees, nearly three hundred Americans, and numerous other foreigners had been killed. But the Lebanese? A hundred thousand people died, Anis told us. "At least," he said. "It's probably closer to two hundred thousand."

"My God," said Bob. "In a country of only three and a half

million. How much hatred from that is still around? Do people still think about revenge?"

Anis looked at Bob carefully.

"Perhaps," he replied. "But the poet is right. We do want to live. And people whose relatives may have killed each other a few months ago are now sitting at dinner parties together—or going to the same art shows." He glanced at his mother with a slight smile. "They are working together, but it will take a long time to forgive and live with our differences."

"Oh, Anis," Hoda said, "don't be so serious."

She turned to ask us if we had noticed the most famous gay personality of Beirut get into his limousine and leave before everyone else. "His silk shirt was a magnificent swirl of flowers," she added. "I don't see how you could have missed it."

"I did see him," said Bob. "Big guy; I thought he was a Samoan diplomat."

THE REBUILDING OF BEIRUT certainly was in process. The Solidère site along the sea was the most dramatic example, a huge expanse of land extending the length of two football fields or more. We toured the site, a veritable moonscape of depressions where dust swirled against the sky from the jackhammers and bulldozers at work. The area was fenced off to keep the general public from tripping over the piles of pipes and cement culverts, from falling into the deep ditches where sewage and water lines were being laid.

Dust. Sand. Noise. Rubble. The Lebanese were finding that, as in the case of many urban renewal projects around the world, much has to be cleared away before the actual reconstruction begins, the hopeful rise of new buildings to replace the ruins of the old.

We could barely see the scores of laborers through the clouds of dust raised by the bulldozers excavating the debris, and the trucks loading that debris to be taken and dumped in a new landfill at the edge of the sea. Mae Zouaine, our Solidère guide, told us that each truck carried twenty cubic meters of rubble and that six hundred truckloads (about twelve thousand cubic meters) are added to the landfill every month.

"We can see how the landfill is growing every day," said Mae. "When I first started showing people around the site, the trucks simply turned around and dumped their loads. Now they have to drive all the way out." She pointed toward the sea. "We're going to set up a new small boat harbor out there," she said.

A square hectare is added to the landfill every month. "It's slow work," said Mae, "but certainly a constructive use for all the rubbish of wartime, those broken cement blocks and bricks. This is part of Solidère's ecologically sound development plan," added Mae. "Even Greenpeace approves of us!"

"Greenpeace?" I echoed.

"Yes," she said, and smiled. "They came to see what we were doing and wrote a report for their international membership. Fortunately, it was a good report. And," she said, "we've asked a lot of consultants from around the world to come here and help us plan so there will be as few problems with pollution as possible."

Our lecture tour was interrupted by shouts from nearby, where a white panel truck, bearing the logo of Lebanese television, had come to a stop near an excavation, raising more clouds of dust onto the group of workers in their hard hats.

"It's the archaeologists!" explained Mae. "They don't like cars or trucks coming so close to their work sites. I don't blame them. Look at that dust!"

Archaeologists? Bob was pleasantly surprised to find his professional cousins at work here, but archaeology, we were told, had become a matter of wide public interest recently, for an unexpected by-product of the Solidère project has been a new insight into the ancient history of Beirut. Here, as elsewhere, builders through the years have tended to erect new buildings on the foundations of the old, never digging down any farther than necessary. Solidère was different, for the plans called for a complete overhaul of the ancient water and sewage systems, which entailed far deeper digging than people had first realized would be necessary. And the consortium's agreement with the Lebanese government contained a clause mandating exploration of any archaeological remains that the construction projects might uncover. We had learned that under the center of the city, untouched for centuries, Hellenistic towers had been found, as well as Phoenician piers, Roman baths, statues of the love goddess Venus from different periods, and a fine medieval Crusader wall of dressed stone.

It was Laila Badr, professor of archaeology at the American University of Beirut, who was shouting at the television truck. She was supervising the scientific excavations that, by law, must precede the coming of the bulldozers and the claw bucket shovels.

"The journalists are mad for this stuff," Mae went on. "But they can't decide whether we're uncovering Beirut's history or destroying it."

We moved closer to Dr. Badr, a lively middle-aged woman in jeans, T-shirt, and hard hat, who was speaking sharply to the television crew. But after chastising them for raising the dust that covered the artifacts and added to everyone's breathing problems, she relented and allowed them to film the students working in the trenches below us. Like all good archaeologists, they were careful, removing the sides from broken jars found embedded in the rubbish, brushing off the earth, slowly collecting and sorting the thousands of potsherds, which, over the centuries of human habitation here, had been smashed and mixed with the dirt and the concrete rubble around us.

"What's the most surprising thing you've found?" asked Bob.

Dr. Badr reflected a moment.

"The Bronze Age materials," she answered. "There has always been a kind of agreement that Beirut was a Phoenician port, going back maybe to 3000 B.C. But no actual evidence has been uncovered, until now. Finding Bronze Age settlement here was rather unexpected. That is so much earlier than the Phoenicians, maybe 4000 B.C., even."

She pointed to a pile of rubble on top of the stone Crusader wall. "We found a Bronze Age burial near there, a child with a small necklace. How it got mixed in with the Crusader wall we have no idea."

"And Solidère is helping with these excavations?" Bob persisted.

She smiled. "Well, yes and no. The design for the city center runs right over these ruins. But the architect's plan was flexible enough so that when we uncovered this"—she pointed to the foundations of ancient buildings nearby—"they could move the lines of the construction and leave this part of the past for us to work in a while longer. How much will be saved for the future is still being discussed."

"An exhibit like this, of the past, wouldn't it perhaps help constitute a sense of nationhood?" Bob asked.

Dr. Badr looked at him questioningly.

"Well," he explained, "you've been torn apart here by religious and ethnic differences. This history can belong to everybody."

Dr. Badr's face cleared. "Oh yes," she said. "It's very important that all Lebanese get to share this new picture of our past. It belongs to all of us!"

Back at Solidère headquarters, Ramez Maluf, the public relations director, lectured us about the value of the project.

"It's happening," he argued, "because the psyche of the country has changed. People are still skeptical—we Lebanese have always been skeptical—but at least they don't laugh in our faces anymore." He was referring to the many wealthy Lebanese who at first had not believed President Hariri would actually sink his own money into this operation. But Hariri had invested millions and now many other Lebanese were following suit.

"What about the squatters?" Bob asked again. "We've seen a few on-site, as we've walked around Beirut. And the legal questions of ownership of those buildings you're tearing up? Those problems are solved?"

Ramez looked directly at us, a bit impatiently, I thought.

"A set of procedures was established to take care of the ownership problem. We have followed those procedures. And," he added, taking off his glasses and wiping his eyes, "as I told you before, the squatters have been compensated and resettled."

We smiled and rose to leave.

"Look, my friends," he said, also standing and walking to open his office door for us, "we're at a crossroads in Lebanon and in Beirut. We're trying to build a city that will be a regional center again. The war went on for fifteen years. People had stopped believing it would ever end. They had gotten used to sleeping outside foreign embassies and begging for visas to get out of here. Now people are coming back—engineers, architects, urban planners. Here at Solidère we have computer specialists working for us and we're doing business with firms all over Beirut."

"Yes," said Bob politely, "and thanks for your help."

"It takes time," he called as we went out the door. "Nothing is perfect. But we *are* rebuilding."

Out on the sunny street, we stared at the old gutted stone buildings on Rue Allenby and Rue Foch, avenues named after British and French colonial leaders, who had ruled Lebanon from the early nineteenth century until its independence in 1941. The buildings were empty, and the avenues were on the way to being restored to new grandeur. But where had the poor families gone, the squatters, who had crowded into these ruined buildings during the war? It seemed certain that they were not going to move back into the splendid edifices that were being rebuilt along these historic streets.

Religious differences have been generally cited as the situation that fueled the long-drawn-out civil war in Lebanon. But some commentators have also noted the gap between rich and poor, a gap that had always been present, of course, but that had widened considerably after 1973 and the channeling into the banks of Beirut of huge sums from the oil-rich countries. If one compared official government statements with on-the-ground realities, it appeared that between the expressed desire to resolve economic as well as religious differences, and the actual movement in that direction, some considerable distance remained.

The squatters in the old gutted buildings were a good example. If Ramez was right, they had indeed been compensated, at about $5,000 per family. But what would $5,000 buy in a real estate market where a luxury apartment cost a million dollars? Where, then, were the squatters heading with their compensation money? Setting up living arrangements outside the city? Perhaps in the old Palestinian refugee camps to the south?

"The camps are closed, we hear," I said to Rosemary Sayigh, who has studied and written about Palestinian refugees in Lebanon for many years.

"Several friends told us this," put in Bob, "when B.J asked about Rashadiyah." This was the camp on the Lebanese-Israeli border where we had filmed *Women Under Siege* in 1981.

"No, no," Rosemary said. "The government won't allow any more camps to be built, true. But there are still twelve refugee camps here, including Rashadiyah. Twelve!"

"Are people living in all of them?"

"Of course. No place else to go."

I looked at Bob. "Maybe we should go down and see for ourselves what's happened to Rashadiyah?"

"Difficult," responded Rosemary. "It's on the edge of the buffer zone—you know, that patch of no-man's-land between Lebanon and Israel. Nobody wants you there, B.J."

Bob asked whether the compensation money from the government had helped the homeless build new houses in the camps.

"Partially," answered Rosemary. "But a basic house, even in a camp, costs about ten thousand dollars these days. And Lebanon isn't allowing UNRWA to build more houses, though they look the other way when individuals do it. That's partly because there's no other low-cost housing for them."

"How are the Palestinians surviving in today's market, then?" asked Bob.

"Not well," allowed Rosemary. "Some of them still live on remittances from abroad—from Canada, Germany, the United States. But it's a big problem, and the refugee working group set up by the 1993 peace accords hasn't yet dealt with it at all!"

"I would think the men would have opportunities to work on the rebuilding," said Bob.

Rosemary smiled. "Yes, but they have to compete with Syrian workers, who come in, live on the building sites, eat bread, onions, and tomatoes, and work for very low wages."

"Syrian workers?" Bob looked doubtful. "Like—how many are we talking about?"

"Some say a million, officials say five hundred thousand. But it's not at all a small number."

Bob looked at Rosemary. "I suppose what you're saying is that Syria is the key to the future of a lot of people in Lebanon."

Rosemary nodded. "Yes. We're all waiting for Israel and Syria to sign a peace treaty, which will get them both out of Lebanon. Then we will all breathe easier."

THE HIGHWAY TO THE SOUTH runs along the Mediterranean coast, dipping in and out of small stands of cypresses and pines, passing oil refineries, new beach hotels, and fast-food restaurants. But closer to Beirut, the view of the blue sea is blocked by miles of wall-to-wall commercial establishments, selling everything from car parts to jewelry. These are the shops set up during the war by the enterprising small merchants whose property was blasted out of the inner city of Beirut, the section now being rebuilt by Solidère. But the plans of Solidère do not seem to include this group of merchants, and accordingly they have replaced their original makeshift carts and shacks with solid walls and roofs. They have added signs, installed electricity and telephones. Even if Solidère should include them, these entrepreneurs say they will not move, for they have made larger and larger investments in their property during the past fifteen years of inner-city insecurity and conflict. Their presence is an embarrassment to Lebanese government officials trying to erase the signs of war, to spruce up and modernize this prime area of beachfront property. But there are other sides to this disagreement.

The seaside area and its inhabitants are also a political problem, for most of them are members of the Shia sect of Islam, the group identified with Hezbollah, the Party of God, which has continued to struggle in the south against the Israeli occupation. As we drove along this stretch of highway, we were presented with a confused collection of banners and billboards. The banners celebrating Shia mullahs, or religious leaders, vied for the passersby's attention with announcements of coming rock concerts and flashy posters advertising new films.

"Now, that mullah," said Hoda, pointing to an oversize poster of a turbaned cleric with a neat beard and a mild expression. "He is shrewd. He knows what he is doing. And he's a friend of mine!"

"Oh, Mother," said Anis. "A friend, really?"

"Really, Anis, we exchange poetry."

"I'd like to meet him," said Bob, craning his neck to get a better view of the man's oversize countenance. "Is he a member of Hezbollah, do you think?"

"Probably," said Anis shortly. "And I'm sure Mother can arrange a meeting if you really want to talk to him, Bob."

"I will invite him to tea," announced Hoda, and settled back into her seat, "when we get home tonight."

"Next time, let us accept invitations from friends closer to home," said Anis a bit testily. He had been driving home from a sumptuous country picnic along this twisted, crowded two-lane road for more than two hours; the sun was hot. We were all tired.

"But they were nice people, Anis," returned Hoda. "Did you enjoy it, B.J.?"

I nodded.

•   •   •

HODA WAS AS GOOD AS HER WORD. She invited Sheikh Hassan al-Amin to tea. "He is very important in the Shia community," Hoda explained. "People always consult him on matters of religious interpretation."

"And you know him how?"

"Poetry. We sometimes find ourselves at these festivals the different groups organize to promote a sort of united front for the future. Like the time I was invited to read at the big Christian shrine out toward Antelias."

"The Virgin on top of the mountain?"

"Yes, that one," answered Hoda. "Maybe I can find the poem to show you while you're here, B.J."

So what did we expect? A tall, frowning religious gentleman, with a beard and a turban, who looked like the posters on the crowded beach road? Certainly not the slight, mild-mannered elderly man in gray trousers and blue summer shirt who sat in one of Hoda's golden velvet French chairs and responded politely to Bob's questions.

After a few general comments, Sheikh Hassan inquired about our reasons for coming to the Arab world. Bob replied that we had first lived in the Shia area of southern Iraq in the 1950s.

Sheikh Hassan opened his eyes with interest. For the next ten minutes he and Bob played do-you-know and we began to see Sheikh Hassan in a different light. He was not the strange other, the poster mullah, a member of Hezbollah, the media-maligned Party of God, feared and hated. He was a friend of our old Iraqi friend and host, Sheikh Hamid, chief of the Al-Eshadda tribe, Iraqi member of Parliament, and leader of the Al-Agra tribal confederation. The conversation between Bob and Sheikh Hassan became even more animated as the talk turned to differences in dogma between the Sunni and Shia sects of Islam and how these differences were important in any consideration of Lebanon's political future.

Lamshiat, Hoda's helper, brought in tea and cookies.

Hoda said, "Now I have to ask you something, Sheikh Hassan, so my American friends can get an idea of what's going on here between us Sunnis and your friends who are Shia."

"Yes, *madame?*" Sheikh Hassan lifted his teacup with a pale, gnarled hand, spotted brown with age.

"I think you know what is always said," she began, smiling and leaning toward him. She wore a modest but chic gown, again black, but this one of silk, with a heavy gold chain around her neck. "Is it true," said Hoda in a pleasant voice, "that the Shia are going to kill all of us Sunni Muslims?"

Sheikh Hassan looked visibly upset, and clattered his cup back into its saucer. "What nonsense!" he said.

Hoda said, a bit archly, "That's what people say all the time. Of course I know . . ."

Sheikh Hassan shook his head in an irritated way. Then he took a deep breath and smiled at her.

"My dear Madame Namani," he said, "what can I say? Such a thing will never happen! But," he added, smiling at her, "if there are problems, you are always welcome, you and your family, to take refuge in my house. Just call me and I'll arrange everything."

He took a deep breath and turned to me.

"You must know, because our hostess tells me you are old friends, that she is a fine poet, a fine poet. And she's on television, too. She and I read poetry together."

He smiled again at Hoda, and, taking a folded piece of paper from his shirt pocket, he proceeded to read aloud to us a poem he had written in Hoda's honor.

She was pleased and flattered and ducked her head. "Ah, Sheikh Hassan," she said, "you must have a coffee now, after that."

"Delighted, *madame*," replied Sheikh Hassan, and nodded to us all.

IN APRIL 1996, after we had returned to Texas, armed confrontations between Hezbollah and the Israelis in the buffer zone broke out again. An Israeli shell ripped into a United Nations center, killing at least one hundred civilians. Hezbollah announced it would lay down its arms if Israel withdrew its forces behind its own border. Israel announced that would be impossible, that it needed to protect itself from the Katyusha rockets that Hezbollah lofted into its bunkers. Israel continued its attacks. Middle East Airlines had to consider grounding its planes again as officials talked about closing the Beirut airport. Despite international objections, Israel continued to shell Lebanon for fourteen days. A cease-fire was eventually arranged, with France and the United States as brokers.

On June 6, 1996, Hoda al-Namani called us from Beirut. I had tried to telephone her for days, but with no success.

"Are you all right, Hoda?" I asked into the breathy emptiness and then the static of a barely successful international connection.

"Yes, yes," she said. "Last week we were not so sure. I *think* we're okay."

"What about Lebanon? Beirut?"

"Oh, B.J.," her voice came through loudly suddenly, "we don't want war. We *don't* want war. We want to live in peace. But will people let us?"

"I hope so, I do hope so," was all that I could think to reply, before the line went dead.

UNITY AND DIVERSITY IN ISLAM

SLAM IS THE NEWEST of the great monotheistic religions. Judaism, Christianity, and Islam all emerged in the Middle East and share a common basis of belief about the nature of God and humans. Yet the differences among them have fueled strife which remains lively—and dangerous—to this day. What are the differences between our myths about Islam and the realities of living in modern Muslim communities?

The first Muslims, of course, were the Arabs, followers of Muhammad, the prophet who lived in Mecca in the seventh century after Christ. Muhammad received revelations that Muslims believe came directly from God through the angel Gabriel; these revelations were set down in the Koran. Jesus is not God, states the Koran. This verse alone was sufficient for the Christian world to view the new monotheistic religion as a heresy, far worse in many ways than "pagan" beliefs that make no reference to Christian doctrine. Eventually, every weapon in the armory of the Christian world was marshaled against the "heresy," including theologians, soldiers, and the thousands of children who marched—and perished—during the Children's Crusade to redeem the Holy Land from the infidel Saracens.

Islam did not originate as an attack on Christianity, however. The Prophet Muhammad is said to have viewed Islam (the word in Arabic literally means "submission") as redressing what he regarded as laxities and depravities that had developed within the religions he knew. Thus, Islam was a reformation of both the practices common to the idol-worshiping peoples of the Arabian Peninsula and those of Byzantine Christianity, with its elaborate ceremonialism and revered statuary.

Muhammad saw the Old Testament of Judaism and much of the New Testament of Christianity as the heritage of Islam, but he rejected many ideas within the scriptures. The idea of the Holy Trinity, for example, ran directly contrary to the Islamic emphasis on one God. Abraham, Moses, and Isaac were revered as great prophets, as was Jesus. But Muhammad did not see them as divine; in fact, he claimed no divine status for himself and insisted that no human being could make such an assertion.

Islam shares with Christianity and Judaism the same fundamental concerns: human salvation, good and evil, heaven and hell. As a total way of life, in which law and politics are no more divorced from religion than are commerce and family relationships, it is closer in spirit to Judaism than to Christianity. And it formed the basis of a new society on earth in the most literal sense of the term.

Conditions for the development of Islam in A.D. 622 were very different from the conditions that existed at the birth of Christianity. Unlike Jesus, who faced hostile, foreign authorities and whose early followers faced charges of insurrection or worse, Muhammad and the people of Mecca and the surrounding desert and oases of Arabia had little to fear externally in the beginning. The social and political problems were internal. Raids and warfare among the nomadic Bedouin disrupted peaceful commerce.

In the past, tribal descent had shaped economic and social status, but by the seventh century, such a system did not match the complex changing roles of wealth and status in the urban life of Mecca. Under the new creed, anyone of any race or social origin who submitted to God's will and became a Muslim had claim to equal footing in the community. The door to personal achievement and success was no longer barred by differences in tribal status. The new religious doctrine was well suited to the capitalist economy of merchants and markets, which had developed by Muhammad's time.

In the beginning, then, Islam was truly revolutionary. The Koran provided a totally new charter for social and political life. It emphasized the equality of all persons within the Muslim community. City merchants and desert nomads were united under the same leadership.

Women as well as men were recognized as Muslim persons, with equality before God and legal status on earth. Women were entitled to veto powers over their marriage arrangements, and to inherit a portion of their husbands' and fathers' estates. Merit was gained in freeing a converted slave.

Less than a hundred years after the birth of Islam, Arab soldiers and traders were moving into North Africa, into Turkey, across the Mediterranean to Sicily, Spain, Italy, France. By the early eighth century Islamic armies were halfway across the European world, and had they not been stopped in France at Tours in A.D. 732, Western history might have taken quite a different course. As it was, the original Islamic community in Arabia had by this time engendered a new empire which reached into three continents. Intellectual life flourished in the tranquillity of Córdoba and Granada as well as in Damascus and Baghdad. Christian and Jewish philosophers made their way to these centers of learning. Indeed, sizable minorities of Christians and Jews lived throughout the Islamic Empire, for the Koran makes special mention of "people of the book," Jews and Christians, as respected and protected minorities within the Muslim community. However, the actual existence of a Muslim state in southern Spain was seen as an intolerable affront by the growing European powers. In 1492 Granada fell to Christian armies under King Ferdinand and Queen Isabella. Muslims and Jews alike were given an ultimatum: conversion, expulsion from Spain, or death. Members of both religious groups fled to Morocco and beyond.

Though 1492 marked the end of the Islamic reign in Western Europe (as well as the discovery of America), the spread of Islam through conversion by no means ceased. During the following centuries it steadily gained strength in Africa, the Indian subcontinent, Southeast Asia, and China. A Muslim community in the Philippines struggles today with the government for some degree of self-governance. American Muslims are said to number more than 6 million. Nearly 800 million people in the modern world consider themselves Muslims. Only one-third live in the Middle East. (The great majority of Middle Easterners are Muslims, though small groups of Christian Arabs and Jews constitute perhaps 5 percent of the total population.)

What is the power of this creed? Why is it the fastest-growing religion in the world today? Islam has a flexibility, a simplicity, an egalitarianism that is seldom mentioned in the Western texts. As Islamicist John Alden Williams has pointed out, " 'Orthoprax' is a far better term than 'orthodox' to characterize Islam; for right practice rather than right theology is primary." Indeed, no generally recognized religious authority declares what is orthodox and what is not; Islam does not have a central ecclesiastic hierarchy. There are no ordained priests or ministers. Rather, communities of Muslims direct their own affairs, through local specialists in Islamic law and theology. Such men (and women) acquire knowledge in the religious schools and universities of their own regions. They are given various titles with some differences in significance depending on local practice: ulema (the group of learned men, including scholars); sheikhs (specialists in aspects of religious as well as secular affairs); qadis (religious judges); mullahs (learned leaders of Friday prayers); muftis and ayatollahs (religious legal specialists). This lack of a central authority, this freedom for the development of practice, is crucial to understanding not only the Arabs but the whole Islamic world.

Outsiders are often puzzled by the variety of seemingly inconsistent behavior. How is it that the Saudi Arabian authorities can stone a princess and her lover to death for adultery while Muslims elsewhere express their horror at such an act? Aren't they all Muslims? Yes; but times have changed since the seventh century.

The consensus on all issues that existed within the small Muslim community during the Prophet's lifetime is no longer universal. Practice differs, from Morocco to the Philippines. For example: the elaboration of mystical Sufi orders found in North Africa, in which pious Muslims take part in weekly *hadras*—meetings of prayer, trance, and meditation—has no equivalent in Saudi Arabia, which forbids such activities. Polygyny, marrying more than one wife, is illegal in Tunisia but not in Egypt. Also, there are seven distinct schools of religious law, each with its own legal specialists and code of precedents; every Muslim is part of one school but respects the other six. How is this latter example possible, since, we are told, all law is based on the Koran and the Koran is believed to be the literal word of God, and hence considered unchangeable?

The earliest consensus among Muslims was shattered soon after Muhammad's death by the issue of leadership succession. Who was to take the place of the Prophet? Shiat Ali (the party of Ali, the Prophet's son-in-law and cousin) argued for succession based on descent through blood ties, a variant of the argument for the divine right of kings. The Sunnis (so called because of their following of the Sunna, or proper path of conduct) argued for leadership based on ability and proven merit. Disagreement over this issue continues into the twentieth century: for the Shia sect in Iran, the idea of leadership carries with it the idea of divinity. The Sunnis find this view blasphemous.

What, then, are the central doctrines and beliefs that can be seen as unique to Islam, that distinguish it from other great religions, and that form the core of beliefs on which all Muslims, of whatever sect or practice, agree? All Muslims believe in one God, Allah (the Arabic word for God). All Muslims must assume the five duties (or pillars): profession of faith, prayer, fasting, the giving of alms, and the pilgrimage to Mecca (if the believer can afford it). All Muslims believe in the centrality and divinity of the Koran as a guide to everyday life and a basis for law.

In addition, they rely on the *hadith*, a collection of the traditions and sayings of the Prophet during his lifetime. Here there is room for theological differences. Local groups interpret the *hadith* differently and see some *hadith* as more valid than others. Individual communities often interpret the *hadith* to fit changing times and local situations, so that in 1972, for example, the grand mufti of Jordan could issue a *fatwa* (an opinion or judgment *for his congregation only*) which states that the use of contraceptives is in no way against the teachings of the Koran, and that Islam allows abortion if the health of the mother or the good of the family demands it.

The issue of *jihad*, or holy war, is another point of concern and Western misunderstanding. Some Muslims would argue that a sixth duty, or pillar, exists, and that is the *jihad*, the duty of the holy war. While the protection of the Islamic community is cited as the religious reason for a *jihad*, social and political reasons are varied, just as in European wars. Far more holy wars have been declared by leaders and would-be leaders than have actually been fought; and far more Muslims have ignored the call to such holy wars than have answered it. But certainly Islam, like Judaism and Christianity, may be used to justify war. Islam probably has about as much to do with conflicts between Sunnis and Shias in Iraq and Iran today, or among religious groups in Lebanon, as Christianity has to do with the tragic conflict in Ireland. In all cases, religion may be used as justification and encouragement for struggles that stem from other circumstances, ranging from economic distress and political oppression to the personal ambitions of secular leaders.

Much orientalist scholarship emphasizes the fixed, static kind of society that Islam supposedly produces. Yet nothing could be further from either the original statements of the Prophet and the Koran or historical practice throughout the ages. The tenets of Islam provide no divine sanction for the development of any form of social hierarchy;

Islam encourages rather than restricts social mobility. This is not to say that many forms of social stratification have not existed in the Middle East in different times and places, however.

Today new class societies are in fact developing in many Muslim countries. In this regard, it is important to remember that Islam in the seventh century posited two bases for Muslim everyday life that appear to have some relationship to our American views of equality and democracy: *tawhid* (oneness) and *ijma* (consensus). Though these two concepts have not always been honored in Islamic historical practice, they are now receiving increasing attention. The great Islamic thinker and reformer Muhammad Abdu published his celebrated essay on *tawhid* in 1897 and suggested then that modern political and scientific ideas were not antithetical to but rather at one with Islamic principles. *Tawhid* means literally "declaring the oneness of God"; to some modern Muslims, declaring the oneness of God implies the equality of all those who so declare that oneness and, by inference, the responsibility of all human beings for each other—a sense of universal brotherhood. *Ijma*, the sense that one is in accord with the needs and ambitions of one's followers, is the ideal to be sought by a political leader. As new middle classes begin to emerge in countries such as Egypt, Tunisia, Algeria, and Saudi Arabia, these concepts are taking on new meanings. Both ideas are being called on by leaders, supporters, and opposition groups who, in different countries with varying social, economic, and political conditions, are attempting to evoke Islamic ideology to construct new societies in the modern Arab world. Colonel Muammar Qadhafi, for example, cites *tawhid* as the basis for what he terms Islamic democracy; President Anwar Sadat, on the other hand, some say, was brought down because he failed to take seriously the need for many new groups in Egypt to be considered in the construction of a national consensus.

Islam, then, is a monotheistic religion, with a fixed center of belief, but with enough flexibility to allow it to adapt to changing times and the needs of its believers. More than thirteen hundred years ago Islam began by legitimizing a new association of people of diverse social and racial origins. Today it continues to legitimize new and developing forms of community life.

II Jordan

Waves
bow
before
the shore
courtiers
to their king
and then
withdraw

Unknown, ninth century

Men cannot save those
Who cannot learn from Time.

Abid ibn al-Abras
LAMENT FOR AN ARAB ENCAMPMENT

THE BUS CARRYING US TO King Hussein's palace for tea suddenly stopped dead. Ahead, through the rapid crisscross strokes of the windshield wipers, we could see the palace gates through streaking rain—formidable wrought-iron structures, guarding the entrance in the high spiked protective fence that encircled the turreted residence of the Hashemite ruler of Jordan. From this stony hill upon which the palace had been built we had been told there was a fine view of the seven hills of Amman, a view of the countryside and of all approaching persons and vehicles. A hilltop bastion for a much-beleaguered king—one who had survived. Once, twenty years before, we had glimpsed the palace hill from a distance. Today, at the gates, we could see nothing but the rain pouring down out of a heavy dark sky on this late winter afternoon in Amman.

"What's going on?" We craned our necks to see.

The bus driver was shouting out of his side window. The uniformed palace guards were shouting back. The driver revved his motor, but the bus remained immobile.

"I think the bus is too high to get through," volunteered the man in the seat behind, a retired diplomat, one of the Americans, like us, invited here to a post-Christmas conference on Arab resources and foreign policy by the World Affairs Council of Amman and the Center for Arabic Studies at Georgetown University.

"Oh no," sighed one anxious wife. "So we have to run out in the rain?" She had emerged from the hotel hairdresser's only an hour before, her new coiffure created in honor of the meeting with royalty.

The arguing went on, but nothing happened. Two eras of technology, it turned out, were colliding. The protective gates had been set around the palace long before the advent of the Jordanian tourist trade and the development of luxurious air-conditioned buses. The neatly streamlined box on top of our bus, which held the coils and condensers for the air-conditioning system, kept tourists cool on the long hot drives through the desert in summer, through the Jordan River Valley to the Dead Sea; to the hidden rose-red city of Nabataean Petra; to Aqaba, Lawrence of Arabia's country. But the box was strung up on the palace gates. The bus was too high. And that was that.

The rain continued to pour down. A gray wet vista at least two hundred yards long stretched ahead of us, and there seemed to be stone stairs beyond, many stone stairs blurring into the distant rain. In a rush to the door, we would all soak our modest finery, donned in some excitement at this invitation to have tea with royalty. For how many kings and queens were left these days to have tea with? Bob and I had said to each other, pleased at the idea. We had written postcards to his mother, to our children; they would get a kick out of it, we told each other. "And," I added, "pageantry has its place, and it's fun for everyone." "True," answered Bob. "And this king really reigns." Now, however, with the rain streaming down the windows of the tourist bus and the light slowly fading, the prospect of much pageantry seemed a bit dim.

But the king's minions came to the rescue—a procession of dark-suited young men bearing helpful large black umbrellas. They shepherded us up the steep, curving, slippery palace walk, rushed us up flight after flight of wet stone stairs, and through a heavy oaken door. Here our coats were taken politely.

We stood in a long wide hall, hung with portraits. I recognized Emir Abdulla, founder of the Hashemite dynasty, the strong face and short beard framed by the agal and kaffiyeh, traditional headdress of the tribes of the area. Abdulla was Hussein's grandfather. Another, darker-toned portrait was of Talal, Hussein's father, deposed for reasons of health in 1952, when Hussein was sixteen years old.

The invitation had read: "You are invited to have tea with His Majesty King Hussein and Her Highness Queen Noor, on Sunday at 4:30 P.M. promptly." Well, we had been prompt, because the bus ordered to take us had been prompt. The conference had started promptly, after the prompt arrival of all the delegates on Royal Jordanian Airlines, courtesy of Ali Ghandour, the energetic and charismatic president. His airline was one of the success stories of the modern Arab business world. Ali Ghandour had come to Amman from Lebanon ten years ago, and had made Alia (Royal Jordanian Airlines) the most efficiently run and popular Arab-owned airline in the area.

Like many conferences, this one had been a mild success, allowing for an exchange of views and papers by American and Arab participants. And the king and queen's tea party was to top it off, so to speak. Where were they, though?

The polite, dark-suited young men suggested we might roam about the apartments until the entrance of the royal couple. To warm us, presumably, against the cold dankness of the rainstorm we had just run through, we were served tea, very sweet, in tiny glasses banded with silver, not the gilt-painted glasses of Arab coffee shops and homes, but real silver as befitted a real monarch. Hussein of Jordan had survived numerous attacks on his life, several threats to his crown, and the demise of almost every other leader in the area over the past generation. Even King Hassan of Morocco, the only leader to rival him in staying power, had come to the throne in 1961. By 1981 Hussein was the only leader who had been in power when we first went to the area in 1956.

How had he survived? Not by barricading himself in the palace tower, obviously. A combination of astute political moves and assistance from the West, yes. But also a recognition on the part of his subjects of his legitimate claim to the throne. Hussein, after all, could trace descent directly from the Prophet Muhammad. He also represented Arab nationalism—as the son and heir of a dynasty that had led the Arab revolt against the Ottoman Empire at the beginning of the twentieth century. Lawrence of Arabia may have gotten the publicity during the revolt, but it was Hussein's ancestors who assumed leadership. In an area of conflicting powers and interests, Hussein's kingdom looked more secure and prosperous than others; he seemed genuinely interested in social and economic development, and his personal courage and honesty had earned him respect.

"The new queen has redecorated these rooms," said a voice at my elbow. A gray-haired Jordanian woman in a dark wine suit, lacy blouse, and gorgeous pearls, she was one of the local participants who had accompanied the American group to the palace. "What do you think?"

"They're very pleasant, certainly," I answered politely. We sat down on a beige and white textured sofa, comfortable, under a glittering French chandelier, its polished crystal drops reflecting and refracting the subtle reds, saffrons, and blues of the old Persian carpets that covered the floor. "Is it all new—I mean, since the marriage?" amending my question at the amused yet kindly look in the lady's eyes.

"These rooms, yes," she said. "Upstairs, the bedrooms, who knows?" She smiled again. "Different wives, of course, have different tastes."

Hmm. The king's first wife had been an Egyptian princess, Dina Abd al-Hamid al-Aun. The second, an Englishwoman, Antoinette Gardiner. The third, Alia, a Palestinian. Where were they now? Alia was dead in a plane crash, the Egyptian divorced and remarried in Cairo, the English woman reported still living in comfort in Amman with her children. Certainly, no traces of that past were evident in the room where we sat. Long, full, heavy biscuit-colored drapes, drawn against the rain, looked new, as did the pleasantly silk-lined walls. Decorative objects of many different cultures and periods had been placed carefully on polished tables of dark wood: miniatures, inlaid boxes, silver cigarette lighters. Against the main wall stood a shelf of signed photographs—photographs of the king smiling beside distinguished world leaders who had visited the palace in recent times: Giscard d'Estaing of France looked out of a silver frame; so did Sultan Qabbous of Oman; Fidel Castro of Cuba; Queen Beatrix and Prince Claus of the Netherlands; Pope John Paul II; President Saddam Hussein of Iraq, the country once ruled by Hussein's own second cousin, Faisal; Helmut Schmidt of West Germany. A strange company, those leaders, their visits testimony to the precarious yet central position the tiny Kingdom of Jordan held in the Arab world of the early 1980s.

The palace where we now sipped our tea was a fortress within a fortress. The agricultural and nomadic peoples of ancient Jordan first came into contact with European culture when the armies of Alexander the Great passed through in the fourth century before Christ. Afterward, the Romans came, and the Arabs bringing Islam from Arabia, and the Ottomans from the north, until the West took over again, carving up the Arab world into new countries and distributing them to France, Britain, Italy. The new "country" of Transjordan became a British-mandate territory after World War I, a fully independent nation by the 1950s. In recent years Jordan seemed to be an armed oasis in a vast desert of sand, wind, barren hills, and sectarian struggles, a fortress barricaded (with the help of the West) against hostile neighbors: Syria, Iraq, Israel. Dismissed as a British invention, a pseudo-nation, when Hussein was a seventeen-year-old king, Jordan had emerged as far more than that as it had held on to its sovereignty and independence during a half century of violent political conflict and change.

"Well, Ronda . . ." Another Jordanian lady's voice brought me back to the drawing room, where we awaited Their Majesties. "What do you expect? Isn't she a decorator, the American queen? Didn't she get some kind of degree?" The woman sniffed audibly, causing her diamond earrings to swing above her subtly striped silk blouse and beautifully cut black suit. "If she's a professional decorator, the rooms *should* look pleasant if she's doing her job properly."

The first lady, older, smiled kindly. "Of course. But remember the queen is young. And also nice, very intelligent."

Although I had not asked, she went on to answer the unspoken question that hung in the air with the words "professional decorator." Queens, the implication was, were not ordinarily, in royal Jordan at least, professional decorators. "Yes, I would say people like the new queen. But we would all be dishonest if we did not admit that any of us"—her gesture embraced the half dozen well-dressed Jordanian matriarchs present—"would have been delighted had one of our own daughters become queen."

The lady in the black suit nodded. "Yes, you are right. And we must remember that the king has had a difficult time. Very sad, his last wife, the Palestinian, dying in an air crash. Politically, that was very important for the king—that she was a Palestinian, I mean."

The topic of the Palestinians was one bound to raise hackles of one sort or another, for the development of a Palestinian guerrilla movement had nearly led to civil war in Jordan; Hussein's own strong support for the Palestinian cause was challenged by the growing strength of the PLO. During 1970 the radical popular front for the liberation of Palestine within the PLO called for the overthrow of the king and radical revolution. The day of Black September, marking the defeat of the Palestinian uprising by Hussein's army, had not been spoken of at the conference. Everyone stressed the need for unity these days, but the old scars obviously remained.

"Here the room is slightly more personal, I think," the kindly lady in the wine suit said. "A sort of vision of what a royal Bedouin leader would have in the way of what you call a recreation room. The idea is American, is it not?"

The royal rec room was the last of the three public rooms: past the entrance hall with its family portraits; past the large reception room where the chandelier glittered and the sounds of all footfalls became whispers in the thick pile of Persian rugs; and past a smaller, salmon-pink reception room, paneled in the French style, where, we were told, the audience would be held. The informal room was fairly small and comfortable, with low couches along the two walls, covered with cushions embroidered in the traditional Arab cross-stitch. Here presumably the royal couple relaxed a bit. Bedouin saddlebags decorated the walls; there were a new stereo and a cabinet of records, a shelf of books: volumes on military maneuvers, on planning, a few contemporary English novels, and Jane's huge and classic concordance of military arms and equipment.

A rustle, a movement in the general direction of the hall, was a signal, communicated along the length of the apartments, that the royal couple was arriving. We moved forward to see them descend the stairs, as monarchs should, preceded by the leader of the polite, dark-suited umbrella brigade which had escorted us through the rain.

Queen Noor, née Lisa Halaby of the United States, M.A. Princeton (urban planning), the fourth wife, was slightly taller than her husband, King Hussein ibn Talal ibn Abdulla. It was Hussein's grandfather Abdulla and his great-uncle Faisal with whom the Allied powers had dealt after World War I. In the chaos of promises given and promises fulfilled and unfulfilled, Faisal and Abdulla had negotiated and bargained hard. Britain doled out territory: Iraq as a mandate under Faisal as king; Jordan as a mandate under Abdulla as king.

The present king smiled graciously and bade us welcome. The queen did likewise. Two circles formed for the audience in the formal salmon-pink drawing room. I found myself in the queen's group; Bob had gravitated to the king's.

Hussein's hair was gray. His neat mustache was also gray, but he was fit and slim, walking quickly, almost eagerly, to greet his guests. In a dark pinstripe suit and white shirt with dark tie, he looked older than his forty-five years. He had been only fifteen, after all, when he had seen his grandfather, Emir Abdulla, cut down before his eyes by a follower of the then reigning mufti of Jerusalem, Haj Amin al-Husseini. That was 1951. One year later, when King Talal was deposed because of illness, Hussein became king. He had reigned for nearly thirty years.

"You are most welcome," the queen was saying. She smiled, a quick smile that vanished as quickly as it had come. She seemed a serious young woman. "We cannot offer you the sophistication or the sights of Paris and London," she said evenly. "We can only offer you ourselves and our hospitality."

"Oh, look at her belt!" whispered a woman behind me.

What a belt it was! The principal piece of jewelry the queen was wearing, the belt was perhaps six inches wide and fashioned entirely of broad scalloped links of massive gold. I stared at it, as every woman in the little circle must have stared at it, in pure astonishment and envy. My eye kept going back to it throughout the brief audience, not only because of its opulent golden gleam but because the queen kept unconsciously fingering it, pushing the great buckle down, gently, from her waist, over and over again. The scallops, curving inward, must be pinching, I thought. Oh well, that was obviously the trouble with solid-gold belts: they were simply too uncomfortable! Yet it *was* lovely, that belt, especially over her midcalf-length afternoon dress, brown chiffon with a gold stripe woven into the fabric. Ruffles at sleeves and neck, a bracelet or two, rings, dark stockings and shoes.

"Yes," answered the queen. Yes, she said, she had strong feelings about her own Arab identity, through her father, Najeeb Halaby, former chairman of Pan American World Airways.

"When I first came to Jordan," she continued, "I was fascinated by the differences between Arab and American society."

American society was "finished," she said, too clean, too ordered; the "homogeneity" of American society left her feeling discontented and she found she welcomed the "complexity" of Arab society when she first came to Amman to work as a designer (score one for the black-suited lady in the reception room).

"What are the differences you feel most strongly, Your Majesty?"

"Well, I can tell you better when I explain how I argue with my father," she answered. The quick smile came and went. "He believes that rational approaches to problems, as exemplified by the West, are the only way. I disagree with him." She smiled again, lightening the intensity of the expression on her young face, framed by shoulder-length blond hair; she had worn her hair pulled back in a neat ponytail at the formal opening of the conference two days before.

"I am interested in other approaches to problems," she went on earnestly, "alternate approaches." She did not specify what they might be and none of us asked.

The circles began to shift. Waiters in white coats were handing around tiny sandwiches on silver trays: egg salad, cucumber, tomato. Someone asked about the queen's interest in indigenous art and artists, her newly established National Gallery.

"We are all pleased," she said, and pushed down that massive golden belt again. "It is a beginning." She sighed slightly. "We cannot compete with the national galleries of the great powers, of course, but it is a beginning."

Others asked questions.

"Your Majesty!" I heard Bob's voice rising above the series of questions being posed in the audience circle. Was his voice louder than the others', so that the queen's circle also paused to listen, or was I just conscious of it since it was my husband's?

"I am a cultural anthropologist," began Bob, "and I would like to

ask whether tribal loyalties and alliances are still important in the political life of the Kingdom of Jordan."

I looked at the king. He had furrowed his brow slightly. I deduced
that this was not the usual question he received from American visitors. But then, how could he know that Bob had lived for two years
with a tribe in southern Iraq, that we had been guests of the sheikh of
one of the largest settled groups there, a sheikh who traced his ancestry, as Hussein did, to the desert, to the seat of the holy places of Islam?

"If you are asking me about Arab character, I am certain," said
the king smilingly, "that it is surviving, and surviving well."

The audience laughed lightly in acknowledgment and apprecia-
tion of the king's parry, but Bob was not going to stop there.

"Your Majesty," he persisted, "I am certain that Arab character
will survive. Your own reign is evidence of its strength, and this pleasant afternoon is evidence of its warm hospitality." The king inclined his
head. He thought Bob was finished. But he did not know Bob. "What I
am asking is whether territorial ties and loyalties, tribal ties and loyalties, still have any importance in modern Jordan."

The king paused. He looked directly at Bob for the first time.
"Yes," he said finally. "Certainly. They have some importance. Even
today."

He looked over us to where the polite, dark-suited young man
was gesturing. "Ah yes," he said, "please." And his gesture indicated
that the audience was over.

We moved through the salmon-pink drawing room into the reception room, where silver urns of boiling tea and a magnificent tea
cake awaited us: a confection of strawberries and cream in the middle of
January. Truly a royal fantasy. We shook the hands of the queen and
the king and thanked them profusely. The Hashemite ruler and his
American bride walked ceremoniously down the hall, away from us,
past the portraits of the Emir Abdulla and mad-eyed Talal, and headed
up the stairs, presumably to kick off their shoes and she to unclasp that
pesky, if magnificent, golden belt.

The umbrella brigade was stationed by the palace doors. We were
shepherded once more through the rain and dark to the formidable
palace gates where our air-conditioned transport, product of the latest
technology, had been forced to wait outside. In the warmth and light of
the enclosed bus, the group burst into sudden conversation.

"I couldn't resist asking the king that question," said Bob. "Do you think it was rude?"

"No, no," I replied. "But he seemed a bit surprised."

"Well, yes. But he owes his life to the Bedouin tribesmen of Jordan and they say the tribesmen are his most loyal supporters today. However, I would guess 'tribe' is not part of the vocabulary of modern kings, at least not in the presence of foreign businessmen and diplomats."

"What did you think of that *belt*?" said one of the wives, turning around in her seat ahead of us.

"Worth a bundle, I'd say," chuckled her husband. "Solid Hashemite gold."

We drove on through the dark rain, and the turrets of the walled, protected bastion of the king's palace receded into the night behind us.

THE RUINS OF THE ANCIENT Roman city of Philadelphia lie under present-day Amman. Once Rabbath Ammon, biblical capital of the Ammonites, the city was conquered by King David in the eleventh century before Christ but regained its independence from the Israelites under King Solomon. Ammon was renamed Philadelphia by Ptolemy II, son of Alexander the Great's general who had become Ptolemy I. And as the Philadelphia of the Fertile Crescent, it prospered and grew until the fall of Rome signaled decline for all the Mediterranean and Near Eastern outposts of the empire. By the seventh century it had been captured by the Arabs and converted to Islam, but it was only a village in 1921, when Emir Abdulla chose it as his new capital.

"So it is really a new city we are living in," explained Amer Salti, a Jordanian banker of Palestinian descent who had invited us to his home for lunch. He had earned a Ph.D. in Arabic literature from the Sorbonne and had also studied in America but had found banking more profitable in the bustling economy of modern Jordan. We were enjoying now one of the results of his labor, a fine new modern house with floors of local marble and wide windows open to the surrounding hills.

In 1960, when Bob and I passed through on our way back to Cairo, Amman had a population of 100,000, but now, a generation later, in 1981, the ruins of Philadelphia were covered by houses and office buildings, makeshift shelters, markets, tents, and grand villas. The king's palace, where we had been guests the day before, stood high above the plain, and the city itself was spreading across its seven hills and beyond, down into the valley.

"They say a million people are clustered nearby," said Amer.

"A marvelous view," I said.

"Oh," joked Rebecca, Amer's American wife. "Every house in Amman has a marvelous view. It's one of those cities, like San Francisco, with built-in views."

"But Amman's is new, in the best and worst sense," added Amer. "It has few remnants of tradition to live up to, no wonderful medieval architecture like Cairo and Baghdad, where you have lived, Bob. But that can be good as well as bad, you know. New people, new ideas, to meet new needs."

"So many people, though," said Rebecca earnestly, "coming and coming."

We lunched on excellent kebab and kufta prepared by Amer's mother, who lived with the Saltis and helped with the two young daughters while Rebecca worked full-time. I looked around the table. Mother. Mother-in-law. A traditional extended household. Not quite. Most extended families focused on one set of grandparents, though not always. I glanced at Rebecca's handsome mother, younger looking than she probably was; at Amer's mother, dark hair graying, fine aquiline features. The way she moved back and forth from kitchen to living room, the way she helped the younger daughter cut her meat, exuded a sense of authority. Here she was, indeed, in charge.

"Mother has just come from Damascus," said Amer. "In time to meet you."

"You're Syrian?" I asked.

The older woman shrugged. "I am an Arab," she said shortly. "Before, we never needed all these permits and passports to get from here to Beirut or Damascus or Jerusalem. It's ridiculous. People are getting crazier every day."

"Well, you know why, Mama," said Amer evenly. "It's the whole business of the Palestinians, and where they are supposed to live."

"Aren't they Arabs, too?" shot back his mother. "What is happening to you, Amer? I thought we were all supposed to be one nation in this life. But people say, are you Syrian, and are you Palestinian, and are you I don't know what."

"We are all Jordanians now, Mother," her son replied. "We are lucky."

What could one say politely about the issue of Jerusalem, the city whose fate was a major stumbling block to a permanent peace in the area? Revered by all three monotheistic religions—Christianity, Judaism, Islam—the name of the city itself evoked wonder, awe, pride, and fierce factionalism. Internationalization of the city had been suggested as the only solution honoring all factions. But at the word "internationalization," Israeli leaders left the bargaining table. The idea that Israeli authorities were controlling the Muslim holy places, second only to Mecca in importance, was a constant goad to Arab emotions.

"We *are* lucky," repeated Rebecca, "to have a decent place left to live, ourselves, with our families. That should be enough."

"But it's not, is it?" burst out Amer's old mother. "Respect and pride are also necessary." She then rose and, with a fierce look at her handsome banker son, took her younger granddaughter by the hand, excused herself briefly, and left the room.

"People move to Amman, Bob," said Amer, "partly so their children can go to the free government schools. There still aren't enough schools in the countryside and today you just can't get anywhere without an education."

"But that's not the only reason, Amer," rejoined Rebecca. "They come to make money, this is a real boomtown." She paused. "And it's safer here than a lot of other places nearby. Be honest. It is safer."

BOB'S QUESTION EARLIER to King Hussein about the importance of tribal loyalties seemed not to be such a dumb or rude question, after all. In the final two days of the conference, we were entertained twice— once at the new Yarmouk University and once at the American Embassy. In both places tribal affiliations and traditions seemed to be a factor, but in different ways. At Yarmouk we were given a splendid *mensif,* the traditional feast of the desert.

At the American ambassador's residence a varied group had been assembled to meet the conference participants from abroad: members of the diplomatic corps from many nations, Jordanians, other Americans living in Amman for business purposes. But the most striking were the tribal sheikhs in their voluminous robes, fine black wool abas bound with gold, and black and white kaffiyehs, or head scarves, crowned with the traditional agal, or circular rope of black and gold thread.

I caught Bob's eye in the throng and moved over to him. "Do you remember ever seeing sheikhs in their robes at diplomatic functions in the past?"

He shook his head. "Well, some of the Iraqi sheikhs were members of Parliament before the revolution, but they often changed into English suits for affairs like these. Apparently attitudes have changed."

The sheikhs were numerous. They sat on overstuffed sofas plying amber worry beads between their fingers, eyeing the moving throng. They lounged by the Western-style buffet, looking at the finger food laid out for guests: carrot sticks, deviled eggs, tiny rolls, meatballs to be speared with colored toothpicks. Men drifted past the buffet table in dark suits, women in silken dresses of peacock colors. Here and there one glimpsed a Moroccan caftan fastened with silver, a printed shimmering sari from India, a Sikh turban.

A tall young Jordanian woman in a long-sleeved, high-necked dress tried out her English on me.

"You have children?" she asked.

"Three."

She wrinkled her brows. "They are with you?"

"No. They are in America, in universities."

She took that in. "They are in America—and you are here. Why are you not in America with them?"

"I am here with my husband." I pointed Bob out, talking in a corner to a stout gentleman I did not recognize.

"Ah." She nodded. "Your husband. He agrees to leave them there? And he wants you to come here with him?"

I nodded.

She peered at Bob again. "I see," she said, and laughed heartily. "Of course. He is young. My father is old. But he is good. And of course powerful."

"I would like to meet him."

"Sheikh Abdulla, my father," she said, and smiled. Her pride in him was also obvious.

I shook hands with the sheikh and said in Arabic that I was honored to meet him and that my husband also would be honored to meet him. We had friends in Iraq, I went on, and felt that I was babbling as I stared into that dark face; I realized I was trying to explain that our friends in Iraq were tribal leaders and therefore—therefore what?

Sheikh Abdulla turned to Bob, who had joined us. They shook hands. Bob tried out his twenty-five-year-old Iraqi Arabic dialect.

"Ah yes," said the older man. He smiled slightly. His false teeth shone. "I am from the north, the leader of many tribes, but we in Jordan are far from Iraq, and not only in geography these days, my friend. It is sad."

"Well," said Bob later. "Tribes are important here, obviously, but it's not a topic anyone wants to expound upon. The sources of power are secrets in any society, of course; it's hardly a thing you take up lightly at a party like this. He's a tough old man, Sheikh Abdulla. I would guess that King Hussein is lucky to have his allegiance in these troubled days. A palace guard is never enough to meet serious challenges."

Bob was articulating what we both felt, but had not stated, during our visit to Amman. For despite the signs of growth, the building and expansion, in the city and its outlying suburbs, despite the warmth of hospitality extended to us and the king's obvious determination to hold on to his nation, there was uneasiness in Amman, fear of the future. The thousands of people flocking across the borders, often illegally, from Syria, Lebanon, Israel, Iraq, were gathering around the king, the palace gates. Yes, they were coming for education, for economic betterment. But they were obviously also coming for protection. The king had been tested and tried for thirty years, as Jordan developed from a dependent mandate to a complex and quickly growing nation in the vulnerable center of the Arab world. He was perceived as a stable, honest leader with ancestral roots deep in the desert, in Islam. He was trying to hold out.

The prophet Jeremiah (49:2) cried, "I will cause an alarm of war to be heard in Rabbah of the Ammonites; and it shall be a desolate heap, and her daughters shall be burned with fire: then shall Israel be heir unto them that were his heirs, saith the Lord."

King Hussein was a presence that defied the prophecy and suggested that Amman, though beleaguered, would not be destroyed, but would live as a peaceful, prosperous city in the shadow of the towers and turrets of the Hashemite palace. Like ancient Philadelphia under Ptolemy II.

COLONIALISM EAST AND WEST

W E AMERICANS, unlike the Arabs, tend to regard our colonial period with pride and nostalgia. Colonial Williamsburg, for example, is a pleasant symbol of the American past. For the thousands of tourists who visit its restored workshops, houses, and gardens each year, it represents the admirable qualities of the early American colony. Americans see demonstrated there the ability to make a living on a new land and to adapt old technologies to fit the needs of a new country—all the virtues of pioneer invention, strength, perseverance, and innovation.

Given our pride in our own colonial past, it is often difficult to relate to the Arab world's reactions to *their* colonial past: rage, shame, anger, the kind of anger that erupted into protest marches, peasant revolts, strikes, terrorism, and guerrilla warfare, which culminated in conflicts far more violent than the struggles of colonial America in its revolution against the British. The American Revolution was fought fiercely, but the residue of bitterness dissipated rather quickly, and by 1785 Great Britain and the new United States of America had established diplomatic and trade relations. The two countries share a long history, a common language, a common religion, and bonds of kinship. We tend to forget that our ancestors, the colonial Yankees of whom we are so proud, were in their time also colonial invaders—of a continent peopled by American Indians. These native Americans may better be able to understand the Arab attitude.

Historically, however, the Arab world has had a far more complex colonial experience. Before the Europeans, the colonial rulers were the Muslim Turks of the Ottoman Empire, who dominated most of the area from the fourteenth through the eighteenth centuries. Then came the French, the English, the Italians, the Spanish—all of whom were far more foreign than the Turks, however disliked Turkish rule may have been. European colonials in the cities and villages of Iraq, Egypt, Algeria, Morocco, and the Levant spoke a language very different from Arabic and practiced a different religion. Unlike many of the English in

America or the Turks in the Arab world, the new European colonists in the Arab world did not settle down, intermarry, and become part of the local population; these Westerners stood apart and looked down upon their Arab subjects or at best considered them as "other." They were strangers as well as foreigners. There was no shared culture, but rather a long history of conflict going back to the seventh century and the fall of the Christian Byzantine Empire before the victorious Islamic armies. Thus, every reason for misunderstanding existed between the Arab and the European, who had centuries before struggled against each other in the bitter wars of the Crusades.

European imperialism in the Middle East is seen by some historians as in part a reaction to America's success in revolting against the British and buying out the French through the Louisiana Purchase. The declaration of American independence changed the balance of power. Britain and France were deprived not only of taxes but also of a source of cheap labor and raw materials as well as a market for European goods. The Arab lands, so much more accessible than North America, took on new attraction. When Napoleon landed in Egypt in 1798, nearly twenty years after the American Revolution had ended, some trade agreements had already been established in the Arab world by foreign powers. By 1853 Sir Richard Burton could write, "Egypt is the most tempting prize which the East holds out to the ambition of Europe." The Suez Canal Company was formed by Ferdinand de Lesseps with a majority of European stockholders in 1858. France conquered Algeria in 1830, Tunisia in 1863, most of Morocco in 1912, and proceeded to bring in French settlers to displace local farmers. Italy invaded Libya in 1913 and later expropriated local farms for the use of Italian settlers. In contrast, virtually no English farmers came to Iraq and Egypt; Britain aimed at political control and economic exploitation, rather than settling its people in the Arab world. Exclusive trade relationships and a guaranteed source of raw materials, such as cotton to supply the textile mills of Manchester, were of greater interest to Britain than agricultural settlements.

All the colonial powers, however, were interested in education to different degrees; the United States was no exception. The French Jesuits established a missionary school in the Levant as early as 1734, another in Damascus in 1755. French and British schools were opened in Egypt in the early nineteenth century, and by 1860 the American missionaries alone were operating thirty-three small schools in the Levant. Robert College was opened in Turkey in 1863, the French University of St. Joseph in Beirut in 1874, the American University in Beirut in 1866. It was not enough to merely seek economic gains in the Middle East. Souls were to be saved and the curse of "Mohammedanism" lifted from the ignorant. The missionary effort, seen as part of the "white man's burden" in Africa and Asia, reflected an unshakable belief in the superiority of Christian Europe and in the general need to "uplift" the Islamic world to the level of the West.

The curious mixture of political ambition, idealism, economic greed, and Eurocentric religiosity that constituted colonialism in the Arab world bears little resemblance to our perception of colonialism in American history and is far more complicated. There were some benefits. The new missionary schools and hospitals in the Arab communities provided help and encouragement; indeed, some say the American missionary schools' tradition of freedom of thought encouraged the development of anti-imperialism and Arab nationalism. But overall, the foreign presence had a more corrosive effect on Arab society than was apparent to either side at the time, or than is even recognized today by many former colonials, more than a generation later.

Why was it corrosive? Certainly, a limited amount of basic infrastructure was developed, in the form of roads, dams, communication systems, and modern government institutions. What, then, was wrong with this introduction to the conveniences and conventions of the West? As many colonial administrators said at the time, "We are really helping these people. Why aren't they more grateful? Why don't they appreciate all that we are doing for them?"

To comprehend something of the feelings of the Arab people who were colonized, we need to recognize that the rule of powerful foreigners meant a devaluation of indigenous political institutions, language, laws, religious practices, arts, methods of trade, agriculture, and irrigation. Traditional technologies were disdained as backward and primitive; new Western methods were introduced, forcibly if necessary.

In many cases changes under European rule fundamentally upset local patterns of social and economic relations. In southern Iraq, for example, the British surveyed the countryside and registered all land in the names of the sheikhs of the tribes. But the sheikhs had not owned the land as individuals; they managed it and arbitrated disputes over its uses, together with the senior members of their tribe, for whom they spoke. Much of the land was for grazing and used by all the members of the tribe. By registering the land in the names of the sheikhs, the British created a class of large landowners in southern Iraq; as a result, individual tribespeople and their families were impoverished. The old system of tribal ownership was destroyed and traditional patterns of tribal authority were undermined.

In Algeria much of the land held and cultivated by local communities of farm families was simply taken away from its users and allotted to individual French farmers with the justification that the French would cultivate the land more efficiently and scientifically, thus contributing to the overall good of the country. Even though some compensation occurred, many Algerians ended up working as laborers on what they considered their own land. So while European technological know-how was often respected and aspects of the European life were emulated by the small elite of foreign-educated Arabs, colonial expropriation of land, devaluation of local ways, and interference with local practices and beliefs were deeply resented and ultimately harmful.

There were other problems. Arabic, the major language of the area, admired by Arabs for its beauty and revered as the language of divine revelation in the Koran, became almost a liability for Arabs with political and economic ambitions. To obtain employment or to conduct major business with the colonial administrators, an Arab needed French, English, or Italian; the occupiers did not learn the language of the occupied. Thus, ambitious parents sent their children to the missionary schools to learn the foreign languages so that they might better compete for a high place in the new social order. From these schools emerged many of the leaders of the new nationalist states a generation later. Yet the missionary education was offered to only a few, and was expensive; only the wealthy could afford to send their children to such schools. Thus, the colonial schools educated an elite, a tiny percentage of the population, which because of its privileged knowledge could enjoy many opportunities inaccessible to most of the people. In 1956, when Morocco gained its independence after forty-four years of French and Spanish rule, there were exactly forty Moroccan university graduates in the entire country.

Religious belief was also devalued by the colonizers. Islam was seen as stagnant, fatalistic, a religion in decline. "The dead hand of

Islam" was something to be cast off, in the view of many colonial administrators, so that the Arabs could enjoy the new advantages offered by Western civilization. There were few converts to Christianity from Islam, however. Instead, proselytizing Protestant sects from Europe and America had to be content with converting local Christians, members of Orthodox and Coptic congregations. Such Christian minorities found special favor with the colonialists and often filled white-collar positions in embassies and trade missions. Islam was so generally depreciated that many members of the elites educated in Western schools turned to a kind of general secularism which discounted all religion as useful in the struggle toward modernization and eventual independence. The result was a serious breach between the religious practices of these elites and those of the majority of the faithful, a breach that has only begun to be bridged in the last decade.

Reactions to the colonial presence took different forms. Many large landowners, traders, and wealthy merchants who constituted the local elites in North Africa and the Near East welcomed the French, British, and Italians, seeing in colonial interests a way to improve their own positions. But small businessmen and artisans, the backbone of local mercantile capitalism, were often shut out of the colonial economy, owing to lack of capital and inability to speak foreign languages. Moreover, their children did not attend foreign schools, for they were needed to work in the family enterprises, and so there was little chance that a second generation would break into the closed colonial circle. As for the poor, who constituted the great majority of people in all Arab countries, they simply retreated, closing their doors literally and figuratively against the foreign presence. While the poor could not avoid the economic consequences of colonialism—or the political consequences— they took care to keep foreigners away from their families and out of their homes. It was only after 1912, for example, when the French took over the governing of Morocco and were present in daily affairs, that Moroccan women began to wear the all-enveloping jellaba and the face veil, to hide themselves from the gaze of these strangers.

Not all resistance and resentment were so passive. The Mahdist 1885 defeat of General Charles Gordon at Khartoum and the following thirteen years of Sudanese independence until Horatio Kitchener recaptured the country in 1898 showed that the British were not invincible. In Libya the Sanusi religious brotherhoods established a powerful network of Islamic education and trade centers across the southern desert, centers that became bastions of resistance against the Italian colonialists. Demands for independence were voiced not only by Islamic figures such as Muhammad Abdu in Egypt but even by the Westernized sons and daughters of the rich old elites who were less enchanted with the foreign presence than their parents had been. The British were forced to resort to bombing unruly tribal settlements in southern Iraq as late as 1932, in a decade that also marked uprisings in Palestine and Morocco. Such revolts required larger and larger numbers of European troops to "pacify" the countryside and made foreign occupation increasingly costly.

It was the Versailles peace talks of 1919 that marked the real beginning of Arab nationalism. During World War I the Western Allies had vied with the Germans and Italians for the support of the Arabs, each side promising the Arabs in exchange greater independence after the war. As a result, the growing rebelliousness of the area was temporarily restrained. But the peace bargaining table did not produce the promised independence.

Instead, mandates and protectorates over Arab lands were handed out among the victorious Allies as spoils. The Europeans claimed that the Arab people were still not ready to assume the direct governance of their countries. But in the view of the Arabs this was largely an excuse to permit the European powers to secure their own future interests. Egypt and Iraq were to be governed by the British, and the Levant was carved up into the countries of Transjordan, Palestine, Syria, and Lebanon under British and French supervision. North Africa was divided between France (Morocco, Algeria, Tunisia), Spain (Morocco), and Italy (Libya). Thus, independence, so enthusiastically promised before World War I, turned out to be politically inexpedient when the battles were over.

The division of the Arab world among the European powers did not pass without protest. In 1919 demonstrations took place across the Arab world. Peasant men and women tore up the railway tracks in Lower Egypt to prevent the British troop trains from running. Cairo was the scene of massive demonstrations and a boycott of British goods. In Iraq a Shia revolt against the British took place in 1920. In Morocco Abdul Krim's Rif tribesmen rose against the Spanish colonialists in 1921 and marched on to disrupt French markets and attack French outposts. In Turkey Atatürk defeated the sultan and the Turkish republic was born—an inspiration for many through the region.

For the next forty years, people throughout the Arab world rose up again and again against the European presence from Fez to Cairo. By the 1950s a group of young intellectuals had emerged, advocating local independence, following the example of earlier nationalists such as Jamal al-Din al-Afghani and Saad Zaghlul. As Frantz Fanon said, "What is given is not the same as what is taken." The people of Algeria took him seriously; they would retrieve from the French, they said, the land that had been taken from them. Every Arab country, with the exception of Saudi Arabia (which had never been occupied by Europeans), struggled with varying degrees of violence throughout the fifties for self-determination. Some replaced mandate-appointed leaders with more popularly backed candidates, while others rose to push the colonial powers out of the seats of government by force. By 1962 most countries of the Arab world had declared themselves independent. France, Britain, and Italy withdrew from all direct rule in the Arab world, yielding to superior force, changing priorities, or, in some cases, international presence. It was the end of an era. But eras do not end tidily. Arabs felt they had scores to settle and that they must secure their economies against foreign domination. In Egypt Gamal Abdel Nasser began to tax foreign companies, insisted that official business be carried out in Arabic, and abolished special courts to try foreign offenders. Nasser's supreme act of independence, however, was his nationalization of the Suez Canal in 1956, twelve years before the French concession would have run out. The British and the French, together with the Israelis, protested Nasser's audacity with troops and bombers, but the United States refused to support the attack and called for an end to the aggression.

The wave of strong anti-Western feeling throughout the Arab world was accompanied by a period of nationalistic concerns. National image became more important; every new country instituted its own airline service; foreign products were out and local products in. New health services and widespread free public education in Arabic became matters of primary importance. Pride in the Arab past was reflected in the arts and literature, which in the fifties and sixties appeared to be entering a new renaissance based on a combination of indigenous and Western models.

Today foreign rule is absent, but the colonial presence remains, albeit in different forms. The West is present through the thousands of tourists who are essential to the economies of many Arab countries, through the Western television programs that fill the screens in many Arab homes, and through the Western consumer goods that flood the markets. The rich Arab countries must reach economic agreements with foreign powers in order to sell their oil; the oil revenues themselves are then invested in those same foreign countries. Poorer nations, to attract the capital necessary for industrialization, must mortgage crops and products for years in advance to foreign countries. The Western presence is also felt in the American support of Israel, which in the eyes of many Arabs is seen as a new imperialist power, one that has already seized Arab lands by force and that has stated aspirations to extend its rule as far as the border of biblical Judah.

Thus, what seems to be emerging in the 1990s is a new stage in the colonial encounter. Many citizens of the Arab world feel their nations have traded the status of colonies for that of Third World countries, still tied to their colonialist rulers by a world economy over which they have little control. Egyptians under Anwar Sadat felt that only the end of financially ruinous conflict with Israel could bring any hope for independent national development. Other Arabs privately agree that peace in the Middle East is essential but remain far from convinced that either Israel or the United States really wants peace. People of the Arab world are now affirming areawide commonalities such as religious identity as a statement of pride in historical tradition. Such a statement is also a defense against what they recognize as a remaining vulnerability to Western interests. Some countries, such as Saudi Arabia and Libya, are even forbidding tourism and restricting the use of Western television programs, in an effort to reduce foreign influence.

Colonialism, then, is both an idea and an experience. In both respects, American and Arab colonialism have differed markedly. No gracious monument like Williamsburg, Virginia, is likely to be built to honor the colonial past in the Arab world today. The bitterness is too deep and the process of independence still unfinished.

A sun of grass and two doves singing
Before the beginning and after the end
of time
They burn in the branches
of the transparent willow

Muhammad Abd al-Hayy
A SIGN

THE LANDSCAPE OF THE Hashemite Kingdom of Jordan varies wildly
and dramatically, from the vast arid Syrian deserts in the east to
the precipitous Shiraa mountain ranges in the south, from dry wadis,
or ravines, between mountain ranges to rushing streams along the
widening fertile valleys. In Amman, the capital city, the landscape also
varies. The distinctive hills and valleys define the city for its people, not
only physically but symbolically, bearing in their names—Jebel
Weibdeh, Jebel Amman, Wadi Saqra—the history of human settlement
in the area. Archaeologists believe that human beings have been living
around Amman for about six thousand years, grazing their flocks on
the hillsides, cultivating grain in the valleys, wearing down the mountains and the fields. They quarried stone to build houses and fortresses
on the hilltops, for the hills were easy to defend against marauders.

The residents of Amman in the 1990s still use those names—
Jebel Weibdeh, Jebel Amman, Wadi Saqra—to refer to the sites of the
original villages that crowned the high empty slopes and marked the
valleys of cultivation. But Amman has grown since 1950 from a small
capital with a population of 100,000 to a bustling metropolis of a million and a half, expanding from a handful of hilltop villages to a dense
mass of houses, shopping malls, banks, museums, small industrial com-
plexes, schools, and hospitals. The old place-names are beginning to
fade.

Still, the hilltops remain the choice building sites. King Hussein lives on one, in his walled castle with his fourth wife, the American-born Queen Noor. The king has reigned for forty-three years now, longer than any other Arab leader; he and Queen Noor have four children—two boys and two girls. And many of the older, more established families continue to live in the heights, far above the newcomers, the refugees and the squatters, who started by camping in the wadis and then building houses as time passed. In 1981, the last time we had visited Amman, the long slopes of sand and pebbles were topped with stout enclaves of stone houses. But by 1996 the sand and pebbles had been completely covered over. From a distance the hills seemed to be paved with stone, so closely were the houses built next to each other.

In the fading light of a clear winter day the hills seemed luminous and opaque, as the sun caught corners and roofs of houses, built of biscuit-colored stone and that rosy-veined limestone found only in Jordan, the color reminiscent of the sandstone that delights the eye in the temples of the ancient city of Petra.

Amman has become a booming, dynamic capital, and yes, the old nomenclature of hills and valleys, of jebels and wadis, is disappearing as people begin to identify themselves in terms of new districts, Abdoun and Sweifieh, and landmarks such as mosques, churches, hotels, pharmacies, and embassies. But despite new street names and new maps, Amman is growing so fast that the directories and maps, to say nothing of the people themselves, cannot keep up. For example, Marcelle Wahba, the public affairs officer at the American Embassy, and her businessman husband, Derek Farwagi, lived in a gorgeous new house on a small street that bore one name at the bottom of the road and a second name at the top.

"You just tell the taxi driver to turn right after the Al-Kiima pharmacy," explained Marcelle, who was kindly putting us up during our stay. "Don't even try to get into the street-name game. Nobody, including us, has it figured out yet."

The shepherds who used to graze their flocks of sheep on the hills of Amman haven't figured it out, either, but, finding no food for the sheep on those luminous stone slopes, they have meandered farther and farther down into the wadis. That first morning in Amman, as Bob and I sat at breakfast with Tom Hartwell, who had come to take photographs, we saw through the kitchen window a large flock of shaggy brown sheep move into view. They were ambling across the empty lot between Marcelle and Derek's house and the neighbor's walled patio, nibbling bits of grass that sprouted between the stones. The combination of the modern houses and the traditional shaggy sheep, guided by the kaffiyeh-wearing shepherd, was too much for Tom.

"I see a picture," he said, and within minutes he was circling inside the flock, his camera in hand.

What no one had counted on was the sheepdog, a faithful and vigilant presence who saw a stranger intruding on the peaceful eating habits of his sheep, and immediately sank his teeth into Tom's leg.

"He was only doing his job, Tom," said Bob as they prepared to set off for the hospital for rabies shots.

"Damn it, Bob, I was only doing my duty, too," said Tom rather snappishly, looking at the blood on the back of his calf where the dog had managed to bite through his heavy jeans and socks.

"At least it wasn't your lens arm," I said, and Tom glared.

"A little sympathy, B.J.," he said, "before I get shot!"

SINCE OUR LAST VISIT TO AMMAN, a series of momentous events had catapulted Jordan into a position of international as well as regional importance. After years of struggle over whether the king or Yasir Arafat was the proper representative of the Palestinian people, King Hussein had given up his claim. Theoretically, this had already happened with the 1974 Arab Summit declaration that the Palestine Liberation Organization was the only true representative of the Palestinians on the West Bank. Still, legal and administrative ties remained from the time the West Bank had been part of old Transjordan, and it was only in 1988 that the king formally cut those ties and recognized the PLO.

In 1990 Saddam Hussein of Iraq invaded Kuwait. King Hussein refused to join the U.S.-led anti-Saddam alliance, stressing that Arabs should resolve their differences among themselves. The Gulf War and its aftermath was a difficult period for Jordan. The United States, Saudi Arabia, and other Gulf States cut off private and public economic aid. In addition, remittances from Jordanian workers in the Gulf, which had added significantly to state revenues over the years, came to an end, as the workers were expelled from jobs in the Gulf as punishment for their king's support for Iraqi Saddam Hussein.

During the fall of 1990 and the winter of 1991 at least 700,000 men and women streamed into Jordan. The majority of them stayed, and began to look for work in their own country.

The 1995 estimate of unemployment was 15 percent. The per capita income remained low, at $1,240, and the World Bank estimated that about one-fifth of Jordan's population of 4 million to 4.5 million lived below the poverty line.

After the Israelis and Palestinians signed the 1993 Oslo accords, Jordan concluded its own peace treaty with Israel. In July 1994 the king officially agreed to end the state of war that had existed between the two countries for nearly half a century. By 1996 Jordan's King Hussein had brought his country back into the good graces of both West and East with his support for the Israeli-Palestinian peace accords, a support that many Jordanians felt was "too much and too wholehearted."

"He could have gone to Yitzhak Rabin's funeral, but did he have to make such a complimentary speech there? He was the only leader from the Arab world to do so," said a well-known journalist.

But King Hussein is in a complex position, living as he does in a small kingdom bordered by Saudi Arabia, Syria, Israel, Iraq, and Egypt, all major players in the long-running conflict between Israel and the Palestinians.

He is still host to more than a million Palestinian refugees, some of whom have been living in ten UNRWA camps in Jordan off and on since 1948. And he and his people struggle with ethnic issues, such as "Who is a Jordanian?" Officially, there are no "minorities" in Jordan, but clear differences do exist. Recent censuses have found that between 65 and 70 percent of all Jordanians identify themselves as of Palestinian origin, which may be partly attributed to the high rate of marriage between Palestinians and Jordanians. Within the majority of Sunni Muslims, small groups retain pride in their Circassian and Chechen roots. Religious issues have become more important in recent years, however, as the Islamic revival has reached Jordan. The Islamists have chosen to work within the system, a relationship for which King Hussein is given much credit. They have regularly run for office, and in 1996 they occupied one-fourth of the seats in Jordan's Lower House of Parliament. About 8 percent of Jordan's 4 million citizens are Christian, and over the years, Muslim-Christian relations have remained generally cordial. It is understood that a Christian will probably never be prime minister, but each cabinet usually contains one or two Christians, and a number of parliamentary seats are filled by Christians and Circassians, elected in proportion to their numbers.

The key to maintaining accord in this complex, multiethnic kingdom, a fortress or bridge in the center of the Arab world, is economic well-being. Thus, the Middle East and North African Economic Summit, held in Amman at the end of October 1995, where Israel was a major presence, turned out to be a kind of triumph for King Hussein.

"Everybody came that was invited," said Marcelle, "all the different leaders, and the general result was that a working plan for joint economic action is now on the books."

Accounts of the summit cite new initiatives in trade, tourism, and banking already in progress. The European Union was an active player in this meeting, as was the United States, and offices for economic cooperation now exist in Algeria, Cyprus, Egypt, Israel, Jordan, Lebanon, Malta, Morocco, Palestine, Syria, Tunisia, and Turkey.

"What was particularly interesting," said another diplomat, "was the attitude of the Jordanians. Unlike some of the other Arab countries, such as Egypt, Jordan's representatives were not at all shy about approaching Israelis and proposing joint ventures."

The general sense was that joint economic activity is on track, even as political negotiations between Israeli and Palestinian leaders falter, founder, and sometimes seem to approach breakdown.

"I think it's because Jordanians don't have the hang-ups of some of the other Arabs," said the diplomat. "They have been dealing with the Israelis for many years, *not as suppliants*, but as equals."

This point of view was also expressed by our old friend Amer Salti, the Palestinian-refugee-turned-philosopher and finally affluent and influential Jordanian banker. We went to see him and his wife, Rebecca, at their home in Amman. Amer is a great golfer, and when Jordan signed a peace treaty with Israel, he decided he wanted to be the first Jordanian to play golf on the highly touted course at Caesarea, near Mount Carmel, which lies within Israel's borders. So he set off, his car loaded with the paraphernalia of the respected game of golf. But, despite the peace treaty, the border between Jordan and Israel still has checkpoints and Israeli Defense Forces personnel, housed in a tall cement bunker near the Allenby Bridge. The guards looked at the golf bag and asked Amer to take it out of his car. He did so. "What is it?" asked one of the young Israeli soldiers, looking suspiciously at the heavy leather bag with its clutch of clubs, their heads protected by individual chamois bags.

"Golf clubs," answered Amer, who told us he could not help smiling as he said it. "And then the soldier looked really alarmed," he added. They asked him to take the clubs out of the bag and the chamois covers off the clubs. And there they were, a collection of strange instruments, with long metal handles, their heads shaped into what the golfer would call a mashie, a driver, or a niblick.

"The soldiers had probably never seen a golf club," volunteered Tom.

"Thought they were weapons, probably."

"Well," said Amer, "they banned golf in Scotland in the fifteenth century for some such reason. Anyway, we stood there at the crossing. I guess they were waiting for the explosion but of course it didn't come. Finally, the guy asked me what I did with them."

Amer had explained that it was just a game, and to prove his point, set a golf ball down on the checkpoint tarmac and proceeded to tap the little white ball gently with his mashie. Other travelers on both sides of the bridge watched this display from their cars, in some bewilderment and amusement. Eventually, after a phone call to a higher authority, the young Israeli guard let Amer put the little chamois bags on the heads of his clubs, put all the clubs back in the bag, and cross the bridge into Israel.

"So did you finally get to play?" Tom asked.

Amer smiled broadly. "Oh yes," he answered. "Once I got to Caesarea itself, everything went very well. When the word got out that I was a Jordanian, the manager of the club came over and insisted that this round was on the club. They wouldn't let me pay. And since I'm a pretty good player, soon the Israeli golf pro, a very nice woman from New York, came and asked to go a round with me. And we are still friends."

"Still?"

"Yes. The next year she came and stayed with us, with her two sons, and we played golf in Jordan."

Rebecca, Amer's wife, nodded. "I liked her," she said, "though I must say I didn't expect to."

Amer's mother sat near us. She was old now, not as vigorous as when we visited in 1981. She had cooked a magnificent lunch for us then, a traditional Arab feast there in the Saltis' modern new house, with its view over the sandy, pebbled hills down to the wadi.

"It's Amer's mother who has made it possible for me to work all these years, now on the Dana Project that you'll see tomorrow," said Rebecca, looking at the old woman with affection. "She's cooked for us and helped raise our girls, just as she raised her own children after her husband died, and they had to make do. Those were bad years, weren't they, Ammi?" She spoke the last few words in Arabic and Amer's mother responded.

"Yes, but I have been blessed now with good years and good grandchildren," she said. And then, in English, she called the girl who had been hired to help in the household in her old age, a quiet Pakistani girl who brought us juice and small bowls of delicious "hors d'oeuvre soup," Rebecca called it.

"Equals," said Amer. "We need to treat each other as equals before we can have real peace in the Middle East. It's beginning, but we have a long way to go."

THE GROWING POPULATION of Amman and all of Jordan has put great pressure on the country's resources, especially water and land. "There can be no freedom for anyone if there is no water to drink in the household taps," Anis Muasher told me when I went to see him about his lifelong concern with conservation, and specifically a three-year-old project at Wadi Dana, which had been recently praised by an official of the World Bank, James Wolfensohn. Rebecca Salti, who had arranged the interview, accompanied me.

"He actually told us that Wadi Dana was one of the best World Bank projects he had seen," said Mr. Muasher with a pleased look. A middle-aged businessman in a gray suit, Muasher interrupted the flow of customers, associates, and accountants streaming in and out of his office to order coffee for us and to talk in a gentle but surprisingly intense voice about the love of his life, Wadi Dana.

"My friend Leila Sharaf, who is a member of Parliament, jokes that the Dana Project is like my second wife," he added. "I suppose she is right. But my wife is interested in it, too." He smiled, a bit self-consciously.

"What's so special about Wadi Dana?" I asked, hoping to provoke him, and I did, for he talked steadily for half an hour about the beauties of the area, the importance of its ecosystems ("not one, but twelve ecosystems, *madame*"), and the opportunity posed by Wadi Dana for Jordan to make a real contribution to global concern over the deteriorating environment—land, species, water, plants.

"Those species are just like us," said Mr. Muasher, "in danger. But they can't do anything about it. We can. And we are trying to do it."

Mr. Muasher's no-nonsense desk sits in front of a window, and the right side of the office is filled with books and papers, neatly filed. A large placard framed in gold hangs over the bookshelves, announcing "God so loved the world that he didn't send a committee." I considered making a quip to the effect that with the World Bank, he was certainly into a committee, but decided against it.

"I can't really say that I understood the environmental issues when we started our first little outdoor club," said Muasher, taking off his steel-rimmed glasses and wiping his eyes with a large clean, white handkerchief. "There were several of us. We used to enjoy camping and hiking and riding, getting to know our own country, back in the fifties. Then we began to see how fast things were deteriorating—the gazelles and the bustards were almost gone. In the eastern desert, green areas were disappearing from overgrazing, and too much hunting was going on. Things were getting out of control."

"But how did you move to an organization?" asked Rebecca.

"Well, Rebecca—" He stopped and turned to me. "Rebecca is doing good work on our project." He smiled at both of us. "Okay. One day six of us got together at my house and decided to start a small conservation club. That's maybe as far as we would have gotten except that it happened at the same time a group of English naturalists came to Jordan and had an audience with King Hussein—people like Sir Guy Montfort and Julian Huxley, who wrote *Portrait of a Desert.* The king knew about our little group and asked us to meet with the English naturalists. And that was how it started."

"Wadi Dana?"

"No, Wadi Dana is only three years old as a project. Lots of things happened before then. There was no legislation for conservation, and so we took the legislation designed to protect agricultural lands and expanded it to include wild areas. First we set up the Azraq Wetlands

National Park, that was in 1966, established as a research station. From that work we could begin to see that our little problem in Jordan was part of a much bigger international problem."

The king agreed to be patron of a chapter of the Royal Society for the Conservation of Nature (RSCN), Muasher told us. Then Muasher and Wasfi Tel, an early political backer who was assassinated in 1971 while serving as prime minister, struggled to get the planks of the RSCN platform accepted by the government. Muasher himself took over the work after Tel's death.

The society was set up, he said, to enforce the laws that had already been passed to preserve and protect wildlife, especially endangered species; to establish structures to manage the protected sites within Jordan; and to create public understanding of the need for conservation of nature. "It was hard going in the early years," said Mr. Muasher. "People just didn't get it. But in 1978 we were lucky. We became famous because of our part in saving that beautiful animal the Arabian oryx. The society took on four males and four females, and by 1983 there were over thirty thriving wild oryx . . . here, here in Jordan!" Muasher thumped on his desk. "We hit *The Guinness Book of World Records* and we celebrated in the Shumeri reserve, where the oryx are living. King Hussein and Queen Noor came, and that helped a lot. We started to form conservation clubs in the schools, and the queen was very supportive, starting reforestation projects and so on."

"The Dana Project," I prompted.

"Ah yes." Mr. Muasher put his glasses back on and leaned over the desk to speak to us. This is important, his gesture said.

"Ah yes," he repeated. "The Dana Project. It is very beautiful. And so when we decided to ask for funds to start a new conservation movement in Jordan, we chose Dana!"

"Why?"

"Why?" Mr. Muasher stood up and brought his hands together in a soundless clap. "Why? You must go, *madame*, and see for yourself. Take her, Rebecca."

"We're going tomorrow," said Rebecca.

"Good. Good. See what we are doing there, *madame*. We are crossing all kinds of boundaries in Dana—political boundaries, too. You go to Dana. And I must go back to work." He punched a button on his desk, the phone began to ring, and the door opened to admit a young man bearing a fistful of faxes.

"Thank you!" I said.

"You will see the beauty," he called to us as we headed out of the office, down the stairs, and onto the top of one of the old Amman hills, now become a new business center—Jebel Amman.

THE DANA PROJECT is an ambitious multifaceted conservation effort spreading across 185 square miles of diverse natural terrain. The nature reserve, a protected area for wildlife since 1989, is only one part of the project, which includes a campsite, six hiking trails, and a visitors' research center, situated at Dana Village, on the rim of the Wadi Dana.

Wadi Dana lies a hundred miles or so down the King's Highway, which follows a nearly straight line from Amman to the port of Aqaba, on the Red Sea. This is part of the Great Rift Valley, which sweeps down from Turkey through Jordan and on south to central East Africa. The valley plunges to the lowest spot on earth, the Dead Sea, 1,312 feet below sea level, and rises to heights of 5,500 feet, in the Shiraa Mountains. From a mere cleft between rugged rocks, as in the entrance to Petra, the forgotten ancient city of Jordan, the valley sometimes opens out to arable plains several miles wide. These lowlands are rich in mineral springs, and the highlands, which include the hills of Amman, are hospitable to fruit trees as well as vegetables and grains.

Conquerors and invaders have left their marks here, the Nabateans in the hidden rose-red city of Petra, the Romans in Jerash as well as Amman itself, the Crusaders in their southwest castle of Shobek. Petroglyphs on the rocks in the wadis testify to the presence of people in prehistoric times, people who recorded the presence of the animals who shared their environment—the oryx, the gazelle, the hyena.

As for Dana Village, the average tourist, Jordanian or non-Jordanian, probably would not stop there, for it is situated off the King's Highway, in a mountainous area known best for the presence of a new cement factory. But Rebecca, who came here twice a week as part of her job as coordinator of the Dana Project's socioeconomic activities, was hardly the average tourist. She turned sharply off the main road at the town of Qadessiyah and shifted into lower gear. We began to climb out of the desert valley, up, up, up, over one rising hill after another. Rock formations loomed on the horizon, and peaks beyond, cutting darkening fretted shadows against the clear blue sky. Then there was a large puff of smog—the cement factory.

"Not too much farther," said Rebecca, "and then you will see the place of which I suppose you could say, B.J., that we are excessively proud. Oh dear, that's an awful sentence, but you know what I mean." Rebecca's enthusiasm was infectious, and we looked around and ahead, at the rapidly changing landscape.

"Of course, the fact that the World Bank thinks it's great makes us even prouder. We're doing something that *matters*."

"But . . ." I peered at the cement factory, three hills across from us, spewing noxious smoke high into that blue sky which was turning gray near the buildings.

"But what, B.J.?" asked Rebecca, skirting a pothole and bouncing onto the gravel shoulder of the road.

"I don't understand how you can have a gorgeous environmental project so close to that . . . industrial complex."

Rebecca was philosophical. "We can't just dismiss the cement factory," she said. "This is one of the poorest and least developed parts of Jordan, and until the conservation project came along, the factory was the only place where people could earn enough money to stay alive."

The village, I had been told, had been an agriculturally self-sufficient community in Ottoman times, at least two hundred years ago, and archaeologists think there was cultivation in the area long before that. Why were these once prosperous villagers so destitute that they had to go to work in a cement factory?

"The water holes dried up," said Rebecca matter-of-factly. "Didn't Anis tell you? I'll get you some stuff to read. But anyway, there used to be a lot of water holes in the mountains, and these watered the land, with occasional rain and snow runoff. But we've had droughts and the vegetation has been overgrazed. So both folks and animals have had to leave."

We rounded the last hairpin turn, and Rebecca stopped the car, skidding slightly on the loose pebbles. There, across the valley, were those dark, fretted peaks, their shadows darkening the rock walls of the valley. Below us was the village of Dana nestled on the very edge of a hospitably flat hill, a line of tall poplar trees marking its boundaries, the gray stone houses surrounded by dense greenery. Wild oaks, olives, pistachio trees, and pines grew here, we were told, and I recognized as Italian cypresses the black, tall trees in the center of the community.

"It's beautiful!" said Tom, who got out of the car with his camera, still favoring the leg that had been gnawed on by Marcelle's neighbor's sheepdog.

"It's more beautiful from a distance right now," Rebecca told us, "because the village was more or less abandoned—no reason to stay there when you can't make a living. And some houses collapsed and the paths were grown over, and some of the fields, too."

"Is there enough rebuilt so we can take pictures?" asked Tom.

"Oh yes. The Friends of Dana, a group of Jordanian women, has raised money to help rebuild sixty-five houses. The villagers help. And they asked for a mosque, so one has been built there."

We had driven on and now Rebecca came to a stop on a circular road which faced the wadi and pointed upward, where, as we got out of the car, we saw a neat mosque, newly built of rosy stone, set high like the rest of the village to face outward toward the mountains.

The village of Dana, up close, is on the very edge of sandstone cliffs that rise from the floor of the wadi, opposite the peaks of the Shiraa mountain range. But at this hour of the early afternoon, the famed red and white sandstone cliffs we had heard about were dulled; sun and shadow together had created another range of colors—blues, grays, midnight blue shading down into black as the cliffs dropped thousands of feet into the wadi below.

"The Grand Canyon of Jordan?" suggested Rebecca lightly.

"Not quite the same, Rebecca," answered Tom, checking his light meter, "but still beautiful."

"Welcome, welcome!" A small man in a *dish-dasha* came out of the visitors' center to help Rebecca unload supplies. Rugs for the floor of the visitors' center, said Rebecca, and for the rooms of the researchers; wires and tools for the Dana jewelry-making operation; boxes of books, plastic bags, and labels.

We shook hands with the small man who sported a mustache and had merry, sparkling eyes. This is Muhammad Musa Na'aneh, known, he said, as Abu Basil. Abu Basil, one of the original settlers of Dana Village, is currently headmaster of the local school. Economic circumstances, he told us, forced him to spend seven years abroad, working as an English teacher in Abu Dhabi and Oman.

"But I always came back to Dana, because we loved it so, and now it looks as though we can really live here again."

"How?" asked Tom, who was out on the bluff, looking at the view; I was not far behind.

Abu Basil, with a glance at Rebecca, who was listening carefully, said, "Let us go inside, and I will explain."

Rebecca looked pleased and ushered us into the visitors' center, built like visitors' centers in many national parks throughout the world, to take advantage of whatever view was going. But this building also housed visiting researchers—zoologists, botanists, ecologists. Designed by Jordanian architect Ammar Khammash to fit into the pattern of the old village, the two-story structure is of local stone and angled toward the canyon.

"Welcome! Welcome!" Abu Basil repeated, coming up the stairs where he and Rebecca, with Tom's help, deposited the boxes and rugs.

"Do not bother taking pictures," he told Tom, "until you can see from outside." He looked pleased and secretive at the same time, like a parent about to give a beloved child a present. We followed him out onto a wide stone terrace with an iron railing, which seemed to extend out over the valley itself. The dark escarpments, the valley between, and the high peaks blocking the opposite sky were spread before us in an incredible scenic panorama, unlike anything I had ever seen before in all our years in the Arab world. We stared and stared. Abu Basil smiled happily.

"Now I will explain to you why we are coming back. Okay, Rebecca?"

"Of course, Abu Basil."

"Perhaps Rebecca has already told you, but the project for conserving nature does not only involve animals and trees, but us, the people in the village."

He went on to tell us the history of the village, the good work of the Friends of Dana, the villagers' delight in their new mosque, the various activities that were bringing new income, like jewelry making, collecting and packaging herbs and dried fruits. Then he said, "Now I would like to give them the tourist spiel, okay?"

"Okay."

"English or Arabic? I would really like to practice my English."

"Okay."

Abu Basil rested his arm on the railing of the balcony, cleared his throat, and gestured with the other hand toward the splendid landscape. His eyes sparkled as he said formally, "Here, my friends, here you see that the scenery is spectacular and diverse."

We were clearly in agreement and he went on to talk about Dana, "this natural treasure in the heart of the Great Rift Valley." I thought to myself that Anis Muasher would be delighted with Abu Basil's "tourist spiel."

Researchers, it seemed, had already identified 555 species of plants, of which 55 are "medicinal and beneficial." There were at least 350 species of animals and birds, but he added, "I do not begin to count the insects."

Would tourists really come to Dana? we asked.

They were already coming, replied Abu Basil a bit huffily. They were filling the campsite at Rumanna, halfway down the bluff, on a green meadow where "twenty-two large tents, with three beds each," plus barbecue grills and bathrooms had been set up. Another campsite was being developed at the edge of Wadi Dana, near ancient Feinan, where copper has been mined since 3000 B.C. "The Romans had slaves there," Abu Basil told us. "No more, thanks be to God."

"And those who do not think to make reservations at the campsites can spend their days on the hiking trails."

The visitors' center, where we now stood on the terrace, admiring the "spectacular and diverse" scenery, is the site of research into the area's several ecosystems, and also the site of workshops, where we were led to see young women fashioning pins and necklaces and earrings out of silver and a strange blue stone, which is, geologists say, a combination of several semiprecious stones found only in Dana. The Dana stone.

The jewelry was featured in the center's souvenir shop, which looked much like souvenir shops in most national parks and museums, offering maps and posters bearing the slogan of the project, "Helping Nature Helping People," the Red Sea guide to diving and deep-sea fishing, and a new travelers guide to the six nature reserves of Jordan:

Dana, Shaumari, Wadi Mujib, Zubia, the Azraq Wetlands, and the Aqaba Marine Reserve. Colorful postcards depicted local species of animals under protection: the Arabian oryx, the gazelle, the onager, the ibex, even the wolf. And the birds, such as the great gray shrike, the little egret, the goldfinch, the cream-colored courser, and a special breed of nightingale which was new to us—the yellow-vented bulbul.

Rebecca pointed out the villagers' products.

"What makes Dana special is not just the conservation bit, B.J. That usually excludes people. In fact, in some countries the conservation has put people out of house and home. What we're trying to do here is put it all together, getting the people who live here to benefit from this as well as the onagers and the oryxes and the nightingales."

"I can see," said Tom, "that the silver jewelry might be a big seller and support those few women who make it. But who else gets a slice of the pie?"

"Well, all the guides are to be local people, like Abu Basil," continued Rebecca, "the guards of the campsite, and the people who are employed to care for the area. Some people should eventually be able to make a living with tourism. And then we've developed other small projects that make people money." She showed me the fragrant bars of olive-oil soap, the packets of organically grown herbs, the jars of apricot jam, and parcels of "Jordan Trail Mix," which includes raisins and nuts from the village. All were for sale in the souvenir shop.

"The women have dried raisins on their roofs forever," said Rebecca. "We just got them to package them and sell them this way. We can't keep up with the demand. It's amazing, really. I think this is just such a special area everyone wants to save it, *and* the people who live here."

A rough form of hand-modeled local pottery was also sold in the shop. "Abu Basil was the one who brought the woman in," said Rebecca, "a very old lady, the last in the village who made pottery. When people in Amman saw it, they thought it was antique, it looks so much like the pottery archaeologists turn up around here." The old woman had now been hired to teach others to make this pottery, which sold well.

Rebecca had thoughtfully brought a picnic lunch from Amman, and we sat in the visitors' center living room, off the terrace, from which we could still see part of the spectacular view. The tables and chairs are of that beautiful rosy marble, with legs and fittings the green of recycled iron. "Ammar Khammash calls himself the Iron Age Company," said Rebecca.

"It looks good, too," said Tom, munching his tuna sandwich. Abu Basil sat down with us, and his son came in with another visitor, a young man in jeans and blue shirt and beard. This was the government representative, one of the border patrol who watched for smugglers and poachers and illegal hunting. He smiled and apologized for not shaking hands with Rebecca and me, "because I am a strict Muslim." Some strict Muslim men, like some Orthodox Jews, do not usually shake hands with women.

Rebecca offered him an apple. He declined but took tea, which had been prepared and brought by Abu Basil's son.

The government guard, whose name was Ahmed, explained that most of the people who hunted illegally did so "because they need the meat, they are hungry. And"—he turned to Rebecca—"what are we going to do with the people in the valley? How can we tell them not to graze their sheep and goats? That's all they have to live on."

Rebecca said crisply, "You know we are thinking about that, Ahmed. We're not going to drive them out."

"Yes. Yes." Ahmed looked at her, looked at us, looked away. He stood up. "*Salaam alaikum,*" he said. "And God be with you."

"What Ahmed is asking is of course the challenge of the project," explained Chris Johnson the next day. He has been appointed by the World Bank to oversee the work at Dana. "That's why I'm here really." The project is funded through the Global Environment Facility, a funding mechanism created by the World Bank in response to the Rio summit on crises facing the planet.

He explained what we should already have recognized—the fact that most conservation projects around the world focus on the flora and fauna, but often exclude the human beings who earn their living in the areas being conserved. "Antisocial, I guess you'd call them," he said, a self-contained young British ecologist with a pleasant manner.

"What the Dana Project is trying to do," he said quietly, "is reverse this situation, try to relate conservation to the development of the local economy. Simply said, we are trying to build a bridge between protecting and fencing off a valuable area of ecosystem diversity and improving the local economy. Your comment from Ahmed, the forestry guard, is right on. What are we going to do?"

A good question, and a difficult one. More than six hundred families live in the Wadi Dana reserve, and their traditional lifestyle of nomadic pastoralism is threatened by the conservation measures proposed and authorized under the World Bank's long-term plan. In the next five years the tribes will presumably have to move or find other means of support. "It's tricky," said Chris, "trying to help create that bridge. Rebecca's working on rug making among the tribal women—that's a big source of income. But what about the men? We hope to involve them in the part of the project concerned with tourism. For they know the area, every plant and insect, better than anyone else. They've lived there all their lives. They could help tremendously.

"Tourism, handicrafts, and new approaches for agriculture—these are the income-producing activities we are working on," he said, "and that Rebecca has helped develop," he added with a quiet appreciative look at Rebecca. She was sitting up straight in Chris's living room chair, drinking the English tea brought by his wife, who was "also an ecologist," Chris told us. "We're working on our kids now." And he smiled proudly.

We had seen agricultural efforts in the village itself, where some people had begun to farm again, subsistence crops like onions and tomatoes, which they could eat, selling the surplus. But the amounts they could raise in the small terraced plots were so small they found it difficult to compete in the larger market. The project staff had brought in agricultural extension agents, who pointed out that the villagers could do much better financially if they grew organic herbs like mint, bay leaves, and thyme, which were in demand in the increasingly sophisticated and specialized markets of Amman.

"They'd make four or five times as much for the herbs as they make for the tomatoes," Rebecca had said. "But people are slow to change. This year, two people agreed to plant half their plots with thyme and mint. If they do well financially, next year other people will follow. We hope!"

A noble experiment, the project. Dana is only one of the six nature reserves that are part of a long-term program of conservation in Jordan. More than four hundred nature and conservation clubs are active in the schools, and Queen Noor has personally sponsored a series of afforestation campaigns organized by the Royal Society for the Conservation of Nature. But it is Dana that has captured the imagination, not only of the World Bank but of Jordanians themselves. The campsite is usually full, and for holidays, reservations for families must be made long in advance.

Anis Muasher, the energetic businessman who helped start the entire effort to save the Jordanian environment from deterioration, had said:

"Perhaps these young people who are hiking and camping today will soon come to appreciate, like my friends and I did when we were young, the wonders of life in the wilderness of their own country. Then we will have a real national cause. It will work!" He had added, "But we have to work at it, too!"

I continued to rhapsodize about my visit to the Dana Project at a dinner party the next evening, for I found myself unexpectedly seated opposite Leila Sharaf, the attractive member of the Jordanian Parliament who had supposedly told Anis Muasher that the Dana Project was like his "second wife."

"It's true. I said it." Madame Sharaf smiled, showing charming dimples in an expressive heart-shaped face, and dark eyes that sparkled beneath a fashionable halo of short black hair. Her navy suit was piped in white, and her hands, manipulating the silver knife and fork, were bare of rings. I had been told that her husband had died tragically young and she was now raising several children on her own, as well as serving in her country's legislative body.

"Anis is totally obsessed with Dana," she continued. "But Dana is probably worth it. It's very important for us, for everybody, what they are trying to do there in the mountains. Did you, *madame*, in all your trips to the Arab world, ever see mountains like that before?"

I confessed that I hadn't.

Rami Khouri, writer, publisher, talk-show host, and oftentimes government gadfly, leaned across the gold-embroidered tablecloth and said to me, "Don't be deceived by all the rosy pictures people like Anis and Leila paint for you about Jordan. We have lots of problems, real problems. You need to write about them!"

"Problems with Dana?"

"No, no." Leila Sharaf laughed. "Not about Dana. Rami doesn't think about conservation. He wants to talk to you about political problems, about . . ."

"Censorship!" finished Rami.

"Censorship?" I echoed.

"Yes," said Leila, and she did not laugh. "They've taken him off the air now and then, over the years, when he becomes too critical of what's going on."

The American diplomat on my right said, in a puzzled way, "But I thought, Mr. Khouri, you were going to be on television this coming week—on that talk show you do."

Rami looked at him, pushing up the bridge of his dark-rimmed glasses that matched his dark eyes and his neat dark hair. He was a big man, but fit, and his words came out carefully measured—for us, the foreign audience.

"That's right," he said. "The government is letting me speak again."

"So who's your first guest?"

"This lady here beside me," replied Rami, indicating Leila and pushing up his glasses again. The party was large and noisy and the room was getting warm. Leila took a drink of water and positively twinkled at us.

"So what is the topic?" asked the diplomat.

"Democracy, democracy," replied Rami, flourishing his fork high in the air and favoring us with a big sunny smile.

The diplomat looked a bit surprised, but he pulled himself up in his chair and launched into an appreciative lecture.

"I'm delighted to hear it," he said. "We at the embassy are always interested in democracy, that's what the United States is all about, after all. And it's good to hear that the *idea* of representative government is taken seriously here."

Rami shook his head from side to side and looked a bit annoyed.

"We have *always* had representative government here," he said, "tribal councils, rule by consensus—that is a tradition in Jordan."

The American diplomat begged to differ. "Not quite the same thing. But," he added, "your country's new Parliament does appear to signal a step in the right direction, toward the American, Western concept of democracy."

"Yes?" Leila had finished her dinner and pushed her plate aside and now sat with her elbows on the table, propping up her beautiful expressive face. She looked intently at the diplomat.

"Yes." The diplomat warmed to his subject. "I suppose the real question we should all be asking is, can the American example of democracy be grafted onto the Jordanian experience and result in a really, truly representative government, such as we all aspire to?"

Rami opened and shut his mouth. For a moment I thought he was going to disagree, and disagree sharply, with the tone as well as the substance of the diplomat's statement. But Leila took up the topic, cleared her throat ostentatiously, and Rami shifted his attention toward her instead, turning all the way around in his chair so he was not looking at me or the diplomat, but only at Leila.

"What an interesting notion!" she said sweetly, looking at the diplomat with a rapt air that should have softened the hardest of hearts. "Grafting democracy. You mean like grafting fruit trees?"

The diplomat smiled and nodded yes.

Rami said, "What I think is . . ."

But Leila put her hand gently on Rami's arm, and he stopped in midsentence.

"Grafting fruit," she repeated. "Doesn't it sometimes happen that when one grafts an apricot, say, with a peach, the result is a completely new and delicious fruit?"

"Sometimes that does happen," I put in. "My grandfather used to say that."

"Thus, Mr. G.," went on Leila, "perhaps we will, by grafting American democratic ideas onto old Jordanian patterns, produce a new and wonderful form. What do you think?"

Mr. G. was intelligent as well as diplomatic, and Leila Sharaf was a force to be reckoned with in Jordan, I had been told, both personally and politically. "Something to think about, certainly, Madame Sharaf," he said.

Rami banged his spoon on the table, in his delight causing us all to turn our attention back to him. "Great line, Leila," he said, beaming. "Will you say that on my television show this week?"

"Well," said Leila, glancing at me with a merry smile, "if you ask me the right questions, Rami, I might."

•   •   •

THE STAFF MEMBERS of the Dana Project say they are trying to practice ecotourism, a new and trendy concept that has begun to filter into the proposals and activities of ecologists around the world. It is particularly relevant in the Middle East and other areas once ruled by colonial representatives of the West. For in the old days, people say, tourism may have brought in hard cash, but it was also associated with colonialism and imperialism, the advent of foreign invaders who robbed countries of their natural resources, made the women into prostitutes and the men into pimps or soldiers in foreign armies. Tourism was equated with earnings, yes, but at great cost to local pride and identity, as well as to the environment and its historical monuments. The Roman amphitheater in the center of Amman still bears graffiti from tourists throughout the ages, and bits and pieces of Petra's rosy stone pillars as well as more valuable antiquities can be found in the homes of many European travelers and wealthy Jordanians, displayed among family mementos on bookshelves and in curio cabinets as travel souvenirs.

Ecotourism is something else, its advocates insist, tourism that honors people as well as environments. Today ecotourism has also become a means of peacefully negotiating common environmental problems shared by not-so-peacefully-inclined governments. ECOPEACE, a regional association of nongovernmental organizations, was established in 1994, and by 1996 Egypt, Israel, Palestine, and Jordan had joined the group. The organization has spawned smaller gatherings, such as those held without public fanfare over the past two years between Jordanian and Israeli conservationists. Anis Muasher, Chris Johnson, and Rebecca Salti were enthusiastic about the possibilities of such joint efforts. "They begin with a common language," said Anis Muasher.

"A common language?" I echoed.

"Yes, zoologists, botanists, geologists, they all speak the same language. Latin! We have to begin somewhere."

THE ECOPEACE MEETINGS CONTINUE, but political tension still exists in the Hashemite Kingdom of Jordan over the issue of how much consorting should go on between Israelis and Jordanians, the issue of "normalizing relations." Several professional groups in Jordan protest that things are happening much too fast, before a real peace is operating. The Jordan Writers Association, for example, expelled two of its members, one for giving an interview to Israeli television and another for performing political comedy in Israel. The medical and engineering associations banned their members from participating in the economic summit. And the situation has become worse since the April 1996 Israeli bombing attacks against Hezbollah forces in South Lebanon, and the resulting loss of over a hundred innocent civilian lives. Several Jordanians, both in and out of politics, expressed sorrow that the bombings had not been condemned more soundly. "And the Israelis could have apologized," said a journalist, adding with a sigh, "I guess it's not their style." Amer Salti's golf experience seems relevant. For as Amer said, "When Israelis and Arabs treat each other as equals, then we'll have peace." That is still not the case.

The isolation that Jordan experienced from almost all Arab states in 1990 and 1991, when King Hussein refused to fight Iraqi leader Saddam Hussein, is almost over. In fact, the king seemed to have bent over backward recently to underscore his opposition to the Iraqi leader when he gave political asylum to Saddam Hussein's defecting brother-in-law and son-in-law. Jordan's diplomatic relations in the Arab world with Arab states were broken off during the Gulf War, but now have been restored. King Hussein himself combined religious pilgrimage with political intent when he visited Saudi Arabia in February 1996. Jordan has even reopened its Kuwait Embassy; air, postal, and other communication services are being reestablished and the Jordan Information Bureau has announced that Kuwait's diplomatic presence in Amman is being upgraded to ambassadorial level. Arab state affairs are returning to normal. But in a curious twist of political fallout, Jordan remains the only legal port of entry to the besieged country of Iraq, still under United Nations embargo.

ARAB LEADERSHIP

AMERICANS WHO NOTICE are often surprised, even bewildered, by political leadership in the Arab world. How is it that a rather grubby-looking, unshaven man like Yasir Arafat has enjoyed so much loyalty while an attractive and well-groomed gentleman like Anwar Sadat turns off his former followers? In our media-oriented country, where makeup and hair dye are as much a part of the politician's image as proud parents and adoring wives (or attentive husbands), a man like Arafat, who speaks to the United Nations in fatigues and five-o'clock shadow, makes little sense to us.

Of course, one cannot very well generalize about all Arab leaders, ranging as they do from the president of a country of 60 million people (Egypt) to the reigning emir of a small principality of 600,000 in the Persian Gulf (Bahrain). But it is reasonable to talk about some of the features of Arab leadership that, at all levels and in all places, seem to contrast with patterns of leadership in the United States and Western Europe.

High office in the United States is associated with celebrity; we want and expect glamour from our politicians, whether mayor or president. There must be a bit of excitement attached to the pressing of the flesh in a campaign tour. Even if bulletproof Plexiglas and tough-looking escorts with bulging suit coats keep us at a safe distance from the star, a public appearance remains an occasion, an event, and the more hoopla associated with it, the better. Indeed, many a political appearance is preceded by warm-up entertainment, like any other first-class act.

In the Arab world it is still necessary that the leader be approachable. While modern measures of security may make this more difficult, the poorest and most obscure Arab man or woman expects to be able to call the leader's name and ask for his help. This is especially true if the person has been the victim of injustice. The king of Saudi Arabia still holds court regularly, open to all Saudis, in which petitions may be presented and where the king often acts directly to solve the problems.

A big smile and a shake of the hand will not do; in fact, such hype is largely missing and would be regarded with considerable suspicion. On his visits to Egyptian villages, the late President Anwar Sadat was expected to sit down and talk with the villagers about their problems; total authority means total responsibility, and Middle Eastern rulers must act on the most local issues if these are brought to their attention. For example, President Hosni Mubarak of Egypt, accompanied by the foreign press corps, visited the Sinai Desert to open a new development project. Arab Bedouin, herders of sheep and goats, interrupted his public address to shout out complaints about the way in which their interests had been overlooked. The president promptly asked the press corps to leave the assembly, which then became an open hour-long discussion between Mubarak and the outspoken herdsmen. At the conclusion of the private session the press, heels well cooled, was asked to return.

If this quality of personal concern for personal problems is successfully projected in the Middle Eastern political scene, other issues having to do with foreign and domestic policies are likely to be of far less general interest to people than is true in the States. At least this has long been the case so far as villagers and herdsmen are concerned. The Egyptian urban public is generally more sophisticated these days, however, and the growing middle class of high school- and college-educated Arabs is certainly no longer so easily satisfied as in the past.

Along with the quality of personal concern for his subjects, the Arab leader is expected to exemplify, albeit in somewhat grander form, the values and traditions of the people he leads. Thus, the ceremonialism of the court or presidential residence is seen as only a more elaborate form of the hospitality expected of any household head in the Arab world. And, like their followers, leaders are expected to appear regularly at the public mosque to participate in the Friday prayers. Although today these appearances are surrounded by security precautions, they are expected nonetheless.

Middle Eastern leaders also do well not to move too far from the personal styles of their followers, or to do so in a most discreet fashion. King Hassan of Morocco keeps luxurious homes in France and Switzerland where, it is rumored, all kinds of goings-on take place. In Morocco, however, he behaves like the saint-king he is supposed to be. President Nasser always appeared in the uniform of his fellow officers or in a modest business suit. Libya's President Qadhafi is seen in uniform or simple leisure suits. King Hussein of Jordan also favors the military uniform of his army, the major source of his political strength. In the absence of personal popularity, it will not do to become enamored of the extravagant trappings of royal rule, as the deposed King Farouk (and the late shah of Iran) discovered.

An Arab leader is still perceived, by many followers, as a kind of superpatron, and the patron-client relationship can continue indefinitely, as long as the necessary duties are performed. (In much the same way, an American senator is kept in office through satisfying his constituents.) Thus, Arabs have traditionally felt quite comfortable having their leaders remain in office for as long as they exhibit basic competence, proper conduct, and what is perceived to be concern for the needs of their subjects. Age and wisdom are still considered to be related and experience is highly valued. The Americans' regular shift of presidents, on the other hand, is an alien idea to Middle Easterners, who find the rationale difficult to understand. Why does an American president have to leave office after four or eight years? Doesn't he learn anything? These are the kinds of questions Arab friends have asked us over the years.

Today Arab central governments are far stronger than was true at the end of the colonial era, and the leaders are accordingly more powerful than before. At the same time, the state and its leader are now obliged to perform more duties than any leader in the past. This is also true in terms of the American presidency, where the responsibilities of that office have surely outgrown the mental capacities of any single person, leaving us to wonder who actually makes the decisions.

As the nation-states of the Middle East grow older, the styles of leadership will change and diversify in response to local conditions and expectations. However, many elements of traditional forms of leadership still remain, and those elements are very different from leadership qualities in other parts of the Third World, such as Latin America.

In the nineties it seems less likely that a single head of state will speak to and for most of the Arab world as, for a time, Nasser seemed to do. Still, the length of tenure in office of a number of current leaders (Hussein, Hassan, Qadhafi) is noteworthy, as is their domestic popularity, relatively speaking. Though not subject to popular recall, these leaders still seem to be fulfilling the expectations of the majority of their followers in the ways that count. Occasional abuses of power, such as the Iraqi government bombing of its own Shia village of Dujaila, are a familiar part of history in the Middle East and less surprising to Arabs than Americans. However, Egyptians, Tunisians, and Moroccans all took to the streets in recent years to protest violently when their leaders, pushed by international lending agencies, it is said, tried to raise the price of subsidized bread by a cent or two. Arab people have never failed to express disapproval when the issue at hand was deemed important enough or the leader incompetent enough. The question is what form those expressions of approval and disapproval will be able to take in the years ahead.

||| *Morocco*

> *A magic castle,*
> *A gate of light*
> *Opening on a time of legend,*
> *The palm of a hand stained with henna,*
> *A peacock ascending through the heavens,*
> *Its rainbow tail spread out.*
>
> Ahmad Abd al-Mu'ti Hijazi
> CAPTION TO A LANDSCAPE

THE JACARANDA TREES were blooming when we first saw Marrakech in late spring 1971. The purple blossoms flared before the red walls of the houses and against the red medieval gates of the city. Heat hung in the air, the heat of an inexorable approaching summer, but it had not yet settled on the wide treelined streets of Gueliz, the newer, French-built section of the city; on the narrow winding streets of the medina, or old city; or on the great square of Djemaa al-Fna, which bridges the divided provincial capital. Standing in the square, in the warm clear twilight, against those fabled red walls, we watched acrobats and snake charmers, fortune-tellers and dancers, and a man who walked barefoot over the sharp, bright green shards of smashed Coca-Cola bottles.

We were hooked on Marrakech from the very first moment of our first visit. Bob had a Fulbright research fellowship to expand his Middle East anthropology experience from east (Egypt, the Fertile Crescent) to west (North Africa). We could have settled in Fez or Rabat or Casablanca, but we came to Marrakech instead. It was all very well to say that it was an important bridge city between the Sahara and the Mediterranean, that Marrakech had been a stop on the caravan route between Timbuktu and the Barbary Coast. It was true.

It was important to remember, as Bob pointed out, that as an oasis city Marrakech lay between the agricultural plains and the tribes of the mountains, a good place to observe rural-urban relations. He was right. But we were as soft on fantasy and exotica as all other Westerners who had ever visited Marrakech. We'd read those books, those poems, those tales about the Dionysian city of the south. So we moved to Marrakech with our three children and settled down in a traditional house on Rue Trésor, in the old city.

A few weeks of marketing, doing the laundry, and looking for schools for the children dispelled somewhat our first impression of fantasy and exotica. The tinsel in our heads went up in smoke as we tried to deal with the problems of everyday life. Marrakech may have had red walls and purple jacarandas in the spring and jugglers in the square, but it was also a city adapting to the difficult realities of life in a newly independent nation, a nation only fifteen years old after a long period of French, Spanish, and Portuguese rule. Slowly, we made acquaintances and friends, we listened and began to learn about the Marrakech that lay behind those legendary red walls. As we learned more, our view of the city changed, but we never lost the sense that Marrakech, mysterious and romantic, would never reveal all of its secrets to us, the strangers.

Hajja Kenza, a rich widow, was our landlady. She lived next door with her only daughter, Naima, and gave us plenty of advice, whether we wanted it or not. And she came in unannounced until Bob finally asked for—and got—*her* key to *our* house.

Aisha Bint Muhammad worked for us. She and her husband, Khaddour, and their four children, Saleh, Abdul Krim, Youssef, and Najiya, lived across the street. Aisha was a sharifa, a descendant of the Prophet, a fact she disclosed quite early in our acquaintanceship. Hajja Kenza, though rich, was not a sharifa, Aisha said. With Aisha's help I began to find my way in the often bewildering byways of the old city; I learned to market; she took me to religious festivals and introduced me to many of my neighbors.

Bob was aided greatly in his discovery of the city by Omar, son of a jellaba merchant, and came to know, through Omar, many of the merchants and traders in the great central Semmarine market. Omar's father, Si Abdulla, explained that the family had lived in Marrakech since the Moors had been expelled from Spain—around 1500, he said carelessly. He was not a descendant of the Prophet, Si Abdulla said, but his wife, Lalla Nezha, was, yes, indeed, so therefore his children were fortunate enough to be so endowed.

And there was Abdul Aziz, the first Moroccan to be allowed to teach French at the local Mission Culturelle Française, where we went with the children each evening to improve our language skills. For the first thing we had learned was that French was the language foreigners were expected to speak; Arabization was under way, but much business was still conducted in French. Bob found he needed French to do his interviewing throughout the city.

All of these people, in different ways, tried to explain to us what it meant to them to live in an independent Morocco.

"Our government is a Muslim government now at last," said Aisha.

"The officials we pay our taxes to are just as mean, but at least they speak Arabic, even if the papers are still in French," said Hajja Kenza.

"The schools are full," said Abdul Aziz. "People are thirsty for education. Did you realize that in 1956, when we got independence, there were only forty Moroccans in the whole country who had graduated from universities? The French did *nothing* but try to keep control."

And Omar had said, "We are in a new age, the age of a free Morocco."

Yet by 1971 the early euphoria had passed and signs of discontent were visible. Marrakech particularly was bitter about its students and teachers who were still in jail as a result of the 1965 riots against the central government. Students and teachers from Fez, Meknès, Casablanca, and Rabat had been tried and most of them released. Marrakech was different, an old imperial city, lukewarm in its allegiance to the central government, thus a potential scene for trouble, Omar thought.

"He won't come to Marrakech, the king," said Aisha. "He won't dare."

Aisha's feelings notwithstanding, King Hassan II did come to Marrakech during the year we lived there. He was a sharif, too, a descendant of the Prophet, an heir of the three-hundred-year-old Alawite dynasty, son of Muhammad V, the beloved sultan who in the fifties had rallied the recalcitrant tribes as well as the urban nationalist intellectuals against the French. He had been exiled for his actions, a fatal error on the part of the French, for exile bestowed the mantle of martyrdom upon him. He returned in triumph in 1955, to become the first king of modern Morocco.

Muhammad V found a country temporarily united against a common enemy but historically divided. In the first flush of freedom he promised everything: a constitutional monarchy complete with Parliament; political parties; free public education; free health care; and quick economic development.

Promises are easy to make, as all politicians (including kings) know, but harder to keep. Muhammad V died in 1961 and his thirty-one-year-old son inherited the promises. They had not, could not, all have been kept during the first few years of Hassan's reign, but it was hard to explain that to the new politically conscious citizens.

In 1971 we could see the school problem on our own doorstep. We had taken Laura Ann, David, and Laila to the local public school, thinking that it would be an important experience for them to attend class with children from Rue Trésor, to learn Arabic in the process. After we had spent ten minutes in the crowded hallways, talking to the polite but harassed administrators, it became obvious that our children's presence would only aggravate the press of people demanding their right to education: over forty in a classroom, often two children sharing a single seat. And, despite the expressed aim of returning Arabic to its rightful place as the national language, the classes were not held in Arabic. Why?

"Well," said the young principal, drumming his fingers nervously on his desk, "not enough teachers have yet been *educated* in Arabic. We have to have teachers, so we use those that are available."

"So?"

"So," he said, "some classes are in French, some are in Arabic, and some"—he paused and smiled engagingly—"some are taught in a mixture of the two!"

Abdul Aziz, when Bob told him this story, explained that of course many details had to be sorted out. "We are trying, Bob. Give us a chance."

Abdul Aziz was right. The government was trying very hard, training teachers, building schools, planning curricula. And despite all the problems, it was doing a good job. Perhaps too good a job. The number of children in school at all levels had quadrupled in nine years (from 320,000 in 1956 to 1,283,000 in 1965). A fantastic achievement! But thousands of young people who had studied and taken exams successfully were now beginning to find that there were no jobs for them in the white-collar positions and professions to which they aspired. They did not want to go back to the farm. They wanted to stay in the cities and lead a better life.

"That's what the 1965 riots were about in the beginning," Abdul Aziz explained. "Too many degrees and not enough jobs. But that is not the fault of the Ministry of Education. That is the fault of the Ministry of Economics and the Ministry of Labor."

"But things are calm now. Are there more job opportunities?"

"Well, yes and no." Abdul Aziz was patriotic, but he was always honest. "A lot of people work part-time, you see, but things are better; of course, we had excellent harvests in 1968 and 1969."

King Hassan II must have breathed a sigh of relief, we thought, as those bumper crops were stored in silos. He had dissolved Parliament in 1965 after the riots and was counting on the army as his principal support. It therefore came as a nasty shock when the army organized the palace coup of July 1971 and tried to assassinate the king on his own birthday.

But that coup also failed. Hassan II, strengthened by his near escape from death, was back on the throne when we settled in Marrakech. But, we discovered, the word "rule" was defined differently in Morocco, and the process of governing could not be compared to, say, Egypt's, any more than Egypt could be compared to the United States. Like many new nations in the second half of the twentieth century, the Moroccan nationalist independent government consisted of old elements, in new combinations. The old elements, according to the political science books we had read, were the *bled al-makhzen*, or territory controlled by the central government, represented, above all, by the sultan or king; and the *bled al-siba*, literally "dissident territory." In the latter areas the rural tribes had existed for centuries more or less independently of the *makhzen*. In the sixties and seventies, however, some fresh yeast was evident in the old brew, the ideas and ideals of the young people trained in the West or educated under the new national system. The young idealists came from both the *makhzen* and *siba* areas; they tended to put loyalty to the nation ahead of loyalties to the old units.

"One has to be realistic," said Abdul Aziz, "but here I truly believe that realism can be joined to idealism. The old *can* be joined to the new. But some things must change. Land system, for example. Taxes on property must be raised."

The new combinations of old elements seemed evident in Abdul Aziz. He was an Arab city boy (from the *bled al-makhzen)* who had married a Berber tribal girl (from the *bled al-siba).*

At first Abdul Aziz had explained that it was necessary for Berber and Arab to unite, to marry, so that the old divisions between groups, so evident in the ethnographies and studies we had read about North Africa, could be erased. But then it turned out that his wife, Zaynab, was actually distantly related to Abdul Aziz. Ties between city and country, between Arab and Berber, had always existed, on some levels anyway, despite what the books said.

"Of course, the city and the country work together," said Aisha. "How can Marrakech live without the farmers? If the crop is bad, the city has no bread. And the villages can't buy the other things they need."

Thus, in addition to the traditional *bay'a,* or pledge of recognition by which the tribes would on ritual occasions publicly express their allegiance to the sultan, there was another, older, more subtle tie between country and city: the economic one. A complex web of relationships had developed over the centuries between country people who brought their sheep and goats and cows into Marrakech and the artisans who made the hides into beautiful soft Morocco leather, who wove the wool into fine rugs; between the traders who brought in knives and tea and bolts of cloth from Japan, India, and more recently Europe, and the farmers in the villages and the mountains who hauled sacks of barley and wheat into the cities to make into flour.

The *makhzen* and the *siba* territories could not survive for long without each other, clearly; political acts of swearing fealty, such as the *bay'a,* simply reinforced the economic connection. And it was these economic ties Bob had decided to study. In his year in the markets of Marrakech, talking to and interviewing merchants, farmers, middlemen, and auctioneers, he developed new respect for the way the traditional methods of personal negotiation still persisted even as the tourist trade continued to reorient many of the goods and services.

"What's really interesting to me is that the old ways still work," Bob said to Omar. "The merchants adapt to new practices; they adjust, change a bit here, a bit there, use calculators instead of abacuses, speculate on the money market rather than on the crop productions, but still rely on the old contacts, the old routes."

"The old ways work better today," Omar pointed out, "because there isn't so much trouble. When the Pasha Glaoui ruled Marrakech for the French, there was always trouble."

"Which was bad for business," said his father, Si Abdulla. "Trouble is always bad for business."

"King Hassan has *baraka* [God's grace]," Aisha said in 1976, the same Aisha who had insisted five years earlier that the king would not dare to come to Marrakech. "Something has saved him *twice*. Of course, he is an Alawite, a descendant of the Prophet, like me. I should remember that."

IN 1976 I WAS IN Marrakech alone, for the first time since we had closed our door on the Rue Trésor behind us. I had come back with Melissa Llewelyn-Davies, a director with Granada Television of London, to help make an ethnographic, educational film about Muslim women.

The acrobats and the fortune-tellers were still there in Djemaa al-Fna. But many of the musical groups, Aisha said, were from religious organizations, or *zawiyas*, bearing witness to their beliefs and hence recruiting for the lodges. There was an upsurge of interest in religion among young people, she said, and Omar confirmed it.

"It's the Green March that's done it," he said when we went to lunch at his house. "The king is very clever, he has put religion and politics together so everyone likes it!"

We had read about the Green March to the Sahara in the American newspapers, watched the television coverage of the unarmed volunteers walking south, green flags waving high. The king himself led them, their religious as well as their political ruler. "We are only asserting our just rights," Hassan II had declared on television when he asked for volunteers to occupy the phosphate-rich territory of the Spanish Sahara.

It was the fall of 1975. The International Court of Justice in The Hague had issued a long-awaited advisory opinion on the legal status of the Western Sahara, a Spanish colony. The court stated that legal ties of allegiance existed historically between the sultan of Morocco and some tribes living in the Western Sahara, but that these ties were not equivalent to Moroccan territorial sovereignty over the entire area. The king took the position that the historical legal ties constituted a legitimate claim, and that it was therefore only right that Moroccan citizens, volunteers from all the nation's provinces, should march peacefully to the south and further that claim.

Abdul Aziz had written Bob about the event and had sent us a book that the king had written, *Le Défi*. "A good book," his letter said. "You will understand the situation in the Sahara better after reading it, Bob, and," he had added slyly, "it will be very good for your French, which I am sure you are losing in America!"

This from Abdul Aziz was high praise for the government, since, in 1971 and 1972, Abdul Aziz, though supportive in principle, had often been extremely critical of the king's policies.

When Melissa and I arrived in the spring of 1976, the popular song about the Green March, "Al-Ayun," still echoed back and forth across Djemaa al-Fna from the tape recorders and transistor radios carried by the young men of Marrakech. The cloth merchants continued to do a brisk business with their Green March designs for caftans (gold and green for the sun and the grain). But the Green March was not working out as planned. The tribal people of the Sahara had not all bowed down to the king and sworn fealty. Many had pulled back, regrouped, and announced that they did not want to be part of Morocco; they wanted their own independent country. Algeria and Libya offered aid to these peoples, through the Polisario Front for Saharan self-determination. Thus, a war was actually in progress in the south.

"But it is nothing serious," Omar insisted. "Merely skirmishes. It will be finished in a few days, a few weeks, but you should not try to film in the south, B.J., it is too dangerous, you must think of your children."

"We are focusing on the women's point of view," explained Melissa, "so it won't be necessary to head south."

"Ah," said Omar, smiling charmingly. "You must speak to Mme Aisha, B.J.'s good friend."

"We have," I said. "And she is going to work with us. We're going to her village tomorrow. Did you know she was a landowner, Omar?"

"I am glad to hear it," said Omar.

IN THE YEARS WE HAD KNOWN Aisha and her family, we had never visited the village of her birth, though she had many times invited us. Her husband, Khaddour, went back and forth, and cousins came and stayed while shopping in the big city. Once several sacks of grain had been delivered to the entrance of the passage where Aisha and her family lived in three tiny rooms off a central courtyard. The grain, Aisha explained proudly, was her annual share of the crop from her own land. We had said she was most welcome to spread the grain out on our roof (Hajja Kenza's roof, of course), and she did so, picking out and discarding the stones and bits of dirt, turning the precious wheat over carefully to let it dry properly before taking it around to the flour mill in Bab Agnaou. City and country. Each was indeed tied to the other, through people.

Aisha's village is small and not on the map. It lies near Sidi bou Othman, a town twenty-four miles north of Marrakech on the Casablanca road, where the rural market is held each week on Mondays. The town is named for the holy man to whom the two shrines are dedicated. The guidebook states that Sidi bou Othman is famous for other reasons. First, Moroccan tribal soldiers made a last stand against the French here, in 1912; they lost and the French broke through to Marrakech. Sidi bou Othman is also the site of a twelfth-century dam, which held the mighty waters of the nearby river in check and stored it in cisterns against the years of drought, cisterns that still exist and that, archaeologists say, must have held nearly half a million gallons of water.

Today the river is only a narrow cut of shallow water beside clumps of old, wild jujube trees, but it marks the way to Aisha's home, the village of Sidi bin Slimane. Our rented taxi took off from the road and followed the river, as she directed (leaving the jujube trees behind and heading across what seemed a barren plain). There were tufts of grass and some prickly bushes, a solitary donkey. Aisha rolled down the taxi window to look carefully at the donkey but announced that she did not know the rider.

"If Aisha's land is out here, it won't do much for her," Melissa remarked crisply. I agreed inwardly. It was pretty desolate.

We bounced over a slight rise, and a whitewashed dome was visible, set into a little grove of trees. "There it is!" cried Aisha. "The shrine. The *moussem* festival is in August, after the harvest. You should stay and make the film then. It is a wonderful *moussem!*"

The excitement in her voice did not seem justified by the landscape. Except for the shrine and the surrounding trees, there was only a row of mud-brick houses, laid out along a low hill, the same color as the ground upon which they stood.

"There! There! There's my sister's house!" And she jerked the taxi driver's sleeve to indicate where he was to turn, beside a metal door. The door swung open as we approached; a tall woman stood just inside.

"Hajiba!" Aisha cried, jumping out of the taxi and embracing her sister. She was home.

Aisha beckoned to us peremptorily to come in. Here she felt clearly in charge. She settled herself on the carpet in a long room in her sister's house, indicated that we were to sit beside her, called for more pillows, ordered tea.

"This is B.J.'s cousin," explained Aisha, introducing Melissa. "They're going to make a film about women in Morocco."

Aisha had made Melissa my cousin just to keep things simple, perhaps, and, I thought, to forestall any objections that her sisters might voice about strangers and cameras. She was already our advance agent.

"A film! Like on television?"

"Like on the television!"

The sister smiled delightedly. "And will she turn the camera?" pointing to Melissa.

"No," said Aisha. "Other women will be coming to do that. They will come on the airplane when we are ready for them," she added airily.

The sister nodded. She was a bit taller and plumper than Aisha, her face more wrinkled with sun and age, but she had the same upright bearing, the same high cheekbones.

Others had entered, another sister, two older women identified merely as "relatives," and a younger woman, very beautiful with black hair and red cheeks and a flowered caftan tucked up partially around her waist, her hands behind her back to support a baby in the traditional sling. Aisha introduced her as Rabia, her brother's son's wife. They kissed each other warmly.

"I am very close to her," said Aisha to me, touching the younger woman's rosy cheek lovingly. "She's like my second daughter, B.J. It's her husband that works my land for me, and I give him part of the crop."

"Film," "cinema"—the words went around the group, were discussed, taken up, put down, discussed again.

"You mean a film about real people and not a story?" asked the beautiful Rabia.

"Yes," I answered. "Why do you ask?"

She laughed. "Because if you want a story, you came to the wrong place. We don't have any good stories here, just work in the fields, and children, and sometimes a wedding or a feast."

When I translated that for Melissa, she looked pleased and said to tell Rabia that was exactly the kind of thing we were interested in. "So the West doesn't think there are only belly dancers and camels here in Morocco," I added. I thought I was being diplomatic. I was wrong.

"We used to have some camels!" cried the older sister. "And we could use them now. Donkeys are so slow and small. But camels are too expensive.

"Do you have rooms as nice as this one in America?" she asked.

I looked around for a moment. It was a very pleasant room, long, low-ceilinged. Whitewashed walls below the log and thatch roof, red rug on top of carefully swept reed mats where we sat against the multicolored pillows and drank tea. A sitting room like many others in Morocco except that here someone with a good deal of natural talent had covered the whitewashed walls with murals in bright colors. Red flowers and green trees, white-domed shrines, a man hoeing in a green field, a donkey being unloaded for market.

"Look, B.J., that's the shrine of Sidi bel Abbas, in Marrakech."

Aisha pointed it out. "See the green roofs, and there is Moulay al-Ksour, where we went to the *hadra*, remember, and then you know the Koutoubia by Djemaa al-Fna."

I had seen wall paintings in many parts of the Middle East—in Nubia, particularly, and in Upper Egypt. Berber houses often had finely painted geometric designs on the wooden ceilings, but I had seldom seen scenes as finely executed as these.

"Does everyone in Sidi bin Slimane paint their walls?" Melissa asked.

The older sister shrugged when the question was translated. "If they feel like it," she said. "You don't have to. Some do. Some don't."

"Who's the artist?"

The older sister looked up. "Why, Khaddour, of course. Aisha's husband. When he came to fix my roof, he would paint when it was raining and he couldn't work."

Aisha looked proud and pleased. Khaddour. I could hardly believe it. That big, lumbering man of few words whom Aisha referred to only as "he." Who had no steady job and picked up money from time to time by loading and unloading crates of vegetables and tinned goods in the market. Who had a vacant look in his eye and seemed, though pleasant, to be a born loser, unable to deal with the world of the new, changing Morocco. Khaddour was an artist of no mean achievement; the lively colorful scenes showed that.

"Well," said Aisha, "that can be one part in your film, B.J., Khaddour painting. I'll hold the paints." She laughed and the ladies in the room laughed with her. "And then we take pictures of my sister with the chickens." The sister giggled, pleased.

Aisha went on planning the film while we walked through the village, and Aisha indicated the single tree, the hedges of prickly pear, the line of stones that marked off the plots, hers, her sisters', her brothers'.

"You still think of it as your land?" Melissa persisted.

"It *is* my land," Aisha said doggedly. "It is my right. That is what the Koran says. That is what my father taught me. And I'll give it to my daughter, Najiya, when I die."

"Not to the boys?"

"No. She needs it more," and to me, very low, "because of her health." She and I both knew she meant Najiya's tragic deformity, the

Young PLO soldiers visiting a cemetery, Beirut.

Photo by Thomas Hartwell

Children of squatters in a
ruined building in Beirut.

Photo by Thomas Hartwell

Hoda al-Namani, Lebanese poet,
near her home in Beirut, 1995.
The wall was shelled and destroyed
in the Lebanese civil war.

Photo by Thomas Hartwell

Couple dancing in a Beirut nightclub, 1995.

Photo by Thomas Hartwell

Amman, Jordan, the crush of
buildings filling the famous hillsides.

Photo by Thomas Hartwell

Model of the future center of Beirut, as planned by Solidère. Now under construction, the new city is scheduled to be completed in 1998.

Photo by Thomas Hartwell

Member of the royal guard at the mausoleum
of King Muhammad V, Rabat, Morocco.

Photo by Thomas Hartwell

At the Feshawi coffee shop in old Cairo,
near Al-Azhar University, one of the oldest universities
in the world, founded in the tenth century.

Photo by Thomas Hartwell

Film poster and ticket lines for a cinema in Cairo.
Poster features Adel Iman, Cairo's favorite comic actor,
in a spoof called *The Terrorist*.

Photo by Thomas Hartwell

hunchback that had frozen her height at an early age and deprived her of the beauty her face promised.

"Thank you, Melissa," Aisha said carefully in English as we settled into the taxi for the return trip to Marrakech. "Tell her"—she poked me—"that I enjoyed the visit. It's good to see my sisters and to see that things are going right."

Melissa smiled. We sat quietly, looking out at the sparse landscape, the tufts of grass, the prickly pear, the low outlines of Sidi bou Othman far in the distance.

"Ah, B.J., we will make a very lovely film together," said Aisha. And she pounded my knee affectionately as her sister had done.

HAJJA KENZA. I had been putting off the call to Hajja Kenza, because I still found it difficult to face the fact that the house on Rue Trésor, where we had lived in 1971 and 1972, was no longer our home, nor anyone's home. It was a hotel! The Hôtel d'Ouriké. When I first saw that sign above our old door, I found myself perilously close to tears. Get a grip on yourself, I admonished myself firmly, stop behaving like a sloppy old lady returning to the sentimental scenes of her youth. It's Hajja Kenza's house, not yours. If she wants to dynamite it, she has every right. But I still would have found it easier to accept the dynamiting than the fact that she had turned that beautiful house into a hotel.

What fuss, what fury, had exploded on Rue Trésor while we still lived there, when another neighbor had reputedly dickered with a hotel company that wanted his house. Hotels were bad for the reputation of the neighborhood, stated the petition that went around. Hotels attract bad people, such as strangers and tourists. The good housewife who brought the petition to my door allowed that yes, we were strangers, but we weren't tourists, and since we'd lived there so long, we were not *as* strange as some might be. We had signed the petition. Hotels would have nefarious influences on the children. Yes, we agreed. But that hotel had opened despite neighborhood efforts to stop it; and now here was Hajja Kenza, the loudest complainer of all in those days, running a hotel herself, a *public place*, as the good petitioning housewife had defined it, speaking as though the words might corrupt her mouth and rot her teeth.

"It's just because Hajja Kenza got so mad," Aisha had explained during my first visit to her after my return. "The people who took the house after you got a lawyer and sued her."

"Sued her? Why?"

"About the water heater. They said it was included in the contract. But when they got in the house, it was gone. Hajja Kenza took it out after you left and sold it."

I suppressed a smile. Why was I smiling? It had not been a laughing matter at the time; the issue of the ownership of the water heater had caused harsh words between Bob and Hajja Kenza, between me and Hajja Kenza. Aisha had gotten caught in the middle, and I had always regretted the stormy scenes because, in the end, it was Aisha who had been hurt, whose relationship with Hajja Kenza had suffered.

"It was awful, B.J. They took her to court and in the end she had to pay for the lawyer and for the judge and for the water heater, too! She was so mad for so long we thought she might just have a fit and die. I kept trying to calm her down, but it never worked."

"Still—a hotel?"

"One day she just said she was finished with renters. She was going to open a hotel and make real money."

"Does she?"

Aisha had nodded, somewhat reluctantly, I thought. "She seems to be doing well."

"So you and she are on good terms again?"

Aisha sighed. "Oh yes. It wasn't just you, B.J. She's always been a hard woman. I see her from time to time. No bad feelings. But I refused to work for her in the hotel. I'm not *that* poor."

I told myself that what had happened five years before lay long in the past. I was here this time to do a job, to help make a film about the women of Marrakech. And I had thought of Hajja Kenza. If one wanted a character in the film that belied the Western public's stereotype of the passive, hidden Muslim woman, who better could one find than Hajja Kenza, the widow, the independent entrepreneur, amassing wealth by her own hand, albeit with a little initial capital from her father, her right under Islamic law, like Aisha's plot of land in Sidi bin Slimane. Thus, I was on my way to pay a call to Hajja Kenza, who was not at home, but in her place of business—the hotel.

"Come in, come in." I scarcely had a second to glance into the courtyard and register that the fountain was still there when a door opened directly on my right, where no door had been before. The double window of different-colored panes of glass—blue, red, green, amber—the window of our living room, had given way to this door to Hajja Kenza's office.

"*Ahlan wusahlan!*" Hajja Kenza stood up, in a neat beige caftan, an elegant brown scarf, and behind her in the small office were, no, it couldn't be, yes, it was—two strange men!

Well, what had I expected? I was not sure, but it was certainly not this. Our former landlady, who had complained of bloat and cramps and pains, who had looked drawn and ashen only five years ago, looked rejuvenated. She was slimmer, straighter, her complexion faintly pink, her eyes—was Hajja Kenza wearing eye makeup? No, it couldn't be, she would not let her daughter wear lipstick, go swimming, ride a bicycle without covering her head, her body to the ankles. But it did look as though Hajja Kenza was wearing very discreet eye makeup. If anyone had wanted an advertisement for the tonic effects of work, here it was, and I would bear witness. She would be wonderful, I thought fleetingly, on film.

Hajja Kenza was speaking. She was pushing me along toward the two strange gentlemen like a child that is being taught to say hello.

I shook hands, as instructed.

M. Sefraoui, tourist administration.

Captain Hamid, police.

They were tall, dark gentlemen, not young. They seemed to know Hajja Kenza, at least from the looks that went back and forth between them, the golden smile that flashed from Hajja Kenza's obviously newly capped teeth.

Hotels were indeed good money, it seemed. But what were the men doing here, I wondered—inspecting the premises?

Hajja Kenza, without getting up, opened the door and hollered "Tea!" in the general area of the courtyard.

The thin old servant knocked and brought in a tray, bearing a teapot, a kettle of hot water, four glasses, and a bunch of mint. Hajja Kenza waited until the old servant had shut the door behind her and then reached down to a ring of keys attached to her belt, a pleasantly braided concoction of beige and brown, matching the beige and brown trim that bordered the sleeves and neckline of her caftan. Middle-aged chic. Ah, Hajja Kenza, you *are* doing well, I thought.

With a large key she unlocked a wooden box on the office desk. It looked as though it might have held papers. It did hold papers, but she burrowed under the first pile and came up with a black lacquer canister of tea and a box of sugar lumps.

"You have to watch everything these days," she said happily, as though she enjoyed the process. "Otherwise people steal you blind."

The man in the dark suit cleared his throat. "You are a tourist, *madame?*" he asked me. "You have stayed in Hajja Kenza's hotel?"

"Tell him what a good housekeeper I am," Hajja Kenza rushed in before I had a chance to answer. "And how I abide by all the rules—"

"The ministry is of course very concerned about hotels," the dark-suited gentleman went on, ignoring Hajja Kenza's interruption. "It is for your protection, of course. Tourists are considered important to Morocco by our nationalist government and by His Majesty King Hassan II, may God keep him safe."

"I understand," I answered, "and I—"

"Tell him. Tell him!" prompted Hajja Kenza, smiling that gold smile again as she spooned the tea into the pot. The keys at her waist rattled and clinked.

The dark-suited man took hold of the conversation. "And your husband? Is he in Marrakech with you?"

"No, he is in America, but he will be joining me soon, and my oldest daughter also."

"Ah." The dark-suited man said something under his breath to the man in the uniform.

This did not seem the moment to raise the issue of filming with Hajja Kenza. In fact, it did not seem the moment to raise the issue of filming at all. I resolved to drink my tea quickly and leave as soon as I could politely do so, without getting involved in whatever Hajja Kenza might have in her head.

"Do you speak French, *madame?*" Up to now the conversation had been held in Arabic.

"Yes."

"Most Americans do not," he answered conversationally in French. "I understand that in America people speak nothing but English, what a tragedy for them." He smiled. I stole a glance at Hajja Kenza and saw her expression change, her mouth harden at the sound of these words that she could not understand. I was tempted to goad her further, to go on speaking French, but remembered that I was a guest. It is rude to speak when other people cannot understand what you are saying, my mother would have said. I switched back into Arabic, stealing another glance at Hajja Kenza as I did so.

"Yes, it is a shame. We need to know more languages."

I was right. Hajja Kenza had relaxed. She was pouring out the tea.

So I finished my glass, excused myself to M. Sefraoui, Captain Hamid, Hajja Kenza. And left.

IN THE END WE DID NOT film Hajja Kenza at all. When I went back, first by myself to discuss the film possibility and the second time with Melissa to see what might work, she welcomed us into her office and ordered tea. She was superpolite, even effusive, as she explained that she had inquired about the process of cinema from "people who know." She had been told that movies cost a lot of money. Budgets, she had been told, were very large, into the millions of dollars, she said, her eyes actually rolling in anticipation.

"So," she said. Her eyes glittered. So what? I thought.

"I would be happy to appear in your film, B.J., five minutes for only ten thousand dollars. This is a special price for you" (hand on my arm, mouth stretched out in that fake smile). "Tell your friend, the director."

I translated Hajja Kenza's offer to Melissa, whose reaction was immediate and expected. She laughed.

Melissa was moving toward the door. Hajja Kenza gave it one last try. She held on to my arm firmly and gestured upward to the balcony where we had sat on summer evenings, where the children had raced around the second floor, playing tag.

"Isn't it beautiful? Tell her!" she hissed. "I could come down to five thousand dollars; you don't realize, B.J., you are new to this game. Movies have lots of money, even in Morocco—"

"No, no," said Melissa.

And I repeated, "No, no, the boss says no."

"Sorry," I said, and extended my hand. Hajja Kenza shook it absently, her eye on Melissa's retreating back.

"Beeja," she whispered conspiratorially. "I *might* come down to three thousand."

I had had enough. It was not only seeing our house cut up and destroyed, it was Hajja Kenza's unabashed greed.

"Hajja Kenza," I said, "we were going to do *you* a favor. It is only because I suggested it that Melissa was even *interested* in the hotel. You would have gotten a lot of free publicity. Many people would have come here. So you should be paying *us* for the privilege of filming *you!*"

She stared at me. Her mouth actually fell open.

"Me pay *you?*" Hajja Kenza just couldn't believe it. She laughed disdainfully. I was obviously mad. "I never heard of such an idea."

Melissa was calling from the street.

"Goodbye, Hajja Kenza. Give my best to Naima."

When I turned back to close the door behind me, Hajja Kenza still stood there, staring after me and muttering.

IN AUGUST THE FILMING WAS FINISHED. We had taken part in a wedding and made a pilgrimage to a distant mountain shrine. Omar's family had invited us to film a *hadra*, or religious ceremony, held in their house. Aisha had taken us to her village, and the camera had recorded Khaddour's paintings on the whitewashed room and Aisha's description of women's land rights guaranteed by the Koran. Bob had come to Marrakech to spend a few days with me before we all left for home. Abdul Aziz, our old teacher of French, had come to call. He had been away while we were filming, in France on "a special project," he said. "Education. Lectures."

"It was an experience, Bob," said Abdul Aziz.

"How do you mean?" Bob himself had just come from six weeks as an academic guest in France, an exchange scholar.

"Well, for me, you know, a Moroccan, it is strange. All my life I have been taught that France is the fountain of civilization; in school, in literature, in the audiovisual course that you and your wife took."

Yes, I thought. I remembered the stories and pictures of the Thibault family, their boring children, Paul and Sylvie, and their holidays in the country with the grandparents where they played in the attic—a concept that poor Abdul Aziz had had difficulty explaining to his Moroccan students, born and raised under flat roofs. But Abdul Aziz was talking again.

"Now . . . I cannot explain. This feeling of attraction for the beautiful city of Paris, and at the same time I felt upset. I disliked it."

"Why?"

"Well, Paris is full of migrant workers, you know. Moroccan, Algerian. Sixty percent of the men in the Moroccan Rif area work in France. They are everywhere. Is that independence? They come to parks and wander around silently. They walk by cafés and don't sit down. They are poor. No one speaks to them."

"Paris is like that," said Bob. "Even French people don't speak to other French people they don't know."

"But at least they are the same color. They don't call them 'monkeys.' "

"Someone called you that?"

"Oh no," said Abdul Aziz earnestly. "Everyone was polite to me and applauded my lectures. Education in Morocco. Social change. That sort of thing. And I quickly learned to wear jeans like you, Bob." Abdul Aziz laughed heartily. When he laughed, his earnest manner dissipated and his face looked younger. "It is only the poor workers who wear the dark suit and tie, as I did when I taught your class."

I served coffee. Abdul Aziz apologized for not bringing Zaynab, who was up in the mountains visiting her family. He picked up the coffee cup, set it down again, and shook his head, as though ridding himself of bad thoughts.

"It's silly to talk about France," he went on, "when we are Moroccan. But then, we are still tied to France. We have to face it."

Bob looked surprised. "Most of the French have left Morocco. How are you tied?"

"Economically, of course. French cheese in the market, French clothes in the stores in Marrakech, haven't you noticed? Who else will we deal with? The king was educated in France, you know. Oh, I support the king, I am proud of what he did in the Green March, but sometimes I wonder where Morocco is going."

"It's hard to do everything at once." Bob was trying to be considerate, as Abdul Aziz's pain was evident.

"About France . . ." He returned to the subject, unable to stay away from it. "It is racism I am talking about."

"We have racism in America, too," Bob pointed out.

"It's different, it's . . . I mean, even I had nothing in common

with those Moroccan workers in Paris . . . I feel ashamed of that feeling . . . I have not said that to anyone . . . In America how do you
get away from that—"

"We haven't, we haven't."

We drank our coffee and discussed children, music.

Abdul Aziz said that his work was going well, that he was writing
a new book of instruction for preschool children, to combine Koranic
education with some of the "more advanced childhood education
precepts of the West. Have you heard of Piaget?"

"Yes," said Bob admiringly. "If you can combine Piaget and the
Koran, Abdul Aziz, you will have solved the problems of social change
all by yourself."

"You are kidding me, Bob." Abdul Aziz laughed.

"Only partly," said Bob.

Bob and I went around together and said goodbye again to old
friends: Aisha, Abdul Krim, Najiya, Youssef, Saleh.

Hajja Kenza wrung Bob's hand and told him that I still did not
understand the world. "They cheated her, Bob, she is too good-hearted,
those movie people have *lots* of money, they just told her they didn't."

Bob smiled. "Yes, Hajja Kenza." She showed him the hotel and
he nodded absently. "A good enterprise," he observed. "You are doing
well."

"Yes, I'm doing well, thanks be to God."

"And to your hard work."

She smiled appreciatively. "Your husband knows what life is
about," she told me, and flashed a final golden smile.

Bob insisted on taking Omar to dinner in downtown Marrakech.
We ate by the swimming pool of the Hôtel le Marrakech and discussed
the future of Morocco.

"It is just beginning to work itself out," said Omar. "Come back
again and see for yourself."

We said that we would.

*Don't throw out the old fire until
you have found the fire maker.*

Moroccan proverb
from the High Atlas

THE DROUGHT HAD ENDED. It was raining in Marrakech, a gentle steady rain that had been falling since our arrival the night before. The members of the 1982 Smithsonian study tour that I was leading looked crestfallen as we checked into our first-class hotel. *Rain* in Marrakech, and the climax of the trip.

"Oh, but it's wonderful!" The hotel desk clerk was almost rhapsodic. "Three years of drought, ladies and gentlemen. It has been terrible. Thank God it is broken. Thank God for the rain!"

In the years since 1976 the letters from our friends in Marrakech had spoken of the drought but not the Green March. The Green March had lost its glory. The skirmishes in the Sahara dragged on, a war neither won nor lost that was draining the nation's resources. Morocco's population had doubled in a generation, and the country that had once exported wheat was now importing 70 percent of its grain.

"People are becoming desperate because of the drought," Omar had written. "I have been to see your friend Mme Aisha and she is in good health but her family in Sidi bin Slimane is not doing well." Omar's message meant that no sacks of grain had been coming from the village to Aisha's house on the Rue Trésor for the past three years; rather, Aisha and her family were contributing to the rural family budgets.

But now it was raining. Winter wheat gleamed green in the fields as the tour bus crossed the plains. Rain had come earlier, and again now, a crucial moment in the growing season. It began to look as though there would be a good harvest.

"The rain," said the bellboy who took up our bags, "is a gift from God."

Even without an umbrella the gentle rain felt good as I walked toward the medina to visit Aisha. Her daughter, Najiya, had died three months before; I was leaving the tour group briefly to make the customary call of condolence. Rue Bab Agnaou seemed more crowded than I remembered: what looked like a population explosion was pouring out of the cinema, and another seemed to be pushing to get in. Horns honked, donkeys brayed, and people shouted as the traffic snarled, screeched, stopped. I was glad to turn off into the narrow Rue Trésor, our old street, where the wet, uneven stones gleamed and the rose-red walls of the houses were blotched with blessed patches of damp. I looked up and stopped dead. The street was literally festooned with signs. For a festival? Hardly. These were hotels, new hotels, *six*, I counted them. Hôtel d'Ouriké, Hôtel des Îles, Hôtel Essaouira, Hôtel Ramzi, Taroudant Hôtel, Aziza Hôtel.

Six hotels. Our old street was obviously no longer residential. The bakery was still there, that wonderful aroma of fresh bread cutting through the damp, the smell of the drains. There, too, was the public bath, horse and cart drawn up as usual beside the door, men unloading logs of wood for the fire that heated both the bakery oven and the water for the bath. Years ago, to entertain our children, Bob had made a lesson in conservation out of the fire that served two purposes at the same time. And men were going into the bath. Business was probably booming, given the spate of new hotels. It seemed doubtful that any of them had private baths. Knowing Hajja Kenza, she had probably sold our bathtub to some "French person" at a good profit.

The rain poured down in a sudden burst, and a bicyclist whizzed toward me, under the multicolored hotel signs, splashing my legs as he passed. Why was I standing in the middle of the street getting drenched and indulging in reveries about the past? There was Aisha's passage where it had always been, opposite our house, now Hajja Kenza's splendid new enterprise, the Hôtel d'Ouriké. Go in, go in, I told myself. This is why you've come, to offer your sympathies to your old friend Aisha.

Quickly, I ducked out of the rain into the low passage, dark and wet underfoot. I put my hand on the rough stone wall and groped my way ahead. Eleven years since I had first met Aisha; six years since I had last seen her. How would she have taken this blow? A terrible blow. Her only daughter. Dead at twenty-eight.

When I had come with Melissa to make the film six years ago, Najiya had helped us, as had Aisha. It had been a difficult project, trying to create for a Western audience a documentary about traditional Muslim women's lives in Marrakech that would be accurate, honest, personal. At one point Aisha and Najiya had even taken me to our old fortune-teller friend Saadiya, "to make you feel better," Aisha had explained. "My treat." And Saadiya had droned, in her deep rich voice, "Ah, your path is strewn with great rocks, iron rocks, but if you work hard and persist, all will be well in the end." A judicious fortune, the kind for which Saadiya was famous, a prediction applicable to everything from difficult pregnancy to a documentary film!

But Saadiya had proved right. The film had turned out quite well. Aisha had helped. And Najiya. Six years before. And now Najiya was dead.

The door at the end of the passageway was closed. Strange. Aisha's door had always been open, except late at night. I knocked, but there was no answer. Had she moved? Where would she go? How would I find her? I knocked again. I could hear somebody inside rattling pots and pans. I pounded a third time. The door was decrepit, light filtering through cracks in the worn wood.

"Aisha?" My voice rose. I hadn't meant it to.

"Who's there?"

"Me. B.J. From America."

The door creaked open. A familiar small figure stood there in the courtyard in the gentle rain. I had forgotten how small she was, Aisha my friend. She wiped her hands on a towel, her caftan tucked up neatly around her waist as always when she was working around the house, revealing the striped bloomers below. A greenish head scarf, much faded, was tied carefully around her head.

"Welcome! Welcome!"

I stepped down into the court and she reached up and put both arms around my neck. We embraced in the rain, and then Aisha recovered herself. "Come, come, what are we doing, it's pouring, come in, come in," pulling me across the court toward her little sitting room and shutting the door behind us.

"There!" She smiled at me, an exercise that eased the new deep lines in her forehead, down both cheeks. Aisha looked much older.

"Oh, Aisha!" I blurted out. "I'm sorry, so sorry about Najiya," and embarrassed myself by bursting into noisy tears.

Aisha began to cry, too, but in a more dignified and quiet way. While I rummaged for a tissue to blow my dripping nose, she arranged herself cross-legged on a flowered cushion on the floor and began to tell me, as though we had met only last week, about Najiya's last days.

"It was winter, she had just come home from work," began Aisha. "Not yet dark, She liked the work . . . it was good . . ."

"What was she doing exactly?" Najiya had done well in her exams and had been offered teaching jobs in Agadir, in Errachidia, but she had never wanted to leave home. I dried my eyes and tried to listen calmly to Aisha, but I did not feel calm at all. Najiya had been dead three months, yet the details of her last day were so vivid in Aisha's mind they could have happened yesterday.

"She was working in the municipality, in the office," Aisha answered proudly. "A good salary. And people were polite, she said they were very polite, they never . . . never—" Her voice broke.

"They never bothered her about her health problem, you mean—"

"Yes, yes." In the eleven years I had known her, Aisha had never once mentioned specifically Najiya's "health problem," her hunchback. The closest we had come to discussing it was once, years ago, when she had invited me to go to the fortune-teller with her and Najiya. "We are going for a special reason," she had explained, "and I'm taking two chickens."

"Chickens?"

"Chickens," and she opened her market basket to show me two live, fine-feathered hens, their feet tied together, their eyes still slightly open.

We had waited in the courtyard of Saadiya's beautiful house in the Kasba, a courtyard far larger than ours, with a pleasant garden. Fortune-telling was a lucrative business in Marrakech, it seemed; times of change and uncertainty created anxiety, wasn't that what the social psychologists told us? And what better way to dispel anxiety than with a nice comfortable prediction about the future? "Your way is strewn with iron rocks . . . success in the end," etc.

"What are we waiting for?" I had asked Aisha.

She had frowned. "Shh" was all she said. One of the chickens in the basket clucked feebly.

Saadiya herself, large and dark and imposing in white caftan and scarf, opened the door of a room on the courtyard and beckoned us in.

"Sheikh Ahmed," she introduced us to a man standing in the room beside her.

Aisha proffered the chickens. Sheikh Ahmed nodded and the chickens went back out the door, presumably to a waiting assistant. We sat down.

Saadiya whipped out a filmy bright green scarf and laid it over Najiya's head and shoulders. The sheikh, a tall thin man in white like Saadiya, with a green turban and a walleye, launched into a chant, a litany, with Saadiya as his respondent.

A single fly buzzed in the small room. Aisha and I were slightly to one side of the ritual trio, but I could still see Sheikh Ahmed's head clearly, his walleye, with a pupil that wandered across his eyeball, then jerked quickly back like a tic. He put his hand on Najiya's covered head and spoke, he put his hand on her shoulders and spoke. He put his hand finally on the rounded hump on her back, the heavy unmentionable lump of bone and flesh that had telescoped her poor back. The language was heavy with rhetoric and words I could not understand, but he seemed to be asking God to release the "tightness," to ease the pain, to mend what had been broken.

"*Ameen*," intoned Saadiya.

"*Ameen*," whispered Aisha next to me. She was clutching her knees tightly with both hands.

A laying on of hands. At the time, I had wondered what the treatment was expected to produce. Did Aisha believe that the hump would melt away under the green scarf and that Najiya would emerge, like the princess in the fairy tale, transformed into the beautiful woman she was meant to be, her back straight as a young tree?

"It's her headaches," Aisha had said to me suddenly.

The séance ended. The sheikh departed. We were to wait a bit till Najiya woke. After a time, Saadiya removed the green scarf and Najiya sat up, rubbed her eyes, and smiled. The hunchback was once more revealed.

"You feel better, my daughter?" Aisha asked quickly.

"Of course she feels better," Saadiya said shortly. "Sheikh Ahmed's gifts are great."

"Yes, I feel better," Najiya had said.

Headaches. Had that been a sign of something? She had always had bad, blinding headaches, even eleven years ago. We had assumed the headaches to be a result of stress. For Najiya, though she had always been self-conscious about what Aisha called "her health," had nevertheless determinedly pushed herself out into the world to get an education. Eleven years ago she had been in secondary school, and from our bedroom window I would see her emerge from the dark passage on rainy mornings, walking her bicycle. Her face set and anxious above the neat jellaba, under the stylish scarf tied beneath her chin, she would look carefully up and down the Rue Trésor before mounting the bicycle awkwardly and pedaling off slowly to class. Perhaps the students mocked her? The headaches had always seemed to come on after school.

Aisha touched my knee, bringing me back from my ruminations about the past. ". . . She had just come from work and I asked her if she wanted tea, but she said no, she was cold, she'd just lie down and cover up and watch the television and have tea later."

"So I left her and came out to reheat the meal. I'd made *harira* soup that day. It's good in the winter."

(I remembered Aisha's *harira*. I sometimes made it in Austin on winter evenings; take a half pound of meat, brown it, add chickpeas and lentils, and beans, an onion, lots of turmeric and pepper and coriander and salt, some water. Cook slowly. Put tomato sauce in later, to thicken it. Delicious!)

"And I turned the gas down on the *harira* so it would warm slowly and not burn. Saleh was coming soon from teaching, and Abdul Krim. Youssef was working late, her father too. I came back to this room where the television was on. Najiya looked at me, and she shrieked once, and then—" She stopped and could not go on.

"And then?"

"I couldn't wake her." Aisha broke down. I put my arms around her.

"Aisha."

"She didn't speak to us again. Ever. Just that one shriek."

A massive stroke? It sounded like it.

"When the boys came, we got a taxi and took her to the hospital

and they said a crisis of the heart, but there was no hope, take her home
and keep her warm, they said, and we did, but . . . four days later''—a
slight sniffle—''she died, B.J., she just died. She died right here.''

Aisha was crying.

''I still can't believe it, I just can't believe it, Najiya, my daughter.
And she had just gotten the job and she liked it and it seemed everything was coming out well for her and—'' She put a finger to her eyes
and wiped the tears away, one by one, gently, turning her face from
side to side as she did so.

''And the boys?''

''They're all right.'' Aisha, with effort, stopped crying. ''Saleh got
his teaching job back. I work two or three days a week cleaning. Najiya
wrote you that, didn't she? We make it, but it's hard. Specially because
of the drought. No grain last year from Sidi bin Slimane.''

''Najiya's letter said that Abdul Krim didn't go on the Green
March because he was sick?''

''Yes, he's sick.''

''He can't work?''

''No. He can't work.'' She paused. ''But there is no work anyway.
So even if he weren't sick, he couldn't work.''

''And Youssef? He was doing so well in school.''

Aisha stood up. ''Let's have tea.''

She left me abruptly and closed the door against the rain, which
no longer beat on the uneven pavement of the courtyard but was dripping slowly and gently, like Aisha's tears. I looked around me at the
little room where Najiya had died, where Youssef and Abdul Krim and
Saleh had studied their lessons, at the neatly tucked piles of bedding,
the mirror, the pictures on the wall: Muhammad V, Morocco's first
''independent'' monarch; Aisha's father, a mustached man in a skullcap;
Aisha and Khaddour at marriage; Youssef as a little boy; Abdul Krim in
his warm-up suit at a high school gymnastics tournament; and the
pictures of my own children, pictures that Laila, Laura Ann, and David
had given Aisha before we left Rue Trésor ten years ago. The pictures,
discoloring from age, were curling at the corners, Laila at ten with two
blond ponytails; eleven-year-old David, laughing at the camera; Laura
Ann, serious, nearly thirteen. How long ago it seemed. The door
banged open.

Aisha busied herself with the tea tray. She handed me a glass, one so full of fresh mint that the glass shimmered green in my hand. Then she settled back with her own glass, one knee up to support her elbow.

"Youssef," I repeated. But Aisha did not answer immediately.

"Is it sweet enough?" she asked.

I sipped the tea. "Oh yes."

Then Aisha sighed. "Youssef. Poor Youssef."

"What's happened?"

"Well, they opened another bakery two streets over, and the baker wanted an apprentice. Steady work. Youssef wanted to do it. I begged him not to quit school but he did."

"And is he doing well?"

She shook her head and looked at the ground, holding the steaming tea in one hand.

"The bakery went broke in less than a year. Youssef's out of work, and now he can't go back to school, either. Once you've gone, you can't go back."

"Oh, Aisha, that's bad."

She turned the palm of her free hand up in a gesture of hopelessness.

"Where is he now?"

"He goes out every day to look for work. Some days he comes home with a few coins; I think he works in the market or finds a tourist to take round Djemaa al-Fna. And Abdul Krim just sits in the room. He is so sick. His hair is falling out."

"His hair is falling out? Oh, Aisha, you must take him to a doctor. Let's go tomorrow. I'll get the names of some good doctors tonight."

This was something to do, something I could do, to break through the sense of hopelessness, death, inertia, that seemed to fill the tiny room.

Aisha said, "Thank you, B.J. But we've already been to the doctor."

"Oh, but maybe not the right *kind* of doctor," I insisted. "It sounds to me as though Abdul Krim needs a specialist," and I used the French word, to emphasize the importance of my point.

Aisha sighed again. "Well, all right, we can try again."

A knock on the door preceded the arrival of Abdul Krim himself.

He shook hands and smiled at me, a ghost of the old lighthearted Abdul Krim.

He did look ill. His face was puffy and pale, not the cheerful, healthy face I remembered. I told myself that perhaps he was just balding early and needed some vitamins and some hope. If he sat about, idle, all day, how could he not be ill—Abdul Krim who had been so full of life, working out at the gymnasium by the hour, winning ribbons in the gymnastic meets?

Najiya's death. Abdul Krim's ill health. Youssef's failure. At least Saleh was still teaching French in secondary school. The situation had seemed desperate for a while, when Saleh had been fired along with hundreds of other teachers who had demonstrated against the king in the troubled years after 1972.

"No, they will not get their jobs back," Abdul Aziz had written to Bob, in response to our inquiry. "It is too sensitive an issue and many hundreds of graduates are waiting to take those posts."

Saleh was lucky. He was taken back. He earned about four hundred dollars per month, Aisha said. This sum, with minor assistance from his mother and his father, was supposed not only to feed, clothe, and house his own family of six people but to contribute to the support of the extended family in Sidi bin Slimane. In 1982, an economist friend told Bob, the average salaried worker in Morocco supported eleven people. Saleh was supporting more than that. The benefits of economic development were distributed unevenly, social scientists had concluded. Yes, indeed. Certainly, in Morocco the war in the Sahara, the three-year drought, the rising inflation, did not help.

"Have you seen Hajja Kenza?" inquired Abdul Krim, settling himself on the banquette beside me and accepting a glass of tea from his mother.

"Not yet. I'm hoping to stop by tomorrow."

"The hotel isn't doing too well."

"Really? I thought she was getting richer." I smiled. "At least when we were here to do the film, things looked good."

"Yes, but—" began Aisha.

"Mama . . ." Abdul Krim cautioned her, then turned to me. "There have been complaints against her. The government is investigating."

"Money, money," burst out Aisha. "She has so much, why does she want *more?*"

"Is Naima still doing the books for the hotel?"

Mother and son glanced at each other across me. Aisha looked down. I remembered then an evening during the 1976 filming, when I had come to see Aisha, in despair because it seemed that none of Melissa's and my plans for filming were working out. It was summer, and we sat in the courtyard, Najiya, Aisha, and me, Abdul Krim slightly out of the circle, reading. Naima, the daughter of Hajja Kenza, who lived across the street, had suddenly appeared. After a barely perfunctory general greeting, she had plopped herself down beside Abdul Krim, putting her arm quickly around his neck and leaning her head on his shoulder in fatigue.

Abdul Krim had set his book aside and put his arm around her bent shoulders.

The two young people had sat there, in the shifting light of the summer dusk, like lovers, like brother and sister, dark, good-looking, comforting each other. Naima had grown prettier in five years, shapely, tall, with fine eyes. She had worn a sleeveless short shift that night and had obviously just come from home; for no one, no woman who cared about her reputation, walked about on the streets of Marrakech in a miniskirted sleeveless dress. But I told myself she *was* at home here, and always had been, slipping across the street to Aisha's house for warmth and tea and acceptance, as I had done that day, as she had done ever since she was a small child.

And Abdul Krim had patted her shoulder and said, "Now, Naima, you work too hard."

She had laughed shortly, without enjoyment. Aisha offered tea, but she refused. Lovers. Brother and sister. Brother consoling sister. An old pattern, for some say that the tie between brother and sister is the most important emotional tie in the Middle Eastern family structure, rivaling in importance the tie between mother and son.

Still, it looked strange to me, the outsider. A public embrace. Abdul Krim and Naima were not actually brother and sister, but the society considered them so. No Moroccan observing that embrace would have found it strange, if they knew that Aisha had nursed Naima with Abdul Krim when they were both babies, for Hajja Kenza had had no milk. It was that gift, that milk tie, that responsibility, that was still a bond between the two women, Aisha and Hajja Kenza, a bond that my presence had threatened years ago. The milk tie prevented Abdul Krim and Naima from ever considering each other as potential mates, even though that evening they had looked like lovers.

Naima. Abdul Krim was talking about her again, but it was not summer now. It was 1982, a rainy winter night. And Najiya was dead.

"Naima nearly got married last year. A good man. But at the last minute it was called off."

"Why?"

"Hajja Kenza was against it."

"But that was what Hajja Kenza always said she wanted, that Naima marry a good, rich man. She even asked Bob to approach Omar, our friend in the jellaba market."

Abdul Krim opened his eyes. He laughed outright, a pleasant sound in the room. "She didn't!"

"Oh yes she did. Bob asked Omar, but he wasn't interested. So what happened to call off this new marriage?"

"Everything was going on well with the negotiations, but Hajja Kenza wouldn't shut up, you know how she is, talk, talk, talk. She had her finger in everything, back and forth. Well, when the contract was drawn up, and the qadi read it to her (she can't read, you know), she found the groom had said that she, the mother-in-law, would never be allowed to live with the couple."

"Really?"

"Really. And she was so furious she tore up the contract on the spot and that was that."

"And now?"

Mother and son looked at each other again, across me.

"Naima doesn't do much of anything now," said Aisha slowly. There was something in her glance, in the way she spoke, that said more, but she did not enunciate whatever was in her mind. If she had stronger opinions, perhaps they had been mitigated by the realization that Abdul Krim wasn't doing much of anything now, either. Although his reputation, his honor, would not suffer as Naima's would, quickly and sharply, when she was seen walking the streets, eventually Abdul Krim's reputation, his honor, would be diminished also. A man is self-supporting; he is a provider; he marries and has children. A real man does not lie about on the bed in his mother's house all day and watch television—unless, of course, he is sick.

"I'm amazed at all the new hotels on Rue Trésor," I said. "What's happened?"

"The street is becoming commercial," said Abdul Krim. "It's valuable property, so near Djemaa al-Fna. They're raising our rent and trying to sell the house and make a lot of money from the developers that want to come in."

"That's why the courtyard looks so bad," said Aisha. "And you saw how the door's cracked. The landlord won't fix anything."

"We need to get out of here," said Abdul Krim. "They're going to sell the roof over our heads. It's only a matter of time."

"Yes," I said, "I can see that. Aisha wrote me." I gulped and pushed on. (It had to be said.) "I *wish* I could help you buy a house, but we just don't have that kind of money. Our children are in college, and my mother, and . . ." My voiced trailed off as I met those two pairs of eyes, one young, one old. What could I say?

The dilemma was not new. They had written for help several times during the drought, when Saleh lost his job, before Najiya found hers. I had sent some money, what I could afford. Now how could I expect them to believe that I did not have enough money for anything, when here I was again, coming to Marrakech on a long expensive airplane trip with no apparent hardship to myself. Six years ago I had come with a crew of young, eager film technicians from England, bringing thousands of dollars' worth of expensive equipment to make a film for schools, for television. No wonder they looked at me that way when I said I did not have $10,000 to help Aisha buy a house, away from the commercialized growing center of Marrakech, to give her some security in an uncertain world. "What I pray to God is to give me a place of my own," she had said in an interview in the film. I had not forgotten that interview, that message. I could not respond adequately to that plea. I did not have $10,000, or even $1,000, to give her. And she could not quite understand why I didn't.

All people, of course, form reciprocal kinds of relationships, every year of their lives, whether in Morocco or America. But people who live in the same culture, even if their positions are unequal, can usually find a mutual understanding, for some shared understanding of the ramifications of each other's economic position exists. But cross-culturally, it is harder. To Aisha I seemed incredibly rich, and in comparison, and by Moroccan standards, I *was* incredibly rich.

During 1971 and 1972, when we lived on the Rue Trésor and Aisha worked for us, we paid her a regular salary. When we left, the salary ceased. When we came back to film in the spring and summer of 1976, I suggested, and Melissa agreed wholeheartedly, that Aisha be put on regular salary, as a member of the crew. When the filming ended, the salary ended. But the relationship had not ended with the end of the jobs. There was more between us—concern for each other, friendship. But probably there had been different expectations from the beginning. Or had there? Was the issue here simply money? What I felt as a responsibility, almost a duty, toward Aisha and her family was not duplicated with Omar and his family, nor with Abdul Aziz or Hajja Kenza. Omar's family had offered us their house as a location for one sequence in the film. They had invited the crew to lunch. Omar and his sister Malika and his brother Ibrahim and even his mother, Lalla Nezha, had told us more than once how they had enjoyed the experience. "Why don't you make a film about the jellaba business now?" Omar had suggested half-jokingly. "Maybe we can get Omar Sharif to act the part of my father. He's old enough now." But Omar's family was well-off. Aisha's family was not.

"How is Lorrie Ann, and Laila and David and Mister?" Aisha was consciously, politely changing the subject. "And Melissa, how is she?"

I described my children's activities, produced new pictures, which were passed to Abdul Krim. "And Melissa has a little girl," I added.

"Didn't Saadiya say so when you were here and had your fortune told?" cried Aisha triumphantly. "She is very good, Saadiya, she knows spirits, if only . . . Najiya—" and she broke down again.

"Now, Mama." Abdul Krim looked embarrassed. He tried to comfort her, but Aisha would not be comforted. The tears came again, slowly, and she wiped each tear away again, delicately, with a single finger.

"It's . . . that I miss her so much," she said, seeing me out across the wet courtyard, through the low passage to the Rue Trésor. Night had come and the rain had stopped while I had sat with Aisha and Abdul Krim. A cloudy sky lay above us, illuminated by a single lightbulb above the sign that Hajja Kenza had installed to advertise her unsuccessful hotel. The door was shut tight. The door of Hajja Kenza's own house was also shut, as was the window where her pot of white geraniums had sat on the sill long ago. What was it a Moroccan friend had said? "Some people are like good bread. Some people are like stones." Aisha. Hajja Kenza. Their relationship was unequal, too. Where did I stand in that friendship, which had started when the two women were children, had continued when Aisha nursed Hajja Kenza's only daughter, Naima, who now did nothing much at all? What responsibility did I bear? Had I helped to sour the relationship? I could not face the myriad of possibilities at the moment. I repeated the ritual words of condolence once more and said goodbye. We were to meet next day to take Abdul Krim to the doctor.

UNFORTUNATELY, the doctor whom we visited the next morning proved to be too busy to see us. But Aisha and her family were still very much on my mind when I set off to lunch with Omar's family that day, although I was unsure whether I should say so.

I had received the invitation early in the morning. "Come to the shop at one," it said, and was signed by Omar. The rather superior desk clerk at the elegant hotel where the Smithsonian group was staying had handed me the note in a very deferential fashion.

"Is everything all right, *madame?*"

I looked at him, surprised. "Yes, thank you."

He shook his well-groomed dark head. "It is only that—is M. Omar a friend of yours?"

"Oh yes, we've known his family for a long time." I smiled pleasantly, I hoped.

"Ah, I see." He smiled back. "Well, *madame*, he came himself, you see, to look for you . . ."

"Yes . . ."

What was all this about? The clerk was going on and on. "So, if there is some problem, please let us know, and we will try to rectify it."

I nodded, a bit puzzled. When I repeated this conversation later to Omar, he had laughed.

"Ah!" he said importantly. "You have forgotten my duties, B.J. Remember, I am in charge of the office which takes care of tourist complaints about hotels. *That's* why he looked so worried. I handle complaints against Hajja Kenza's hotel; why shouldn't I also slap the hands of the people who own the most elegant hotel in Marrakech? We are a free country now, Morocco; every complaint can be investigated and offenses punished!''

Omar had suggested I meet him at the family jellaba shop, and he would take me from there to his house for lunch. I had followed his instruction and gone to the market at the appointed time. It was raining again, a fine drizzle, as I crossed the square of Djemaa al-Fna and passed into the covered market, down the wide street of the Semmarine, the street that never failed to dazzle me, no matter how many times I walked through its displays of silks and velvets, its caftans laced and bordered with gold and silver. At the herbalists' corner I turned off, not having time today to peruse the jars of powdered verbena and chamomile, the bottles of orange water, the secret dark jars of stronger cures, dosages: belladonna, crocodile tails, and other specialties. Si Abdulla's narrow jellaba shop was just beyond. But Omar was not there as he had promised.

Ibrahim, his brother, came forward. ''Omar had an important case to finish in the office,'' he said. ''He'll be late. I'll take you home, and he'll be there in time for lunch. We're living at our uncle's place because we're redoing the house.''

''Your uncle and aunt are with you?''

''No, my uncle has another house, a rent house that is empty at the moment.''

Ibrahim pulled down the wooden shutter door and locked the shop. The rain had ceased, and the clouds were moving fast across the sky, pulling apart from time to time and letting the sun through. We set off, deeper into the labyrinth of the market, past the woodworkers' corner, fragrant with the odor of argan wood. One of the luggage merchants had decided to nap in his shop and snoozed against the stock: painted tin trunks of blue, pink, red, piled up on each side of him, like multicolored walls. The rows of leather shops gave way to the specialty belt and ribbon and scarf shops. Here hung the braided ropes of imitation amber beads mixed with colored wool and glittery sequins, the fringed scarves waiting for Berber women customers who wore the ropes around their heads, their waists.

''You are completely renovating your house?'' I asked politely.

''Yes, the wiring had to be redone. We have two television sets now and my mother wants a washing machine. So we decided to do the whole thing—new bath and so on."

"I see."

"But Omar thinks we should build a villa outside the city."

"Omar?" I was surprised. He had always defended the medina for its convenient location, its comfort and quiet, its easy access to shops and mosques.

"That's what he says." Ibrahim paused. We had reached the fork that leads to the shrine of Sidi bel Abbas, the patron saint of Marrakech. The green-tiled roofs were just visible down a narrow alley.

We turned left, away from the shrine, toward the family house. The streets were beginning to feel familiar.

"We all want to stay in the medina, *madame*, except Omar. Maybe he wants to marry and has not yet told my father." I thought he smiled to himself. Ibrahim of the brooding eyes, as we had named him, did not often smile. He was not happy with his assignment in the family business while his brothers branched out to tourism, customs, away from their father.

We were walking now in a quiet residential area. There were no more shops, only long stretches of blank walls plastered with the red clay that is distinctive to Marrakech. Massive wooden doors were set into the red walls, doors with brass knockers, silver knockers, all in the shape of a hand. Since Roman times the classic symbol to ward off evil, the hand is called in Islamic countries the hand of Fatima, the Prophet's daughter.

It did not seem that ten years had passed since Bob and I and the children had walked these streets.

Ibrahim, after his outburst, was silent. I did not feel it appropriate to comment on the possibility of Omar's secret marriage plans or the suggestion that father and sons were divided about where the family house should be established, or reestablished: in the old city or the new burgeoning upper-middle-class suburbs—not Gueliz, with its French memories—but the newer areas near the palm groves and the Agdal Gardens. I wondered why he was confiding in me. We were friends of the family, it was true. And of course my presence was temporary; I would be leaving again in a day or two; I could be confided in, therefore, since I had no permanent place here, to help or to hinder whatever might develop.

"My father sold some of his land in Bab Doukkala," said Ibrahim, adding more to the picture. "That's maybe why he might agree to a villa, but keep the medina house, too. We could rent the medina house. Marrakech is growing so fast."

So that was it. The family was getting into real estate development. But even in the past Si Abdulla had always had many strings to his economic bow. The jellaba shop was only one of several enterprises. Ten years ago Omar had explained to Bob that his father believed in diversifying his financial interests. "It's better for business. And for taxes. Also, if the jellaba market is bad one year, the leather market may be good."

Bob had said, "Ah yes, diversifying investments, otherwise known as 'not putting all your eggs in one basket.' " (How much sillier that sounded in French, Bob added.)

A similar Moroccan proverb existed, Omar had declared happily. "But not everyone is smart like my father," he had pointed out. "Look at our friend Muhammad, the rug merchant. He's made a big mistake. He's expanded his shop so it looks like a French store."

We had noticed that in 1976.

"He'll be sorry," Omar had predicted to Bob on that earlier visit. "The foreign tourists may like it, but they come and go. Only once has he had a famous movie star like Burt Lancaster in his shop. Tax collectors are always around and his rate has already gone up. Everyone can *see* he's getting richer."

"That attracts the evil eye?"

Omar smiled. "Yes, the evil eye. You foreigners are fascinated by the evil eye. But what *is* the evil eye? A symbol of bad luck, is it not?"

Bob agreed that it was.

"For Muhammad the evil eye is the eye of the tax collector," he finished triumphantly, and laughed at his witticism. Then he became serious. "But you see, Bob, the point is, it is not magic, it is real life. I have told Muhammad, but he does not pay any attention."

"I'm surprised," said Bob. "I always thought Muhammad was eminently practical."

"Maybe," allowed Omar. "But he's from the country; he doesn't yet understand the big city."

"How many generations does it take to become a Marrakshi?" asked Bob, smiling a bit. "Muhammad was born here, you know."

"He's learning," Omar had admitted, "but he still has a long way to go."

Afterward Bob had repeated this conversation to me. "Interesting, isn't it?" he said. "The process of succeeding in business is seen so differently in different cultures. What does an up-and-coming young businessman do in America? He buys a house with a twenty-year mortgage, a new car he can't afford, a three-hundred-dollar suit, all to advertise to the world that he is doing well, with the idea that this will attract more business. Here it's just the opposite. The old ways militate against public display. Why? To protect what you have against less successful relatives, greedy tax collectors, thieves, and other unpredictable forces. Here people have been capitalists for centuries without the encouragement and protection that capitalist governments provide."

"I thought things were changing in the new Morocco," I had offered.

"Omar says some things are changing, but not the tax collectors!" Bob had replied.

I was brought back to the present by Ibrahim, who had stopped at one of the tall doors. For a moment I felt as though I still *was* in the past, entering Omar's old house. The general plan of this house was the same: the short dark dead-end foyer, the spacious tiled central courtyard open to the sky, rooms opening around it on all sides.

But the kitchen was to our left, rather than the right; the courtyard was not strictly symmetrical, narrowing at one end, perhaps to accommodate an older house next door. And the door frames around the courtyard were plain dark wood, not carved and painted, as at the other house we had known.

"Please." Ibrahim held open a door. Two young women stood up to greet us from their places on the banquettes against the wall.

"Malika!" I said.

Omar's older sister smiled.

"Welcome," she said. "This is my friend Tahiya from the college."

"How do you do?" The friend, dark-eyed, dark-haired, eyed me curiously and extended her hand. *"Comment allez-vous?"*

So this part of the conversation would be in French.

"Tahiya is from Fez. She is in my class at college; she lives with

us during the school year,'' explained Malika. Both girls were fashionably and carefully dressed, Malika in a gray crepe de chine mandarin-
style blouse, a gray flannel skirt, a gold Koran on a chain around her
neck; her friend Tahiya in a black sweater and skirt with a silky crimson
print overblouse.

''In the medical school?''

Omar had written of Malika's acceptance to medical school, where
places were reserved for those who scored highest on the competitive
government examinations.

''It is wonderful!'' Omar had written. ''The whole family is honored.''

''The family succeeds, not the individual,'' Bob had commented.
''Omar, a minor clerk in the ministry, his older brother in the customs
house, another brother in the shop selling jellabas, and their *sister* gets
into medical school. In America I'll bet the brothers would have been
piqued.''

If Malika was in medical school, why was she in college here in
Marrakech? The medical school was in Rabat.

But Malika, it turned out, had not chosen to attend medical
school. She had decided to go into research medicine and was working
on her Ph.D.

''What did your father think about that?''

Malika smiled, fingering the tiny gold Koran on the chain around
her neck. She looked across at her friend.

''Our fathers both were a bit surprised,'' she acknowledged. ''But
they have opened up a science program here in Marrakech and I can go
on for my doctorate right here.''

''And at the end we are guaranteed good jobs,'' said Tahiya. ''The
country needs scientists, in all fields, especially medical science.''

''So our fathers agreed,'' said Malika.

The door opened, and a tall young man came in, smiling.

''*Bonjour, Mme B.J.*'' We shook hands.

Malika looked from him to me. ''You don't recognize Ahmed, my
younger brother, B.J.''

I had to agree that I didn't. He had been in elementary school in
1972, when we had come to dinner. I had a hazy memory of a small
dark-haired boy who had played with his baby sister.

"He is into computers, too."

The young man stopped smiling and became earnest and eager. "It is the way to the future," he said in the tone of the true believer. For five minutes he lectured me about the benefits that computers could bring to his country.

"Now, now, enough of this school talk!" It was Lalla Nezha, Omar's mother, a bit older, a bit plumper, but smiling and bustling in the same no-nonsense way.

We embraced and she inquired after my family. I produced the pictures of Laura Ann, Laila, David, and Bob. Lalla Nezha passed the pictures to her computer-enthusiast son.

"Why don't you study computers in America, Ahmed, instead of France? See how nice B.J.'s girls look, how pretty they have become."

Ahmed's expression changed; strain was evident in the way he was holding his hands, directing his words. "Yes, Mama, they are very nice indeed, but you know it is already arranged for me to go to France."

"France! France!" Lalla Nezha looked annoyed. "France used to be our enemy, the enemy of Morocco. Now suddenly France is our friend. What has happened to change everything? Your mother hasn't been to school, my dear, she doesn't understand."

"Mama," said Ahmed, once again in that careful voice, "we have to be realistic about our relationship to France, we have to think of the future, of trade—"

He was interrupted by the arrival of Omar, who burst into the room, shaking hands, kissing his mother, and apologizing.

"I am so sorry, B.J. How is Bob? I had this difficult case that had to be written out and submitted, because it goes to court next Wednesday, some doctors conspiring with the biggest pharmacy in the city to overcharge for some medicines . . . You won't believe it, Malika . . . The typist had to do it over *three times. Bonjour, Tahiya.* Ahmed, can you get me some matches, please?"

He sat down. Ahmed, as younger brother, was sent to serve his older brother. The lecture about the future of Franco-Moroccan relations was suspended in favor of lunch. For it turned out that the father of the family, Si Abdulla, had also arrived. He came in, leaving his slippers at the door. Ahmed was dispatched a second time, to bring his father a glass of water.

Lunch. Ah, lunch. Once more Lalla Nezha had outdone herself. There was couscous. Dishes of salads. Cabbage with fennel. Chopped beets with vinegar and pepper. Tomatoes with cumin. Lalla Nezha excused herself, she would not sit with us, she said, she had something that must be finished, but she would join us for tea later. But everyone else gathered round the big table in Uncle's house: Malika, her friend Tahiya from Fez, Ahmed, Ibrahim, Omar, and eleven-year-old Faneeda, the baby with whom David and Laila had played so happily ten years before. I felt warmed, cheered in this prosperous Marrakshi household, only regretting that *my* family was not at the table as well. Si Abdulla sat beside me, offering choice pieces of the day's main dish, a delicious chicken *tajine* with olives and pickled lemons.

"Your children are grown, *madame?*" Si Abdulla inquired between bites.

"Yes, thanks be to God."

"Thanks be to God," he repeated. "Children are the heart of life. That is what we work for, do we not?"

"You are right, Si Abdulla."

I looked around the table and thought that Si Abdulla had a right to be proud of his family, all of them, in various ways, adapting beautifully to Morocco's independent new society. The problems of alienation, of stress, which was so much discussed in the texts and monographs on social and cultural change, were distributed unevenly, just like the benefits of economic development, it seemed. They were not apparent here. Perhaps with enough property, enough resources, it was possible to adapt to any new situation and turn it to one's advantage. But it was as a family that these new adjustments were being made.

The same relationships existed between Aisha and her family in Sidi bin Slimane. The difference, of course, was that Aisha's family did not have as much to share. They had survived, but barely, during the recent drought, on reciprocal relationships. The simple truth was that the effects of rapid social change were more immediate and devastating if one was poor. And if one had less to lose, like Saleh, one demonstrated against the status quo. No one in Omar's family had felt the need to march in protest against the king.

I made a quick decision. I broke the comfortable silence and told them about Aisha's son and the unheeding doctor, about Najiya's death, about Saleh, who had lost his job for political reasons and how he had regained it, about Youssef and the disastrous bakery apprenticeship. And I asked for Omar's help, to ensure that Abdul Krim would get to a good doctor. I would be leaving Marrakech the next day and would not be able to go back to the doctor with Aisha.

There was a silence at the bountiful family table.

"Wasn't Mme Aisha here when you filmed in the house?" It was Malika.

"Yes," I said.

"She's a sharifa, too, like Mama," said Omar.

"Well, of course you must help," said Malika in French.

"I will, I will, I promise." Omar looked at me keenly. His hair was thinning, too, I noticed, but the pallor of despair did not hang about him as it did around Abdul Krim.

"It is our duty, as good Muslims, to help others," said Si Abdulla, rather pompously, I thought. Though his manner tended to run to the rhetorical phrase, the ritual gesture, his actions often belied his style; and I was relieved.

"Yes, Father," said Omar. To me, in French, "You have always been a good friend to Mme Aisha."

"And she to me," I responded.

"That is true," he replied.

"Please be sure to give our regards to your husband, and his family, and also to your family," said Si Abdulla, rising.

"Thank you," I answered. "And now you must think of coming to America and visiting us. It is our turn to entertain *you*. You would be most welcome in our house."

He inclined his head and went to the courtyard, where he sat down with Lalla Nezha to drink mint tea before siesta, the traditional way to settle the stomach after couscous and *tajine*.

With the departure of Si Abdulla, the conversation around the table became more relaxed. Ahmed started in on computers again, Malika asked about biochemistry in America, and Omar could not resist telling me that he had received more complaints about Hajja Kenza. As for her daughter, he shook his head.

"*La pauvre*," he said. "With a mother like that . . . I would walk the streets, too."

"Come and watch television," said little Faneeda, taking my hand. "I will come and see you in America, shall I?"

"Faneeda!" Malika scolded. "Don't be rude."

"No, I would love to have her," I answered sincerely. "My own children are grown now, remember."

"You can see television in America," said Omar. "I want to show you how we are renovating the house."

Omar, Ibrahim, and I walked down the narrow street to their old house. From the outside it had not changed. But once past the door, it was unrecognizable except for the courtyard floor. The slate-blue and white tiles were still there. But the rooms were gone, the tiles ripped from the walls, exposing the wooden struts laid in as support against the mud bricks plastered outside with Marrakech red clay. Pieces of wire, parts of pipes, hung from different levels, as though some giant beast had been nibbling at the walls. Two workmen were sitting in one corner of a wall, eating lunch in the sunshine. I was not certain why Omar had brought me here, with Ibrahim.

"It is good to do a big cleaning like this to change things, to get rid of the past," said Omar. "But it costs money."

"Yes." The sun had come out and a bright haze rose from the courtyard floor. The tiles were steaming as the rain evaporated.

"At least you'll keep this floor," I said, relieved.

"Oh no, that will go when the rewiring is finished and the new water pipes are in."

"You will keep *nothing* of the old house? It was such a nice house, Omar."

"B.J., we're keeping the basic structure. See." He drew out a rough plan, and it was true, the basic structure would be the same when the renovation was finished. "We are rebuilding from the inside. And we'll have new tiles, from Moroccan factories, not from Spain like before. I would be interested in your selections. What do you think of these?"

I looked at the samples. They were certainly not Spanish. One pale gray with a pattern of roses, rather French in feeling. Another flower motif in blue. Some geometric patterns, white and green; and the last sample was an adaptation of old Berber wooden ceiling designs: brown etched diamond shapes and whorls on white. I had noticed similar designs on the new mosques throughout the countryside, high in the mountains. White-plastered minarets with these same patterns of diamonds and ovals in brown, or in green, the Prophet Muhammad's color.

"They are very nice. I like the brown and white, the Berber one," I said.

Omar smiled. "So does Malika. She and Ibrahim want this tile in one of the salons. My father and I prefer the green. My mother says she doesn't care but she wants the rose tiles in the kitchen and maybe in the bath. Why not one of each? Brown Berber design in one salon, the green and white in the other. They are all Moroccan designs."

"Even the roses? They look rather French."

Omar looked pained. "We have beautiful roses right here in Marrakech. You see them in the market every day."

Omar went to speak to the workmen before we left. "What do you think, B.J.?" Ibrahim asked, in Omar's absence.

"I liked your old house very much," I said truthfully.

"She liked the old house," Ibrahim repeated to Omar as we headed out the door.

"Well, but it was worn-out, it had to be replaced. One has to change with the times, and thank God we have the money to do that."

"What about building a villa in the palm groves?"

Omar's eyes flickered. "In the future, maybe. First we have to restore what we already have. Whether we live here or not, it's a good investment for the future—fixing up the old house for the new times."

We shut the door of the old house behind us and stood in the street where the beggar had sat, years ago. He was not there now.

"I must go. Thank you for everything. Come visit us in America."

"God willing. Regards to Bob. Be sure and tell him we miss him."

We shook hands, Ibrahim, Omar, me. "Thank you again," I said. "And please don't forget Aisha."

"It is my duty," said Omar. "I won't forget. I promise."

And we parted, Omar cutting through to the modern city and his office in the ministry, Ibrahim back to the jellaba shop in the traditional market of the Semmarine, where merchants had traded in Marrakech for nearly a thousand years.

•   •   •

"IT'S NOT OUR AFFAIR, you know," Bob said later. "I mean, I'm sure Omar and his family feel they have enough responsibilities without taking on Aisha and her family—just like we do."

"Yes, but I felt I had to try to do *something*, Bob."

"Just so you aren't kidding yourself."

"Kidding myself?"

"Yes—into believing that charity and good works and all that will solve all social inequities. It won't, you know. If it did, the Salvation Army would have taken care of things long ago."

"Bob—"

"It's true."

"I know. But it helps some."

"And *you* feel better."

"Yes," I admitted.

Bob smiled, a bit wearily, I thought. He reminded me that our Muslim friends had a far more realistic attitude toward charity than we did. The Bible says very clearly that an act of charity benefits both giver and receiver. But in Muslim tradition it is still true that the giver, not the receiver, benefits the most from giving, for he has fulfilled his duty, both to God and to his fellow human being.

THE BUSINESS OF MARKETS

T HE STATEMENT is frequently made that Arab-world economies are
becoming increasingly Westernized. Presumably, this is a good
sign, a statement of approval. Western economies, after all, are based on
industrial capitalism and this means the things with which we are familiar: factories, corporations, supermarkets, banks, stocks and bonds,
international cartels—the institutions that have made the West what it
is today. The assumption is that Westernization is improvement, but
we do not consider what kind of economy is being replaced in the
process of Westernization. We can imagine what Arab society is getting, but what is it losing? More important, what consequences may
this loss, this replacement of one economic formation by another, have
on the patterns of life in the Arab world?

This is too wide-ranging and complex a question to answer in a
few pages of discussion; it is central to the whole structure of Middle
Eastern society and the relationship of these societies to the world
economy. However, one aspect of the process of Westernization affects
the most commonplace activities of daily life in Arab communities and
can be appreciated without benefit of economic theories or complex
statistics. We refer to the part played by traditional markets in Arab
communities and the consequences of the Westernization and transformation of those markets that is in progress today.

In fact, the changes that are taking place in this everyday activity
affect the whole rhythm of community life and the legitimacy of its
political processes. Much more is changing than merely the way in
which groceries and clothing are bought and sold. If we understand
change in the market, we can begin to see why the Westernization of
Middle Eastern economic life has far-reaching consequences, many of
which have not yet been fully integrated into Arab communal life.

From Saudi Arabia to Morocco, a great many Arab cities and
towns today have two distinctly different shopping districts in their
centers. One is much like that to be found downtown in a European or
an American city: straight, wide streets along which are ranged, in

orderly rows, large glass-fronted stores, office buildings, and specialty shops of various kinds. Signs indicate the contents of each building. In these districts an American visitor finds little that is particularly "foreign" except the language of the advertising—Arabic—and often English or French is added to help the visitor along.

But nearby perhaps, or in an older section of town, will be found another market center. Here, to the visitor, confusion seems to reign. Rows of small shops, side by side, open-fronted, are filled with what seem to be the same goods; there are few if any signs; narrow lanes twist and turn in a bewildering way in all directions; and above all, there are noise, confusion, and milling crowds. To visit the Muski in Cairo or the great medina markets in Marrakech or Fez for the first time is a formidable experience for the Western tourist, but the same kind of market is to be found in smaller cities or villages, with fewer shops and probably less commotion. Such markets are still a ubiquitous feature of the Arab world, even though in big cities such as Cairo or Baghdad they are no longer the centerpiece of urban life. Indeed, such "Arab" markets are to be found with local variations throughout most of Asia and Africa and in parts of Latin America. They are a feature of the so-called Third World, but they should not necessarily be considered a sign of poverty or "underdevelopment." Such market forms are rather a historical development of considerable antiquity and resemble in many ways European markets as they were before the Industrial Revolution. Some scholars see in them what remains of the central manifestation of mercantile (as opposed to industrial) capitalism. Adam Smith found them inspiration for his views of free enterprise. For these markets are not just different in terms of scale (small versus large stores); they are part of a whole way of life that is intensely personal, competitive, and open to public knowledge and participation. They are also the arena for much of the political and religious life of the city.

The traditional or preindustrial type of market was highly personal in the sense of providing its patrons with the opportunity, indeed, the necessity, of developing face-to-face relationships with a cadre of merchants and artisans whose goods and services provided the necessities of daily life. A cloth merchant in Marrakech described his regular customers as "fish." "You need to attract them but you must also provide them with something if you expect them to come back," he said. This includes not only the product itself but also the conviction that the product they have purchased is a good one at a good price. The merchant's personal responsibility is to provide such a conviction so that the customer will at least start at the same store the next time he or she has similar needs. For the traditional market provides the convenience of many shops together; it is always easy for the customer to walk a few feet farther and look at the same, or nearly the same, goods offered by a different merchant. Competition exists on the spot and the merchant must be alert to deal with that phenomenon. The traditional market is actually a collection of markets, each one devoted to a different category of goods: cloth, spices, baskets, copperware, radios, pottery. The Marrakech market has over thirty separate markets for different goods and several smaller markets located at different points in the city where the same goods are sold.

"Picturesque, yes, but what an inefficient system," the foreign tourist remarks, arriving back at the hotel after visiting the traditional market, walking long distances, and purchasing few items. "The bargaining is so difficult, far too personal as a steady diet." Americans express discomfort at what they feel is the hard sell. We are used to being left to ourselves when we make most of our purchases; most clerks would be taken aback if asked to express an opinion about a vegetable or a set of dishes. To the Marrakshi merchant and his customers, however, personal advice is part of the business, something they expect.

Business on a personal scale also has other advantages. The merchant/proprietor can handle it himself, both literally and figuratively. He knows his customers, his sales, and his inventory, and if he has need he is not far from the source of supplies. For the market is usually within walking distance of his home and/or small storage rooms where additional inventory is laid away.

It is also true that merchants in these markets tend to regard partnerships, which might permit a larger operation, as a source of trouble, and prefer to have members of their own family working with them, their sons if possible. Such family relations in business do not mean that the market is entirely closed to outsiders. "The games of the marketplace are open to anyone who can buy ten dollars' worth of potatoes and push them around on a cart," said a Marrakshi friend. "A bit of luck and the next day you may be able to start out in the morning with an inventory worth twenty dollars." Many merchants began their careers as peddlers or shop assistants, often at a very early age.

Merchants depend upon, as well as compete with, each other. If the customer wants something he doesn't have, the merchant may go to one of his fellow merchants to find the style or size required. The other merchant will expect similar favors another day—or may share in the profits. Merchants stand together in matters of taxation and import duties, in concern for the physical condition of the market, in all matters of common interest. In Marrakech those selling the same kind of goods belong to an organization with a recognized head who can speak for the group and who will arbitrate disputes between members of the organization should the need arise.

So the merchants are on personal terms not only with regular customers but also with each other. Not surprisingly, standards of behavior exist in such a setting that are violated only at the risk of ostracism by the fellow merchants with whom one both competes and cooperates. For instance, trying to lure away a customer engaged in looking at a neighboring merchant's goods is considered very bad form—though a sly wink may pass without remark. The merchants' collective scorn is reserved for the peddlers with goods over their arms, selling scarves or dresses or baskets, perhaps, at cut-rate prices. Such salesmen, in fact, along with those selling from carts or offering goods on blankets laid upon the ground, are often confined to the outer edges of the market area. There they depend on a loud voice and a convincing manner to catch the customer before he or she plunges into the main market. But many dignified, established merchants passed from such humble beginnings through several metamorphoses before reaching the prestigious splendor of the cloth bazaar with its clean, well-swept stores and often luxurious merchandise.

A traditional market such as that in Marrakech serves not only the people of the city but also Moroccans from the plains and mountains of southern Morocco and tourists from around the world. Agricultural goods arrive daily from within a radius of a hundred or more kilometers around the urban center. Many of the people from both city and country who visit the market come not only to buy but to sell the goods they have produced, for the market is a production outlet for the same region to which it sells. Manufactured goods, both local and foreign, are sold and country products bought—not only vegetables, grains, and animal skins but items like rugs and wood carvings.

All the merchants have a keen sense of their customers' tastes, depending on origin and age. A rug merchant specializing in foreign tourists knows that the Danish prefer the flat kilim rugs, while the French like thick-pile carpets; he also is aware of the rug size limits for foreign air travel. He selects his stock accordingly, when he visits villages looking for handmade rugs or assesses those brought to him from homes in Marrakech where families are involved in rug weaving.

On the other side of the Arab world in northern Saudi Arabia, in the city of Hail, a town of approximately seventy thousand people, there is also a traditional market of small shops and stores, though it has recently been rebuilt, its lanes straightened and cemented. Hail is a market town serving dozens of surrounding agricultural oases. Bedouin families drive to market in their pickup trucks, stopping first in the animal market to sell a few sheep, then proceeding on to the food or dry goods markets to buy supplies for the next week or two. The gold jewelry market is always crowded with women, putting their extra money into that safest of investments or selling a bracelet to meet the extra expenses of a wedding or a trip. The old mud-brick market was torn down and rebuilt by the government as one of the development projects that have transformed Hail into a modern city. Here the shops are all taken and there is no indication that the old style of marketing is disappearing even though Western-style shops have opened in other parts of the city. Families, both nomad and settled, say they are more comfortable in the traditional more private setting. On the edge of this market (as in Marrakech) veiled women sell used clothes, and in the vegetable market they are also to be found sitting on the ground selling ripe produce from crates. Women play a secondary role as merchants in traditional markets, but they are there. And everyone comes to the traditional-style market, rich and poor, young and old, male and female, a mix of gender and age not so apparent in the large stores in the modern downtown area.

The consumer goods of these "traditional" markets, whether in Morocco or in Saudi Arabia, are by no means limited to handcrafted or homegrown local products. On the contrary, all these markets offer goods of foreign manufacture, in greater or lesser quantities. In Hail, for instance, it is difficult to find anything made by hand these days, and Yakima, Washington, apples are as common as in American Safeway stores. High-tech products, such as video and TV sets, calculators and digital watches, are available in great profusion. Such is the result of the high standards of living made possible by oil wealth. However, in the less affluent Moroccan society of Marrakech, handmade items are still available. The best jellabas (the colorful, full-length garments customarily worn by Moroccans) are hand-tailored and sewn from handwoven cloth and decorated with handmade cording. The division of labor in the market involves both families and hired labor. The work includes people of all ages and both sexes. (Women do a great deal of sewing for the market in their homes.) Perhaps the best-known products are leather ones, which begin as damp skins carried through the market from the slaughterhouse to the tannery, where they are prepared for cutting and sewing by different sets of specialists. Moroccan leather has been famous in the markets of the world for centuries, and the craftsmen of Marrakech still turn the skins of the sheep and goats from the Atlas Mountains into everything from fine book bindings to leather hassocks.

The traditional market is more than simply an alternative to the American system of retailing, from malls to convenience stores. In the Arab world the market was the center of social life before it began to be replaced by its Western counterpart. This is still largely the case today in a market like that of Marrakech. Mosques and religious shrines are part of the market landscape, permitting visitors and merchants alike to stop and pray during the day. The newest mosque in Hail has been constructed of marble and tiles alongside the modernized traditional market. Lawyers and scribes along with barbers and blacksmiths had (and still have) offices and shops in the market. Entertainers perform in Djemaa al-Fna, the open square near the Marrakech market; some are actually witnesses for their religious organizations and are raising funds for their lodges. Blind beggars stand at the market entrances accepting the alms of the faithful. In a market like that in Marrakech, boys are socialized into adult roles, learning how to manage in the world of commerce, taught such skills as tanning, leather design, tailoring, or metalwork. Girls learn to sew for the market working with their mothers at home.

Of perhaps even greater importance was the role of the traditional market in providing an arena for the development of public opinion and an opportunity for men to win their standing in the community in a public manner. A man's reputation was earned on a daily basis doing business before the community at large. It was merchants who constituted the majority of the "respected men," those whose counsel was sought by the pasha or sultan in time of trouble. Trust and accountability were highly valued qualities in the traditional market; a man's word sufficed and the system managed without the profusion of written contracts and legal proceedings so necessary in our contemporary Western business world. Indeed, while rulers, often appointed in distant capitals, came and went, the merchants constituted the local elite. For a landed gentry was lacking in much of the preindustrial Middle East, unlike in preindustrial Europe, where merchants often did not enjoy so high a standing.

Thus, in exchanging new forms of markets for the older form, more is lost than simply a variety of handmade objects, a style of buying and selling. What is being lost is an important center for the formation of a community: of leadership and of consensus over matters ranging from religious and political concerns to the proper conduct of business. With the disappearance of these markets other means must be developed for these purposes. The problem is becoming easier, perhaps, with the increase in literacy and the spread of radio and television, but these sources of opinion are also more easily subject to authoritarian control than is the word-of-mouth communication of the market setting. The development of newly rich middle classes is of great importance in this regard, but it is also the source of new problems. The two styles of markets, as in Saudi Arabia and Morocco, can only reinforce the growing gap between rich and poor. And in this changing setting, the sources of community consensus remain unclear as the traditional markets give way to the Westernization of the Middle Eastern economy.

L'écume de la vague envoie son premier
communiqué:

A nous le pain et la terre.
Nous réinventerous le soleil sur carte perforée
par la liberté

Marrakech se reléve

Tahar Ben Jelloun
MARRAKECH L'OEIL

R AMADAN, the Muslim month of fasting whose time/place is determined by the lunar, not the Gregorian, calendar, fell in March during 1993. We were not prepared for this, since Western calendars do not announce the months of the Muslim, or indeed the Judaic, religious year. Thus, it was with some surprise that we noted, in the late afternoon of our arrival, a hush on the usually busy streets of Marrakech, the southern imperial city of the Kingdom of Morocco. Few taxi drivers or even horse carriages awaited the arrival of the late train from Rabat, where we had spent a few days with friends en route.

A harried young taxi driver with a bushy black mustache, clearly on his way somewhere else, finally responded to Bob's calls and managed to get us to the Hôtel Imilchil at lightning speed, scarcely pausing for the lone policeman's upraised arm (Stop!). The fare was not even a subject for argument. He took Bob's proffered notes, dropped them on the seat beside him, and roared off in the brown Fiat with black bands that is the "official" taxi of Marrakech. We were left unceremoniously, with our two pieces of luggage, at the door of the hotel, a modest establishment chosen for its convenient location—halfway between the old city, the medina where we had lived twenty years earlier, and Gueliz, the French section of villas and wide treelined streets. Bob had not been back since 1976, when he came at the end of the film shoot for *Some Women of Marrakech*. I had been back briefly in 1988. Now we had come back to revisit old friends and take a look at the city's reputed economic and artistic renaissance. But it seemed we might have chosen a more opportune time, not when everyone was indoors, sleeping through the fast, praying in the mosque, or eating on the dot of sunset at a family *iftar* feast.

"No one seems to be here," pronounced Bob, banging on the hotel door. "Can the hotel be closed?"

A spanking new hotel in Marrakech, the tourist haven, closed? It surely was not possible. But after knocking on the door, separately and then together, we began to wonder. The skies above us were darkening above the Rue Echouhada. A band of gold lightening the edge of the horizon indicated that the sun had nearly set. Unknown birds, twittering and chattering, settled in the palms and dark cypresses and cottonwoods along both sides of the avenue.

"Well, what do we do now?" Bob asked somewhat testily.

I shook my head. "One more try," I suggested.

Bob banged again on the door, and suddenly a face appeared, the bolt of the lock was drawn, the door was flung open. A grizzled gentleman of indeterminate middle age, in a dark coat and tie bespeaking "clerk," was wiping his face with a napkin and beckoning us in.

Aha. The *iftar*. Our appearance was cutting into the meal ending his day-long fast. No wonder he hadn't answered our first knocks.

Bob rose to the occasion, rather grandly, I thought.

"*Ramadan karim,*" he intoned, the phrase that indicates, all at the same time, respect for the religious requirement of fasting during the holy month; admiration for the person who is fulfilling the religious requirement; and recognition of this tenet of Islam.

"*Allah karim*" (God be praised), replied the hotel clerk, and he smiled before dabbing at his mustache once more with his *iftar* napkin. "You have reservations, yes."

He quickly led us to our room, pressing a key into Bob's hand.

Fasting during the month of Ramadan, one of the five duties of good Muslims, is like the *hajj*, or pilgrimage to Mecca, a situation that creates community among the faithful. As Bob says, fasting means holiness, the triumph of spirit over flesh, of godliness over earthly impulses. We, the tourists, feeding ourselves during Ramadan, are, despite our well-cut clothes and affluence (we can afford to stay in a good hotel), surely inferior to the lowliest citizen of Marrakech who is fasting. A certain success is celebrated nightly at the time of *iftar*. Right over wrong—East over West—justice over injustice. Poverty over wealth.

No one is too poor to fast. And in Morocco at any rate, no one is too poor to afford at least one meal a day. *Iftar*, the breaking of the fast, usually involves the same general pattern of foods, designed, we have been told, to soothe and not overload the stomach after twelve hours of not ingesting either food or drink. A few dates, some yogurt, followed by a bowl of *harira* (bean and lentil soup), perhaps a hard-boiled egg with cumin, certainly a steaming glass of milky tea. This kind of repast was delivered each evening at sunset to the old man who sat in the guard box of the government court building opposite the Hôtel Imilchil. I watched the daily scene from our narrow balcony. The unknown birds twittered again in the darkening trees, dipping and skittering between the television aerials that clustered on the rooftops like strange bare narrow trees of crossed metal. The sky turned from gray and gold and rose-red, like the roofs and walls of the city itself, to a darker gray. Then a young girl would appear from inside the courthouse, bearing the *iftar* tray. Head scarf in place, apron tied around her waist, the girl clop-clopped across the newly paved sidewalk. The old man would take the tray, go inside his cubicle, and shut the door, presumably to murmur a kind of grace, *Bismullah* (in the name of God), before breaking his fast in peace.

We would sit on the balcony together before sundown on those first gray evenings of our return visit to Marrakech watching moving forests of bicycles, carts, donkeys, motor scooters, and horse-drawn carriages head home, together with a few buses and cars. Time for all, fasting or not, to head for home, as the sunset hour approached. This crucial time was calculated to the minute by the religious officials in the mosques, taking their cue from each other and then sending, to be published each day in all the Arabic and French newspapers in Morocco, the exact times of the prayers. On March 17, 1993, the announcement was as follows:

Al-Fajr (the first prayer before dawn) 5:10

Ach-Chourouq (dawn) 6:36

Al-Dohr (noon) 12:44

Al-Asr (sunset is coming) 4:05

Al-Maghrib (sunset: time for *iftar)* 6:44

Al-Ichaa (last prayer before sleep) 10:08

Sundown. Traffic stops. Silence descends on the city, except for
the twittering of birds. One evening we went down at 6:30 to find the
hotel desk empty and our friend, the clerk, nowhere to be found. He
was discovered eating in the breakfast room. Bob unconsciously glanced
at his watch and the clerk leaped up, dabbed his mouth with his napkin
again, laughed, and then explained (although we had not asked) that
the hours of prayer printed in the papers were the hours in *Casablanca.*
Marrakech was two hundred miles farther south. So sunset was a wee
bit earlier here.

"Of course." Bob smiled back, and we walked out to dinner along
Rue Muhammad V, the artery between the old and new cities, which
was at that time almost empty. A lone couple, holding hands, walked
near us and settled on a park bench. Hmm. This was new—not much
evidence twenty years ago of young people embracing in the park when
they should have been home praying and then breaking fast in their
parents' homes. We walked on, heading toward the new city. This was
to be an evening of planning—how to find our friends Aisha and Omar.
Aisha had worked for us twenty years ago. She had taught me the
rudiments of Moroccan Arabic, how to make *tajine,* how to find my
way through the tangled maze of streets in the old city. Aisha had
become my friend and Omar had become Bob's friend, introducing him
to the merchants, who explained the ways of the market, welcoming us
into his home.

La Jacaranda, a small provincial French restaurant in Gueliz, was
our destination, but the neatly lettered placard on the door announced
it would not open until 8:00 P.M.—a mark of respect for Ramadan.
Thus, we settled for a glass of lemonade at the Café des Négociants,
across the street, gradually filling again with patrons. It was 7:30 by
now: the young men and a few women promenading by were clearly
out for a turn after *iftar.* For Ramadan nights are nights to enjoy—
consciences clear, duties fulfilled, time to revel, albeit mildly, until
dawn; certainly, this dictum is taken seriously by the rich, who can
afford to sleep most of the day, less so by the poor, who must work on
empty stomachs.

"Maybe we could look for Eva Lehmann, the German painter," I suggested. "She lives around here. And she's supposed to know where Aisha has gone." We had been told that Aisha had moved, leaving no address.

We had a half hour before the restaurant opening, and we set off through the back streets behind the Café des Négociants, searching for Rue Ibn Aisha, the written address of Frau Lehmann, who had kindly over the years served as a conduit between us and our small contributions to Aisha's well-being. Rue Ibn Aisha, a fitting name for someone who would hopefully lead us to the new address of our old friend, Aisha herself.

But Rue Ibn Aisha was not to be found. The streets were darker than we remembered. "Perhaps the man who turns on the streetlights is still enjoying his *iftar*," suggested Bob as we stumbled around the streets, looking for street signs. There were no street signs. We asked directions. A boy pointed.

"That is Rue Ibn Aisha."

We dutifully walked along, peering at gates. Eva Lehmann lived at number 31. There was no 31. There was number 39, and an old man opened that door and looked up and down the street.

"Excuse me, sir," Bob asked in Arabic, "is this Rue Ibn Aisha?"

The old man stared at us, shook his head, slammed the door.

"Well, maybe it's my bad Arabic, and maybe he meant this *isn't* Rue Ibn Aisha, but whatever, he wasn't exactly welcoming," muttered Bob.

We had reached the end of the street. There were no more houses. The streetlights had still not been turned on. A boy, or girl, whipped by us quickly, laughing, and was lost in the shadows.

"Let's turn back. There's nothing here," said Bob, and we wandered back the way we came, but lost our way in the dark empty streets, having on the first try failed to find Rue Ibn Aisha, Eva Lehmann, *or* Aisha. It was 8:30 by the time we reached the light, laughter-filled restaurant La Jacaranda and were awarded the last table in the house. A good omen.

The restaurant owner, daughter of the former proprietor, was sympathetic to our search. We ordered her recommended specials: fresh fish en brochette, calamari in tomato sauce, and *tarte au citron meringue* for dessert. We enjoyed this delicious meal, made even more delicious by our two-hour wait (one could not call it "fast," as we had had a reasonable lunch of *tajine).* But she could offer little information about Eva Lehmann—or, of course, our friend Aisha.

IN THE MORNING, the sun was shining into the room where we drank *café au lait* and considered our next move.

"Maybe we could find someone on our old street who would know where Aisha has gone," Bob suggested.

"Well, I was told that several people have tried that and it didn't work."

"It can't hurt. Come on. Anyway, wouldn't you like to see what our old house looks like?"

I was doubtful, both about the likelihood of finding Aisha this way and about revisiting our old house. But I kept silent. I knew, for I had been here in 1988, that our beautiful tiled house on Rue Trésor had been made into a tourist hotel; I told Bob this, but he probably didn't believe me—or wanted to see for himself. He was right, though, about one thing: if we were serious about trying to find Aisha, we didn't have much choice.

When I visited her in the old street in 1988, she was talking about leaving. The landlord was raising the rent; the owners wanted to sell the building; "big people" in Gueliz wanted to tear down these old structures and develop them into shops; the street was close to commercial traffic and would be much more profitable if it were like an American shopping mall and not cut up into tiny little apartments like hers. I had heard all these arguments before, in 1972 before we left; in 1976 when we were making the film *Some Women of Marrakech;* in 1982 when I came through with the Smithsonian tour. And each time nothing had happened. At least not until two years ago, when mutual friends wrote that Aisha had indeed gone from her little house and was nowhere to be found, though our mutual friend, Jim Miller, still thought Eva Lehmann might have some idea where she'd gone.

Back on Rue Muhammad V, we walked toward Djemaa al-Fna, the minaret of the ancient Koutoubia mosque signaling our direction. Across from the *baladiyah,* or town hall, the public park extends from Rue Echouhada to the Koutoubia. It was a late Ramadan morning— nearly 11:30. The public garden was full of people, strolling through the clusters of palm trees, the ubiquitous oleanders, the dark olive trees, mimosa trees not yet in bloom. Families sat on the benches of red adobe, the same color as the city's rose-red walls and houses, adobe benches set in cement and hence immovable. Toddlers in caps and bonnets and sweater suits (the wind was cold in a graying sky and dust was rising) staggered off their mother's laps, crawled onto their father's knees, chased each other on the garden paths. A father looked at his watch, holding his jumping son by one hand. Twelve noon. Six more hours till sunset and *iftar*. Ramadan *is* blessed, is it not? A young woman walked the paths near us, reading a book as she walked. Other young women and men were doing the same. Studying for exams? Reading from the Koran? A useful way to pass the hours of the fast.

The Koutoubia seemed to be under construction or reconstruction. The building near the mosque that housed the old crippled-children's home, the Cheshire Foundation, had been torn down. Why? No one knew. Rows and rows of wooden planks were piled on the site where the crippled-children's home once stood. But as we got closer, we saw that the planks were red, the same rose-red tint as all the other buildings of the city. So clearly these planks were not wood, but brick baked into the shape of wooden planks. Something else was being built here—offices for the mosque? A visitors' information center? No one could tell us. Aisha might have known, but we could not find her.

We crossed the dusty green square known as Parc Foucauld, named after an early French governor of Marrakech, and headed to Rue Bab Agnaou, just as we had for the year and a half we lived in Marrakech: the children ran home along Rue Agnaou from the bus stop on Rue Foucauld, Bob came back from his research visits to the market along Rue Agnaou, I crossed to Rue Agnaou after grocery shopping near Djemaa al-Fna. And the street looked unchanged. The Chevron station, the Grand Hôtel Tazi, and the rows of stores offering Chinese-made crockery, aluminum pots and pans, coffee, sports goods (soccer balls, fishing poles). The pharmacy and then the cinema. Just before the cinema was a turnoff into a small street where we had lived. But the street sign that used to be nailed on the wall high above pedestrian heads, "Rue Trésor" on a blue metal ground, was gone: the nail holes were still visible in the wall. What was the name of the street now? Was it our old street?

"Oh yes of course, B.J.," said Bob impatiently. "There's the bakery and the bath. And the pavement's still not been repaired."

A motorbike scooted past us, setting up small spurts of dust, and we were in the street, surrounded by signs. Not street signs. But signs advertising hotels, many hotels. Hôtel de Sud. Hôtel d'Ouriké. Hôtel Ait Melloul. Hôtel Tiznit. Hotels. Hotels. Hotels.

I bit my lip to keep from saying, "Didn't I tell you?" as Bob stood, staring up at our house which had now become the Hôtel d'Ouriké. The entrance had been painted white, and the half-open wooden door refinished and varnished to a fine clear gleam to attract customers (when we lived there, the door was always closed).

Bob knocked, and a round woman's face appeared, her complexion the color of overworked dough. Not our landlady. Nor her errant daughter.

"Want a room?" she asked. "Got lots."

"No," said Bob clearly. "We lived here. We want to look in."

The woman shook her head. Either she didn't understand our Egyptian Arabic or else she thought we were mad. Two middle-aged foreigners lived *here* on this narrow dusty street?

But Bob pushed through and we stood on the threshold. The woman's disbelief was understandable. The cluttered space before us bore no resemblance to the wide courtyard, floors, and walls tiled in geometric shapes of blues and greens. The courtyard where we sat and drank tea or read, listening to the soft splash of the central fountain, or to the children reciting their French poetry homework.

> *Des oiseaux gris viennent de passer—*
> *Vol! Vol! Bel oiseau, vol . . .*

Bob took a deep breath. "Well, at least the fountain's still there," he said. But it was dwarfed by an ungainly staircase, of black and brown tiles, which wound from the fountain sideways up to the second floor, its dimensions wholly out of proportion to the space in which it had been erected. And rooms, surely small ones, had been built out *into* the courtyard from the far wall (where the *djinn*, or benevolent spirit, lived, Aisha used to say, though from her tone it was not clear whether the spirit was benign or not; it had to be placated, at any rate, one way or the other). The whole effect was claustrophobic, doors and stairs higgledy-piggledy, seeming to push out against a little piece of court-yard floor left near the door.

The doughy-faced woman stood in front of the stairway, her stance a watchful one as though we might storm up to the second floor—to do what? Plant explosives? Steal the beds?

"Is Hajja Kenza here?" I asked finally.

"No, gone out."

"Let's go, B.J.," said Bob, turning away, and we were out on the street, opposite the narrow entrance to Aisha's tiny den, opening on a courtyard around which several other families lived. But we knew she was not there now.

At the entrance stood a bucket of garbage, the bucket handmade of old automobile tires, waiting for the daily pickup. We remained there for a moment, looking up and down the narrow street. Expecting what? Our own children coming from school, their French schoolbags on their backs? One of Aisha's sons beckoning? Aisha's hunchbacked daughter, Najiya, on her bicycle? Hardly. Najiya was long dead, our children had graduated from college in America, Aisha and her boys didn't live here anymore.

A woman came out of the narrow passage, with a handful of carrot and potato peelings to add to the contents the bucket. She was of medium height, wearing a faded green nylon caftan over a long-sleeved brownish sweater, the pushed-up sleeves and tucked-up skirts indicating she was in the middle of her household chores. Her eyes were small in a plump face and she wore a white head scarf. She stared at me. I stared at her.

"Uh, er—"

"Speak up, B.J." It was Bob, who had walked away slightly, not wanting to intrude on the woman's privacy.

"Is Madame Aisha here?" I asked a little too loudly.

The woman dropped her vegetable peelings into the bucket and wagged a finger at me.

"Nope. She's gone."

"Where?"

She shrugged her shoulders, scratched her head at the edge of her head scarf, turned away, and disappeared down the dark passage.

Bob and I looked at each other uneasily.

Now what?

"Let's walk down this side alley," he said. "We can't just stand here. It looks strange."

The side street, or *zanka*, that used to house a distinguished Koranic scholar, bore still another hotel placard and a luminous Day-Glo pink sign announcing that car rentals and *"voyages touristiques"* might be arranged inside (Follow the arrow to the door!).

Discouraged, we turned back to find the plump-faced woman smiling at us from the entrance to Aisha's old house. She pointed at me.

"You!" she fairly shouted. "You used to live there, you and M'sieu" (a finger indicating Bob, who was shifting from one foot to the other in the street).

I smiled back. "Yes. We came to see Aisha."

"All the way from America?" she asked in amazement.

"Yes, my husband had work here and we came to Marrakech for a holiday."

"Well, if you want to see Aisha, you came at the right time."

"What do you mean?" I felt vaguely alarmed.

She nodded and smiled to reassure me. "It's Ramadan," she said.

"Ramadan karim," I replied.

We smiled at each other and then fell silent.

She then said, "Where are your children?"

"In America."

"Why didn't they come with you? Aisha always liked them."

"They're grown-up. Two are married."

The woman's smile broadened. "Good. Good!"

Bob interposed, "Why not ask her to take us to Aisha? I'm sure she knows."

But before I could ask, she offered.

"I can take you to Aisha. It's not far. Give me a minute."

She gestured and was gone once more down the dark passage.

Bob and I waited, on our street that was no longer our street and no longer even had a name, while I mulled over the woman's strange remark about arriving to see Aisha at the right time. Was Aisha ill? Dying? What was going on? And who was the woman? Was she one of the granddaughters of Rakosh, the strong matriarch of the extended family that had occupied most of the house where Aisha lodged? Perhaps one of the half-grown girls who shouted gleefully at our daughter Laura Ann from the opposite roof, where she sorted grain with her cousin in the sunny fall afternoons.

A woman on a motorbike zoomed up the street, her jellaba slit high on the sides to allow some legroom. Two young men in leather jackets sauntered past, eyeing us curiously; everyone in Marrakech seemed to be wearing leather bomber jackets, black or brown.

Out came our friend and erstwhile neighbor, now clad in a brightly printed jellaba—green, pink, and blue with white clasps and frogging. A clean white head scarf but no face veil.

"Where are we headed?" Bob asked me to ask.

"Near the Mellah," she answered with a sidelong glance at Bob.

We set off, our guide in front, me close by, Bob slightly behind us, along Rue Bab al-Jedid, toward the Bahia Palace, the gold market, and the area called mellifluously in the Guide Bleu *le place des Ferblantiers*, the tinsmiths' quarter. A long winding street offered useful everyday products one might need to furnish or refurnish a house or an apartment or even a hotel! In one, a young man sat on a bale of green hay reading the morning newspaper, presumably to gather strength to stuff one of the flowered mattress cases with that fresh hay. Yes, it was a mattress place! See your mattress made before your eyes so you can be sure the mattress maker doesn't slip in wads of paper or dirty hay! Unconsciously, I could almost hear Aisha's voice from the past telling me this as I was trying to have new pillows made for expected guests.

"You have to stand there," she had said. "At the mattress place. And watch. The (wool, feathers, hay) might be dirty, might have bugs," she explained rather pettishly. Did she think I was laughing at her?

"Of course," I had rushed to reassure her.

This street looked much the same as it had twenty years ago. The mattress stuffers and other small artisans had not been incorporated into a modern shopping mall at all. Half-counters on the street offered us the same mix of material possessions we could have bought in the past: sections of forged iron for gates, brass doorknobs, that tinware made by the *ferblantiers*, bolts of mattress ticking, batteries, small car parts, lamps and shades. Every fifth store also seemed to purvey the goods called "notions" in old-fashioned American department stores: colorful hair bows and clasps, needles, thread, key rings, scissors, ballpoint pens.

On the other side was the government building where, while we were away, Bob's mother, Alta, had taken our children in a carriage in the dead of night to ask that our apartment's electricity be turned on. And between the government building was the secondary school that served as the old Mission Culturelle Française, where we had gone to evening French classes.

"How much farther?" I asked.

Our guide tut-tutted. "Haven't started," she said. "We're not even to the Mellah yet."

As we rounded the corner that led to the Bahia Palace and enclosed the gold market, a crowd of women was gathered by the walk, talking together excitedly, gesticulating, as they sat on the street in groups. A woman in a gray jellaba and hood raised a hand on which many finger rings sparkled and glittered in the shifting sunlight. Another woman with a baby asleep in a sling on her back reached for the rings. It looked as though she had paper money in her hand.

"What's this?" Bob asked behind me.

"Used gold, used silver, who cares, if it's used it's money," responded our guide, laughing a bit.

"Wasn't here before," I murmured. "They did their business inside."

"Yes, yes." She took me by the arm. "But you see, today there are more people in Marrakech. So more business. Inside *and* outside. Not room for everybody in the gold market that wants to buy and sell!"

All along the walk, the bargaining went on. If one wanted to raise money in a hurry, here was the place to do it, to bring your jewelry, buy, sell, trade. Cars were parked nearby, with well-dressed men at the steering wheels. "Are their wives buying and selling?" I asked.

"Of course," said our guide. "Can't you see?"

When I tried to pause to listen to the bargaining, she pulled me along.

"I thought you wanted to see Aisha, not buy gold," she said, and we headed into another souk, with more shops and more goods and more motor scooters whizzing by, between the press of people coming and going on this late Ramadan morning. "We're in the Mellah now," our guide prompted. "You can see even *here* it's crowded. Lots more people than when you lived here."

"What are we going to do if we actually do find Aisha?" Bob said from behind.

"Give her something for the feast, I guess."

"But we won't eat or drink."

"No. Ramadan after all provides us with a good excuse."

We both knew that Aisha, well schooled in the Arab traditions of hospitality to guests, would use the last of her meager resources or even borrow cash to offer us tea, biscuits, fruit, whatever, despite the fact that it was Ramadan. She knew that we were not fasting—we were not good Muslims, we were the other, nice enough, perhaps, but other. But we were still guests.

"Is Rakosh, your grandmother, dead?" I asked, hoping to find out whether this woman was indeed one of the neighborhood girls of twenty years ago.

"Yes, yes, maybe for two, three years." She held up fingers to make sure I understood. She sighed and added, "She was very, very old."

"And you?" I asked. "How is your health?"

A deep sigh as we continued to amble through the Mellah. And another sigh.

"I've been sick a lot. I had an operation. They cut me here"—she stopped and pointed to her stomach—"and took out the sickness, or most of it. It was the liver."

I wondered privately how they could possibly have removed her liver, or even part of her liver. Surely I had misunderstood.

"Your liver? You were in the hospital?"

"Yes, yes. The government hospital."

"For how long?"

She thought. "A long time, maybe ten or fifteen days. Now I'm on a *régime*. No fat."

Ah, it was something to do with the liver at least.

"Was it a good hospital?"

"Oh yes, *very* good, *mzaynbezzaj*."

I needed to identify this woman, but my memory failed me. She was clearly Rakosh's granddaughter, but there were four. She looked as old as I, but she couldn't be more than forty. A hard life and a bad liver will take it out of one.

"You're married?" I asked tentatively. It was ridiculous to be walking along with this nice woman, pretending I knew her and yet didn't.

She stopped in the street and looked at me accusingly.

"Of course I'm married. You know that."

So she was married while we lived in Marrakech. Aha! She must then be Fatima!

"How is your husband?"

Another sigh. "Not good. One day he's sick, one day he's better. He had an operation, too. A big operation. Two operations, really. They cut him here" (indicating her back under the flowered caftan) "and here" (indicating her chest).

"Two? Why?"

She pulled on my arm again and looked directly at me. Her eyes were small but they were sharp with intelligence.

"It was his heart. His heart was full of junk. So they cleaned it out. They blew out all the little pathways to his heart. So his heart would work." What a great description of a double bypass operation, I thought to myself.

"That's wonderful," I replied. "Those operations are done in America, too."

"He's still not well," she answered, "he can't work. So the kids work. They had to leave school."

"What do they do?"

"One works in a coffee shop and one in the souk, helping in a shop, and one is . . ." She paused and found a living representation before us, along the street. "Like that."

A gesture to the bench along the street where two men, one old, one young, were engaged in the tricky business of applying the final tiny stitches to the edge of a splendid gold and white caftan: the boy held four wooden handles that kept taut the lengths of the four golden threads the tailor was using to finish his work. "Thank God my sons have *some* work," Fatima added.

"Did you see that?" Bob called from behind.

My friend turned around and bobbed at him. It was the first time she acknowledged his presence.

"Aren't we nearly there?" he continued.

Fatima realized what he was asking, and reassured me.

We were through the Berrina Gate now, coming out onto the

open space in front of the old walled Jewish cemetery, its high gates locked, the Hebrew sign unchanged, clearly readable in the early afternoon sun. The Mellah, once the old Jewish quarter, was now home to Muslims.

Past the bath, several small all-purpose grocery stores, and into a side street where Fatima banged on a gray metal door set into a high stone wall.

"Aisha seems to have done well," remarked Bob, looking around the reasonably well kept street. "It looks better than the other place."

Bang! Bang! Bang! A voice from the other side.

"It's Elizabeth and M'sieu, come to visit Aisha," shouted Fatima. "They're here from America."

The door opened. Aisha's middle son looked out. It was Abdul Krim, looking gray and cavernous, his hair tousled; he had clearly been sleeping. This meant he was still out of work. Oh dear.

He shook our hands. "We knew you'd come," he said. "I told my mother you would."

Fatima pulled on my sleeve. "See," she said, "I told you you'd come at the right time."

Bob and I stood there, perplexed. Right time for what?

Abdul Krim sensed our confusion. "My father died only three days ago," he said. "We knew you'd come to offer condolences."

Death. The father dead. Died in the village of Sidi bou Othman. Sick a long time. We did not know. How could we know? Who would tell us? Eva Lehmann, whom we searched for in vain? Omar, whom we had not yet found? Jim Miller, who had not been in Marrakech for a year? How could we have known? Yet we were expected.

But this did not concern Aisha, who swept in, dressed all in ceremonial white. She had been taking the ritual bath suggested in the days after death. She greeted us enthusiastically and ceremoniously, discarded her new white *ship ship* shoes, and sat us down in the spacious room of her new house. Our sympathies and condolences were offered and accepted, as was our gift for the feast to come. News of family was exchanged. Pictures of our children were presented and admired.

We commented on her new lodgings. Two large rooms and a water closet.

"Yes," she said, "it's cheaper than Rue Trésor. Bigger and cheaper. But no courtyard. And not much water."

"You're still better off," ventured Bob.

"We-ell," Aisha began, and her face wrinkled in lines of worry. I could think of nothing to say. In the silence Aisha said, "You must have tea." She kept on her white outer jellaba, only proper in the presence of Bob, though she had not done this while working for us. It must be the presence of Fatima; perhaps she was keeping up appearances during the ritual period of mourning. Abdul Krim sat beside her, on the banquette, his hands loose between his knees. He looked dreadful and was turning gray.

"No, thank you," said Bob. "*Ramadan karim.*"

"But you're not fasting," said Aisha with a touch of her old mischievous spirit.

"No, but you are," Bob replied.

"And I am, too," put in Fatima, whose presence had been forgotten in the flurry of reunion, the phrases of condolence.

"You should be, though, Mr. Bob," said Aisha crisply, laughing a bit, and it was not clear whether she was being ironic or not.

"Yes," replied Bob, "but you see, we are not Muslims. So we must leave you to prepare your *iftar.*"

We stood up. Aisha commented on the rightness of our being in Morocco at this time, to perform that most important of social duties, the condolence visit following a death in the family.

"*Ramadan karim,*" said Bob again, and held out his hand to Abdul Krim.

But six-foot Abdul Krim drew back. He produced a passport from his pocket.

"Look, I have the papers. My brother helped me get them. Now find me a job in America!" It was not a request, but a demand.

Bob took the proffered passport, looked at it, gave it back.

"Sorry, Abdul Krim," he answered. "I could ask for a visa, but you'd have to be able to do a job that no American can do."

"I can teach gymnastics," said Abdul Krim, drawing himself up.

Rather gently, Bob said, "But to teach, you need to speak English."

Abdul Krim drew his mouth down as though he had just tasted something unpleasant. "You do not want to help me," he said.

"Now, now," Aisha broke in. "They came for the *azza*, Abdul Krim, on the death of your father."

But Abdul Krim had turned away. He did not even say goodbye.

Aisha bustled forward. "Thank you! Thank you! Thank you for coming!"

We embraced, Aisha and me, Aisha and Fatima, Aisha and me again. Bob shook her hand and slipped some more money into it, a lot, I hoped. This was appropriate for an *azza* visit.

All the way back to our old neighborhood Fatima was silent. When we parted, she said, "Tell your husband not to worry about that son of Aisha's. He thinks he's too good to work. My boys don't act like that, thank God."

"Thank God," I repeated. "Thank you for taking us, Fatima. I hope things go well for you."

She nodded, a quick dip of her head, and then she looked up at me out of those small bright eyes. *"Bslama,"* she said. "I liked seeing you and M'sieu" (with a nod in Bob's direction).

And she was gone, into the narrow street where we had all once lived, Aisha, Abdul Krim, Fatima, and her grandmother the matriarch Rakosh. Bob and I and our children, David and Laura Ann and Laila. The street once called Rue Trésor, now the street without a name, the street of hotels.

DEMOGRAPHERS WRITE THAT Marrakech has nearly tripled in size in the past twenty-five years. At first, this did not seem possible to us. Surely, the demographers had overstated their case. During the day, when we walked out from our hotel, the streets seemed less than crowded and the wheeled traffic not much heavier than it had been when we lived here in the 1970s. We reminded ourselves that it was Ramadan, and people were fasting. Of course, the streets would not be crowded; people worked, rested, stayed at home. And we noted that in the evenings the sidewalks were filled with men, women, and children taking promenades after *iftar*. And the traffic roared up and down and around us, just as the demographers had stated.

But physically, central Marrakech did not seem to us to have changed much. Orange trees still lined the Rue Muhammad V, between the medina and Gueliz, and flags still flew in front of the *baladiyah*, the town hall, set back from the street, across from the park, in an elegant garden. A few French shopkeepers in Gueliz had gone, but the shops still retained their French signs, some carrying as well the new Moroc-can owners' names. Policemen in black and white uniforms and black berets still choreographed the movements of cars and trucks and horse-drawn carriages from their wooden platforms raised high above the traffic circles.

"I don't think there are as many carriages as in the old days," pointed out Bob.

The post office remained a busy place, with a few tourists like us, but mostly local residents. No longer was it jammed with European and American nomad-hippies, camped inside the building or lounging out-side on the steps, waiting for remittances from abroad (parents, hus-bands, wives, agents) to allow them to continue their nomadic exis-tence.

The food market in the center of Gueliz, crowded with customers, retained some of its former culinary splendor: fresh carrots with bits of earth clinging to them, tiny Belgian endives, specialty greens like lamb's-tongues; wonderful oranges; cheeses and butter from Europe. The prices of meat were staggering, however, at the same level as Texas markets at home. But people were buying, shopping for *iftar* and the late Ramadan meal that is usually served before midnight.

"Would Madame like a basket to carry groceries?" The old mer-chant in skullcap and ancient sweater sat at the side of the food hall as always, proffering sturdy handwoven baskets of natural fiber, decorated with dyed bands of crimson and green.

Madame would indeed like a basket, but not, sadly, to carry gro-ceries home to Rue Trésor. That time was finished, for better or for worse. But yes, I did want a basket to carry back to the hotel my purchase, a plate from the coastal town of Safi, where pottery had been made for hundreds of years. And some bread and cheese and fruit for Bob's and my lunch, since restaurants were closed during Ramadan.

WE HAD BEEN LOOKING FOR OMAR, but, it must be confessed, some-what halfheartedly. His old shop in the Semmarine was occupied by a stranger who claimed to have no knowledge of Omar or his family. And after the drawn-out search for Aisha, the emotional but somehow un-satisfactory visit, we both felt a certain reluctance to look into other past relationships.

"We did what we could for Aisha," said Bob. "I gave a gift for the feast. It was fairly generous."

I was silent. Yes, we had been generous, but what of the future? How was she to continue to live? She had been working for a Peace Corps family in 1988, but they had gone. Abdul Krim was clearly a drain, an unemployed and depressed member of the household, and no mention had been made of any present work or of the third, absent son.

"I must stay home for the first forty days after his death," was her response, deflecting my question about her employment.

As if reading my thoughts, Bob said, "Well, Omar was hardly poor, so that's not the problem for him. His family owns real estate in the medina. So let's go by the shop once more."

I have never met anyone who is not affected in some way by the ancient bazaar called Semmarine, with its center street, broad enough for two donkey carts to pass, winding past rows of shimmering silks and satins, antique rugs, jewelry, jellabas and burnouses handwoven of goats' and sheeps' wool. Some visitors are frightened and want to leave immediately. Perhaps it is the noise, the confusion, the press of people. Or perhaps it is the strange sense of unreality, produced by the light and the absence of light, the sudden semidarkness that descends after one turns in from the wide-open sunny space of Djemaa al-Fna, toward the covered souk, past the spice merchants, the sellers of dried dates and apricots, the stalls that hawk colorful Safi pottery and *tajine* dishes, what every Marrakech housewife needs: those unique covered cooking vessels of reddish-brown fired clay.

We had visitors clamor to leave before they even got *into* the covered bazaar. And we had other friends who exulted in what the bazaar has to offer, striding in and often losing their bearings after a moment or two. That of course posed still another problem. One friend, enchanted but suddenly lost, stopped dead, said she looked around, could see nothing familiar, and felt panic rising in her until Laura Ann's blond head emerged from a shop ahead of her.

Perhaps the pungent scents—of cumin, coriander, cloves—combined with the strange semidarkness, create a sense of unreality, of being in another time, another place. At the bottom of a well, or in a closed capsule beneath the sea. Just as deep-sea divers report bits of sunlight sparkling through the surface of the water, so is the darkness of the Semmarine punctuated by minuscule dots and bars of sunlight, filtered through the woven rushes of the roofs covering the old bazaar, and falling like dusky golden coins on the packed-earth passageway in front of the visitor's steps.

Even the grand shops that line the passage contribute to the strange light, for though they use blazing electric bulbs and winking fluorescent tubes to illuminate their wares from China, India, and Timbuktu as well as Morocco, they often turn this fluorescence off to save money, turning them on only as a prospective buyer approaches. The abrupt switch from light to darkness and back again discomfits the novice visitor.

Historically, the Semmarine has made its residents incredibly wealthy and occasionally poverty-stricken. Tax collectors periodically raid the great market, in search of merchants who have evaded, through diversifying their resources, the bite of whatever government has been in power. And word that the tax man was making a regular visit spread like wildfire through the souk, occasioning the closing of shops, the slamming down of shutters.

"That's why my father has several little holes-in-the-wall, and not a grand *magasin*," Omar had explained long ago. "It attracts less attention."

The French tried to close the Semmarine and they did succeed in appropriating for a Club Med part of the land on which the bazaar stood. The French-trained city planners proclaimed the necessity of tearing down all of the "retrograde structures" in favor of more modern premises for trade. Dangers were cited—fire, bad sewage, terrorism—all to no avail.

It is true that the Semmarine is a good place to hide, for political dissidents, thieves, runaway wives. And I remember one day, when Laura Ann and I were bargaining for some green silk, that a cry passed along in front of us.

"Make way! Make way!"

Two young men in jeans and T-shirts were tearing through the Semmarine, veering left and right, to disappear in the direction of the famous mosque and lodge of Sidi bel Abbas, the patron saint of the city. Would they have sanctuary there? I asked Omar, for it was he we were buying from that day.

Omar had smiled. "They will not be there," he said. "The policemen might as well give up."

And indeed, when two black-uniformed policemen came trotting down the broad passage five minutes later, they looked as though they knew the game was up. Their pace, Laura Ann pointed out, was too slow for a chase.

"So what are those young men?" I'd persisted.

Omar, folding up the green silk, inclined his head.

"Who knows?" was his reply, meaning of course who wants to know, better keep silent, the government may be after you next.

Now in 1993 we were in the Semmarine once more, drawn into the strange light, the pungent scents, the cries and calls of merchants, the illumined banks of silks, the clops of a donkey behind us. We headed once more for Omar's father's old shop—the flagship shop we called it, for his other numerous enterprises: leather, brass, dry goods, as well as ready-made jellabas for men and women.

No Omar. But a middle-aged man stood up behind the glass counter and yes, he did know the family, and yes, they were still in the Semmarine, he thought in the large area where imported silks were concentrated. He would send his child assistant to lead us there.

The child took off down the street and we hurried after him, past the turnoff I had never been able to resist, the turnoff to what Marrakshis call the Berber market, where one can buy amulets against the evil eye and beads to hang over the door or around the neck of a beloved and endangered child. One can also buy sponges for the bath and hand-made local toothbrushes of walnut bark. The narrow little alley opened out to the banks of shops called "the pharmacies" by Aisha. Here men experienced in the practice of traditional medicines would prepare powders for stomach woes and soothing herbal teas, all things I had noted and lingered over during the time we lived in Marrakech, but which I never had the nerve to buy or try. But I had seldom paused before the shelves of green and gleaming glass bottles containing strange preserved objects of unknown provenance, guaranteed to increase (or decrease) health, virility, fertility, those basic needs for the continuation of life everywhere.

"Come on, B.J.," called Bob, "come on," and I ran to catch up with him and our child guide, who was now busily counting shops to the left—one, two, three, four, five. He pointed us to a large establishment and skittered away.

We stepped up, two steps, and into the shop, which was surely

large enough to be called a *magasin,* or large store, the kind Omar had
so scorned in the old days. The walls and ceiling were hung with ready-
to-wear caftans—gold, peacock blue, crimson, jade—which shimmered
in the bright neon, creating an opulent background for the handsome
wooden counter. There a pair of young women in sober jellabas were
engaged in serious business with the two salesmen, judging by the
number of bolts of silk unrolled before them.

One of the salesmen looked up. He was not too tall, mustached,
and nearly bald.

He dropped the bolt of printed silk he had been holding and came
forward.

"Bob!" He smiled. And yes, we could see. It was Omar, a good
deal older, but Omar.

Handshakes, embraces, invitations—tea, lunch at home, coffee.
No, no, no. *Ramadan karim.* No, we leave tomorrow noon. Then we
must at least tour "new" developing Marrakech, the new suburbs in
the Agdal Gardens, then have *iftar* as his guest in a restaurant of our
choice. We must, he said.

I looked at Bob.

"Thank you, Omar, we'd love to," he responded.

"I would take you home, Madame B.J., but my mother is away
this week," he said.

"No matter. Please give her my greetings," I answered, wondering a bit. In all the time we had known Omar and his family, his
mother had never been away from home. Her family came to her, for
she was the wealthy and hence more hospitable relation. But of course
it is Ramadan, I told myself. Maybe she's not away at all, but Omar is
making polite excuses so he won't have to ask her to cook lunch for
nonfasting infidels. Still, what about *iftar?* Didn't Omar go home anymore, like all dutiful sons, to celebrate the breaking of the fast with his
parents and his brothers and sisters?

"Bob, you were right about many things," Omar was saying as
he escorted us through the Semmarine and out in the direction of the
Mouassine. He had shaken hands with the two sober ladies bargaining
for silk, turned the negotiations over to his assistant.

"How are you?" asked Omar. "Madame B.J.?" He smiled at me.
And at Bob. "How are you, my friend?"

He steered us through the Mouassine and out onto the parking lot in front of the police station, where the sun shone on the peddlers selling oranges and lemons, and on the row of black horse-drawn carriages waiting for passengers. An old man, the self-appointed car watcher, sprang forward as Omar approached his Fiat.

"Yes, Bob, you will see how Marrakech has changed, how big it has become." Omar turned sharply to avoid a loaded donkey that was plodding on directly in front of us. Omar's shout at the driver woke the man up, who stared at us and shook his head in irritation. His donkey continued forward.

"It's Ramadan," he continued. "Have to be careful." He thrust a small bill into the hand of the car guardian, who guided us into the main street, then saluted.

"Omar," said Bob. "Would you call that guy, the car watcher, employed or unemployed?"

"He is semiemployed," said Omar.

"And is the semiemployment rate up or down these days?" persisted Bob. "And the employment rate?"

Omar smiled at Bob. They had had many of these discussions in the past, in our house over coffee, in Omar's shop over tea, in Omar's house over one of his mother's bounteous meals. "Down and up. Up and down. The new development projects need many workers. Sometimes it's hard to find skilled workers. That's one reason so many new houses are not finished."

"Where?"

"All over. People are building all around Marrakech. We have nearly a million people now. They have to have somewhere to live!"

"Well," said Bob, "if there's so much work, how come all these men are hanging around in the souk, doing nothing?"

"They're not doing nothing," protested Omar. "They're doing *something*, part of the time at least, even though you, a foreigner, with your own set of ideas, may not see it."

Bob was not to be put off. "So," he said, "would you call those people employed or unemployed?"

This was an old argument between Bob and Omar, how to define employment or unemployment in a society where working part-time at several jobs is more common for most men than having a full-time salaried job.

"Like the farming life a lot of these men in the souk come from,"

Bob went on. "You work at different tasks, fields, animals, and in some seasons of the year you don't work at all!"

Omar laughed. "It's good to see you, Bob," he said.

"Good to see you, too, Omar," Bob answered, "but let's get back to the question of employment."

Omar did not answer directly. "You were right in your prediction about the *huntas*, Bob."

"The *huntas*—the guilds? What did I say about that?" Bob forgot his question in his surprise.

"You said that the government would make the traditional head of the guild, the *amin*, into a government official and that would combine the new allegiance with the old. And they did."

"Really?" Bob was intrigued.

I looked around me. We had come through Bab al-Doukkala, the northern gate of the old city, and were heading through Gueliz, past the Lycée Victor Hugo, where our children had attended school.

"Will the lycée stay?" I asked.

"Of course, *madame*. People still need to know French. But the mission near your old house is closed, so if adults want to study French, they need to come to the mission here, near the lycée. And," he added, "now everyone learns English. The French are not pleased."

"I bet," said Bob, a little too vehemently, perhaps remembering difficulties our friend Ruth Ann Skaff had encountered when she set up the American Language Center twenty years ago.

"Oh yes, English is all the rage. You should speak to me in English."

"All right," said Bob. "I will. Where are we now?"

Omar held up his hand. "Enough, enough," he said, laughing. "Maybe I should come to America."

"Fine."

"I'm only joking," said Omar. "Too much to do here."

"Tell me about your new shop."

"Later, later." Why the resistance? What was wrong with the partnership that had produced that surprisingly grand and apparently profitable *magasin* in the old souk? Long ago, Omar had insisted that such displays of wealth were not good business. Something had changed. Something was different. But what?

North and east of the city lay the old palm gardens, the *agdal*, and this was where we were heading. Yet the palms were gone, having given way to the unmistakable signs of extended suburban development. The French might have designed this, I thought, frustrated in their attempts to bulldoze the medina, with its narrow streets that wound about and into dead ends, with its own logic that did not fit the French view and the Francophile-Moroccan view of rational planning for the future.

"You see, Bob and Madame B.J., the new medina," proclaimed Omar, gesturing toward the small city in the process of being built even as we watched.

"But where are the beautiful palm trees?" I cried without thinking.

"Well, there are still a few," temporized Omar, indicating one or two lone trees in a tuft of grass on broken ground. They stood at the corner of what could only be called a ring road, paved, two lanes, circling the new constructions. House after house, shops like corner grocery stores in French towns, a mosque, and more houses. The whole expanse of the Agdal Gardens had become an upmarket housing development.

"Who lives here?"

"It is just beginning," explained Omar. "We have bought houses here, my family and I. Let's look at them. They are very beautiful, very modern."

True, they looked beautiful, modern, new, but they all looked exactly the same, two-story villas of rose-red adobe brick, set a few feet apart to allow for small gardens, *à la française*. Carbon copies of each other.

"The garden replaces the courtyard in the old houses of the medina," explained Omar. "Do you not find that attractive?"

I nodded mutely.

He looked so proud of his new urban suburb I could not bear to say what I thought, that the old spacious courtyards of the medina allowed both privacy and openness to the sky within the house itself. That the old houses were unique—beautiful adaptations to the environment of a walled city, comfortable and convenient within walking distance to the place of work, energy-saving, space-saving. All those characteristics now so desirable for pleasant living today. The new two-story suburban villas had none of these unique characteristics. They were late-twentieth-century imitations of late-nineteenth-century European architecture.

Bob, perhaps guessing my thoughts, broke in with questions about the number of new houses, the dimensions of the area of land occupied by each house and by the whole development, the ratio of shops to houses. Omar answered eagerly; he had clearly spent time researching the pros and cons of this opportunity, an opportunity available in different proportions to all members of Marrakshi society, he explained.

"One buys the land, lays the foundation at one's own expense, and then it is possible to get loans from the government banks for the rest. Anyone can do that, if you have the money. But this area"—he smiled—"is restricted to those who can pay cash for the land. It's a very good investment."

This would explain the half-finished state of the majority of the houses and the obvious fact that they were built on the same grand plan. We had learned that the same conditions had been fulfilled by some friends of friends—young secondary school teachers—but their land was in Daoudiate, an older suburb west of the central city, where house size was not specified and cost and restrictions not so high.

A good investment, in a good neighborhood, and, it would appear, a rich neighborhood. This might partly explain Omar's enthusiasm. For although property in the medina was still very valuable, there rich and poor lived side by side, as they had for centuries. This new suburban development was clearly restricted to the very wealthy, an additional attraction perhaps to up-and-coming affluent families in Marrakech, just as it was an attraction in the United States and many other countries of the world.

We wandered into Omar's own partially built house, were shown floor plans, rooms, stupendous bathtubs waiting for water lines, carved wooden doors propped against walls, waiting to be hung. His parents' house next door was a mirror image of his.

"So you're going to sell the old house and move here?" I asked.

"No, no, it's not finished here yet. And we haven't really decided. My mother doesn't want to move."

I bet she doesn't, I thought. Far from the market, her mosque, her friends, isolated and dependent on her husband and sons to drive her where she wanted to go.

"But it is a good investment."

"Yes, Omar, I see that," said Bob.

While we had been wandering from room to room of Omar's house, watching workmen applying sculpted plaster to the border of the salon, noting painters working over the wood trim, the sun had dropped. The sky had begun to dim and then darken. The painters quickly plunged their brushes into cans of the local equivalent of turpentine, removed their spattered coveralls, nodded politely, and bolted. The sculptor-craftsman climbed down his ladder, rather more slowly. A cannon sounded in the distance—the sign that the sun was down. The fast was over for the day. *Iftar* time!

"Dinner, dinner!" called Omar, and we took off through the unfinished streets, leaving the denuded palm gardens far behind.

Later, much later, over the remnants of a roast chicken and salad in one of the old Gueliz garden restaurants, Bob returned to the subject of investment and Omar's new venture.

He lit a cigarette and inhaled deeply before answering.

"I don't know how to explain, Bob," he said slowly. "It is a long story."

"Yes," said Bob, prompting him, "and our friendship is a long story, too; but," he added hastily, "if you don't want to talk about it, fine."

"No, no." Omar looked down. The top of his head was bare, except for a few graying hairs carefully combed across the dome. His mustache, too, when he looked up, had changed to pepper-and-salt from its former exuberant black. Omar, like Bob and me, was getting old.

"You see, my family has ousted me."

Bob opened his eyes. Surely he had misunderstood. Omar was the trusted oldest son in a large extended traditional family. He had been thrown out of the family? Why?

"I am no longer welcome at home. I'm living with my brother and his wife till my new house is finished. My father accuses me of stealing, misappropriating, a lot of his money." He stumbled over those words—stealing, misappropriating—as though even to speak them aloud was shameful, which indeed it was in any society, but even more so here—where family honor was cherished and protected, where family reputation was all. Omar? Stealing? I could not believe it.

Seeing Bob's shocked expression, Omar rushed to say, "But of course I didn't do that at all. My father wanted to invest in the Agdal and to do that he had to declare all his business assets. And so I said I'd try to do it for him."

"And . . . ?"

"And I did. But of course it cost something to do that, go through his confused books, fulfill the government regulations for the loan—this means taxes, more forms, on and on. He could not believe how much it cost, and he was furious about the taxes—he's been paying peanuts for years. Well, you can imagine. He's a very rich man, but never faced it before."

"He didn't throw you out for that, did he?"

"No. I told him the best way to avoid future taxes was to invest in some modern ventures. Computers are very big here now, so he gave me money to invest in a computer company in Casablanca, and I did it."

"He should have been pleased," said Bob.

"*You* say so, I say so," said Omar, "but he's not. What's more, he expected to get his investment back within the year. He doesn't understand the *principle* of large investment, and when he didn't get it back, he accused me of stealing it. And that's the story."

He stubbed out his cigarette and called the waiter for coffee.

"I'm thinking of leaving Marrakech," ventured Omar. "But it's my home. I grew up here. Everyone I know is here. I don't want to leave."

"Can't your brothers explain to him?" persisted Bob.

Omar nodded. "They have tried. He just flies into a rage and threatens to throw them out of the family, too. Even my sister has not been able to get through to him and she's his favorite, you know, Ph.D., science professor at the university, all that."

"How old is your father?" I asked.

"Eighty-two." Omar smiled bleakly. "And healthy as a horse. He'll probably live to a hundred, and outlive *me*."

"I'm sorry," Bob said, and I echoed him.

"Yes. I'm sorry, too. What to do? The worst thing is he goes round telling stories to people in the souk, trying to ruin my reputation so I can no longer work there. Most people know the real truth and don't pay much attention, but still it's not good. Why do you think no one in the Semmarine would tell you where my shop is?"

Omar asked me if I would have *tarte aux pommes* or *crème caramel* for dessert. He clearly wanted to change the subject. I ordered the *tarte*, which was good, and we talked of politics, of King Hassan's renewed respect among his people, of the improving economic climate in Morocco, of problems in America, of the Western media fixation on the Islamic fundamentalists, and on a possible Islamic revolution.

"Islamic revolution?" Omar laughed out loud. "Oh, Americans. Don't they realize that Morocco already *is* a Muslim state? What else do we need to do to prove that? Ramadan, for example, is really observed by most people."

I thought of explaining that people in America had little understanding of Islam itself, let alone Ramadan, that we ourselves had not been aware that this was the month of Ramadan when we bought our tickets to come to Morocco. But I kept silent, and thought instead of Omar's dilemma, a very real dilemma which threatened his hopes, his success, his entire future. The family, it is said, provides support, economic and emotional, for all its members, in exchange for allegiances during times of marriage, birth, and death. But what about radical changes in the functioning of a society? What is the family's role then? What if the dominant member of the family, the father, fails to understand and appreciate the need for new approaches? What if the father is unwilling to give up any control to his children? What if he tries to destroy his children, as Si Abdulla was trying to destroy Omar? Then clearly the family is neither solace nor support, but a detriment to its members.

Omar was obviously not the only son to suffer from the whims of a tyrannical elderly father, but he had experienced a particularly painful blow: blame for what he perceived as good work well done.

"I will drive you to the train tomorrow," said Omar at the door of the Imilchil Hotel. "And by the way, this is a good hotel. I still have my hotel inspector job but my father's trying to get them to fire me."

"Omar, don't bother to drive us. It's quick with a cab," said Bob. "We-ell—"

"Yes, yes. You're fasting, too. Thanks. Take care. Come visit us." Bob proffered his new professional card.

Omar took it and inserted it carefully into his wallet.

"Goodbye, my friends."

"Goodbye, Omar. *Ramadan karim*. God be with you," I said. "And do greet your mother and your sister Malika for me. I am sorry not to have seen them."

Omar peered at me and smiled his old smile. "I will, Madame B.J.," he said. *"Ramadan karim."*

THE IDEA OF THE FAMILY IN THE ARAB WORLD

THE FAMILY IS FREQUENTLY CITED as a human institution common to all peoples. Middle Eastern families, for example, have often been compared to families in preindustrial America, when men, women, and children worked together in order to survive. Today, as the Arab world becomes increasingly urbanized, family members may still be contributing to the household income, but they are more often working for others, outside the home. In this sense, families in the Arab world appear to be becoming more and more like modern American families. But there are still some important differences between East and West, in function but also in the way people think about the institution.

The family, not the individual, until recently has been the major unit of political, economic, as well as social life in the Middle East. In America the reverse is true. This difference can be seen in the way the term *ahl* (family) is used in each society, the group of people to whom it refers. "Family" in America has come to mean many possible combinations of people and households; many of them are new, such as single parents, stepparents and children, parents and adopted offspring, divorced parents with two sets of children. The term is also used to refer to groups of people who hold periodic reunions—and try to figure out how they are related to each other. In American public life, the word "family" takes on very different spins in the speeches of politicians, the sermons of ministers, and the plots of TV soap operas.

In the Arab world, the word *ahl* or family also denotes different sets of relationships, but these, unlike the American case, are not at all new. The most common usage refers to a single-family household, but *ahl* may also mean "relatives, kinfolk, clan," and, in a more metaphoric sense, "inhabitants, companions, partisans," and other groups of closely associated people. Characteristic to all these forms of *ahl* are shared ideals about the responsibilities of kinship, and a shared public identity and reputation; all people are known by their *ahl*. Most American families have no such inclusive public group identity; members are often scattered about and frequently change their place of residence. At school, at work, most of us are known as individuals, not as members of families. In the Middle East, by contrast, family names and reputations are of long-standing common knowledge in villages, towns, and urban neighborhoods. When someone is mentioned in the Middle East, he or she is always identified by their family connections.

Nor do Arab world households share the same diversity of composition as those in America. An Arab household is almost always headed by a male. Few women live alone and single-parent families are unusual; if a woman is divorced, she frequently returns to her own family, her parental home, where her father is in charge. Families are patriarchical; they are governed by religious canons that have legal standing in matters of marriage, divorce, and inheritance, all of which favor males. Moreover, the Koran and the Bible are seen as guides to everyday life. Such admonitions are taken very seriously by most people.

Above all, families must be seen to stand together, against others, though how the lines may be drawn, who stands with whom, may not always be the same. Thus, in the past, and even today, government authorities who wished to talk to a family member often contacted the family head. If a member misbehaved, punishment and correction were often left to the family. For a family's honor, its public reputation was and still is every member's responsibility and legacy. And, in exchange for the allegiance of its members, the family group has served as employment bureau, insurance agency, counseling service, older folks' home, source of credit, hospice for the disabled, and marriage broker. The Arab family reckons its members through male descent, but ties with other families through marriage are important. And marriage between cousins is also often common in the Middle East, tying family branches together.

The Arab family has long contributed to the stability of the Middle East, providing a safety net in a world that has lacked other dependable forms of security. How else could high rates of unemployment continue without riots or famine in poorer Arab countries that lack unemployment compensation and credit agencies for the poorer classes? Government programs of food subsidies are more common these days, but in times of need most families still provide essential help for their less fortunate members.

Of course, the Arab family has never been a perfect system, but in the 1990s it is under more stress than ever. A growing middle class questions the need to help poorer relatives; with a new lifestyle, middle-class urbanites say they can only afford to care for their own children and parents. In countries like Egypt, government public assistance is falling behind individual needs. Public schools are overcrowded and middle-class families must pay for private schools or after-school tutoring. Reformist Islamic groups have responded to such pressures by offering help in times of disaster, charity to the poor, and free medical clinics in the mosques, services which have gained them support among both poorer and wealthier Muslims.

The realities of everyday life are thus changing attitudes toward the family among both women and men. In countries such as Morocco and Egypt, from which thousands of men immigrate for foreign employment, many women are in fact running their households, perhaps supporting it, though their absent husbands remain the symbolic head. Working women are now commonplace in much of the region, though many men still argue that a woman's proper place is in the home. Given the increasingly large number of families that depend on both female and male incomes, however, moving Arab women out of their jobs in most cases seems highly unlikely. All the same, the responsibilities of the family versus the responsibilities of the government for the individual's well-being has become an issue of general concern and public debate.

Americans discovered at the time of the Great Depression sixty years ago that a family could no longer be a security blanket for all its members. With the New Deal, the American government took over economic and social responsibilities that had previously been family-managed. The Middle East experience has been very different. As it has become clear that neither the traditional family nor the government can provide for individual needs in the modern era, other structures are forming, modeled on the family paradigm. Using family networks to find jobs for unemployed members remains a universal practice, but women are forming familylike ties with neighbor women when their husbands are absent, offering each other limited personal assistance. Men and women from the same rural communities form solidarity groups in cities to provide what before were always family services (such as burials). Some migrant groups may rent rooms in cities to provide recreational opportunities for the young (such as TV sets and pool tables). Furthermore, political party membership and family ties often overlap; in Beirut during the recent civil war political ties between related families were all that prevailed in the absence of effective government. And, for both men and women, membership in a religious group may be considered a relationship of brotherhood and sisterhood, just as compelling in terms of mutual obligations as those of shared kinship. Simulated family ties may thus replace or at least supplement relationships of kinship.

Are these family and familylike organizations in the Middle East going to persist and continue to provide an important degree of social stability and security in the face of governmental limitations? The chances for this seem much better in the Middle East than ever was the case in the United States. Ethnic, regional, and class diversity in America curtailed, almost from the beginning of our history, a common national understanding of the family. But in the Middle East a consensus around the idea of the family still appears strong. The population of Arab countries remains far more homogenous than the United States, even with the rise of the new middle classes. Moreover, the educated younger people of the region, who once might have been more attracted by foreign ideologies, are now far more likely to be actively interested in Islamic thought and practices.

The enormous strength of Islamic identity now provides the basis for a common discourse, a language for young and old, urban and rural, within which differences of opinion can be addressed as changes in styles of life are accommodated. This broadly shared ideology gives the Arab world an enormous advantage. But can urban family and familylike bonds, even though reinforced by the rising strength of religious identity, be sustained by future generations without the material bases of the older family structures—especially shared interest in land and real estate? As urban populations continue to grow and grow, the long-term effects of current urbanism and industrialism on the traditional Middle Eastern family group, and the consequences for the future stability of the region, are perhaps the most compelling problems Arab people will face in the next century.

> *We need an angry generation,*
> *A generation to plow the horizons,*
> *To pluck up history from its roots,*
> *To wrench our thought from its foundations.*
> *We need a generation of different mien,*
> *That is not forbearing, and forgives no error,*
> *That knows no hypocrisy, and falters not.*
> *We need a generation of leaders and of giants.*
>
> Nizar Qabbani
> WHAT VALUE HAS THE PEOPLE WHOSE TONGUE IS TIED?

W E ARRIVED IN CAIRO at the end of a revolution. Seven years have passed since the Free Officers' Revolt, which had been, as revolts go, a rather decorous occasion. Little blood was shed, and the king abdicated peacefully. King Farouk, descendant of another soldier, Muhammad Ali, an Albanian who wrested power from the Turkish Ottoman rulers in 1811 and assumed control of Egypt, was allowed to sail away on the royal yacht, carrying as much personal treasure as his vessel could hold.

Egypt was now a republic, under the presidency of Colonel Gamal Abdel Nasser, son of a rural postal clerk. Three years had gone by since President Nasser had nationalized the Suez Canal, causing international outrage and disbelief. He said at that time that he had acted because of the sudden withdrawal of American and British loans promised for the construction of the High Dam at Aswan, symbol of the new Egypt. The Suez war followed, the British-French-Israeli attack on Egypt to regain the Suez Canal. The United States intervened and hostilities had come to an end after eight days. All these events lay well in the past. It seemed to us that the worst uncertainties of the revolution were over and the time of building was under way.

Bob had accepted a three-year contract to teach anthropology at the American University in Cairo; I was seven months pregnant with our first child. After two years of research in southern Iraq and a year at the University of Chicago while Bob wrote his dissertation, we had decided to go back to the Middle East, rather than to Kansas or Wisconsin. We liked the Middle East, we liked the people we had met, and we set off for Egypt with high hopes and great enthusiasm, despite dire warnings from colleagues about the dangers of burying oneself in the lotus-eating atmosphere of foreign climes.

"It's just a good excuse not to do any work," said one anthropologist friend lightly, and "You'll be far from the cutting edge of the field," said another. So our farewell parties in Chicago had been ambiguous in tone. It was obvious, people joked, that we had opted for travel and adventure rather than serious academic endeavor. Bob replied a bit defensively that for an anthropologist interested in the Middle East, three years of employment in the area was a great opportunity to be a participant observer, particularly at a time when the area was changing so rapidly.

"We have a chance to see Egypt in the process of building a new nation," Bob said a bit sententiously. "A chance to witness revolutionary change firsthand."

"Some revolution," commented a critical colleague. "Nasser is just another two-bit dictator."

Bob shook his head. We did not think of Gamal Abdel Nasser as a dictator. He seemed to us like a new kind of leader in the Arab world, the first indigenous leader in centuries. Even Muhammad Ali had been a foreigner. When we had stopped in Cairo in 1958 on our way home from Iraq, the Egyptians and the expatriate Americans and British we met spoke of Nasser with respect. "The nationalization of the canal was one thing," said Geoffrey Godsell, a correspondent of the *Christian Science Monitor*, "but now Egyptians are running it themselves at new levels of efficiency, thank you very much; that's what's giving people pride in being Egyptian." Godsell had lived in Egypt and knew the country well. "I think it is going to grow," he said, "that pride, that self-respect."

Western commentators at the time who were concerned with East-West relations viewed with alarm President Nasser's new alliance with the Soviet Union, which had stepped into the breach and offered aid for the Aswan Dam. But it was withdrawal of American aid that had resulted in the alliance in the first place. What else, we said to ourselves and our doubting friends, was Nasser to do?

Egypt, it seemed to us in 1959, was demonstrating a more positive form of postrevolutionary development than any other Arab country. Morocco, Tunisia, Lebanon, Syria, Iraq, Sudan, had all gained their independence from colonial powers by the mid-fifties. Algeria was still battling the French, but the others were fledgling nations, and Egypt, we thought, was a model for those nations. In 1959 and 1960 Nasser's pro-Arab movement was attracting supporters all over the Middle East. Nasser had taken another revolutionary step when he joined with Tito of Yugoslavia and Nehru of India in declaring that the so-called Third World countries must get out of the cold war. "Why should we be drawn into the quarrels of the superpowers? World peace can be better served by our neutrality," they said.

Omar, a young Egyptologist who befriended us early (he had gotten his Ph.D. from the University of Chicago, too), echoed Geoffrey Godsell's remarks about pride. Nasser's greatest achievement by 1960, Omar said, was not just schools or clinics or land reform or legal secularism or the Aswan Dam, though these were indeed important. His greatest achievement had been to give Egyptians self-respect. It was no accident, Omar continued, that President Nasser was allocating more funds for improving the Egyptian Museum, for restoring and preserving the pharaonic and Islamic monuments, that he personally insisted museum admission should be free on some days so that all Egyptians could learn about their own glorious past.

"The new Nile Hilton has picked up the pharaonic theme, too, I noticed," said Bob.

Omar nodded. "And why do you think they hauled that enormous statue of Ramses II all the way from Memphis and put it up by the railroad station?"

"I thought it had always been there," I answered. "It seems to fit, with the fountain and all."

"No, B.J., it was only put there in 1955. And remember, it is of Ramses II, the great builder pharaoh. And where? Not in the museum or the university but near the train station, in the center of the working city, where everybody passes by and sees it every day."

"Come, come, Omar," said his sister, Aziza, lightly. "Don't get carried away. A symbol, yes. But it's too much, that statue. Too *big*."

Omar was from an upper-middle-class landed family, but he supported Nasser in those years. His sister, Aziza, who had kindly taken me around Cairo to upholsterers, drapers, and picture framers while I tried to furnish our first home, was not so enthusiastic.

"All of our past belongs to all of us," Omar would say earnestly.

"Yes, I agree," Aziza would say, sipping tea in our new half-furnished study and nibbling on the good raisin pound cake that Abbas, our Nubian cook, had prepared. "But—"

"But *nothing*, Aziza. We must reclaim our past. After all, we have been colonized by foreigners for hundreds of years, and they looted our riches, not only the natural resources like cotton but our cultural treasures too. First the Ottomans, then the French, the Germans who stole Nefertiti's statue, then the British—"

"And now the sons of postal clerks," put in Aziza rather sharply, "destroying the old Egypt while they say they are building it up. Taking away people's property, nationalizing the land. For whom, Omar?"

"For everyone, Aziza," said her brother, glancing about somewhat uneasily as though someone might be listening on the other side of our apartment walls. "It must be done."

"Radical change is never easy," put in Bob. "In revolutions, they say, the losses always seem greater than the gains—at first, anyway."

"Well, the whole country is losing—"

"Aziza!"

"It's true, Omar. Lots of people who are losing their property are leaving Egypt for good."

"Let them go—the rich . . . the king's family—"

"Not just them. Many other well-educated people who have much to give . . . Nasser is trying to move too fast—"

"But the problems are overwhelming," I said. "Poverty, health. He feels he has to show results."

"He's not moving fast *enough*." It was Omar, glaring at his sister. Bob and I might not have been present at all. This was obviously a family argument that could be going on in many upper-class Cairo households in those days. "Would you really like to go back to the days of the thirties, Aziza, when Egypt was owned by foreigners—French, English, Italian, Greek—when there were special *laws* for them, so they didn't have to pay taxes or even go to jail for crimes committed against *us*, the real Egyptians?"

Aziza tried to laugh. "Of course not, Omar, you know that. It's just that you've been away a long time in America, where things are different."

"All right," said Omar, facing his sister. "But you can't have *any* improvement in people's lives here when a few big landlords own most of the country. That's what Nasser is trying to avoid."

The arrival of other guests, less well known to us, put an end to the discussion. Open criticism of the government was a foolish risk in front of strangers. But Aziza and Omar were not alone in their feelings. Not surprisingly, many better-off Egyptians were divided on the issue of nationalization, sequestration of property, and land reform. Landlords who had lived comfortably off their estates for generations, going and coming to Europe and America, did not like the controls being placed on their travel and their capital by the strict financial measures of Nasser, who was keeping a tight rein on the country's economy in an effort to balance the budget. Those Egyptian landlords who had applauded the nationalization of Greek and Italian and British enterprises were not pleased when similar measures were taken against themselves. Yet Nasser was not quite as headstrong as Aziza implied. He had allowed each Egyptian citizen to keep a maximum of two hundred feddans (a little more than two hundred acres); in a large family where each member was allowed those two hundred feddans, many estates were hardly touched. This was not sentimentality on Nasser's part. He knew that he needed the agricultural expertise of the old landlords if the fields of the Delta and Upper Egypt were going to continue to produce food and high-quality cotton.

But many people were leaving, especially foreigners, Europeans who had been in Egypt for generations. With the abolition of their special law courts and their nontaxable status, many merchants and industrialists felt Egypt was no longer a profitable or safe place to do business. The landed aristocracy—pashas and beys, many of Turkish origin—also were leaving. Every week the newspapers advertised auctions of their belongings.

An entire economy was being forcibly transformed from one of peasants, landowners, and foreign merchants to something else, though just what the shape of the new society might be wasn't yet clear. Certainly, it was more *Egyptian* than under King Farouk. But a lot of the old bureaucracy was still in place; most of the old elite, even if they had lost some land, still had lovely homes, lots of servants, automobiles.

President Nasser, himself an army officer, gave privileges to the army. Army officers were in. Or were they? What was left of the upper class and the descendants of the pashas took care to keep the less important army officers out of the sacrosanct rooms of the Gezira Sporting Club, the Muhammad Ali Club (now the Automobile Club). So the army officers formed their own club, a far more splendid edifice than the aging Gezira Club. The engineers and other groups such as lawyers did the same, and a plethora of new professionally based family clubs sprang up all over the growing city of Cairo.

With General and Mme Muhammad Fahmy, the parents of an Egyptian friend in America, we went often to the Police Officers' Club, where excellent food was served and, on holidays, the best entertainment in town. One feast day we were lucky enough to witness an early performance by a young dancer named Nagwa Fouad, who charmed both sexes of all ages into participatory clapping and singing, with her sensuous combination of beauty, dance, and wit. We discovered early that belly dancing is family entertainment in Egypt.

Our own parents were far away in America, like the Fahmys' children, and thus the surrogate roles we filled for each other were a source of comfort for us both. Also, we were foreigners and Mme Fahmy was of Greek descent, while General Fahmy was an Egyptian Muslim. Under Nasser's new laws, army officers could no longer marry foreigners; thus the Fahmys, like us, were somewhat anachronistic in the new Egypt.

It was Mme Fahmy who stood up as godmother for our firstborn daughter, Laura Ann, when she was baptized in the Roman Catholic chapel of the German nuns' school in Bab al-Loukh, another remnant of old colonial times.

General and Mme Fahmy also belonged to the Gezira Club, but, said the general's wife, "the food is really much better at the Police Officers' Club, even if the clientele is a bit arriviste."

"Now, Jenny," cautioned her husband gently. Retired from the army, he supported President Nasser, while at the same time expressing some reservations about his methods.

"Well, I have no one to talk to here," explained Mme Fahmy reasonably. "So many of my old friends are gone."

"But it is a comfortable place, don't you think?" General Fahmy asked Bob. We looked around the large lounge, heavily carpeted, with easy chairs arranged in family groups so that mothers and children and other relatives could drink tea, play games, and chat as though they were in their own private living rooms. New Egyptian-made materials, printed with lotus and papyrus motifs, in the clear colors found in pharaonic tomb paintings, had been used for the drapes and the slipcovers.

Mme Fahmy sniffed. "They are trying, but they have not yet quite developed a modern patriotic style," she said, smiling a little, and I tended to agree with her.

"It all takes time, Jenny," said her husband. "Took France hundreds of years."

"Yes," agreed Bob, and finished his Egyptian beer before rising for lunch. "The beer, I will say, is excellent here."

"It's a German process—" began Mme Fahmy.

"—but Egyptian workmanship," said the general, leading the way to the dining room, "and it's Egyptian water. You know what they say about the waters of the Nile, Bob?"

"I certainly do," said Bob. "Whoever drinks of the Nile will always return to Egypt."

"But there's something else," persisted General Fahmy as we waited on the sunny patio for a table to be readied. He smiled. "The Nile, my friend, is supposed to have great powers of fertility." He slapped Bob on the back. "But I see you already know that."

It was true. I was pregnant with our second child.

Taste. Decor. Although some things were changing, much seemed the same. The auctions of the goods of departed aristocrats and foreigners always attracted the army officers and their wives. Louis XV love seats, old china, Persian rugs, silver plate, English and Italian furniture, European bibelots or paintings of any school—all commanded enormous prices. The taste of a departed elite was still the preferred style. In fact, the standard technique of the auctioneer, when he saw the bidding begin to flag, was to mention the names and titles of the goods' former owners. Names. Titles. The sound of those words stimulated the bid-

ders and the prices would immediately rise again for such items as
Prince H.'s desk or Mme C.'s dressing table mirror.

One winter morning I saw twelve Haviland fruit plates and a
matching footed epergne, the property of a departed French family,
fetch a thousand Egyptian pounds. The Haviland was old, true, and the
epergne quite beautiful. But a thousand pounds? I turned to Aziza and
shook my head.

"The family was important," said Aziza, and shrugged. "Mme
Gaudet gave very exclusive dinner parties."

A thousand pounds for a memory? For the thrill of trying to
participate vicariously in the social activities of a foreign elite? An elite
whose private lives had been closed and forbidden to Egyptians, and
who had now disappeared forever? Whatever the reasons for the high
prices, a small percentage of each auction's proceeds went into Egypt's
republican treasury, where it was needed badly.

Newly prosperous wives could be seen in the flower shops along
Kasr al-Nil and Suliman Pasha streets, buying enormous arrangements
of roses in the fall, huge sprays of almond and apricot blossoms in the
spring, bunches of tuberoses in the winter, whose insistent fragrance
perfumed the entire shop. They lingered in front of the show windows
where Egyptian shoemakers were displaying good copies of Italian and
French designs. They flocked to the boutiques where French embroidered baby clothes and English-style smocked children's dresses were
still for sale. Though the new Egyptian Ministry of Industry was pushing locally manufactured goods, those goods often imitated familiar
European patterns. Even in the delicatessens and pastry shops, European influences continued. More indigenous pastries like baklava and
kunafa were available from the "Syrian" bakeries near the Opera
House and the Ezbekiah Gardens, but Simonds in Zamalek and Heliopolis and Groppi's in central Cairo were crowded with people vying for
essentially European delights: meringues, pound cake, napoleons, lady-
fingers, chocolates in beribboned boxes, marrons glacés wrapped indi-
vidually in golden paper—the sweets of a vanished European population. Fresh Italian ravioli and French pâté could still be purchased,
together with fanciful sugar Easter eggs, for the Egyptian Coptic, Greek
Orthodox, and other Christian groups, as well as the small foreign
population (which now included us).

In Groppi's tearooms, where we drank café viennoise hot in winter and cold in summer, we saw the old class and the new class meeting, but now speaking. Army officers' wives, in new clothes, very high heels, and bouffant coiffures spooned ice cream confections next to elderly men in old-fashioned suits of excellent if shabby tweed, who might nurse a single Turkish coffee throughout an entire morning. The ancient waiters in Groppi's, I noticed, never tried to run these old men off for holding on to their seats too long. They knew well that such men had probably had their apartments sequestered and their furniture auctioned, and were economically useless in the new Egypt. But they still had stature of a kind recognized in Groppi's.

"Let's take Laura Ann to the puppet shows," suggested Aziza.

Aziza was finishing some courses at the university but had a lot of free time "while I think about when I want to get married," she had once explained to me in a burst of confidence. Thus, she had taken me around the city and had "adopted" Laura Ann almost from her birth.

So Laura Ann put on her best dress (from one of those Kasr al-Nil shops) and was taken by Mama and "Auntie" Aziza to the puppet show, *Imad al-Din and His Donkey*, the dramatization of an old Egyptian folktale that was drawing full houses, of adults and children, to the theater in downtown Cairo. "It is part of the new Egyptian culture," Aziza said.

Laura Ann, aged two and a half, watched entranced as the puppet donkey plodded along the stage, maneuvered from below, and the puppet peasant plodded along beside him. And she laughed delightedly when the puppet donkey brayed in a most convincing manner, "like ours," she said.

"What?" Aziza cried.

"Ours," responded Laura Ann.

"I think she means the donkey that pulls the garbage wagon," I explained. "It's her donkey as much as the garbageman's, she thinks, since it goes by our house and stops by the *ganeena*, the park where she plays every day."

Aziza looked a little taken aback, but I said quickly, "I guess she's learning about all aspects of Cairo, Aziza."

A new indigenous dance group, the Reda troupe, was formed to choreograph and produce authentic Egyptian folkloric programs; a large tent, the Balloon Theater, was raised in the Dokki district of the city, so many people could watch the Reda troupe perform variations on traditional Egyptian themes. The troupe, begun by an engineer, was distinguished also by the fact that the engineer's own daughter was one of the dancers, a breakthrough in a nation where, until recently, female entertainers were called *artistes*, a word often used as a synonym for prostitutes.

The legitimate theaters were refurbished, revitalized, like the cinema industry, "like the poetry, the literature," added Omar. "It is a cultural renaissance for Egypt." So it seemed.

And foreign policy somehow became a part of that renaissance as European powers vied with each other to offer Egyptians the best cultural events of their nations: Russia sent the Bolshoi Ballet for three weeks, with Ulanova or Plisetskaya dancing every night. Germany presented fine string ensembles. Bulgaria and Rumania sent folkloric troupes and invited the Reda troupe to tour their own capitals. Italy provided a season of opera performed in the local replica of La Scala, built in 1869 for the Empress Eugénie's projected visit to Cairo in conjunction with the opening of the Suez Canal; Verdi was asked to write *Aida* for that occasion. France sponsored a season of new films; Britain sent a Shakespeare repertory company. The United States sent choir and jazz groups.

We went to many of these star performances, benefiting from the cultural by-products of the cultural cold war. And afterward we would sit with friends on the Victorian porch of the old Semiramis Hotel, beside President Nasser's new riverside Corniche: drinking Egyptian beer and tea with Omar, Aziza, Nicholas Millet, an archaeologist from Chicago, Susan Spectorsky, an Arabist from Radcliffe, Mona and Abdul Latif al-Shafei, then of the American University of Cairo. And while we contemplated the eternal Nile, we felt that we were truly fortunate to be in Egypt at this time. The river, black and gleaming by night, remained the same, but Egypt was changing: an ancient nation was being reborn, we believed, awakening from years of domination by others to assume responsibility for its own destiny. At the time, we recognized that there would be some problems along the path to progress. How could there not be problems?

President Nasser went further. The nationalization and sequestration of lands, he said, should not be limited to foreigners and Egyptian large landholders. He struck at another establishment interest in the old system: he nationalized religious property. By creating a ministry to handle the management of Wakfs, religious endowments, he hoped to remove the dead weight of real estate, often some of the best property in Cairo, which was frozen in charitable trusts and could not become part of the modern economy. In so doing he also ended any semblance of an independent religious establishment. From then on, mullahs and sheikhs were government employees, paid out of the national treasury like the majority of other middle-class Egyptians.

President Nasser's new entente with the religious establishment was demonstrated in a historic 1962 television broadcast on the issue of family planning. By then, the good news from the health care programs indicated a decline in the death rate. Fewer babies succumbed to dehydration, fewer children and adults were dying of smallpox and cholera. But the bad news was that, partly owing to the declining death rate and an improvement in diet (and, people whispered, new hope for Egypt's future), the population had grown from 21 million in 1956 to 26 million in 1962. Nasser, however, appeared on television, flanked by the rector of Al-Azhar University, the leader of the Islamic community in Egypt, to declare that family planning was necessary for the good of the nation. Nothing in the Koran or in Islam forbade family planning or the use of contraceptives, said the rector, provided that these measures were used not for sinful purposes but "to improve the condition of the family," the most important institution in the Islamic world. President Nasser said that the population increase needed to level off, or Egypt would not be able to keep its promises to its people: hospitals, housing, food, and schools for everyone.

The government's drive toward free education for everyone had made spectacular strides. In ten years, between 1950 and 1960, the number of primary schools had doubled (from 1,530 to 3,330). And the number of primary school students had also doubled (from 1.3 million to 2.6 million). Yet the momentum was slowing—partly for economic reasons, partly because of language. During the colonial period, Egypt's business was conducted in French or English, not in the indigenous language, Arabic. Hence, thousands of teachers had to be trained to teach in their own native language.

Bob and I found that educated people did not want to speak Arabic with us but preferred to keep up their more fluent English or French (foreign languages, though currently out of fashion, could be useful in the long run). But since we both felt strongly about keeping up our

Arabic, and improving it from our Iraqi days, we hired Sheikh Ali, who came twice a week to our apartment for tea and lessons.

"God be praised," Sheikh Ali would intone when he sat down in our apartment, slowly developing from five bare rooms with electric wires hanging from the ceiling into a kind of home. Winter, spring, or fall, Sheikh Ali requested politely that all our windows be closed, "because of the dangerous breezes," so we would shut the front windows reluctantly, the windows that looked out over the balcony, to the ganeena, where Laura Ann and then David, our newborn son, went each day for recreation, and across the cottonwood and casuarina trees to the limpid, gleaming Nile.

"The breeze brings disease," Sheikh Ali would explain, blowing his nose ceremoniously on a white handkerchief which he secreted somewhere inside his many layers of clothing: overcoat, suit coat, vest, shirt, and long underwear (the edges showed white outside his shirt cuffs). Whatever the season, he wore that underwear and the high black laced shoes of my grandfather's day. In winter he added a sweater, and spring meant no overcoat, "but one had to be careful." All seasons, however, he wore what in the past in America we would have called a Shriner's hat, a red fez; here, he explained, it was called a tarboosh, and there were still special men in the markets who steamed and cleaned tarbooshes, Egyptian hatters who blocked the tarbooshes on tarboosh molds that looked like overturned flowerpots.

"The tarboosh is worn by the middle class," Sheikh Ali explained to us, and we realized he was speaking of the past. Few people wore the tarboosh anymore, that sign of Turkish days, when the Ottoman *effendis*, or white-collar workers, wore tarbooshes to indicate their government rank.

"True, young people no longer wear the tarboosh, but they do not deserve it," he would add, while he drank thirstily two or three cups of hot black tea with plenty of milk and sugar which Abbas provided for our "lessons."

We learned many things from Sheikh Ali, and we probably learned some Arabic, too, though his methods of teaching were, to say the least, unconventional, if not innovative. Faced, during his entire lifetime, by a stream of American and British missionaries who wished to be tutored in Arabic, Sheikh Ali had developed the parable approach.

After his opening statements, blessing the occasion, remarking on changing times, he would launch into one or another of the parables in his repertory: Bible stories shared by Christians, Jews, and Muslims, stories of the Old Testament that could not ruffle the feelings of anyone but a Goliath supporter. We sat politely in our newly furnished study, closed to the view of the Nile, listening while Sheikh Ali told us the tales of Daniel in the lions' den, Samson and Delilah, Joseph and his many-colored coat. Each of the parables contained a wealth of new, if not always useful, vocabulary words: lion, bars, growl, green, yellow, scarlet, purple, pillars, temple, passion. We listened, and we asked questions, and he corrected our grammar between parables. But when the session was almost over, signaled by Sheikh Ali passing his hand over his eyes beneath his heavy horn-rimmed glasses to get a surreptitious look at his watch, Bob would leap into the pause and ask questions about Egypt of the past. Sheikh Ali would reply reluctantly.

"In the old days, foreign people like you came to Egypt, too. But they stayed. Not here for one year, two years. The Vandersalls have been here twenty-five years. *Their* Arabic is excellent." (We felt properly humbled.)

"Then we knew each other, all peoples, Christians, Jews, Muslims. We believed in the same God, but we worshiped differently," he was going on. "Now Cairo is full of strangers, Russians, Japanese, people from Yugoslavia. Who are they? What are they doing here?"

Whatever we may have felt about Sheikh Ali's opinions, we were provoked enough to comb our Arabic dictionaries in search of the right words so we could answer him; for his great virtue—tarboosh, Bible stories, and all—was that he spoke no English. Or at least if he did, we never knew it.

"But things are now improving for everyone," Bob insisted, "not just for a few."

The American University, where Bob was teaching, was one of the institutions that mirrored change, resistance to change, and the lessons of the past. For it had only declared its commitment to secular rather than religious ideals a decade before, and the atmosphere of a missionary school still hung over the university, as it did over the American Girls College, a preparatory school in Heliopolis, from where many of Bob's students had come. But the religious atmosphere seemed to bother us more than it did our Egyptian friends. "There young people learn good English and are preparing themselves for the Egypt of tomorrow," General Fahmy explained to us. "The Koran says, 'Educate your children for tomorrow,' and as Muslims, we feel our faith is strong enough to deal with the issues raised by other faiths."

As President Nasser's campaign for free public education gathered momentum, the Egyptian universities—Cairo, Ein Shams, Alexandria—increased dramatically in size. Some say that university attendance in Egypt jumped 500 percent in one generation. By 1960 over 100,000 students were enrolled in institutions of higher education; the total had tripled in a decade. Here, if one passed the government examinations at a sufficiently high level, one could obtain professional education (engineering, law, medicine) as well as the Ph.D. (social science, science, humanities) at no cost whatsoever. These unprecedented opportunities were seized by thousands of bright young people whose parents would never have been able to afford to send them to college or university. And from these graduates a new kind of elite was emerging, upwardly mobile, intelligent, and supportive of President Nasser's regime (after all, hadn't he been responsible for their success?). Young, hopeful, dedicated, they began to inject new enthusiasm into a tired bureaucracy, new ideas into an intellectual establishment devoted until recently to Europe and Europe alone, new forms into arts and letters, new plans into the architecture and public works of the city. Sawsan, one of our friends from Cairo University, came from a family of seven children whose father had been an assistant gardener at King Farouk's Abdine Palace. Ten years later Sawsan had become an anthropologist, her sister a film producer for Cairo television, her four brothers an engineer, a librarian, a doctor, and a short-story writer and reporter on one of Cairo's daily newspapers. Cairo University offered a system of competition based on merit, not only family ties. It also offered coeducation. Cairo University was becoming the great leveler.

But coeducation meant something else in Egypt, which after all was an Islamic state. It meant a relaxation of the close supervision usually accorded to young women. Going to the university became not a duty, but an honor, and a redefinition of women's role and place began to be attempted. No one in the middle and upper classes of Egyptian society had been veiled for years. That had disappeared in the

1920s, with the dramatic public unveiling by Hoda Sharawi and Seza Nabarawi and the subsequent formation of the Egyptian Women's Union. Though peasant women still wore long loose-fitting dresses and wrapped a black *milaya* around their heads and shoulders when they went out, middle-class and upper-class Egyptian city women wore Western dress. Yet dress of the West did not necessarily equal freedom of the West. Boys and girls did not date Western style, and marriages were arranged by families. Before 1952 the educational level of women was very low, no matter what they wore, and work laws and family laws still favored men. The opening of schools taught in Arabic and President Nasser's public statements about the duties of all citizens, men and women, in the new Egypt gave impetus to the participation of greater numbers of women in education and in the workplace than had ever been involved before.

But parents of a more conservative generation were often not ready to give their daughters the run of Cairo University, with its great mass of students from all parts of socialist Egypt; for them, the American University provided an acceptable alternative. Further, one did not have to pass government-administered examinations at a high school to be admitted. One of President Nasser's own daughters, Hoda, had not done well on her exams, so he sent her to the American University, which admitted her on probation. Fairly small (fifteen hundred students), fairly expensive (and thus beyond the reach of all but the well-to-do), the American University was reputable academically, but its degrees were not yet accredited by the Egyptian Ministry of Education. Thus, the American University, by default, directed its graduates to nongovernment jobs in what remained of private enterprise, in the worlds of banking, tourism, public relations, and private schools where good English or French was still as much an asset as a degree from the new national university. Thus, the university, American missionary school though it may have been in the 1940s, had become a different place by 1960 with an international flavor (forty-eight nationalities), a kind of private-school cachet, and a more pluralistic even if more elitist student body than other educational institutions in the country.

Our two children grew and prospered in the Egyptian sunshine, in spite of the "noxious" breezes Sheikh Ali so abhorred. They prospered also in the Egyptian social climate, where children are universally desired, indulged, and adored. Several years later, in Cambridge, Massachusetts, Laura Ann came home from her first-grade class each day with a glum look on her face. "What's the matter, dear?"

"People are so mad here."

"What? What do you mean?"

"Well, nobody says hello. When I say hello, on the street, they just look mean at me."

Poor Laura Ann. It was difficult to explain to her that she was missing a whole attitude, a whole culture, that was hospitable and affectionate to all children, in a way that her own society was not. But I tried.

Then she said, "Even the ganeenas here aren't the same."

She was right. The parks in Cambridge were larger and greener and had far better play equipment than the small garden outside our house in Cairo, but the people were not as friendly. What I, brought up in America, found perfectly natural, Laura Ann, brought up in Egypt, found alien. The mothers and fathers in the park, good Bostonians, did not speak to all the children, and certainly did not bounce strange babies on their knees or comfort any passing toddler that was crying, as the good-hearted Egyptians in the ganeena did without thinking twice about it. "Our" ganeena in Cairo was a kind of school, though we did not realize it at the time, socializing children in the ways of play and affection and what could be expected from adults; socializing country girls, new servants for the newly well-to-do, in the ways of city nannies. The ganeena also served as an employment bureau for the female servants, at a time when the old ways of hiring help (through relatives) were changing, and new families that needed and could afford servants had appeared alongside some of the old ones.

Parks. Public gardens. Ganeenas. They had existed in Cairo long before Nasser's time, but not in such profusion, and not without the restrictions of entrance fees. The new public gardens were free, another demonstration of Nasser's belief that Egypt belonged to all Egyptians. And he had appropriated more urban space for parks. Early in his presidency he had begun by leveling the British army barracks that had occupied a vast area beside the Nile. The old military parade ground was planted with trees and flowers, transformed into walkways and parks which led into the Corniche, a new tree-shaded esplanade that wound along the river from the Kasr al-Aini bridge in the south to the northern edge of the Boulac district, allowing ample space for public picnicking, strolling, and just sitting beside the river. The private gardens of the aristocracy came next. Princess Fawzia's garden in Zamalek became a children's playground; the Manyal Palace, the Abdine Palace, and the king's summer palace at Ras al-Tin in Alexandria were made into public grounds and museums. Like all the other parks, the ganeena below our apartment was free, but not to everyone. Only women and children were admitted. This seemed strange to us at first, but eventually friends made it clear that this was a protection for women in a society where reputation was still crucial, and where being seen talking to a strange man could ruin a woman's reputation—and life—forever.

My own feelings about the ganeena were mixed, for although it looked like any children's playground anywhere in the world, it was not. The ganeena was really not for mothers and children to take the air; it was for *nannies* and children. When I had adjusted to the fact that the nannies in the ganeena were vaguely unfriendly when I spoke to them (after all, wasn't I letting the side down by not providing a job for one of them?), and when I decided that a good Egyptian nanny could both increase the amount of care and affection my own growing family would receive and give me some time to write, I departed from the ganeena forever. I occasionally observed the children from the balcony, but I let Farida, our nanny, take Laura Ann and David to the park. Everything changes, Sheikh Ali had said—including us.

PRESIDENT NASSER RETURNED from an international meeting of the nonaligned-bloc leaders. He was cheered by thousands as he rode through the streets, standing upright in an open car, smiling, waving his hands in recognition of the applause, the shouts of adulation—"*Ya Gamal! Ya Gamal!*"—that greeted his progress. "He has diabetes, you know," said an Egyptian colleague who stood with us above the crowds on the roof of the American University to comfortably watch the triumphant cavalcade pass. "He is not well. And I'm sure you've heard about Vice-President Abdul Hakim Amer. Corruption, the old story."

"But not Nasser himself?" asked Bob.

"No. No one criticizes him personally. But the people around him, that is another matter."

By 1962 President Nasser had been in power for nearly ten years.

The plans were familiar and promises were coming due. The industrialization program had been a moderate success: Egyptian textiles, furniture, plastic dishware, cosmetics, refrigerators, drugs, appeared in limited supply. The Egyptian-made small car, the Ramses, built in cooperation with Fiat of Italy, was seen on the streets. But food prices were rising, the agricultural reclamation program was lagging, and so many new college graduates were being turned out that Nasser was having to add staff to the already crowded offices of the government bureaucracy to keep his promise of a job for every young Egyptian B.A.

Yet the biggest promise of all, the key to future advances, was the High Dam, that oft-dreamed-of, constantly discussed engineering miracle that was meant to change the face of Egypt by providing more arable land, more hydroelectricity, and insurance against disastrous floods. The High Dam was the subject of newsreels at every local cinema, of gossip, of more jokes, of party chatter at every social gathering. Could Nasser pull it off?

Thumbing one's nose at the West and taking on the Soviet Union was no joke. And it was rumored that Nasser had mortgaged Egypt's cotton crop for many years to repay the Russian loans. It was a great, costly gamble, and as the years passed, the dam became more and more a symbol of Nasser's aspirations for a new Egypt.

But word had reached Cairo that many unforeseen problems had developed around the dam. It would take longer to finish than expected. Costs were mounting. The Russians were having trouble working in Upper Egypt's intense heat. And our friend Sawsan, whose brother was one of the Egyptian engineers employed on the dam, said there were "differences in temperament" between the Egyptians and the Russians. "The Russians are so serious," said Sawsan. "They won't listen to us. And my brother says they never laugh, except at silly things that aren't jokes at all. Very heavy-blooded, the Russians."

The dam had many implications. When the structure was complete, the backwaters would form a lake, flooding the Nile Valley south of Aswan into northern Sudan. Magnificent pharaonic monuments, including the temple of Abu Simbel, stood in the path of the floodwaters. Their plight was attracting international attention. UNESCO appropriated funds for a giant project to save or to document all the monuments before they disappeared forever.

Omar, our Egyptologist friend, was delighted by the international attention. "My nation is finally being noticed again in the world of art and culture," he announced at a dinner given by his parents for a visiting French archaeologist. "Abu Simbel is a word known today around the world, Bob."

"What about the people who live near Abu Simbel?" asked Bob. It was a large dinner, elegantly presented and served, and most of the guests seemed to be concerned in one way or the other with the archaeological monuments of Egypt.

"Who? Oh, you mean the Nubians. Nasser," said Omar, "is making arrangements for them, too."

"He is?" Bob sounded interested.

"Yes. The government is taking care of it all, I think."

"Hmmm," murmured Bob, then, a bit louder, "I suppose they are, but I've been wondering if anyone is interested in *their* life and culture. It would be interesting to find something out about the plans for the Nubians."

"Go to Dr. N. in the Ministry of Social Affairs," said Omar. "He will tell you."

Bob was staring intently at Omar. "Okay." Then to me, he said, "Don't let me forget his name, B.J. Dr. N. in the Ministry of Social Affairs."

"Why don't *you* do something about it?" John Wilson, the late great Egyptologist, had said. "Fifty thousand human beings moved! A whole culture changing! You're young and vigorous."

"Me?" Bob had gotten his Ph.D. only two years before. Cairo was, after all, his first teaching job.

"Why not?" John Wilson returned.

"We could do something through the center," suggested Dr. Laila Shoukri al-Hamamsy, director of the Social Research Center of the American University.

John Hilliard, Ford Foundation representative in Cairo, came to share our concern for the Nubians. And so the Nubian project became a reality, a three-year ethnological survey before the High Dam was finished. Anthropologists, sociologists, geographers, architects, statisticians, a photographer, and research assistants became project members.

Americans and Egyptians worked together, recording the culture of the Nubian peoples and coordinating efforts, wherever possible, with the Egyptian Ministry of Social Affairs, which had been given the task of resettling the fifty thousand Nubian men, women, and children who were living in Egypt. About the same number of Nubians in the Sudan were being resettled by the Sudanese government, because of the rising High Dam reservoir.

The Nubians were already petitioning the ministry on their own behalf. A census was taken. Surveys were conducted. Did the Nubians want compensation for the loss of homes and land? No, they wanted communities, with new houses and new land. Thus, New Nubia was planned, a twenty-four-mile-long crescent of government housing north of Kom Ombo, to replace the string of villages along the Nile that would be drowned by the coming flood.

Nubia turned out to be a far more diverse region than we had at first realized. There were three separate social groups, to begin with, each speaking a different language. The Kenuzi in the north spoke one language; the Arabs in the central area spoke Arabic; and the people in the south, near Abu Simbel, spoke a third, Fadija.

Hassan Fathy, the celebrated Egyptian architect, recorded his own feelings of amazement when, with a group of artists and writers from the Ministry of Culture, he first visited this southernmost region of his own nation. "It was a new world for all of us, whole villages of houses, spacious, lovely, clean, harmonious. . . . Each village seemed to come from a dream country . . . from Atlantis itself it could have come. There was not a trace of the miserly huddle usually seen in Egyptian villages." But, as we came slowly to understand, this clean, sparkling, and dreamlike look of Nubia was due in part to the fact that the villages were not involved in the messy business of making a living: that was done largely by absent males working in Cairo and Alexandria, whose lives became another segment of the study.

Arrangements were made to have members of the project in each of the three language areas, and Bob settled in the south with two research assistants. I went down with Laura Ann, then two and a half years old, and David, then one and a half, for the winter of 1961–62. We lived in one of the villages of Ballana, near the Abu Simbel temple, and shared one of those spacious lovely Nubian houses with Saleh, his two wives, Dahiba and Hanim Ali, and his niece Khadija.

The house, high on a sand dune, above the valuable arable land along the river, was indeed lovely and spacious and the scenery below us was marvelous, the river flowing past the green strips of cultivated land, and palm trees forming a verdant frame for the worn, ancient, tabletop mountains on the opposite bank.

But the living was not easy. Bob was excited about the research, but also tense with the responsibilities of three field camps, diverse assistants and colleagues, many of whom had never lived outside urban, comfortable Cairo before. I might have felt more adventurous if I had not been four months rather heavily pregnant with our third child, and had the responsibility of Laura Ann and David. On the other hand, though baby food, in fact all food, was a problem, rapport in the village was no problem at all. It was quite obvious that I was a woman in the family way and my sniffling children behaved no better and sometimes worse than Nubian children. This gave the Nubian matrons plenty of opportunity to observe, chide, and tease me for my permissive child-rearing methods while at the same time expressing genuine kindness and helpfulness toward all of us.

"See," Khadija explained kindly to me, "if you just tie Davy's ankles together lightly, with a cloth, he will sit in one place longer and won't crawl into the dirt."

She demonstrated with her own son, Abdul Nasr, but I also noticed that Abdul Nasr's proud grandparents watched him fondly getting *out* of his ankle sling craftily, and applauded his cunning and strength. I could not bring myself to tie David's ankles. He wheezed and sniffled with asthma so badly that I was happy to see any movement on his part.

"Taking him to Nubia can't make the asthma any worse," my Cairo pediatrician had advised. "The dry air might improve it. The Nubians call it a blessed land, you know."

"Yes," I said. "I know."

But for us, Nubia did not seem a blessed land at all, at least at first. My feet and legs swelled ominously from so much plodding in the sand, Laura Ann's eye swelled shut with eye infections from the flies, and David's asthma seemed to grow worse every day.

"Maybe you'd better go back to Cairo, B.J.," Bob said as David's breathing failed to improve. He smiled a little wryly. "Maybe it's because we're not Nubians. The benevolent spirits of the land are not with us."

"Sometimes I feel that way," I confessed. When the children were asleep, we would sit out on the *mastaba,* or bench, along the front of the wall of the house; the stars blazed in the quiet sky. "You know, Bob, Muhammad's mother, Shemessa, really has it in for me, and for David. She doesn't want me down there giving Muhammad's twin sons those antibiotics. I hate to go."

"I know, I know," Bob said, and sighed deeply. "But Muhammad is my best friend here. He asked me as a special favor to have you do that, because he says his mother doesn't believe in modern medicine and throws it away, and his wife is not strong enough to stand up to her."

"How can she?" I returned. "Nezla has to take care of all those children *and* iron Muhammad's beautiful galabias every day so he can march around and look impressive, and then she's supposed to stand up to his old mother, too? Sometimes I think that old woman is a witch, putting a hex on me and poor David."

"B.J." Bob put his hand on my arm. "You're crazy. You probably should go back to Cairo. This life is hard on you, too."

I tentatively agreed to return, but then David came down with pneumonia and was too sick to move. For days we watched hopelessly beside his crib, and our friends brought things they said would help: *karkaday* herb tea; a kind of thick oily paste to rub on his chest; a blue bead to hang on his bed and ward off the evil eye. It was Nezla who proffered the blue bead, and I took it as a good omen: she knew Shemessa's virulent moods and tempers better than anyone, and I felt she was trying to thank me for caring about the twins. Shemessa did not come, and I was glad she stayed away. I did not want her around David's sickbed.

Our Nubian adventure had a happy ending. Either the spirits changed or I had been overanxious about Shemessa's influence in the blessed land, but one night after the crisis of the pneumonia, David suddenly began to breathe normally for the first time in months. He was cured—miraculously, it seemed. And the asthma never returned. Our pediatrician later confessed he didn't know why, but our friends believed they did.

"It was the *karkaday,*" said Khadija.

"It was the blue bead I gave you against the evil eye," said Nezla.

"The antibiotics finally took hold," Bob stated.

Whatever had done it, it was done, and I thanked the gods—and Nubia—for our son's restored health.

When we returned to Cairo, Bob wrote a series of papers, based on the preliminary research, for the Ministry of Social Affairs. These papers dealt with the problems of resettlement from the Nubians' point of view and included some suggestions about how the problems might be solved and possible dangers to the community averted.

The camaraderie of the project staff continued even after we had all left the field camps and come back to the city. Our third child, Laila, was born, and Nubian as well as Egyptian friends came to call. I went to visit Dahiba, Saleh's wife, in the Kasr al-Aini hospital, where she was having a cataract operation. Then Sawsan became engaged and I had a bridal shower for her. Amina, one of the other research assistants, invited us for a weekend at her family's *ezba*, the country estate of her father, a member of the nineteenth-century landed gentry. Her brother took Bob around the farm and talked about some of the serious agricultural problems that had yet to be solved in Nasser's Egypt.

"It's not the land reform," he had said. "It's overirrigation, bad crop planning, village-to-market problems."

We were settling in to Egypt, and our parents, apparently deciding that we were there to stay for a while, came and visited. I began to write a book about our earlier experience in southern Iraq.

"How can you justify what your government is doing in Palestine?" Karim, who had worked with us in Ballana, would ask and ask. Himself a Palestinian, he was more sensitive than most, but everyone asked that. "And why don't they invite Nasser to the White House?"

"America still thinks of Egypt as inferior, that's what it is," said Hassan, another research assistant. "A second-rate African country." He was laughing, but he was not joking.

They had touched a nerve and they knew it. We were good enough friends now that we could be teased about our behavior or U.S. foreign policy and be expected not to take offense. But we had become extremely sensitive on the issue of our country's record in the Arab world. It was becoming harder and harder to explain America's indifference and even hostility to the nonaligned bloc of nations, of which Nasser was a major leader. America, from our point of view, at least where we lived in Egypt, did not seem to be paying much attention to the new nations in Africa and the Arab world.

In 1962 Algeria's ten-year struggle for independence ended finally, with the departure of the defeated French. But this historic occasion did not seem to us to get enough attention in the American press. Yet it had been John Kennedy, while still a junior senator, who had been the first member of the U.S. Congress to raise the issue of French torture and imprisonment of Algerians. Although this action earned Kennedy the undying respect of the Middle Easterners, it was considered a real faux pas at the time by many Kennedy supporters. France was an old and trusted ally, after all, and Algeria only a North African colony.

John Kennedy's popularity in Egypt at that time was apparent in every newspaper kiosk, where his photo could be bought for pennies, along with photos of local leaders like Nasser and public figures such as the great singer Um Kulthum. When Kennedy was assassinated in 1963, strangers came up to us on the streets of Cairo, tears in their eyes, to shake our hands and offer condolences.

Like other Americans both at home and abroad, we were stunned by that event and had no more explanation for it than did our Egyptian friends. It just wasn't the sort of thing that happened in America—or was it?

Yet even though Kennedy had been widely admired as a person and a president, U.S. foreign policy, even under his presidency, was not. At best it was felt we were naïve, and being used by the Israelis and European powers for their, rather than America's, best interests.

"What are we doing here, anyway, B.J.?" Bob asked one night in late 1963 as we sat on our balcony enjoying the cool breeze from the Nile after dinner guests had departed. The children were soundly asleep, our cook, Abbas, had departed for the night, the ganeena was empty, we were finishing another year as strangers in Egypt.

"It's true we are strangers, always will be," I ventured, "but aren't we doing something that may be valuable in its way?"

"I hope so," said Bob. "But I'm beginning to have doubts about living as an expatriate anywhere. What has to be done has to be done by the people who live here, the Egyptians. We're just freeloaders really."

"And lotus-eaters? Adventurers? Copping out from the responsibilities of our own society?"

"Well, not exactly," worried Bob. "But it seems that America is changing fast, or faster than Egypt, and we should go back there before we become strangers there, too. And the children need some kind of roots. Laura Ann is four now."

"Yes, but wait until next year," I replied. "You have to finish your contract—"

"And teach in Alexandria."

Bob's mood suddenly shifted. "That should be interesting, talking to engineers about community development!" The Ford Foundation was sponsoring a graduate program in community development, and the dean of the faculty at Alexandria Agricultural College had asked Bob to give a weekly seminar. His students would be the young Egyptian engineers and planners who would be working in the first tracts of reclaimed land to be opened to small farmers. He had enthusiastically agreed on the spot, even though he would teach in Arabic, imperfect as his still was. "Sheikh Ali will be shocked." Bob smiled. "I have no correct verbs—and no shame!"

THE NUBIANS WERE MOVED NORTH in several stages, and in 1965 we visited our friends in their new homes above Kom Ombo, barely one year after the final resettlement. It was a very painful experience. The government-issue cement-block houses were raw and ugly, some still unfinished. Many old people and children had died. Markets and schools were not yet operating. Lack of fodder had decimated the animal stock. And the sugarcane crops that the Egyptian government wanted the Nubians to raise were unfamiliar; the farm development was not proceeding as rapidly as expected at any level. Much of the agricultural land allotted to the Nubians was still unirrigated. And small family savings were dwindling in the new situation.

"We have to buy everything in the store, here," explained Khadija, "even *sand* for the courtyard floors."

"But it's the river we miss the most," said her aunt, Hanim Ali, who still wore on her fingers, as she had in Old Nubia, a number of strange and curious rings. "Look, B.J., there's no view at all. We brought some palm trees and planted them but it will be years before there is shade.''

"We're making out, though," Muhammad told Bob. "It will get better. We'll fix up these awful houses. Give us time."

"Yes," Galal Moursy had said. "We'll do all right. The government is trying. And the lake is filling up. We'll go back when the lake reaches its new banks.''

Many Nubians said the same, but most of the researchers on the project, though they nodded pleasantly, did not believe it was feasible.

"A dream, not practical," they said. "Much too difficult. The government will never give them permission to go back, even if they want to.''

By 1964 PEOPLE IN CAIRO were worried about the high prices of food and the growing authoritarianism of the regime. People spoke of the secret police, of the torture of dissidents, of long incarceration of political prisoners in faraway oasis prisons. The nonaligned bloc of nations did not seem to be developing into the influential force people expected. President Nasser's attempts at Pan-Arabism, his short-lived federation with Syria, his military adventures in Yemen, had come to naught. But he apparently felt he held one trump card: the High Dam.

That summer the Nile rose and flooded the land, as it had done every summer for thousands of years. The farmers watched the precious silt pile up in the fields as the waters withdrew, and the television cameras recorded the occasion, which would soon, said the commentator, be an event of the past, a part of history. In his dark blue business suit and sober striped tie, the commentator extolled the advantages of a new controlled Nile. But was it our imagination that his voice broke a little as he spoke? The Aswan Dam was rising, and when it was complete, the Nile would no longer flood the land. Was this a good thing or a bad thing?

President Nasser insisted in his speeches and on television that the dam was a marvelous thing for Egypt. Whatever drawbacks it might have would be more than compensated for by the new areas of land that could be farmed, by the electric power that would be generated to bring lights and television to every Egyptian village. Man could harness nature, Nasser asserted, to make it work for the good of all the people. His strong face stayed full in frame until the sequence faded and Abdul Halim Hafiz came on to sing the song of the sixties, "Sud al-Ali," the Song of the High Dam. An orchestra of drums and violins and flutes and ouds backed him onstage and the audience clapped enthusiastically until the music ended.

When we went home to the United States in 1965, the High Dam was still not finished. The structure, however, was growing higher and higher and the waters of the Nile had covered all of Egyptian Nubia except for the tops of the palm trees.

DOMESTICATION OF THE NILE

*T*HE RELATIONSHIP BETWEEN the Nile and the people of Egypt has radically changed since the completion of the High Dam in 1971. No longer is the river an unpredictable variable in the equation that determines the size of the harvests. Its water now flows steadily all year long, and its slight rises and falls are easily accommodated to the agricultural cycle. The mighty Nile has become a large irrigation ditch.

Unquestionably, the High Dam has had positive effects. Two and a half million acres of land in Upper Egypt are now cultivated two or even three times a year; this is possible thanks to a system of irrigation ditches that has replaced the basin method of catching the floodwater behind a dam and then releasing it after the soil is soaked. Nearly 950,000 acres of formerly unusable desert land have also been reclaimed for agriculture (although there is little net gain owing to the loss of farmland through urban expansion and shoreline erosion along the Mediterranean). Turbines at the High Dam are producing 4 billion kilowatt-hours of electricity per year and are presumably able to produce again that much. This has permitted the electrification of most of Egypt's villages. With the population (62 million) at nearly double its size when the High Dam was completed, it is hard to imagine how Egypt could do without the dam.

Yet the radical transformation of the flow of the Nile has had many other effects on the lives of the people who depend so entirely on this river they now control. The Nile no longer contains itself within its banks but seeps constantly into the land around it, waterlogging and salinating the alluvial deposits its floods once carried to the sandy plains. In the past, though the untamed Nile would sweep away hundreds of acres of land from one bank, at the same time it deposited as much or more fresh soil somewhere else. Any living river does the same. In the past, farmers never knew which bank would come and which might go and thus riverside cultivation always held an element of chance. With the dam, that element of chance has been eliminated. But the constant presence of the water is slowly melting away the banks, dissolving the Nile's own container, and often requiring cement reinforcements, the costs of which are far beyond the means of the river users.

Further, the river can no longer keep itself clean. Before the dam checked its flow, the Nile scoured its own bottom, flushing excess mud into the alluvial fan it had deposited at its mouth on the Mediterranean Sea. Today the Nile carries nothing to sea. Its old bed is full of mud islands near the shoreline, its waters used up in the irrigation ditches of the Delta. The Mediterranean, unchecked, is eroding the shoreline and threatens to break through the land that divides the sea from the fresh-water lakes on the edge of the Delta. If this happens, it will be a disaster for local cultivation and for fishing.

In Upper Egypt, eight hundred miles to the south, the constant presence of the Nile waters has permitted the change from basin to ditch irrigation to take place, but the lack of free flow is becoming a dangerous convenience for farm families. Constant exposure to the standing ditch water, which is used for drinking, sanitation, laundry, and the washing of animals such as water buffalo, increases the possibility of infection by water-carried diseases, particularly the debilitating schistosomiasis. Before the High Dam, these diseases were generally only found in the Delta, where ditch irrigation had been customary for centuries. Today schistosomiasis and intestinal parasites threaten the health of the population, which, before the dam, drew its water directly from the free-flowing Nile rather than from standing water. Projects to provide piped water for drinking purposes will help but will only partly reduce the human health risk from this new, more intimate involvement with the river.

In the millennia during which the Nile rose and fell according to the amount of rain several thousand miles away in the mountains of Kenya and Ethiopia, the Nile was the center of year-round attention among Egyptians, whether city dweller or farmer, rich or poor. The changing color of the river, the beginning of its summer flood, the wonder at its power, or the mourning at its failure to rise was the subject of constant conversation, the reason for major ritual and economic activity. Among the ancient Egyptians the Nile was a focus of religious attention. Around the river they wove a complex web of mythological expression based on their need to have this source of life and to explain its unpredictable behavior. Indeed, the ancient Egyptians were so involved in the life of the Nile that they described rain, another unpredictable natural phenomenon, as an "inundation from heaven."

However, the end of pharaonic ideology did not result in the loss of the material circumstance it reflected. Thus, throughout Egyptian history the Nile has remained central to a rich body of folklore and legend; it forms part of the proverbs and idioms in every Egyptian's vocabulary, and it is the object of local rituals, such as Sham al-Nessim, which have remained separate from the orthodoxy of the great modern religions.

Since 1971, the Nile has no longer provided the seasonal rhythm, the pulse of tension and release, that once animated Egyptian society. The color of the water stays more or less the same, the wild spaces of new floodland no longer appear. Egyptians still worry about the future of the Nile, but not, as in the past, in terms of the next cycle of seasons. They worry about an indefinite future in which this new tamed Nile, now part of the local economy, dominated by the imposing technology of the High Dam, will grow older and develop more problems with increasing age, like any one of us. There is no annual relief from this worry, and hence nothing to celebrate.

Egypt was the gift of the Nile. Its floods brought the alluvial soil that fertilized and renewed the agricultural land its water irrigated. That gift was given on its own terms, however, and people had to manage as best they could. Now, as a domesticated resource, the Nile is dependent for its health as a river on those who use its waters. Like houseplants or pets, the Nile can be no better than its owners. Soon the Sudan will be building dams and expecting its share of Nile water. Competitive needs and claims may arise and lead to new international quarrels.

But the Nile will not be able to settle international disputes any more than it can clean its own riverbed. The days when the Nile was a wild, unconquered part of nature already lie in the nostalgic past. Today the question is whether the Nile can survive its domesticity.

> Our pallid Egypt
> The sun scorches and scourges
> with bitter-and-spite-laden arrows
> and exhausts it with thirst and disease.
> Our sweet Egypt
> in a gay fair
> gets drunk, forgets, and adorns itself, and rejoices
> and scorns the tyrannical sun.
>
> C. P. Cavafy
> SHAM AL-NESSIM

CAIRO, THE PRESENT CAPITAL of Egypt, lies on a site that has been continually inhabited for as long as historical records have existed. The ancient Egyptians called it Khere-ohe, "place of combat," because it stood on a legendary battleground where the god Horus, beloved son of Isis and Osiris, took on the god Seth, his wicked uncle, in order to avenge his father's murder. The myths are not clear on the outcome of the battle; some say the city of Cairo contained and absorbed that superhuman struggle, a struggle that supposedly still goes on to maintain a balance in the universe between the forces of good and evil.

The Greeks called the city Babylon, and it remained Babylon under Roman rule, when it served as headquarters for one of Augustus's legions. But when it was captured in A.D. 641 by the victorious Muslim army of Omar, the second caliph, General Amr ibn al-As called his new city Fostat, literally "surrounded by trenches." The capital was extended, away from the old Greek and Roman fortress, toward the Nile, where the Nilometer was built to measure the annual flooding of the river, and north and east where the great mosque of Ibn Toulun was raised.

"Cairo" as a name came later, when the Fatimid caliph took over in 969. While the cornerstone of the caliph's new residence was being laid, the planet Mars—Qahir (Victorious) in Arabic—crossed the meridian of the new city. "Call it Al-Qahira after the planet," the caliph is supposed to have shouted, "for we are indeed victorious." And Al-Qahira is the name it bears to this day.

In 1981, when we returned to live again in Cairo, it was the old name of the city, Fostat, that was painted in dark blue letters on the white prow of our temporary home: the boat where Bob and I settled in on the edge of the Nile. The *Fostat* was an honorable if slightly run-down old *dahabiya*, a once-elegant passenger river steamer retired from its former duties as a Thomas Cook's tour boat in the twenties and thirties, and as a Nubian archaeological expedition headquarters in the sixties and seventies. It now served as a hostel residence for the American Research Center in Egypt and housed fellowship students, the Library of Congress representative, and professorial nomads like ourselves. Outside the hectic bustle of the city center, yet close to the riverboat commuter stop in Giza, the *Fostat* was for us an ideal temporary residence.

Bob and I were alone, as we had been when we first arrived in Egypt in 1959. Our children were grown. Bob had support for further study and research in the region; I had a grant to make an educational documentary film about social and political change as seen from the local women's point of view. Part of my proposed film involved Palestinian women; another segment, I believed, should be shot in Cairo. Both Bob and I were traveling frequently in and out of the city, interviewing, meeting people. It did not seem feasible to set up housekeeping, gather cooking gear and furniture, hire a servant. We lived on the *Fostat* in one comfortable room with an adequate if quirky bath attached. Nescafé, eggs, and bread could be prepared in the downstairs galley kitchen; a meal of sorts was cooked each evening by a resident cook; and despite the cool winds of winter that blew from the Mediterranean, we had an unparalleled view of the Nile.

Now, after a week in Cairo, I sat with Bob on the *Fostat*'s deck and tried to make sense of my violent and unexpected reactions to the new Egypt. I was appalled at how much the beautiful city I had so loved had changed. Cairo had a population of 12 million, more than double its size of 5.5 million when we had left in 1965. Every place, every institution, every part of the city, reflected that increase and strained against it. The city was noisy, dirty, jammed with people.

Bob had been in Cairo for four months already and was now a seasoned visitor. He had even taken steps to conquer the transport problem in new Egypt and had bought himself an Indian bicycle with balloon tires. He kept it downstairs near our boatman's tiny bunk room at night, and by day he scorned the taxis and buses, pedaling his way triumphantly through the choked, stuttery traffic of a city that not only was spilling out over all of its boundaries but had difficulty moving through the streets that already existed. He seemed to like it.

"I hope this gloom or lady's vapors or whatever will soon get over with," I said. "I don't know what's wrong with me. I hate it!"

"What's wrong is that we lived here for six years and we loved it, or at least that's what we remember, and now we're back and it's not the same, that's what's wrong," answered Bob. "You have to look at Cairo for what it is now, the most enormous improbability. It's amazing that it runs at all. Don't look for it to be what it was."

He was right. Yes. He was absolutely right. I knew it. But the images kept running through my head, over and over. A mixture of old memories and new experiences like moving snapshots, black-and-white for the past, color for the present.

Garden City, for example. The image machine in my head stopped there, in that quiet quarter where we had lived for six years. I was standing, much younger, on the balcony of our comfortable apartment looking out toward the Nile, across the children's playground, the ganeena where baby Laura Ann (with nanny) jumped and shouted enthusiastically in her blue pram. *"Garagoz! Garagoz!"* cried the traveling puppeteer, who came into focus and began setting up his stage. Then bang, he was gone! And we had a slide of Garden City today, a building site. Houses had been turned into places of business and the streets were lined with small plastic billboards, advertisements mounted along the pavement, like stationary flags on flagpoles, testifying at every step to the new entrepreneurial purpose of Garden City. Clearly, Sadat's open-door policy, after Nasser's tight controls, had attracted Western enterprise. Pasha N.'s heirs, owners of the house, had been given a fortune by IBM, we were told.

The image machine stopped, reversed. We were back in the black-and-white past: the daughters of Pasha N., in white frilly dresses, hair ribbons, and curls, came out of the mansion and got into an old black limousine. Past. Gone. Forward again.

Boom! Boom! The image machine had added sound to its reper-
toire: the sound of a technological marvel, a pile driver, that operated
within a great gash in the earth, a block-square chasm of Technicolor
mud and rocks that stood to the right of our old apartment building, on
the edge of the ganeena. *Boom! Boom! Boom!* A makeshift fence
around the chasm had been painted red, and a sign announced that an
international business and recreational center would soon rise out of
the chasm in the earth.

Click! We were back in the past. A black-and-white snapshot of a
palace, the palace that had once stood in the chasm. An old stone mansion with a wrought-iron balcony on the top floor commanding, we
supposed, a superior view of the Nile. When we sat on our own balcony
across the ganeena, having tea in the good weather, we would often
observe activity on the palace balcony. A very old gentleman would be
wheeled out. In a red fez, covered by a lap robe, he, too, would drink tea
and look out, like us, at the marvel of changing colors on the river. The
sun would go down suddenly, in tropical glory, and the flocks of kites
would rise screeching and calling above the nearby rooftops before settling for the night in the branches of the cottonwood and casuarina
trees in the ganeena beside the palace. The image machine switched off.
The palace disappeared into the hole.

Cairo friends assured us that sunsets these days were more dramatic than ever before, owing to the dust and smog on the horizon. But
the old gentleman in the wheelchair was not there to see the panoply,
and we had yet to find a proper spot to herald the new spectacle.

We visited our old apartment. Not for sentimental reasons, actually. We had been invited for cocktails by the assistant cultural attaché
at the American Embassy, who just happened to live in our old building, though in a grander flat. The doorman greeted us as old friends; he
was the same man we had known twenty years ago.

"How are you, Am Taher?" Bob and I shook his hand.

Am Taher, older, grayer, broader, turned to me. How were the
children? Fine. How were his children? Fine. He reported that our old
cook, Abbas, was in Kuwait, making "much money," and Farida, our
nanny, was still in Cairo, but her health was not good.

"Please tell her I'm here," I said. "Where can I find her?" I had
sent a letter ten years before that had been returned with an "unknown" notice stamped on the envelope. Am Taher shook his head. He

did not know her address, but would tell her where to reach me if she came by.

A tall dark-haired boy in jeans and navy T-shirt appeared through the door that led to the building's bank of mailboxes. "My son," said Am Taher proudly. "He is in the university."

We shook hands again and smiled at each other. It was Am Taher who broke the impasse by striding up the wide marble stairs to open the elevator doors for us, as he had done hundreds of times in the past when we had come carrying flowers, groceries, presents, bearing the babies home from the hospital. The same elevator. We got in and closed the door and moved slowly upward. It was then that it happened, an entirely unexpected outburst. Tears. A flood of tears. Tears for what? For the past? For a vanished time in my own life? For children once small and lovable, now grown and gone? For youth? It was true that in the crowded bus we had taken from the other side of town, I had been surprised when an old man gave me his seat. Was I old? Of course not, but, yes, I was well into middle age, not *really* old, though, I told myself.

What had triggered the tearful reaction? The smell of the elevator, perhaps, a good smell of wax and furniture polish, the same smell as long ago when we rode up in that elevator with one child or another, Laila in her stroller with the yellow sunshade, Laura Ann and David in their Port Said nursery school uniforms, those uniforms they were so proud of, a pink pinafore for Laura Ann, a blue coverall for David.

"We could just leave, B.J.," suggested Bob.

"Yes," I answered.

We had walked out toward the river, past the darkened ganeena. One corner of the garden now held a long rectangular building, the *hadana*, or nursery school, Am Taher had told Bob. Another corner held a different kind of nursery, where potted plants were raised for use in government offices.

"The plants help pay the salaries of the people who work in the ganeena," Am Taher had explained to Bob. "And the *hadana* is open to all kids. Mothers can leave them for six piasters a day. A great bargain." Indeed a great bargain. Low-cost day care in pleasant surroundings.

End of tears then! Nostalgia begone, I told myself. A new era is dawning in Egypt, it is ridiculous to romanticize the past. Eight hours of child care for six piasters, less than ten cents. Servants and idle mothers have had their day. Now it is the era of working mothers, most working not out of some need to fulfill themselves as individuals, but to help put food on the table. Bread was subsidized heavily in Egypt, but meat now cost five dollars a pound.

We headed out to the Corniche, the broad treelined river walk that Gamal Abdel Nasser had presented to his people as a gift. It still stretched along the Nile, but we followed its meanderings with some difficulty, for parked cars filled the sidewalk, all the way from the Nile Hilton to the Meridien Hotel, near that great gash in the earth, where the palace had once stood. The pavement was buckling from the unaccustomed weight of the cars, and as we walked, the broken cement pointed upward and caught at our shoes, stockings, ankles.

A fine cloud of dust rose everywhere, settling on the buildings, then sifting down again to mist the streetlights and blow against the hundreds of yellow eyes of headlights on the automobiles rushing up and down the Corniche. The old Semiramis Hotel with its Victorian porch was gone, and in its place was another immense pit in the ground, where a sign on still another makeshift board fence announced that the new four-hundred-room Semiramis Hotel would open in 1981. But 1981 had already arrived and the new Semiramis was not even a shell of its projected grandiose self.

At the Kasr al-Nil bridge we dipped down below street level to the new pedestrian underpass that protected us from the many lanes of traffic entering and exiting over the bridge. On the other side, we could see that the bridge was still protected by its stone lions, shabbier now, encrusted with smog and dirt from the cars and buses that wound down and up and around the cloverleaf channeling the evening traffic toward Zamalek, Roda Island, Giza, the suburb of Maadi. The noise was deafening—insistent honking of horns which meant "Move over, move over," squealing of tires coming to sudden stops to avoid collisions and fender scrapings, backfiring of imperfectly tuned engines, and the thunder of the overloaded red buses, leaning dangerously to one side or the other depending on which side carried the most passengers as hangers-on.

We ate dinner in the Swissair restaurant in Giza, a new eatery where Sadat himself was rumored to dine on the cook's night out. His residential palace was only two blocks away. He ate upstairs, however, in the luxury establishment; we ate on the ground floor, where the good but unchanging *table d'hôte* menu attracted many middle-class Egyptians as well as foreigners in business, the media, the diplomatic corps.

An old friend had suggested that my gloom might be due to coping with the empty-nest syndrome, a suggestion that Bob greeted with a hoot of laughter. "We're the ones who flew away," he said. "We left our children and the dog to take care of the house and came off by ourselves."

"You left—"

"The children are nineteen, twenty-one, and twenty-two years old," I hastily said to the shocked look on the Egyptian woman's face.

I did not really believe that the nostalgia I felt was for my years of motherhood that I had spent in Egypt, happy as they were. I liked my life now and would have found the old responsibilities tough to take on again. What I thought I was feeling was a much more general sense of regret and loss as I looked around, walked through, experienced life in Cairo in 1981. I could not convince myself that the thousands of new cars, luxury hotels, foreign banks, flashing neon lights and billboards, the flood of consumer goods, were an adequate exchange for clean air, leisurely crowds, lovers walking on the Corniche, and the poor but proud attitude which for a time was fashionable among Egyptians of *every* class.

We walked home along the Giza side of the Nile, away from President Sadat's heavily guarded palace, past huge new apartment buildings in the process of construction, where guards and workmen slept on pallets in the shadow of the scaffolds, past the Turkish Embassy, where police kept watch in their little closet-size black billets. Fewer cars raced beside us. It was nearly midnight by the time we reached the *Fostat*.

In 1981 the United States was heavily involved in Egypt's economic life, its struggle to come to terms with the modern industrial world, not only because President Sadat's open-door policy had made it possible for many American firms to invest in enterprises but also because the Camp David accords included large bundles of aid for both signing parties, Israel and Egypt. United States government aid to Egypt was estimated at a billion dollars a year, not including arms and military equipment. Most of the billion dollars was allocated for economic aid projects administered largely by Americans or American companies. The projects were initiated and approved by joint U.S.-Egyptian committees: agriculture, education, sewage, water, garbage disposal. An entire office building was devoted to the U.S. AID mission. By January of 1981 nearly five hundred Americans were associated with the official American presence in Egypt; they constituted the second largest U.S. mission, it was said, in the world. This was a far cry from the small community at the embassy that had existed during the sixties. By 1981 the embassy and the AID mission were both protected by walls, computers, electric eyes, and automatic doors as well as by U.S. Marine guards and Egyptian police. The Iranian hostage crisis and revolution had sent shock waves all the way across the Persian Gulf and up the Nile. Our more pessimistic friends talked about Egypt as the next Iran. Sadat was not as popular in Egypt as he was in the United States. Things were not good. But both American and Egyptian businessmen were making millions from American AID contracts. Most Americans in Egypt seemed to feel that Sadat was immortal.

Sadat's *infitah,* or open-door policy, had indeed brought rapid wealth to many Egyptians, even some from the middle and lower classes. But its effects were uneven, and the growing differences between the new rich and the still poor were very conspicuous in a crowded city where both groups constantly looked at each other.

For us personally, Egypt had also changed. Many of our friends were gone. General Fahmy had died. Sawsan, a Muslim, had married a Copt, to both families' dismay; the young couple had compromised by moving to Paris. Dr. Laila was working for the ILO in Geneva, and several of our Egyptian coworkers on the Nubian project were teaching at universities in the United States. Omar had gone into the diplomatic service after the UNESCO documentation of pharaonic monuments was finished; he now served as cultural attaché in an Eastern European capital. His sister, Aziza, was married but still living in Cairo, in her parents' apartment, in fact. She invited us for lunch to meet her husband, a pleasant middle-aged lawyer.

"Hello, Bob! Welcome back!" It was another Egyptian archaeologist, older than we, who had worked for the Department of Antiquities but was now retired. He and his wife were Aziza's other lunch guests.

"Do you find Egypt much changed?" asked his wife, Nawal, younger than her husband. She was not a close friend, but I remembered her well from parties at Aziza and Omar's, from lectures at the French Institute, the Italian Cultural Institute.

"Much," said Bob, dutifully stating the obvious. "There's more, more of everything, people, cars, problems."

"Yes, yes, yes," the archaeologist agreed. "The city is bursting, it is true, but don't you find it more luxurious than in Nasser's time?"

I could not hide my surprise. "Luxurious?"

"Ah, B.J.," said Nawal. "It is the outside of Cairo you are thinking about. Cairo was always shabby, more or less, on the outside. But you know people in Egypt care more about their *own* space, the inside, their homes." She gestured vaguely around the dining room where we sat, its antiques well kept and gleaming, the paintings sporting tiny new spotlights.

The archaeologist's wife's gesture was eloquent. She was right, this house had not changed, had perhaps even improved; weren't the spotlights on the paintings new? In the collapse of the old upper class, Omar and Aziza's family had emerged as survivors. Education had helped. Omar was well placed in the diplomatic corps, and his younger brother had gotten an engineering degree from a British university and now held a good job in an engineering firm owned by Sadat's brother-in-law.

"I have good memories of the old days in Cairo," I said. "I remember a marvelous *cheveux des anges* that we ate at this very table years ago. Weren't you here, too, Nawal?"

Nawal smiled and nodded, and Aziza, serving the chicken tarragon, turned toward us, a bit plumper, graying slightly, but still smiling mischievously, as she had done in the past.

"The *cheveux des anges!*" Aziza laughed and looked at the archaeologist's wife. "She has the most amazing memory," she said lightly, with a sideways glance at me. "*Cheveux des anges*. Maybe she'll put us in one of her books, Nawal. Do you suppose?"

"*Cheveux des anges,*" Nawal was reflecting. "What a wonderful dessert. I used to ask for it on my birthday when I was a little girl." She sighed. "No more. No cooks. The servants are all gone," she said to me.

"To the Gulf, I suppose," I said politely.

"Yes," said Aziza, "to do construction work. So we have simple food today. No frills."

We had heard that thousands of Egyptian workers had migrated to Saudi Arabia, where they earned several times the salary offered in Cairo or Alexandria.

"Our old cook is in Kuwait," I put in. "Earning hundreds of dollars a month."

Aziza nodded. "They get enormous salaries there. But some old family retainers have stayed on to help. Muhammad, for example, B.J., is still with us."

"That's because he's too old to migrate, my dear Aziza," said Nawal rather bitterly. "It's not because of loyalty. That's all gone the way of progress."

"All gone? Twenty years ago you said that would happen, Aziza."

She looked at me hard. Aziza, in a purple silk dress that became her matronly years. "That's true, I did. And it's happened. The people who run things in Egypt now, Sadat and his crowd, those are people we had never even heard of."

"But at least Sadat is so much more understanding, Aziza, than Nasser was," insisted Nawal. "He lets everyone keep more money. And there aren't all those horrid controls on travel and imports. These days"—she turned to me—"you can occasionally find quite nice foreign blouses and stockings, and cheese comes in from Europe regularly."

Aziza made a face. "Yes, but at what prices."

The conversation became general: prices, inflation, taxes.

"But you see, Bob, the government still subsidizes basic foods for the poor people," Aziza's husband was explaining seriously. "Tea, sugar, oil, meat, they can buy at the *jamaiiyas*, the government cooperative stores."

"And we buy there, too," put in Aziza.

"Yes, that's true, my dear," said her husband. "It is a good policy for everyone."

"At least the rich Saudis and Kuwaitis that come here for vacation don't go to the cooperatives," said Aziza crisply. "They have too much money, so they don't care."

"They spend it all in the nightclubs on the pyramids road," added the archaeologist. "Those clubs really are something of a scandal. A bad influence on young people. They should be curbed."

Bob and I had noticed those nightclubs one night on our way to an Indian restaurant near the pyramids. But the road was so crowded we decided we were on the wrong street, and had driven miles into the country before realizing our mistake. The old pyramids road had become a major urban highway. It was no longer empty, as in the old days, a straight line in the middle of the alluvial plain, leading from Cairo to the mighty mausoleums in the desert that were one of the Seven Wonders of the Ancient World. Twenty years before, a few country houses hugged the sides of the pyramids road, modest embellishments to the impressive vista of the looming pyramids in the sand ahead. By 1981 that vista had disappeared behind rows of high-rise apartment houses, brightly lit Las Vegas–style gambling casinos, and sumptuous many-storied villas.

"How are the children?" We moved into the salon for coffee, and I sat down with Nawal on a newly upholstered satin settee to exchange photos and bits of news about our grown and growing progeny.

"Life isn't the same," went on Nawal. "It won't be the same for the children, I think. They'll have to deal with different problems than we did." Her voice held an edge of irritation.

"At least your daughter isn't covering her head with one of those awful scarves," said Aziza, "like Najat's girl at Cairo University. Be grateful for something, Nawal."

"Najat's daughter is wearing what they call Islamic dress?" I asked.

Nawal sniffed. "Islamic dress. What Islamic dress? The Koran does not prescribe a particular kind of *dress*, it says be modest, show respect."

"But many girls seem to think that covering up is the way to do it—at least that's what I've heard," I added quickly.

"They are just frustrated, I think," said Aziza lightly, a little too lightly; "a neurotic reaction to traffic and so on. They want to hide from the world so they don't get pinched on the bus."

"Where?" said her husband.

"On the bus!" said Aziza sharply. Bob laughed.

Lunch was splendid even if simple. We told Aziza truthfully that we had to go home and take a little nap, as in the old days. She and her husband smiled and bade us goodbye.

The newspapers gave the 1981 International Book Fair all the attention due a spectacular public event, and indeed it seemed deserved, as we watched thousands of people streaming into the gates of the fairgrounds in Giza and lining up to enter the exhibit halls where ninety-seven nations, the handout said, had sent their printed wares, their records and audiovisual materials, to tempt an obviously eager population.

The greatest crowds were milling about the specialized religious book exhibits from many different parts of the Islamic world: exhibits of Korans, editions of the *hadith*, philosophical essays. Mostly young, mostly neatly dressed, these young Egyptian Muslims were attired in a variety of what Aziza denied was "Islamic dress." The women wore head scarves, some in simple babushka style, others folded and tucked over their foreheads to cover every strand of hair. Some wore long flowing gowns and wimples like the nuns of an earlier age, though these gowns and wimples were not black and white but multicolored: blue, green, yellow, plaids. Less dramatic were the simple toques and turbans; the skullcaps and beards of the men.

"Nobody dressed like that when we were here before," I volunteered. "At least I don't remember it. Do you, Bob?"

Bob shook his head. We had decided to eat lunch at one of the scores of picnic tables set out on the fairgrounds. Kebab, turnip pickles, and bread constituted the standard fast-food meal.

"There were some getups like that when I first got here in 1978," declared Tom Hartwell, our friend from Texas now living and working as a freelance photographer in Cairo.

"New images," I mused. "For the film maybe. New self-images," I explained in answer to Bob's and Tom's questioning looks.

In the sixties what was called "Islamic dress" was not apparent at all. At that time more and more young women had been wearing Western dress, not only upper-middle-class and professional women like Aziza and Dr. Laila but the new group of high school graduates who had gone out to work as shop girls, secretaries, government employees, bank clerks. In 1965 traditional long, full gowns, tight head scarves, and wraparound *milayas* were worn by peasants and the more conservative so-called *baladi*, or country women in the cities, particularly in poorer districts. Even in those areas, however, Western-style dress was often worn under the *milayas* and was a sign of upward mobility. The new 1981 style of Islamic dress bore little resemblance to the traditional *baladi* style. It was a most dramatic visual addition to the crowded streets of Cairo, to Alexandria, the new universities in the Delta. Bob said he had also seen it during his fall trip to Aswan.

"Are they counterparts of the Muslim Brotherhood, a kind of sisterhood?" I asked. As puritanical advocates of theocratic rule, the Muslim Brotherhood had constituted a political threat to many of Egypt's leaders, from the 1920s on, and Nasser had been no exception. In Nasser's time the Muslim Brotherhood had been suppressed, many jailed, some executed.

"No, no," said Bob. "It seems to be a much more inclusive statement of Islamic identity than that."

Tom looked unconvinced. "Come on, Bob. You know people say these guys—and girls—are really into politics." He indicated an especially pious-looking young man in a kind of Nehru jacket and trousers of unbleached cotton. "That costume is supposed to be a political protest against Sadat."

Against Sadat? Yes, said Tom. Lots of complaints against Sadat. Stories of corruption, of high living, of favoring the rich, of turning the gardens Nasser had opened to the public back into personal palaces, à la King Farouk. But, I said, in America we heard of Sadat as a brave political genius, at least in foreign affairs, who had taken the initiative in the Arab-Israeli dispute and maneuvered a peaceful settlement at last.

"You think Sadat gets brownie points with Egyptians because he made peace with Israel, B.J.?" Tom asked me incredulously. "You should know this country better than that."

"Yes, Tom," put in Bob. "I know they don't like Israel, but I get the feeling people are delighted to have peace. Last fall I talked with people all over the Delta and in Upper Egypt who told me they were not interested in going to war anymore."

"But do they have a choice?" interrupted Tom.

"They have to be considered," insisted Bob. "Any leader worth his salt will think twice before getting into more adventures. Really, Tom. Everybody I met had lost a son, a brother, or at least an uncle or some relative in the wars of '48, '56, '67, '73. Egyptians have taken the brunt of all the fighting and they're tired of being shot up. And besides, war is damned expensive. It has drained this country."

"But all the Arab world has pulled away from Egypt, Bob, Egypt that used to be its leader, and—"

Tom stopped himself. "Look over there," he said suddenly. Near us three young men occupied a table for ten while around us the picnic tables were jammed. Good-looking, dark-haired, they wore fashionable jean suits. A television crew, obviously, by the equipment, the Nagra sound recorder and the booms, the camera with its peering, protruding lens. I had just spent two weeks in London looking over equipment like that.

"Why are they hogging the whole table?" asked Bob.

"Not their choice. It's an Israeli TV crew. Nobody will sit with them. Peace? Yeah. Maybe. No love lost on either side."

It was true. Two years after the Camp David accords had been signed, peace was still just the absence of war as far as most Egyptians were concerned. Double police details were stationed around the Israeli residence and the Israeli Embassy. Arab guests tended to leave parties unceremoniously when Israeli diplomats arrived. The Egyptian lawyers' syndicate had staged a protest rally on the anniversary of Camp David.

The situation was not improved by braless Israeli female tourists wearing T-shirts with "Shalom" written across their chests—not necessarily from a standpoint of decorum or morals (Egyptians have seen the worst as well as the best), but because of the implied contempt. Yet bus service had been instituted from Midan al-Tahrir for the eight-hour trip to Tel Aviv, and El Al planes flew regularly in and out of Egypt. No one reported any overtly unpleasant public incidents, and many Egyptian merchants and hotelkeepers were very welcoming.

This was part of the setting in which Islam and the statement of Islamic belief were generating enthusiasm among all groups of people. Twenty years before, when we had lived in Egypt, Egypt called itself a Muslim state, but that identity was not so publicly demonstrated. Now the new style of dress for women and men was only one such kind of overt statement. Most taxicabs and private cars carried Korans in velvet cases on their dashboards rather than the Kewpie dolls and teddy bears of yore. Jewelers in the gold and silver markets had developed an entirely new range of medallions engraved with Koranic verses. And a large selection of religious magazines and books was to be found in every newspaper kiosk and bookstore. New mosques had opened all over the city and more were under construction. Some people, we had been told, had even gone as far as to "claim" unused land as places for community prayers. One of the most popular local programs on Cairo television was hosted by Sheikh Sharkawi, a religious authority who sometimes gave short talks on morals, sometimes presented formal sermons, but always answered the studio audience's questions about faith and practice.

When I visited the television building in connection with my forthcoming filming, I was surprised to see small areas set aside on each floor for employees to say their daily prayers.

"It's become a requirement," Bob said. "You'll find them in factories, ministries, offices, everywhere."

On Friday, the day of worship, the mosques were overflowing. For those who could not make it into the mosque, the public address system broadcast the prayers and homilies over loudspeakers, and people came out of shops to pray on mats laid out on the public sidewalks, not just in the more traditional parts of town, but on the main streets of the city, even Kasr al-Nil and Sharia Talaat Harb, the focus of Westernized luxury shoppers in the 1960s. The public prayer in the streets was accepted and accommodated by the nonpraying passersby.

There had even been an upsurge of Islamic political activism two years before. A group that called itself Repentance and Holy Flight had plotted against Sadat, been uncovered, its members jailed, its leaders executed. But most of our Egyptian friends said that Repentance and Holy Flight was a fanatic exception to the general rule. It was not representative, not part of the general interest in Islam expressed by many Muslims, especially younger people.

"Does it surprise you, these 'born-again' Muslims?" Bob asked me. "It seems important to include in your film."

"Yes and yes," I answered. "It surprises me, and yes, it should be included in the film."

We sat on the deck of the *Fostat*, our refuge from the frantic activity of the city. The gleaming pewter-gray water of the river, rippling toward us and away, muted the noise of automobiles, buses, trucks, and people, buried the city dust in its moving depths, carried debris past us, north to the sea. On the opposite shore stood the new Salah al-Din mosque, sand-colored by day, golden at sunset, when the muezzin's call to evening prayer marked the moment for scores of electric lightbulbs to be flashed on, outlining the minaret and dome in a pulsing radiance, casting a glow over the entire edifice.

"Why are we surprised at this return to religion?" asked Bob. "It's even happening in America. Ask yourself why it's happening in America. Some of the same reasons may be here."

"I guess we thought Nasser was promoting secularism when we were here before. People talked about Egypt in terms of nationalism, or maybe anticolonialism and so on—not in religious terms so much."

"Yes. One thought of Saudi Arabia as religious, maybe, but Egypt—as what? Progressive? Socialist? Too political, maybe?"

"Are the two contradictory?"

"Religion and politics?" Bob laughed ruefully. "We used to think so."

Many people used to think so. A quarter of a century earlier, when we had first come to the Middle East, social scientists used to measure what they called progress and what they called political maturity by the degree of separation between church and state. Just as in America. Insofar as the Arab world appeared to be separating itself from its "outmoded religious attitudes," adopting a more secularist, pluralistic Western-style stance, so then was it seen by such scholars to be progressing, socially and politically preparing, at least, for economic development.

Even in the sixties the annual *mulids*, or birthdays, of Sayyidna Hussein and Sayyidatna Zaynab were celebrated in Cairo, along with the *mulid* of the Prophet Muhammad himself. In old Cairo, near the Khan al-Khalili bazaar, lies the mosque that bears the name of Sayyidna Hussein, son of Ali and grandson of the Prophet. Here the activities of his *mulid* would take place, beginning with a parade of the Sufi brotherhoods, complete with flags and banners. The brotherhoods would then set up their tents in the shadow of the mosque, to receive members and guests from city and country. For several days the mosque would be filled with the faithful, praying and attending *hadras*. Singing and other entertainment went on far into the nights. The *mulids* were religiously based holidays that had, over the years, incorporated other functions, for they were in essence minipilgrimages, social and economic.

For the 1981 *mulids* the crowds everywhere were greater than we remembered, not only at Sayyidna Hussein but at the *mulid* of Sayyidatna Zaynab as well. Around both mosque shrines the nearby shops and streets were festooned with colored lights, and the booksellers, the nut vendors, and the peddlers of balloons, cotton candy, and souvenirs thronged the neighborhoods. Was it that we were more conscious of the celebrations than before, more sensitized by published descriptions of the Islamic resurgence? No, friends both Egyptian and American assured us, more people *were* attending the *mulids* now. Not just the poor, for whom the *mulids* had always constituted great festivals, but also middle-class and professional people who had previously not taken part. Had the newer members of the middle class discovered, in their march forward toward modernity, that they did not need to leave behind their traditional religious practices? Had Egyptians decided to reject outdated Western measures of "modern" behavior? Was it a political expression? A personal search? We asked these questions and received a variety of answers. Yes, it was a search. No, it was not an anti-Western movement, for that would be seen as negative in tone; it was rather a positive pro-Muslim stance. Politics? Partly. Not just one reason, but several.

It was Nabila in the end who made that cliché phrase "Islamic resurgence" a reality for me. Nabila was a secretary for the Egyptian National Insurance Company, and I went to see her, in her place of work, to deliver a letter from a mutual friend and invite her to tea.

"You are interested in Islam? Tim wrote to me in his letter that you are," said Nabila in rather slow and stilted English. We sat in the garden of the American University, in old rattan chairs, drinking tea; it seemed a good compromise between Groppi's (Nabila would never go there, Tim had told me) and our houseboat, which was rather far from Nabila's office. She was a small girl, lovely, with huge dark eyes.

"Yes," I said. I explained about my plans for a film, about our previous years in Cairo.

I asked her about "Islamic dress," which she herself was wearing, a pleasant costume in tones of peach, a cream-colored scarf clasping her throat and fastened on each side, behind her ears, with small pearl-tipped hatpins.

"It is out of respect," she said gently, looking up at me with those great dark eyes, measuring me, I felt. She looked down at my book, at the cover, a drawing of the famous Egyptian singer Um Kulthum.

"You see, in your book, Um Kulthum, too, wore Islamic dress."

Um Kulthum, however, had taken off her head scarf and sung without it for years, though her dress was always modest. I made no objection, though, not wishing to begin an argument in our first five minutes of acquaintanceship. "Respect for God or for others or for oneself?" I asked instead.

"It is all together," said Nabila very gently, bringing her hands together and clasping them tightly. "Like this. You see?"

I nodded. We looked at each other once more. Nabila, I felt, was still measuring me, searching for whatever dark spots might lie upon my soul.

Nabila began again. "It is simple," she said. "This is the dress God says we should wear, and so we wear it." Her hand was raised again, in self-deprecation, but her smile belied the deprecating gesture. Nabila believed in God and in herself as well.

Thus began a series of meetings that took me all over Cairo to witness the phenomenon of Islamic resurgence from Nabila's personal point of view. I visited Nabila at home, where her father, a government civil servant, told me how proud he was of his youngest daughter. We attended a women's study group in one of the newer city mosques. I was introduced to Dr. Zahira Abdine, medical director of the Giza children's hospital and the leader of the Muslim Women's Association.

"We speak of Islam and belief, but we also mean service," said Dr. Zahira carefully and slowly. "Service to others. We have many young women and men doctors volunteering their time in these clinics for the poor."

"Where are they?" I asked politely.

"They are in the big mosques in districts where medical care is unavailable. Nabila will take you, won't you, my dear?"

Nabila took me to a clinic at the Sayyidatna Zaynab mosque. She also took me to some Koranic schools that were modeled along "modern lines," she said. In one of these Nabila herself was a volunteer teacher.

Dr. Zahira said she would be happy to help me in trying to present Islam to the West on film.

"For they have misunderstood Islam, I think," she said. We sat that day in her home in Zamalek, a luxurious apartment not too far from Aziza's house.

"The West, that is," she continued. "You think of Islam as restrictive, but it is actually flexible. This is an advantage and a disadvantage, as it can be pulled in many directions. But Islam is really for *people;* it should be an expression of the best of the human spirit."

I visited the five-story building of the Muslim Women's Association. The plump, kindly lady in charge showed me the dormitory for women students attending the university, the day-care center for students' children, the Koranic class for schoolchildren.

"And we help the girls," she said. "We have a cooperative, you know, like the government cooperatives. But ours is our own. The girls can borrow small sums of money for books, we help them with doctors; the cooperatives are all over Egypt now. It is very good, our work."

Nabila told me that Dr. Zahira was important in the lives of many young Egyptian women. "She is—like a—"

"A model?"

"Yes. This is what women in Islam should be."

"But what about politics?"

Nabila looked pained. "All Americans ask that. That is all you are interested in. Do you speak of Repentance and Holy Flight?"

I nodded.

"They did not understand the spirit of Islam. One must not put oneself above one's family, above other people, above one's duty to others. God does not want that. No, I am not with that group. That is not Islam."

I perhaps did not look convinced. "They say that in the West people believe our religion is bad, is that true, B.J.?" Those dark eyes searched mine again, testing for flaws, for bad intentions.

"No," I said firmly. "But—"

"Yes?" Her small, gentle face was troubled.

"But sometimes—sometimes we believe religion can be *used* by bad people for bad purposes."

Nabila smiled triumphantly. "But so can anything," she said passionately. "It is the *intention* that is important. You understand?"

"Yes, Nabila," I answered. "I understand. We will talk about all this in the film, and with Dr. Zahira, too."

"Oh yes." Nabila looked very pleased. "It is important to do that. When will your technicians come?" she asked. "I will do what I can."

NUBIA, 1981

ONCE UPON A TIME a great and good prince was beset by evil enemies. He had no recourse but to try to escape, and so, taking his sword, he fled north from caves and rocks deep in Africa. He began to run very fast, trailing his sword behind him. He turned this way and that, to avoid his enemies who were close behind him, and wherever he ran, wherever his sword touched the ground, the earth opened and a silver river flowed to protect him. When he reached the Mediterranean Sea, he disappeared. Many people have waited for the return of the good prince; but he has never been seen again. The river still remains. It is the Nile.

The old fairy tale about the creation of the river Nile is no longer told by Nubian mothers to their children. A man, Gamal Abdel Nasser, interrupted the natural course of the Nile. By 1971 the structure of earth, rocks, sand, clay, and cement known as the High Dam was finished. More than two miles wide and 130 feet high, the dam was changing the face of Egypt, molding its contours, filling its hollows in patterns not foreseen by the old storytellers. A huge lake covers the old "blessed land" of Nubia—Lake Nasser. We could see it from the plane that morning in February 1981 as we circled Aswan, on the way to visit our Nubian friends once more.

"The lake's supposed to have filled up long ago," said Bob, "but they didn't expect so much water to be lost through evaporation and seepage." He leaned across me in the seat to look down where before only a shining slit of river had been visible: now a wide expanse of silver water stretched below us, said to be at least three hundred miles long, six miles wide, and covering a total area of three thousand square miles.

"It doesn't look like a lake, it looks like an enormous uneven leaf," I protested.

"What did you think, it would be round, like a pool? It's bound to be uneven. It's backed up into all the wadis that used to cut into the river from the desert. Lots of water surface; the shoreline varies from place to place."

"How can it?"

"Well, the water slides away from the desert, half a mile or more in some places, when the water level falls in the winter and spring."

Now, below us, the water shimmered in the early afternoon sun and lapped gently out in all directions, as though deliberately pushing out for new banks, propelled by forces deep beneath the earth. Wherever the water came to rest on the land, a fringe of green was visible, the new foliage tracing boundaries of fertility, suggesting possible new areas of cultivation. Had this eventuality been predicted by the Russian engineers of the dam, the Egyptian planners? I asked Bob.

"Yes, of course," he answered. "They always counted on the shores of Lake Nasser to offer new agricultural land. And you've heard the stories. Nubians are actually already going back."

"They knew before everyone else that the land would be good?"

"No, not really. But some of the Nubians have always wanted to go back. And now they've gotten permission from the government. They're there. Four settlements! I've visited them. Pioneers, they call themselves."

The government settlements north of the High Dam in Kom Ombo had been much improved since that sad time in 1965, said Bob, just after the move. He had been down earlier in the year, to see the land allotted to the Nubians by the Egyptian government. They were growing sugarcane, as the government wanted them to do, but the Upper Egyptians had to help with its cultivation, something the Nubians had never done themselves. Often women were supervising the farms, since many men were working abroad, as migrant laborers.

"They can make more money in the Gulf, I suppose," I said.

"Yes," said Bob. "Labor migrants, like before. And there are lots of educated Nubians now, teachers and engineers as well as cooks and waiters. They're making big bucks and sending it home to brighten up the home villages. You'll see."

"Mmm."

"And they're anxious to see you, B.J."

"In Cairo people said many of our friends were dead."

"True, but many are still there. The only thing they won't understand is why we didn't bring the children," he said. "I explained to Muhammad, though, that we couldn't afford both education *and* airfare for expensive trips. Muhammad understands, everybody understands, the high costs of educating and raising children these days."

"I just dread seeing his mother, Shemessa," I finally brought out.

"She used to scare me really, when David was so sick and she'd glare at me in that evil way when I went down to dose the twins."

"You still think about that after all these years?" asked Bob. "I don't believe it."

"Well, not all the time, obviously," I said defensively, "but—" and I subsided in a fit of coughing. We both had bad colds.

Bob blew his nose as we landed. "Maybe the dry air will be as good for our old chests as it was for David's," he said hopefully.

And, coughing and sniffling, we filed out of the plane onto the tarmac. We were in the new boomtown of Egypt—Aswan.

The effects of the High Dam and the great silvery Lake Nasser were not much in evidence on the ground, among the rocks and dusty dunes beside the road from the airport to the center of the city. But there was a great traffic circle on the outskirts, and colorful signs proclaiming the benefits of the dam. "Peace," the signs said, and "Prosperity."

"There's also a new soccer stadium, and many more schools, and lots of luxury shops along the Corniche. Plus new first-class hotels. They say it has a hundred thousand people."

"Aswan?" I remembered Aswan as a small sleepy town in a beautiful riverside setting.

Bob's old friend Muhammad was waiting for us at the airlines terminal. I had known him, of course, when we lived in Ballana in 1961 and 1962, but I had seen more of his wife and mother than of him. Thus, I was somewhat surprised, though not displeased, to be engulfed in an enthusiastic bear hug.

"Well, you're like a member of the family, B.J.," announced Muhammad, almost as though he were surprised at himself. He drew back, and there he stood, impressive and dignified as ever, in a flowing immaculate blue galabia (who ironed it today? I wondered), a wide white turban, and fashionable black sunglasses.

"Welcome back to Nubia!" he said in English. We shook hands and exchanged news of our respective children. Our David had been very ill and near death in Nubia, Muhammad remembered. His twin sons had been very ill and had died in Nubia, I remembered.

He took off his sunglasses to wipe his eyes, and I could see that he now had an unmoving, artificial eye, his own lost from infection. Handsome Muhammad, who was once the best hunter, the best tambura player, in southern Nubia. What was he doing these days? He managed his new sugarcane land, he said, and he had plans for a Nubian cultural center in Aswan. He had also, Bob had told me, been one of the forces behind the pioneer settlements, pushing the requests to the government, to President Sadat himself, that had finally resulted in permission being granted for the settlements to legally exist. He had become a well-known spokesman for his people.

"And your mother, Muhammad?"

"She's fine. She went to Mecca."

"Wonderful."

"But she's old now, B.J."

We looked at each other, standing there in the road, Muhammad, Bob, and I.

"You're staying at the Cataract Hotel?"

"No," said Bob, "at the old Social Research Center apartment."

There was a slight pause. "Let's go to the Cataract, though, and have some tea," suggested Bob. "We can talk there."

"We're going back to Old Nubia," announced Muhammad, swinging in step along with us up the steep hill where the Old Cataract Hotel, built during the days of British rule, commanded the best view of the river. "Did Bob tell you?"

"Yes, he did," I answered. "And I also read about it in the *New York Times*, a big American paper."

Muhammad looked pleased. "It's important to go to the old blessed land," he said. "But it's really hard getting started. Hard going." He turned to Bob. "You saw it, Bob. It doesn't pay for itself yet. But it will."

We were nearly at the top, the river swirling down on our right, new buildings rising on our left.

"My son is in New Nubia, B.J.," added Muhammad.

"You must be very proud of him."

"I am. And David? Bob says he's working in the Texas oil fields. Why?"

"He says he's taking time off from the university until he figures out what he wants to do."

"Ah." Muhammad nodded. "Here we are not so lucky. The students, particularly the Nubian students, must work extra hard to make high marks on the government exams the first time so they can go to college at all. Then it's free."

"Well, it isn't free in America," put in Bob. "It gets more expensive all the time."

"People in Cairo say the Nubians have done very well in the new schools, Muhammad."

"Yes, they have. We hired tutors for the boys and girls so they could do well on the exams. The schools are really too crowded. It's the only way to be sure they get an education these days."

College educations on the one hand, and on the other a movement back to a faraway agricultural settlement on the banks of Lake Nasser. The two efforts seemed contradictory. But the Nubians had always selected well from what was available to them, fitting bits and pieces into their own plans wherever possible, discarding what would not work.

"Here we are." We came out on the open terrace of the Old Cataract, the splendid setting for the film of Agatha Christie's *Death on the Nile*. The Victorian verandah's Moorish-style carved pillars framed a magnificent view of the Nile, of ancient Elephantine Island, of the sailboats on the water, the tomb of the Aga Khan glistening white, high on the opposite bank. The cataract for which the hotel was named tumbled over the rocks below.

The tea came. Heavy white ironstone china, lemon, sugar, an extra pot of hot water. Scotch shortbread on a plate. The English habits lingered on.

"You see all kinds of tourists in Aswan these days," offered Muhammad conversationally as he poured hot milk into his tea, an old Nubian custom. Half milk. Half tea. Nutritious, Khadija had explained to me. "Mostly French and German, but some Israelis, too."

He sipped his tea, became serious. "We can get tourists to come to the Nubian cultural center when it opens."

"When it opens." Bob smiled appreciatively at his friend's audacity. "Here you have just designed postcards to raise money for the center and you're already talking about opening it to tourists?"

"Why not?" asked Muhammad. "We'll have baskets and things for sale, Nubian music and dances. The tourists will learn something. You have to think this way, Bob, I'm serious."

"Okay, Muhammad, okay." Bob paused and then went on. "They say Aswan was an important city thousands of years ago. Maybe it's becoming one again, thanks to Gamal Abdel Nasser and the Aswan Dam. And John Foster Dulles," he added mischievously.

Muhammad was indignant. "Dulles. The American. What did he do?"

"Made Nasser so mad he signed the contract with the Russians and got the dam built."

"Okay, Bob, okay."

The three of us were silent for a moment.

The view from the Victorian-Moorish terrace encouraged musings, silences, contemplations on the past, on fate. Perhaps because it was so unexpectedly and wildly beautiful, the dark rocks flung down into the gleaming Nile, the river water bubbling and boiling up around them, first light and then dark, as the legendary river must have bubbled up to protect the legendary prince from harm. And then, just in front of us, the river became calm again, and the feluccas in full sail, like heavy wide-winged swans, moved silently with the wind, up, down, and around the islands.

Muhammad broke the silence. "Nasser did the dam, you're right, Bob, but he didn't live to see it finished. Sadat opened it in 1971. And he's the one who has given us money for a new pump down in the pioneer settlements."

"Who will want to live in the settlements, Muhammad?" I asked. "Other than the pioneers," I added hastily, and Muhammad turned and faced me. "I mean, with all the young people doing so well in school and all . . ." I finished lamely.

"They will," asserted Muhammad with conviction. "At least some of them. The good ones. We'll have modern farms down there, owned and run by Nubians. We will raise vegetables for the Aswan market." He gestured with his teacup. "Tomatoes, eggplant, okra." He set down his cup carefully in the saucer. "But though the farms will be modern, we will all speak Nubian together. And we will have Nubian houses."

Nubian houses. Those beautiful structures that Hassan Fathy had described as pristine and dreamlike were very different from the government-issue houses we had visited in New Nubia in 1965. Cement-block structures, a small court open to the broiling sun, an animal shelter and a toilet side by side in the court, leaving little room for the human occupants.

"The houses in Kom Ombo weren't very nice in the beginning, I grant you," Bob said.

Muhammad nodded vigorously, his wide white turban teetering slightly. He adjusted it carefully and said, "We've fixed those houses up properly. You'll see when you come to us, B.J."

Bob looked at his watch, then out to the river, where the sky was filling with dusky color. "We should get to the apartment before dark," he said. "We can come back here again and look at the view."

The hill beside the Cataract had been landscaped into a public park set with benches and chairs where several young couples sat decorously drinking Coca-Cola and munching cookies. At their feet small birds with black and white faces hopped about hoping for crumbs. The sky had become a clear, glorious red.

Bob turned to Muhammad. "We didn't see young people holding hands in public in the old days."

"They are not Nubians," said Muhammad rather crisply. "Nubian women don't hang around like that. Or Nubian men either. Our girls go to school, but then they come home and help their mothers."

"Your girls are all in school?" Muhammad, for all of his interest in the outside world, had never been too interested, I thought, in allowing his own daughters or his wife much share in it.

"Two are. The others are needed at home," he said, then added, almost gratuitously, "My mother, Shemessa, is very old now, you know, B.J."

Hmm, I thought to myself.

"Many teachers are women," went on Muhammad as if in answer to our unspoken question. "And you know, Bob, Mekki's daughter is running his shop in Aswan now. She inherited it from her father."

"Come on, B.J.," urged Bob. "You know how fast the sun sets here. We have to get to the apartment before dark so we can turn on the water and electricity. It's been so long; I'm not sure I even remember where the place is."

"Oh, I do," said Muhammad airily.

Dark was coming, dulling the sky as we turned in from the river, toward the large government housing block where Bob had rented an apartment years ago for the Nubian project. Twelve Egyptian pounds per month, for four rooms, bath, and kitchen. Headquarters for the project staff who had taken part in the initial three years of fieldwork and the follow-up studies after resettlement. The Social Research Center had kept the lease all these years.

It was here that we would stay at night while we spent our days in New Nubia. Fourth floor. Walking up the outside cement stairs. Opening up the door. The first time in a long time. The air inside was stuffy. I moved forward to open windows. Bob turned on the bright unshaded overhead bulbs. The quick tropical darkness had come down upon us, as he had predicted.

"When will you come to Ballana? Tomorrow?" asked Muhammad. "Everyone wants to see you, B.J. They've already seen Bob." He laughed.

"The day after tomorrow," said Bob. "We're both tired and have bad colds. You know Cairo these days. Everyone has colds. We need a day just to rest."

"Fine, okay." Muhammad nodded. "I'll see you, then, on Friday for lunch."

The door shut. Bob and I were alone in the old apartment. Neatly piled sheets, towels, blankets, were covered against the dust with yellowing newspapers, copies of *Al-Ahram* nearly two years old. The windows had been blocked with paper to discourage the desert dust that blew hard during the *khamsin*, the sandstorm season. The furniture was simple but adequate; we had bought some of it ourselves. New beds, refrigerators, cupboards, all made in Egypt, the first fruits of the ambitious industrialization program of Gamal Abdel Nasser. "Keep Egypt independent," he had urged, and he had pushed for the manufacture of consumer goods for the new Egyptian middle class. "Ideal" was the proud Egyptian brand name. And here still were the old Ideal refrigerator, the Ideal cupboards and beds. The refrigerator still worked well, and it began to hum when I turned it on. Bob was moving through the rooms, opening windows, folding papers. In one metal cupboard lay mimeographed interview schedules in English and Arabic: name, age, number of children. The little balcony that gave onto the river was just wide enough to hold laundry lines. Its view of the Nile was cut in half by the corner of the apartment block in front of us.

Nineteen eighty-one. I had not been in Aswan since 1965. Sixteen years. Why did the apartment seem so familiar to me, so loaded with memory? It was plainly furnished for working, not for leisure. I had stayed here only briefly, twice. Yet when I opened the dining room cupboard and laid out the teacups—a gray and white calico pattern with a pink rose overlay—my heart thumped strangely. All the clichés about remembrance of things past rushed into my head. It was not the length of time we had stayed here, perhaps, but the quality of that time for us, for our Nubian friends. And although we had changed, the apartment had remained the same. I could almost hear the voices. Nineteen sixty-five. With some of the research assistants, we were getting ready to spend the day in New Nubia, our first visit after resettlement.

"Are you going to take Laila?" It was Fadwa al-Guindi, who had worked in the Kenuzi villages.

"Well." It was myself, younger, more worried, more uncertain. "I don't know. Farida wants to keep her here." Laila was only three then, and Farida was our nanny, whom we had brought with us on this brief trip to Aswan.

"No, no, Fadwa." It was Hassan, one of the research assistants. "Leave Laila here with Farida."

"They could both come for the day," suggested Fadwa.

Hassan made an inarticulate sound of annoyance. "Fadwa," he said, "you *know* that wouldn't work. Nubian women don't work for other people as nannies. They would be rude to Farida."

"But everyone will want to see Laila," insisted Fadwa. "You were pregnant with her when you lived in the village, B.J.!"

"Take a picture of her!" Bob, younger, brusque, in a hurry. "No discussion, it's a waste of time. Leave Laila here. Come *on*, B.J., aren't the other children ready yet?"

"Bob . . ." It was Fadwa again, laughing. She had a wonderful laugh that often successfully masked other emotions. "Remember that old Egyptian saying, words are like whips! Give us a break. We're coming."

The calico cups with roses. Farida was gently pulling those cups out of Laila's fat little fingers . . .

"B.J., you're too quiet," said Bob. "You're thinking sentimental thoughts about the past, right?"

"Right."

"Good times those. Bad times, too. We nearly lost David, but think what the Nubians lost."

"Yes, I know. Everything."

"But just think," said Bob, "what life was like in those doomed villages, people doing what they'd always done, all the while knowing that in a few months everything would be covered with water."

"They didn't really believe it, though," I answered. "The women told me they thought it would never happen."

Our open window showed a strip of Nile, darkened, new lamp-posts lighting the Corniche, along which people walked and cars drove. A much larger Corniche, widened since 1965.

"And when it did happen," Bob continued, "when the boats came and took the people away, they say everyone cried and some old people actually died of shock."

"Now *you're* talking about the past, Bob."

He nodded. "But still, we know all this, but we didn't actually live it. It has to be lived and suffered through, I think, to—"

"Bob."

He stood up. "You're right, we're run-down from bad colds. We need to sleep, not go on and on about the good old days."

"We weren't," I insisted. "We were trying to put it all together. It's strange, coming back like this."

"Good night, dear."

We fell down on our Ideal beds and slept. And I dreamed of the past, of Fadwa and Hassan and Farida and Laila and Laura Ann and David and of Shemessa, Muhammad's mother. Old Shemessa in her traditional *gargara*, the full black pleated dress that trailed behind her in the sand when she walked, appeared and reappeared in the dream, snatching a cup out of my hand. Shemessa who glared at me when I appeared at her house with the bottle of medicine for the twins. "Babies that are meant to live, live," she had said to me then. "It is God's will." "Yes, Shemessa, but sometimes God helps those who help themselves." "Ha! And isn't your own son sick?" "Yes, he is." "And do you give him that medicine?" "No, but his sickness is different." "Ha!" Shemessa's face seemed to become the calico cup, growing larger and larger to the edges of the dream.

Then Muhammad's wife appeared. Nezla, kind, pleasant, pretty, not up to the iron backbone of her mother-in-law. Nezla smiled at me in the dream and told me she was pregnant. And I woke up, shouting, "It's Muhammad's fault! It's his fault."

Bob called out, irritated. "B.J., wake up, you're talking in your sleep. What, for heaven's sake, is Muhammad's fault?"

"I was dreaming."

"But what was his fault? Now I'm awake, you might as well answer the question."

"Well, in the dream Nezla got pregnant, so how could she expect to nurse the new baby *and* the sick twins, of course they would die. And so that is why . . ."

". . . it was all Muhammad's fault? Well, it takes two to tango, as they say. Now go back to sleep."

Bob was snoring in a moment. After tossing and turning, I got up and went into the dining room and sat at the table in the dark. The calico cups were back in the cupboard behind me. The shutter on the riverfront window was half-open and I walked toward it, toward the tiny laundry balcony. The Nile, that part of it I could see around the neighboring apartment house, was black and still, the streets below me empty. All sensible people were asleep.

Never go back, the poets said. It is not the same. It is never the same. Well, I don't want it to be the same, I said to the anonymous poets. But there is something to settle with Shemessa. Some vague dark frightening feeling. It is better to see her, to banish the unreasonable nightmare fancies in which she occurs and recurs as nemesis.

Our sentimental journey to New Nubia began with the muezzin's call to Friday prayers. We set off in a rented taxi, in order to reach Ballana by lunchtime. The taxi driver, an old man, had his wife beside him and a Koran on the dashboard, as we had often seen in Cairo. He said he would like to turn on the religious station and listen to the prayers celebrating the holy day of Friday and the recitations from the Koran that would follow.

The chant rose and fell through the cracked speaker of the taxi as we passed by the older Kenuzi villages, settled in the 1930s after the first Aswan Dam was heightened by the British. A man in a white galabia, his beard as white as his garment, was climbing up the rocks on our right, toward the little mosque at the top of his village. The walls of the barrel-roofed Kenuzi houses were painted with flowers and animals, but the mosque was pristine white. The rim of the road was shaded by heavy old acacia trees, and clay *zirs*, or water coolers, hung from them, like giant Christmas tree ornaments.

"Ah yes." The wife of the taxi driver turned around in answer to my question. "The *zirs* are *bénéfices*, in thanks to God for a vow, or a wish granted." She used the French word for a good deed, but I wondered who would drink from the clay containers so suspended among the nodding leaves of the tree. Birds? Djinns, the spirits of the trees, the earth, the river?

The narrow fingers of land between the road and the river, and between the road and the rocks upon which the village lay, had been plowed and planted. It was winter wheat, Bob said, and alfalfa. Makeshift scarecrows, rags on crossed sticks, stood in the rows of onions, the fields of rounding gray-green cabbages. A gasoline truck roared ominously behind us, and the old taxi pulled over onto the road shoulder to let it pass.

"You have friends in Ballana?" asked the driver politely.

"Yes," said Bob. "We lived in Ballana long ago before the water covered everything."

The old lady turned around to look at us. "The land was beautiful there," she said. "The river was beautiful, too."

"Yes," I answered. "Where are you from?"

"We are from Kalabsha," she said. "The big temple. It is gone, too."

We talked about our children, about the farming. "They want us to grow sugarcane," said the old man. He spat out the window. "Who knows how to grow sugarcane? We rented our land to some Saidis. They know how."

"And our son is in the Gulf. He sends us money," added the old lady. She turned around full in her seat and smiled a gap-toothed but contented smile below her black head scarf. "He is a good son," she said.

"Yes, we do all right," said the old man.

In the south the river's banks had disappeared under Lake Nasser, but here, below the dam, they seemed much the same as in the past. The river still served as a main transport route. A huge flat barge was chugging slowly along on our left carrying, of all things, sand, to the north. The river thronged with feluccas, large, small, one close enough so we could see its striped mast of orange and green, its banded boxes and cartons piled abovedecks. Acacias and cottonwoods edged the tiny fields, giving shade, and a few date palms had been planted among them. The donkeys being driven along the side of the road by small boys carried wide loads of dried palm fronds. The Nubians were cultivating their beloved date palms again. We had seen hundreds of palm shoots from the trees of Old Nubia lining the banks of the Nile in 1963, shrouded in their own fibrous netting, waiting to be transported to Kom Ombo by government boats. Other trees had been brought to the new settlement by the Nubians themselves, to plant near their new homes. The actual fruit of the tree, the date, was only one of the many products of the palm that were used in everyday life. Dried palm fronds like those loading the donkeys beside the taxi could be woven into roofs for the courts of the new houses, into fences for the animal shelters, and into mats for the floors. The bits and pieces could be used for fuel, and thin strands of fiber served as the base material for Nubian baskets and plates. The fronds were more valuable now than ever before, since the old stands of date palms lay under water, and the new trees were just beginning to bear fruit.

"I believe in peace," said the taxi driver suddenly. "That's why I bought this dove for my taxi; peace is what the Koran says is best. Nubia was always a land of peace. That's why it was blessed."

The old man was right. There had been practically no crime in Old Nubia. When the government policemen assigned to Ballana Province had occasionally stopped by our house there, they complained of boredom. Bob served them tea and discussed the ways of the world with these homesick men from Cairo who were at a loss to explain the total absence of crimes of violence.

"Of course there is a little smuggling, we know that." The policeman had smiled knowingly at Bob.

"Of course," Bob would answer. Everybody knew about the smuggling of tea and cigarettes from the Sudan. A lot of people were in on it, too, including, some said, the police. But petty smuggling was accepted; nobody considered that a crime. Even a policeman likes Italian sunglasses.

"Well," Bob had added, "there's bad feeling between some families, but the only crime I ever heard of was a man last year who went stark raving mad and started running through a northern village with a butcher knife. He had to be taken to a mental hospital in Cairo."

"I remember that case," said the policeman. "But, you know, he didn't hurt anyone!"

There must be some dark places in Nubian culture, I had argued with Bob and the other research assistants. Circumcision. Yes, everyone agreed that female circumcision, which was still practiced in the area, did not fit into the idealized picture of peace, contentment, and love that was the local cultural ideal. And here the radical, or pharaonic, circumcision was common. Not only did the operation cause physical pain and long-term discomfort to women in their sex life and in childbirth, it also caused frustration and concern among the men, Muhammad had confided to Bob. Where did it come from, this seemingly bizarre and cruel act? How did it fit into the picture? No one seemed able to answer except to explain that it made women "more feminine," that it had "always been done."

Bob and the driver were speaking. "We have another hour to go," Bob said to me. "We should be turning off soon, away from the river."

I hoped the sweets I had brought as a present to Muhammad's family were adequate, appropriate. But why was I worrying? They were old friends.

"The candy should be given to his mother, Shemessa, I think," said Bob. "We'll be having lunch with them."

"Shemessa?"

"Yes," he said firmly. "And stop being so silly about the poor old lady."

We turned east, away from the river. A clear empty sky. An empty landscape of hills. Bits of broken grass tufts rolled toward us, against the car, like tumbleweeds. This was the moment we had dreaded in 1965, leaving the riverside. Over a ridge the villages appeared, rows of houses, boxlike as before, but now as we came closer, we could see that the cement had been covered with smooth sand-colored plaster, the fronts of the houses had been adorned with mud-brick benches, or *mastabas*, and the walls and the doors of the houses were ornamented as the old Nubian houses had been, with geometric designs in white, with flowers picked out in red and green and blue on the smooth matte surfaces. An occasional wall was illustrated with scenes of everyday life, of travels. A donkey carried a load of grain, a taxi returned from Mecca, a plane was bound for London. The scenes were meticulously painted and signed, with the name of the house owner. The women had done the painting in Old Nubia; was it the same in New Nubia?

"Here we are!" The taxi came to a stop beside a gas station. A school building rose behind it. We got out and I shook hands with the driver's wife through the open car window. Bob paid our fare and we said goodbye.

"See, B.J., doesn't it look better?" Bob had taken my arm and we walked down the streets, swept clean of trash, decorated with great mud-brick tubs in which small palm trees flourished. Soon they would be big enough to replant in the fields. Potted palms, no less! I smiled. The children running ahead, behind, and to each side of us gave one reason to smile. They looked much stronger and healthier than the children I remembered in Old Nubia. Their eyes were clear, too, of the suppurating infections that had been the bane of the old villages, that had caused our own children so much trouble and had cost Muhammad his eye.

"*Ahlan wusahlan!* Why didn't you tell me you were getting off at the gas station? I would have come to meet you." It was Muhammad, greeting us warmly and literally propelling us down the street to his house, into the salon where a center table was covered with a white cloth and a new television set was turned on immediately for our pleasure.

"Where are Nezla and your mother?" I asked politely, after we had watched an Egyptian soap opera for about five minutes. The old pictures were on the wall again, the picture of Muhammad with his tambura, photographed by a French newsman before the temple of Abu Simbel. I felt as though I should get up and go into the women's quarters myself, but it seemed more polite to inquire, in case they were not ready to receive visitors.

"Come, B.J., they're out here." Muhammad opened the door of the guest room and Bob handed me the big box of candy, mouthing as he did so, "Shemessa."

There she was, all in black, the center of my recent nightmares, Muhammad's mother. "Ah! Ah! *Ahlan wusahlan!*" That high cracked voice was the same, a little thinner perhaps but still the same tentative welcome—"Ah . . . Ah" came first, as though signaling that she was not quite sure she *wanted* to welcome me. I shook myself inwardly and remembered my promise to Bob not to be silly.

"Sit down, then, will you?" Shemessa said, and I did so, while she eased herself down beside me, on a mattress covered with a green spread and carefully placed in the shade in the coolest corner of the courtyard.

"Soraya! Pillows!" she shouted, and a young daughter came running, a flowered pillow in each hand.

I presented my box of sweets.

"Ah!" said Shemessa. She did not seem nearly so malevolent in person as I had conjured her up in my dreams. She was a feeble, very old lady, her eyes milky with cataracts. Could she see me? Did she even know who I was? Her hair, the bit that peeped out from her tightly tied black head scarf, was sparse, the gray mixed with the bright orange tint of henna.

"Ah!" repeated Shemessa, clearing her throat once more, loudly, and pushing her scarf back a little, loosening it slightly, scratching her head. After all, she was at home, she could relax. Then she enunciated, finally, the traditional greeting of welcome in the Fadija language.

"*Mascagna!*"

"*Mascagna!*" I replied. "And how are you, Shemessa?"

"Not bad, nah, not bad." A clearing of the throat again, and she stretched out her old legs on the mattress, grunting with the exertion as she did so. "It's my knees," she said. "Ahh!"

"*Mascagna!*" It was Nezla, Muhammad's wife, who had come forward to shake hands, older, plumper, but still smiling, gently, kindly, wearing a flowered-print housedress without the old-fashioned Nubian black overdress, the *gargara*.

"*Mascagna!*" I answered. "How are you, Nezla?"

She nodded, a kind of *comme-ci, comme-ça* reply.

"Come and see my new stove. And our house. We have fixed it up."

She gave me a tour, proud of it all: six rooms around the wide half-roofed courtyard: the guest room where Bob and Muhammad and several other men were presumably still watching the Cairo soap opera, a kitchen with a white enamel gas stove, two bedrooms, a storeroom, and an immaculate toilet off in a far corner, where the sun beat down fiercely, "to kill off the smell," she explained.

"We put a wall in here, B.J.," she pointed out, "see, so the animals stay on the other side. Can you imagine such a filthy thing—who would put animals in a house with people? I've been in Cairo and I never saw *that*."

It was true that many farmhouses in rural Egyptian villages had animals stabled in them, but the government architect who had designed these houses for the Nubians had probably never been south to see the beautiful old Nubian homes. Even if he had, it was unlikely that the government would have been able to afford to build such spacious residences for the resettled people.

"We have a washing machine, too," said Nezla proudly, and she demonstrated. "First we got the washing machine, then the television. Next, I hope, a refrigerator. Ah, I fought with Muhammad to get the washing machine first, he wanted the television. We got both."

The little girl, Soraya, hanging onto Nezla's skirts, smiled at me.

"Soraya was born here in New Nubia," said Nezla. "So were Mona and Latifa. I have all girls except the oldest, the boy."

"And the others?"

Nezla turned from me, gracefully folding back her sleeve to stir the stew on the stove.

"They died," she said shortly. "The twins died first, then the little boy that was born after, when I was pregnant and you were pregnant with Laila in Old Nubia. And my daughter with the growth. You remember, you came to see us in the hospital in Cairo."

I remembered.

"Ha! Nezla! Beeja!" It was Shemessa calling us from the mattress in the shade.

"Go sit with her, B.J.," said Nezla. "She's old now."

"But still strong, I think," I offered tentatively.

"Yes, God knows," she replied, the daughter-in-law, and turned back to her pot.

"Nezla needs to get her eyes fixed," said Shemessa shortly when I had settled myself beside her again. "She's getting old."

"Nezla?"

"She's got a skin over the eyes, like me." Shemessa demonstrated, pulling up her eyelid so I could see where a grayish milky cloud was forming over the lens, the cornea. It was a cataract. "In the hospital in Aswan they do it in two days, peel it off like a grape. Ha!" She smiled a toothless smile. I didn't remember ever having seen her smile in Old Nubia.

"Soraya! The whisk!" Soraya came running with a horsehair fly whisk and Shemessa began to apply it lightly, back and forth across her shoulders.

"Ah! Ah!" Shemessa was flicking the nonexistent flies away. Her feet, stuck straight out in front of her, were seamed and wrinkled, and the skin, decorated with patches of healing henna, was shrinking inward, creating hollows around each instep.

"I've been to Mecca, Beeja," she said. "You can call me *hajjiya* now!"

"Congratulations," I said. "That's wonderful, Shemessa!"

"I went with Hanim Ali."

"Ah!" I responded noncommittally. "We went on the plane, that was great," said Shemessa. "But it was very hot in Arabia. We went around Mount Arafat, like the Prophet says we must do, around and around, from the morning prayer until the afternoon prayer. We prayed all the time. We were half-dead but it was wonderful! And now I'm a *hajjiya!*"

Slap. Slap. The whisk went back and forth. Shemessa, my nemesis all these years, was obviously not a witch at all, but only a very old woman who had done her duty as she had seen it, all her life. Crotchety perhaps and certainly domineering but hardly a witch. Perhaps she and I had become the objects of each other's anxieties back in Old Nubia.

For I had been very insecure in those days, worried about the children, worried about the baby I was carrying, worried about my fatigue, my feet swelling as I plodded over the sand, worried about the progress of Bob's project. Worry that could not be assuaged, as Shemessa's worry about the twin boys could not be assuaged. And we had therefore fixed on each other as the focus of our discontents. I was an obvious target for Shemessa's antagonism, a stranger bringing unknown medicine, doing things to the babies that she did not understand, an instrument of possible harm to her family.

"Hanim Ali will tell you she stayed a month in Mecca," went on Shemessa. "Don't believe her. She only stayed three weeks. I stayed a month. But then, that's Hanim Ali, always pretending she's better than she is. Can't trust her. Look at the way she carried on over her niece Naima's wedding."

Naima's wedding was the occasion for which Hanim Ali had fought, had bargained for special dates, first-quality henna, for extra-special music, good fat lamb, and for dancing. The dancing had been memorable. She had danced herself, at the end, Hanim Ali, with all the other Nubian women, young and old, celebrating the joining of two families, the strengthening of the community.

". . . and just because the Begum Aga Khan gave money for a present, that was all Hanim Ali was interested in . . ."

Old grievances. Shemessa had been spiteful then, and was now.

"Oh, I don't think so, really, Shemessa. She always wanted Naima and Jabbar to marry. It wasn't just the money the Begum gave—"

"It's always money," interrupted Shemessa. "Or maybe God. We had both in Mecca . . . thanks be to Him." She pointed the whisk at me. "Hanim Ali never bore any children of her own, you know, that's what was wrong with her . . ."

The whisk went back over the old shoulder, covered in two layers of black, like the shoulders of all good Nubian elderly ladies. "Well, we leased our land," she said. "The boy is working in the south . . . we make it . . ."

Looking around the courtyard, at the pattern of pleasant dappled shade cast on the neatly swept plastered floor, Nezla bustling back and forth between her storeroom and her kitchen with its new gas stove, hearing the television blaring in the guest room, where Bob and Muhammad were now watching the soccer match, I thought, yes, they are making it. And now they are returning to the old land, trying to make it there, too. The material comforts offered by the new settlements—washing machines, flyless courtyards, television sets, schools, clinics—were not quite enough, it seemed. Other things were important: pride, sentiment, independence.

"Praise be to Him," muttered old Shemessa, half to herself.

Slap. Slap. I was being lulled into half-sleep when the old woman suddenly sat up straight and said, sharply, clearly, in another, younger voice, directly into my ear, "They died. The twins died! Your son lived, but the twins died. And it was *you* that brought the medicine when they were sick. You. You . . ." The rest of her sentence was unintelligible, but the intent of those words was not benevolent. Could she be cursing me? Something seemed to flash through the clouds of those whitening eyes. I had never been cursed before. And my heart chilled, as it had years ago in Nubia, when David, aged one, lay in a high fever, rasping and coughing, and old Shemessa had hissed, "Your son is no better, is he? Who knows where the evil eye hides, hey?"

"Come and eat, B.J." Bob and Muhammad were standing before us in the court, Bob greeting Shemessa at that moment. I wanted to work out, if at all possible, whatever remained unfinished between us. Her outburst had been so unexpected, so vindictive, after our earlier, peaceful conversation about Old Nubia, Mecca.

Bob shook his head. "Muhammad says if you eat with us it's easier on his wife. She won't have to serve formally twice. Also I think the men would like a look at you. Jalal and Ahmed are here. Jalal came especially from Aswan."

I looked back at Nezla, standing at her kitchen door, Soraya by her side, at Shemessa, who was flicking her whisk again, not even looking at me. Nezla gestured me toward the salon. "We'll have tea later," she said.

The television was turned off as I walked into the room, "in your honor," whispered Bob. "Be pleasant." I went around, shaking hands with Jalal, with Ahmed, an older man whom I did not know but who had come back to Nubia to retire after living in Paris for many years. It was strange to shift so quickly to this formal gathering of men, from the courtyard where old Shemessa flicked the flies and little Soraya ran about to do her grandmother's bidding. Although men and women had never been strictly segregated in Nubia, as in Iraq, women tended to spend more time together since their tasks were different from men's. Bob had visited like this, in the formal guesthouses; but I had sat with the women and did not know Jalal and Ahmed except as appendages to their wives and children.

"How is your family?"

"They are fine, thanks be to God."

The conversation moved around and past the London Nubian club, the children, the price of meat. But in a little corner of my mind, Shemessa's vindictive face with the cloudy eyes remained. And the two moments of malevolence came together—the one long ago when David was so sick, the one today. What were my children doing at that moment? Was David all right on that oil rig? I hadn't had any news for a month.

"You must go visit your other friends," Muhammad was saying, picking up our empty plates and loading them on the tray. "Khadija and Hanim Ali will be mad at me for monopolizing you, B.J."

So off we went, down the street. Wherever we stopped, I found myself enfolded in the voluminous black garments that women wore, garments redolent of the marvelous odor of sandalwood.

"*Mascagnu.*" An embrace, a kiss, three times lightly on each cheek.

"*Mascagna,*" I replied, and was embraced again.

"Come have tea, B.J." "How is baby Laila?" "Why didn't you bring the children?" "We are so sorry to hear your mother died." "Your hair is still short, why?"

I was unreasonably glad to see everyone, Hanim, her children, Naima, Naima's sister from the other bank. It was reassuring, after Shemessa.

"How do you like my salon, B.J.? I did it myself, but Hanim Ali gave me lots of advice." Khadija giggled. "You know Hanim Ali!"

The salon was painted light blue, with a border of darker blue simulating a panel two-thirds of the way up the wall. The ceiling was white and the floor covered with a new imitation Persian rug. "An elegant room, Khadija," I said.

We smiled at each other, then my hostess covered her mouth in embarrassment. She had lost her two front teeth but otherwise was still the village beauty, plumper and with a new hairstyle, frizzy curls framing her face all around her head scarf.

"It's like an Afro," she said, touching the front curls. "We see those American Afro hairdos on TV. And the tiny braids all over the head. Just like the little girls used to wear in Nubia, remember?"

Khadija put her hand on my arm. "If we don't go to Hanim Ali's," she said, "she'll kill me. Naima and the others will come there."

Hanim Ali looked much the same, more dried-up and wrinkled, perhaps, but henna had been more artfully applied to the wings of hair escaping from her head scarf, so it didn't have the bizarre orange and gray look of Shemessa's. And when she embraced me in a cloud of sandalwood, her old strangely wrought rings pressed into my arm. I kissed her, in the Nubian way, lightly, three times on each cheek, and the evil memory of Shemessa faded.

"Did Shemessa tell you she went to Mecca and stayed a month?"

"Yes."

Hanim Ali shook her head. "Don't believe what Shemessa says. She's getting old. We both stayed three weeks."

Yes, I thought. That's it. She's getting old. Doesn't mean what she says.

"This year we watched the *hajj* on television," said Hanim Ali proudly. "It's wonderful, television. In that little box we see Africa and America and London and Egypt and Syria and Saudi Arabia. We see wild animals. We see people. And we see that the cows in America are fat and *white*. Tell me, do you make good yogurt out of those white cows' milk?"

"Yes," I said. "It makes good yogurt, but you can buy yogurt in the stores in little containers now."

Hanim Ali sniffed. "You can buy it in Aswan like that," she said scornfully. "But it's not like what we make at home. In America I believe you have machines do everything."

"No. Not everything."

"Well, sometimes machines are *better* than people, they make life easier. Do you remember how we used to wash clothes? Look at my hands."

I looked at those old, scarred, cracked hands, and I remembered well how they used to wash clothes; the women first had to haul water up the steep dunes from the river, in cans gracefully balanced on their heads. A picturesque ethnic sight for photographers, but hardly pleasant for the women who had to haul those heavy cans of water once, twice, sometimes three times a day.

"So it's better here," I offered.

"Some things are better, some worse," allowed Hanim Ali. "The water comes out of the tap, that's wonderful. But you know, in the beginning many died, many animals died, many people, many children—"

"I know, Hanim Ali, I am sorry." Her own husband was dead, her cowife, and the three children of Muhammad.

"Beeja," said Hanim Ali. "We saw on the television a program about the black people in America, and we see that there is trouble between whites and blacks in your country. Why?"

"It is better now, Hanim Ali," I began, "but . . ."

I was rescued from having to explain the history of racial conflict in America by the others who came in—Naima, Hanim, and the grown-up children whom I did not recognize but who recognized me. They wandered in smiling, to shake hands, ask after the children. What had I been dreading? That Nubia would be dying, that people would be sick, some dead? Some were dead. Times had been bad. But things were better now than they had been in 1965. The Nubians had taken what was offered—a government house, a piece of land, help in moving— and had made it into a base for something better. Many men had gone to work in the Gulf, just as they had left Nubia in the past to work in Cairo, Khartoum. In their absence, the womenfolk had leased the land to Saidis from Upper Egypt, who farmed it as sharecroppers. The men told Bob that at first they made up to six hundred dollars or more a month as migrant laborers, but now they got less, since the migrant population in the Gulf had increased and wages had fallen somewhat. In Nubia itself, the women said, it was possible to live well for a hundred dollars a month. The children were almost all in school, many, like Abdul Nasr and Elias, going on to universities.

The warmth of our reception, the hopefulness of our friends, cheered us both. I decided again I had been imagining things with Shemessa and made a point of asking for her when we went back to Muhammad's house to say goodbye.

"Shemessa's taking a nap, B.J.," said Nezla. "She's tired out."

"Nonsense," Muhammad replied, and strode into the bedroom. He came out again more quietly and closed the door softly. "I'm sorry, B.J. She *is* asleep. You know how mothers are, Bob," he joked, with a sidelong glance at me. "She's getting old. You must forgive her. She still has bad memories of Old Nubia."

"Yes, Muhammad," I said. "I understand."

I thought I did understand. The work of Bob and his colleagues, the many publications that had resulted from the Nubian project, was important to the Nubians, for it documented and recorded their heritage. Bob had contributed to their community as they had contributed to the success of his career. But our relations with the Nubians and theirs with us were a much more personal matter. Shemessa and I, full of anxiety as we both were in those days in 1961 and 1962, had become the personifications of each other's problems. Time had not changed that.

All reasonable discussion with Bob notwithstanding, I was not surprised when we got back to Cairo to find a letter from Laura Ann. "Don't worry, Mama. The worst is over. David had a bad accident on the rig, the pipe slipped. It weighed about a ton, so he was lucky not to lose his hand when the pipe came down. His hand is broken and swollen up like a boxing glove, but the doctor says they can save his fingers. He says to send his love."

The heavy pipe came crashing down on David's hand that last week in February, when we were in New Nubia. The day that Shemessa cursed me? Astrologers and psychic readers and fortune-tellers make much of the confluence of good and evil vibrations. I discounted such ideas, rational Westerner that I was. So did Bob. But I could not forget Shemessa, the flash from those clouded eyes. The dark corners of the human heart have yet to be explained away; they are there. Violence. Passion. Hate. And all can be activated when unbearable situations arise in which the protagonists feel powerless. Whatever I might feel, Shemessa felt greater grief, greater hate. For my son, David, was alive. Her three grandsons were dead. And in her bitterness she struck out, she still blamed me for their deaths.

"Coincidence is the gadfly of the imagination" was all that Bob would say.

Before we had left for Cairo, Muhammad came to Aswan bearing a proposal for a Nubian cultural center in Aswan. "Do you think the Ford Foundation would finance it?" he asked. "They supported your project."

"Why not try?" said Bob. He took the proposal back to Cairo and gave it to John Gerhart at the foundation. Muhammad himself came two weeks later for an interview and discussion. Bob in his denim suit, Muhammad in blue galabia, and Jalal in a new brown safari suit made up the delegation.

The grant was awarded in the fall of 1981, to help develop "a Nubian center that will allow all peoples the opportunity to view the best of Nubian culture." By the summer of 1983 the foundations of the building had been laid. Muhammad and Jalal had launched a drive for more funds to complete the construction.

LONG AFTER WE LEFT NUBIA, I remember Hanim Ali's description of "that little box," the television set where she had seen Africa, America,

Asia, and white cows cavorting on a distant green pasture. Egyptian television was just beginning in the 1960s. Now more than half of all Egyptian families owned their own television sets, and nearly two-thirds of the entire population watched television regularly, either at home or in the local coffee shop. As the advertising copywriters might have phrased it, Egyptian mass media had made a quantum leap forward. The National Television Corporation occupied an entire building along the Nile, near the center of Cairo, a ten-minute walk from the Hilton. From that single giant twelve-story building emanated the news, the soap operas and talk shows, the religious and educational programs that filled the Egyptian television screens for at least eight hours every day.

Sheikh Sharkawi dispensed homilies and religious advice; school-teachers offered special tutoring sessions in mathematics and science, to compensate for the crowded classrooms where individualized instruction was not possible; Egyptian playwrights, poets, and filmmakers were interviewed, their latest works discussed. The soap operas, or "family serials," enthralled viewers with daytime romance and tragedy (the handsome young doctor falls in love with a poor patient in the hospital and deserts the rich and socially prominent girl his parents have chosen for him; a child ill with an incurable disease brings estranged members of his family together before death); President Sadat opened many news broadcasts with a long "chat with the people"; and the news was also presented in English and French. Then there were the imported shows: *Roots* and *Little House on the Prairie*; the Monte Carlo entertainment show from France; *Edward and Mrs. Simpson* from Britain; and finally, the most popular of all, *Dallas*.

Dallas was the one phenomenon that in 1981 brought traffic virtually to a standstill in downtown Cairo for the hour of its transmission; it kept children from their homework and ruined the conversations of many dinner parties. Money, sex, and power. Ingredients to appeal to any society; the *Dallas* combination had the added titillation of being foreign, Western.

"I must say I like to look at the decor, the sofas and the curtains," said one Cairo matron. "And of course Sue Ellen's clothes."

"It shows our people what they must avoid in the West," said an earnest young painter. "It is instructive to watch an evil man like J.R.

and see that he is the *real* American, not like the ones we have romanticized in the past."

"I don't agree," said an Egyptian army officer with whom I sat at dinner. "I do not let my children watch it. It sets a *bad* example for them."

"You don't watch *Dallas?*" I asked, amazed. I had yet to meet an Egyptian who did not.

The army officer smiled, shrugged. "Well, yes, I watch it myself. By myself. But my children"—he raised his finger and wagged it at me—"never!"

The television management, canny and public-minded, chose to put their most important public service announcements close to *Dallas*. And these included spots promoting family planning.

Family planning, barely being discussed in the sixties, was now in. President Nasser's 1962 broadcast urging family planning had been seen as a landmark. Now President Sadat also backed family planning, though not as enthusiastically as his wife. Still, a vigorous and expensive government campaign was in progress, backed by USAID and other foundations, and promotion was attempted not only on television but on radio, on billboards, and in hundreds of clinics through the country. By 1970 there were three thousand family planning centers in the twenty-five governorates of Egypt. Their effectiveness, however, was less impressive than their numbers. Even after ten years of the campaign, contraceptive use remained as low as 2 percent in some rural areas.

For the segment of the film I was making in Egypt, I thought it vital to document not simply the government's efforts at family planning but women's and men's personal and individual reactions to what could be viewed as an attempt to regulate the most private aspects of their lives. This was a society, after all, where children were universally desired and admired, as our own son and daughters had happily learned during their years in Egypt. Here neither men nor women were considered mature adults until they had produced children, children who were a source not only of pride and affection but of economic assistance, insurance for parents' old age, and, last but not least, a continuation of the family line.

The Cairo Family Planning Association and the Media Campaign

Personnel were very hospitable, and I was invited to several clinics, both in the city and in the country. In one Delta village an impressive experimental program was in progress, based on a cooperative effort between the overworked woman doctor at the government clinic and Sadika Mahmoud, a local woman, described in the experimental program brochure as the "volunteer village leader."

"I can't imagine anybody not wanting children," said Sadika, a warmhearted, intelligent mother of three, wife of the local elementary school principal. "Everyone wants them. But these days, you know, times are changing. Many women tell me that they don't really want more than three or four. They can't afford to feed them."

She spoke as though this were a new idea, and in some sense it was. She wanted sincerely to help women limit their families to a more manageable number, and her work was showing results. In her village, thanks to the cooperative program, the number of women using contraceptives had risen from 3 to 30 percent in two years. A hopeful sign locally, but it would have to happen nationally—and fast—if it was to make any difference. Though the average number of births per woman was falling slightly, the downturn could not overcome the inevitable cycle of multiplying births that had begun a half century earlier. Egypt's population was growing at a staggering annual rate of 3 percent per year, and the projected population for 1985 was 50 million.

"We can only try," said Sadika when I talked about the national figures. "Three or four children in a family is better than it used to be."

She was right. In 1965, for example, women in one rural area averaged thirteen pregnancies each, but only five of those children survived. The death rate had declined since then, but the memories of an earlier generation were still fresh. Fear of loss of children led to larger families, much larger than the total of three or four that Sadika was trying to promote in her village. And even though half of Egypt's people had become city dwellers, and hence children were not needed as laborers on the farms, they could still work in the cities. More children could mean more incomes, however small those incomes might be.

The only way to deal with the growing population was to increase the productivity of the nation, President Nasser had said, and President Sadat had concurred. The two leaders had gone about it in different ways, Nasser opting for control and central organization, Sadat trying out free trade and encouraging foreign investment and private business.

And over the years since 1959, the gross national product had increased. The industrial plant was also impressive, but the results had not been as glorious as had been hoped. In fact, after initial early improvements, the overall economic situation had slowly worsened. The Egypt that could feed itself in 1964 was by 1981 importing 60 percent of all its food. And the 1981 trade deficit was estimated at $4.8 billion. Of course, there were signs of prosperity everywhere—the cars, the consumer goods, the well-dressed Egyptians in foreign banks and luxury hotels. But this was deceptive, if only because it was seen just in those places most frequented by foreigners. Millions of Egyptians were no better off than they had been when we had first come a quarter of a century before. The Egyptian economy seemed to have come to a standstill, like the apartment blocks and luxury hotels that stood unfinished throughout Cairo, waiting for a new injection of capital so building could begin again.

In 1983, when we returned for a brief visit, Egypt, on the surface, did not seem to have changed much since 1981, except for another great chasm in the earth, this time right in the center of town. Midan al-Tahrir, the traffic circle that commemorated Nasser's time, was being excavated to make way for a modern subway! The traffic was still frantic, but efforts had been made to improve the flow with the completion of several new overpasses and cloverleafs. Even the pedestrian walkways were painted in bright greens and blues. Painters and builders had been at work in downtown Cairo refurbishing stores and buildings, in defiance of the dust that still settled everywhere, like a fine film of decay that disappeared at the first light wind, only to settle somewhere else. The television had kept its nightly audience, but the annual birthrate had dropped slightly, from 3 to 2.9 percent. Islamic dress was still evident on the streets, among both men and women. Whatever the excesses of the fundamentalists who declared their responsibility for Sadat's assassination, the majority of Egyptians had separated that act from the other, more personal aspects of Muslim identity. And more mosques had been illuminated, many with green neon lights that shone brightly in the dark quarters of Cairo's new suburbs.

President Sadat had been dead for nearly two years, and the shock of his assassination had subsided. Hosni Mubarak, his successor, was a different kind of man: low-keyed, quiet, almost self-effacing. But he began his term of office by dealing firmly and effectively with the young army officers who had killed Sadat, an act that some saw as a bizarre and twisted replay of the Free Officers' Revolt in 1952. President Mubarak had attacked corruption, bringing to trial Sadat's own brother. These were highly visible actions, much approved by the general populace, it seemed. The economy, sluggish and slow, was tackled next. Mubarak cut back on imports, particularly cars, by increasing import taxes. And he reduced government subsidies of many food items, such as imported cheese, olive oil, and beer, which had been consumed principally by more prosperous citizens. But he did not advocate checks on free enterprise, either in industry or in any other private sector, and this included agriculture. Indeed, by 1983, the government was offering generous subsidies in both spheres, rather than direct government control as in Nasser's time.

Government subsidies were helping many people, including, to our surprise, Murad, a young college-educated friend of Tom Hartwell's who had worked for CBS in 1981. Murad, a handsome and eminently urban young man, had resigned from CBS and gone back to the land.

"The farm is a lot more interesting than television journalism," he said, laughing a little. And when Bob and I looked slightly skeptical, he invited us to come to his *ezba* and see for ourselves.

"We'd love to come," said Bob.

Murad came to collect us one morning in his old Toyota, on the way to the farm with some refrigerated serum against Newcastle disease, a common malady of chickens raised in chicken houses rather than in chicken yards. Murad was being cautious with this batch of five thousand chicks, he said, because the last time had been a disaster. One thousand young chicks had died in an hour in a heat wave, halfway through their six-week growing cycle. Chickens were profitable, he said, but chancy; if all went well, he could expect to clear $2,500.

"Not bad for six weeks' work," commented Bob.

"Yes, *if* all goes well. But heat or disease can wipe out my profits and leave me with interest that has to be paid. Poor people can't take the risk!"

The government subsidies helped the larger farmers most, he said, subsidies for chicken feed and fertilizer and price supports when the chickens were marketed.

"Economies of scale."

"What, Bob?"

"The bigger the operation, the greater the profit and loss margins."

Murad nodded absently, swerving quickly to avoid a bicyclist balancing a large box on his head, who had veered suddenly in front of us.

For an hour we pushed through the heavy morning city traffic heading east toward Heliopolis, once the center of religious life for the ancient Egyptians, now a middle-class residential suburb that gave way to housing projects and to textile factories on the north, military training schools and barracks at the northeast. The international airport lay straight ahead.

Murad pointed out a complex of condominiums ahead of us as we turned off the main Cairo road. "One of Nasser's last promises," said Murad. "*Alif sukann.* The project of a thousand houses. Still not quite finished. Like a lot of his plans. But, you know, Bob, he was a good president. He really tried. Mubarak's trying, too, with private enterprise, like in America. That's how I got my loans, he's opened things up."

"But will it be enough?" asked Bob. "Can you raise enough food?"

Murad shrugged. "Maybe not. But what else can we do but try?"

We had suddenly left urban life behind. After the blare of automobile horns and the roar of buses, the noises of the countryside were like a balm, a release from irritation: the bray of a donkey, the whine of an occasional mechanical waterwheel, and the gentle twittering of small birds dipping down and rising above the fields. The green land, stretching away on each side of the road, was marked off by banana trees that rustled in the morning breeze, by stands of palms, heavy now with clusters of dates in different shades—yellow, red, and brown—waiting to be harvested. A cart ahead of us, its wheels creaking, and donkeys, loaded with baskets of newly picked dates for the village markets, moved over for our Toyota to pass.

"Why do they have to have the date market exactly where it's always been, right in the middle of the bridge?" Murad asked testily as he maneuvered around the approach to the narrow bridge, where scores of men and women sat close together offering baskets of dates for sale. The road spanned a large feeder canal, the focus of the village, and here the harvested dates were everywhere.

"Beautiful! Look at that!" I murmured, looking down as we crossed the canal, where enormous clumps of violet flowers grew outward from the grassy banks and stood in the water.

"You may think they're beautiful, B.J. Not me!" said Murad. "They choke up the canal and cut down on the flow of water we get for the crops. And nobody wants to clean them out. They're like elastic or something. I clean my part, but the others won't cooperate. It's a real headache."

"Problems, problems," said Bob lightly, eyeing the new Murad, who until recently had appeared to be a dedicated playboy and who now worried about water hyacinths and canal cleaning.

Murad laughed. "Well, it *is* more interesting than working for television," he said. "And I can still go to Cairo on Fridays and see my friends."

Tomato plants were sprouting in the field nearest us. The fall wheat was coming up, row upon row of green shoots, and yellow mustard burgeoned in the fallow furrows. In the distance one field seemed to be dotted with white blossoms, but as we came closer, I saw they were rows of small white birds pecking at the earth.

"Ibis? The sacred ibis?"

"No, B.J. They're something else, I can't remember the English word. We call them the 'friend of the fellah'; they eat bad bugs. Maybe you've seen them on TV, sitting on the water buffalo's backs and eating the fleas? Egrets," he brought out triumphantly. "That's what you call them!"

To our left a large rambling house was visible, shaded by thick trees, protected by high walls.

"Nahas Pasha's house. Muhammad Naguib has been there for years, under government supervision. His son is there, too. But Naguib is sick, in and out of the hospital."

"Naguib? I thought Nasser had let him stay in town."

"Maybe," said Murad. "I don't know. But anyway Mubarak is different. Naguib is an old, old man. He probably likes the country better. Nicer here than in Cairo now."

"Yes," I answered.

Still, it seemed ironic that General Muhammad Naguib, leader of the 1952 Free Officers' Revolt that unseated King Farouk and such leaders of Parliament as Nahas Pasha, should now live out his days in the country retreat of his former political enemy.

Murad turned a corner quickly into a driveway, with a yellow stone house and a garden on one side, a farm compound on the other.

"Here we are!" he said. "And there's Ahmed. He helps with the chickens. Now we all have to work fast to get the serum into them. Do you want to help?"

We said we would be glad to help.

In the new, modern chicken house, screened and airy, Ahmed and Murad mixed the vials of serum into the barrels of water, and then each of us, bearing tin cups, began to fill the water trays, narrow rims along the red plastic cone-shaped trays that hung like lanterns in rows from the ceiling. One by one, we lowered the trays after they had filled, so the chickens could drink, five thousand of them, half-grown, softly chirping and peeping and following us or rushing from us in waves of moving white feathers as we walked across the newly cleaned floor.

"Don't let it down too low, B.J.," cautioned Murad.

"It's so they can drink more easily."

"Yes, I know, but that's what I'm trying to *avoid.* I want them to work a little," he said, "stand up straight, stretch a bit to eat and drink. That strengthens their legs, gives them a bit of muscle, improves their appetite."

"So they gain more weight and you can sell them for more?"

"Exactly."

"What kind of chickens are they, Murad? My aunt Mary used to raise white leghorns. These look like them."

Murad, tall, dark, and handsome, answered, "Don't know. They're French, they're white, and the Ministry of Agriculture is pushing them this season."

Five thousand chickens stretched their legs to drink, pecked at the scientifically mixed food that Ahmed and Murad put in the feeders for them.

"They're thirty days along in their forty-five-day growing time," said Murad, pleased with himself, "gaining weight and feathers, as you can see," and he picked up one white cheeping example to show us the fattening thighs.

This was obviously another kind of *ezba.* Another kind of farmer.

No need for ritualized entertainment of guests (leisurely coffee, then luncheon served by old family retainers, followed by a tour of the grounds). Nothing embarrassing about honest work; you and your guests rush to the chicken coops together and administer serum to five thousand chirping, cheeping, half-grown white fowl.

It was a pleasant estate house, utilitarian and comfortable. A workmanlike compound, stable, barns, housing for the hired men. And a small mosque, newly built so that the doors and windows looked not inward to the stable yards, but outward, to the fields, where bright blue morning glories spilled over the mud-brick walls.

"It was my duty to build a mosque here, Bob, for our help," Murad explained.

We did have a tour of the grounds, however, for Murad wanted to show off his much prized water buffalo, all twenty-eight of them, who gave the richest milk in the neighborhood, Murad said proudly.

"They're a big investment, two thousand dollars *each*. And they're strong. Independent. You have to have one man to stake out and work with every three buffalo. And I have to pay each of the men at least a hundred and twenty dollars per month. In the old days around here, we'd pay fifteen cents a day."

"There they are!" He raised his arm and pointed to the fields beside the farm road, where the great beasts stood, their curving horns vaguely reminiscent of Texas longhorn cattle, though these animals were heavier, broader in the beam. They were staked out on long ropes, but one (at two or three tons of weight) had already managed to pull up her stake and wandered forward, nuzzling into the earth for choice bits of grass, and pausing occasionally to raise her head and stare at us as we walked slowly down the dirt road, separated from the beasts in the field only by a narrow irrigation canal, where the troublesome but beautiful water hyacinths grew.

"We didn't own a lot of land—my father's family, I mean," explained Murad. "My grandfather had a little land in Zagazig, but he was a judge there. When my father came to Cairo, during Nasser's time, he sold the Zagazig spread and bought this."

"It's lovely here, Murad," I said. "Nicer than Cairo in many ways."

He nodded. "I'd like to stay on, I think. But now my father wants to sell at least part of this land to developers."

"Developers. Here?"

"Yes, they're already on their way. See those houses over there? See that fence? All that land has already been sold, and the plots marked out for houses."

"People who would work in Cairo and commute here?" from Bob.

"Exactly. But I say to my father, what will they live *on* if all the land is used for houses? They're already scraping the loam off up along the river and making it into bricks," Murad said bitterly. "Spending millions to reclaim land up north, and here they're burning up the best soil. People are crazy."

"But that's illegal, to use the farmland like that."

"Yes, sure, but they do it anyway. The workers come back from Saudi Arabia with money and they want good brick houses. Houses are more important than food? What're they thinking about?"

He had walked to the end of the road, through the dappled shade of morning cast by the cottonwoods and palms, and now turned back.

"It's called progress, I believe," said Bob.

"Mmm." Murad did not answer. After a bit, he said, "This land still belongs to my father. He can sell it if he wants to. I have to make a good enough profit on the chickens and the *jamoosas* [water buffalo] together so I can buy some land myself, and convince him it makes more sense to farm than sell."

"The *jamoosas* aren't profitable?"

"Oh yes, I make about a thousand dollars per month from the milk, but the profits aren't as much or as quick as chickens. *Jamoosas'* profits are like *jamoosas* look: sure, steady—and slow."

Ahmed came out of the chicken house to wave goodbye. We set out for Cairo, past the date market, more crowded than before.

"If I could build a milk-processing plant here," Murad was saying, "I could do a lot better on the *jamoosas*. I'm trying to get Ali to go in with me. Then I could pay back my loans to the Agricultural Bank and buy a lot of land before it's gone forever."

Bob said, "Why not?"

Murad sighed. "There may not be time," he said. "There aren't many people like me out here. Most people say to hell with it and sell out to the developers. It's easier. You don't have to work, you don't have to mess with the government, this office, that form. I had one guy who put pressure on me just last month to do a scam on the Ministry of Agriculture—''

''And—?'' said Bob.

''And of course I refused. I'm not into that. But I had to refuse very carefully, because I still have to do business with that guy all the time.''

''Corruption even in the chicken business?'' asked Bob.

''You said it,'' answered Murad. ''Not me.''

We drove on, through orange groves, past fig trees, grape arbors, planted in full sun.

''But you know, Bob, all that propaganda about people going hungry in Egypt. That's not true. There's enough here. Look at this beautiful land. But it has to be used right.'' He paused. ''They should sell it to me, not to the developers. The developers aren't developing it, they're destroying it. It's the *farmers* that develop the land, that make it work.''

''Yes.''

Murad laughed shortly. ''Sounds like I think I'm important, doesn't it? I don't. I like what I'm doing. It's interesting, and I'm making good money. But I'm Egyptian, too, you know, and I think the land is important. If it goes, so does Egypt.''

We had reached the crossroads beside the unfinished thousand houses. Behind us lay the *ezba*, the fig trees, the lemon and orange groves, the stands of date palms laden with ripe fruit, and the newly planted fertile fields where the small white egrets presumably still sat and quietly ate insects. Was it possible that such land could really disappear, be scraped up and burned, and its remains filled in with asphalt so that a few hundred more cars and a few hundred more houses could be fitted in where the tomatoes and wheat were now growing?

''It's possible,'' said Murad.

Murad's optimism, the busy country date market, the lush fertility of the countryside around his *ezba*, were difficult to reconcile with the dismal statements about Egypt's economic condition published in the foreign press and in academic journals. According to these analysts, Egypt was an economic disaster area that would collapse if outside aid from Saudi Arabia or the United States should cease.

Yet Egypt did not look as if she was teetering on the edge of disaster. With all the overcrowding in Cairo, the barely adequate public facilities, great strides forward had been taken in improving basic services such as electrification and piped water. New overpasses and bridges had begun to relieve some of the worst bottlenecks in Cairo traffic by 1983. Cairo still had one of the lowest crime rates in the world. To us, and to many more privileged Egyptians and resident foreigners, the decline in the quality of life—pollution, lack of services—was a sign of decay. Yet there was another side. In 1983 some Egyptians who had begun life as poor as many of their fellow countrymen were making money and enjoying material comforts. Asian labor was actually being imported into Egypt, as Egyptians found better jobs abroad. Even if upward mobility was still exceptional, if only one out of twenty Egyptians had been able to buy cars and TV sets and approach the "good life" so explicitly depicted on local TV soaps, the example served to encourage hundreds of thousands of others.

Egypt has tried state socialism and free enterprise and, under President Mubarak, a more careful mixture of both. It has experienced foreign rule and foreign patronage under the Turks, French, British, Russians, and now the Americans. "Can we survive the Americans?" one of our old and more sanguine Egyptian friends asked at a dinner one night.

"You mean because of the peace treaty with Israel?" an American student asked.

"No," he said. "I mean because of the corruption, the money being made on AID contracts, the get-rich-fast attitudes."

But not all the money flowing into the pockets of Egyptians comes from American assistance; most of this aid, under U.S. law, must be used to buy American goods and services in any case. By 1983 over $3 billion of hard currency was estimated to be coming into Egypt each year from migrant workers, an amount greater than any other source of foreign exchange. Although the male migration rate was leveling off, the female migration rate was rising, as the demand for teachers, nurses, and maids in the oil-rich countries increased. This unexpected injection of wealth had the added virtue of bypassing governments and going directly into the pockets of the people who earned the money. The resourcefulness and ingenuity of Egyptians has always made a difference in the unfavorable ratio between the resources of the country and the needs of its people. Of course, the inevitable result of labor migration spending, labor shortages, and higher wages is inflation. Millions of Egyptians are hard-pressed to maintain minimum standards of living and as a result depend on government subsidies of basic food as well as on their own arduous efforts to keep whole families at work, often at several jobs at once. A slight rise in the price of bread resulted in rioting in Cairo in 1977 with the burning of nightclubs and other symbols of wealth. The specter of uncontrollable disorder was clearly presented to Sadat's government and its American security advisers. Thus, it seems doubtful that a rise in basic food prices will be permitted again.

American patronage has been a limited success so far, providing capital for joint business ventures, foreign job openings, opportunities of making money in foreign banks, and a limited range of other possibilities in the local economy's Westernized sector. But Egypt is not a Western country and never will be. In mosques and private homes hundreds of thousands of young men and women look with disfavor on what they regard as the moral corruption associated with Western-inspired prosperity. They regard peace with Israel as a betrayal of Muslim brotherhood, and they see the Israeli presence as a return to infidel colonialism, with only token differences. The mild optimism we sensed among working- and lower-middle-class Egyptians we knew, as well as among the younger, educated men like Murad, could quickly disappear, given a loss of job opportunities abroad, a decline in Egypt's current limited prosperity.

The Islamic advocates of radical reform, of return to government based on Islamic principles, are waiting in the background for an opportunity to press their case. Whether their outlook is practical or hopelessly utopian has yet to be determined. But their case is not unappealing to the majority of their fellow citizens. For in many ways the Egyptian community is a classic example of human strengths and limitations. Hard as they might try to expand their economy (and they have tried with the High Dam, with the renovation of the Suez Canal), Egyptians have limited national resources. In the modern era of great-power struggles and international market systems, Egypt as a country has little control over its fate. A drop in international oil prices, for example, would send Egyptian workers home, a prospect that looked possible by the summer of 1983.

But Egypt, after all, is not only rocks and sand and fertile fields.

Egypt is its people, who are, one official quipped, the burden of Egypt as well as the bearers of that burden. However, the Egyptians whom we had known in the sixties, whom we had seen again in the eighties, did not seem to have fallen into despair when contemplating their own personal futures. They were all—Omar, Aziza, Murad, Muhammad, Nabila, Dr. Laila—doing their best to survive creatively in circumstances not of their own making. In 1983 Egyptians were still finding places in the crowded city to have family picnics by the river, they were still telling ironic jokes about themselves and their leaders, they were still trying to achieve a stable and pleasant life for themselves and their families. Perhaps this personal hope bodes well for the nation.

Yet Egyptians as individuals can only do so much, and they know it. As Nabila once said to me, "We are all guests of God on this earth," and guests have responsibilities as well as privileges, not only to their hosts but to each other. Nabila and many others of her fellow citizens are beginning to wonder whether those responsibilities are being fulfilled as class differences increase in moderate Egypt.

LABOR MIGRATION, OLD AND NEW STYLES

*T*ODAY IN THE ARAB WORLD millions of people are traveling back and forth across national boundaries each year in search of work. This movement—labor migration on a historically unprecedented scale—is probably of greater long-term importance to the future of the area than the Arab-Israeli conflict, but it has thus far received little attention in the Western press. In the last two decades, oil wealth has transformed human labor in the Middle East into a marketable commodity to a degree that was scarcely foreseen a generation ago. At least three million Egyptians are working outside their native land; over a third of the Saudi Arabian labor force is made up of foreigners from many different countries. And the movement is not limited to blue-collar workers. Migrants include electricians, architects, stonemasons, farmers, doctors, teachers, plumbers, librarians, engineers, and administrative and clerical workers, as well as servants.

No planning preceded this new movement. Contemporary Arab labor migration is a grassroots phenomenon of unexpected scope and far-reaching consequences.

In 1959 it was commonly stated that Egyptian *fellaheen,* or peasants, would never leave Egypt, though the possibility was raised even then as the population crisis loomed. But in those days labor migrants were defined in roles already recognized in the area: traders, servants, artisans. Migration of the Arab population from the eastern shores of the Mediterranean, for example, was well established before the beginning of the twentieth century. Syrian-Lebanese traders were among the first traveling salesmen in the Third World, the first to transport and sell industrial manufactured goods to customers in Africa and South America. As front-line representatives of the new capitalist mercantilism, they worked shoulder-to-shoulder with the missionaries and the colonial administrators. Some of these traders eventually returned home to retire in Lebanon or Syria. But others settled permanently in colonially administered lands and new nations, where they live to this day; in Spanish settings they are still called *sirio* or *turco* families.

Mercantile migration has also been a long-standing pattern among Yemenis, who shipped goods by dhow to the shores of East Africa and across the Indian Ocean in export-import businesses that were family-owned and -operated. Within Egypt, nineteenth-century records show that Nubians came to Cairo and Alexandria from their homes a thousand miles away in the south. They worked as servants, cooks, doormen. Saidis, natives of Upper Egypt, became the fruit salesmen/brokers of Egypt's northern cities. But these highly traditionalized forms of labor migration, preindustrial in origin, created little stir, as the numbers were relatively small, the practice developed gradually, and the resulting social contacts were limited.

Modern Middle East migration bears little resemblance to these earlier forms. To begin with, the number of people involved is enormous, some say up to four million or more. Secondly, the migrants' wages are high, often two or three times an average home-country salary. And demand exists for all skills. Rich countries such as Saudi Arabia, Kuwait, and Libya want the advantages of advanced technology and science now, and they want the services that must accompany such technology, so that the material benefits can be enjoyed to the fullest. They are willing to pay well. Thus, farmers from the Nile Delta, paid two hundred dollars a month plus expenses, work side by side with Saudi Bedouin who are trying to establish new farms. Before the Gulf War, a skilled construction worker from Egypt could earn forty dollars a day in Iraq, an unskilled worker nineteen dollars. Egypt is also the only Arab country with a surplus of college-educated men and women, thanks to Gamal Abdel Nasser's open-door university policy of the sixties. Thus, Egyptian schoolteachers, along with many displaced Palestinians, still staff the thousands of new schools and universities that have opened in the oil-rich states during the last two decades.

The new labor movement that has been developing since the mid-seventies is also radically different from the post–World War II pattern of Arab migration to Europe from Algeria, Morocco, and Tunisia. North African migrants, like all workers moving from less developed to more developed countries, have generally filled blue-collar jobs and therefore have had limited relationships with the resident population. Arabs in France live within communities of their own, in low-income districts. In Aix-en-Provence, a rich provincial town in the south, social intercourse between the Arabs and the French is at a minimum. The

Algerians and the Moroccans clean the streets and perform much of the town's heavy menial labor but, except for taking orders from their employers, have little opportunity for social exchanges. Even the workers' special needs in terms of food and bread are filled by small Arab-run stores. An Algerian man or sometimes an entire Arab family may occasionally occupy a bench in the public squares and parks of the city, but none are found in the chairs of the chic cafés that line the Cours Mirabeau. While some cross-cultural contact does take place among younger people, French residents and foreign tourists can live in Aix, as in many other cities of France or Belgium, practically unaware of the significant Arab component in the population. A similar pattern is found with regard to Turkish workers in Germany and Scandinavia.

But in Saudi Arabia the situation is very different. Representatives of many nationalities, who often share the same language or religious faith, encounter each other every day. In a Saudi Arabian city the barbershop may be staffed by an Indian from Madras while the corner grocery is owned by Pakistanis, as is the nearby catering service. A Yemeni may run a restaurant next door to an Egyptian establishment. Shirts are tailor-made by Delhi Indians. School is taught by Egyptians and Palestinians. All day Pakistanis in bright yellow uniforms patrol the streets, picking up trash, including throwaway plastic and glass bottles which have no more value in Saudi Arabia than in America. Throughout Saudi cities, houses of reinforced concrete and cement blocks are being built, plastered, wired, and painted by Tunisians and Egyptians. A Palestinian doctor, educated in Lebanon, does physical checkups; an Algerian dentist fills teeth. Business in the offices of a government that dispenses money to its citizens through a complicated system of grants and subsidies may be conducted jointly by a Saudi citizen and an Egyptian administrator, though the supervisor will always be a Saudi. In short, Saudis are in constant contact with people of many nations, and Saudi public life is filled with male foreigners, mostly alone, and most of them in the prime of their lives. (Thus, it is perhaps not surprising that the present king has assumed a more conservative attitude toward the already limited public roles permitted to Saudi women.)

The new pattern of migration of all kinds of workers has had different effects on the migrants' home countries. Egypt is suffering from severe labor shortages, particularly of skilled artisans such as plumbers and electricians. Construction sites remain unfinished. And although the loss is perhaps less obvious, some of the finest intellectual talent has left for better-paying jobs in other parts of the Arab world. The family life of migrants is obviously affected. Wives whose husbands are abroad on two- or three-year contracts find themselves running households, shops, or farms alone for the first time, as well as managing a significant cash flow of remittances. Other male members of the absent husband's family, however, are likely to be more involved in spending those remittances than would be customary in the United States. In Egypt the consumerist binge has become a part of life at all but the poorest levels of the society. Egyptian television, now accessible to more than two-thirds of the population, has primed the consumer demand with its commercials and its soap operas depicting prosperous Egyptians living in comfortable homes filled with modern appliances. Migrant workers' earnings are often used to buy cars, refrigerators, washing machines, television sets. Mud-brick homes in rural villages are being replaced with cement and fired-brick houses. The infusion of foreign salaries has fueled the rise of inflation, and many local incomes have not kept up with the cost of living. Thus, talented government workers find themselves tempted to join the ranks of labor migrants or, failing that, must take on two or three jobs in Egypt to make ends meet.

Labor migration in the Middle East today is distinctive in still another way: it exists outside of direct political control. Though some border restrictions are enforced, particularly between Egypt and Saudi Arabia, and migrants are supposed to have official work contracts and visas, thousands of workers slip across borders each month. Even the deteriorating relations between Libya and Egypt did not affect the flow of labor migrants, nor did the diplomatic freeze placed on Egypt by other Arab countries after its recognition of Israel. Before the Gulf War, scores of workers lined up at the Iraqi Interests Section in Cairo each day to apply for work visas. International labor migration has become a necessity for both giver and receiver countries, a reality with which Arab political leaders must live, whether they like it or not.

The result of this massive new movement of human beings will be, in the view of one Egyptian social scientist, "a new social order." The sharing of everyday life by people for whom no language barrier exists and among whom Islam is a common faith is producing a new international Arab community of a far more substantive nature than that conceived by Gamal Abdel Nasser, who popularized the idea of political Pan-Arabism. Public opinions are currently being created which every Arab national politician will have to consider in the years to come. A recognition of common economic interests and a sense of common Muslim identity are becoming evident. In the future, such developments may come to supersede sectarian and national differences.

In this way night dies
with the sun springing to mount the sky
and the streets inhaling
the sounds of din,
braziers of light spilling
illumination to make shadows
piercing the stones.

Salah Abd al-Sabur
EXPECTATIONS: NIGHT AND DAY

THE CAIRO SUBWAY has now been in continuous operation for nearly ten years, confounding the critics who said it could never happen. This pioneer system, the first in the Middle East and Africa, carries close to a million passengers each day along its twenty-five miles of well-maintained lines. It cuts north and south, sometimes pushing deep underground, but more often climbing up, into the sunlight, to race along what used to be the bed of the old Cairo tramlines and commuter trains.

As with subways in other great cities of the world, the names of the subway stops not only indicate places (Maadi, Marg) but also mark old and new institutions (Ein Shams University, the Sayyida Zeinab mosque). The stops also note Egypt's recent history. Riders who alight and depart at the Saad Zaghlul station are reminded every day of the man who led the Wafd Party and the Egyptian independence movement and became, in 1923, the first popularly elected prime minister in Egypt. (His name is also attached to a whole series of popular adages for survival. In the face of calamity, the victim is reminded that "Saad Zaghlul said . . . ," presumably a solution to whatever problem has been posed.) And the three central subway stops carry the names of those men (Gamal Abdel Nasser, Anwar Sadat, and Hosni Mubarak) who have ruled Egypt since it cast off monarchy and British protectorate status in 1952 and declared itself a republic.

Given this pattern of naming, it is not surprising that the hub of the subway lies beneath Midan al-Tahrir, Liberation Square, the marching field of British troops which Nasser converted into a public square. It was then bounded by the river Nile, the Egyptian Antiquities Museum, the Kasr al-Nil bridge, the old Semiramis Hotel, and the American University. The new Nile Hilton Hotel went up soon after Egypt's declaration of independence, and Nasser added to the Mugamma, or people's gathering place for official business. Thus Midan al-Tahrir was an obvious place from which the new president could deliver his regular speeches to the Egyptian people, standing high on a central platform, which we expected, like everyone else in those early heady, hopeful days of the fifties and sixties, would soon boast a ceremonial bronze statue of the father of modern Egypt.

But before a statue could be raised in his honor, Nasser suffered a series of disasters. His popularity declined as the process of state socialism did not proceed as planned, and as he then began to silence his critics with ever more stringent arrests and jailings—even torture, it was rumored. One of the last jokes told about Nasser before his death in 1970 dealt with his growing reputation as a dictator who cooked the ballot box and brooked no public expression of opposition. The joke goes like this:

Nasser is irritated at his critics. He asks the secret police to find the man who is making up jokes about his declining popularity, about the problems that ordinary citizens are encountering. After a long search, a very old man is found, and brought to the Presidential Palace.

"So," says Nasser, "you're the one who makes up all these jokes?"

"Some of them, yes, sir."

"Some of them?" thunders Nasser. "Did you make up the one about the price of meat?"

"Yes, sir."

"And the army officers?"

"Yes, sir."

"And the one which said I won the popular vote of the Egyptian people by ninety-nine and forty-four one hundredths percent of the vote?"

"Not that one, sir. You made that up."

After Anwar Sadat came to power and opened up the economy to foreign investment, creating an early illusion of economic and political freedom, people said, "Sadat is the one who'll have the statue in Midan al-Tahrir, you watch and see." But it did not happen. Nor is there a representation in the square of Hosni Mubarak, who succeeded Sadat after his 1981 assassination, and who still, as of 1996, rules Egypt. The pedestal in Midan al-Tahrir was actually removed, with the lawns and flowers of the square, to make room for the construction equipment that signaled the beginning of the subway.

Today the Midan has no real symbolic center; it has been given over to traffic, a gesture toward solving the public transportation problems of the exploding city. The underground stairway to the subway is marked on the western perimeter, and taxis and buses throng the traffic circle, turning into the scores of bus lanes, marked with small green and yellow awnings to shade the passengers, who wait, at all times of the day, to get a ride home. The subway fare is about eight cents, but the bus is half that, the cheapest and most crowded ride in town.

But pedestal or no pedestal, Mubarak, Nasser, and Sadat are immortalized (at least for the moment) by the subway stops, which is more than can be said of Egypt's earlier rulers. The subway history is a selective history: there is no station for Abdine Palace, where the kings of the Mohammed Ali dynasty lived, and none for Mohammed Ali, or King Fouad, or the last king of Egypt, Farouk, peacefully deposed in 1952.

The success of the subway is a salutary lesson for those old observers and residents, Egyptian and foreign, who, like ourselves, laughed when the subway project was proposed a quarter of a century ago.

"Subway!" I remember myself saying, though I am embarrassed to report it now. "How can they do it?"

"By tunneling under the center of the city," returned our British friend Christopher, who added, "but they can't do it. No way. The word is there's no map of the utilities and sewer lines put in by my countrymen. Look at the problems without the subway!"

Several people had pointed out what seemed obvious at the time. If the Egyptian authorities could not locate enough of the system to stop the regular explosions of sewage in the 1960s and had to cover them with five-foot-high towers in the middle of the streets, how were they going to be able to track a path for a complex subway?

Despite such dire predictions, however, the subway project was launched with some fanfare in the eighties, and the trains began to run in 1987, after many problems, as expected. The tangle of utility, water, and sewage lines under Midan al-Tahrir had not been mapped, it was true. So the engineers simply set about doing it.

"Take a ride on it," friends said to us in 1996. "Or are you still afraid it will collapse?"

"Not at all," replied Bob stoutly, and we accordingly took the stairs down to the Sadat station in Midan al-Tahrir and tried to buy tickets for Maadi.

"Where in Maadi?" asked the ticket seller politely. "There are three stops there."

Bob had to explain exactly where we were going, and the ticket seller advised us to get off at Sekanat al-Maadi.

Three stops in Maadi? How could that be? We remembered Maadi as a quiet, treelined suburb, where foreigners, particularly foreign nationals, chose to live, because of its distance from the center of Cairo. We had turned down an opportunity to rent there, because we wanted to be nearer to the center of the action. But some of the same Egyptians we knew then had moved to Maadi, because, they said, "the air is cleaner." It was farther from the noxious auto fumes that rolled up into Cairo's morning-blue sky and turned it dull and smoggy by noon.

The subway walls were bare of advertisements and also of graffiti. The entries, the stairs, and the platforms were so clean they easily put the New York subway to shame.

"Police patrol this place seriously," said Ted Swedenburg, a professor at the American University. And I remembered that one of our students in Texas, while studying Arabic in Cairo, had actually been fined fifteen pounds, about four dollars, not a trifling sum, for spitting into the ditch through which the tracks ran, gleaming, over the dark earth.

I declined to sit alone in the women-only carriage, but joined Bob and Ted in a full car, where we stood up, holding onto leather straps attached to the stainless-steel rails (also clean). We were the only obvious non-Egyptians in the car. At the second stop, the Sayyida Zeinab mosque, an old man in a crumpled suit stood up and offered me his seat, glancing reproachfully at the younger man next to him, who sat without moving. But when I slid onto the bench with a heartfelt thank-you, the young man rose, making his way to the back of the car. That empty seat was quickly occupied by two teenage girls, one in a head scarf and one without, who squeezed together into the single seat, stared openly at me for several minutes, and then struck up a conversation.

"How are you?"

"Fine. How are you?" I replied.

"What country do you come from?"

"America."

They giggled. "You speak Arabic?"

"A little."

They giggled again. "Why?" asked the one in the head scarf. "Don't they speak English in America?"

"Yes, but we have lived in the Arab world, so we tried to learn Arabic."

"Did you live in Egypt?"

"Yes, for six years."

The girl without the head scarf wore beige. Her black hair curled all around her face and reached to the center of her back; she clapped her hands over her mouth. "Six years! And you lived in other Arab countries?"

"Yes. Morocco. Iraq."

The two girls whispered together. "Which country," said the one in a head scarf, white, over a black and white print dress, "which country is the most beautiful?"

The train slowed its smooth progress and slid into the Mar Girgis station, the Coptic church of St. George. This was where I had brought my mother and my aunt Mary long ago to visit the nearby church of St. Sergius, where, according to legend, the Virgin and child had taken refuge after their flight to Egypt, and supposedly spent a month in the church's crypt. I stared out the window, but of course there was nothing to see except the neat platform, the blue sign lettered in white, like the Paris Métro, and crowds of people moving forward, their forms blurred by the movement of the train.

"*Madame?*" The girl's voice brought me back to the present.

"Yes?"

"So which country is more beautiful, Egypt, Morocco, or Iraq?"

This was a question that had been posed to us hundreds of times in our many years of travel and residence in the Arab world, and we had a stock reply.

"Each country," I said, "is beautiful in its own way."

The girls nodded and smiled. "She's a diplomat, a politician," said the one with the long, curling dark hair.

"Like Mubarak," put in the one with the head scarf. She giggled and waited for my response. "You don't know Mubarak, *madame*?"

"Yes," I answered. "He's president of Egypt."

"And he loves America, they give him lots of money, right?" persisted the girl in the head scarf.

I caught Bob's eyes, as he stood there holding onto the subway strap and looking amused. How was I going to reply to this one?

"Well, that's what they say," I finally got out.

The two girls looked at each other, smothered more giggles, and turned back to me.

"And where do you go now, *madame*, with your husband?" said the girl with the long, dark curly hair.

"Sekanat Maadi, to visit friends," I answered.

"We live in Helwan," said the one in the head scarf. "We work there."

"And," said the other girl, "here's your stop, *madame*. Have a nice time in Egypt!" She got out the last phrase in an accented English such as guides use with tourists. Well, I told myself sternly, we *are* tourists now, no longer residents, and have not been for many years.

Helwan is the town south of Cairo where in the fifties President Nasser chose to situate the first iron and steel factory. The factory not only signaled Egypt's debut as a member of the modern industrial world, it created thousands of jobs for immigrants to the city.

Those were the years when people were pouring in from the rural areas, attracted by the possibility of wage labor, daily wages that would replace the uncertain income from the agricultural land that had fragmented into smaller and smaller plots, through the divisions of inheritance. Even Nasser's land reform program, taking from the large landowners and assigning land to peasants, did not stay the migration to the city for long. By 1996 Helwan was a city of 350,000 and marked the farthest southern stop on the subway.

The northern branch of the subway ends at Marg, a prosperous village which was once the home of King Fouad's sister Princess Nimet, who had lands and houses there. The lands have long since been reassigned and the house of Princess Nimet is now a government agricultural cooperative office. Hassan Aziz Hassan, nephew of Princess Nimet and one of our friends who most derided the idea of the subway, announced that he had actually ridden out all the way to this relative's former home.

"A very nice ride, really, one has to say so," Hassan told us. "But I could not believe how all that country, that used to have trees and grain fields, is now covered with houses, and more houses."

"They're making baked brick out of the farmland," pointed out Bob. "A real tragedy."

But what to do? People need houses, and according to present scenarios, agriculture should no longer be the principal means of subsistence.

Latest government plans call for an extension of the subway into the northwest working-class section of Shubra, and southwest to Giza, on the road to the pyramids. Construction has already begun to help ease the continuing and acute problems of human transport.

The success of the Cairo subway also challenges the received wisdom about Egypt: *"plus ça change, plus ça reste la même chose"* (the more things change, the more they remain the same). This old French adage is often quoted by international consultants, travel writers, and even by Egyptians themselves. It suggests that nothing changes in Egypt, home of the pyramids and the sphinx; Egypt is eternal (but also static).

Egyptians, however, like our old friend Aziza meant something quite specific when they quoted this adage. It applies to the people, she would say. No matter what physical changes take place, no matter what new challenges they are forced to accept, Egyptian people will remain the same—adaptive, resilient, creative, hardworking, and above all, humorous. "Egyptians," Aziza would tell us, "in contrast to most other people, have *dem al-khafeef*, or light blood." Having *dem al-khafeef* means that one has a wry, good-humored view of the world, a view that includes an ability to laugh at oneself.

"Russians have *dem al-thageel*, heavy blood," Aziza would explain.

"And Americans?"

She would eye me in a good-humored, *dem al-khafeef* way and allow that Americans were in between. "Some are lighthearted, and some are not."

It was this characteristic of self-mockery, Aziza felt, that gave Egyptians their special—and she felt unchangeable—quality.

But international planners and policy-makers with business to do in Egypt use the adage in a less pleasant way to comment on what they see as Egyptian inability to fully participate in the modern, industrial world into which they have been thrust by global politics. The sharpest example of the way this assumption is implemented in actual practice is the way in which USAID is administered.

In 1979, when the Camp David peace treaty was signed between Egypt and Israel, the United States, in recognition of the fact that peace has a price, promised each country $3 billion in annual aid, a grant that continues until this day. Equal allotments. But not equal implementation. Israel receives its $3 billion in a single check at the beginning of each fiscal year, a check that may be deposited immediately and that accrues valuable interest. The underlying assumption is that Israelis know how to use the money in rational and useful ways of which the United States would clearly approve.

Egypt, on the other hand, is not given a single check. It must earn its $3 billion, by writing and submitting scores of small proposals to justify its projected spending. The United States must approve each request, and thousands (a whole army) of American administrators and clerks and grant writers now live in Cairo to deal with this one AID program. The underlying assumption is that Egypt is incapable of rationally planning for the "proper" use of its AID grant, proper (as defined by the United States) for a country that is still, as one AID administrator said at a party, "corrupt and in the dark ages when it comes to understanding its country's needs." Is Israel, then, not corrupt? The point, of course, is that the United States sees itself as knowing Egypt's best interests better than Egypt itself, a country still stuck in the past, encumbered by that old deterrent to progress, the dead hand of Islam.

Bob and I told ourselves that it was our dear friend Aziza with whom we agreed on this issue. Obviously, Egypt had changed, Cairo was not the same, but the Egyptian people had not changed. But, as we walked about the streets of Cairo and crossed the bridges on the walkway over the Nile, we began to realize that we did not want to face just exactly how drastically Cairo, and Egypt, had changed. We should have known that memory, misted over as it often is with the sentimentality of youth, was a faulty lens through which to view the changed city, its tumultuousness, its complexities, its troubles.

Was it true that thirty-six years had passed since we arrived in Cairo on a hot summer night, the city where our three children were born, where Bob held his first teaching job, where we had observed with interest and participated indirectly in what we thought then, like many others, was the birth, under Gamal Abdel Nasser, of a new kind of Egyptian society, proud, independent, self-reliant?

What had happened to that hope, that idealism? And what had happened to the city? Cairo was familiar, yes, like our second home, but it was hard to discern any traces of that calm, hopeful city of the fifties and sixties in the overcrowded, blaring, noisy, smoggy metropolis, with its multiple bridges and overpasses, where cars could not always manage to move along the streets, which were clogged with pedestrians.

Huda Zurayk and Barbara Ibrahim of the Population Council were quick to point out, when I asked this question, that 5.5 million people had occupied that calm old city in 1965. By 1996 the population had swelled to 15 million.

"That's the official figure," said a young researcher at the Population Council. She went on to explain that yes, perhaps 15 million was the number of people who actually slept in Cairo every night, but that at least 1 or maybe even 2 million more commuted into the city every day from nearby towns and cities. Bob's old friend Adel al-Zein, an Alexandria businessman, came to Cairo once a week, boarding the bus to Cairo, doing his business, lunching with old friends in the Automobile Club, and returning to Alexandria in time for a late dinner at home. It wasn't just clerks and blue-collar workers who commuted.

"Yes, it's bigger, it's exploding even, physically," said our friend Dr. Laila Shoukri al-Hamamsy, retired now both from her job with the International Labor Organization and as director of the Social Research Center at the American University. "But the people are the same. This is an old, old culture."

She was repeating what Aziza had said years ago.

"Doesn't it seem, Bob, rather remarkable to you," she continued, "that in this hot, noisy, overcrowded city, people are still relatively polite? Do you see any fights on the street, I mean?"

Bob shook his head.

"And you're still safe on the streets here, even at night. Our crime rate is some incredibly low figure, I always forget exactly what it is."

"Yes," I agreed. "I do feel safe here, even with the so-called Islamist attacks."

Dr. Laila tossed that one off. "The government is handling that, finally. After all, not one incident took place during the recent international population conference. And there were hundreds of foreigners. *That's* quite an achievement for any government, Islamist or not Islamist."

"But, Laila, nobody seems to tell jokes anymore."

Laila laughed. "Well, maybe not to you, my dears, most of the new Mubarak jokes are, as they say, unprintable. But let me tell you the one about . . ." She proceeded to regale us with several stories which caused the dignified diners in the old Automobile Club to glance in our direction, we were laughing so loudly.

The elderly waiter paused and told her that a special dessert was available today. Laila ordered it for all of us.

"An Egyptian specialty, they say it's from Turkey, you must try it."

It came in small clay custard cups, still warm from the oven, a pudding with a base, not of eggs and milk, but pumpkins and raisins and spices. Pumpkin crème brûlée, maybe? We savored it silently. How many years had we been in Egypt and never even heard of this dessert?

"And, Bob," said Laila in parting, putting her hands on Bob's arm, "don't underestimate the Egyptians today. On any count. Even the jokes . . . they're everywhere. Sign of a really sophisticated and ancient culture that knows itself well enough to laugh at itself."

"Everywhere?" I echoed.

"Yes, in the cinema, in the drama, in the literature, in the newspapers every day. Look at that comedy *Zaim*, about an unnamed ruler. It's been playing for two years in a theater on the Giza road."

Of course, she was right about jokes in the media, and in the cinema, about the Egyptian penchant for satirizing themselves and their leaders, for mocking pomposity, in order to make light of the problems facing them. *Terrorism and Kebab* was a good example, one of the most popular films in recent Egyptian history, which ran for nearly two years in Cairo before traveling to the provinces. We saw it one night in Cairo.

Terrorism and Kebab made fun of three current issues troubling all Egyptians: the government's struggle to deal with the Islamic opposition; the high price of meat; and the difficulty of accomplishing any official act that requires a visit to the Mugamma, the so-called people's building which rises twelve crescent-shaped stories on Midan al-Tahrir. The Mugamma is where births and deaths are recorded, where visas are issued, where resident permits are given and taken away, where political asylum is granted to foreigners, where the average Egyptian must come if he wishes to do something as small and important as changing the school assigned to his or her children.

The story of the film was simple but revealing. Adel Iman, Cairo's most popular comic actor, played a sober middle-class family man trying to get official permission to shift his children from one school to the other. But at each visit, clocked in by gate guards, maneuvering the labyrinthine stairways and crowded passages of the Mugamma, our hero fails to get the attention of the proper official. Why? That gentleman is constantly praying, and hence cannot be disturbed. After numerous polite attempts have failed, the hero becomes so enraged that he grabs the Islamist gentleman's staff.

"Terrorism!" cries the holy man, setting off a chain reaction that eventually isolates Iman and several other disaffected petitioners on the top floor of the Mugamma. When the police and the governor and the terrorism squad gather below in Midan al-Tahrir to ask the terrorists to enunciate their demands, the characters look at each other and realize they are hungry! They demand "kebab, made from the best-quality lamb meat." The officials deputized to deal with "terrorism" are sure that this request is a hidden message of some sort, but eventually the "terrorists" get their kebab, and the movie ends happily. Everyone files peacefully out of the building, no one is jailed, and one of the petitioners murmurs to Iman on the way out, "Well, at least we got a decent meal of kebab out of it!"

Humor and courtesy have always been two Egyptian methods for dealing with the travails of everyday life, methods that are recorded at the time of the pharaohs. But of course they do not solve the problems they ridicule or gently chide. They merely make those problems bearable. And today many Egyptians, particularly young Egyptians, are arguing that stronger measures than satire are needed to improve what they see as a worsening economic and political situation in the country. Per capita income is still an estimated $750, as opposed to $1,100 in Jordan and $2,300 in Syria. The compulsory free education that was such a heralded and much appreciated plank of Nasser's government plans, which was to give Egypt the highest literacy rate in the Arab world, has slowed. Overall literacy is about 48 percent, below Jordan's 80 percent and Syria's 64 percent. Young people have found their earlier expectations of social mobility frustrated. The advent of television has brought images of luxury consumer goods into every Egyptian home, stimulating the desire for better shoes, clothes, furniture. It is clear to everyone in Egypt that something must be done to strengthen the beleaguered middle class, who are often working at two or three jobs to keep families and lifestyles together; and to stop the widening gap between rich and poor which Nasser struggled so hard to reduce forty years ago. The question at issue is the means to achieve this end.

"Islam Is the Answer" was the slogan used on the banners of opposition candidates in the 1995 parliamentary elections, echoing the sentiments delivered in sermons, in the mosques, and published on bumper stickers. The stated goal of the Islamists, they said, was to achieve a just society, and the means they offered to reach that end were twofold. First, Egypt must reject the Western secularism that has enslaved the nation for a century, causing a long decline in the indigenous beliefs and moral strengths that had earlier led to Egyptian political as well as moral ascendancy. Second, Egypt must embrace Islam as the basis of all life—government, law, economics, and social interaction.

The Islamist candidates' posters were not hung in Zamalek or Dokki, the presumed bases of the rich secularists and leftists, but were plastered on walls in the old quarters of the city, near the Al-Azhar mosque, in the back streets of Jamaliyah, and in working-class areas like Shubra and Imbaba. The majority of the candidates pictured on the posters were men in neat beards, some in skullcaps, and the qualifications listed on the broadsides included medical degrees, doctorates in engineering, philosophy, theology. The bona fides cited by the candidates suggested to the voters that they, the candidates, had succeeded in combining Islamic religious belief with Western technological knowledge, both needed to bring Egypt into the modern world.

But on the streets of Cairo it is not men, but women, who can be said to visually represent the idea that Islam is the answer, women in head scarfs, long, flowing loose dresses, and a few with face veils.

"Do you see more Islamic dress than when you were here before?" Nawal Sirry asked me when I went to visit her. She was the news director for Egyptian television, whom we had interviewed in our 1982 film *A Veiled Revolution*.

I shook my head. "Not really." Then I paused. "But maybe more head coverings like yours."

It was true. Nawal Sirry did not cover her head when we interviewed her on film, but her head was covered now, even in her sitting room, where we drank tea and ate excellent chocolate nut cakes!

"Yes, I decided to at last," she acknowledged with a smile. "It took me a long time, but I am happy now that I am doing it."

"I haven't seen the complete cover-up, though, with veil and gloves, like I did in 1981."

"That's kind of died down," admitted Mrs. Sirry. "There may be a few but they tend to stay at home."

I showed her an article from the Western press, stating that nearly ninety percent of Egyptian women were wearing Islamic dress! She read it carefully. "Where did they get these figures?" she asked.

I said I had no idea.

She smiled. "Of course, I'm sure the Islamists would be happy if this is true," she said. "But it's not. And as a journalist myself, I object to this kind of undocumented presentation. How can they call themselves responsible?"

"What percentage would you say?"

Mrs. Sirry got up and walked around her small parlor, looked out the window, came back, and sat down.

"Fifty percent covering their heads, that's kind of a given now," she said. "It's taken for granted. And maybe another ten or fifteen percent who go further, covering up more, but ninety percent? No! Absolutely no!"

And not all women covering up are like Madame Sirry, who took seriously the decision of whether or not to wear Islamic dress.

Many women good-naturedly admit that pragmatism is an underlying motive; "One receives respect if one covers one's head," said a student. In the crowded city, that is important in the workplace, at the university, and on the bustling streets.

"But would all those women vote for Islamist candidates?" I asked a political analyst at Cairo University.

"No, no, not at all. And some who do not cover might! Cairenes are still very independent in these matters. We're a majority of Muslims here. Not everyone thinks the same! That's one of the problems the West has. I am continually asked," he added, "what is the typical Egyptian?"

"And what do you say?"

"That it's a silly question. There is no typical Egyptian." He smiled. "But maybe it's easier to think about this complicated place if you can put people in pigeonholes."

"No typical characteristics?"

He laughed. "I know what you are expecting," he said. "And you're right. All Egyptians tell jokes—but not, B.J., about religious belief."

Militant Islam? Another wave of violence? The general feeling among Egyptians and foreign observers is that this militancy is declining at the moment. Not surprising considering the time, effort, money, and brutal methods employed by the Mubarak government to put it down. But the issue of Islamist-based political representation has not gone away; the Islamists want a share of the action, a say in the direction of Egypt, "which is indeed their right in a democracy, is it not?" asked Bob.

"What do they want, though?" returned Egyptians, young and old.

The paradox is that the Islamists criticize the secularists who hold power under Mubarak for being too Western. But the secularists insist that they are Muslims, too, and, with a small minority of Coptic Christians, want to govern Egypt in a more open and liberal way than that which the Islamists propose. However, the degree of complexity greatly exceeds this paradox, because there are many kinds of so-called secularists and many differences in political views among Muslims. And of course, Egypt is still controlled by its military.

Of central concern to both sides, secularist and Islamist, is the state of the Egyptian economy, and all of the political candidates bemoaned its sad state. It came as something of a shock to us to hear Egyptians still refer to their country as "an economic basket case," the epithet derisively applied to Egypt in the past by the British, the French, and then the Americans. We heard the phrase in 1959, when we arrived in Cairo, and again in 1981 and 1991. Surely this could not be seriously said about a country of 62 million people that has, in our lifetime, changed from a rural agricultural society to a primarily urban-based economy, and one that is now, for better or for worse, part of a regional and global economic system.

I posed the recurring "basket case" stereotype to Dr. Heba Handoussa, executive director of the Economic Research Forum, a new regional consortium funded by both public and private money to take a long-term look at the economy across the Middle East, from Morocco to Iran and Turkey.

Dr. Handoussa had agreed to meet us because we are friends of her old school friend Laila Ahmed. "You don't remember, but I met you both in Oregon at the MESA meetings in 1992," she said. "Laila introduced us at the panel on E. W. Lane's work."

I was embarrassed to admit that I didn't remember that specific moment, but Dr. Handoussa did not seem too offended.

"Economic basket case?" she repeated. "Yes, people do ask me about that view, and my answer is 'What do you mean by the phrase?'"

I thought for a moment. It seemed obvious. "It means that Egypt is on the verge of bankruptcy, I guess."

"And the corollary?"

"The corollary?"

"Since Egypt is on the verge of bankruptcy, it needs the West, the International Monetary Fund, the World Bank, to tell Egypt how to get out of her own mess, right?"

"Well." This was not quite the way I had expected the interview to proceed. "Let me rephrase my question."

Dr. Handoussa smiled. She was a slight, dark-haired woman in sober silk. Her dark deep-set eyes conveyed a formidable intelligence, but no emotion whatsoever until this smile. "No, no, my friend, that's all right. I just wanted to try that one out on you. What you must do, when you hear people speaking of Egypt as an economic basket case, is to ask what they're comparing it to? Russia? Japan? Latvia? Chad? The United States?"

I nodded. How obvious, I thought. Why don't people apply that criterion? I shook myself mentally, for Dr. Handoussa was talking.

"I remember," she said, "that the British used that figure of speech in the nineteenth century as an excuse to justify the takeover of Egypt. They said it was for the country's own good, of course, and it was true, that after the Khedive Ismail died in 1879, the country was greatly in debt."

"A lot?"

"Yes, indeed. Close to a hundred thousand pounds sterling, and that was a lot in those days."

"So the Brits had a point?"

Dr. Handoussa settled back in her chair and smiled that lightening smile again. She propped her elbow on the arm of her desk chair and rested her chin on her hand. I had the feeling that she was enjoying herself.

"Oh," she said. "The Brits. Yes, they pride themselves on their rational approach to the world. But what they ask for is not usually what they want. In this case, I think what they wanted was to get hold of the Suez Canal."

"And they did," I prompted.

"Until Nasser took it back in 1956. Remember how the Europeans fulminated when he did that? I was just a little girl then, but I remember my parents talking about it. It was big news for us!"

I remembered well the world media coverage at the time, 1956. We were on our way to Beirut, on a ship that was not allowed to dock in Alexandria harbor because of what was termed "riots in the streets over President Nasser's unprecedented action." The *Newsweek* story quoted the British canal administrators reassuring European stockholders that they were not to worry. "The gyppies won't be able to run it, too complex for their Eastern minds. They'll come running to us in a bit, you'll see."

"Yes, yes, I agree, whatever you say," joked Jillian Foster, Dr.

Handoussa's colleague, who came in with a tray of those delicious cups of Turkish coffee that all visitors to Egypt, like us, look forward to. "How's Laila Ahmed?" she asked. "We were all in school together, Heba and Laila and I, at the British School. Her book about women in Islam is good, don't you think?"

"It's good," I answered, but before we could get into that discussion, Dr. Handoussa brought us back.

"I'm just explaining to our guest," she said, "why that old chestnut, Egypt as economic basket case, makes me so mad!"

We both turned to her, sipping our coffee, as she sat forward in her chair.

"Everything must be seen in historic terms," she went on. "It's true that in those few years when the khedive died, and there was so much debt, Egypt might have been termed a kind of basket case. But there was nothing structurally wrong with the country. In fact, it was a land of opportunity in the Arab world, much as the U.S. was viewed by Europeans at the time."

She smiled again. I took notes busily.

"So structurally the place is falling apart now?" I knew I was being provocative, but Dr. Handoussa did not seem to mind.

"Structurally? We have a huge crisis in the twentieth century. Laila tells me you lived here . . ."

"Yes, in the Nasser years. We've been back regularly, though."

"When?"

I began to enumerate on my fingers the times: 1971 for a resettlement conference; Bob's research year in 1980–81 during which I made two films; Bob's year among the Nubians in 1990–91; and Bob's three years as chairman of the board of the American Research Center in Egypt, during which he came to Cairo annually, for a month.

"So you've seen things change?"

"A lot."

"And you still believe in that old adage of the French residents of Cairo, *tout ça change, tout ça reste la même chose?*"

"Not really," I said. "In the early sixties we studied Arabic with an old sheikh, and he once said, don't believe the French. Everything is changing. Egypt will never be the same!"

"Thank God!" enunciated Dr. Handoussa. It was her first expression of emotion. "Think what it was like long ago." She rummaged on her desk and came up with Lord Cromer's *History of Modern Egypt.* "Look at this sometime. Terrible poverty, and inequality, in a comparatively rich and lush country."

"Poverty and inequality are still there," I persisted.

Dr. Handoussa looked at me searchingly. "But not like it was in Cromer's time," she said. "Surely you don't believe that things have not improved."

I agreed that things had improved, but it seemed to me, coming back after five years, that things were getting difficult again.

"It's the structural problems I was talking about earlier," she offered. "We've had a kind of lopsided growth between population and every other national resource, like water, land. Every effort that is made is swallowed up quickly. There's very little room left to develop on . . ."

I asked about the new lands, the resettled areas and reclaimed areas west of Alexandria, about the Peace Canal that is supposed to allow several thousand more acres to be cultivated in the Sinai, considered in biblical times the most hostile environment in the world.

"Good signs. Hopeful signs. But water is still a problem. Look yourself as you go around and see old friends. I even think I've read something you or your husband wrote, somewhere . . ."

I was flattered, and said so.

"About the family network being at the root of the economic and social and political system here. It's true, you know. That's what has kept Egypt together but it's now being shaken up. That's what one must watch—the hopeful signs you've mentioned and the situation in the family. And water. Those are some of the future trends we are analyzing."

AGRICULTURE IS seldom mentioned in modern analyses of Egypt's economy, and crops and fodder are not the topics of conversation at elegant Cairo dinner parties. The talk there, among the elite, is of the Cairo stock exchange, of computer technology, of the possibility of more offshore oil strikes. It is true that the United States provides surplus wheat shipments to supplement Egypt's grain production, but one-third of the nation's foodstuffs are still raised in Egypt, and nearly half of the sixty-two million people live in the countryside, where they earn a living by working part-time or full-time as agriculturalists, as *fellaheen*. Bob had been told that since the High Dam farmers were being given water year-round, this had forced changes in the old agricultural techniques. What were farmers doing about it?

"Well, they're adapting," said our old friend Murad, when Bob posed the question. "They've been farming for thousands of years, so they're resourceful, don't worry."

"But what are they actually doing?" persisted Bob. "About drainage and fertilizer and new cropping patterns, for instance?"

"Come and see what I've been trying," Murad answered. "You and B.J. want to see the farm anyway, don't you?"

We nodded, pleased to be invited once more to the family *ezba* in the country, which nowadays seemed to be Murad's, not his father's, responsibility. In the early days, when Murad had given up his job in television production and expressed his desire to farm, his father was dubious and had insisted on being involved in almost every decision about the land. But no longer.

"My father's getting old," Murad said as we headed out of Cairo early one morning. "He doesn't do much with the farm these days. But you know my mother never was interested in it, anyway. She'd rather stay in Cairo and play with the grandchildren, my two girls and my sister's kids."

"So you're in charge?" Bob prompted.

"More or less," Murad agreed.

His hair was grayer than it had been fifteen years ago, but he was tanned and fit. The outdoor life clearly suited him.

"I'm farming the whole piece," he went on. "Some of my brother's and sister's land as well as mine and Father's. Almost fifty acres, a big spread in this part of the world. The soil's so damned good, it gives good return. Local small farmers can make it on three acres. I know an American probably wouldn't believe that, but it's true."

He added, laughing, "But I've given up chickens, Bob."

"Not profitable enough?"

"Profitable, but risky." He smiled at me in the rearview mirror. "And messy. You remember, B.J. You helped with the food and water when you were here before."

"So you tore down the chicken hatchery?"

Murad shook his head. "Why would I do that? It was a big investment. I've rented it out to a local guy, and he's raising chickens there now. The market's still good."

"And what are you into?"

"Rice, wheat, basic grains," said Murad. "Berseem as fodder for my water buffalo. I still have about thirty. I raise them for meat, not milk, now."

"They're still profitable?"

"Oh yeah. But the grain is the big challenge, with everything different since the dam. You'll see."

We were making good time on our way to the *ezba*, much better time than we expected, for Murad had nixed the morning snarl of traffic through central Cairo and taken the ring road, a new four-lane highway that circles the city and intersects, on the northeast rim, the highway to Ismailia and Suez.

"Big development plans for this area," remarked Murad, and I remembered Dr. Laila had talked about people building condominiums out here, and country houses. We passed a huge billboard advertising the Katawiya Heights Golf and Country Club and other signs offering land for new house development (fifteen-hundred-meter plots "at competitive prices"). A group of warehouses for the Egyptian army loomed up large beyond the projected golf club. Murad explained that we were on the border between Cairo and the governorate of Ayyoubia.

"Thank heavens, the farm is in the Cairo governorate," said Murad. "The Agricultural Ministry folks in the Cairo governorate are much more receptive to farmers' complaints than the ones in Ayyoubia."

"So what are you complaining about?"

"Big development, as usual," said Murad. "This time I think we've nailed a guy. He was really stupid. He was trying to build and sell houses fast, and he built over an irrigation canal, which affected the flow of water to several people's land, including mine."

"Maybe the guy didn't understand the agricultural process—if he was a city slicker, I mean," offered Bob.

Murad snorted. "Come on, Bob. Is there anyone over the age of six in any country who doesn't know that crops won't grow without water? He knew, all right. He just didn't want to bother checking the plans, and then it was too late." He paused. "But I registered an official complaint, along with several of my neighbors."

"Will the ministry people really do something?"

"Oh yes," said Murad. "They're coming next week, with lots of men, to break open the blocked canal. It'll be a big deal in the neighborhood. Serves him right."

"I'm surprised they'll do anything," said Bob.

"Land, my friend, is still sacred around here. And water. You're not supposed to hurt the land or the water supply, at least not let anyone see you doing it." He paused. "But it would have been so easy for him to just build a cement rise over the canal. It wouldn't have cost much. And it would have saved him a lot of trouble. Why didn't he do that?"

We had reached the turnoff, Burka al-Hajj, which Murad said was named for the *hajj*, the pilgrimage to Mecca. In the days of the camel caravans this bustling village was so far out of Cairo that it served as the first stop for Muslim pilgrims and their camels on their way to the sacred city. And then we saw an enormous sign, KAJMA, "a Japanese company," Murad explained, "which is working to renovate the Great Sphinx. They needed a place to warehouse their stuff, the machinery and everything. So they rented this man's land. Good deal for him. No work. But plenty of money."

"Murad," said Bob, "I thought you enjoyed farming. At least that's what you used to say."

"Yes, Bob, you're right, I do. But it's damned hard. Coming out here every day and then back to my family; I want to see my wife and kids every day. And if I don't get out here, the help thinks I'm being lazy, so they get lazy, too. It's interesting work, but no picnic."

"You're making money, though?"

"Not starving" was Murad's laconic comment as we maneuvered down the narrow dirt road that led to his house. I was almost thrown out of my place on the backseat as he pulled sharply to the right and off the road to avoid a farm cart, traveling fast, wooden wheels rattling over the ruts, two healthy donkeys pulling, two girls in the cart. One was standing up, driving, in a flowered ruffled dress and red head scarf, her pigtails flying; the other sat in the wagon with a baby. They shouted, and Murad shouted a greeting back.

We pulled up and parked near the house, which looked much the same as it had fifteen years earlier. Two stories. Yellow stone. Balconies with, I remembered, a fine view of the surrounding countryside. A rose garden, still there, but somewhat overgrown. Utilitarian outbuildings. Judging by the sound of cheeps and peeps from the hatchery, it was full of hungry growing chickens. The small mosque had a new brick minaret. Inside the house, the furnishings and mementos were reminders of Egypt's foreign relations over the past forty years, for Murad's father had been a diplomat under Nasser. He was in Africa for many years, which explained the tiger skins and the carved ebony figures; and in Thailand, where he bought the chairs of teakwood carved into the shapes of elephants.

Murad took three Pepsis out of the fridge and we sat down outside, on wicker chairs, shaded by a woven roof screen of palm fronds.

"Doesn't the mosque have a new minaret?" asked Bob as we drank our Pepsis.

Murad nodded. "Well, not really. It was here before, you just don't remember. Maybe the brick exterior is new."

"Your neighbors must admire you for what you do, Murad. The mosque. Serving the complaint, that helps you all . . ."

Murad looked at him. "Well, I doubt it. They don't understand what I'm doing. But I don't understand them either, scraping up this wonderful earth to make houses! So maybe we're even."

"Ah, Ali!" Murad said. "Good. Come meet my guests." It had taken Murad less than three minutes to down his Pepsi. He stood up, towering over the young man who had come up to us. Ali wore a white galabia and a scarf around his head.

"This is Ali," said Murad. "I'm training him as a kind of field foreman."

Bob stood up and shook the hand of the young man, who nodded at me and looked away. There was a short silence.

"I fired the other one," said Murad, though Bob hadn't asked. "He was stealing from the help. Bad person. He thought he could get by because he didn't steal from me. His mistake."

Ali was saying something about a pump.

"Okay." Murad turned to us. "I'd better go look at the pump. You're welcome to come if you want."

We took a last gulp of cold Pepsi and followed Murad and Ali along the dirt road, which followed the canal and was bordered by great old trees offering pleasant dappled shade on this rather warm late spring morning. Feathery white cattails grew along the damp slopes of the canal, high enough to reach the sturdy young palm trees, "palm kids," Murad called them, which were hardly recognizable as trees because they had been tied up in swaths of green banana leaves to give them support in the first stages of their growth.

"You want to see pollution?" said Murad. "There's pollution."

He pointed to the canal, where the water ran thick, a dead white color. "It's from the houses upstream. But you'll see, B.J., when we get up ahead, the water's clearer, nice and green."

"Why?"

"It comes directly from the Nile up there," said Murad.

From the road we could see that in nearby lots several houses were going up. Two and even three stories, in different stages of construction, the buildings stood awkwardly in the green fields. On each house, clusters of structural steel stood up like candles on a birthday cake, awaiting the next load of bricks, the next construction phase.

Murad followed my eye. "They start building," he said. "Then they run out of money. So they wait until they get some more money from their jobs in the Gulf, and they build another room."

"They're not farming at all?" asked Bob. "Just using the land for a house lot?"

"Oh no." He pointed to a family group in a nearby field. The old man straightened up in his galabia and raised a hand to Murad. Two women and a boy continued to bend over the earth. "You can see that the women help, and the kids. The young men are the ones working in the Gulf. But everybody else, including the grandfather, works on the farm. They hang on to the land and they use every bit. They plant alfalfa around the palm trees, and I do the same. They get two or three small crops every year."

"And you?" Bob asked.

"Two," answered Murad absently. We were approaching the silent pump, and his attention was drawn there. Ali doffed his galabia, revealing work pants, a white shirt, and a bright green vest; he climbed into the ditch. "A valve is broken, I think," he said.

Murad straddled the ditch, then joined Ali in the space taken up by the pump, where he proceeded to fiddle with the mechanism.

"Looks like it's just clogged up," he announced, "but we'll see."

Ali produced a pocketknife; the two men took turns cleaning out the pump innards.

A moment passed. Several minutes. Murad pushed something in the back of the pump, pushed it again, and the pump came to life.

Chucka, chucka, chucka, it sounded, and the water spurted out merrily, propelled from one canal into another, where it would gradually spread over the nearby field. Murad and Ali were clearly pleased with themselves, as they should have been.

"I've got wheat in the left and right plots. See the lines, Bob?" Murad pointed along the land where the early wheat was green, and to the brown middle plot which was recently plowed. "The middle is going to be the nursery for the rice plants. They'll grow there for forty-five days and be replanted."

"Replanted?" echoed Bob. "Replanted where?"

"In the other two plots, because by that time the wheat will be harvested. By April fifteenth, all the land will be in rice," Murad finished, adding, "*Inshallah*" (God willing), and he took off his baseball cap, scratched his head, and replaced the cap.

The sun was warm, but not unpleasantly so. March and April were good months, and June, too, sometimes, said Murad. "It's July and August when we all cook out here."

He bent over and took up a handful of earth to show us.

"See how easily it breaks up. It's because I've started to use natural organic fertilizer. The chemical stuff sets it in chunks, hard to plow and plant, hard for the salt to drain out."

Bob nodded. Salinization of the land is a major problem in irrigated agriculture, as on the alluvial plains of Iraq. It never used to be a major problem in Egypt, but since the river no longer floods and falls, salt is creeping into the Delta, too, taking its toll on the land's productivity.

"Salt is getting to be a big problem here?"

"Not too much—for me, anyway." Murad smiled. "Come on, Bob, I thought you were going to ask me why my neighbors don't understand me . . ."

"But you said you'd show us!" from Bob.

We walked through the fields to the canals, which surrounded the land like life-giving frames. A pair of black crows rose from the ground in front of us, calling brokenly to each other as they soared above. Twittering white birds—egrets or ibises—and scores of white butterflies seemed to be wafted about by the slight breeze. I could see that purple clover was sprouting in the unplanted center field, with small white flowers like miniature morning glories. An occasional clump of wild arugula cast a dark green shadow on the brown earth, and a tall border of sunflowers burned yellow in the distance against the wide sky, which was bright blue, not the gray, smoggy shade that passes for sky color in Cairo. It was hard to believe that we were less than an hour from the crowded city, with its deafening noise of people and automobiles and chugging overburdened buses. Here the silence lay like a balm, in the biblical sense, upon the spirit—the human silence, that is, for the birds continued to twitter and call, the pump turned over, and one heard the occasional bell of a passing farm cart.

I could see why Murad was angry with his neighbors for selling their land to developers, for using it to make the bricks for their houses. For since the raising of the dam, there is no more precious silt deposited each year on the land by the river as a gift to the Egyptian farmers from a benevolent nature; that gift has gone forever. And the land they have before them, under their feet, is all they will ever have. This is the stuff they have to work with, to make do.

Chucka, chucka, chucka. The machine wheezed and turned and kept on pumping. This water was much clearer than the dead white stream near the house. Was it from the Nile, then, I asked Murad, one of the offtakes, not the stream that ran past the village houses? Murad agreed.

"Come on, Bob, you know about irrigation and all that. What am I doing differently?"

He smiled slightly at Bob as he stood there, a tall figure in his baseball cap, on the corner of the canal where on one side lay Murad's early wheat, and on the other a neighbor's plot stretched away.

Bob looked back and forth, at the pump, Murad's wheat, the neighbor's field. Then he smiled, too.

"Yes," he said. "You've leveled your land and raised up the canals so they're smaller and more shallow than before. Not true of the neighbor."

Murad nodded, delighted. "And I've lowered my drainage ditches. It's working, but not perfectly."

"To do what?" queried Bob.

"Well," said Murad, taking a stance by the pump rather like that of a college professor about to begin a lecture. "We get water eleven months of the year now, as you know. So everything is different."

"How?"

"Remember what we used to do? We flooded the land during the annual rise of the Nile. We had to soak it then because the water level fell so far when the flood season was over. We don't have to soak it anymore. In fact, it's bad. Soaking saturates the soil and brings up salts."

Bob paused and looked at the land again, the neighbor's uneven field and Murad's flat and furrowed land. "Let me see, you don't need so much water, so the field canals are now shallow, bringing just enough water to reach the furrows where the crops are planted."

"You got it, Bob." Murad paused. "And you know, the salt has gone down a lot since I started this all about five years ago. And the leveling . . ."

"For more uniform irrigation?" suggested Bob. "So the water that you do use is spread evenly?"

"Yes," said Murad. "But," he added, "the leveling's not quite finished. I work on it a little more every year."

I was puzzled. "So if what you're doing is better for the land, why do your neighbors think you're so strange?"

"Well, for one thing, it's a hell of a lot of work to do what I've done, B.J.," responded Murad seriously. "I buy organic fertilizer, which isn't cheap. The chemical stuff is. And I buy clean seed through the Ministry of Agriculture. That all takes time—and money. Sometimes the local *fellaheen* don't have enough of either."

We were stumbling over the recently plowed field, on our way back to the house. I bent down to rescue a flash of white from the brown clods; it was a snail shell, pristine against the dark earth, but an ominous sign of the other curse of the Delta—bilharzia (or schistosomiasis), the debilitating disease passed through the snail to the farmers who work barefoot in the canals.

Murad saw me pick it up. "Yes, B.J., I know what you're thinking," he said. "But more people know about bilharzia now. They try to wear rubber boots in the canals. And really, people are doing a lot better than they used to. Their health is better."

"Making a living, you think?" Bob asked.

"Yes, on two or three feddans they can make a living, growing two crops a year. Berseem and/or rice; alfalfa and corn or rice and wheat. Rice is where the money is."

We had gained the road, Bob giving me a hand to leap over the dead white stream of polluted canal water.

"But your neighbors must see that your crop yields are better," said Bob.

Murad nodded. "Yes, they're beginning to see that. They're impressed with that. One or two have actually started to raise the level of their own canals."

"So—you're helping change the system, Murad, to deal with the new conditions produced by the High Dam. Conditions no one foresaw or at least never said anything about, at least as far as I remember."

Murad laughed a bit self-consciously. "Big talk, Bob," he said. "I'm just a farmer, remember?"

At the house he took us up to the balcony and then went off to finish some errands in the village.

Chucka, chucka, chucka. The pump was still working, bringing up the water to irrigate the fields, which now, thanks to Murad's resourcefulness in the face of new dangers to the precious farmland, were being revitalized and beginning to produce even more than before. From the balcony we could see the family group still working their field below, the clumps of structural steel still standing up like birthday candles atop the half-completed houses. When I leaned over, I saw that Murad's mother's rose garden was indeed overgrown, though the pink and white rosebushes stood up proudly in the weeds. But the white climbing rose had taken off on its own, to grow through the tangle of shrubbery that formed a natural fence between the front of the house and the farm road bordering the canal. The white rose was now quite wild, it appeared, but it continued to blossom white against the stiff bamboo, the bright green banana trees, and the brown stalks of the date palms.

The estate was indeed a new kind of Egyptian country *ezba*, as we had said before to Murad and to his family. It was not just a refuge for the rich from the bustle of the city, but a middle-class farm, managed directly by the owner, who drives his own tractor and works side by side with his farmers. Now it was becoming something more—a model of how to overcome the new challenges posed to Egyptian agriculture by the side effects of the High Dam.

"Murad's a model," I said to Bob, in the stillness that fell over the land after the noon call to prayer had sounded from the minarets in the many nearby villages. "God is great!" they had cried.

"A model!" repeated Bob. "Well, don't tell Murad that. You'll only embarrass him."

"But he is. Don't you think so?"

"Yes, he is. He's a post–High Dam farmer!"

THE KHEDIVE ISMAIL, who piled up enormous debt during his tenure as ruler of Egypt from 1863 to 1879, was also the moving force behind the construction of what used to be called modern Cairo. In complete contradiction to the 1990s Islamists, he believed that Egypt could only take its place in the pantheon of modern advanced nations if it became thoroughly Westernized. "My country is no longer in Africa, it is now in Europe," he is supposed to have proclaimed, and he set about transforming that rhetoric into reality.

Using, as Dr. Handoussa had pointed out, resources Egypt did not have, he bulldozed whole sections of the city. He replaced the narrow streets with wide Parisian-style boulevards, added tramways, bridges, gaslights, waterworks, and public parks. One of the largest was the Ezbekiah Gardens, around which his architects built theaters and book-stalls and a fine new opera house, a miniature replica of La Scala in Milan. The khedive commissioned Giuseppe Verdi, who was already gaining kudos for his work, to write an opera for the opening of the Opera House, which was to coincide with the opening of the Suez Canal.

The opera, which was of course *Aida*, was not finished in time for the opening, but many French stockholders in the canal came anyway, as did the Empress Eugénie, who was driven down the new boulevards in the royal carriage before officiating at the canal opening. It was 1869, and the canal continues to operate successfully into the end of the twentieth century, bringing revenue regularly into Egypt's coffers. So the khedive's extravagance, since it included the Suez Canal, was not entirely foolish.

But the Opera House is gone, burned down in the 1970s, another casualty of the changing Cairo. And the Ezbekiah Gardens have shrunk considerably, to make way for the new commercial developments.

"The Opera House one is sad about," said our old friend Aziza. "But it was a firetrap, remember, B.J.? Still, one misses the lovely gardens where people could stroll, sit down, and have a coffee. All very leisurely."

"And the Opera House was great for the Bolshoi and the Paris Opéra," said Bob. "We loved it. But the cultural events were certainly more European than Egyptian."

"That's what the khedive wanted," put in Aziza.

"Times have changed, sister dear," said Aziza's sister, Laila, who had returned to Cairo recently after many years in England. We were all lunching in the Gezira Club, once the exclusive turf of Europeans and still a kind of high-cost oasis, with its swimming pools, racetrack, tennis courts, and billiard room in the center of the island of Zamalek, conveniently opposite the new Marriott Hotel, which is a renovated old palace.

"All right, all right," Aziza replied to her sister rather testily. "But what does that mean, Egyptian culture, tell me, Bob."

"You tell me, Aziza," returned Bob, not to be put on the spot.

Aziza turned to include her sister. "What do you think?" she asked.

Laila looked interested for the first time. We had never known her well in the sixties, and she had a reputation as a contentious and discontented person. "Egyptian culture?" she repeated. "The English think it's belly dancing, peasant stick dances, maybe our great singer Um Kulthum, whom they don't understand," she added with a sniff.

"Um Kulthum, certainly, I agree with that," said Aziza patiently. "But . . ."

Laila spoke again. She had come to life suddenly. "Well, coming back after so many years abroad, I think I see a kind of hybrid culture, a kind of hybrid art developing here."

"Give me an example," said Bob.

"Well, the music, the art, uses both European and Egyptian forms," said Laila.

Aziza nodded. "But how could it be otherwise?" she returned.

"The khedive sent people to Europe to learn about Western ideas. They came back and opened art schools as well as military schools. So of course we're influenced by Europe."

"But . . ." Without thinking, I had been toying with my food on the paper plate that had been handed to me as I went down the cafeteria line in the Gezira Club gardens.

Aziza was suddenly solicitous. "Is the fish all right, B.J.?"

"Oh yes, yes, very good," I said quickly.

"I'm glad you like it." Aziza's quick smile signaled relief. "We eat here a lot these days," she went on, "since our parents and my husband have passed on." She sighed. "The children are in America, both of them. So Laila and I are making do in the old family flat. It's very grand, but no servants. And I have to confess I'm not a very good cook."

"The fish is good, Aziza, really," added Bob. "I may go back for seconds."

"Not like the old days, though," Laila said, "when we had table-cloths and the waiters brought round those wonderful lunches, kept hot under silver covers."

"We don't have that privilege anymore, and that's probably to the good," said Aziza briskly. "Have to get used to the new egalitarian Cairo. Nobody around to make beds these days, either. But my dear," she added in a harder tone, "you must have learned to fend for yourself all those years in the West, right?"

The exchange was sharper than either of us expected, I think. It was true that these two very different sisters, Western-educated daughters of a distinguished family, were now having to make peace as they settled down to live together in their declining years. And Cairo was a very different place in the 1990s than it had been when they were growing up half a century ago. Past family achievements meant far less now than money and access to the new centers of power, the banks, the foreign aid community, Mubarak's security apparatus.

Aziza turned to me. "Have some dessert, B.J., Bob."

"Coffee maybe," agreed Bob.

"Ask for Nescafé," said Laila. "Nobody in this place knows how to make Turkish coffee anymore."

Aziza took a deep breath. She had always been a peacemaker. And she had given much of her time and money to improving the lot of

Cairo's less fortunate citizens after her children had gone away and her husband died unexpectedly. It was clear that her patience was being tried by Laila, who had unwillingly returned home after ill health forced her to give up her teaching job in England.

"You both must visit the Hanager Center," Aziza said to us. "I do believe it is quite remarkable, a worthy successor to the khedive's Opera House. It's right around the corner. And," she added, with a look at her sister, "you might even see some of Laila's so-called hybrid art there."

Laila chose not to respond, and finished her Nescafé in silence.

THE HANAGER CULTURAL COMPLEX is the Cairo equivalent of New York's Lincoln Center. The new Opera House is the center of the complex, an impressive domed hall of stone, donated by Japan as a gesture of goodwill to Egypt, one nation to another. The thousands of pedestrians, bicyclists, and passengers in taxis and private cars who cross the Nile every day over the Kasr al-Nil bridge catch a glimpse of the Opera House, as its dome rises above the biscuit-colored walls enclosing the garden, and towers over the museums and galleries in the complex. And the Hanager has one great advantage over Lincoln Center. It has on-site parking!

In November 1995 Cairenes and other visitors to the Hanager Center had choices including the Arabic Music Festival, the Cairo Symphony playing Vivaldi, the Cairo Opera Children's Choir, and an experimental theater piece called *Elephants Hide to Die*, which had earlier won an international prize for Walid Aiouni, its producer/director. The Cairo children's puppet theater offered performances on weekends, the first Arab woman's book fair was held in one of the smaller halls, and the Museum of Modern Egyptian Art offered a feast of old and new "modern" artists.

An exhibit on the Art of Calligraphy in the Arab World was set in the Opera House art gallery to coincide with the festival of Arab music; the festival was much anticipated, since troupes were expected from fourteen Arab countries—Saudi Arabia, Lebanon, Palestine, Jordan, Algeria, Morocco, Kuwait, Turkey, Sudan, Libya, Bahrain, Tunisia, Syria, and, of course, Egypt.

When I went to buy tickets for *Elephants Hide to Die*, I was told it had been postponed to December. So I tried for the Arabic Music Festival and said, conversationally, how interesting it was that so many countries were to be represented despite their somewhat ambivalent political relations with Egypt. The young ticket seller pulled herself up and said primly, "This is a cultural event, *madame*, not a political meeting."

And, in case I didn't get the point, she added, "We are the cultural and artistic center of the whole Arab world!"

The Opera House did not include lectures and debates about different forms and combinations of secularism and Islamism, but those lectures and debates take place all over Cairo, in mosques, in religious study groups, in the regular weekly meetings of the Sufi organizations, and on college and university campuses, where students now number over 100,000.

Cairo's newspapers and magazines publish each day not only the establishment position but critical views from every sector of Egyptian society. Even the women's magazine *Hawa*, under its new editor, Iqbal Buraka, has become more serious, with regular columns and interviews on legal and religious issues that affect women. The censorship that silenced writers and performers and speakers in Nasser's and Sadat's time has been lifted, under Mubarak, who has presided over what a friend called "the opening of communications to the expression of alternate points of view." In addition to the eleven daily newspapers (six in Arabic and five in other languages), fifty-three other periodicals are published regularly in Cairo.

But the "opening" of Egypt to alternate points of view was severely tested during the 1995 parliamentary elections; such elections are mandated by the Egyptian constitution to be held every five years. The most recent round of protests began when two new local nongovernmental organizations took it upon themselves to publicly protest what they saw as persecution of journalists who openly espouse an Islamic viewpoint. The Egyptian Organization for Human Rights and the Legal Aid Center for Human Rights took issue with the arrests of Salah Abdel-Maqsoud and Magdi Hussein and the government's stated plan to try them in a military court. The Press Syndicate, of which the accused journalists are members, scheduled a four-hour sit-in on syndicate grounds, which was attended by Maqsoud's own wife, herself a journalist, in heavy veil, and their five children. The children marched about with placards, according to press reports, on which had been written, "Where's my daddy?" and "What's my daddy's crime?"

The arrests were the most recent in a series of government attempts to discourage and harass opposition candidates, particularly those of an Islamist cast. This led to growing concern about the conduct of the 1995 elections, and when the government refused a request to invite international observers to monitor the two days at the polls, a self-appointed group established an Independent Commission for Electoral Review, the first of its kind in Egyptian history. Such a move was perceived as a radical political act, even though Mahmoud Kassem, a former Arab League diplomat and a founding member of the commission, made it clear that the group was "not taking sides." To emphasize its purported objectivity, the committee refused to accept funding from any government or other partisan groups. The budget, a modest sixteen thousand dollars, was donated by individuals and human rights organizations, and was spent to fund the field survey. Six hundred volunteers were hired to monitor the two days of elections and submit their findings and recommendations to the commission. The report was filed on December 12, two weeks after a tumultuous and charged period in which the commission received 1,240 complaints from candidates and voters.

European and American newspapers noted the abuses of the election process, the arrests, the irregularities in voting records, and the violence used by Islamists to forcibly enter women's voting stations in the affluent districts of Dokki and Agouza. But, having done that, and having reported the results of the elections, they more or less dropped the issue. No one mentioned the work of the monitoring group.

What were the election results? No one was surprised that the government National Democratic Party won 317 of the 444 parliamentary seats. Independent candidates won 114 seats and opposition parties won 13 seats. Noticeably absent in the returns were wins by any member of the parties that declared themselves Islamists. And 5 women were elected from a field that included 87 women, running in areas throughout Egypt. The number of opposition party candidates dropped from 47 in 1985 to 13 in 1995, though the independent candidates did much better than expected.

"We're not happy with the results, of course," said our friend Dr. Saad ed Din Ibrahim, who, with Dr. Said al-Naggar and Dr. Milad

Hanna, signed the report of the independent commission. "There is one small sign for optimism, however. Despite serious threats against our lives, the commission refused to give in; we finished our report on the elections and submitted it, as we had promised. It is now public domain."

Democracy, then, in the American sense, is still not present in Egypt. But what is present is an amazing number of grassroots organizations—cooperatives, clubs, and self-help groups—that have risen in response to the needs of different interest groups within the staggeringly large and overwhelming conglomeration of human beings and resources that is Cairo today. Such organizations, which must register with the government, totaled over 21,000 in 1996. This included the 14 political parties, 24 professional syndicates (like the Press Syndicate), and about 4,000 cooperatives, 3,000 social clubs, and over 14,000 private voluntary organizations (PVOs). The PVOs included everything from the Population Council, the Red Crescent Society, and the Association for the Protection of the Environment.

The official total did not include the hundreds of *jamaiiyahs*, or private savings clubs, that, among the rich and especially the poor, have traditionally provided Egyptians with a hedge against financial disaster and a small nest egg to cover special occasions, like weddings and funerals. Nor do they include the avowedly religious organizations, both Muslim and Christian, who fund social services and work toward cooperation among disaffected and competing groups. And the unregistered, semicovert political groups advocating radical viewpoints of various kinds are still vulnerable to political repression.

Several of our Egyptian friends told us that they gave money and time to the organizations that work to keep families together, families torn apart by migrant labor, rural-to-urban movement, divorce, and most especially poverty.

"This is the crucial area for all of us," said Dr. Laila. "Families must continue to bridge political and economic differences."

Nashat Hussein, a bright-eyed young anthropology graduate, has been hired by the Arab League Commission on the Welfare of the Child to work with the growing number of homeless children that are appearing on Cairo's streets.

"We've never seen anything like this," he said. "A few, maybe, but now they tell us it's close to three hundred thousand! I can't be-lieve it."

He is working on a task force with volunteers from religious groups to try to persuade the homeless children to leave the freedom of the streets and move into the schools and health centers that are being set up to receive them.

"Sounds good!" I told him.

"But they don't want to," said Nashat, shaking his head sadly. "Can you suggest someone in America who would know about these matters? It is so new to us. We need help!"

What was it Dr. Handoussa had said? "The nuclear family unit is being torn away from the larger extended kin group. In the West you see that as progress, right? That the ideal family is the nuclear family, independent from the larger unit and ready for geographic and social mobility."

I had admitted that that certainly has been an implied idea in the West for many years.

"And does it work out so wonderfully?" she had persisted. "Chil-dren stuck with one set of parents, or maybe just one parent, without the advice and help of the larger group?"

"Our tradition is different," I had replied, and added, before she could ask, "We expect to live apart from our parents, to live indepen-dent lives without their interference."

Dr. Handoussa had smiled that warming smile. "Exactly. And *our* traditions are different from yours. With women working outside the home and men away, with grown children unable to live near other members of their families, our old traditions are being undermined by circumstances. What works for you in the West will not necessarily work for us."

IN MARCH 1996 Bob was invited to give public lectures at the Ameri-can University in Cairo, where he had first begun to teach forty years earlier. He talked about masculinity and gender studies in the United States. He talked about the assumption that masculinity and femininity are culturally constructed and that those constructions change in re-sponse to new demands. In Egyptian society men's roles and women's roles are already changing in practice, he said, though the stated idea is the same: man as head of the family, woman as nurturer and child-bearer and child-rearer. The audience was silent and respectful, but their questions revealed confusion: was Bob being antifeminist or was he just being provocative? Egyptians are interested in improving the position of women, men, and children, but not yet ready to accept the fact that their ancient patriarchal traditions are already being transformed into new patterns.

After Bob's last lecture, we were honored at an elegant, al fresco supper hosted by the university. It was a beautiful early spring evening, one of those evenings found only in Cairo, in which the thin moonlight filters through the smog and the bright neon lights, and the noise of autos, the call of flower sellers, and the music drifting out of passing automobiles combine to create a sense of anticipation, of pleasure, of great possibilities.

We sat in the university garden with old friends and new friends. Mohammed el-Fikri, who had worked with Bob on the Nubian research project, talked about the Nubians today. Sohair Mehanna described a research project on bilharzia (schistosomiasis) in a group of Delta villages, and a proposal for a study of Egypt's new recycling program.

"And Islamism, is that part of Egypt's future?" asked Bob.

Mohammed and Sohair looked at each other. There was a pause.

"Yes, Professor Fernea," said Mohammed. "We are nearly all Muslims here, you know that. But if you mean the Islamist *debate*, that's been replaced by the debate about female circumcision, right, Dr. Laila?"

"Yes, indeed," said Dr. Laila. "There is a long way to go there. Let's see who gets appointed as the next rector of Al-Azhar University; if he's liberal, that will help those who wish to abolish this harmful practice. If not, it will take time. But at least we can joke about circumcision. One never jokes about religion."

Bob could not resist. "What about men's circumcision?" he asked.

The table broke up into laughter. "But that's a sacred custom. Who would want to abolish that?"

"Still unthinkable, right? Like female circumcision until recently," said Bob. "In America now many people are choosing not to circumcise their boy children."

"I don't believe it."

"Really?"

Sohair said, "Americans! What will they think of next?"

"Well, some things are changing here," said Mohammed, "but not everything. Not that!"

"Are things changing for the better?" asked Bob.

"Better or worse, we cannot tell," responded Dr. Laila. "But it's happening, whether we like it or not. The big question is, do we want to be part of it?"

"Of course we want to be part of it," said Sohair firmly. "We already are. Don't forget that this is our country. And we are proud of it—Egypt!"

6. Comment

NUBIA NOW THAT THE FUTURE IS THE PAST

THE FUTURE IS A period of time best left to science fiction writers, but it is a hard subject for social scientists to avoid. Who, in fact, is not drawn to at least speculating about the future of something that one supposedly knows more about than others. It has certainly been a common practice among cultural anthropologists, and the practice continues from one paradigm to the next. Here I want to take advantage of my own past audacity and look at what I wrote in 1973 about the future of the Nubians.

I was at least modest about predicting the future.

> If the Egyptian government had not undertaken a massive and costly effort to resettle the villagers together and provide them with land to cultivate . . . the more than fifty thousand residents of Nubia would now be dispersed across Egypt, . . . transformed into an urban minority . . . villages [have] remained the dependable check on the process of assimilation, the counterbalance to cities.

In 1973 most Egyptian Nubians were condemning the dam construction which robbed them of their native lands. I judged the dam then according to the "greater good for the greater number of Egyptians." However, most of the Nubians I knew hated the High Dam before and after relocation, and felt great resentment toward the Egyptians who had imposed it on them. So who was I to look at the greater good for the greater number?

I also argued that "the survival of Nubian culture . . . would seem to depend on whether the villages of New Nubia will be able to provide the social functions of Old Nubia." The reasoning is based on the assumption that a culture depends on local reproduction by certain institutionalized practices, which, if lost, means the end of the culture. So when I go on to say that Nubian separation from the Nile will eliminate age-old felucca travel and "the river rituals can no longer be practiced," I am implying that Nubian cultural reproduction will be impaired. Did this happen?

All Nubian rituals and ceremonies, including those involving the river, certainly have been reduced in content and complexity over the past thirty years. In Old Nubia, weddings and funerals involved many days of visiting by kinspersons and close friends from nearby villages. These visitors were fed by the host families, which meant a great deal of expense and work for the hosts. In the early years of resettlement, hosts at weddings and mourning ceremonies were overwhelmed by the increased number of visitors; Nubian participation in ceremonies had greatly increased. Today weddings are practically public events. Hundreds of people, related and unrelated, from the neighborhood, from other villages, cities, and even from foreign countries may attend a wedding with relative ease. But Nubians have adapted their festivals by reducing the number of days, offering simpler refreshments, and dropping most of the ceremonial trips to the Nile.

Furthermore, since 1973, new employment possibilities have developed in Nubian society to replace the ones that have been lost. Felucca sailing is gone, but taxi driving now attracts a number of young men. Taxi driving, rather than agricultural labor or urban jobs, is an independent way of earning a living, at home, in New Nubia.

In 1973 I also noted that the Nubians would have to change their local economy from subsistence cultivation to cash-cropping sugarcane, would lose their palm trees and their waterwheels (eskalay). As all of these aspects of the local economy had much symbolic significance and required different kinds of social cooperation, this also boded ill for the Nubian future.

> On the other hand, as the quality of the new land improves, the villages of New Nubia will be far more viable economically than those of Old Nubia, and the pressure for men to migrate to the cities for work will be considerably reduced.

I went on to point out, however, that in Old Nubia many men who had land to cultivate preferred labor migration. Going to the cities of Egypt to work had become a rite de passage into manhood in Old Nubia; only those few men with salaried jobs in Old Nubia or who were somehow disabled or unfit for city jobs remained in their villages. Old Nubia was a haven, a place for retirement, but not for earning a living. I thought this might change in New Nubia.

My prediction was quite wrong. The old pattern of migration has continued. In the 1990s, for most adult male (and many female) Nubians, New Nubia, like Old Nubia, is still not a place to stay, but a place to visit, to live when unemployed, and to retire to—eventually. Egyptian Nubians made sure they would have claim to a house and land in New Nubia; some managed to claim more than one home, in fact. Everyone understood the advantages of having this new resource. But that did not result in a universal conversion into farmers among Nubians. One can make money from one's land without doing the work. Sharecropping with a Saidi farmer is the most general choice, though some Nubians today complain that they are cheated unless the arrangement is attended to by themselves or a close relative. There is also a government cooperative which manages a member's land and pays him or her one-fourth of the net income from the sugarcane cultivation. But this is the most conservative choice and is generally made by Nubian women with no close male relatives. And it is also true that quite a few Nubian men have become farmers, a choice that is now considered honorable, implying no lack of intelligence or enterprise. Thus, New Nubia is more diverse than in the past, with more options for both men and women.

Yet a dislike for heavy manual labor prevails. Most Nubian men are not farming sugarcane themselves, but are sharecropping. After sugarcane, animal production is today the biggest Nubian cash crop; it was *the* major cash crop in Old Nubia. Now the six-year fallow pattern for sugarcane land has made animal production an even more attractive opportunity, and it is common to see strings of cows and calves being herded daily from Nubian villages to fields. In fact, joint ownership of animals, as in Old Nubia, has become a common form of economic linkage between Nubians and sometimes between Nubian and Saidi partners. Such joint ownership of animals had been a common practice in parts of Old Nubia, where animal power was needed to turn the waterwheels. Today, with modern forms of canal irrigation, this is no longer a necessity, but the older pattern prevails.

In the twenties and thirties the growth of the migrant population in Cairo led to formation of the *gamma'iyya* clubs, where opportunities arose for the development of artistic and other skills that would not have been possible in the old villages. I had hoped for a similar occurrence in New Nubia, a renaissance of Nubian basketry, painting, or perhaps pottery making after resettlement. But alas, the absence of palm fronds has made the once ubiquitous woven Nubian plates scarce in many Nubian households today. And pottery has universally been abandoned in preference for aluminum cookware. Painting, however, has become recognized as an artistic activity requiring special talent. Many homes in New Nubia are decorated with scenes from Old Nubia, painted on the walls by local artists, some trained in Egyptian and European art schools. Houses are also painted different colors, though their exteriors lack the extravagant decoration found on the facades on Old Nubian houses.

An entirely unexpected expression of Nubian creativity (at least by me) has been the development of a Nubian style of popular music which is now recognized throughout Egypt. Nubian music is played on the radio and on television and has become fashionable entertainment at fancy Egyptian urban weddings. Families pay thousands of pounds to the Hilton and other first-class hotels for a "Nubian band" to play as an opening set before an "Egyptian band" takes over. Nubian music is really a new invention, since in Old Nubia music was made with drums and flutes and ribabas. The modern Nubian band is electronic, with many different instruments. The lyrics are in Arabic or one of the two Nubian languages, or sometimes a mixture of both. While some younger Nubians do not understand the Nubian languages, this does not keep them from singing the modern songs. Indeed, classes in the indigenous languages are offered in Cairo and other cities by and for Nubians, and an effort is afoot to persuade the government to allow Nubian languages to be taught in the New Nubia schools. Thus, I was off the mark when I stated that "within two or three generations, it is probable that only the eldest persons in New Nubia will be able to converse in the language of their forefathers." Young people do tend to speak Arabic together, rather than Nubian, but this does not mean that a counterinclination is not also present, and the development of a popular Nubian style of music has certainly helped promote this trend.

In discussing the likely disappearance of the Nubian languages, I gave great weight to the "increased contact between Nubian villagers and Egyptian administrators and institutions." I did not think about the presence of Egyptian television in every Nubian home. I also did not realize how soon Nubian schoolteachers would fill all the positions in the New Nubia schools and how quickly young Nubians would take over administrative posts in most of the Egyptian institutions involved in Nubian daily life. Many of the Nubian schoolteachers are said to be relaxed about allowing Nubian to be spoken in the classroom or on the playing fields; in fact, the new contacts with the institutions of the Egyptian state are less alien to Nubian culture than I anticipated, for they are mediated by the new Nubian middle class, many of whom speak a Nubian dialect.

I should also have realized that the resettled Nubians would be quick to take their place among the rapidly growing Egyptian class of administrators, educators, professionals, and free enterprisers. Even in the 1960s our demographic surveys surprised us by showing that Nubian occupational stratification was parallel to that of Egypt as a whole. In developing a middle class, the Nubians have kept up with greater Egypt; the question now is, how long is the educated middle class going to remain Nubian?

When I was in Nubia in 1991, I watched while middle-class Nubian men, dressed in suits and carrying briefcases, took over the Bayt al-Nubi, the Nubian House, which an older, less educated Nubian friend of mine had tried to establish on the Nile as a tourist attraction. Dissatisfaction with my friend's performance had led to the takeover, which was not entirely without justification (in the opinion of many other Nubians and myself). The new Nubian middle class is now a force in the community as well as in Egyptian and foreign cities. As long as the new Nubian middle class retains its attachment to and interest in New Nubia, Nubians will remain a visible, articulate ethnic minority in Egyptian society. New Nubia shows no sign of becoming just a settlement of farmers, even though agriculture is an important source of income for all Nubians, who are, after all, owners of both land and real estate.

A great deal of money has been invested in New Nubia by the Nubians themselves. Most of it has been used to improve the government-issue houses. These investments have been made by many men who do not now live in their New Nubia houses most of the year, but who expect to do so one day—or who hope to sell them at a good price when, after forty years of relocation, the government promises it will give the owners legal title to their property. Even now, many sales and exchanges have taken place, largely to make it possible for kinsfolk to live nearer each other. Such deals, however, remain uncertified by deeds and titles.

We researchers in Old Nubia did not anticipate the quantity and quality of investment that would occur in New Nubia, nor consider how this would help tie the dispersed community of Egyptian Nubians together. For in addition to improving their houses, the Nubians have funded public buildings—mosques, shops, and guesthouses. The guest-houses are used for ceremonies, for meetings of various kinds, and for bedding down visitors and kin for whom there is no room in the new houses.

In 1971 I mentioned the lost beauty of Old Nubia, "the view of the river, the villages situated between mountains and water . . . high green palm groves," but I added that "aesthetics are not necessarily the basis of a society." Well, yes, but the fact is that the memory of Old Nubia is a precious source of nostalgia for Nubian men and women who once lived there. For the post-relocation majority, these memories are what they have overheard, what they see in photographs and painted on the walls of their homes. The lyrics of the New Nubia songs re-create images of the past, for those who were part of it and for those who were not. Among the 300,000 people in New Nubia, the loss of the land of Old Nubia is perhaps the strongest ideological tie, the founding myth. But how many Nubians these days would reject the present material advantages of New Nubia to move back to the old communi-ties? A few families, after all, have moved back to pioneer communities along the shores of Lake Nasser, though they are not yet self-support-ing.

I HAVE ARGUED ELSEWHERE that Nubians are better understood as an ethnic group than a race in Egypt, even though they are black, and thus distinctive in their physical appearance. Nubians continue to inter-marry with other Muslim Egyptians, including even some of the Saidi of Upper Egypt, who have become their neighbors and fellow workers. Some Saidis now live in New Nubia, and one sees Saidis walking on the streets with Nubian friends. When house sales become possible, I imag-ine that the price offered will be more important than the ethnicity of the would-be buyer. If that is the case, an even greater diversity in the population of New Nubia is inevitable. But before any of my new prophecies are taken seriously, a second contemporary factor deserves recognition: foreign affairs.

Egypt and Sudan are currently on bad terms. The reasons are complex, but one thing is clear: the two countries have competitive interests in the water of the river Nile. The Nubians feel that the Egyptian government identifies them with the Sudanese and is unfriendly on that account. This has helped create a strong us versus them attitude among some Nubians. Nubian intellectuals argue that the Nubians of today are the descendants of the ancient Kushites and hence once ruled Egypt as well as the Sudan. Egyptians are even becoming the butt of new Nubian jokes. Perhaps of greater importance is the fact that some Nubians have relatives among the northern Sudanese; these people have connections with Sudan historically as well as culturally, in terms of common languages and architecture. Thus, Egyptian Nubians, whether they like it or not, now have a connection outside Egypt which is of more importance today than it was before resettlement. This foreign connection may be of great significance for the identity of Egyptian Nubians during the next thirty years.

V Saudi Arabia

> *How often, when the country is barren and dry,*
> *The people are more generous than nature,*
> *Not scorning, coldly, their fellow man,*
> *But giving, as naturally as the wind blows.*
> *Among our lineage, our ancestors, we see*
> *How hospitable were the old ones of the tribe—*
> *We come from a tradition of generosity,*
> *Of riches, nobility and greatness.*

Labid
MU'ALLAQA

THE REAL ARABIA, for romantic Westerners and travelers since the Middle Ages, lies in the deserts of the region and among the nomadic Bedouin, who are believed to wander about in those deserts living in tents and raising camels. Even within the Middle Eastern world, the Bedouin has a special place in the hearts and minds of Arabs themselves, for the word still symbolizes a purity and courage associated with right living and right thinking. The city is the seat of corruption, but the desert is seen as the place where morality is a natural outcome of a lifestyle free of laxity brought about by material comforts and self-indulgence. The Prophet Muhammad was a city man, from the important mercantile center of Mecca in the Arabian Peninsula. But, like many men of the period, he had spent time with nomads as a child, and in middle life he retreated to the desert again to hear the words of God.

Yet the attitude of today's settled Arabs toward the nomads is ambivalent. Generally, nomads and their lifestyle are seen as having no place in modern society. Old resentments also rankle, memories of the days when desert uprisings made travel risky and when Bedouin raids on towns and villages were common occurrences. Townspeople, in some contexts, also characterize Bedouin as ignorant, indifferent in the practice of Islam, and generally unreliable. Thus, the logic follows that

nomads, for their own good, must be encouraged to leave their historic
ways and settle down in one place—preferably as farmers. Like the
forest outlaws of medieval England, nomads may be unequivocally admired in the Middle East only when they no longer exist.

The movement to settle the nomads in the Middle East coincided
with the end of the Western colonial period in countries such as Iraq
and Egypt. Tribes had always played a role in the area's politics, but the
Western-educated Arab urbanites who took control of the new nationalist governments viewed with dismay and distaste the special interest
and attention given to nomad tribes by colonial administrators, travelers, and writers. During the mandate period, English and French administrators had officially recognized sheikhs as tribal representatives
in some countries, and eventually appointed them members of Parliament. Customary tribal law was also recognized in the legal codes of
the time. "Tribes are a primitive form of social organization," said one
Iraqi government official, and another said to Bob in 1957, "What did
the British think we Arabs were, American Indians?" In the newly
independent countries of the fifties and sixties, the official, publicly
stated view of the tribal Bedouin was that they were a remnant of a
primitive past and must be settled as soon as possible.

Today, in most countries of the Middle East, the percentage of
nomadic Bedouin is small, about 2 percent in Egypt, for example. But in
Saudi Arabia, despite twenty-five years of gradual sedentarization, the
nomads still constitute a significant segment of the population, nearly
20 percent. That percentage was considerably larger in 1964, when Bob
went out to Saudi Arabia to conduct a brief socioeconomic survey of the
newly settled Bedouin in the Wadi Serhan, a valley in the northern part
of the kingdom, between Sakaka and Al-Qurayat. An American engineering firm had contracted with the Saudi government to evaluate the
first efforts at government-sponsored Bedouin settlement in the valley.
At that time, a six-year drought had reduced the available natural pasture to almost nothing, and thus the animal-dependent nomads were
welcoming an opportunity to shift to sedentary cultivation. Government policy at the time seemed to coincide with Bedouin needs and
desires.

The early results looked promising. Only fifteen years before, in
1950, the valley of the Wadi Serhan had produced nothing but "dates
and a few tomatoes for the market," Bob wrote. But by 1964 the area

under cultivation in Sakaka oasis alone had doubled, thanks to the opening of new lands by the central government. The government had also provided funds for irrigation, and for administrative personnel from the nation's capital, to help launch new agricultural activity and encourage further settlement. Though a few nomad Bedouin remained in the area in 1964, their plight was pathetic. Bob wrote, "Their flocks are barely enough to keep them alive and several [of the men] said that their children, women and animals had died in the past few years and that they had been reduced to catching rabbits, birds, even rats in order to eat. Most of the people I talked to say they would like to settle down."

Everything seemed poised for the move from nomadic pastoralism to sedentary agriculture. But there were problems. Successful farming in Wadi Serhan depended on the development of new water sources, specifically the new wells with engine-powered pumps, for the water of the oases' ancient artesian wells was already fully used by the settled Arabs of the oases. The government had foreseen the need and had supplied the wells and pumps. But the farmers were inexperienced and pumped too much water onto the oasis land, drowning the spring plants and causing large areas to become so saline that no crops would grow at all. Even some of the date palms, staple plants of the oasis, were dying. Everywhere, Bob and his companions were shown broken pumps whose owners were unable to find spare parts or mechanics to repair them.

Finally, not enough land could be made available to take care of all the nomads who wished to settle down. These early problems led many farmers to hold on to their animals against the possibility of crop failure. Bob noted that most of the farmers in the valley settlements, from Jawf to Sakaka, kept a few sheep and goats near their new houses, and in some cases had farmed out more animals to their kinsmen who were still nomads.

Thus, efforts to settle the nomads in the sixties did not fail because of Bedouin resistance. Drought and loss of pasture were breaking down the old preferences for a pastoral existence. Many Bedouin were already settled and others interviewed by Bob in the sixties expressed hope that they would soon be able to do the same. The problem was that in 1962 the Saudi government simply could not afford to pay the infrastructural costs of a complete changeover. Pumps and land were not enough; support services such as market roads and agricultural extension assistance, as well as pump parts and repair services, were vital, too.

In 1983 Bob returned to Saudi Arabia, again to do a demographic and economic survey of Bedouin, this time in the province, or emirate, of Hail, southeast of the Wadi Serhan, where he had worked nearly twenty years before. As part of his 1963 report, he had written that "development schemes are only worthwhile if they are economically feasible in the specific social and cultural setting of the people they are intended to benefit." The post-OPEC Saudi Arabian government of the 1980s could afford to take such advice seriously and had accordingly hired an American planning and engineering firm to provide a long-range program of economic development for the Hail Emirate. The plan was to take into account the specific characteristics of the Hail population, whether nomadic, agricultural, or urban, and try to forecast the population's needs over the next twenty years. Bob's particular assignment in the spring and summer of 1983 was to survey the condition of the nomadic Bedouin in the area and to try to contribute some information concerning the economic and demographic aspects of nomadic life to the overall planning process. The Bedouin population of Hail fluctuates according to the time of the year and the weather conditions, but it was generally considered to consist of from 10 to 20 percent of the total population. Between the Hail Emirate and the valley of Wadi Serhan lies the Great Nafud Desert, heart of historic nomad life in the Nejd. Through this great desert the Bedouin used to travel by foot and camel each year in search of water and pasture. Bob set off in a Jeep to look for them.

"Things look much better than when I was here before," Bob wrote in one of his first letters.

It is not the stick of famine but the carrot of land grants, generous loans, and subsidies for machinery, housing, and crops that makes farming not only a more attractive but a more secure venture than it was in 1965. And what a wonderful difference to see no more ragged tents, thin people and animals, real dust bowl scenes. People show every sign of prosperity. Now I have to start traveling around in the area to see if my initial impressions can be justified by hard data from interviews.

THE GREAT NAFUD DESERT

July 12, 1983, 1:50 P.M.

Dear B.J.,

At this moment my Jeep is stuck in the top of a sand dune. I am filthy dirty because I had a flat tire an hour ago and had to crawl around in the hot sand to change it; my hands are still scorched from that experience. Lucky I am in good shape or I would have had a heart attack, it was so hot and the tires were so damn heavy. As to my present situation, a Bedu tent with a truck is visible on the horizon about two miles ahead and I think I am on a main track so it seems unlikely I will perish here. The wheels of the Jeep are in sand up to the hubcaps and there is nothing I can do but sit in the cab out of the sun and hope some truck will eventually pass by and pull me out. I am more ashamed than frightened for having driven so badly, particularly because I said I did not want the driver to come along. So goeth pride. However, I intend to stay out here for five days interviewing nomads and I did not want the driver on my hands. Besides, when a native speaker of Arabic is with me all the conversation flows in his direction and no one tries to understand me because of my bad pronunciation of the local Arabic dialect.

Fortunately, I do have a lot of water with me—supposedly enough for the whole trip. It is so hot here (120°F, I suppose) that I can hardly touch the steering wheel. I'll need to drink a lot. I guess I do feel a kind of panic. Though I know I will be found eventually, the space around me is so vast and so fearsomely hot that it is frightening. I think of some of Paul Bowles's stories and get a tightness in my stomach.

One bad thing is that this is the Id, the second day of the big holiday after Ramadan, and all right-minded people are celebrating with their friends and families. I wish I were.

It is very annoying to be within a few feet of solid ground but still unable to move. It happened to me once on the beach in Oregon. I was worried about the tide then, but not as much as I'm worried about the heat here. I also hate the idea of having to confront strangers with my stupidity.

I don't like being here at all, soaking wet, sweat running down my face. I am getting too old for this sort of thing. My heart is racing, just sitting here. I don't feel like writing anymore.

2:15, same afternoon

I doubt I have ever shared such feelings with you, but I have always thought that deserts can provide a particularly horrible kind of death. The idea of hell must come from bad experiences on deserts like this, from stories that big Bedouin tell little Bedouin as warnings against getting stuck out here. The Nubians hated the desert. Their houses faced the Nile, the palm groves, and gardens along the riverbanks. Somehow, when I was living there on the edge of the Sahara, I never thought of the desert behind me unless I walked to the end of the village and noticed the sand which was gradually blowing over the deserted houses there. No way to stop the blowing sand. The Nubians never went out behind the villages except to bury their dead. They felt the desert was full of unfriendly creatures, and since they used to be regularly raided by the nomads, they were right.

At this moment the silence really seems deafening. It seems to hum in my ears. Behind me is sand. Below and ahead of me as far as I can see are rolling hills of sand with widely scattered tufts of brown grass, scrubby shrubs, and that one distant black tent. I am glad that tent is there. If by night no one has come by I will flash my headlights and perhaps the people in that tent will drive over to see what is up—or down. Nobody expects me, nobody is worrying about me, so if I must stay here all night no one will be concerned, except me, that is. I have an orange and half a sandwich. I am beginning to feel better. Perhaps I will just continue to write. We never pay much attention to what anyone is saying but ourselves, so why should letter-writing be regarded as a chore? Too much of a commitment, I suppose. Anyway, I don't feel very wise or smart just now, only dirty and worried.

The desert is still empty. Perhaps I am the only damn fool in these parts who would try to cross the Nafud in the middle of the day. I was here once before but I wasn't driving and you can't get the hang of sand driving without doing it.

Turaba, the town I was heading for when I got stuck, looks like a teardrop on the relief map. It is a flat basin which has remained uncovered by sand because its position is in the lee of a small clump of mountains. The wind blows the sand around the mountains and leaves this clear space. Turaba has no agriculture. It is a service center for the Bedouin. They come in to buy supplies and get their pickup trucks gassed up. When I was here before and stayed overnight with the emir of Turaba, he struck me as a very tough gentleman. He is the voice of the government here and I guess it must have to be a loud one; all the tribesmen I saw last time were armed.

The wind has picked up. The sudden gusts which whip around the Jeep have the effect of voices, indistinct and blurred like those of a crowd which are blown in from a long way away. A single gust comes across like the muffled voice of an announcer at some distant game. I have to leave the windows open or I'd be cooked, but the air burns my neck as it blows through the Jeep. I hope I can get out of this mess without having some kind of rescue mission. I can just hear the authorities asking, "Why did you let him go out here alone?" "Because he is fifty-one years old and we thought he knew what he was doing." I should have taken a lower track over this dune. I should have switched into four-wheel drive sooner. Oh well. Too late now. If I sleep here will a truck come over the hill and run into me in the dark? Should I sleep in the sand? Will a scorpion bite me? A viper? I'd better sign off again. Such nonsense.

3:30 P.M.

Now I am a bit more worried because I just saw a pickup traveling about half a mile to my left. I realize I must have swung out quite a long distance to the right of the main track. I thought I was much nearer the main road. But I've seen many tire tracks around here. I suppose someone will come this way eventually.

4 P.M.

I have just taken steps. I have put long strands of white toilet paper on the top of my radio antenna—a bit of "papering" in hopes that someone will see me. I now realize that my Jeep is almost out of sight from the main track since I've heard at least five or six pickups going by and apparently no one has seen the Jeep. (Did you know that you can hear wind in the distance, before it arrives?) One thing I will not do is leave this Jeep. I may get awfully hungry but I can last for at least four or five days with the water I have. I can't believe I won't get help before then.

A car or truck has just stopped on the main road. I think they have seen me. They can't get over to me from where they are but at least someone knows I am here. How glad I am and how embarrassed will I be. However, I won't leave this Jeep to walk to the tent, even at night. You really can't tell how far away something like that is. Anyway, the lights would probably go off when I got halfway there. It would be crazy.

I can still hear the truck in the distance. Perhaps it will try to find a way to get here—or perhaps it will report me to someone else? The truck is out of earshot now. Just the rustle of toilet paper in the breeze. I think I will try to use my side-view mirrors to flash the sunlight on the main road.

July 13, 6 A.M.

About 6 P.M. yesterday a Toyota pickup turned off and came down my side track. By that time I was standing on top of the Jeep, waving a rag I had found half buried in the sand; it looked like a woman's head scarf. There must have been a Bedouin encampment on the dune a long time ago. The driver roared up this dune at about 60 mph and didn't slow down till he hit firm sand about twenty yards from my Jeep. He got out of his Toyota, walked over, asked if I had four-wheel drive (I did), shook his head at the mess I had made (front wheels turned, in the sand down to the axle). I got half under the Jeep and dug out the transmission while he dug out the wheels a bit; we were both working with our hands, of course. Then he got in, straightened out the wheels, and proceeded to back out of the hole I was in!

Said I should have power steering! But he seemed to take the situation pretty much for granted, as if I wasn't the first damn fool to get stuck like this. He really knew how to drive on the sand. I think I know more about it now too, but I was terrified every time I hit soft sand on the rest of the drive to Turaba and it is going to take a while before I get over that feeling.

I reached the residence of the emir of Turaba last night about 7:30 and had a rather cool reception. He was leaving for Hail early next morning, he said. Why had I come alone, what was I doing? Luckily I had brought some photos of him from the last trip and that warmed things up a bit. After finishing some business (settling a quarrel of some kind, as near as I could tell), he took me to a small gathering at the other end of the village where we met several other men. The emir seated me with a tribal sheikh, on the same rug outside the sheikh's house. We all turned out to be the same age, fifty-one; they said I looked at least fifty-five; I think that was a compliment. I guess I should have said they looked sixty but it didn't occur to me.

The roast lamb and rice were excellent and my companions became very friendly. The big surprise, however, was that one of them knew Sheikh Hamid, our host in Iraq long ago. He said he probably visited the village in Iraq at the same time we were there. Twenty-five years ago his tribal group used to travel from here northeast across the rest of the Nafud Desert and over the border into southern Iraq. There they could graze their animals near the Euphrates River. Not far from where we were living. He said they don't make the trip anymore (seven days by camel) in search of pasture for their animals. No need to, even when they have a dry year here, since the government subsidizes barley for feed. They knew Sheikh Hamid well, he said. "Head of the Al-Agra confederation," they said, "wasn't he?" I nodded. "Lived in Al-Nahra. A big sheikh." The tribes here are part of the Shammar tribal confederation, just like the Al-Eshadda with whom we lived. The sheikh and I realized that we must have been in Al-Nahra about the same time, and here we were, sitting together twenty-five years later, in Saudi Arabia, two men the same age from different parts of the world, and mutual friends of the same man. The coincidence was quite amazing, and we both realized it,

I think. It put me on a quite different footing with my new acquaintances.

It's now early in the morning and I am writing this while waiting for my host to get out of bed. He's one of the local tribal emirs. The Turaba district emir turned me over to him last night and has gone off to Hail, as he said he would. There are many kinds of emirs here just as there are many kinds of sheikhs in other parts of the Arab world. The most important is the district emir, who is appointed by the king. He's the one I contacted last night. However, the government also appoints tribal emirs, who are the official intermediaries between the government and the sections of the tribe. The tribal emirs have a lot of clout since they must stamp all the official papers of their tribesmen: loans, birth certificates, things like that.

I slept outside last night and got badly bitten by mosquitoes. Not surprising, since I've seen standing pools at the big hot spring in the middle of this settlement where the tribesmen fill their trucks with water for their herds. I hope I can start interviewing soon, before the temperature gets up above boiling again. From the conversation last night, it sounded as if my host is supposed to help me. It all depends on what the big emir said before he left. He'll be gone two or three days in Hail. It would be good to finish my thirty interviews before he gets back. *Inshallah.* My stomach feels like it has a brick in it. Oh well. The conversation last night, the coincidence of meeting the sheikh who knew our friend in Iraq, was really great. For a while I felt as though I was back with Sheikh Hamid in the *mudhif* [guesthouse] in Al-Nahra.

3:45 P.M.

I did twelve interviews. My voice is sort of raw but I really learned a lot. I started at 6:30 after my host got up. We went out to interview camel herders who water at the big cement troughs set up for them on the edge of the oasis. They had over a hundred camels there. It was very hard to talk with them. I had a tremendous sense of distance from them. Men who still live with their camels on the high desert, without pickup trucks, without interest in selling their animals at the market, are really the last of the traditionalists out here. Their Arabic is unlike even that of the people I sat with last night; some ancient desert dialect, perhaps, uncorrupted by transistors and Egyptian schoolteachers! Last night there was always someone in the group who understood what I was saying in my mixture of Egyptian and Iraqi dialects, and I had no trouble communicating most of the time today with the goat and sheep herders. With the camel herdsmen I might as well have been speaking English and I needed a lot of help from my host-and-guide, the tribal emir. My host got into the act early in the day and started asking the questions, but finally got bored with the same subjects. Can he drive, though! My God, he just flew across the desert in my Jeep. Each time we started out he broke into loud song, like a war cry, as he pushed his foot down on the gas, far down, let me say. The first time he took over the Jeep and put that foot down on the accelerator, I decided it would only be a few minutes before we rolled over. But then I got caught up in his mood and didn't care if we rolled over or not. In comparison, I drive like an old cow.

We are now taking a midday break. I have my galabia on and he is smoking his water pipe. All is tranquil. In a moment I will try to nap. Today seems like a week, a month, from yesterday. It is so eventful, so full of life and people. We have driven miles from tent to tent to visit people who live by and for their goats, sheep, and camels. There is only animal husbandry here; no agriculture for miles and miles. Only the desert, the Great Nafud.

July 14, 12:30 P.M.

I am sitting under a goat-hair tent awning attached to the tent of a group of goat and sheep nomads. Just finished lunch, consisting of many fistfuls of rice and some lamb covered with tomato sauce. It's been quite a while since I ate with my hand so I was pretty messy but had a lot to eat. There were twelve other men for lunch, although when we first stopped, only a small boy and his mother were here and she was on the other side of the tent partition. Then one after another Toyota pickups rolled up and suddenly there was a feast in front of us. It seems like a lot of visiting takes place at all the tents but maybe it is more these days since it is the end of the big holiday following Ramadan. We are still on the Nafud, about ten kilometers from Troba. My host/guide who drives so well has brought me here. He sometimes complains a bit but seems to be having a good time traveling with me and introducing me around. There is general conversation now—gossip which is hard to follow. I did eight interviews but it was hard to keep attention and get questions taken seriously: they don't think about their herds in quantitative terms, nor do they keep family accounts. No surprise, of course. However, since they buy their supplies in large quantities (fifty-kilo sacks of rice, sugar, etc.) it is possible to get some idea of what is spent for what. From tent to tent there are variations but lots of similarities.

I may have to leave tomorrow as my host also wants to go to Hail and I have no alternative guide in sight. I am not too disappointed. After getting up at 5:30 A.M. and working till late at night I am pretty tired. I am also filthy dirty and very bitten by mosquitoes and last night I was also attacked by ants. But I could manage to stay another day or two, if it works out. Will have to see what develops. It's good to speak nothing but Arabic. A lot of dusty old vocabulary seems to be creeping back into the active zone of my brain. I find myself saying things that amaze me.

The floor of the tent where I am sitting now is covered with a Persian rug. The tent itself is set on reddish sand full of dried sheep droppings. The sides of the tent are up, and in the "room," thirty by thirty feet perhaps, are several oriental rugs, machine made. At the center of the U shape made by the rugs on which we are sitting is a fire pit. An incense burner was carried around after our meal. We pulled our head scarves forward and made a kind of tent for our faces and body in order to get a good scenting; it's very refreshing to take deep breaths of the incense. Rose water was also sprinkled on us every once in a while from a small container that looked like an oil can. We had the local coffee-and-cardamom brew in small porcelain cups and then tea in little glasses. The other furnishings? There are a set of coffeepots of graduated sizes, a teakettle, three storage boxes, brightly colored padded boxes on the rugs beside us to lean against as we sit cross-legged.

We've left the tent with the rugs and are in a neighboring tent. You can't pass by a tent without stopping for a long hello and some tea and coffee. These people are doing all right, I think. For fuel, they use dead wood from the low shrubs or trees around here. The wood falls off as green branches grow in at the top of the plant. The wood is gnarled, twisted, and very dry. Looks like it takes a long time to accumulate. When the grass is consumed and the wood is finished nearby, the people move their tents but still stay within trucking distance of Turaba. There they fill their water bag once or twice a day, depending on the heat and the number of their animals. Some men have to make three trips a day. The bag is a sort of canvas bladder that takes up the entire bed of a pickup truck. Of course, if you are well off, you may have a real water truck to haul water for your herd of goats and sheep—and camels, too. You haul the water to your herds rather than bringing them to the water. It is quite a system. And when you couple this with subsidized barley you can see that these nomads are doing all right; if they get fifty sheep to market they can afford to buy a new Toyota!

3:45 P.M.

Same day. We are back at my host's home—where it seems like paradise. It is hot under those goat-hair awnings with the glare of the sand and the scorching wind. Everyone says it is not as bad as yesterday, which was *hot*. Yes indeed.

Hail July 16

I am back home—at least, back to my own room, with the door shut, the fan and the air conditioning on. A different world from the desert. Today is Friday so the day is mine. I got home yesterday afternoon, with twenty interviews complete plus a pricing of commodities from a little survey I did at the weekly market in Turaba. The trip to Turaba took ten and a half hours, what with the two flat tires and the five hours I spent in the sand dune, but the return trip was only three hours: I hit the right roads (or tracks) and had no mishaps. When I first got home, I was very "high" on my successful adventure but developed a bad headache (dehydration, I think) and sort of collapsed and slept very fitfully all afternoon and night. But I feel fine now. Drank gallons of water. I did have some strange dreams, one in which I was looking for my watch and the hands fell off.

The Turaba trip was quite an experience. It is strange to plunge into another culture like that: everything changes, language, food, ways of relating to people, clothes, even toilet habits. Hard as it was in some ways, both physically and emotionally, I find I am looking forward now to the rest of the summer far more than before this trip. I feel I can handle both the interviewing and the getting about by myself. The hard part is being always a guest, having to drink thirty coffees and teas a day and eat more food than one wants. Twenty interviews meant at least twice that many visits. Sitting and sleeping on the ground also takes some getting used to, though it will be easier next time.

Throughout the whole intense trip I had a very strong sense of déjà vu. Indeed, I was often in the same situations as I had been in twenty-five years ago in Iraq when I traveled out of Al-Nahra with the sheikh's son and visited the different tribal settlements. The people here are far better off than the people in Iraq in those days. However, there is also the same unevenness in their knowledge (from our viewpoint, at least). For instance, in one tent, after a vigorous and critical discussion of American foreign policy ("How long do you Americans think you can be friends of two enemies at the same time?"), I ended up moderating an argument about whether or not the world is round. This was between two men who had more knowledge of U.S. foreign policy than most of our friends in Texas. The teenage son of our host, who was sitting in the fire pit handling the coffee service, offered the accepted scientific opinion about the shape of the earth but was not taken very seriously. The boy and I exchanged glances as the argument moved on to the citation of Koranic verses. But after that same night they asked me to point in the direction of Troba, which way the town lay. I said truthfully I had no idea. They then proceeded to show me how to read the stars and navigate at night, laughing kindly at my ignorance. That is the way it is out here.

More later.

In the months that followed Bob's first trip into the Great Nafud, he traveled extensively throughout the Hail Emirate, an area the size of Oregon. Sometimes he was out for several days at a time, interviewing Bedouin as he found them in their widely scattered campsites.

Historically, the Hail region in north-central Saudi Arabia was the independent domain of tribal groups led by the Rashid emirs, allies of the Ottoman Turks. At the end of World War I, as Ottoman power was waning, Abdul Aziz Ibn Saud, founder of the present dynasty that rules Saudi Arabia, was engaged in unifying the Arabian Peninsula. The British encouraged him to include the Hail region, which would further reduce Turkish influence. In 1921 Hail surrendered, and the emir of Riyadh, Abdul Aziz, gave himself a new title, Sultan of Nejd, and sealed a peace treaty with the Rashid tribe by marrying one of the widows of the tribe. Today the son of Abdul Aziz and the Rashid widow, Fahada, is the head of the Saudi National Guard and second deputy prime minister of the nation. Long before the peninsula was united under Ibn Saud, Charles Doughty visited Hail. In his classic nineteenth-century *Travels in Arabia Deserta*, he describes the escarpments of Hail, which could be seen from a great distance, the jagged mountains which rise, as Doughty says, from "the extreme barrenness of the desert plain, barren as a sea-strand and lifeless as the dust of our streets; and yet therein are hamlets and villages, upon veins of ground-water. It is a mountain ground where almost nothing may spring of itself, but irrigated it will yield barley and wheat and other Nejd grains." A little overdone as a description, according to Bob, since this "extreme barrenness," where "almost nothing" grows, may, depending on seasonal rainfall, support thousands of goats and sheep, as well as camels, on its natural pastures.

Doughty then found what is now Hail City, a large town with "some high buildings with battled towers. These well-built and stately Nejd turrets of clay-brick are shaped like [English] lighthouses." Palm groves, walled then, surrounded the town, which contained a small market souk, some houses, and the palace of the Rashid emirs. Today the town is a city of around 200,000. The palm groves have diminished in size in favor of treelined, paved streets, modern shopping districts as well as a more traditional souk, hospitals, clinics, administration buildings, and an industrial zone. Bob jogged on a synthetic-fibered four-hundred-meter track in the recently completed large sports center. It stands amid the modern villas that have replaced nearly all the mud-brick homes. The "stately Nejd turrets" are now national monuments, some of the older buildings that have been preserved. The Saudi government is attempting to use its oil wealth to benefit all the provinces of the kingdom, including Hail, home of the once fiercely independent al-Rashid dynasty.

Outside the modern city of Hail, hundreds of villages of various size still line the "veins of groundwater" of which Doughty spoke, while on the desert plain around these villages are the tents of the nomads, widely scattered over the area. The herds still graze on the wild grasses and browse on the low shrubs and trees that grow in this arid environment. As Bob traveled about the region, it became clear, however, that the old patterns of nomadism had changed somewhat. No longer are animals produced only for nomadic consumption and limited exchange. The majority of the Bedouin are becoming increasingly market-oriented and are raising their animals with the expectation of selling them to urban consumers. A large animal market exists in Hail along with government-controlled slaughterhouses. Even the proud camel, raised in the past for its own sake and valued so highly as to be eaten only under special circumstances—great feasts or dire emergencies, for instance—now may be seen awaiting the butcher's knife. The demise of the camel was offensive to Bob's romantic soul, but he explained it as a pragmatic answer to the national shortage of meat. Saudi Arabia now imports around half of the meat it consumes. The Hail development plans were to include schemes for increasing meat production among the Bedouin.

He soon found, however, that there were many differences between the Bedouin in terms of lifestyle and standard of living. Tent dwellers near the city of Hail were "suburban tent dwellers," Bob felt. They often had jobs in the city or went to school there. In fact, many Bedouin families stayed within pickup-truck distance of villages and towns where their children could regularly attend the local schools. Others had agricultural land or hoped to acquire land through land-grant programs. So seminomadism was common throughout most of the region south of the Great Nafud.

Not until his last trip in mid-September 1983 did he go back into the Nafud, where full-scale nomadism was most commonly practiced. This region had actually fared better than the desert plains to the south during the rain-short years of 1981 and 1982, since the desert plants with their large root systems managed to grow on the water stored under the surface. As his first letter suggests, the Nafud was a formidable environment for the inexperienced traveler. The British explorer William Gifford Palgrave also thought so in 1876:

> We were now traversing an immense ocean of loose reddish sands [he wrote], unlimited to the eye, and heaped up in enormous ridges running parallel to each other from north to south, undulation after undulation, each swell two or three hundred feet in average height, with slant sides and rounded crests furrowed in every direction by the capricious gales of the desert. In the depths between the traveller finds himself as it were imprisoned in a suffocating sand-pit, hemmed in by burning walls on every side; while at other times, while labouring up the slope, he overlooks what seems a vast sea of fire, swelling under a heavy monsoon wind, and ruffled by a cross-blast into the little red-hot waves. Neither shelter nor rest for eye or limb amid torrents of light and heat poured from above on an answering glare reflected below.

Bob found this an accurate as well as poetic description but was determined to go back to the Great Nafud Desert, not only because of the requirements of his job but also to conquer the fears he had brought back from his first trip. If the travelers of yore had made it on foot and camelback, why couldn't he do it in a Jeep?

JUBBA, HAIL PROVINCE, SAUDI ARABIA

September 16, 1983

Dear B.J.,

I'm off in the Great Nafud again, once more alone, and with a much greater distance between me and Hail than the last time in Turaba. I got stuck again this time, too. The graded road (a paved one is being constructed) came to an abrupt stop at the bottom of a sand dune and so did I. I didn't feel so bad, though, because several other Jeeps were stuck in the same place; you lose your momentum and that's what happens. Another guardian spirit, robed and scented, took charge and let half the air out of my already low tires. After that I could drive myself out. Just hope these tires make it over the rocky parts of this track. You should see me on the sand these days, floorboarding the gas pedal in second gear. Suspend all driving rules and keep it at 40 mph no matter whether you can see over the next dune or not. That's the way you do it!

I made it here to Jubba oasis in about four hours, so it wasn't a bad trip. Just now I've had lunch with the very cordial district emir, who has sent for a tribal emir to help me find the tents in the dunes around here. Jubba is the first place I've seen in Saudi Arabia that comes anywhere near the storybook image of an oasis. Green trees on a white plain right in the middle of red sand dunes. We seem to be on the floor of an ancient lake. This area, maybe two or three miles square, lies in the lee of a mountain, like Turaba, so it doesn't get covered with sand of the Nafud. The sand blows around rather than over the basin. The village is strung out—no cozy cluster of houses nestling among the palm trees. And it is dusty, fine white powdery dust from the gypsum soil. There are lots of cement-block houses built and under construction, replacing the old mud-brick ones. A lot of Bedouin stay here in the winter, the emir told me. It gets very cold; remember the Iraqi winters?

Speaking of Iraq, I'm back among tribesmen of the Shammar confederation, like our hosts in Al-Nahra. But they don't have memories of Sheikh Hamid because they travel north toward Jawf oasis and Jordan from here, not northeast toward Iraq like the Shammar in Troba used to do. In fact, Jubba is on the old desert trail along which people used to make the trip to Amman and Jerusalem; it took five days by camel. Today you can get to the border in seven hours by Jeep, if you know what you are doing; trucks can't make it through the dunes, however. They are too slow and heavy and sink in. But there will be a paved road through here one day soon. Much talk of it in

Hail and the road is already partly finished from there to here. It will make Hail the major gateway to the north.

What with all the construction work going on—a new secondary school and clinic in addition to the houses—the village is full of migrant workers from Egypt, India, and Pakistan, just as in Hail and the other villages I've visited. Labor migration isn't limited to the cities of Saudi Arabia by any means. My host has rather contradictory attitudes toward these foreign workers: he feels that Saudis should learn to do the work and not rely on others. But he thinks the country is benefiting from them too. He seems to be saying, "We shouldn't have them but we can't get along just now without them."

At the moment, it seems I've been stood up. One of the two tribal emirs (at my host the district emir's suggestion) was supposed to send his son to act as my guide. No show. That explains why I am writing to you now, sitting under an arcade in my host's courtyard, where he does his business in the summer. My host finally got mad and sent a man to see what happened to my proposed guide. The deputy, he said, was to convey the message that I'm here on official business and must be looked after. It's obvious that I'm regarded as a nuisance (which I am) and my mission (to ask the Bedouin questions about their animals) of no great importance. But I have acquired good thick skin over the years; I will outlast their polite indifference.

4 *P.M.*

After a bit, the father emir turned up at my host's *majlis* or council, in answer to the emissary. He didn't know what happened to his son who was supposed to pick me up, he said. He didn't seem particularly angry, but he offered to take me out. I could stay with him, he said, and go out to the tents from his place on the edge of the oasis. Our first excursion over the nearby sand dunes produced nothing except views of old campsites. The father didn't drive my Jeep with quite the verve of the younger men, but he did damn well for a man in his fifties or older, who had probably not started to drive until ten or fifteen years ago, when Jeeps began to be common out here. In fact, he said that when he was a young man he would travel by camel with his father to Riyadh to collect their ma'ash [living] from the king; the trip took fifteen days. Today it seems the ma'ash comes here, with the land grants, the feed subsidies, and the other money the government is spending on the people in the provinces. After a fifteen-day slow camel trip, Jeep travel must seem luxurious, but it's very tiring to bounce around so much. And Jeeps last only two years, the emir said, "before they begin to eat you up in repair costs."

The tribal emir and I finally visited two tents belonging to Bedouin families who are building blockhouses below the dune where the campsite lies on the edge of the oasis plain. They are among the ninety-five families to whom the emir distributed land. He says two-thirds of the Bedouin families are still trying to farm; it didn't seem that many to me. Egyptian farmers were working with both the families we visited, trying to get crops started in the sandy soil. When the Egyptians heard me speak Egyptian Arabic, one looked up and we exchanged greetings. He said he was from Beni Suef and would be staying another year to complete a two-year contract. The emir himself has six Egyptian farmers working for him, he said. He also owns a cement factory that is supplying cement blocks for a new school and a new clinic that are under construction. The emir is probably very wealthy, but nothing in his personal style indicates it.

September 16, evening
The tribal emir's house

It is now settled that I will stay in the tribal emir's house for two days and go out from here to interview the nearby Bedouin. His house is much like that of my earlier host, the district emir in Jubba. An arcade, shaded, facing a pleasant courtyard with plots of tomatoes and other vegetables. The wall at the end of the arcade, behind the fireplace, is papered with a ten-by-fifteen-foot beach scene—waving palms, ocean, but no people. At the moment, I've been left alone with an Egyptian worker, maybe thirty-five, who comes from Sharqiya Governorate in the Delta. He acted very "tough" at first, but after some conversation, became very affable. He wants me to interview him as I'm interviewing the Bedouin, and I'm trying to explain why that is of no use (do you produce animals for the market, etc.?—he obviously doesn't, but is here, like other Egyptian workers, to help the Saudis get their farms started).

A videocassette has been turned on for our entertainment. It's an Egyptian feature film, vintage 1963–65, I'd say. Fantastic, really, after just coming from crowded Egypt, to see the streets of downtown Cairo so empty, and the people dressed exactly as they were when we lived there. Only Saʿid, the Egyptian migrant laborer, and I seem interested in the film. The family men have gone into the house.

9:30 P.M.

The men have come back out and we are sitting around informally. Two young Saudi boys, looking like dandies, are sharing their impressions of Cairo with Saʿid and me. They were not impressed and complained about the crowds and the dirt like any other fastidious tourists. One wants to come to the United States to study, but he doesn't speak a word of English. I'm tired. But I can't sleep, with the video on and the conversation as well. But the electricity goes off at 11 P.M., so I should be able to sleep then.

September 17, 7:45 A.M.

Well, the electricity didn't go off till midnight. I watched a super-duper Indian melodrama with no Arabic or English subtitles, which kept a couple of Arab boys fascinated for two hours and a half! This tells me more about Indian-Arab cultural relations than I had ever even considered before. I found the films intensely boring, full of all the old tricks of fades and time extensions. One minute the lovers floated like scarves across the grass toward each other for a long, loving look deep in the eyes; the next moment Indian cowboy types were galloping madly after a train. If I could understand why I found it such a bore and why they liked it so much I could write a fine article. Are film styles a one-way street? Is melodramatic exaggeration now forever hopelessly corny? I should add that technically speaking the Indian film was fully up to Hollywood standards. And the color was good.

I slept in the *majlis* where we watched the Indian film. This morning a veiled lady came in, built the fire, and as I rose from my mattress told me to help myself to coffee. I took the coffeepot out of the hot coals left from the small wood fire she had made. She had left some flat bread and canned cheese. Now the emir has come in and is eating with me. No camel milk here; no camels! I didn't sleep well—mosquitoes and sand flies and it was too hot under the arcade, no breeze. It did cool off around 4 A.M., and I slept a few hours. Now if I can just do my interviewing. One son (of the two young men from last night) has disappeared and the second one is supposed to take me around the Bedouin tents in the area. The emir just asked me if he had shown up yet and I told him he hadn't. The father went out to look for his son. Where is parental authority? He doesn't seem to have much more than I do! The emir says he has a brother studying in America. Although he has been there five years, the emir doesn't know the name of the place where he lives. (I am clearly still a nuisance and it isn't certain to me that I will ever get taken out to the tents. As in Turaba, up here in the Nafud I have to have a guide as I can't find anything by myself in the sand dunes. They all look the same to me.)

11:30 A.M.

The emir took me out, and we spent three hours traveling up one dune and down the next. I only did three interviews in four hours, but the trip was spectacular—fantastic desert landscape—a real calendar scene with sharp-edged dunes and rolling hills of sand. Some sparse vegetation, clumps of green grass and low bushes. Didn't find many people, because the camel nomads have gone north toward Jawf in search of better pasture. Jawf is four hours over a desert trail from here, outside the Hail region of the Nafud, where I must stay.

The new road they're talking about will make a big difference, for it will open up a new stretch of desert to the goat and sheep herders. Now they can't camp more than ten kilometers away from Jubba, because they have to haul water to their herds twice a day in summer, and they can't manage more than forty kilometers per day over these dunes. The trip is just too tough; tires last only six months, for instance. But still, as I wrote earlier, this breakneck cruising over the sand is a real trip. Perhaps the emir threw in a bit of dash this time for my benefit, but I wasn't scared. Lapsed into another state of mind. A real trip.

Water is a problem in this area. But there is plenty of it underground, people say, and as the land is distributed to new farmers, lots of wells are being dug. The government is interested in developing agriculture here and has opened up the area to possible private investment. Government subsidies are also pouring in. The farming development schemes seem to be working.

When we got to the house, the young men were back: the son who was to meet me here this morning says he got here by eight-thirty. But his father and I were here then, and he wasn't. Could it be that the younger generation is going to hell here too? (Like all younger generations, of course.) The errant son has asked the servant if his father is mad at him. The servant boy seems to be a bit feebleminded, somehow not normal. They tease him but he loves it. The video is back on—another Egyptian film. This time a sixties comedy. The family has quite a collection of cassettes. Electricity is on for part of the day since the town has several generators.

It turns out that Abdulla, the son, was in Cairo not as a rich tourist but on business to arrange for five Egyptians to come here to work for his father. One of them is Saᶜid, with whom I talked last night. The son volunteered that Egyptians are liars and thieves.

Four men from Jubba are studying in the States now. The emir's brother is in Kansas, according to Abdulla.

9 P.M.

Tonight the Indian migrant laborers have come to the emir's arcade to watch an Indian film on the video machine. He invites them every week, I'm told, which is very nice of him as there doesn't seem to be much else to do for entertainment. I've found out that there are Egyptian and Palestinian schoolteachers working here. And just up the street are Pakistani dressmakers. They were working late the last two nights, finishing up some fancy ladies' dresses: I saw fifteen or twenty dresses, rather conservative Victorian style, hanging on racks behind the old-fashioned treadle sewing machines, waiting to be picked up.

September 18, 4 P.M.

I've been bumping over sand dunes all morning and have just come back to the emir's house. I've finished fifteen interviews, an excellent sample of all the camp-situation types stretching as far as eleven kilometers from Jubba. But I'm exhausted, and my body feels like something heavy has rolled over it several times. The Bedouin I interviewed today varied enormously. Some had already cashed in on government assistance programs; others had never had any help from the government and hadn't thought of asking. The ones who lived farthest from Jubba looked worn-out; they said they went back and forth all day hauling water to their herds. It sounds good to be using trucks for herding and hauling water, but it's in many ways much harder than the old way, when the traditional nomads had to settle for whatever water they could walk to. Today's nomad is working harder—here, at least. Pastoralism is becoming not so much a way of living as a way of earning a living.

In these intense days, I have been getting to know the tribal emir's sons—there are twelve of them—and like them very much. They are really good sons and help their father a lot, it turns out. Every one of the boys is either involved with his father's interests or in school. Even the one that didn't show up to take me out, as he was supposed to, was apparently out in his truck collecting firewood, nearly a hundred kilometers away.

This tribal emir has a lot of responsibilities beyond his economic interests. The whole family has to help. Like the old sheikhs of Iraq (which is more or less what they are, it seems to me), the emirs have to be ready to receive people all day long, make and serve coffee, tea, and meals, provide lodging for travelers, and look after unexpected problems like myself. My host is very lucky! His strong sons are essential factors in his prosperity.

One of the boys told me that he spent five years in the desert with his father before the emir settled down here in Jubba. He says that the Bedu are *jahal,* literally pre-Islamic, though the word also means kind of naïve, unsophisticated. But he still admires them. "Why is a young Bedu so much stronger than three boys from Hail, even if the Bedu is smaller?" he asked me. "How do you account for their confidence?" He is very ambiguous about them. I said, "You'll never forget those five years with the Bedu." He said, "Yes, you are right. When I went to Egypt and saw all the people crowded together there, I thought about the Bedu out here." But he thinks that in a few years, no Bedouin will be left. "They go to school and then it's all finished," he said.

September 18, evening

I've finished my interviews. We traveled about seventy kilometers today, around the edge of the oasis. It felt like seven hundred in some ways, but there were good moments. I feel I have made some new friends here. Literally. Today suddenly the emir and his sons and I seemed to be on much more personal terms. The older boys are twenty, twenty-two, and twenty-three, but there are younger boys, half brothers, since the emir has had three wives. I really like this family, and only wish I had met more people like them during my months in Saudi Arabia.

The job is nearly done. I will be leaving Saudi Arabia soon to meet you in Cairo. This is my last trip on the desert, the last session of interviews. A good trip to end with, I think. Last night I had a good sleep in the sand, parked high on a dune, and when I woke, from a distance Jubba looked more like a storybook illustration than ever. The construction and farm developments weren't visible, only the palm trees, which seemed to be floating in a bluish white mist (really the dust of the settlement). The people have been hospitable and friendly; they have that reputation, but it was more than I had hoped for or expected. It is an old settlement, Jubba, some say three thousand years. The rocks are covered with pictographs from prehistoric times, so people must have been here even longer than that. The new paved road from Hail is due to reach Jubba in a few months. When the city of Hail itself has changed so much so fast, one can only hazard a guess about how Jubba oasis will change in the coming years. And I wonder how my friend the emir and his twelve fine sons will survive and manage, in such a different future. If the circumstances of their lives change as drastically as they seem likely to do, I wonder whether they will or can continue to be what they are—hard-working, generous, hospitable, the real inheritors of an ancient and proud tradition.

THE ANTHROPOLOGIST IN THE FIELD

CULTURAL ANTHROPOLOGY is distinguished from all other social sciences by the practice of fieldwork, a period of study spent by the anthropologist in a cultural setting other than his or her own. The ideas and concepts that are developed by anthropologists quickly find their way into the work of other social scientists, and anthropologists are just as free about picking up creative contributions from other disciplines. But it is the anthropologist's fieldwork, the research in unfamiliar cultural contexts, that sets the discipline apart from other social sciences. This research in the field, the observations and experiences organized and interpreted, results in theories or models about human thought and behavior. That is the standard view. As a member of a discipline that is concerned with the unique properties of each human culture but yet is devoted to the notion that there are fundamental similarities between them which bridge cultural differences, the anthropologist is faced with contradictory intellectual expectations. Fieldwork is a unique experience, but it must be understood according to some general pattern of interpretation that will permit comparisons. For this reason, no matter how unique and adventurous or mundane and familiar the experiences of fieldwork may be, they must constantly be subject to reflection so that the experiences will find a place within the discourse of anthropology, the conversation of the discipline.

Fieldwork is participant observation. Anthropologists are both actors and spectators in the field. Although this is what is said about the experience, it is not that the anthropologist is sometimes the participant and at other times the observer. From the moment one arrives in a village or suburb, a tribal guesthouse or a local bar, one becomes part of the social scene, whether one likes it or not. In a foreign setting this can be very difficult to manage, not from one's reluctance to take part in the local scene, but rather because one's participation (as a stranger) is potentially so disturbing. No matter how well one learns the language and local customs, the difference between the anthropologist and his or her hosts remains—a plus as well as a minus, for it is within the context of one's strangeness that one observes.

As a human being, however, the anthropologist consciously or unconsciously tries to transcend the participant-observer opposition, however impossible this may be. Such moments come closest to taking place during conversation. Not the ritualistic forms of conversation in which the exchange is more or less predetermined, but the kind of conversation in which both parties, the anthropologist and the other person, are struggling to come to a common understanding about a particular subject. In the areas where I have been fortunate enough to do fieldwork—Iraq, Egyptian Nubia, Morocco, Saudi Arabia, Afghanistan—there has been someone in the fieldwork setting who has been particularly adept not only at understanding my limited speech but also at understanding what I am talking about, what the questions I am asking "really mean." At moments in conversation with such persons the participant-observer opposition collapses and I have felt myself become a person interacting with another within a framework of shared understandings. That is what "really mean" means, of course, not an ultimate truth, but a conceptual agreement. In this regard, while living in another culture, I have never felt comfortable about ending a serious conversation when I felt I knew something the other person did not understand. My best informants—and my best friends—in the field have always seemed to share that attitude. They have been at least as stubborn as I am.

Anthropological fieldwork takes place in different cultural contexts and can have very different intellectual objectives. The latter are usually determined both by the history of research in the particular region of the world where one works and by the intellectual paradigms currently in favor. Just as the problems and approaches that are popular one decade may change to something very different the next (structuralism today has been displaced by various forms of postmodernism), so, too, do the fieldwork situations to which one must adapt change radically from one region of the world to the next. Since fieldwork requires constant involvement in the local scene and a willingness to become part of social events to one degree or another, it is hard to understand how it could be undertaken by a person who really dislikes the situation, the setting, the people. Thus, anthropologists generally stay in their regions of special interest with some degree of emotional enthusiasm for the one of their choice. This is not to say that anthropologists, like everyone else, never have negative feelings about people and living conditions. But the general style of life, of personal interaction, cannot be too irritating or upsetting. The Middle East, for instance, is no place for American men who have trouble being touched by other men, any more than Mexican villages are suitable for male researchers who can't hold their pulque. As a poor drinker, I've always been glad that alcohol is generally not part of the Middle Eastern village scene. And I have not felt threatened when a friend takes my hand. In fact, the measured rituals of traditional hospitality serve to ease the preliminary introductions to a Middle Eastern setting (tribal, village, or urban). Someone is always there to receive strangers, including the anthropologist, and this initial welcome provides an opportunity to make one's business known. The ritual of hospitality, however, requires participation. There is the pleasant obligation, on the part of the guest, to drink tea or coffee and often share a meal; I was astounded once when an anthropologist friend told me he never accepted tea in a field setting out of concern for infections. But he explained that in Africa, where he did his research, such customs did not prevail. The Middle East was definitely not to his taste, it seemed.

Most anthropological fieldwork has been done among people who are on the lower end of living standards, however measured. Why? Because such people are less well understood? Because they are in need of study in order to be helped? Because they are like the majority of people in the world? Because they are the way we all were, in some sense, before the industrial revolution made some of us middle-class? Perhaps all of these reasons motivate some anthropological research. Yet my esteemed colleague Laura Nader has rightfully chided us, her colleagues, for not "studying up," for not looking more closely at the behavior of the rich, the capitalists, the establishment, the upper classes, who call the shots in other societies, as well as our own. It is a point well taken, and today, within the profession, Professor Nader and others are making efforts to "study up." However, the rich in all societies are very difficult to reach. One cannot walk into a village of millionaires and watch them conduct their business; the settings within which they carry on their daily lives are carefully protected from outsiders, including anthropologists. Thus, somewhat by default, the anthropologist often has no choice but to study the poor, the oppressed, the mistreated, the powerless, the neglected people of the world, the ones who are at best manipulated by the rich and powerful. In such studies the behavior of the rich and powerful remains a matter of inference. Anthropologists also study the poor in part because the poor are less able to resist us, less able to tell us to mind our own business and get out. We try to think this is not the case, to discount the possibility and excuse our behavior in various ways, but we have to face the fact that we also benefit from the privileges of class and country, however modest our claims, however noble our intentions.

The difference in class and status, in power base, between the anthropologist and his or her subjects of study in the field leads to charges of exploitation. Anthropologists are deriving personal benefit from their researches, it is said, and are aiding the dominant political and economic forces by contributing to their knowledge of the subject populations. On the other hand, anthropologists are also accused of sentimentality, of wanting to preserve a state of affairs, a culture, that is outmoded, of trying to hold back progress to the detriment of the people they profess to admire. Both charges have elaborate ideological underpinnings. The first implies that we, as individuals, are no more than agents of our class, and the second assumes that a single measure of progress exists. I do not agree with either view. However, it is true that until recently much anthropological research has assumed that the group being studied exists in a kind of isolation, a never-never land of self-containment, which was misleading both for the anthropologist and for those who read the anthropologist's work. If anything of significance has resulted from the controversies mentioned above, it is the recognition that villages, tribes, and urban groups are part of a larger political and economic system, a system that intrudes upon and reshapes the local community wherever it may be. It is the anthropologist's responsibility to convey this reality to his or her students and colleagues.

Edward Said, in *Orientalism*, has illustrated how, in the discourse of scholarship, we describe and analyze other cultures, like the Middle East, with signs of our own historic creation. He suggests that the signs of such scholarship over the last two hundred years have been shaped by the dominant position of Europe vis-à-vis the Middle East and he wonders whether the superior economic and political position of the West is not still inevitably embedded in our contemporary studies of non-Western countries. So it is that terms like "lineage," "tribe," "veil," "peasant," "Islam," acquire meanings of their own in the West and resist our attempts to see beyond them to the "real" subject of our inquiry.

Certainly, the anthropologist, like the literary critic, the economist, the historian, or the political scientist, has his or her own baggage of theories and categories, the intellectual tools of the discipline. But in the field, in the communities and the homes of others, the anthropologist, vulnerable both personally and intellectually, finds him- or herself in an inferior position. He or she is dependent on the help and goodwill or the tolerance of those "others" for information, friends. This position at least offers an existential basis for the development of a new perspective. For though the anthropologist, like other scholars, cannot escape historic intellectual theories and cultural categories, the field-work situation forces him or her to reflect on those theories and categories, to look at them more carefully, to rethink their implications, in personal as well as scholarly terms.

Today fewer and fewer countries are open to anthropological research. Governments of the left accuse us of being imperialists, while those of the right see us as radicals and troublemakers. Fieldwork in other cultures may eventually disappear, along with cultural anthropology as we have known it. This will be doubly unfortunate, for the same authoritarianism that would eliminate this form of disciplined human concern would also put an end to the splendid human diversity that anthropologists have tried to describe.

IN DECEMBER 1996, B.J. traveled to Saudi Arabia for the first time with a group of invited American academics. The two-week trip, sponsored by the National Council on U.S.-Arab Relations, included Jeddah, the ancient port city on the Red Sea; Riyadh, the capital in central Arabia; and Dammam, the oil center on the Gulf coast. Such a brief stay can hardly compare with Bob's lengthier visits in the 1970s and 1980s, but some changes were clear enough.

Saudi Arabia has grown. In two generations a small desert kingdom (population four million) has become a nation of eighteen million people, with an impressive state-of-the-art infrastructure of housing, highways, hotels, schools, and other public buildings. The magnificent airports in Jeddah and Riyadh combine elements of traditional and modern architectural styles, evoking, in Jeddah, the image of clustered Bedouin tents, and in Riyadh, the fountains and gardens of an imagined paradise. The Dammam shopping mall is called "mother of all malls" and certainly in scope, decor, and number of stores is larger than any American mall I have seen.

Educational accomplishments are also remarkable. Since 1970, when Saudi Arabia had one of the lowest literacy rates in the Middle East (15 percent for men, 2 percent for women), government public schools and universities have succeeded in raising these rates to 73 percent for men and 48 percent for women. Today, 3.5 million students are in primary and secondary schools. Of the 142,000 students attending the seven universities, nearly half are women, taught however in separate facilities not always as grand as the men's.

Many modernizing projects were on the drawing boards in 1983 when Bob went to Hail as a consultant for development planning. But by 1996, many of these projects still remained in the planning stage. Saudi Arabia has been running a deficit economy for several years, mainly due to the international fall in oil prices and, more recently, because of the cost of the Gulf War with Iraq, for which Saudi Arabia paid the United States $75 billion in cash.

"We were happy to share the costs," said one Saudi official, "but now why doesn't the United States treat us more as equals? Why are there still thirty-five thousand American troops here at our expense?" The presence of so many Americans creates a general concern about dependence on the United States. And the sudden development of unemployment in a country that in the last decades has had jobs not only for Saudis, but also for thousands of foreigners, was a constant source of discussion with our group. No real poverty was evident to us, but the general mood I sensed was one of unease. We heard stories: of corruption in high places ("and the U.S. says nothing"); of human rights abuses, especially of the Shia minority ("and the U.S. says nothing"); of lack of movement toward a more democratic government—the authorities imprisoned men who signed a petition respectfully asking for a greater public role in national politics—("and the U.S. says nothing"). "I thought you Americans were into promoting democracy," one Saudi professor said, sadly and ironically, it seemed to me.

One-fourth of the American oil supply comes from Saudi Arabia, so protecting our national interests there is no joke. Furthermore, the kingdom controls around 25 percent of all the world's proven oil reserves and thus dominates the market supply. But, for Saudis, fresh water has locally become more valuable than oil. Oil sales pay for expensive water desalination and subsidizes agriculture, which nevertheless produces only a small portion of the national food supply.

So, Saudis are asking, what is going to happen now? How is our country going to become more self-sufficient? How will we use the skills of our newly educated young men and women? How can we persuade the many Saudis who have coasted through life that it is now time to work and often work hard at jobs they may not like? How long will the kingdom remain an absolute monarchy? When will the government change the laws enforcing women's seclusion and supervision (no driving, mandatory full veiling in public, segregated public services)? As the country becomes ever more part of the global capitalist economy, as awareness of changes that have taken place elsewhere in the Muslim world become universal, Saudi Arabia is the only Arab nation to enforce such sex segregation, practices which many Muslims argue are not supported by the Koran.

Saudi Arabian people whom we met were proud of the country's guardianship of the sacred cities of Islam, the annual focus of pilgrimage for 2.5 million Muslims every year. They are also proud of their country's technical modernization. But conversations and interviews also suggested that many people in Saudi Arabia are ready to play a much more active role in the responsibilities for this guardianship and in the political, social, and religious life they will lead in the coming century.

VI Israel and the West Bank

When words stop, the sword begins to speak.

ARAB PROVERB

JERUSALEM. JERUSALEM. In twenty-seven years of travel and residence in the Middle East, I had never journeyed to Jerusalem. Bob had, in 1964, before the face of the city was changed by the 1967 war. Laura Ann, our older daughter, had come to Jerusalem from Damascus, as part of her ten-day visit to Israel in 1978. And in 1961 my mother and my aunt Mary had made a pilgrimage to the holy places of Christendom on their way back to the United States from a visit to us in Egypt. But now we were here. October 1983. Bob and I had come at the invitation of Bir Zeit University, one of four Palestinian universities on the West Bank, for a conference on rural society in the Middle East, a conference sponsored jointly by the University of Durham in England and the University of Amsterdam.

One of the oldest cities in the Middle East, inhabited continuously for perhaps six thousand years, Jerusalem is the home of the sacred shrines of Judaism, of Christianity, and of Islam. For Jews and Christians, Jerusalem is the city of beginnings; so is it also for Muslims, for whom it is the most holy city after Mecca and Medina. The Dome of the Rock is where the Prophet Muhammad is said to have visited during his lifetime, and the place where in a vision, many believe, he ascended from earth to heaven. The Caliph Omar prayed on this spot in A.D. 638, after capturing Jerusalem from the Byzantine Empire. The Dome of the Rock was pictured on many of the posters we found pasted on the walls of buildings in the Palestinian quarters of Beirut, next to the posters of the martyrs. I saw the same posters in the houses of the refugees in Rashadiyah, where I had filmed in 1981, as well as posters depicting the Church of the Holy Sepulcher, sacred to Christians and also to Muslims. A calendar bearing a small colored likeness of the golden Dome of the Rock hung in the living room of my friend Um

Zhivago. Jerusalem was the city to which the people of Rashadiyah longed to return. But they could not, for Israelis rule Jerusalem now. Three and a half million Jews from all parts of the world live in Jerusalem and in the surrounding cities and towns of the State of Israel, many of them refugees from the inhuman Holocaust of the Hitler years. Um Zhivago knows that, of course. But she also knows what we did not fully realize until recently: nearly two million Palestinians also live in or near the sacred city of Jerusalem, 500,000 within Israel itself and 1.3 million on the West Bank of the Jordan River and in the Gaza Strip, which stretches along the sea from Israel to Egypt.

Jerusalem. The sound of the word vibrates in the mind and the heart of every person who has ever attended a church, a synagogue, a mosque, who has read a collection of literature, recited poetry, sung sacred songs, grown up within one of the three great monotheistic religions of the world: Judaism, Christianity, Islam. Western roots lie here, in the East. And the beauty of the city, its unexpected and dramatic setting, its austere majesty, makes its own statement. Stones quarried hundreds of years ago, stained over time with blood and anointed with oil, prayed over by bishops and archimandrites and rabbis and qadis, fought over by knights and barons, by sultans and emperors, pave the roads that wind through the enclosed city. Groves of olive trees rise, gray-green against the sandy-colored soil, on the seven hills that are part of, that encircle, the city. (An olive tree, once rooted, will bear for generations, we were told. Some of the olive trees in Jerusalem are said to date from Roman times.)

The people of Jerusalem, many wearing Western dress, some wearing the distinctive dress of orthodox Judaism, orthodox Christianity, orthodox Islam, walk along the narrow cobblestoned streets of the old walled city, wait for buses on the streets of the new town, shop for tomatoes and bread in the traditional souks, for frozen foods in the modern supermarkets. We were shown the pool of the Greek Orthodox patriarch, the *khan*, or inn, that belongs to the Coptic Church. The massive stone walls that protect the city were completed in 1542 by Suliman the Magnificent, ruler of the Ottoman Empire. There are the remains of a real moat, and a drawbridge that was still operating in the early part of this century. This is the spot where the commander of the British Expeditionary Force in Egypt, Field Marshal Edmund Allenby, stood after capturing Jerusalem from the Turks in 1917. ''Saladin, we are back!" he is supposed to have shouted, thus bringing to a triumphant end the Crusades begun eight hundred years before. Today Muslim and Christian conquerors have been put aside; Jewish conquerors rule the city. But whoever rules, Jerusalem within the walls remains an urban site of multiple religious enclaves: four distinct quarters, Muslim, Jewish, Christian, and a special Armenian quarter. Within these are numerous convents, hostels, offices, and delegations of various sects, watched over by religious congregations in all parts of the world. Jerusalem belongs, both literally and metaphorically, to millions of people who will never visit, much less live in, the city. And the stones, the streets, the buildings, the very niches within the buildings, are charged with multiple meanings, with memories, with the history of many different groups, many different beliefs about the rule of God on earth, about truth, about justice.

Bir Zeit University, to which we were headed, is a relatively new institution of higher learning (1972) which has evolved from an older secondary school. Walled, pleasantly laid out with courts and flowering shrubs, it lies about fifteen miles north of Jerusalem, near Ramallah, a largely Christian town; about two hundred faculty teach two thousand students. While the conference was in session on the campus, the students went back and forth to class, sat on the low benches in the courtyard in the sunlight, talking, laughing, reading aloud to each other. In their jeans and sweaters, their boots and tennis shoes, they looked much like students in an American university. But here the situation differs vastly from that on an American campus.

Bir Zeit (the Arabic words mean literally "well of [olive] oil"), the town and the university, lies on the West Bank of the Jordan River, the area taken by Israel in the war of 1967 and since that time administered by a military government. Seventeen years is a long time for so many people to live under occupation. The people of the West Bank to whom we spoke chafed under the military regime, and we remembered reading about the incidents resulting from such alien rule which were reported in the Western media. Stones are thrown at military jeeps. A Jewish settler is killed in the West Bank city of Hebron. Demonstrations are held at Bethlehem University, which is partly supported by the Vatican and has an American vice-president. Bir Zeit has been closed by the Israeli military authorities seven times between 1973 and 1982, for periods ranging from a few days to three months. The charge:

political activities. The four West Bank universities—Bir Zeit, Bethlehem, Al-Naja, and Hebron—together constitute one of the better university systems in the Middle East. Developed since 1967 under Israeli occupation, the universities in the past have been allowed relative freedom to raise funds outside Israel—particularly in Jordan and other parts of the Arab world. Today the Israeli authorities are apparently having second thoughts about the autonomy of the Palestinian universities. Faculty and staff at Bir Zeit told us that a number of military orders have been issued; these orders, if implemented, could severely restrict the universities' hiring and firing policies and the contents of their curricula.

To us, in October 1983, the West Bank looked outwardly serene, as did Jerusalem. Many of the houses and the domes and spires and towers within the walls of the old city were built of a distinctive local stone, which casts a faint rosy glow into the clear, golden light of the highland fall. The Jordan Valley, where we traveled to visit agricultural settlements, was lush with autumn planting near Jericho, where we lunched in an open-air restaurant under grape arbors, on a local Palestinian specialty: *mussakhan*, chicken grilled with onions and sumac. In the south toward Hebron, the famous grapes of the area, purple and dusky gold, were being harvested from the stone terraces and offered for sale in lean-tos along the roadside by women in the colorfully embroidered dresses and flowing head scarves of their villages. Bob was scheduled to present a paper at the conference about Saudi Arabia. I had agreed to show my documentary film about the lives of Palestinian women in the Rashadiyah refugee camp.

We could not view the West Bank and Jerusalem and Bir Zeit in a neutral light. Like other Americans involved with the Middle East over the past twenty-five years, we had come to be concerned about the Arab-Israeli conflict, about the growth of the State of Israel, about the situation of the Palestinians, both in Israel and on the West Bank and Gaza. The controversy, bitter and long-standing, about rights to the land and to the city of Jerusalem, looked to us in 1983, as we talked with people on both sides, at least as far from settlement as it had looked in 1967 at the end of the war when Israel occupied the West Bank.

Yet everyday life proceeds in Jerusalem and on the West Bank.

People, both Israeli and Palestinian, would describe, politely and pleasantly, their lives to us, lives that to middle-class Americans like ourselves seemed unreal. The Israelis in the more than one hundred legally contested new settlements that are rising around Jerusalem and on the West Bank live in totally segregated communities, in huge, self-contained white-painted housing developments that ring the villages and hills around Jerusalem like fortresses, modern stockades of cement and stone. A Swedish filmmaker whom we met in the American Colony Hotel told us that in some of the settlement apartments a single button closes all windows and doors automatically and that the location of the crucial button is taught very early to Israeli children. We ask Israeli acquaintances against whom the windows and doors are closed automatically and the reply is, "The enemy."

One of the representatives of an international welfare foundation, a British friend of ours, says he feels obliged to present his "solution" to anyone who will listen. Of all peoples in the world, his lecture goes, the Jews and the Arabs would seem the most likely groups to be able to live together in some kind of harmony. Says Hugh, "They have so much in common. They share roots in the same religion, in the same language family, they value the family tie greatly, they have a rich tradition of folklore and literature."

However, there are few social meetings between Arabs and Jews under present circumstances. Instead, these groups of people so divided, so shut off from each other, live together, uneasily and full of mutual distrust, on the same small piece of historically contested ground, and talk about the violation of the ideals of their forefathers.

Israelis explained to us, again patiently and politely, that ideologically Palestinians do not belong in Israel, whether they are Muslim or Christian. Why? They are not Jewish, and Israel is a Jewish state. But they are there, nearly two million, and half of them are under fifteen years of age. Since the great flight of Palestinians from their home in 1948, fewer and fewer have left Israel, partly because of the strict laws that stipulate that any Arab who chooses to emigrate must formally renounce the right to return. Given the close family ties among Arabs in Israel, such a decision is very difficult. More West Bank Arabs leave, to study or work abroad, but even so, only 3 to 4 percent are lost through emigration each year. The lack of employment opportunities for educated Arabs is a problem, however. As a group, the West Bank people have one of the highest levels of formal education in the Middle East.

"What do they think of us in America?" a high school girl at the East Jerusalem YWCA, where we were housed for the conference, asked me. She was a student in one of the classes offered at the YWCA for girls who wish to obtain vocational training after finishing secondary school.

I answered that many people in America, I thought, had sympathy for the Palestinians and hoped that a solution could be found for their problems.

She was about sixteen, dark-haired, plump. She simply stared at me. "I can't believe that," she said.

"Why not?"

"Because everyone says, in the newspapers and magazines, that the Americans think of us all as terrorists, *beasts*. Who has sympathy for *beasts?*"

I started to explain how Americans might get that idea, the way the media referred to the PLO and saw all of its behavior as the acts of terrorists. She heard me out, polite to the end, but I could see she did not believe me. "Thank you," she said, and that was the end of the conversation.

Many Israelis expressed their concern about government policy on the West Bank. "The old consensus in Israel has fallen apart on this issue," said a well-known Israeli professor, a friend of friends. "In the old days, when we came here, we all thought we were dedicated to a common goal, developing a free state, a symbol for the world. It's not true anymore."

"But perhaps that's to be expected," I temporized, "given the growth of the state, the differing backgrounds of the people who have emigrated to Israel over the years."

He was an old man with white hair, a lame leg. He shook his head. "I understand what you are saying, the values of a pluralistic society and so on. But in a pluralistic society people can criticize, complain, have the power to change things. We can still do that here. This is a democracy still. We have a free press, you know."

"Yes," I said. "We've noticed the kiosks—all kinds of newspapers,

Cairo subway.
Sign in upper left says "No smoking."

Photo by Thomas Hartwell

Bodybuilding posters, Baghdad.

Photo by Thomas Hartwell

Nubian women in Kom Ombo,
near Aswan, prepare a meal.

Photo by Thomas Hartwell

Murad Essawy, innovative Egyptian Delta farmer, with Ali, his assistant.

Photo by Thomas Hartwell

Facade of primary school on the outskirts of Baghdad.

Photo by Thomas Hartwell

مَدرسَة صَدام العَرب الأبتدائية

Israeli soldier guarding rooftop in Jerusalem.

Photo by Thomas Hartwell

Riverside, Baghdad, Iraq, 1996.

Photo by Thomas Hartwell

Baghdad, Iraq, 1996. Women selling products on Rashid Street.

Photo by Thomas Hartwell

Men of the tribe gather in front of the new *mudhif*, or men's guesthouse, in the village of Al-Nahra, southern Iraq. Author Robert Fernea is in the front row to the left of the doorway arch.

Photo by Thomas Hartwell

in English, Hebrew, Arabic, expressing all kinds of differing opinions, presumably. Very heartening—and important."

The older man pointed a finger at me. "But it is only the Israelis that really have that freedom, you know. People on the West Bank do not."

"So what you are saying about the consensus falling apart here has to do with the government policy toward the West Bank—"

"Toward the Palestinians generally. How can we, supposedly one of the most idealistic societies in the world—we *were*, you know—"

I nodded.

"—how can we support the policies that do not let another group of people live useful, free lives, live in peace—"

"Do they let *us* live in peace?" angrily, from a younger man. "Isn't that the crux of the issue?"

"Have either of us tried?" asked the old man of his younger colleague.

Peace, everyone says on both sides of the divided city, is what everyone wants. Peace would bring an end to the devastating cost of arms, the draining wars; peace would bring relief to the economy, which, despite years of hard work by Israelis, is not even close to self-sufficient. But the atmosphere of Jerusalem, of the West Bank, is not conducive to peace. Israeli soldiers turn up unexpectedly in the markets, as they did when Bob and I were shopping in the old city, pushing people and goods aside with their weapons. Traffic police may choose to search an entire car that has been stopped for a minor violation, as happened on the Gaza road when we were traveling with our friend Hugh. Life is expensive in Israel, and inflation continues to rise. An automobile, after import duties and taxes, costs three times what it would in the United States. The government subsidizes basic foods, such as bread, but the flat Arab bread is not subsidized. Cars registered on the West Bank bear blue license plates to distinguish them from Israeli cars (yellow license plates). To make it even more confusing, Palestinian cars in East Jerusalem also have yellow license plates. But in Gaza, where more than 400,000 people, the majority refugees, are jammed together on a narrow strip of land and where trouble is reported to be frequent, the license plates of the cars are silvery gray so they can be more quickly distinguished by the police, people told us.

In general, however, any action that is taken by Israeli officials or police must be justified legally, we were told by both Palestinians and Israelis. The courts regularly hear lawsuits brought by both Israelis and Palestinians. Recently, a Palestinian woman scientist submitted a petition to the faculty of the Hebrew University, where she was then teaching, to obtain permission to publish a scientific journal in Arabic, since none now exists. This petition, supported by many Israeli faculty groups, ended up in the courts and was denied in late 1983. The woman also lost her job. Permits must be obtained to grow tomatoes, to buy land, to get a telephone, to travel, to build a house, to register a company, to stay overnight in Israel proper (if you are from Gaza), to plant olive trees or grow plums. (You need not get a permit to plant grapevines or grow plums if you have a deed to your property that has been accepted by an Israeli court as valid or if the grapes or plums are for personal consumption and the plants do not exceed twenty in number.) People on the West Bank must carry their identification cards with them at all times; Jews as well as Arabs who are stopped by police are expected to show their cards of identity.

Westerners in Jerusalem and on the West Bank to whom we spoke exhibited a wide range of reactions to the present situation. For tourists, very little out-of-the-ordinary activity is noticeable, other than the presence of many armed soldiers on the streets. For Americans and Europeans stationed in the area as staff members of the many volunteer organizations, it is a different story. Such organizations would not be there if they did not regard the Palestinians to some degree as war victims, and thus in need of special help. In addition to the U.N. agency UNRWA, at least seventeen voluntary organizations operate on the West Bank, in Gaza, and in Jerusalem; they include CARE, Save the Children, Catholic Charities, Oxfam, the Friends Service Committee, American Near East Refugee Aid (ANERA), German Aid, AMIDEAST.

What do the agencies do? They provide supplies for schools in the refugee camps in Gaza, they dispense grants for piped water, improved drainage, agricultural cooperatives, scholarships for Palestinian students to go on to the university. The voluntary organizations fall into two distinct categories, we were told: those that cooperate with the Israeli government and help the Palestinians on the West Bank by supplying what amounts to welfare services (food allotments, for instance), and those such as ANERA that try to promote independent development among the Palestinians. The latter groups often wait for months, even years, for permission to implement their projects.

"We're here to help, in whatever way we can," said one representative. "I would rather work with the Israeli government because then I know it will be done."

Henry Selz, the representative of ANERA, disagrees with that position. "The only way we can help the Palestinians is to let them rely on *themselves*," he stated. "And the way to do that is give them the means to achieve some economic independence."

Mr. Selz is not always able to fulfill his aims. In the last three years many ANERA projects have not been approved by the military government.

"That's because the early ones were too successful," he argues. White-haired, lean, rangy, restless, he has been working for the American Friends Service Committee and other peace-promoting organizations for most of his life. "The Palestinians are good businessmen and excellent farmers. They organize well. Look at the olive oil cooperative in Tarqumiya, one of the poorest areas on the West Bank. It has twelve hundred members, representing people in fifteen villages. They're marketing the oil. It's working. And the same with the chicken and egg cooperatives in Ramallah. But those products compete against Israeli products in the market."

"And then what happens?" asked Bob.

"They're not allowed to sell the chickens or the eggs or the olive oil outside a small, specified area. Actually, that's not quite true," Henry corrected himself. "They must get a permit. But of course the permit isn't granted."

Henry Selz took us to see the new construction in many parts of the West Bank, to view small industries financed and run by Palestinians. "Look at that," he said as we rounded a curve on the road south. A factory complex of some sort lay in the valley below us. It was empty, closed.

"What is it?" asked Bob.

"A cement factory. Doing very well," answered Henry. "Too well, in fact. So the military government passed an order, required the owners to buy their raw materials at retail rather than wholesale prices. That put them out of business rather quickly."

The situation in Israel and on the West Bank becomes more complex the more one travels, the more one sees, the more people one meets. Not all Palestinians are destitute, nor are all Israelis rich. The diversity in the Israeli population was expected; we had read about the different groups of people, from every class and every country, that constituted the new state. But we had not read as much about the Palestinians, even during our years in the Arab world. The Palestinians we met were as various as would be found in any sizable population, and two million is obviously a sizable population. Poor farmers, rich landowners, college professors, small-scale artisans, unskilled workers. The Palestinians are divided in other ways: geographically, between Israel proper, the West Bank, the Gaza Strip, and the Hashemite Kingdom of Jordan, just across the eastern border of the West Bank, two hours' drive from Jerusalem. Palestinians are also divided on the means to deal with occupation—militant, passive, opportunist, collaborationist. We visited a settlement in the Jordan Valley where the village leader explained to us in Arabic that he preferred to go along with the military government so he could obtain the things his village needed: electricity, a school. "You understand?" he asked anxiously.

We said that yes, we understood.

Hebron, a West Bank town of forty thousand southwest of Jerusalem, is a different story altogether. Hebron is sacred both to Jews and to Muslims as the site of Abraham and Sarah's tomb, and it is called Al-Khalil in Arabic, that is, "friend of [God, or Abraham]." The foundations of the city predate its biblical mention. A sizable Jewish community always lived in Hebron until 1929, a time of strife throughout Palestine, when four to five thousand Jews and Arabs lost their lives. Jews were killed by Muslims and most Jews left the area. Today a small group of Jewish families has come back to Hebron. After first settling outside the town of mostly Sunni Muslims, they are now moving inside the old city, praying in the old Ibrahimi mosque, which developed from a Byzantine church. The joint prayers in the building proceed according to an agreement reached between Muslim and Jewish leaders. However, said Muslims, the Jews who come to pray still refuse to take off their shoes as a mark of respect to the mosque space.

We were sitting in the American Colony Hotel with a Western journalist when this tale was recounted to us. The journalist retorted,

"Familiar kind of situation. Nothing new. Garden-variety colonial problems."

The garden-variety colonial problems looked more ominous when we drove to Hebron, past the outskirts of the town where the potters still produce the flowered painted plates that the Crusaders presumably took home as souvenirs in the Middle Ages, just as the German tour group pouring out of the bus paused on the road was preparing to do. In the center of town, across from the partially destroyed old market area, stands a military outpost, an armed camp surrounded by a high barbed-wire fence and floodlights. An Israeli flag has been planted in the middle of the parade ground, behind the barbed-wire fence.

What is happening in Hebron?

"Fanatics from the Muslim side and the Jewish side," asserted an Israeli professor of history. "The Jewish fanatics are all Americans. Why don't you keep your citizens at home?" Then he laughed. "I am only teasing," he added. "But you see what happens. A Jewish settler was killed. Then in retaliation you have that terrible attack on Hebron University, where three Muslim students were killed and many wounded, up to fifty, they say."

The wife of Rabbi Levinger, who heads the new Hebron Jewish community, was interviewed by a *Jerusalem Post* reporter for a feature on life in Hebron, which appeared on October 5, 1983. Asked whether she was upset by living in a hostile environment, she replied, "Not at all. We had the same problem in New York. There we were in danger, too, from blacks and Puerto Ricans. Here at least we are guarded by Jewish rather than Christian police."

We left Hebron and headed back to Jerusalem. "Would you like to live in Hebron?" asked Henry Selz. "It gives me the shudders whenever I come here these days."

Bob and I said that we would certainly not care to live in the city of Hebron.

JERUSALEM HAS BEEN THE symbolic site of power struggles for centuries, not only between Muslim empires and Judaic leaders but also between Christian groups, between the Egyptian Coptic Christian Church and the Ethiopian Christian Church, between the Russian Orthodox Church and the Greek Orthodox Church, between the Vatican and the Austro-Hungarian Empire. Today it is still a symbolic site, an ancient walled city, governed by Israel, yet fragmented into many small segments that are controlled by Christian, Jewish, Muslim groups. And outside the ancient city lie two other cities. To the west the new modern Israeli Jerusalem stands, with efficient buses, Western shops, art galleries, antique stores, pizza parlors, film clubs offering the newest American and European films. To the north and east of the walls, past the Damascus Gate, morning assembly point for Arab day laborers, lies the Arab city, officially considered part of the occupied territories, and under military occupation. The line seemed vague to us, and we asked people how they could tell where one section (legal) ended and the other (illegal) began. The Palestinians to whom we addressed this question looked at us incredulously.

"You *know*," they answered. "And you carry your identification cards all the time, everywhere. The Jews do, too. It's that kind of place."

As occupied territory, the West Bank is not a country, it is a nonnation, just a place, publicized on Western television by the incidents, the rock-throwing, the demonstrations, the weeping women. How do more than a million people go on living in such a situation?

"We don't all throw rocks," said one Bir Zeit student rather defensively. "But that's all you hear about us in America."

"It's true," said Henry Selz. "Given the provocation under which these people live, I am constantly astounded at how peaceful they are."

"The small amount of violence amazes me," agreed another voluntary agency official.

"We are *samid*," said a Palestinian professor.

"Agreed," said his wife. "It means 'steadfast' in English. We are that."

Many Palestinians told us they were *samid*, steadfast. "It is a policy," they said, a stand, a way to survive with dignity. *Samid* means "I will stay firm. I will not move."

But *samid*, as a stance, did not appear to be as passive in practice as we had expected.

Standing firm also involves standing by one's principles, expressing one's identity. Ibrahim Daqqaq, the elderly chairman of the Engineering Association of the West Bank, heads the Arab Thought Forum, an informal group established after other ethnically based organizations were declared illegal. "In old Palestine we had problems, too," he said, "the individualism of our peasant farmers versus the communal ideal of the society. Here we must think about these kinds of problems, too."

The forum holds regular meetings with speakers; it has established a library. Members are academics, students, and, as Mr. Daqqaq describes them, "more practical persons." Part of the purpose of the Arab Thought Forum, he said, is to "make life bearable under unbearable conditions, to help create identity, cultural ties, combat a sense of despair and nihilism among our people."

The Israelis have talked about expelling or encouraging the emigration of Palestinians, according to Mr. Daqqaq. "But," he said, "getting rid of Palestinians is not an easy job. We try to help our people in the short term and in the long term, too, by protecting and developing Palestinian indigenous institutions."

Samiha al-Khalil, a vigorous dark-haired widow, views *samid* in another way. She is the founder and director of In'ash al-Usra, the Society for the Preservation of the Family, which she sees as the most important indigenous Palestinian institution of all. With a study-tour group of American YMCA representatives, I visited Mrs. Khalil's educational and training center for girls. One hundred and fifty girls a year graduate from the society's programs in sewing, secretarial skills, hairdressing. She has organized support on the West Bank and abroad for children orphaned by the conflict and runs a nursery for working mothers. Mrs. Khalil has been jailed by the military government five times, we were told. When I asked her about her imprisonment, she brushed the question aside. "We want only to live in peace," she said. "Let them live. Let us live. We just want to stay on our land."

As we were leaving the center, waiting to shake hands and thank Mrs. Khalil for showing us the workshops, one of the American representatives of the Young Men's Christian Association of New York State said to me, "Isn't it wonderful to have a Christian woman in a place like this? She can do so much good with her faith, here in this Muslim land."

I turned and looked at the woman, pleasant-faced, gray-haired, well dressed. "But Mrs. Khalil is a Muslim," I said.

"Oh no," said her husband. "She can't be. She speaks about peace."

"You don't think the Muslims want peace, too?" I asked.

The man and his wife looked slightly embarrassed. By now we had expressed our thanks and were standing outside in the midmorning sunshine, in front of the whitewashed building that housed Samiha al-Khalil's Society for the Preservation of the Family.

The man said, "Well, that's not what we hear at home, is it?"

I found myself suddenly angry. "But you're *here*, not at home," I said, and at my tone two or three other members of the group of Christian leaders looked around curiously.

The pleasant-faced wife looked at her husband, at me. She fumbled with the brochure.

"Shall we go back and ask her whether she is a Muslim?" I finally got out, but the couple was already turning away, heading toward the tour bus.

"No, no," they murmured.

And I was left in the street feeling foolish, but still annoyed.

ABDURAHMAN NATSCHE is the director of the University Graduates Union, a kind of student union building/night school/cultural center for Palestinians in Hebron; surely a difficult place these days, we thought, to practice the stance of *samid*.

"Oh no." Dr. Abdurahman smiled. "It is important. We must stay here. The building provides a recreation area for the youth of this town. We had the first library in the area."

"You've been here a long time?" asked Bob.

"Since 1953. We now administer the secondary school examinations of Jordan. We have adapted our institute program to the Israeli public school system here, which lacks history, geography, any sense of local culture, and so on."

"You fill in, in other words?" Bob said.

"Yes," said Dr. Abdurahman, a middle-aged man, heavily built, with a soft voice and a pleasant smile. "We give courses, fill in the gap between the local public school and a good education. A good education equals a good citizen. We try to connect this generation to its roots."

Law in the Service of Man is another kind of *samid* approach, a legal research and information unit, rather like the American Legal Aid Society, which occupies three small rooms on the upper floor of a small

office building in downtown Ramallah. Begun in 1980 by two Palestinian lawyers, Jonathan Kuttab and Raja Shehada, to observe and report
on the way in which international law is administered on the West
Bank, the unit now has the support of the International Juridical Association. Leaflets, written in simple language, have been prepared by the
unit on such subjects as what to do when you are arrested and what to
do if the military government tries to take your land. It was Raja
Shehada's moving book *The Third Way: A Journal of Life on the West
Bank* that was being widely discussed in October, that was sold out in
all the bookstores in both the Israeli section and the Arab section of
Jerusalem. Shehada's account opens with an epigraph which, he says, is
"from the wisdom of the Treblinka concentration camp: Faced with two
alternatives, always choose the third. Between mute submission and
blind hate—I choose the third way. I am Samid." Steadfast.

TWO NIGHTS BEFORE LEAVING Israel we had dinner in a small Arab
restaurant in East Jerusalem, around the corner from the National Hotel and its nearby tourist bazaars offering brass ashtrays, olive-wood
carvings, crucifixes, Arab headdresses, and postcards of the holy
shrines. We were a curious party: Bob and I; our photographer friend
Tom Hartwell; the Swedish filmmaker; the British director of Oxfam
Middle East; and an Israeli army officer who was active in the Israeli
Committee for Solidarity with Bir Zeit University. I had noticed him at
some of the sessions of the conference, tall, imposing, the biggest person in the room.

Human rights. The discussion was of human rights, East and
West, of Israeli and Palestinian films and filmmakers—Jud Ne'eman,
Michel Khleifi, Avram Gitai—of groups within Israel that protest regu-
larly and loudly against the policies of the government toward the West
Bank and Gaza. Peace Now. Israel Left. Committee for Solidarity with
Bir Zeit University. Israel Association for Civil Rights. Oz VeShalom
(Religious Zionists for Strength and Peace). There Is a Limit (Army
Officers Who Refuse to Serve in Lebanon). The evening had begun in a
series of somewhat wary interchanges, since at first we did not all know
each other well, and Bob and I and Tom had not even been introduced
to the Israeli army officer, who was, it turned out, also a member of
There Is a Limit. But the evening developed slowly into a serious dis-

cussion of serious subjects. We ate and drank—shish kebab, stuffed zucchini with yogurt sauce, lamb and vegetables, beer made in Israel from a Dutch recipe, wine from a local Christian monastery—though the Israeli army officer ate only bread and salad, I noticed, and drank a glass of water.

"What you don't realize," said the filmmaker, who had covered Vietnam for Swedish television, "is that the West has screwed both Israel *and* the Arabs."

The Israeli army officer was wearing a red shirt and blue denim overalls. He sat back in his chair, his thumbs under his overall straps. "Easy for you to say," he offered mildly. "Sweden has never taken a position on anything."

"Oh, come now," said the Briton as the Swede opened his mouth to reply. "Let's not blame everything on the British and the Americans again."

"Why not?" said Bob. "Who bears more responsibility? Billions of dollars in U.S. aid means involvement *and* responsibility."

"Yeah, looks that way," chimed in Tom.

"I agree," said the Israeli officer. "But it has become more complex these days. It is an issue *here*, for *us*, in Israel." He banged his finger on the table to emphasize his words. "A moral issue. *We* must solve it, not *you*."

"The Palestinians must also be involved in solving it," put in Bob.

"They already are involved," said the Israeli.

We stood on the street outside the restaurant, exchanging names and addresses. The Israeli was talking about the latest officer to be jailed for refusing to serve in Lebanon.

"But *you're* not in jail," said the Swede suddenly. "Why not?"

The Israeli looked down at the Swede. "I am a famous war hero," he replied. "It would embarrass the government to put me in jail."

WE LEFT THE WEST BANK feeling that most of the Palestinians there were no longer convinced that a military solution to their occupation was possible; they seemed ready for a settlement that would involve their neutrality and independence. Clearly, the present polarized situation, the split society, benefits no one, neither Israelis nor the Arabs.

Rabbi Ovadia Yosef, chief Sephardic rabbi in Israel, said in 1979,

"Under Jewish law, it is forbidden to give back even the smallest parcel of the Land of Israel, [but] if there is any question of life and death, if there is any danger whatever of a war involving bloodshed, for example, then it is surely permitted to hand back areas of the Land of Israel and arrive at territorial compromise anywhere including Judea and Samaria. . . . I am of the opinion that Israel should negotiate with all moderate Arab Palestinians who recognize Israel and accept UN resolutions 242 and 338."

And Raja Shehada had written in 1982, "It is the faces on the West Bank and in Israel that I love, admire, am proud to know, that have pushed aside my nightmare visions. . . . Our struggle is not senseless: it is not yet proven that good never wins the day."

A compromise on the West Bank could reduce the polarization and improve the lives of everyone in this ancient region where Christian, Jew, and Muslim have fought for centuries over land they all love passionately. But what of the refugees outside the West Bank and Israel, 300,000 still in Lebanon alone? Where will they go? Who will concern themselves about them?

Thirty years of conflict, of violence, of rhetoric, have created a fog that, however dense, still cannot mask the two basic facts. The Jewish people were disenfranchised and suppressed in the brutal events of the Holocaust. The Palestinian people were disenfranchised and are being suppressed in the actions of the West to atone to the Jews for the great injustice done *them.* But the Arabs were not responsible for the Holocaust and do not see why they should suffer for the sins of Western civilization. Today both Jews and Arabs suffer.

> *Here in these mountains,*
> *hope belongs to the landscape*
> *like the water holes. Even the*
> *ones with no water still belong*
> *to the landscape like hope.*

Yehudah Amichai
SUMMER EVENING IN THE JERUSALEM MOUNTAINS

> *But they know that my country*
> *has known a thousand*
> *conquerors and they know*
> *that all melted away like driven*
> *snow.*

Tawfiq Zayad
BEFORE THEIR TANKS

*S*CUD MISSILES FIRED BY Iraq's army were still being displayed on-site in Israel when we arrived in March 1991. The Gulf War was barely over, but nightmare memories of the conflict lingered on, commented upon and described in the media, and present in the demonstration sites where fathers took children to get "a piece of the missile" as a souvenir.

We had come to Jerusalem to begin work on a peace film, a film showcasing the efforts of the peacenik community on both sides, the dedication of Palestinians and Israelis who had been working for years to create a social climate conducive to peaceful coexistence. Not surprisingly, when we mentioned the purpose of our visit, people in the airport and in the American Colony Hotel looked at us as though we might be crazy. And we ourselves wondered whether any hard-won trust remained between Israelis and Palestinians interested in peace after the support given to Iraqi President Saddam Hussein by many Palestinians, including Yasir Arafat, during the Gulf War.

This was hardly an ideal time to make a film about prospects for peace. The organizations that had earlier funded our film now raised serious questions, and in January we had made a series of expensive phone calls to Israel and the West Bank, to recheck the current situation with the peace groups we had met earlier.

"What do you mean, is it worth coming?" Hanoch Livneh, the Tel Aviv stockbroker thundered. He was a strong force in Yesh Gvul, the Israeli army officers' group that refused to serve in what they called the Occupied Territories.

"Well . . . with the war and all . . ." I said.

"The war and all is over," said Hanoch. "We're ready to get back to peacemaking."

"Now *is* the time to come," said Khalil Mahshi, principal of the Quaker school in Ramallah. "The war separated the wheat from the chaff. Yes, some summer soldiers broke camp, but the ones who really care about peace are beginning to work again."

I asked about Women in Black. Were they still demonstrating?

"Absolutely," answered Judy Blanc in Jerusalem. Judy was a founder of the group of Israeli and Palestinian women that since December 1987 had kept silent vigil each Friday in twenty-three towns and cities. "We feel it's more important now than ever before."

"A little publicity for our efforts might even be helpful," put in Rita Giacoman, the public health educator from Bir Zeit University on the West Bank. Her husband, Mustapha Barghouti, was a founder of the Israeli/Palestinian Physicians for Human Rights, a team of volunteer Palestinian and Israeli doctors who offered free medical care to West Bank villages without clinic or hospital services.

So we had managed to reassure our funders and had decided to give the filmmaking a chance. But it had become a more complicated maneuver than before. The crew had been hired in December 1990 before the war began (Steve Talley, Los Angeles, director; Ziad Darwish, Jerusalem, camera; Diana Ruston, London, sound; and Yaron Shemer, production manager, and Martha Diase, production assistant, both of Austin, Texas). What was to be done? Could I ask them to keep their own schedules on hold while Operation Desert Storm raged? We did not know how long Saddam could last. But they agreed to wait.

I had taken unpaid academic leave for the semester, and there was no way to turn that around. Still, as I first headed out for Cairo early in February, on an almost empty Swissair plane, I had begun to wonder myself what I was doing. I took off to Egypt to wait out the war with Bob, who was in Aswan doing a restudy of the Nubian community, among whom he had worked in the 1960s. Swissair had charged me an extra five hundred dollars to go to Egypt "for security during wartime." No American company would insure the film equipment and crew, so I had traipsed around London visiting insurance companies known for risk-taking. Diana Ruston, my friend and scheduled sound recorder, had finally taken me to a company that agreed to insure us, very expensively.

But now, aboard the cavernous Swissair plane bound for Cairo, the news was not good. Operation Desert Storm was, so to speak, in full storm. As a protective measure, the Iraqis had just set fire to several Kuwaiti oil fields, causing thick clouds of heavy toxic smoke to cover most of the tiny country. Environmentalists around the world were predicting dire, long-term atmospheric results. Israel had so far restrained itself (at U.S. insistence, it was said), not returning fire when the Scud missiles zoomed into and around its cities. But how long could this go on? Kind friends in London and Washington had warned me about going to Egypt.

"Any Arab country is bound to have complicated reactions to the American military push," they said elliptically.

"You mean I might be suspect as an Arab/American/Israeli spy?" I had replied, half laughing.

"No, no, nothing like that."

"What do you mean, then, by 'complicated reactions'?"

Pause. "Just . . . be careful, B.J."

I was the only non-Egyptian disembarking in Cairo, and I was glad to see the factotum from the American Research Center, who rushed me through visa formalities and customs, put me into a cab, and left me. Where was Bob, then? The unnamed factotum did not know— his instructions were to meet me and put me in a taxi to the new Marriott Hotel in Zamalek. This he had done.

"Good night, *madame*."

"Good night."

The taxi door shut, but it didn't really shut. The door was loose.

The driver ground to an abrupt stop, got out, slammed my door hard, and took off again. Soon I was hurtling through the midnight streets of the city that had been our home for seven years. Where was Bob? Were foreigners, especially American foreigners, being discouraged from hanging about in public during the war and especially in the airport? We had agreed that he would come up from Aswan to meet me, and that we'd stay in Cairo a day or two before heading south to Nubia, where he was working. Why hadn't he come?

The Marriott lobby was empty. Yes, I had a reservation. My husband was indeed here. But—

"Room 2020, *madame*," the clerk had said.

The bellboy banged and banged and finally opened the door with his key. The room was dark, and yes, Bob was there, sound asleep.

"Oh, B.J., you're here, I'm feeling better."

"Better?"

"Well, I've been damned sick. But I'm better. I think I had a touch of malaria."

A wave of relief passed over me. He was not jailed or under political surveillance. He was merely ill with malaria!

"I thought—well . . ." All my paranoid fears and trepidations poured out . . . "Spy . . . darkness . . . foreigners . . ."

"What?" He was half-asleep. "What? What nonsense! Who have you been talking to? Go to bed. We can discuss it tomorrow."

Cairo, in the morning, seemed designed for reassurance, for banishing the nightmarish fancies that had been prompted by the suggestions and innuendos of well-meaning friends. The sun was shining on the complex splendors and miseries of one of the greatest cities in the world, sixteen million people housed along the longest river in the world. Spread out before us, as we stood on the twentieth-floor balcony of the Zamalek Marriott, were the silver bridges, the dusky skyscrapers, and the new highway overpasses channeling traffic up and down and around, under and above the gleaming river. Just there, to the far right, the shadow of a pyramid, the great pyramid of Giza, between the buildings, through a mist of smog.

"The smog is not bad at all today," said Bob in a pleased voice. "I feel so much better today, B.J. Malaria is the pits. But the new medicine hits it in a hurry. I'm also glad you're finally here."

War? What war? The Marriott Hotel was in the midst of a strawberry promotion: strawberry shortcake, strawberry crepes, strawberry sundaes. I thought of the dire predictions in America and England. They did seem like parts of a bad dream.

Yet the war continued. In fact, the ground war began February 24. Saddam Hussein exhorted Iraqi soldiers to "fight to the death." But the only indications of the war that could be seen in Cairo were the empty tour buses and the idle riverboats. And the only bulletins of what was going on were to be found on the CNN nightly news carried on Egyptian television.

When we traveled south, we found that Aswan, although also outwardly calm, was clearly suffering, for Aswan has only three sources of income: the High Dam, the fertilizer factory, and tourism. And there were no tourists. Egyptians were angry at Saddam Hussein or George Bush or both, whomever they blamed for the war. They were also angry with their own government for siding with America against fellow Arabs. Not that there was much love lost between Iraqis and Egyptians.

"It's terrible what the Iraqis did to the Egyptian immigrants during the Iran-Iraq war," a restaurant owner said to us. "And they'd invited the Egyptians to come in and do their farming."

"What actually happened?" inquired Bob.

"They say they let soldiers murder the Egyptian farmers. Then they took back the land."

"What land?" asked Bob.

"You know," said the restaurant owner. "The land they'd been given by the Iraqi government to get them to come there from Egypt in the first place."

Other Egyptians, we heard, had been imprisoned in Iraq at the beginning of the Gulf War, and many others sent home, minus wages and belongings. But in Aswan the major resentment was loss of income, at least among restaurant, hotel, and shop owners.

If I thought of the film at all during this period, it was to worry about the crew. They had all assured me they wanted to wait out the war in the hope of actually doing the peace film. But they had to support themselves. They could not wait forever and the war could go on for some time if the Iraqi population took their leader's instructions seriously and did indeed fight to the death. I sent an occasional fax; watched the CNN news in Aswan; visited Ballana, the village where the people we had lived with in the 1960s had been resettled; worked with Bob on his interviews with Nubian friends; shopped in the new Aswan bazaar.

But one morning we rose to find that the war had ended. CNN showed Iraqi soldiers with their hands raised, capitulating to allied forces. A sense of despair pervaded the screen. The Iraqis looked tired and ill-fed. Back in Cairo the Marriott was full of exultant Kuwaitis, living it up in the restaurants. The contrast was great between the tired Iraqi soldiers, the thin unemployed Egyptians in Aswan, and those well-fed Kuwaitis. Who lost? Who won? Yes, the Iraqis invaded Kuwait. Yes, they did great damage. But would the United States have mounted such a mammoth campaign against them if Kuwait had not been a major oil-producing country? Cynicism was not limited to Bob and me. Our Egyptian friends had no trouble articulating *their* feelings. Western power protecting a source of Western oil supplies: that was the general consensus.

In this climate my desire to get back to the peace film was renewed, as something positive to do in the sour cynical after-war climate. The crew was ready to go. Bob offered to come with me to Jerusalem to give me a hand at the beginning, and I accepted gratefully. I wished he could come and stay, but he had to work at what he had a grant to do, a follow-up on the 1965 Nubian resettlement program. When the Aswan High Dam was built in 1964, fifty thousand people were moved from their ancestral homes to government-issue houses north of Aswan, near Kom Ombo. Twenty-five years later a new generation of Nubians had grown up and Bob wanted to see what had happened.

Thus, less than a month after arriving in Cairo with a war going on, I was en route to Jerusalem with Bob to make a film about peace. We found that we were actually anticipating the uncertain process ahead, even though it was bound to be complicated. From the beginning, people had been dubious. Well-meaning Americans found it difficult to believe that there were Palestinians and Israelis who really wanted peace in what is portrayed in the Western media as a two-thousand-year-old "tribal" conflict involving blood feuds, and hatreds based on ethnicity and religion. How could one combat this deep-held belief and show that the conflict is actually a modern one, less than a hundred years old and based on claims to land! We did not know what we would find, and I was grateful for Bob's support. We had four weeks to finalize plans before the crew arrived.

The American Colony Hotel in Jerusalem, one of the world's most charming inns, had given us special rates for the duration of the shoot. The owner is Mrs. Roberta Vetter, a descendant of the original nineteenth-century family who founded the American Colony. She, too, was intrigued by the idea of possible peace; hence the rates. Had they also given special rates to some of the early illustrious visitors such as T. E. Lawrence? I liked to think so.

The American Colony was spruced up and charming. In its air of quiet affluence, it stood out in the surrounding environment of closed shops, graffiti-covered walls, barbed wire, and rubble. The small Barclays Bank where my film funds were deposited had its front window patched with cardboard. East Jerusalem was clearly suffering. The Palestinian *intifada*, or uprising, now in its fourth year, had led to more Israeli curfews and slowed economic growth.

Now we had to deal with conflicting views. Our cameraman was Palestinian and the assistant camera Israeli, our sound recorder a British feminist. Our production manager was a capable Israeli, our production assistant a knowledgeable American of Palestinian parentage. They all had ideas about what they thought the film should do. Good ideas. Our director from Los Angeles was used to working with a compliant, unquestioning public television crew. Before returning to Cairo, Bob had said my fate was to have to negotiate peace with the crew in order to negotiate a picture of the varied peace movements in the area.

In both East and West Jerusalem we had several leads, several subjects who had agreed to be in the film. At least, they had agreed before the massive interruption of the Gulf War. But now peaceniks on both sides were doubly challenged: they were suspect in their own communities for trafficking with the enemy, and suspect in the opposite camp for the sincerity of their motives. Thus, it took a person with an exceptionally strong commitment to work for peace, and to continue to do so for many years in the face of such pressures. Bob and I remembered well Judy Blanc, whom we had met during our 1983 visit, earnestly explaining to a *New York Times* reporter that her "peace activities" had not come at any great personal cost.

Her husband, the distinguished linguist Haim Blanc, had disagreed. "Now, Judy," he had said softly from his wheelchair. He had been injured during the 1967 war and was now nearly blind. "You know there have been costs."

"Which ones?"

"So many of our friends from the past no longer even *speak* to us, let alone invite us to dinner. With some, it is very hurtful."

This general attitude on the Israeli side was duplicated even more strongly on the Palestinian side. Palestinians felt themselves to be in an especially disadvantaged position, socially, politically, and economically. After all, the Israelis were citizens of a democracy. Palestinians were in no-man's-land, literally; as residents of occupied territories, they had no rights. For example, Mike Levin, an Israeli government employee, and Jad Isaac, a Palestinian agricultural engineer, had both agreed to be in the film. Both had gone to prison for their principles— Mike for refusing to serve in the Israeli army in the West Bank; Jad for leading a nonviolent campaign against Israeli taxation of the West Bank town of Beit Sahour during the *intifada*. But the consequences of the prison sentences were not the same. Mike kept his job, but lost some friends; Jad and his family were put under curfew and special surveillance by the Israeli Defense Forces. Jad's eight-year-old daughter was picked up and briefly jailed for "violating the curfew" when she spent the night at the home of her cousin. The reasons for this difference in treatment were clear. Mike was an Israeli citizen and hence was charged only with civil disobedience, his "right" in a democratic society; Jad was subject to the whims and interpretations of Israeli security law by whoever was in charge of the local defense forces.

"It really does depend on who's the general," Jad had told us. "Things are much easier now. But before . . . !"

He had agreed to talk on-camera about the Palestinian nonviolent tax revolt in Beit Sahour. "No taxation without representation" was the slogan of the movement, and the entire village held firm in their refusal to pay taxes when they had no control over how those taxes were used. Refusal to pay taxes had led to confiscation of inventory for shopkeepers, to loss of household furniture for many residents, and to a curfew and prohibition of trade between Beit Sahour and other villages. To fill the gap in supplies of edible commodities, Jad had launched a victory garden program (he had received his graduate training in the United States and had read his American history well). Backyard gardens were declared a "danger to the security of the Israeli State," and the village nursery of bedding plants was shut down by security forces. Jad went to jail.

"But the plants kept on growing," said Jad, smiling.

"And schools in the homes kept kids off the streets," put in his beautiful wife, Ghada, who, a teacher herself, helped organize home teaching throughout the village. This, too, was declared illegal, but the schools kept moving, from one house to another.

Beit Sahour's struggle did not go unnoticed.

"It was that village and its principles, and the *intifada* generally, that made me, as an Israeli, take Palestinian self-determination seriously for the first time," a Press Bureau official told us over lunch in one of West Jerusalem's outdoor restaurants.

We had spent the morning in the press office, awaiting an exchange of faxes that would prove our bona fides—so that we might be awarded Israeli press passes, a necessity if we were to do any filming at all. The power of the media, the power of film, was clear to the Israelis, who were concerned enough about tiny Beit Sahour's stand to forbid any coverage, national or international, of a peace rally in the village church, attended by Israeli and Palestinian religious figures.

The next stop was at the Palestinian Journalists' Union, to pick up a press pass there. The office was cold and dark, as the electricity had been turned off for repairs, the young man in jeans and sweatshirt explained. But within ten minutes we were served Arab coffee in small white cups.

"We are sorry our director cannot welcome you," said the young man. "But we are authorized to issue the passes."

"Where is he?" I asked.

The young man looked surprised.

"I thought everyone knew that Radwan Abu Ayyash was in jail."

It turned out that he had been in an Israeli jail off and on for several months, but his position remained unfilled, a kind of symbolic tribute, apparently, to Mr. Radwan. We came to appreciate the reasons for that tribute when we interviewed Radwan Abu Ayyash on the last day of our shoot, the day after he had been released from jail.

Modest and unassuming, Radwan walked over to the Friends School in Ramallah where the interview was to be held, holding one of his small sons by the hand. He was charming, yes, but firm and articulate.

"We must end this bloody struggle," he said. "It endangers all of us. But there must be justice with the peace."

This was a note sounded by many Palestinians, peace with justice. By this they meant some equalization of positions, a recognition of Palestinian rights, the release of political prisoners, an end to the expropriation of land, the expansion of settlements, house demolishing, curfews, and unwarranted searches. Israelis, on the other hand, talked of peace with security, and they meant of course security against bombs on buses, knifings in crowded streets, the security to move about without fear in what they defined as their own land.

But contradictory needs and wants lay beneath these statements. There was, for example, the presence of 150 Israeli settlements on the West Bank (Palestinians pointed to this as a threat to *Palestinian* security); and then there was the presence of nearly 100,000 Palestinian workers in Israel (Israelis pointed to these people as a source of *Israeli* insecurity, although they were needed by Israeli business as a source of cheap labor; and Palestinians desperately needed the work). The religious party of Hamas was growing in strength among Palestinians; the religious parties within Israel were growing in strength among Israelis. Both were seen as threats to national security by Israeli authorities.

But we were not dealing with these unresolved points of conflict, I kept telling the crew. That was another film, perhaps. In this film we were trying to show grassroots peace movements among both Israelis and Palestinians, something that had not been shown before on American television and in American classrooms.

For the peace movements were everywhere. A young woman introduced to us at the American Colony Hotel by the hotel's respected owner gave me a list of all Israeli organizations dedicated to making peace with Palestinians which were officially registered with the Israeli government. They totaled seventy-eight! No such list existed for Palestinians, for there was no official way they could register as peace groups. Where would they sign in? But the largest were well known: El Haq, on the West Bank; the numerous youth organizations sponsored by the Friends School in Ramallah; and the Beit Sahour committee. Then there were the joint organizations in which both sides participated: Women in Black and Gesher la' Shalom, the Bridge to Peace.

Dan Lefkowitz, a Texas graduate student in social linguistics doing his research in Haifa, introduced me to his aunt Aliyah Strauss.

"She's invited us to a meeting of Gesher la' Shalom, the first since the Gulf War. She says she thinks you'll find it interesting."

We set off from West Jerusalem's downtown bus station in the late March afternoon, along the highway that runs south, and inland from the sea. I was struck again with the beauty of the landscape, something that is never mentioned in media accounts of the conflict, but that turns up again and again in novels, poems, and memoirs by Israelis and Palestinians. Yes, both sides want this land because it is sacred land to each of them; because of their religious beliefs, because of their respective pasts here. But surely also these conflicting desires are kept aflame because it is so beautiful. The rounded holy hills of Jerusalem give way to the banks of dusky olive trees, to the fruit trees just coming into bloom of pink and white; we were rushing past an ancient forested land of hills and dales, modest mountains and deep river valleys where sheep should be able to safely graze. Surely both sides must feel this way.

"If you think this is beautiful," said Dan, "wait until you see Haifa. High on a hill overlooking the Mediterranean."

At Ra'anana junction we stepped down with scores of men and women returning from work. The housing shortage in Israel is so great that many families commute from major centers like Tel Aviv and Jerusalem to their homes in small towns nearby. Many also live in the disputed settlements on the West Bank, having been tempted by inexpensive government mortgages. A minisized dark blue sedan drew up to the bus stop. "Welcome to Israel," said Aliyah as she opened the car doors for us. She was middle-aged, with an open face that was indeed welcoming. "It's my country, though I was brought up in America."

We stopped to pick up Taghreed R. on the way to the meeting, the good-looking young wife of an Arab construction engineer, mother of four. The children were watching Egyptian television while eating a dinner provided by Taghreed's sister, who was living with them, I learned in a brief exchange of Arabic. Dan and Aliyah looked pleased: I really could speak the other's language! It took me about five minutes more to realize that the people at the meeting were not going to be Palestinians from the West Bank, participating in the ongoing *intifada*, but would instead be Israeli citizens—the Palestinians who had stayed on the land in 1948, rather than fleeing and becoming refugees.

"Taghreed and I met at a Women in Black vigil," Aliyah was

explaining as she maneuvered along the ill-lit roads between the small towns lining the narrow bit of land that constituted southern Israel. Lights on one side were out at sea; the lights on the other were, said Taghreed, in Qalqiliyah, on the West Bank.

"So close," I murmured.

"Yes, we are *very* close to each other here," confirmed Aliyah. "That's part of the problem."

"Aunt Aliyah, be careful, please," interrupted Dan, and she jerked to a quick stop behind a dark shape which proved to be a heavy truck traveling without taillights.

The hall, or *diwan*, of the large Arab-style house was nearly full when the four of us filed in, Aliyah and Taghreed looking to the left and right for friends, and settling next to them. These people clearly knew each other well, and had for many years. This was one of the first dialogue groups established in Israel, according to Aliyah. I was told not to discuss the plight of West Bank residents. The thorny problems of the rights of the 800,000 Israeli citizens who happened to be of Arab descent was the subject of the evening's discussion, the "second-class citizens," as Israeli Palestinians referred to themselves.

"Many people in Israel won't even discuss the *intifada* or the issue of Palestinian self-determination," Dan had said, "but they will work like mad to assure that all Israeli citizens receive equal treatment."

That indeed was the first topic raised—how Israeli Jews and Arabs who were neighbors and friends had reacted during the recent Gulf War. Tears and invective followed calm and not-so-calm questions, answers, and statements. These flowed back and forth and round the large irregular circle of men and women who were all neatly, and sometimes formally, dressed. The Arab and Israeli cochairs wore suits and ties. Some were old enough to remember the days before 1948; others were barely old enough to vote. Everyone wanted to speak and the words poured out, many words, all in Hebrew, which of course I did not understand. But I was lucky. The talk was translated gently in my ear by Aliyah. She did not miss a beat, and I admired the way her translation communicated the rhythms and emotions below the surface of the formal words.

Dan and I were asked to introduce ourselves, as new members. Dan spoke first, in Hebrew. Then before I opened my mouth, Aliyah

said, "She speaks Arabic. She will address us in Arabic. It is only fitting. We must learn to understand Arabic if we really think of ourselves as a bridge to peace."

So I stood up, flustered, and stumbled through a few rudimentary
phrases.

"Why you are here, tell them," Aliyah instructed.

"I'm here to make a film," I explained, "about people like your-
selves, people on both sides who want to see this long conflict come to
an end, peacefully."

"Who will see this film? Who will show it? Who funds you?"

"America," enunciated a man, dark and young. I couldn't tell
whether he was a Palestinian Israeli or a Jewish Israeli. "Yes, America
needs to hear this, but they will never believe it. I know, I've been
there."

"Let her *speak*," said the Arab cochair, a gray-haired man.

And the discussion went on until after midnight so everyone
could speak.

No way to get back to Jerusalem now, averred Aliyah. "You must
come and spend the night with us on the kibbutz. No, no, I *insist*."

I had hoped to talk with Aliyah about the intense evening of
dialogue, but when I woke, she had gone "to her first appointment."
Dan was making coffee, and Aliyah's husband sat with us over a breakfast of bread and fruit.

"You're involved in the Gesher la' Shalom group, too?" I asked
him.

"No," he said, and smiled. He was pleasant-faced, gray-haired.
"I'm a travel agent."

"Business good?"

"Not bad," he answered. Then, "I think it's enough for one
member of the family to be involved in politics, don't you? At least in
this country," he added.

Dan managed a noncommittal reply before we were whisked off
to catch the 9:30 bus back to Jerusalem.

Women in Black. In Akko, in Haifa, in Jerusalem, we heard the
same story. A new kind of organization. No lists, no dues, no rules, no
meetings. Hanna Safran, the dark-haired, pleasant-faced head of the
Women's Center in Haifa, said it most eloquently. "Women's organizations in the past were modeled on men's organizations. That is, they

met after work, in the evenings. But of course evenings are the times women need to be at home, for dinner with husbands and children. Women in Black is different.

"Everyone knows what to do," she said. "At noon on Fridays, go to the designated spot, traffic circle, bus station, intersection, the place selected as likely to get the greatest attention. Wear black, carry a sign ["Stop the occupation"]. Stand there silently for an hour. That's all."

"I had no idea how hard it would be," said Naomi Raz of Kibbutz Shamrat. "People say the most awful things to us. And we just stand there quietly."

"What we do *is* important," Leila Najami of Akko confirmed. "Otherwise we wouldn't get so much flak." I scheduled a film scene.

Seminars and classes for teenagers, Palestinian and Israeli, to talk about mutual fears were the contribution of Khalil Mahshi, the charismatic principal of the Friends School in Ramallah.

"We haven't resumed the joint seminars since the Gulf War," he explained. "But we do have a class in our school which you are welcome to attend."

"Teenagers today are the leaders of tomorrow," he said. "It's so obvious but people don't really think about it. And teenagers, the young, they are the most bitter and angry. They think their fathers failed them. They are the base of the *intifada.* I feel I have to try and reach them." I scheduled another scene.

The Runners for Peace was next. And then the new dialogue group in Beit Sahour, organized by Veronika Cohen, an Israeli music educator, and Ghassan Andoni, a Palestinian physicist. So we went on attending meetings, interviewing members of peace groups. People were cooperative and helpful. Only the Israeli Defense Forces occasionally gave us problems, announcing curfews at unexpected times for reasons unknown to us, curfews that meant that certain villages were closed; we couldn't pass through those villages in our van and we certainly couldn't film.

On one occasion the captain of the forces guarding the checkpoint to Beit Sahour said affably, "Let us know who you are planning to interview, and maybe we can arrange things."

I opened and shut my mouth.

"Your schedule will be helped," he offered.

"No," I answered. "No, thank you. We'll do it another day."

This decision caused a small explosion among the crew, who were tired, hungry, and annoyed. For it had rained all morning and our ambiance shots in and around Jerusalem were not going to be usable.

"Why not take him up on it?"

"He seemed nice enough."

"Come on, B.J."

I became stubborn. "I'm sure he meant well," I finally got out, "but who knows? The people in Beit Sahour have surely had more than enough trouble already. I just don't want to be the cause of more, giving them names to put on lists. Who knows how those lists might be used later . . ."

"B.J., be sensible!"

"No!" I found myself almost shouting.

But next morning, two members of the crew, one Israeli and one Palestinian, came to me privately and told me they thought I'd acted correctly. "One just can't take chances," said the Israeli.

"Westerners don't really understand, they live in a free society," said the Palestinian.

Such complications caused delays, rescheduling. Production costs continued, for the crew had to be paid and kept and fed, whether we shot or not.

Hours, days, curfews, weeks passed; the film went into the cans, was marked, taped, shipped off to labs in London for developing, and for checking that our cameras and sound recorders were operating correctly. Did we have enough material? Long days in the van took their toll on all our tempers, and I found myself, as producer, trying to get away by myself in the evenings. Bad form. Not good for the production. This had to be jointly planned, shot. For film is not an individual, but a community, undertaking. Then my friend Heather Taylor, a photographer, came to take stills, and cheered us up a bit.

Filmmakers, like fishermen, are fond of telling tall stories, the big fish that got away, the incredible footage that *could* have been shot but slipped out of focus/range/time. Of course it's all true.

We got to Akko on Passover. Easter was soon to come. But our cameraman, Ziad, pointed out that on three separate occasions we had passed the three religious leaders of the town, Muslim, Christian, Jewish, on their way to pay formal visits to the other. Great opportunities, but was this "grassroots peace movement" material? Or not? "No," said Ziad, "it's been the custom of many centuries."

In Jerusalem, waiting in the courtyard of the Church of the Holy Sepulcher one day, we saw an astonishing procession of formally clothed Greek Orthodox clergy, in their black cassocks, high black hats, clinking crucifixes. They passed within three feet of us. We were brought to attention because the procession was led by a Muslim cleric, also formally attired in robes and turban, carrying a staff with which he pounded the courtyard in time as the procession moved out of the church toward the street.

"What is going on?" I asked.

"It's a tradition from the nineteenth century," the factotum at the tourist information office explained. "Each year, on this feast, a member of a revered Muslim religious family leads the Greek Orthodox procession."

"Why?"

The clerk shrugged. "I don't know really. Muslim protection maybe? Harm me, harm my guests?"

It would have made a great film sequence, but not in our production.

We had a reception for friends and subjects and crew on the last day before our departure. We had been in Jerusalem for nearly three months, and the first stage of the film was finished.

In the course of the filming, however, the title of the production had changed. "Prospects for Peace" sounded bland to the crew as well as to me, for we had all been impressed by the energy, strength, and vision of our subjects and the difficulties they had faced. Strength particularly. Peace was not going to come easily. It had to be fought for. We all agreed on a new title. *The Struggle for Peace: Israelis and Palestinians* premiered on PBS March 15, 1992.

THE WEST BANK, 1994

BARCLAYS BANK in East Jerusalem had a new door, a new front window, in fact, an entire new facade of slate blue and silver chrome. The manager shook my hand warmly as I once more deposited funds to make a film, this time a documentary about the effects of peace on ordinary people's lives, both Israelis and Palestinians. It had happened. The Oslo peace accords had been signed in Washington, D.C., in September 1993.

"Thank God, times are changing," said the bank manager. "Let us hope peace brings us prosperity, too. When you were here before, we were beginning to wonder whether any of us could go on much longer."

And it looked like it, too, I thought, remembering the windows patched with cardboard, the lines of people desperately trying to cash checks on empty accounts.

Business did seem to be picking up. The travel office next door to the bank was open, its computers clicking and its phones ringing, and Nadia's Coiffures was lighted and half-full of customers. A brand-new store just around the corner from the American Colony Hotel offered office furniture, books, desks, and lamps. Featured in its front window was a splendid director's chair, with a simulation of the new green and red Palestinian flag sewn into its black vinyl back.

"No" was the answer to my request to take a photo of the chair with one of the salesmen sitting in it. Heather Taylor, my good friend, had come back to take stills for the forthcoming film, and we were both fascinated by the director's chair.

"We don't have a Palestinian state yet," said the manager. "This is a beginning. No picture with me in it. We're not there yet."

Still, the display of the flag, forbidden for nearly thirty years, said something about what was going on in East Jerusalem. Peace had broken out in the last eight months, and we had come back to document what was happening.

Bob and I walked through East Jerusalem, where shops had reopened with new stock. We went into the old city, a dangerous place for foreigners in years past, we had been told. But now we were greeted by shopkeepers along the winding narrow streets who, Bob said, were probably praying and hoping that we were the vanguard of a new flood of tourists. During the past years of conflict, and especially during the *intifada*, the tourist trade had dropped off sharply. Americans stayed home for fear of violence, though a few European tourists always turned up in Jerusalem for the Easter Week festivities. Jerusalem, after all, was a city sacred to many people throughout the world, not just Arab Muslims and Christians and Jews.

Like the shopkeepers who had invested in new stock with the signing of the peace accords, we were hopeful that at last a breakthrough had really taken place in this intense conflict that had been in progress for nearly fifty years. What was it someone had said to us in 1983? "Both Jews and Arabs suffer in the standoff." War, as the old sixties poster stated, is not good for children and other human beings. Yes, the Oslo accords were a breakthrough, despite the office manager's statement that no Palestinian state yet existed. But the man had admitted that the accords were a beginning. A beginning was something.

"It won't be easy," an Israeli friend in America predicted. "But there is no going back now. The terms have changed."

"What terms?"

"By recognizing the PLO as the legitimate representative of the Palestinian people, Israel has essentially accepted the PLO as a legal negotiator."

"Which means?"

"They have someone to negotiate with," said our friend in some irritation. "Before, Israel argued there was no one to negotiate with. End of any argument about trying to make peace."

Yaron Shemer and Martha Diase, who had worked on *The Struggle for Peace*, had agreed to take part in the new film shoot. Yaron would be director, Martha the associate producer. We saw the film as an effort to get behind the cheery headlines and try to see what peace had accomplished so far for both peoples, not in the august halls of political leaders, but on the ground, in schools, hospitals, the workplace.

Yaron and Martha and I had been discussing the possibility of a new film ever since that triumphant September headline, "Peace Accords Signed in Israeli-Palestinian Conflict," had flared across the front pages of national and international newspapers. We had watched the historic scene on television, as President Clinton officiated at the symbolic handshake between Yitzhak Rabin and Yasir Arafat before a crowd of thousands assembled on the White House lawn. And the next day the *New York Times* followed up with a three-column picture of a jubilant demonstration of Palestinians and Israelis, marching together in Jerusalem.

"Look," Martha had said. "Isn't that Jad Isaac?"

"And Veronika Cohen?"

"And Jalal Qumsiyah?"

Martha was right. There in the picture of the demonstration celebrating peace were some of the people featured in our earlier film, *The Struggle for Peace*. A sequel seemed to be a natural, and fortunately two of the earlier supporting foundations agreed, though the grants were much less than what we had been able to raise for the earlier film. This puzzled us.

Yaron pointed out possible reasons for the apparent lack of enthusiasm for filming peace on-site. Some reviewers of *The Struggle for Peace* had criticized the film as focusing on people who were actually dissenting figures in their own communities, a small minority, "not really representative of either Israelis or Palestinians."

"Maybe," said Yaron, "they think it is too early to make a film about peace. No one can be sure how it will turn out."

"But this is exactly the right moment to film," said Martha. "An historic moment. It won't come again."

I agreed. And the three of us decided to go ahead, despite the fact that we still had not been totally funded. To cut costs, we elected to shoot on video rather than film, and to hire a Palestinian-Israeli crew on the spot. This would not only save money but, we felt, keep us all honest in terms of presenting alternative viewpoints about what was happening and what was going to happen. I argued that if the people who were actually doing the filming and the sound recording represented different perspectives among Palestinians and Israelis, it might contribute toward a more interesting and localized representation.

"Don't be too idealistic, B.J.," warned Bob.

"I'm not," I answered. "I'm being practical. And it's you, my dear, after all, who argues that documentary filming in the Third World by representatives of the First World is the last colonial encounter, an imposition on people. This way, at least it's the people themselves who are involved as well."

Bob looked at me. "Worth a try," he allowed, and agreed to do our field research in the newly liberated areas of Gaza and Jericho. This would save us time, as we did not have the luxury of a research period before the actual shooting began. We were going to try to accomplish both processes at the same time, in five weeks.

"Risky," cautioned Yaron.

"I know."

"We'll try," said Martha.

It was early May. "Let's start with the folks in the first film," suggested Yaron. "They know us already. The peaceniks."

We found the earlier peaceniks in disarray. Some, like the Runners for Peace and the Women in Black group in Jerusalem, had already disbanded, believing that their goals had been achieved. Others said they had done their bit; it was time to let another generation work on achieving a lasting peace.

The army officers with whom we had worked, the members of Yesh Gvul (There Is a Limit), had changed tactics. Hanoch Livneh continued to campaign against serving in the West Bank, but Gideon Spiro told us he'd organized a new protest group—against the Israeli nuclear plant in the desert, near Dimona.

"We get lots of media coverage for this one," said Gideon by phone. "Lots more than we got when we were organizing for peace. But it's important to keep up the pressure. Are you going to interview in the settlements?" he asked.

"Yes, of course."

"That's the key," he said. "The settlements. Have you noticed how they are creating their own ghettos now?" He laughed, shortly and bitterly. "My parents," he said, "came all the way here from Europe to get out of those ghettos and now people are creating new ones. What is the matter with my people?"

"You tell us," said Yaron, who was on the other line.

"Will *you* be doing the interviews in the settlements?" Gideon asked Yaron.

"Yes."

"Good. You will speak in Hebrew?"

"Of course."

"Ask them about the Palestinian state."

"Yes, I will."

Gideon laughed again. "I'd like to hear how they get around mentioning the word 'Palestine'—because it is still a no-no word, as you say in America."

"Thank you," said Yaron. "He wants to speak with you again, B.J."

"Yes, Gideon?"

"We kept up the pressure, didn't we? And it helped some. But you must keep up the pressure in America."

"Yes, Gideon."

"My brother in America says that is the second key—the attitude of American Jews toward the possibility of peace." And he hung up abruptly.

Yaron and Martha and I looked at each other. Gideon was one for cryptic messages; he always had been.

"But we are *here*," said Yaron clearly, "to film what is happening here . . ."

"And then hope to get it on American TV," finished Martha.

Phase one first. We spent the afternoon looking at tapes submitted by Israeli and Palestinian cinematographers and sound recordists, and selected our crew: Uri Sharon, camera, and Adel Samaan, assistant camera. We had to alternate between two sound recorders, Dan Matalon and Moshe Dor, as they were in demand by the news media, beginning to gather for the triumphal return of Yasir Arafat, scheduled, it was said, for June 15, then postponed to June 20, June 30. Kamal Abu Shamsieh worked as production manager on the Palestinian side; Danny Mottale in Israel. Allison Hodgkins, a graduate student in Middle East studies and public affairs, came with us from Texas to work as our overall production assistant.

What was happening here? Given the new opening for peaceful coexistence, was it possible for Palestinians and Israelis to both begin to move forward? Did the capabilities and the will exist so that joint enterprises of mutual benefit, political as well as economic and social, could develop? Or were Palestinians hopelessly behind their Israeli counterparts in technology and education, unprepared to assume equal roles in this new setting? These were the questions we asked ourselves as well as the people we interviewed, as we set out to try to create a visual picture of the new possibilities that peace offered to people in Israel, the West Bank, and Gaza.

The economy. That was the crucial issue, said people in Jerusalem, Tel Aviv, Ramallah, Gaza. And schools and hospitals. It was all very well to say that Israel had ceded, or partially ceded, the governing of Jericho and Gaza to the new Palestinian entities (no one used the word "state"). How were people supposed to eat? How could they get attention for their sick babies when there was only one working incubator in the entire city of Jericho? How could children learn in the crowded classrooms with the overworked teachers in the underfunded schools?

In Gaza, families were allowed access to the beaches after twenty-eight years of occupation, and we filmed families picnicking and children playing on the sand. Resourceful entrepreneurs had begun to make bumper stickers with the dove of peace wearing a Palestinian kaffiyeh, key rings with miniature replicas of the Palestinian flags that were flying everywhere in Gaza and Jericho. But these were minimal efforts; what was needed was large-scale economic development. This was what advisers on both sides asserted.

The economy, then. While Bob traveled into the West Bank, visiting factories and cooperatives, talking to directors and workers and chief financial officers, we began to set up interviews with members of the old peace groups, and Yaron began to investigate the possibilities of filming in the settlements.

Although the Women in Black group of Jerusalem had disbanded, the group in Tel Aviv continued to stand. Our old friend Aliyah Strauss, who had taken me to the Gesher la' Shalom meeting three years earlier, explained it thus: "Our job isn't finished. It's only a partial peace. Gaza and Jericho. What about the rest? What about a Palestinian state? No, we must continue to keep our vigil."

The Tel Aviv Women in Black had been joined by an opposition group, who, we were told, called themselves the Women in White. Men and children had joined the vigils, which were now peaceful confrontations. On Fridays the two groups demonstrated across from each other on a busy Tel Aviv thoroughfare, so that passersby and bus and taxi passengers were treated to weekly statements of both positions on the establishment of a Palestinian state—pro, with Women in Black; con, with Women in White.

Khalil Mahshi in the Friends School in Ramallah was moderately hopeful about the future, he said. He had helped organize several new youth efforts—sending Palestinian and Israeli teenagers together to a peace camp in Europe. "It seems to be useful," he said in his quiet way. "Some of the young people have remained friends and keep in contact with each other. It can't help but do good.

"But it is bound to be difficult," warned Khalil. "Over thirty years of hatred and bitterness. How can that be dissipated with a single signing of a paper? No, it will take a long time."

As we traveled, we could see that the early jubilation about peace had subsided, and old fears resurfaced.

There were marches of disaffected Israelis who had been support- ive in the beginning, but now were less enthusiastic and had begun to worry about their own security again. Palestinians expressed anger about the slowness of the Israeli Defense Forces withdrawal and pre- dicted an ominous future if three basic issues were not faced: the status of Jerusalem; the state of the settlements, which continued to expand despite the peace accords; and the perennial problem that no one wanted to face, the status of the two million Palestinian refugees who were now in diaspora just as the Jews had been. Half the refugees still lived in refugee camps in Jordan and Lebanon as well as in Gaza; others had immigrated to America, Europe, Latin America, Australia, and Af- rica.

But still a mood of cautious optimism prevailed and, we found, a feeling of relaxation. This was evident in the hospitable way we, as a film crew, were treated on both sides. The commanding officer in the headquarters of the Palestinian authority in Jericho offered us a guide to take us around, to set up interviews with the men on the joint patrols. This was an important development. Heretofore it was peaceniks from both sides who had joined together in a common cause, but now army officers, trained to fight each other, had been ordered to cooperate, to ride together in the army vehicles that did indeed patrol the highways in and around Jericho. An orange flag was the signal that a joint patrol was passing.

"We would like to interview two officers who do this together," said Yaron, and the director said fine. But when we went out to begin the interview, the Palestinian was doubled up with cramps. "I'm just too sick," he said, and he clearly was. "Come back next week and we will do it." (But we were never able to. By the time we got back to Gaza three weeks later, new rules had been laid down, including one that stipulated "no interviews of men on joint patrols.")

Allison, our overall production assistant, was the one who pointed out that these former enemies in the joint patrols were bunking in the same buildings, on opposite sides, of course. But they had planted trees in the middle of their joint compound, "for a peaceful future," one of the Israeli soldiers told Allison. And a dove symbolizing peace next to Israeli and Palestinian flags had been painted on the compound.

Despite the joint patrols and the return of many Palestinian men from exile in Libya, Iraq, Lebanon, and Jordan, formal Palestinian authority had not yet been totally established in Gaza and Jericho. The checkpoints were still there, continually checking the comings and goings of Palestinians into Israel. There were still Israeli soldiers present in the newly freed areas, partly, it was said, to protect the settlements of Jewish families in Gaza itself, settlements that covered significant amounts of land in Gaza.

An air of expectancy lay over Israel and the West Bank. What was going to happen? Who would be in charge finally? How would Yasir Arafat settle into his new position as a head of state, rather than the leader of an armed struggle? For Yasir Arafat had yet to return to Gaza and claim his leadership position.

In this period, authority on both sides had yet to be redefined. No guidelines had been set down about press protocol or media travel through checkpoints or the areas allowed or disallowed for the general public. At first, Bob, who was in Gaza to set up shots, worried because there seemed to be no one to say yes or no to his requests. However, it soon became apparent that this would be to our advantage. Almost everyone was willing to talk to us, for and against the peace accords. Everyone was interested in the possibility of having their views presented on American television. For we believed the film would be shown on American television, as *The Struggle for Peace* had been. Several stations had actually stated their interest before we departed for the field.

We traveled to Gaza and Bob went to call on Omar Ismail, a friend of a friend, who worked as an economist in the United Nations Relief and Works Administration office. We lunched at a brand-new fish restaurant, just opened on the beachfront by three Palestinian workers who had returned from abroad after the accords had been signed.

"It is wonderful to be back," said the young owner. "And I believe we are the first enterprise to open in what will be the great tourist area, don't you think so?"

"Looks good," Martha replied, smiling.

When Bob explained that we wanted to portray in our film the obstacles as well as the openings for peace, Omar offered to help.

"Well," Bob said, "American audiences should know about which issues divide Palestinians. I presume," he added, "that not everybody in Gaza is enthusiastic about peace."

Omar laughed shortly. "Not this peace, maybe."

"Okay, this peace. I suppose you don't have many Hamas friends, right?"

Omar had looked at him, at us. "What do you mean, Bob? Of course I do. One of my neighbors, who's also a good friend, is a strong Hamas advocate."

"Would he be willing to talk on video? With members of rival groups, like Arafat's party, for example, or the socialist PFLP?"

"Of course," said Omar. "Everybody is dying to talk. We could set up a discussion group in my garden, and you bring the cameras!"

So we did.

Reaching the Israeli settlers was more difficult. All contacts with the press had to be channeled through the Settlers Council, whose public relations director, Datya Herskovitz, was an efficient young woman. Yes, she would give us an interview herself. But she was uncertain about permission to go to the settlement Yaron had requested: Netzarim. This small settlement was actually in Gaza, only a few miles from the garden where we interviewed Omar Ismail and his friends about the peace accords. The Netzarim settlers had declared themselves as a kind of symbol of Israeli determination to stay on the land despite the accords.

But Yaron was persuasive. We wanted to interview families. Children, he pointed out, are always sympathetic figures on television. We just wanted the settlers to express their views, about what they saw as the future, their future, in the newly forming Israel. Datya agreed.

While Yaron, Uri, Moshe, and Adel continued to shoot, Martha and I were busy with the arts groups, schools, and hospitals, with cooperative organizations like the Workers Hot Line in Tel Aviv, which took on cases of Palestinian workers who had not been paid by their Israeli employers. Martha also visited the office of the Israeli-Palestinian Physicians for Human Rights and set up a day of shooting in a clinic on the West Bank. We wanted to include these groups as well as others that had been working for peace long before the 1993 accords, groups like Peace Now, the Interns for Peace, and Givat Haviva.

In the first rush of enthusiasm after the accords, many joint arts projects had been initiated on both sides. *Romeo and Juliet*, in an Arabic/Hebrew translation, was playing in West Jerusalem, the first joint production of Israeli and Palestinian theater troupes. But the Israeli Defense Forces refused permission for one of the Palestinian actors to travel to Jerusalem regularly from his hometown on the West Bank. So performances were often canceled, rescheduled, delayed.

Bilha Maas, an Israeli producer specializing in children's drama, invited us to *Oozoo Moozoo*, a musical based on a fairy tale about two brothers, once close, who had, after a quarrel, built a wall between them. The musical play had been running in Tel Aviv for five years.

"It's an effort," said Bilha, an attractive dark-haired young woman, "to say that walls are a bad thing. We have to talk to each other. We have to get over the walls."

The play ended with the wall coming down, a hopeful omen for the future, Bilha stated.

In my daily walk through East Jerusalem, I noticed an announcement of a joint art exhibit of work by Israel Rabinowitz, an Israeli sculptor, and Suleiman Mansour, a Palestinian painter. I tracked them down, and they said they would be happy to be interviewed.

And four women, two Israelis and two Palestinians, were presenting *Cycles*, a multimedia drama about commonalities in women's lives. In performances in East and West Jerusalem, they found their use of Arabic, Hebrew, and English to be especially appealing to audiences on both sides of the city.

Were these joint cultural efforts enough to help start erasing the long record of bitterness and fear? Clearly, they were helpful, everyone said so, but the economy remained the key.

"When people can provide a decent life for themselves and their children, only then can they begin to relax, to think about others," we were told.

So we were back to our original supposition. Cultural cooperation was very important, but we had to remember that the groups we had interviewed were groups of peers, of equals, where economic security and personal security were not the issues.

Yaron felt strongly that we needed to show the state of the Palestinian economy and its relationship to the Israeli economy. So we visited the office of the Israeli-Palestinian Center for Research and Information, near the Damascus Gate of the old city. Gershon Baskin, the Israeli-American economist who heads the center, immediately agreed to a "talk" sequence, in which Palestinians and Israelis would debate the state of the economy before the camera. "Because," said Baskin, "the economy is the key to everything. And one has to look at the gulf that divides them, in almost every way."

"As, for example?" queried Yaron.

"Well, to begin with," Baskin pointed out, "Israel has a total annual gross national product of sixty billion dollars, whereas the Palestinian economy has an annual GNP of only three billion. It's like comparing the economy of an elephant with that of a fly! But we have to get those economies working together if there's going to be long-term peace."

"Would you say that on film?" Yaron asked. Baskin agreed that he would.

"And we should take up other issues in the film discussion," Baskin went on. "How can Palestinians get their produce into Israel, with the laws the way they are? Israeli products can be sold in Palestine, that's not a problem, but the other way around? No! That has to change!"

Bob described his visits to successful Palestinian business enterprises in the West Bank, modern factories we had not known even existed.

"You didn't know they existed?" repeated Baskin. "I thought you all were Middle East specialists."

Bob said, "Well, I suppose we have this recurring media image in our minds, the image of the downtrodden Palestinian unable to come to grips with a modern industrial economy. This film is a chance to show more of the real picture."

So Bob took taxis to towns in the West Bank like Tulkaram, where Bassam Badran presided over a textile factory with 250 workers. It turned out there were twenty-eight small factories in Tulkaram alone, and their machinery looked as up-to-date as that in most European and American enterprises. Badran's was the biggest, Bob said.

"Of course, I work as a subcontractor with Israeli companies,"

Badran said, reminding us of the long-standing relationship, almost ignored in Western media accounts, between Israeli and Palestinian workers and managers. "But it is an unequal relationship," he said. "I fill the orders they give me, for the materials they want to use, in the patterns they have decided on."

"And where does the stuff go?" Bob asked.

"Mostly to the American market," replied Badran, "like Liz Claiborne, Calvin Klein, Chadwick's of Boston. And it is hard . . ."

"Because of the unequal relationship?" suggested Bob.

Badran, sitting in his efficient office in his efficient factory, looked at Bob. "Yes, of course," he agreed, "but the real reasons are the difficult working conditions."

Bob had looked around at the orderly rows of machines and workers.

"Difficult working conditions?"

"Yes. Limited hours of work. Arbitrary closures, if there has been an incident anywhere. How can one do good business in such an atmosphere? And then we are penalized if we don't finish the contract work on time."

Sudki Ebaido produces shoes in Hebron, in an impressive automated factory that does not accord at all with Western media images. Hebron is usually presented on television as a tense divided city, site of Abraham's tomb, where a barbed-wire enclave protects four hundred Israeli settlers from masses of Arab residents.

But here in Hebron was a shoe factory making, Ebaido told Bob, all kinds of shoes. "Imitation Nikes. High heels. Did you expect only sandals with this high-tech equipment?"

"No, no," said Bob.

Ebaido was a young man. He smiled, but not cheerfully, when he explained why it had taken so long to start up his enterprise.

"I bought the machines in Italy," he explained, "but the Italian engineers wouldn't come to Hebron to set them up. They were too afraid of terrorists, so I did it myself." The last remark was casual, almost a throwaway, but one look at the massive automated machines made Bob look twice at this modest factory owner and realize, he said later, that Ebaido "is the very model of a modern capitalist."

"He looked a bit sad, actually," Bob said. "He told me that he was only producing a quarter of what these machines are capable of. That's all the market can take—in Israel and the West Bank, he said. He's not allowed yet to export outside the area."

"But maybe peace will bring that for you," Bob had said to him.

"I hope so," he answered. "We've made the investment. We're ready to expand."

Even the Palestinian agricultural sector was prevented from selling their produce in Israel. This explained why we found tomatoes rotting in the fields. The Ramallah chicken cooperative, a large-scale enterprise dating from 1974, had been successfully manufacturing and selling fifty tons of chicken feed per day, but was not allowed to export into Israel. They also needed chicks for their farmer members to grow for meat and eggs. Kibbutz Yavne had stepped in to provide the chicks. "Thirty percent of our production is sold on the Palestinian market," said Moshe Gellis when we visited the kibbutz.

Clearly, the potential for joint production and distribution is present in Israel and Palestine; personal initiative has created those links over the years of occupation. But Baskin pointed out that new laws had to be enacted to support those joint efforts. Up until now, Israel had taken advantage of the peace accords not to eliminate barriers in economic relations with Palestinians, but to expand their own markets throughout the Arab world. Authorities in Beersheva confirmed to Bob that Israel was already selling drip irrigation systems to Saudi Arabia and had succeeded in making trade agreements with Oman in the Gulf. Israeli businessmen were enthusiastic participants in the Casablanca summit of 1994, the Alexandria, Egypt, regional business conference in June 1995, and the Jordan economic summit of November 1995. Such moves only served to suggest to Palestinians that the peace accords were designed more to open up the Arab world to Israeli exports than to establish a Palestinian state as a trade partner.

And, Palestinians pointed out, the flow of labor and goods from Gaza or the West Bank into Israel was still entirely at the disposition of Israeli authorities. The so-called Palestinian entities had no control over the border closures, which were usually enacted after a bombing or suicide attack that killed Israeli civilians. The closures often punished those who had no role in the violence; they created hardship and resentment among Palestinians and left Israeli firms without workers for long periods of time. (Israeli firms had begun to hire workers imported from other parts of the world.) And the closures were not minor affairs; they affected thousands of people on both sides. Gershon Baskin estimated that over 100,000 Palestinians worked in Israel at good periods, but this flow was reduced to 20,000 or 30,000 after a threat to Israeli security.

"We have to show this," said Yaron, "the process, I mean."

He accordingly took the crew out before dawn one morning to the Eretz checkpoint between Gaza and Israel, to film the long lines of men waiting in metal-screened tunnels, the search for weapons, the electronic scan of official identification papers, before the workers were allowed to pass the checkpoint and board the buses and taxis waiting to take them to their jobs in Israel.

"Look at us!" shouted the men, young, old, middle-aged. "We're like cattle! Cattle!"

"Every day we lose two hours of work time this way," said one. "We wait! Wait! From four-thirty in the morning!"

"And it's worse than before," cried a young man as he moved along the line. "More checkpoints! More searches! Is this peace?"

Was it? Uri, Danny, Adel, Yaron, and Martha were silent with exhaustion after this session, but also silent, I surmised, with their own private thoughts about what they had witnessed.

And at the small synagogue outside Jericho, in the one part of the Jericho-Palestinian entity that is still considered Israeli territory, Uri warned me not to speak to the settlers there.

"Because you're American, B.J., and a woman besides, so they might hassle you," he said. "Don't answer their questions. I don't anymore."

"But what do you say?" I was curious.

"I tell them I have to earn a living, and that's why I film. But my opinions? Forget it. I don't have any."

The settlers in the Jericho synagogue were guarded by Palestinian soldiers, representatives of the new Palestinian authority, and Yaron had in mind a sequence in which the Palestinian soldiers talked to the settlers over the fence that bounded the ancient synagogue. It sounded great as a vehicle for showing the new interrelationships.

But it didn't work. The Palestinian soldiers, smiling, said they would be glad to cooperate, but the Israelis wouldn't come near the fence. Allison and I, as women, were not welcome in the synagogue either, but one of the recent settlers, a Russian immigrant, came out to talk to us in the courtyard.

"What are you doing here? Who pays for you?" he demanded.

I explained that our film was designed to document the new process of peace as it unfolded between Israelis and Palestinians.

The Russian shook his head. "Not to happen," he said. "Listen to the settler now being interviewed by your chief!"

But the interview was being conducted in Hebrew, and it was not till later that Yaron explained that the settler (a recent émigré from New York) had indeed, as Gideon Spiro had predicted, refused to mention the name of Palestine or Palestinians.

"So how did he get around it?"

"He talked," said Yaron, "about this 'people which is not a people.' He said the settlers intended to stay; they were there by divine order."

The settlers in Netzarim were similarly adamant about their resolve to stay on the land, despite the peace accords. Netzarim had already been attacked by young Palestinians, angry at the continued Israeli presence within the Gaza Palestinian authority area. They had thrown stones and tried, unsuccessfully, to storm the heavy metal gate that protected the settlement from any unauthorized incursion.

"But aren't you worried?" Yaron asked. "About the future? With your families here? Is staying worth the risk?"

Yechiel Hamdi, the settlement spokesman, had replied quickly, firmly, without hesitation. "What do you mean, worth it? It is our absolute conviction that if, as a result of our efforts, Netzarim, Gush Atif settlement, and all of the Gaza Strip remain in Jewish hands, then it is worth the risk!"

Yet despite opposition from both Israelis and Palestinians, the peace activists continued to work, setting up new dialogue groups. It was Ghassan Andoni and Veronika Cohen who spearheaded these efforts, as they had the first dialogue group in Beit Sahour. There was now an official Reconciliation Center in Beit Sahour.

"What is hopeful is that young people are joining," said Ghassan. "We need young people. We need to have more dialogue groups, to at least help repair the damage that has already been caused by the leadership on both sides."

"People have to understand how the other side is feeling," put in

Veronika. "If we can make a contribution to that end, we are not working in vain." Both said that much work remained to be done to establish a real and long-lasting peace.

We traveled with the group to Nablus, often considered the center of violent anti-Israeli sentiment. "The fact that we are meeting in Nablus is very important," said Judith Greene. "Five years ago, no Israeli would have set foot in Nablus."

The 1994 meeting was in two parts—one meeting for children, one meeting for adults. We interviewed the children, focusing on an Israeli girl, Hannah Greene, and a Palestinian girl, Raya Sowalha. Their sentiments were telling.

"How did you find the Palestinian kids when you first met them, and how do you find them now?" Yaron asked Hannah.

"Before, they seemed in another world," said Hannah. "Now I think of them as people, as Palestinians."

And Raya, interviewed by Martha, said, "We teach the Israeli kids things they don't know, and they teach us things we don't know. But," she added, "I don't tell my friends I meet Israeli kids."

"Why not? Are you afraid?"

"No." Raya paused. "When the Israeli kids came here, they were very afraid. I don't tell people because I don't want them to hurt the Israeli kids, or hurt us because we meet with them."

Yaron suggested that the encounter between the children's peace groups, the adults of the future, was a good way to finish the film on a note of hope. And we did that.

We all realized that opposition to the present accords existed on both sides. But we also came to realize that ideological opposition, such as that expressed by the settlers and by the Islamic party of Hamas, was the province of a small minority of Jews and Arabs. For most, the state of the economy was the thing that mattered. And security. And schools. And hospitals. And the environment, as Jad Isaac said in an eloquent interview staged before Solomon's Pools, on the now neglected Ottoman water system. But we could not put everything into a one-hour film, Yaron and Martha kept reminding me. "We have more footage than we can possibly use already," said Yaron.

The crew had worked together remarkably well, despite their differing cultural and political views, and at the farewell dinner we all spoke about what had impressed us as we had traveled throughout this ancient land called Zion, called Israel, called Palestine, and Canaan, the land termed the promised land in the Old Testament, a text common to Judaism, Christianity, and Islam.

"Promised to whom? That's the question," said Danny Mottale, Israeli.

"The Palestinians are ready to take their place in a new society," said Nidal Amoos, the Palestinian driver who had become a participating member of the crew over the four weeks we had worked together.

"And many Israelis are willing to share, to build that new society," said Yaron.

"Yes, you're right, Yaron," said Martha. "Some are. But some are not."

Moshe Dor said, "I never worked with a Palestinian before. I was afraid it wouldn't work out. But it did. That impressed me more than anything else."

"I never understood until now what you and Yaron were trying to do," said Zvitka, our part-time camera assistant. "We were taught in film school that you can't have a good film without conflict. Conflict is what makes film interesting. I think now I see that you are trying to make peace interesting."

Had we made peace interesting? Something people wanted and were willing to work for? Back in Austin, Texas, Yaron and Martha and I sat in the postproduction studios at Metropost, cutting the miles of video. There were obvious areas of continuing conflict: the settlers' determination to stay in the Palestinian authority area, the opposition to the accords by the Islamic party of Hamas and the socialist PFLP. There were many obstacles to free economic relations across Palestinian and Israeli boundaries; there were serious problems with education and medical care. But there was also an enormous amount of goodwill among some people on both sides. Enough to make the accords work? We cut, edited, translated, wrote subtitles, commentary, recorded music. We began to think we had a good film, which gave a reasonably accurate picture of what was happening.

But on November 4, 1995, one month after our film, *The Road to Peace*, was finished and shipped off to the public television stations that had asked to view it, Prime Minister Yitzhak Rabin was shot by a Jewish theological student. The student said that his religious conviction had given him the right to shoot Rabin, who was giving away the land of Israel. The public outcry in Israel against the crime seemed to increase rather than decrease the hopes for peace. Shimon Peres was cited as a clear favorite to be elected to Rabin's post.

Then four bombs went off in crowded Israeli settings, buses, shopping centers. Estimates of those killed reached a total of sixty. Citing the steady number of Palestinian deaths occurring since the peace accords as well as the expanding settlements, Hamas took responsibility for these violent incidents, claiming that Yasir Arafat was giving away the Palestinian homeland and had betrayed the Palestinian people. Shimon Peres, faced with mounting opposition, apparently okayed a series of bombings in Lebanon to counter the attack by Hezbollah rockets into the zone Israel had established inside Lebanon to serve as a buffer for its own security. More than a hundred Lebanese civilians were killed and hundreds more wounded in the sixteen days of shelling. Benjamin Netanyahu was elected prime minister of Israel, promising to further expand the settlements and establish Jerusalem as Israel's capital. He won by less than 1 percent of the vote, but he won.

The future is uncertain. But we think of friends on both sides, who continue to suffer.

"We're tired," said an Israeli. "We want peace. But it must be peace with security."

"We're tired," said a Palestinian. "We want peace. But it must be peace with justice."

Perhaps our film was too optimistic. We didn't think so. It is currently being distributed by First-Run-Icarus films in New York for classroom use, as a document of a particular period in Israeli and Palestinian history. But it was never shown on television.

"It's past history now," wrote one television program director. "Nobody knows what the future holds."

RELIGIOUS FUNDAMENTALISM

"FUNDAMENTALISM" has been a term much used recently, applied by our media (with considerable abandon) to religious phenomena in both the Middle East and the United States. Indeed, there do seem to be some basic similarities between the born-again Christians, modestly attired, and the born-again Muslims, bearded or veiled. Both are attempting to return to their own versions of God's truth, based on what is felt to be a literal acceptance of His word, whether in the Bible or the Koran. Thus, whether in Egypt or in America, this means the rejection of certain behavior felt to be contrary to God's will and the injection of a religious consciousness into many areas of daily life previously regarded as secular or even profane. Is there not something analogous between the American boy who says he lifts weights for God and the Egyptian girl who studies engineering veiled, gloved, and totally robed? Are not both a form of fundamentalist behavior?

Such apparently similar styles of behavior must be related to the contexts in which they occur. For while we cannot examine the inner states of mind that accompany such forms of piety, it is reasonable to ask what significance such acts may have as a form of social communication. What do the conspicuous signs of godliness mean to those who adopt them and those who in daily life observe them?

In the United States, signs of godliness are announcements of preference for a more conservative pattern of social behavior. At least among high school and college students this is very important. A person who is "born again" cannot be teased or ridiculed because he or she drinks little or no alcohol, smokes no pot, and refuses to engage in sexual intercourse after a couple of dates. Indeed, such behavior, seen as evidence of newly important religious faith, earns respect and support, even from many sinners. The nonbelievers find it prudent to keep their cynicism to themselves. Fundamentalism provides a high road through the new and uncharted frontiers of post-Pill sexuality, HIV infection, and street-corner pharmacopoeias. It's a way to say no and it is the basis for warm friendship among fellow believers as well as political ideology.

For the young Middle Eastern man or woman the contemporary social scene is also new and unprecedented if compared with that of parents and grandparents. In Cairo, scene of one of the strongest Arab Islamic fundamentalist movements, the middle-class standing to which ever-larger numbers of Egyptians aspire certainly cannot be obtained or sustained without wage-earning by wife as well as husband. In the last thirty years this has meant the assumption of Western dress by both men and women and the association of male and female employees who are unrelated to each other. Brotherly and sisterly terms of address are often used in work situations, suggesting that forms of mutual respect may be developing between men and women. But riding the bus and walking the crowded streets mean constant and often very close contact with strangers. One has only to observe the respect with which the modestly dressed workingwoman is treated in Cairo today to know how rewarding this must be after a few (or many) experiences of her being shoved, pushed, and often manhandled in short skirts, Western style.

So, insofar as conservative dress is concerned, it is the public situation that is changing for the better for women in a city like Cairo. In the United States it is more the problems of private relations in private settings that are made less complicated for the young, unmarried woman by the new fundamentalism. In neither case are born-again Christians or conservatively dressed or veiled Muslim women returning to some old-fashioned, traditional form of behavior. For many of the grandmothers (and even some of the mothers) of the middle-class workingwomen in Cairo today would not have appeared in the street in the past, veiled or otherwise. Nor would many of the great-grandmothers (or grandmothers) of American girls have been allowed to party with boys without benefit of chaperones. At least for many Egyptian and American women, signs of religion solve two quite different sets of problems, one public, the other private.

But this is only one aspect of Christian and Muslim fundamentalism today. The movements involve both genders and speak to wider issues. Recently, in Dalhart, Texas, we watched a well-produced TV program in which two ministers, one white and one black, calmly explained why films such as *E.T.* and *Poltergeist* were to be avoided by good Christians. Why? Not because evil spirits, demons, and other nonhuman creatures such as are portrayed in such films do not exist. Indeed, they do exist, the ministers insisted, and they cited passages in the Bible to support this contention. Such films are satanic because they show extraterrestrial Muppet-like beings curing wounds with a touch of their inhuman (and ungodly) fingers, while mediums and other spiritualists (rather than the ministers of God) are shown driving out demons.

The restatement of orthodoxy in America has, of course, been extended to schoolbooks and libraries as well as films. For those who do not share the sense of what is godly and what is not, such attempts to order the world are most unwelcome: we cannot accept the religious significance that some but by no means all fundamentalists would attach to forms of entertainment and intellectual interest.

In the Middle Eastern context the more militant forms of Islamic fundamentalism carry a far different set of concerns. Basic to those concerns is an overall criticism of the socioeconomic status quo from what has historically been an irreproachable position: religious faith. It is not the poor of Egypt who adopt, on religious grounds, a critical stance toward the rich and powerful. Rather, it is the men and women of the fledgling middle class (women in modest dress, men in beards and white robes) who implicitly and explicitly condemn the excesses of the Western-style nouveaux riches.

For Americans who have not lived in Egypt, it is difficult to appreciate the overwhelming quality of the Western presence, especially the American presence. The American Embassy in Cairo is one of the largest in the world; the total American population in Egypt is close to ten thousand. Along with our technology go our sales techniques, administrative methods, ideas about investment and economic growth. Accompanying these methods and ideas are rock music, bars and nightclubs full of alcohol and fashionably dressed women and men. In the more European areas of the city, high-priced prostitution flourishes. To the fundamentalist Muslim (and many other Muslims, it must be emphasized) this general pattern of behavior is not only sinful, it is seen as the herald of a new phase of Western domination. And it also signals the loss of Egyptian, Arab, and/or Muslim ways of life—a shameful loss of independence, respectability, and honor itself.

If the militant fundamentalists in America share a concern for the "right" way of life, it is essential to understand that in the United

States this means imposing on one another forms of orthodoxy about which there is no agreement but about which our differences of opinion are as old as American society. The "right" way of life is seen here as one that existed in our own historical past and to which we must return. In the Middle East the concern is somewhat different: many Islamic fundamentalists see their enemy as Western in origin, a force from outside their society, one as alien as the weapons for their armies and the sexy, violent American videos in the rental shops. And it is this alien force that needs to be criticized, even fought against, so the "right" way of life may be reestablished, so that honor and independence may be restored.

IN 1996 THE RASH OF NEW BOOKS published in America on "militant Islam" and the constant flow of stories about "Islamic terrorism" in the press would lead the reader to believe that religiously motivated violence is an everyday occurrence in the Arab world. This could not be further from reality for the people who live there. Even in Algeria, where people gathered under Islamic banners to protest corruption, the current violence was sparked by the incumbent government's refusal to accept the Islamists' success in the national elections of 1993. Certainly in Egypt the lack of public support for violent behavior has helped the police arrest and suppress its practitioners in recent years. This does not mean that violence has disappeared, but rather that to see it first as some form of religious fanaticism is to overlook the underlying circumstances that provoke such behavior.

What, then, are the issues that incite so-called Islamic fanaticism? Of primary importance is government corruption plus fear of domination by Western cultural, economic, and political interests. But in addition, what is constantly discussed in the media, the home, and the workplace are issues such as the rising cost of living, unemployment, housing shortages, the growing need for improvement in education and health and in the position of women and children. People now raise questions explicitly as Muslims, to ask whether or not national leaders are following Muslim principles and to discuss what these principles must be. Such questioning, however, does not constitute an endorsement of any universal forms of Islamic fundamentalism. Instead, reference to Islam legitimizes such critical public discourse in Islamic countries just as reference to Christian principles has done in some Western countries.

The newly reawakened sensitivity to religious identity in the Arab world is complemented and has been sustained by the historic presence of religious expressions in all forms of discourse. Anyone who has read direct translations from Arabic speeches knows how they are usually laced with so many religious references and terms as to make them seem excessively pious or, conversely, blasphemous to the Western reader. In the Arab community the insides and sometimes the outsides of houses are adorned with religious icons, including calligraphic inscriptions of the names of God, portrayals of the life of the Prophet and His Companions, and sometimes depictions of the resident's own religious pilgrimage to Mecca. Copies of the Koran sit on the dashboards or under rear windows of taxis, trucks, and private cars; the Koran is part of every solemn ceremony and occasion. Koranic recitations are daily occurrences on the radio, television, and public address systems of the mosques. In ordinary conversation hardly a statement is made without praising God or accepting His Will. In America, religious representations have not so thoroughly infused daily public and private life for many years, but they have never been absent from the Islamic world and are increasing in number.

"What is the most Islamic answer to this political or social question?" is a far more important question in the Arab world today than it was during the period of Western colonialism in the Middle East. Christian rulers, having discovered that Muslims could not be converted, made a point of instituting secular governments where they could, and that is what Europe left behind. Today Arab peoples are claiming (or reclaiming) a place for Islam in public discourse. This does not mean that the social and economic problems of the day are instantly solved or that anyone expects them to be. So, for instance, female circumcision is debated among Muslims in Egypt somewhat as abortion is debated among Christians in America. Such practices are perceived in different ways by members of both Christian and Muslim communities. In neither case, however, are medical knowledge and questions about women's rights and needs excluded from the discussion.

If we are to grasp what is going on in the contemporary Arab world, we must set aside the repetitious and often inflammatory prose about Islamic militancy. We must learn to recognize the difference between the terms of the discussion (religious) and the issues that are being addressed (political, social, economic). When acts of violence occur, Western newspaper headlines trumpet "Islamic terrorism," while the stories that follow are peppered with atavistic words such as "fanatics," "blood feuds," "tribal politics," and the like. Such rhetoric suggests a return to some dark and evil past rather than confrontation with the problems of the modern Middle East—which are our problems, too, as the periodic deaths of Americans in the region so tragically demonstrate.

"Islamic militancy" has become a commodity on the Western market, something that sells books and newspapers and television specials. It is a new spin on old stereotypic oppositions, in which the West is scientific, rational, and progressive, while the Arab world is superstitious, irrational, and backward, caught forever in its own past. But by looking at the Arab world in this way, we are captives of our own past, unconsciously reproducing the attitudes that have accompanied the many attempts of the West to dominate the Middle East. This razzle-dazzle obscures our understanding of the serious human problems that now confront the Arab world and in which the West is deeply involved. Only by moving away from judgmental positions and alarmist outlooks will we be able to gain a more compassionate understanding. "Religious terrorism" may sell papers and popular books, but such flashings of frightful visions and ancient memories have little to do with honest attempts at understanding the contemporary world. But then, stereotypes require much less thought than analyses, and violence has always sold much better than compassion.

VII Iraq

1. Baghdad and Al-Nahra, 1956, 1983

> *O Iraq!*
> *O Iraq! I can almost glimpse,*
> *across the raging seas,*
> *At every turn, in every street*
> *and road and alley,*
> *Beyond the ports and highways*
> *Smiling faces that say: "The Tartars have fled,*
> *God has returned to the mosques with*
> *the break of day,*
> *A day on which the sun shall never set."*

Badr Shakir al-Sayyab
AN ODE TO REVOLUTIONARY IRAQ

IT WAS NOVEMBER 1956. Bob and I were in Baghdad. The pastries we were nibbling were crescent-shaped, stuffed to bursting with finely chopped nuts, sugar which seemed to have crystallized in the baking process, and plenty of cardamom. Delicious. The tea was strong. We sat gratefully around the Aladdin kerosene space heater on which the kettle hissed and steamed, for outside, along the partly paved streets and between the unfinished houses of this new part of Baghdad, the winter wind from the desert gusted, rattling the windowpanes and pushing against the freshly stuccoed camel-colored walls.

The Kirtikars' house, where I had taken a room while Bob traveled through southern Iraq, searching for a hospitable village in which to conduct his anthropological research, was new and drafty. The thick Persian carpets and the green and wine velvet upholstery on the furniture did not totally absorb the wind, nor the dank, bone-creeping cold that came up through the cement floors, directly from the chill, damp ground.

Bob had rejoined me in Baghdad for the weekend. "And why did you come to Iraq, sir?" asked the young man with sandy hair and a sandy sweater under his British tweed jacket. (In those days the old Spinney's stores sold tweed jackets and Marks & Spencer underwear in addition to canned brussels sprouts and English biscuits—provisions for the ex-colonial civil servants who still lingered behind in the employ of King Faisal, and for the American Point Four assistance families who had arrived, it seemed, to take their place.)

"I came here to learn," said Bob. "It's part of my studies in anthropology, to do research in the field."

The young man looked at Bob with a mixture of astonishment and pity. But then, we already knew that Baghdadis thought we were crazy. Anyone who would voluntarily go off to live in southern Iraq, much of which was without electricity and running water, half the time cut off from the rest of the world by impassable muddy roads, anyone who would do that had to be mad. And to be interested in tribespeople . . . there were no tribes in Iraq anymore, not according to the newly rewritten British laws, anyway. But then, everyone had ulterior motives. "It's very strange," said the young sandy-haired man, nibbling at his pastry. "All of us"—looking around at the Kirtikar family—"all of us have been here too long. We would like to leave, and you come all the way from America. I don't understand."

Bob began to explain, about the important relationships between America and the West and the Middle East, about reclamation of new lands, about technical assistance and international cooperation. He spoke eloquently and I was quite impressed. Not so the Kirtikars, nor their visitor, the sandy-haired young man, invited to meet us at this afternoon tea honoring Bob's weekend visit to the big city. (The cardamom crescent-shaped pastries were for Bob, Ms. Kirtikar had shyly explained to me.)

The two Kirtikar girls, one pretty, one plain, listened to Bob and turned to each other and giggled. Their mother gave them a sharp look and they subsided. Mr. Kirtikar looked as though he might speak but decided against it. Our naïveté or our ignorance or our own duplicity was apparently too boundless to contemplate.

"Sir, I beg your pardon," said the sandy-haired young man. "There is nothing here. You don't seem to understand. The Middle East, all of this, this is nothing." He gestured around the new living room and toward the window, where we could see a half-finished house, obscured in the fading winter light by a haze of blowing sand.

"The Middle East," he said, firmly taking another crescent, "is just a corridor, a pass-through for great powers. Always has been. Throughout history. Even more now."

"But the Golden Age," I protested. "The Arabian Nights."

"That was centuries ago." The young man laughed disdainfully. "Do you see any magnificent palaces in Baghdad today?"

"Where are you from, please?" I asked politely, trying to head off what seemed to be developing into an unnecessarily unpleasant afternoon.

"Me? I am a Christian from Syria originally, but my family has lived here for about a hundred years. Mr. Kirtikar is from India, but his wife is a cousin of mine, from Damascus."

"But surely if people come from Damascus and all the way from India to Baghdad, there must be something here to come for," Bob observed. "Otherwise, why bother?"

Mr. Kirtikar set down his biscuit-filled plate. "Ah, Sami," he said to the sandy-haired young man. "You're not being fair to our guests. We are all here, my friend, because there is work to be found. What you mean, my dear Sami, most probably, is that you do not see a long-range future for yourself here in Baghdad."

"Why?" asked Bob. "Is it politics? Religious discrimination against Christians? East-West tensions? The Arab-Israeli conflict?" Bob came out with it. The company looked slightly embarrassed. Mrs. Kirtikar offered more tea. There were more cardamom crescents and also large round thick cookies with whole almonds pressed into their centers.

Sami nodded. He had apparently decided to take this strange American seriously. "All of those things," he replied. "Yes. I would like to go to America. Maybe you could give me a list of places where there are scholarships available? Because," he rushed on, "well, in addition to all of those things you mentioned, you must remember that this is a poor area, a poor country. Without resources such as you are accustomed to taking for granted." He laughed, bitterly, I thought. "Nomads. The desert. Living off the goats' milk. You have surely heard of all that, even in rich America."

"But what about oil?" Bob asked. "You have plenty of that."

Mr. Kirtikar sniffed. "The British take most of it. Iraq gets only a small share. But, you see, the British made a great investment and they are the ones who brought the technology that made it possible for Iraq to exploit their oil. So they deserve the largest share.''

Was he serious? I stared at him. He was, and he was not finished talking.

"And the Arab-Israeli conflict, that is not such a problem. It will pass with time." He sounded a bit as though he were reciting a lesson.

"Mr. Kirtikar," Bob said, "you've just built a new house. Why, if there is no future here . . .''

Mr. Kirtikar shifted in his overstuffed chair and looked uncomfortable. "One must live as well as one can in the present circumstances that are open to one," he said stiffly.

"What about Mr. S. across the street?" pressed Bob. "The Iraqi UNESCO officer who has come home and built that big house, the one with the Ping-Pong table on the porch?"

A look passed among the company.

"Well, of course," said Sami. "He is a Muslim."

Mr. Kirtikar sat forward. "That is not the only thing, Sami. Being a Muslim is important, but he also has a degree from Oxford and a lot of money. His servant is a Muslim, too, but there is no future for him except as a servant. Just like us. We live in a poor area," he repeated, "a poor country."

In our freezing-cold cement room later, Bob and I discussed that conversation and could not decide what to make of it. What the Kirtikars and Sami were saying simply did not make sense to us. The Baghdad Pact had tied several nations together in a protective alliance against Russian encroachment. With the advice of English and American experts, the Iraq Development Board was pumping millions of dollars from Iraq's small but growing oil revenues into irrigation projects, drainage schemes, land-reclamation projects. New homes were being built all around Baghdad, new hotels were under construction downtown. The political discontent among some of the intellectuals we had met was hard to take too seriously. They all seemed prosperous enough, well dressed, and with good jobs. It was true that the Parliament was handpicked by the prime minister, and democratic elections were still not established. But they were surely on the way; it was only a matter of education. What could our landlord possibly mean, that this was a poor area and there was no future here?

But while we huddled in our cold little room in Baghdad, events had already been set in motion that would transform the Middle East and change the relationship between the West and the Middle East forever. After centuries of wooing and fighting, like old lovers, the West and the Muslim world were about to part again. But Bob and I were too close to see what was happening, just as were the Kirtikars and the tribespeople in the south and Sami the Syrian and Mr. S. of UNESCO. We all had our own rather myopic points of view.

Bob and my meeting in Baghdad that November 1956 was a kind of reunion for us, as the October rioting that followed the Suez war had separated us from each other and from the rest of the world for several days. Bob had been in Diwaniyah, a small southern Iraqi town, and the local irrigation official, fearing for his safety—or perhaps because of orders—had confined Bob to the government rest house for his protection. There were demonstrations in the city streets, guns fired and stones thrown, protesting the Israeli, French, and British attack on Egypt, in an attempt to retake the Suez Canal. No matter that Bob was an American and America was trying to call off the troops; one Westerner looked like another, said the irrigation officer bluntly. For several days Bob's only contact with the outside world had been the rest house guard-servant, Ali, who brought him food and bits of news with each meal. "Russia has bombed New York" was one of Ali's first cheerful messages, making his subsequent report that it was only the American *Embassy* in *Baghdad* that had been burned, a welcome relief. Ali was full of news which was a mixture of radio broadcasts and street talk. Fortunately, most of what he reported to Bob was pure imagination— or wishful thinking.

After five days, Bob managed to get to the public phone in the Diwaniyah post office and called me at the Baghdad YWCA, where I was living until the Kirtikars' room was finished. Our conversation was full of mutual concern. Who had worried the most? I reported rather tearfully that I, with several other foreign ladies, had stayed in the YWCA building and its walled garden. We had been cautioned not to go out. We had been told that the tribes of the south were rising against the government. Bob had heard that Baghdad was in flames. Now that the situation was settling down, he promised to try and join me as soon as possible.

Ali had been Bob's source of knowledge during the troubles; I had had the YWCA director, a slender Englishwoman of uncertain age. The noise of gunfire plus the shouts of marching mobs which reached us occasionally from nearby streets apparently stimulated her to reminisce in graphic terms about the terrible events in Africa during the Mau Mau rebellions, which she had witnessed.

"The natives went quite berserk," she had reported cheerfully in a high, thin voice. Her audience—me, two Sabena airlines secretaries, a German nurse, and an Iraqi woman teacher—listened without comment. "We could do nothing to stem the evil tide," she continued. "But we drank tea every afternoon. Kept up the routine, just as we are doing now, ladies." Her smile seemed slightly superior.

In fact, it was Bob and I who felt superior. After all, President Eisenhower was taking a firm stand against the British as well as the French and Israelis. It was infuriating to be identified with the English and their repression of African rebellions, as if America were also to blame! By helping Egypt, America, we thought, was now being true to its own origins as a once beleaguered colony.

The curbing of Israel and the old colonial powers in the Suez war, with U.S. help, seemed very significant to us at that time, marking the beginning of a new era in the region, the true end of foreign domination. Egypt under Nasser seemed to be setting a new pattern of independence and self-determination. While the remnants of British authority were still to be found in Aden and the small Gulf States, it was clearly only a matter of time till this would end. To us, the United States now seemed solidly on the correct side, supporting national independence for countries that had once been colonies, just like ours.

Even the Arab-Israeli conflict did not seem so far from solution in the late 1950s, nor did America's role in the Arab-Israeli conflict seem particularly important. Of course, many Palestinians had been displaced. We had seen the Palestinian refugee camps in Lebanon. But we had also met many prosperous middle-class Palestinians in Baghdad, doctors, teachers, and government civil servants. We supposed that in time both groups would merge with the local populations as the need for jobs and the possibilities of intermarriage completed peacefully the migration that the Israelis had begun by force. The Israelis would become more "reasonable," perhaps, offering compensation for the lands they had seized, so that both sides could become reconciled to the status quo and learn to live and let live.

Of course, what the United States had done to the Palestinians by helping the Zionists wasn't right, but one had to be realistic about such things. After all, what our ancestors had done to the American Indians wasn't right either. All we could do now was to push the Israelis to provide compensation, and our government had stated its support of this principle. Surely, anyone could see the need for that; after all, Israel was an isolated country whose people were greatly outnumbered by the surrounding Arab populations. It had to make peace with the Arabs for the sake of its own survival.

The tense five days in Iraq during the Suez fighting was only part of the "transition" period, we felt, a slight danger for us as our life in Iraq began, but a clear sign to the Western world that a new era had begun in the Middle East. The demonstrations by the Iraqi people had been a statement to Iraq's Prime Minister Nuri Sa'id and his British advisers that a pro-Western policy in Iraq could not proceed in the face of Western aggression in other parts of the Arab world. This was a sign of Arab nationalism, the spirit of the times.

We were exhilarated by our own involvement in this event and felt slightly heroic, just to be Americans, on the right side. Bob as an anthropologist was devoted to the idea of cultural relativism, and we felt this included the right of each nation to set its own course and develop in its own way. But dearest among our unspoken assumptions was the belief that democracy would be the ultimate choice.

How, then, could the Kirtikars and Sami say there was no future in the Middle East? Coming from abroad, we had a clearer perspective. We could see that the future held a great potential indeed for the West, the East, for Arabs, Israelis, for everyone. The dark colonial period had passed, economic development was under way, and America was involved in improving the lives of the people who had been colonialized. Baghdad had been the center of a great Golden Age of civilization a thousand years ago. Another Golden Age, we firmly believed, was about to begin.

Bob settled finally in Al-Nahra, a village near Diwaniyah in southern Iraq. The sheikh of the major tribe in the area, the Al-Eshadda, lived on the edge of the village and had offered us a small mud-brick house to live in; we accepted his hospitality with pleasure. I bade goodbye to the Kirtikars and set off, with Bob, one winter evening in December 1956. For the next two years we lived in Al-Nahra as the guests of the sheikh. Sheikh Hamid traced his ancestry to the Shammar, the groups of nomadic tribes of the northern Arabian Peninsula; his tribe had been settled in southern Iraq for nearly a hundred years. In the 1930s the Al-Eshadda and the other tribes who formed the Al-Agra confederation had been the last groups to surrender to British troops engaged in the "pacification" of the Iraqi countryside. The dissident confederation had held out until the heat of midsummer, when the British cut off their irrigation-canal water and bombed their villages. (The average temperature was over 100°F in the shade.) While we lived there, from 1956 to 1958, the women I knew still spoke of that incident, though it had happened twenty years before our arrival.

"I dream that I go down to the irrigation canal," said my friend Laila, the niece of Sheikh Hamid. "And the canal is dry. In my dream I am very thirsty, but there is nothing to do about it. I sit there on the banks of the canal, but the water doesn't come back."

Bob's research, for his doctorate in anthropology from the University of Chicago, was a study of the relationship between irrigation and central authority; he was interested in the idea that "oriental despotism" had arisen from the need to create a bureaucracy to organize and direct water use on the farmland. He traveled with the men of the tribe, interviewed in the village market, and talked with the central government administrators in town.

My life was different, spent almost entirely with the women of the tribe and of the town, for Al-Nahra then was still a sexually segregated society. Honeymooning in a mud-brick house in a remote village of Iraq was not something I had exactly anticipated, and it was not easy in the beginning: the isolation, the difficulty in learning Arabic, and the need to wear the local ladies' garment, the abbaya, to cover up whenever I went out. We settled gradually in our little house with its walled, wild garden, a house that the sheikh had built for the youngest and fourth wife, Selma. Selma the beautiful, I used to call her, and she became a good friend to me, someone to whom I turned for help in those years. For I was often lonely at first.

Bob, as a Western man involved in research for a foreign university or government, was a reasonably familiar figure in the area, for he looked much like the British colonial civil servants who had administered the Diwaniyah region until very recently. But I was an oddity, a Western woman who did not sit in the sheikh's guesthouse, the mudhif, with the men, as Gertrude Bell had done when she visited Al-

Nahra in the twenties. And yet I had none of the personal or social attributes an Iraqi woman was supposed to have: no children, no gold jewelry, no women relatives as company, no skills as a housewife. I was a sad figure by local standards, and if it had not been for the kind-hearted ladies who took pity on me, I might have led a miserable life, or simply left the field, decamped to Baghdad, and waited for Bob to finish his work. The women of Al-Nahra felt sorry for me and took me in; they taught me how to cook rice, how to embroider my pillowcases with the proper Arabic proverbs, how to improve my halting and broken Arabic. They took me on a pilgrimage, taught me poems, and tried to introduce me to a new world. They taught me by their example that there are many ways of organizing one's life, one's society, and that the diversity of human life in this world is one of its strengths rather than one of its weaknesses.

In many ways we were privileged in those years, though we were not really aware of it at the time. Privileged to witness a system that was coming to an end, a system that for better or for worse had served the peoples of southern Iraq since long before the British mandate began in 1920. The settled farmers, the town merchants, the government administrators, and the tribal nomads had lived in a relationship that was probably thousands of years old, since human beings first began to settle in Mesopotamia, the legendary site of the Garden of Eden. Al-Nahra was close to that site, which, according to myth, lay near the confluence of the Tigris and Euphrates rivers.

Bob's closest friend in Al-Nahra was Jamal, the irrigation engineer, a tribal boy himself who had gone to the university and risen through the new bureaucracy instituted by Nuri Sa'id, who ruled Iraq then under King Faisal II and the consultancy of the British government. Jamal appreciated the old tribal system, but he felt it had to go—and would go—in the new democratic Iraq that would arise from the revolution, a revolution, he said, that was just around the corner. Here we were much closer to Iraqi everyday life than we had been among the members of the foreign community of Baghdad, and we could see that the system as it stood had serious flaws. Life was hard, and people were hungry despite the highly publicized development board schemes that were supposedly transforming Iraq from a subsistence agrarian society to a more prosperous industrial nation. After the revolution, Jamal said, farmers would own their own land rather than be in constant fiefdom or sharecropping debt to the sheikhs, and the government would take on the task of cleaning and desalinating the land as well as distributing the new centrally pumped irrigation water. More equal laws would be passed, and women and men would work together in the new Iraq, Jamal added. He enlisted us to help his sister, Khadija, who kept house for him, adjust to the new Western mode, in which unrelated men and women would sit together socially, without the veil or the all-enveloping black abbaya. In those days all women of Al-Nahra covered themselves in public, and I had followed their example.

One month after we left Iraq, in July 1958, the revolution did take place, as Jamal had predicted, toppling the monarchy and the regime of Nuri Sa'id. Abdul Karim Kassem became premier; the king was executed; Parliament was dissolved; sheikhs were outlawed. Our host, Sheikh Hamid, was clapped into jail for a brief period but soon released upon the intercession of one of his own sons, Hadi, who had demonstrated against the Nuri Sa'id government in 1957 and 1958, while a student at the university. Hadi himself had been jailed while we were living in Al-Nahra, and released through his father's intercession. But Sheikh Hamid had at that time refused to support his rebellious son at the university any longer. It was Hadi's mother, my friend Bahiga, who had sold her gold jewelry so that Hadi could continue his studies. Now the political tables had been turned. Hadi eventually received a generous fellowship to do graduate work in chemistry in the United States.

Bob returned in 1964 to Al-Nahra, where he was received, as he said, "as though I had been absent six months rather than six years." By that time I had borne three children, and the women of the sheikh's family sent back a present to my youngest child, Laila, a gold charm set with tiny turquoises such as children in the village wore to protect them from the evil eye. The village had benefited from the revolutionary government's development programs, with improved roads and a new intermediate school. Sheikh Hamid was back in the village, receiving guests in the mudhif, and all seemed, in the village at least, much as it had been before. Construction had resumed on the nearby Mussayyib irrigation and drainage scheme, a project begun in the fifties that was to benefit the entire southern alluvial plain eventually. The soil was to be leached and thus desalinated, the canals were to be cleared of the dread schistosomiasis-bearing snails, and water would be delivered on a regular basis to the farms. The big difference in the area was that the large estates of the sheikhs had been broken up under the new land reform laws, and thousands of acres distributed, under government supervision, to small farmers.

Abdul Karim Kassem had fallen. Another central government took over the administration of the new Iraq. In 1967 Bob stopped in Baghdad on his way to Afghanistan. He did not have time to go down to the village, but his good friend Nour, Sheikh Hamid's oldest son, came to Baghdad to see him. People were still farming in the Al-Nahra region, Nour said, though many other agricultural areas were almost deserted, as hundreds of farmers had left the countryside for Baghdad in search of urban jobs. The situation generally was not good. The Mussayyib project had been stopped again. Sheikh Hamid had died of a heart attack while police guards stood outside his hospital room, for he had been accused of unpatriotic activities, unspecified, relating to his years as a member of the Parliament in the old Nuri Sa'id government. "But he was well treated," said Nour, "in spite of everything." Bob felt that Nour's visit to see him was taken at some personal risk, the political situation being so volatile in those years, and both of us felt some reluctance to correspond with our friends for a time, in case their connection with us, as Americans, placed them in difficulty.

Thus, we were more than pleased when Hadi called us from California one day in 1973. He was nearly finished with his Ph.D. and had heard, he said, that I was scheduled to lecture at a nearby university. "Bob," he said, "I know you don't want your wife staying alone in a hotel room, it wouldn't be proper, so I've arranged for her to stay with a good Iraqi family. Don't worry about her at all. I'll be staying in the same house. I will meet her at the airport and take her back when she leaves."

At first I was somewhat taken aback. I had not seen Hadi for years and had indeed scarcely known him in Iraq, though I had known his mother and sisters well. I had been rather looking forward to the privacy of a California hotel room for a day or two. But then I remembered that to my friends in Al-Nahra, the greatest misfortune that could befall any person was to be alone, without kin, and among strangers. And I was moved and touched that, after all these years, Hadi still considered me enough like a member of his family so that he had gone out of his way to make my stay more comfortable and more respectable.

The Iraqi family welcomed me warmly. The lecture went well; I asked Hadi to make a few comments about his own experience, and he did so with grace and charm. The day I was to leave he invited me to visit his laboratory, where his thesis was in preparation. I protested that I knew nothing of chemistry, but he insisted. When we got to the laboratory, I saw why. Instead of demonstrating the complicated experimental equipment he had set up for his thesis, he showed me photographs. Dozens of photographs of the family and the tribe—the children that had been born since we had left in 1958, the new wives and husbands, the sons and daughters who had graduated from high school and college. One of Hadi's own sisters, the sheikh's daughter, was teaching in a boys' school in Diwaniyah, something that would have been unthinkable when we were living in Al-Nahra. At that time girls of the sheikh's family had only been attending the village school for five or six years. It had been Selma, beautiful Selma, herself a secondary school graduate, who had encouraged her husband, Sheikh Hamid, to send the girls to school.

"The revolution had many good effects," said Hadi. "If we look outside of politics, we can see that. Lots of schools. The girls are really becoming independent."

"And do they marry outside the tribe?" I asked, remembering Laila's long-ago explanation of tribal purity. The reluctance of the lineage to give its daughters in marriage to strangers outside the clan meant that many girls of the Al-Eshadda did not marry in those years. For the boys had started school before the girls; many had gone on to college and often did not wish to marry their illiterate cousins.

"Well . . ." Hadi temporized. He paused, took off his glasses, wiped his eyes. He was tall and dark, with a look of his mother, but with the height and breadth of his father—a big man. He had the high cheekbones and aquiline features of the desert Arab. "Not yet," he said, put on his glasses, smiled at me. "Maybe I will arrange for one of my younger sisters to be the pioneer."

"*Inshallah*" (God willing), I replied rather mechanically. Things hadn't changed too radically in Al-Nahra, at least not yet, I thought.

When I left, I thanked Hadi profusely for his help and chided him for not visiting us in Austin. "You must come before you go back to Iraq," I said, "or it will be *ayb* [shame], on our house if not on yours. What will people think if you spent all this time in America and we never had you in our home?"

Hadi shook hands with me, nodded rather formally. Had I not insisted enough? It had been fifteen years since I had lived in Al-Nahra. Perhaps I had forgotten my Al-Nahra manners.

"We would really like you to come," I said again. "And my husband, Bob, would like to see you."

Hadi inclined his head slightly.

"Have you ever stayed with an American family?" I tried another tack.

"No," he replied.

"Well, then, Hadi," I said firmly, "you must come. That's terrible. What kind of ideal of Iraq would we have had if we had only stayed in Baghdad and talked to Americans?" I rushed on, "And you must meet our children so you can report back to your mother that I'm really okay. She and Selma and Kulthum were so good to me when I was there, and felt so sorry for me because I was childless."

Hadi smiled then and nodded, much less formally this time. "I will try, B.J.," he said. "Though I cannot promise," he added, "that I will convey your news *personally* to Selma. I think my mother still does not like her very much."

"Yes," I said. Yes, I thought. Selma was the fourth wife, very beautiful, replacing Bahiga in Sheikh Hamid's affections. How could she like her very much?

Hadi spent a week with us in Austin. It was a good time. Returning, even briefly, the hospitality that had been offered us so generously years ago by Hadi's father was a great pleasure. Having someone from Al-Nahra see us in America, in our own setting, somehow completed something, closed a circle we could never quite complete while we had been in Iraq.

As a guest in our house, Hadi was able to talk about those times with us, the role of Nuri Sa'id and the king, the prerevolutionary demonstrations, the imprisonments, his father's displeasure and anger. Time had softened his own resentment of his father and all he represented. "But still, I was not wrong, Bob," said Hadi, "in opposing the system then. It was a bad system. They tell me that the Ba'ath Party is really improving things in Iraq now. That's good, if true. I'm looking forward to going home—"

"But—" Bob interrupted.

"But what?"

"What about politics?" Bob asked. "You were always into politics, Hadi. It sounds like it might be dangerous these days."

Hadi set his jaw. "I have resolved not to meddle in politics," he declared, "but only do my research and teach at the university."

"And will you marry?" I asked.

"Yes," said Hadi, and, suddenly turning to Bob, "I will not behave toward my wife in the macho way many American men do."

"Macho way . . . ?" Bob looked surprised. "Compared to Iraq in the old days?"

"Yes!" said Hadi vehemently. "Why, even you, Bob, are . . . somewhat that . . . way . . ." He trailed off and looked anxiously at Bob. "Don't be upset, it's just—"

"I'm not," said Bob. "I'm just surprised, that's all."

"You see," said Hadi, "when you were in Iraq studying us, we were studying you, too, you know. And we watched you very carefully to see how you acted."

"You did, did you?" Bob said, half smiling.

"Yes. We learned that some things in the West are good, and some things are not."

"Like . . ."

"Like marriage and relations with women and so on. Your system is a good one, but you do not take marriage very seriously. Marriage, I believe, is to found a family," he said.

"Well." Bob gestured around our house. "That's what we tried to do, wasn't it, B.J.?"

"Yes," I answered.

Hadi nodded. "But there are some things that you could improve, Bob, in the way you *treat* your family. That's all I mean."

"You're right, I'm sure, Hadi," said Bob a bit stiffly. Then, "But did your father treat your own mother so well, marrying Selma and all?"

"That was the system at the time," Hadi said. "Unjust. Your own system in the West seems to me to be more just to women and men.

But it differs from one person to another. It can be abused. But I think it can be wonderful, if one works hard at it."

"Yes," I said. "Now let's have dinner."

We took Hadi to San Antonio, into the Hill Country around Austin, and down to the LBJ Ranch, which he wanted to see. He was particularly fascinated by the contrast between the tiny house where President Johnson was born and the great sprawling house of the ranch itself.

"And the big house belonged to his mother's brother, not his father's family?"

"That's correct."

"And he grew up here, in this little house, seeing that big house, all the time, and knowing that it wasn't his?"

"Yes," said Bob.

"Now I see," said Hadi quite seriously, "what drove Mr. Johnson to his ambitions. He wanted his uncle's house and had to get rich enough to buy it. He couldn't inherit it, right?"

"Right," said Bob without hesitation.

IRAQ, 1983

WE HAVE NOT HEARD DIRECTLY from our friends in Iraq since Hadi left Austin in 1974, on his way home. And we have not written, being advised by Iraqi friends in England, Egypt, and the United States that it is better not to draw attention, these days, to individuals of the Shia sect. The Iran-Iraq war, which has been in progress since 1980, has disrupted civil life in Iraq, for it has drawn attention to the historic religious differences that have always divided the country, between Sunni Muslims in the north and Shia Muslims in the south. The Ottoman Turks, who were Sunni, encouraged the Shia-Sunni split, as did the British administration that followed, using tactics of divide-and-conquer as a means of more easily controlling a subject population. In general, it has been Sunnis who have ruled Iraq. But after the 1958 revolution, efforts were made to heal the traditional breach, and Shia as well as Sunni figures were named to cabinet posts and other positions of importance in the new revolutionary hierarchy. That entente has been eroded by the current war.

Despite the tensions between Shia and Sunni, all of our sources, including both Iraqi friends and American archaeologists who have spent part of each year in Iraq for the past twenty years, insist that great economic improvement has taken place throughout the country. The new Iraqi antiquities museum in Baghdad is described as a jewel among museums. Slum sections of the capital have been torn down and public housing erected. Villas, luxury hotels, and modern public buildings surround the new public squares. In preparation for the 1981 conference of nonaligned nations scheduled in Baghdad, a full-scale urban renewal program was launched. A convention hall was built, parks landscaped, high-rise housing for conference delegates begun. Labor was being done by Iraqis in cooperation with migrant workers from Turkey, Egypt, Korea, Pakistan, and India.

And although the government may be questioning the loyalty of its Shia citizens in the south, at the same time it has been spending a great deal of money to improve the area. The Mussayyib irrigation development scheme is almost complete. Diwaniyah, a sleepy provincial capital in 1958, now boasts an automobile tire factory, a plant that produces heavy-metal machinery, and several brick factories. Industrial smog hangs over the roofs of the town. Al-Nahra itself, where we lived in our mud-brick house, has tripled in size. The market is larger and the mosque has been refurbished. Fewer women wear the abbaya and veil than in the past. Today many foreigners live in the village, since migrant workers from Egypt, Turkey, and Pakistan are present even there, two hundred miles from the capital.

The tribal system officially ended in 1958 with the revolution, but some of the trappings and traditions of the system apparently still survive. Another sheikh from the Al-Eshadda lineage succeeded Sheikh Hamid after his death, and the mudhif, or tribal guesthouse, where Bob spent so much of his time in the years we lived in Al-Nahra still stands, on its slight rise, near the outskirts of the village. Modern brick houses have been built next to the mudhif, friends say, but they are dwarfed by the majestic proportions of the mudhif, constructed of reeds and mats in a distinctive arched style reminiscent of ancient Sumerian temples.

A new railroad is under construction from north to south Iraq, and an eight-lane highway, the autobahn of the Fertile Crescent, is being laid from Jordan to Kuwait. When finished, it will pass within two miles of Al-Nahra, ending whatever remnants of isolation the village might have had.

The stain of poverty seems to have been erased. People in Iraq are not hungry anymore. Thanks to OPEC, the country's oil revenues have risen far beyond any limits that our old friend Mr. Kirtikar could have imagined twenty-five years ago when we sat in the drafty living room of his new Baghdadi house. Actually, few Western or Arab observers predicted the extent of the oil wealth that was to change the Middle East in one generation from a backwater, a corridor between continents, into an area of major importance in international affairs. A goodly portion of Iraqi oil revenues has been used, as was promised by one revolutionary government after another, for capital improvements, for development of human resources.

But all the urban renewal, the construction of railways, highways, and irrigation projects, has come to a standstill in recent months. The war between Iraq and Iran has changed everything. Fears of bombing caused the nonaligned nations conference to be canceled. The economy is being drained, to the point, friends report, that women have been asked to contribute their gold jewelry to the national cause. Battle casualties are rising. The war drags on, a conflict not so much an outcome of colonialism as one that goes back much further, to the ancient rivalries between Persian and Arab, which were expressed later in the differences between Shia and Sunni Islam. Oil revenues today are being used to buy munitions and food.

Clearly, no new Golden Age can begin in Iraq as long as conflict, such as the Iran-Iraq war, continues. At the end of 1983, prospects for peace looked brighter. And Iraq was making overtures to American companies once more. Perhaps the time is coming when we will be able to return to Iraq and visit, without risk to them or to ourselves, the old friends there who taught us so much about the world of the Middle East when we were still young.

THE BODIES POLITIC

*B*AGHDAD IN 1996, UNLIKE OTHER Middle Eastern cities, does not feel crowded. On the spacious streets Saddam Hussein has created on the west side of the Tigris, there is no crush, no press of bodies. This was not surprising, for there are few stores or offices in the district. The deluxe Rashid Hotel, temporary home to foreign visitors like B.J. and me, is in a large block flanked by wide streets and fronted by a six-lane boulevard. We had no trouble crossing those six lanes of traffic, dodging the few cars and pedestrians.

Even on the other side of the river, along Rashid Street, in the older part of Baghdad, there were no shoulder-to-shoulder crowds as one finds in Cairo, and relatively few women. Mostly, the streets are full of men, who seemed smaller and thinner than I remembered from forty years ago, in their tight slacks and shirts. I felt conspicuous at 5'11" and 160 pounds, and not because I was an American. Few would have guessed my nationality, since Americans were not expected to be wandering around in Iraq. It was rather the size of my body I felt self-conscious about, my size and my appearance of well-being. I remembered the ironic way my grandmother used to describe somebody as being "disgustingly healthy." That was how I felt on the streets of Baghdad, "disgustingly healthy," next to the thin men and boys who plied their trades and shopped along the principal thoroughfares.

My sense of conspicuous well-being in the public spaces of Baghdad came in part from being stared at. In America, as an older man, I was used to being glanced at and dismissed. But in Baghdad, I felt I was stared at, admired, or even envied. I felt unsettled, more as I had felt sometimes in public when I was much younger. What I had expected was the pleasure and security of being treated as an elder in a country that respects age. But in Baghdad I looked too healthy for that.

The exceptionally large number of crippled men on the Baghdad streets, men with only some sections of their legs left, was also disturbing. These men were not begging. They were just moving along with the rest of us, going in and out of stores, visiting the outdoor markets. They wore many kinds of prostheses. Some used a crutch under one armpit. But most wore a metal strut, shaped to hold the leg stump and to brace itself against the upper body. If only a foot was missing, a man might use a straight cane and a false foot or peg. Men lacking both legs were on roller sleds. Like the shiny poster pictures of Saddam Hussein, the men's metal braces caught my eye, and one of them was nearly always in sight.

Of course, the Iraqi men in the lobby of the Rashid Hotel were not thin and had all their limbs intact. They were well dressed and young and sat about on the many leather chairs and couches in the lobby under the crystal chandeliers, filling the ashtrays on the coffee tables in front of them. These young men appeared plump under their double-breasted suits. From time to time I noticed them chatting with each other or with the hotel personnel. Sometimes I saw them leaning their chubby bodies against the shiny cars, visiting with the drivers in front of the hotel. But they seemed most interested in visitors like us and, when Iraqi friends came by to visit us, they often moved to a couch nearby. Since we saw these well-fed young men several times a day, I began to offer Iraqi greetings but they did not respond. In their crisp shirts and handsome ties they were far better dressed than I, much more like the well-groomed European businessmen and diplomats whom I surmised were the usual hotel patrons. When I wore my old slacks and jacket, I felt slightly defiant as I walked through the lobby. I presumed somehow that I irritated these elegantly attired young men, for I wasn't properly attired for my splendid surroundings.

In contrast to the scene in the lobby of the deluxe Rashid Hotel, there were very few elegant Western-style suits on the streets of Baghdad. And very few men wore traditional dress. The black-and-white-checked head scarves and long brown cloaks of the Arab south and the turbans and baggy pantaloons of the Kurdish north had practically disappeared from the center of the city. In fact, before we went south to visit Al-Nahra, I had begun to wonder whether such clothing had passed out of fashion and whether my old friends, if anyone had survived, would also be dressed in tight pants and shirts. It was true that few of the young men in Al-Nahra wore tribal clothing, but the older men were dressed exactly as before, in full-length cotton gowns (*dish-*

dashas) over baggy underwear, long vests, and covered by generous ankle-length capes, abas. Such an outfit puts space around a man, adds to his stature and dignity. Even a thin man appears to fill out in such garments.

Nour, the sheikh's eldest son, was my closest friend in the village. When he rushed out of his house to greet me, he was bareheaded and wearing only his *dish-dasha.* Of course I recognized him, but I was shocked by a large tumor on his neck, the dark circles around his eyes, and his stooped posture. We are about the same age. But he was obviously sick and he seemed much older. He told me that his government ration of insulin was not enough to control his diabetes. "Well, if I can come again, I'll bring . . . ," I started to say. He stared at me. I dropped the subject.

Nour's half brother, Feisal, had been only eight when we left Al-Nahra. Now he is middle-aged and was wearing a well-tailored tribal suit. His figure was full, in fact it was portly, which was common in the old days, but now exceptional enough that I noticed. It was he, not the older half brother, who seemed to be in charge. I didn't remember him at first, but he was friendly and deferential toward me; after all, I had been his father's guest long ago. I was not aware he was now *primus inter pares*, first among equals, in the company around us, though his physical well-being should have been sign enough to let me know.

Sayid Muhammad, our young servant and social adviser during our bewildering first months in Al-Nahra, was then thin as a rail and also mostly dour. Now tall and smiling, he warmly embraced me, and it was clear that Sayid Muhammad had filled out over the years. He took us to meet his ample wife and he showed off his first grandson, a fat infant. Why haven't you lost your teeth, I wondered? How did you and your family stay so healthy? How is it you appear so prosperous when you were once so poor? But, of course, these were the personal questions I couldn't ask, not after so many years apart. But I did inquire after his younger brother, Abad, whom we had helped put through secondary school in Diwaniyah. There was a short silence, then suddenly tears in Muhammad's eyes. Abad is not conclusively among the quick or the dead, it seems. He is not here or anywhere else. He disappeared . . . his body has not been found. There is suddenly an empty space next to us.

Mallala was the only close friend I had from the *ahl es-suq*, the market people of Al-Nahra. I often discussed local affairs with Mallala either at his store or in a nearby coffee shop and I valued his knowledge and his point of view. But I always felt a bit intimidated by him, even though he was a few years younger than I. Even then he was a stocky, bullish sort of man, who used to speak to me with his finger on my chest and his face close to mine. Forty years later, when he came to the tribal mudhif to take me to his house, he again practically overpowered me, pulling me along and pushing me into his car. He drove me the short distance over the Al-Nahra canal and on to his new house on the edge of the village. Mallala was still heavy and strong, not portly like the sheikh's son Feisal.

But it was not just Mallala's size and strength that had increased: his voice volume was now on high. He shouted at everyone, at me in the car, at his family in the elegantly decorated living room of his house. His voice was so penetrating I wanted to put my hands over my ears. But then I realized he was deaf, probably stone-deaf, and that his affliction had begun long ago. When I first knew him, Mallala had talked loudly to hear himself and now he shouted much louder; neither then nor now did he seem to be able to realize how boisterously he was speaking. "Saddam Hussein is a great man!" he hollered at me. "Our greatest leader!" "Ramsey Clark is a good man!" Ramsey Clark? It took me a moment to connect the former attorney general's early opposition to the Gulf War to Mallala's overwhelming proclamation. "Yes," I shouted back, "Ramsey Clark is a good man." But Mallala did not hear me and he continued to lean toward me and shout versions of the same message until his middle-aged son came across the room and put his hand on his father's solid shoulder. Later, when we got ready to leave, Mallala pulled me against his chest in a great bear hug. I felt overpowered again, but happy. We could no longer talk together, but we were still good friends.

Given the number of maimed veterans, and the almost anemic men on the streets of Baghdad, it was surprising, almost shocking, to see the well-muscled male figures on posters announcing a bodybuilding contest. Iraqi bodybuilders? Where did they come from? Did they get special rations of food? Were they members of the Republican Guard or some elite units of the armed forces? Were they all officers?

The only men who looked like they might be into bodybuilding were the guards we saw around Saddam Hussein when we watched television in our hotel room. These were burly men in open shirts, who accompanied the president on his seemingly endless tours around the country. The president himself also seemed in quite good shape. Did he lift weights?

But those bodybuilding posters reminded me of *Pumping Iron,* Charles Gaines and George Butler's book, in which they describe a trip to Baghdad by some of Arnold Schwarzenegger's friends. That was in 1972, the year the government had nationalized the Iraq petroleum industry. *Pumping Iron* records that the Iraqi Weightlifting and Bodybuilding Federation sponsored the Asian and World Bodybuilding championships that year at the Al-Nasr Cinema in Baghdad; this was a week-long affair before sellout crowds of three thousand or more, carried on television inside and outside Iraq. On the last night, when American bodybuilder Ed Corney beat his friend Mike Katz for top place, the two finalists were almost mobbed by admiring crowds outside Al-Nasr Cinema. For these Americans to be treated like celebrities was an amazing experience, since in the United States bodybuilding contests were still considered freak shows by most of the public; Schwarzenegger had yet to achieve his fame and fortune. But in 1972 bodybuilding was the second most popular spectator sport in the Middle East; only soccer could draw bigger crowds.

Bodybuilding is still a spectator sport in the Middle East. And now, in the United States, millions of middle-class males lift weights themselves as their favorite athletic activity. When we were in Baghdad, I saw no bodybuilding contests, only posters. But every night we did see the president and his broad-chested bodyguards on television. At each location, at each school or celebration, Saddam Hussein would move forward, between his guards, to wave at crowds and kiss young children. His muscular companions stood close by, looking for any signs of trouble, filling the TV screen.

In modern Iraq, power is in the hands of a few. Health and strength are generally tangible attributes of political as well as economic success. Physically, the weakness of the masses is a reality, an aspect of daily life. So are the nightly television portrayals of the leader surrounded by his bastion of muscular guards, and the spectacle of those enormous concrete molds of Saddam Hussein's forearms and hands holding immense swords high above parade grounds. The Iraqi people are permitted to gaze each day at these virtual embodiments of power, but spectators they must remain. Attempting to appropriate any of this power, to make this a matter of doing, rather than just viewing, seemed highly unlikely to succeed.

> In Iraq there is hunger.
> At the time of the harvest the crop is winnowed
> So crows and greedy locusts will be fed.
> But the people still stand in the harvested fields,
> And the mill grinds them with the gleanings and the stones.

Badr Shakir al-Sayyab
SONG OF THE RAIN

> *The state of this city is greater than can be described. But ah! what is she to what she was! Today we may apply to her the saying of the lover: "You are not you, and the houses are not those I knew."*

THUS WAS THE CONDITION of Baghdad in March 1184, as described in his travel memoir by Abu al-Husayn Muhammad ibn Ahmad ibn Jubayr, secretary to the Moorish governor of Granada.

More than eight hundred years later, in March 1996, we looked out over Baghdad from our tenth-story window in the luxurious new Rashid Hotel and silently agreed with Ibn Jubayr's sentiments. The vista before us did not resemble in any way the city we had known.

In 1184 Ibn Jubayr was decrying the decline of Baghdad, known then as a center of religious learning, arts, and sciences. All that glory had faded, he wrote. We, on the other hand, saw Baghdad as far more splendid and much larger than the small and dusty provincial city we had known in the 1950s, before the 1958 revolution, before the rise of the Ba'ath socialist party in 1968, before the ascent of Saddam Hussein to the presidency in 1979, a post he still held.

Ibn Jubayr had stopped in Baghdad on his way home from making the pilgrimage to Mecca, something he had longed to do all his life. We were on a kind of pilgrimage as well. We had come east to Baghdad from America after an absence of forty years, to see once more the Arab country where we had first lived after our marriage, where Bob had done his anthropological research, the country that had changed our lives and launched us both into a lifelong interest in the Arab world.

"It's hard to believe we're really here," said Bob, standing by the hotel window. "Look for yourself, B.J. Can this be Baghdad?"

Tom Hartwell, our photographer friend who had come with us, joined Bob at the window. "And it doesn't look much like the bombed-out ruin they showed on CNN after the Gulf War, does it?"

It was true. We could see no evidence of the ravages of war. The capital city of twentieth-century republican Iraq extended, vast and orderly, as far as we could see. From this height the geometric plotting of city space was clear. A complex series of intersecting circles and lines made up the road system that enclosed the monuments, the hospitals, schools, apartment blocks, and office buildings that rose out of the dark groves of date palms, and stood, tall and golden, in the early morning light, against the clear sky. Five bridges spanned the ancient river, the Tigris, which had watered the alluvial plains for millennia and made this piece of the world inhabitable.

A new city. From above, it looked like a magic city. Ibn Jubayr would have reveled in it.

"Why are we so surprised to find Baghdad looking like this?" asked Bob over breakfast, the meal we were required to take and pay for at the hotel. Eggs, bread, excellent orange juice.

"And coffee, please," added Tom.

"Coffee is extra," said the waiter.

Bob said, "Okay. We'll pay."

The waiter shook his hand. "Sorry, sir. No coffee. We have no coffee." A magic city of Arabian Nights fame without coffee? Problems. Problems under this golden facade.

We drank tea.

"You two haven't been here for ages," Tom pointed out. "Saddam Hussein has been building like mad for twenty years."

"Do you remember what you used to say, Bob?" I asked. "How different the country would be, how it would really take off, if only Iraq got a decent percentage from the sale of its own oil?"

"Not me. It was Jamal who used to say that."

Jamal. The irrigation engineer in Al-Nahra, the Iraqi village where we had lived. Jamal, who had been Bob's close friend during his two years of research, had insisted that the reason Iraq was poor was that it had no control over its own resources. When the old regime came down, said Jamal, and Iraq got a fair share of the oil revenues, then justice and prosperity would prevail. "The will of the people is there, Bob," he would declare.

In the fifties, certainly the potential for improvement was there, not only in the newly discovered natural resource of oil but in the people themselves, their hard work, their resiliency. We had read about the Iraqi people's historic ability to deal with almost every sort of demanding situation, from invasions, floods, and earthquakes to autocratic rule, from Genghis Khan to British colonial administrators.

So we should have been prepared for that urban vista we viewed our first morning in Baghdad, just as we should have been prepared for the careful scrutiny by government personnel that had managed to land us in this particular hotel. Iraq, we knew, was a police state, and all comings and goings, particularly of foreigners, were closely monitored. Tom had told us that the Rashid Hotel was known for its sophisticated surveillance equipment. "If you put all the foreigners together in one place, you can save on electricity and labor!" he pointed out.

We had actually tried to register at the Baghdad Hotel near the South Gate, a hotel we remembered from long ago. Friends in Cairo had said the Baghdad was less expensive than the deluxe Rashid, and we felt we had to be careful with the money we had brought: all transactions were on a cash-only basis, no plastic, no checks. The hotels took only dollars. The gray-haired clerk at the Baghdad was friendly, and Bob came to get me, from the taxi, to look at the room.

"Cheaper than the Rashid," said Tom. "Centrally located. Why not?"

But when all three of us returned, the clerk said, "Sorry, we have no rooms."

"But we were just here, and you said you did," protested Tom.

Across the check-in counter, we could see the rows of mail slots, all empty, the unused keys hanging on hooks. No one was staying here, clearly.

"We have no rooms," the clerk said forcefully. "Don't you understand Arabic?" Then she had added, "Why not try the Rashid? They welcome foreigners such as you."

Here we were then, in comfortable rooms, overlooking the new city after forty years. I had not been back since we had departed in June 1958, one month before the July 14 revolution.

Bob had made two short visits, one in 1964 on his way back from a consulting job in Wadi Serhan, Saudi Arabia; the other when he passed through Baghdad on his way to Afghanistan. That last visit was in 1967, a month before the 1967 Arab-Israeli war.

Still, we had maintained ties with Al-Nahra, the village where we lived in southern Iraq; and one of Sheik Hamid's sons, in the process of earning a Ph.D. in plant physiology in the United States, actually visited us in Texas in 1973. But since then our communications with old friends had dwindled to occasional secondhand or thirdhand reports or to mere reflections in papers at academic conferences like the 1989 reevaluation of the 1958 revolution held at the University of Texas and sponsored by Bob and the historian Roger Louis.

We had actually been advised to stop communicating with friends as United States–Iraqi relations rose and fell, so as not to place our Shia friends in jeopardy. "Security people may wonder why someone in a Shia village is getting letters from an American," said the sheikh's son.

In 1981 we had come closest to a return visit. The Iran-Iraq war was not yet in full swing, though Western media reported Iranian bombing of Basra in retaliation for Iraqi attacks on Teheran. Bob and I decided we would be willing to take the trip when we were invited to a conference in Basra itself, sponsored by the Center for Gulf Studies at the University of Basra. Sadly, our visas were apparently sent to Texas rather than to Cairo, where we waited, and by the time the visas reached us, the conference was over.

The Iran-Iraq war dragged on until 1988, at great cost to both parties. Estimates were published in the press of a million casualties over nine years (100,000 dead plus uncounted wounded). There was no possibility of visits in those years, for friendship or research.

In 1990 Saddam Hussein invaded Kuwait, claiming historic territorial rights. This triggered the military operation known as Desert Storm, which brought the United Nations and Western powers together in a joint effort to reverse the Iraqi move. Saddam retreated, finally, after thirty days of intensive bombing and four days of ground warfare. Iraq suffered, it is said, between 50,000 and 100,000 casualties; over 80,000 men were taken prisoner. The economic sanctions placed on Iraq after the 1991 defeat were still in force in 1996, as we arrived in Baghdad.

When we had contemplated visiting Iraq to update this book, we were told that the country was off limits. American passports were the property of the United States government, not of American individuals, and could not be used to visit what was still considered an enemy nation. And this enemy nation was still politically isolated and econom- ically punished by a strict blockade enforced by the United Nations with strong American backing.

But we noticed that several journalists had managed to get into Iraq, for we read their accounts. Emboldened, we wrote the Iraqi office at the United Nations, requesting visas. No response. Telephone calls from friends assured us that the visas were on the way, but they never came.

"You know too much. You've been there before," Bob was told by several Iraqi exiles. So in June 1995 we gave up. At a dinner party in Cairo we mentioned that, to our disappointment, we were not going to be able to include in our book an update about Iraq, since a year of trying to obtain visas had produced no results at all. "That's ridicu- lous," said the Iraqi wife of our host, and she marched to the telephone while we sipped after-dinner Turkish coffee. She came back and handed us a small piece of paper. Numbers and names.

"Try one more time," she said.

So our last day in Cairo we found our way to the Iraqi Interests Section in the new district of Muhandaseen. We stated our request through a narrow aperture (it couldn't be called a window) set into a side entrance of the building to screen visitors and suppliants—and, we supposed, possible hostile attackers.

The tall mustached man invited us inside.

"*Ahlan wusahlan*," he said, producing a ring of keys with which he opened a series of locks. We passed through and he slammed the metal gate behind us.

We filled out applications, submitted pictures, and showed copies of our books. Then we sat quietly, looking around us at the colorful posters adorning the walls of the reception room. The Arch of Ctesi-

phon by moonlight; a view of modern Baghdad skyscrapers; the recon-
structed Ishtar Gate in the ancient city of Babylon; a portrait of Iraq's
leader, Saddam Hussein, in army uniform, eyeing us solemnly.

"We don't know how things are going these days," said the inter-
viewer, an attractive young woman. "But we will let you know."

Four months later I found a small square envelope, without a
return address, in our Austin, Texas, mailbox. The message was hand-
written on thin, crinkly airmail paper bearing no letterhead whatsoever.

The message was short and simple. "Dear Mr. and Mrs. Fernea,
You have visas to visit Iraq, whenever you wish. Please pick them up in
Cairo as soon as possible."

Cairo? We had just come back from Cairo and had no plans to
return. And no money.

"Well," Bob had said sadly. "That's that."

But the fates or serendipity intervened. Bob received an invitation
to present the annual Distinguished Lectures at the American University in Cairo, where he had taught anthropology and done research in
Egyptian Nubia from 1959 to 1965. The university would also pay "the
spouse's way," i.e., me.

"We can go on to Iraq, then," we agreed. "Cairo to Amman to
Baghdad—that we can afford," said Bob. "Maybe Tom would come
along and take pictures. We'll need new pictures. When have you seen
a picture of daily life in Iraq?"

ON MARCH 19, 1996, we agreed to pay two hundred dollars for a taxi
to take us from Amman, Jordan, to Baghdad, on the highway that is
still the only legal access to Iraq.

We left the hills of Amman at six in the morning, in a thick fog
which blankets the houses and the hills of Amman. As the taxi wound
down into the valley, the fog began to lift and we could see day laborers
lining the streets, waiting for transport to their construction jobs in and
around the expanding city. But fog still swirled around the palace of
King Hussein on the hill above us.

We were riding in a 1984 Chevrolet Caprice, its burgundy upholstered seats worn, but clean and comfortable. Our driver, a middle-aged
Jordanian, recommended by Tom's journalist friends in Amman, made

this run two or three times a week, we were told. He was a quiet man. He did not even play the radio on his dashboard.

The driver stopped on the outskirts of Amman to stoke himself up with coffee for the fourteen-hour stretch to Baghdad. We did the same. Then he opened the trunk, where our two suitcases and our bag of presents were stored, and stuffed in two large plastic bags, each as wide as a small round table, full of flat bread.

"Do you think we should buy some, too?" asked Tom. "Maybe there's a shortage of bread in Baghdad these days."

We had been told that there was a shortage of everything in Baghdad, but particularly medicines like aspirin, and ibuprofen, and vitamins for children. We had brought medicines and vitamins as well as Nescafé and chocolate for friends and friends of friends. Perhaps we needed to buy bread as well. We did, following the driver's example.

Just before the border, where the four-lane highway would supposedly become a superb first-class six-lane highway (can it be true?), the driver stopped again. "Lunch," he muttered laconically. But while we sat in white plastic chairs, exactly like those for sale at Pier One in Austin, Texas, eating ta'amiyah and egg sandwiches proffered by an Egyptian restaurant owner, we could see the driver in his dark blue dish-dasha and kaffiyeh passing down the row of shops set up for travelers such as us who wished to lay in supplies for the voyage ahead.

What was for sale? Presumably everything that was needed or wanted in isolated Iraq, goods stacked from floor to ceiling of the stores. We followed the driver as he bought dried milk for babies; packets of biscuits; large tins of halawa, tea, coffee; six crates of Pepsi-Cola; Marlboro cigarettes; ballpoint pens, light globes, pads of writing paper. The trunk was now so full of new purchases that our suitcases had been transferred to the roof of the car, where the driver roped them tightly to the luggage rack. I found myself buying six more pens, five packages of mint Life-Savers, and three spoons, which I stuffed in my purse.

"Why are you buying spoons, B.J.?" asked Tom.

Why indeed? But what if there was little to eat in Baghdad, and we were forced to eat our own purchases: the halawa, the peanut butter, the bread, the biscuits? Maybe we would need spoons. We had heard so many dire reports about the scarcities in Iraq that I had fallen into a camping trip mentality.

We had hashed and rehashed the pros and cons of coming here; if the political clamps were so tight on the people of Iraq, wouldn't they refuse to talk to us? And if they did, wouldn't they risk imprisonment or some other horrible fate? So, if no one would talk to us, why go at all? Sitting in a hotel would hardly provide us with insight about what was going on in Baghdad and no news at all about our friends in Al-Nahra. Iraqi exile friends in the States had warned us we probably would not be allowed to travel south, where we had lived in the fifties. Al-Nahra, they pointed out, was in a Shia area, not too far from Kerbela, the holy city where I had gone on pilgrimage with my women friends in 1957. Kerbela had been the site of an armed revolt in 1991, immediately following the Gulf War. Shia rebels rose up in response to President Bush's promise to help them overthrow Saddam Hussein. But American help never arrived, and the rebellion was mercilessly suppressed by government troops, who even blasted the holy mausoleum of al-Hussein, where the rebels had taken sanctuary. The protective sanctuary of a holy place meant nothing to Iraq's Ba'athist leadership, but word was that the shrine, like Baghdad, had been rebuilt.

We were not too sure we really even wanted to try going south after reading a *New York Times* account of journalists robbed and kidnapped on the highway near Hillah. But we had finally decided that just getting to Baghdad was worth the trip, to see once more the city where we had first met the Middle East. So here we were at last, looking out the window of the Rashid Hotel. Our hotel room closets were now full of our border supplies. We had eaten a late supper in our rooms: bread, peanut butter, and *halawa* (yes, with my spoons). And we had paid off the driver who had taken us to the bazaar to change money. The rate was 750 Iraqi dinars to one American dollar, down from an earlier rate of 3,000 Iraqi dinars to one dollar. In 1956 the Iraqi dinar was worth one pound sterling—nearly three dollars.

IBN JUBAYR DESCRIBED the twelfth-century Baghdadis he met as "vain and proud. Strangers," he said, "they despise, and they show scorn and disdain to their inferiors, while the stories and news of other men they belittle." Now that we were actually here, we wondered how we would be treated. We were unofficial representatives, whether we liked it or not, of the United States, a country that had bested and humiliated Iraq in war and that still prevented the country from receiving enough food and medicine, spare parts for machines, and all other consumer goods. If they acted toward us in the way Ibn Jubayr predicted, who could blame them? Expecting the worst, but hoping for something better, we had written in advance to Iraqi friends, exiles in America and England, offering to call their families, deliver gifts, whatever. Some had written back thank you, but no thank you; one wrote to say his family was so paralyzed by fear that a call from a foreigner, an *American* yet, would scare them to death. Other friends, however, sent phone numbers of relatives, packets of goodies to deliver, and assurances that our calls would be welcomed.

The first telephone call we made from the Rashid Hotel, to a local businessman, contradicted Ibn Jubayr and was more in accord with our own happier past experiences in Iraq.

"Welcome to Baghdad!" said Mr. W. "My friend wrote you were coming. Are you free today?"

Bob replied that we were free, yes, indeed, we had no plans.

"I'll come pick you up in an hour, then," he announced. "We can take a tour of the city, and afterward you must come home with me for lunch."

Tom and Bob and I looked at each other. Ten minutes earlier traditional Arab hospitality had been almost more than we could have expected, but now seemed perfectly natural.

"Well, well," said Tom. Then he stopped as I pointed at the ceiling where we presumed the bugging devices recorded our conversations.

"I think a gift is in order," said Bob, "but somehow I don't have the feeling this man needs a big sack of bread."

"Let's take a tin of *halawa*," suggested Tom. "That's a nice present for anyone."

He raised his voice on the last phrase and we turned toward the presumed bugging devices.

"Come on, guys," I said as we walked out into the dim hall. The Rashid seemed to suffer from a light globe shortage. "We've been here less than twenty-four hours, and we're already getting paranoid."

"Is it paranoia?" Bob asked.

"Think how the average Iraqi must feel," returned Tom.

Mr. W., the businessman, was round and cheerful. He shook

hands, opened his car doors for us, speaking genially to the car watchers as he did so, and we were off for a ground-level look at the new city of Baghdad we had viewed from our hotel room on high.

"This city," Ibn Jubayr told his readers, "has two parts, an eastern and a western, and the Tigris passes between them. Its western part is wholly overcome by ruin. . . . The bridge [was] carried away by the river in its flood, and the people have turned to crossing by boats." Those unique Iraqi round boats made of skins were still in use in 1956 by poor people. But in 1996 not a boat of any kind was to be seen on the river, which we crossed on a four-lane bridge, with wide pedestrian walkways on each side.

"I thought all the bridges were destroyed in the bombing," said Bob.

"You have to look for the war damage," said our host. "He's rebuilt everything exactly as it was before. You have to give him that." And almost as an aside, he added, "He would have made a great minister of development." We sped over one bridge, circled the traffic loop, and headed into one of the districts where new government buildings had been erected. "Here is the Ministry of Defense, and there's the new medical complex," Mr. W. pointed out. "They had everything there before the war to do any kind of operation. Not anymore.

"Now we're going on, to Kadhiman, golden domes, very famous Shia mosque." The men in their brown abas and the women in black abbayas looked like figures I remembered—all the people in Al-Nahra dressed that way. We saw more mosques, tiled, plain, some with minarets dating from the twelfth century and some from the twentieth. Parks. Convention halls. Museums. Baghdad had become a new city.

"There are five bridges now," said Mr. W. "The old travelers would never have believed it."

"Travelers like Ibn Jubayr?"

He glanced at me in the rearview mirror. "Ibn Jubayr. You know the work of Ibn Jubayr, *madame?*"

"A little," I admitted. "His book of travels. But only in translation. My Arabic's not good enough to read it in the original."

"But you speak some Arabic, I'm told, you and your husband?"
We agreed that we did.

"I'd love to take some pictures of that Jewad Salim sculpture," said Tom, pointing at the great banner of granite stretched across Liberation Square, the principal roundabout for the new roads of the city. I peered at it, too, the dark sculpted metal figures marching, moving, battling across the gray granite background toward a final resolution of peaceful figures enjoying the fruits of their land.

"Jewad Salim? Didn't we meet him once, B.J.?"

"Yes, I think so."

Our guide said, "Jewad Salim was a very famous Iraqi sculptor. But," he said to Tom, "you can't take any pictures anywhere in Baghdad without approval from the Ministry of Information. Rules. Those are the rules."

"Yes," said Tom. "I know. I've been here before. I'm taking these folks with me to the ministry tomorrow."

Our friend drove us to a rise from which we could see one of the new palaces of Saddam Hussein, currently under construction, complete with private lake. We'd read that the Baghdad water system was in crisis and that the sewage plants had broken down due to lack of spare parts. Wasn't building a palace complete with private lake a bit extravagant? Our host laughed. "And now you're going to ask me about the recent and untimely deaths of our leader's brother and son-in-law," he said.

There was a pause.

"We feel," said Mr. W., "that what leaders do among themselves is no concern of ours. We are glad to stay out of it."

"Good approach," remarked Tom rather laconically.

We were retracing our route now, across the Tigris, through central Baghdad, past the Jewad Selim monument again.

"The big issue is food," said Mr. W. "Can the leader feed his people? If he can't, he can blame it on the United States, not on himself. So why the embargo?"

"Theoretically," said Bob a bit stiffly, "it's supposed to erode the power of Saddam Hussein."

Mr. W. laughed again. "Yeah. Sure. Look around you. The embargo has exactly the opposite effect—it's actually helping our leader maintain his control."

Bob said nothing. Tom looked out the window.

"We thought you Americans were too smart for that."

Bob could not let that pass. "Yeah," he said, "but remember that we smart types can't control our foreign policy any more than you can control yours!"

Lunch was a pleasant affair, served family style in the dining room of Mr. and Mrs. W.'s modest home. The house stood in a row of similar modest brick structures on a quiet street in what our host termed the officers' district. Chicken. Rice. Vegetable stew. Veal cutlets. Mrs. W. was slight and dark-haired, with a cheerful expression and lovely eyes.

Mr. W. continued our earlier conversation. He held forth on the problem of feeding Iraq, a country that at the best of times produces only a third of its food, he said. We waited for a detailed condemnation of the United States for continuing to impose heavy sanctions, but it didn't come. Instead, we were treated to a fascinating and rather sad tale of the imposition of food rationing, and then of the search for alternate ways to feed the population of 20 million people.

"Our leader," he said. This was a phrase to be repeated over and over again during our visit to Iraq. People did not say "the president," they said "he" or "our leader." Portraits of the leader hung everywhere, on billboards, on the sides of buildings, painted on banners strung across the public squares. He was depicted in a uniform, in a white suit, with a beret or a turban, in a casual shirt, smiling. But no one mentioned his name.

"Our leader," said our host, "imposed food rationing fairly and squarely." A ration book had been issued to every man, woman, and child, books that entitled them to specified regular amounts of twenty basic commodities, like flour, sugar, tea, rice, lentils, cooking oil, soap.

"Some people got more, don't forget that," put in his wife.

"Yes," he admitted. "Those close to our leader, the army officers and such people, they got extras. But everyone, everyone received the same basics. That's the truth."

His wife rose and cleared the table. I helped carry the plates into her kitchen, which, like her neat house, was modern but modest. No dishwasher, but a nearly new gas stove and a large refrigerator. Through the kitchen window over the sink, I could see a small vegetable garden and a row of rosebushes, pink and white, in bloom. She followed my glance. "My really beautiful roses are in front," she said.

"Now that the children are grown-up, I can use the front for flowers. Let's have tea on the porch where we can smell them. And the jasmine is in bloom."

"I love jasmine," I said sincerely. I associated the sweet scent with summer nights in Cairo in the gardens of old friends.

"And let's change the subject and talk about our kids, okay?" she said to her husband as she set down the tea tray on the glass-topped table. The scent of jasmine and roses drifted to us across the freshly watered lawn.

"Yes, my dear." He smiled. "But I just want to tell them one more thing, it's important."

She shook her head at him, but she smiled. "Okay," she allowed.

"You see, Bob," he went on, "at one point things got really bad, and some scientists at the university came up with data that showed guess what, the pits of dates contained important nutrients. Well, you know that Iraq has more dates than anything else, except maybe oil, and we can't sell that right now, thanks to you Americans."

Bob smiled ruefully. "I suppose," he said.

Mr. W. smiled in return. "So we thought, fine, but how can we get people to eat the pits?" He looked at us. "People made a joke about it, but by that time a lot of people really were ready to eat anything, even if it was the pits."

Tom let out one of his great hooting laughs, and Mr. W. smiled his acknowledgment. "So what did you do?" asked Bob.

"We ground up the pits very fine and added them to the flour," proclaimed our host triumphantly. "It didn't help the taste of the bread, but it helped us get through some bad times."

Bob cleared his throat and said we'd imposed on our new friends too long, and we should head back to the hotel.

"I suppose the Rashid's full of journalists?" queried W. "Here to cover the elections day after tomorrow?"

"Nope. Not that we've seen."

"They expected lots of foreign journalists."

"I don't know why," said Tom. "Nobody's here but us chickens."

TWO FRIENDS OF FRIENDS called early in the morning and offered to accompany us to the Ministry of Information "to make the visit easier." This was another surprise, as was the relative friendliness we met at the ministry. What was our program? What would we like to do? Bob made up a list:

1. Travel to Al-Nahra, in Diwaniyah, now Al Qadissiyah Province, to visit old friends.

2. Walk and take pictures along Rashid Street, in the older part of Baghdad.

3. Visit the Gailani mosque.

4. Visit and photograph monuments.

We were interviewed by one of the Baghdadi women journalists. Why were we here? We produced our books again and talked about our life in the village before the revolution.

Tom came out of one of the rooms of the Press Bureau to say that he thought there would be some delay in getting our program approved. But we were free to go to Rashid Street today and to observe the election process tomorrow, if we wished.

"Rashid Street, by all means," said Bob.

"But we have to take somebody from here with us," said Tom, "and I think I have met a nice guy."

And that was how we met Hadi.

"I will be, I think, stuck to you from now on," he said with a smile. He was a slim, rather dapper young man of moderate height with a mustache, a modest manner, and a B.A. in comparative literature from the University of Basra. When I volunteered that I was a professor of English, he said, "We must discuss then, *madame*, the great Russian critic Bakhtin!"

"Well, well!" said Bob.

On our way out of the Press Bureau, Bob stopped Hadi.

"What do you think about permission to go south," he asked, "to visit the village? That's really our first priority."

Hadi's dark eyes betrayed no surprise or particular concern. He said smoothly, "That will be decided soon."

But he added in a different tone, "Even if they say yes, you know we can only go for the day. It is forbidden for foreigners to spend the night anyplace in the south between Baghdad and Basra."

We digested this piece of news in silence. An hour and a half driving down, an hour and a half back, over the good new roads. That would mean less than half a day in the village, since we had to be back in Baghdad before dark. Why the restrictions?

"For your own safety," said Hadi, as though we had spoken.

"Okay!" said Tom briskly. "Rashid Street! Let's go!"

"Where do you wish to begin, Professor Fernea?" asked Hadi rather formally. "Rashid Street, as you will remember, is a long thoroughfare."

"I want to find someplace familiar," answered Bob. "From what we've seen up to now, I wouldn't know this was Baghdad at all. But I'm sure it's here somewhere . . . covered over, or . . ." He glanced at Hadi and added, "It's hard to explain. Let's go to the South Gate, to Bab Sharqi."

The rented taxi parked at Bab Sharqi, and we walked north, along the colonnaded sidewalks of Rashid Street, which seemed much wider and less congested than we remembered. "Maybe because there aren't any more two-decker English-style buses roaring up and down, taking up the whole street," Bob suggested.

There were rows of small shops, as in the past, opening onto the shaded sidewalks beneath the colonnades, and selling shirts, sweaters, camera equipment (but no film), hardware that looked used. Some shops were closed, their steel shutters pulled down and locked to the sidewalk with large padlocks. While we waited for the driver at a small juice bar, the smell of coffee reached us from across the street.

"It is very expensive," cautioned Hadi.

We passed up the coffee shop, in favor of continuing the walk.

"What do you remember, Professor Fernea?"

"That department store! What was its name, B.J.? Isn't that it?"

"Yes, it is. It's . . . Orosdi-Back!"

Hadi smiled. "Now a government cooperative, where people can come to use their ration cards."

"Let's take a picture of the ration process," said Tom.

But it didn't work. The manager of Orosdi-Back, now a government cooperative, was not interested in having foreigners photograph the nearly empty shelves in the dim establishment over which he presided, where movements in and out were carefully monitored by guards standing beside the heavy iron entrance railings that only permitted us to enter single file.

"And what are *they* selling?" I pointed to two women in worn abbayas seated on the street outside Orosdi-Back, hawking small sacks of rice and flour, cans of cooking oil.

Hadi looked closely. "Extras, from their own rations, I believe," he said elliptically.

Rashid Street, the principal artery of the city in the past, had always been lively, boasting a great variety of stores, some with offices and hotels above, some new structures, some old. It was still lively. But the shops appeared more run-down and shabby than we remembered, despite the new covered market halfway to the North Gate, featuring household goods and ready-to-wear for children and adults. Bookstores had limited goods to sell, for they were unable to import new stock, and local publishers were hard-pressed to produce books, Hadi said, because of a shortage of paper. This must, we thought, be hard on Iraqis, who before the Gulf War constituted the largest reading audience in the Arab world, and a big market for books. The literacy rate, we learned, had reached 90 percent, the highest in the area.

Tea in the cafés still came in *stikans*, those small glasses, with gold stripes painted round their rims. And a half-grown boy, clanking his ladle against a large metal basin to advertise his wares, was selling, yes, it was *shinina*, that refreshing mixture of water and yogurt.

"Not expensive," said Hadi. "Would you like some, *madame?*"

I looked at the chunk of gray ice floating in the white *shinina* and shook my head. But I was sorely tempted, remembering how cooling the drink was on hot summer days and nights in Al-Nahra.

No one hassled us on our long walk, no one shouted insults, no one cursed us as far as we could tell, but people did stare at us. Foreigners were clearly strange creatures in Baghdad these days. Of course Hadi was with us, but it was doubtful anyone on Rashid Street recognized this thin young man as an employee of the Ministry of Information, sent along to "mind" foreign visitors.

Even when Bob and Tom visited one of the many outdoor flea markets one afternoon, no one bothered them. They wandered among the displays of used electronic equipment, watches, and radios, where the traders were Somalis and Sudanese as well as Baghdadis. Tom bought, for a journalist friend in Amman, a watch with the face of Saddam Hussein; it was an old army watch, the salesman told him. But we had no time for a visit to the thieves' market, under the ramp of one of the principal bridges, where, we were told, anything stolen the previous night could be repurchased the next day if the owner had enough cash to pay for it.

And we also resisted buying anything from the dozen or so specialty shops in the Rashid Hotel, some selling items on consignment for Baghdadis now in need of cash. There were chests of old, initialed family silver, feathered fans, czarist memorabilia, old and new jewelry, china, rugs—everything at incredibly inflated prices by any standard. Some of these luxury goods were reported to have come from Kuwait as wartime booty.

Overall, Baghdad appeared calm, not quite the golden magic metropolis we had viewed from the Rashid Hotel, but still orderly, though showing wear and lack of upkeep around the edges. There were no soldiers in the streets, no guns mounted in the traffic roundabouts to control a restless populace. After reading the horrendous reports about malnutrition and medical shortages, we had feared we might see throngs of beggars or starving children on the streets. The United Nations estimated that more than 100,000 Iraqi children have died since the end of the Gulf War in 1991.

We did not see any obviously sick children, however, since we did not visit the hospitals or schools. There were none on the street, and almost no beggars, only a few poor women sitting in shady spots along Rashid Street. That was all we could see.

"I think they don't realize we are Americans," said Bob, and gave as evidence his recent shoe shine, and the skepticism of the shoe shine boy when he said no, he was not Polish, he was American. "The expression on the guy's face said it all," Bob recounted. "Americans? No way, José!"

"Now where?" asked Hadi. We had been walking for two hours, and our mentor was beginning to look tired. So were we.

"One last thing," I said. "Abu Nawwas Street. I'd like to look for a little gold charm, to replace the one I lost, the one the sheikh's wife gave me long ago to keep my children safe."

Bob was somewhat impatient. "You won't be able to find the exact same pattern, B.J. Forget it!"

"Well, let me try," I said defensively. That small bit of gold, cut in the shape of a hand with tiny inset turquoises, the traditional amulet

to ward off the evil eye, was a treasured memento of my long friendship with the village women. It had disappeared two years ago.

"Maybe we'll see something similar," suggested Hadi, and he
began to help me search in the narrow shops along Abu Nawwas Street,
where cobblestones created a pleasant walkway, a definite improvement
over the rutted and sometimes muddy lanes of old.

We looked at delicate gold chains of different lengths hung from
hooks, at gold bracelets positioned in tempting piles of threes and fours,
at gold wedding bands in velvet-lined boxes, a few small Korans and
crosses. But there were no charms for babies of the sort I remembered.

"There is a special place for such charms," one of the goldsmiths
told Hadi, and explained how to get there. We set off, all four of us, in
search of my charm, and I realized that we had begun to relax in an
atmosphere that was far more friendly than we had expected.

"It's quite far," pointed out Hadi, "that place the goldsmith suggested."

"And aren't we due for lunch at two P.M., in Azamiyah, B.J.?"
from Bob.

I nodded. Azamiyah was a long way from Rashid Street, in an
area known in the past for large estates and gardens, the property of old
Baghdadi families.

Hadi stiffened. "You are lunching with Iraqi friends?" he asked.
His forehead wrinkled a bit.

"Yes," said Bob. "At the Gailani house."

Hadi did not comment, but I could almost feel him memorizing
the name, though he was too polite to bring out his notebook and write
it down. Was this paranoia?

"I suppose he'll be asked," Tom pointed out later. "That's his job,
isn't it? To tell people where we are and what we do, and to mind us
while we're doing it."

After a delicious lunch at the home of Madame al-Gailani, we
proffered thanks and goodbyes and set out for the Rashid Hotel. But it
took a ten-minute walk to find a taxi, an old car with an old man
driving, a small boy curled up beside him in the front seat.

"Rashid Hotel," Tom said authoritatively, and then, to the
slightly puzzled look on the old man's face, was surprised to find he
must explain carefully just where our home away from home was lo-

cated. The child turned around and stared at us. He hung on more tightly to the driver, presumably his grandfather. Tom, who has a five-year-old son himself, tried a smile, but the child did not respond. He burrowed down into the seat, into the shelter of the driver's arm, out of the sight of us, the strange and frightening foreigners.

We drove and drove in the wheezing old car, and the man apologized before stopping for gasoline.

"At least gas is cheap," remarked Tom, with a glance at the pump.

"I had no idea that Azamiyah was so far away," Bob said.

"Almost there," said Tom. "There's the hotel. Stop, please."

"Here?" queried Bob. "In the middle of this big boulevard?"

"Yes, yes," said Tom. "We can walk across the traffic easily."

The old man stopped obediently, but while we were getting out, a belligerent young policeman came down from a nearby guard box and began berating the old man.

"Forbidden!" shouted the policeman. "Forbidden to stop here! Where is your license?"

"What is forbidden?" Tom was already out of the car, standing by the driver's seat where the old man was practically weeping, pleading with the policeman while he scrabbled in the glove compartment for whatever paper had been demanded of him.

"Leave him alone!" shouted Tom in an angry voice that has gotten him into trouble at other times, and other places, in the years we've known him.

The policeman raised his arm, as though to strike, but Tom continued to shout. "He's an old man. Leave him alone."

Bob moved in to intercept what might take place next, took the policeman's hand, tried to calm him down. A couple of Iraqi onlookers had moved toward us by now.

The policeman finally relented, but not before the old man grabbed his hand and began to kiss it in an obsequious way, his tears falling on that official hand until it was unceremoniously snatched away. The policeman marched back to his post, and Bob pressed money into the driver's hand. The old man looked at it without counting, his eyes still wide with fright. "For the fare," said Bob.

The child sat up and looked back at us as the old taxi wheezed off, and the two Iraqis plus Tom finished their discussion.

"So what was all that about?" I asked as we crossed the highway and made our way through the Rashid Hotel garden to the automatic doors. The doors were not always automatic these days; they were opened instead by a doorman got up in Arabian Nights costume, towering at least seven feet in his baggy trousers, embroidered waistcoat, and giant turban.

"Oh, the policeman was going to take the old man's car permit away," Tom said. "That's his livelihood!"

"But why?" asked Bob. "I still don't understand what he was doing wrong."

"The taxi driver stopped where he wasn't supposed to, on the wrong side of the street, that's why. Those kinds of cops make me sick, whether they're in Cairo or Baghdad or Austin."

"Yeah," agreed Bob, "but for a minute there I thought he was getting ready to put you in the slammer with the old man."

It was easy to admire the calm and order that prevailed in Baghdad and forget that it was a police state ruled with an iron hand. The policeman who had hassled the old taxi driver was only a small cog in the complex machinery of regulation and surveillance that covered every aspect of Iraqi life. We had been welcomed by the Gailanis. But they had wealth and a long and distinguished family history which helped cushion them from official displeasure. But there were several families in the city who had not responded to our phone calls, who were clearly afraid to see us, despite the assurances of their own relatives in exile. What were their daily lives like?

"I have the feeling we'll not be allowed to go down to the village," said Bob.

But he was wrong. The next day we woke to find that Tom had gone off at dawn, in the company of a Spanish journalist, to cover the elections. We walked over to the Press Bureau, in case they might be open for business, passing families in their best clothes, out for the election day holiday to cast their votes in the ballot boxes set up in their respective neighborhoods. Our businessman friend, Mr. W., had said, in answer to our question, "Of course Parliament is controlled, but there are some differences between the local candidates. Better if your representative is someone you know." He had added, "And it is always wise to be recorded as having voted."

The Press Bureau was open, and as we walked in, the director came out of his own office and smiled.

"Well, you're free to go to Al-Nahra tomorrow!"

"Great!" Bob almost jumped up and down in his delight, but I could see him restraining himself. "Really? That's great!"

"Hadi will go with you, of course, and a driver."

"Yes, of course."

"And," he said, "you have permission to spend the night there if you like. I know you want to spend as much time with your old friends as possible."

This was a real surprise. How come? We didn't ask, we just said thank you and headed back to the hotel, almost exultantly.

WE WERE ON OUR WAY BACK to Al-Nahra, speeding south on Route 8, the new six-lane highway with interchanges and driver-friendly green signs in English and Arabic that stretches from the Jordan-Iraq border, in the northwest, all the way to Basra on the Persian Gulf. Travelers' facilities had been installed along the road: gas stations, rest stops, and cement picnic tables and benches under metal awnings. The facilities, however, seemed unused, if the grass growing up between the picnic tables and chairs was any indication. But they were a big improvement over the past, when the two-lane highway, dark and isolated, was a dangerous place, especially at night. Jamal, Bob's irrigation engineer friend, had been killed, together with his new bride, when he crashed into a heavy truck, sitting without lights on the road in front of him. The accident went unreported for hours. The road was considered so dangerous, in fact, that in the old days most people took the train, as we had, a four-hour clunking journey from Baghdad to Diwaniyah.

The road site itself, from Baghdad to Hillah (near Babylon), then southwest toward Mecca or straight south to Samawa and Nasiriyah, was very old, dating as far back as archaeologists have been able to trace the history of transport in Mesopotamia. Hillah was a stop in the pilgrimage routes as well as the caravan trails heading for Baghdad and then north to Damascus and the Mediterranean Sea. Ibn Jubayr traveled this road, in 1184, and he had high praise for the road facilities funded by Zubaydah, wife of Haroun al-Rashid, who had ordered the creation of a series of wells, pools for watering animals, and storage tanks to conserve rainwater. "The facilities and useful works have been of service to all," wrote Ibn Jubayr. "But for [Zubaydah's] generous action in this direction, the road could not have been traversed."

Early biblical scholars in Europe placed the Garden of Eden near the confluence of the Tigris and Euphrates rivers, the area we were now crossing in our modern Chevrolet sedan. I had even found an old map once in London, on which the word "Eden" had been printed in careful flowery script over the land between Baghdad and Basra, roughly the place where Bob and I had lived, the village of Al-Nahra. This gave me a lighthearted line to use in Christmas cards in those days, sent to relatives and friends in Chicago, Portland, and Milwaukee. "We honeymooned in a mud-brick house," I had written, "but it was in the Garden of Eden."

The village where we lived in the hypothetical Garden of Eden was actually not far from Nippur, the intellectual center of ancient Sumeria, though we did not hear much about Sumerian civilization in our classes in ancient history at Reed College; in those days people still believed firmly that civilization, real civilization that is, began with classical Greece. But without Sumer, where the wheel and writing were invented, where settled agriculture was established, there would have been no Greece as we know it today. Even Ibn Jubayr does not mention Ur, or Nippur or even Babylon, in his travel account, though he was certainly acquainted with the achievements of classical civilization in Greece. It was hard to believe that these ancient and renowned cities lay unknown under the alluvial plains we were now crossing, even in Ibn Jubayr's time, the Golden Age of Islam. Nineteenth- and twentieth-century archaeologists uncovered the royal treasure of Ur, the stele bearing the law code of Hammurabi, the thousands of stone tablets that, when deciphered, included the earliest heroic epic, the Epic of Gilgamesh, that recorded the history of this place, successively known as Sumer, Babylon, Mesopotamia, Iraq, where we had come in 1996, searching for pieces of our own past.

The highway we were speeding down may have been the site of past glory, but the fields spread out on either side seemed deserted. No stands of winter wheat or barley, not by any stretch of the imagination the "broad and fertile lands" noted by Ibn Jubayr, which were in his time "watered by canals and shaded by the foliage of trees in fruit." On the contrary, water stood in unregulated swaths in the fields, and the dark groves of palm trees were only visible far away, on the horizon. And there were, as Bob enunciated it, no sheep grazing, no camels moving, no tribesmen mounted on horses.

"No animals," Bob had said. "Why?"

Hadi turned from his post in the front seat. "There is a law, I think," he said.

"What kind of law?"

"Lots of disease, I'm told. Not much food. The government had to destroy most of the horses some years ago, and since then, they ask people to concentrate on cultivating the land, not raising animals. We need food very much these days."

"Not even *jamoosa?*" asked Bob. The *jamoosa*, the water buffalo, were always said to be immune to most of the local diseases and gave good value in meat and milk.

"Not even *jamoosa*," repeated Hadi. "Not here, anyway."

Bob was silent, and I remembered his description of the historical pattern of life on the Mesopotamian plain. When the land was flooded or salted up, people turned to nomadic pastoralism, scratching a kind of living, as the Bedouin did, by grazing animals on the fields that provided some growth, but were not fertile enough to produce crops of grain. But that nomadism had only been possible before the rise of large-scale urbanism, which meant cities full of people to be fed.

"We seem to be riding much higher than the land," Tom pointed out.

He was right. "Looks like they have scooped up the farmland to make the roadbed, to build it above flood level," Bob suggested. "If you look further out, the land itself seems to rise."

No animals. Standing water. Not a good recipe for prosperity. I felt my stomach tighten involuntarily and realized that my heart was full of anticipation, but also of anxiety. What awaited us in the village? Ruin and starvation? I told myself the Ministry of Information would never have let us travel down here if that was the case. But who would remember us after such a long absence?

"Did anyone from the ministry tell the village we were coming?" asked Bob.

Hadi shook his head. "I don't think so."

"So," said Tom, "you don't know whether you'll be welcomed with open arms or shunned as enemy Americans, right?"

"Come on, Tom," Bob answered.

Hadi spoke. "If it is too difficult, we can simply return to Baghdad."

We not only feared that our friends might be leading an impoverished life, we worried about what might have happened to them in the recent political uprisings. Al-Nahra was relatively close to the important Shia religious centers of Kerbela and Najaf. In the 1950s Najaf had been a center of opposition to the British-mandated government headed by Nuri Sa'id, the prime minister, and the young King Faisal II. The underground Communist organization had been strong during the time we lived in Al-Nahra. Jamal, the irrigation engineer, had presented Bob with pamphlets printed in Najaf that had attacked our presence in the village, and especially Bob's activities, talking to tribesmen and going out on horseback to survey the network of irrigation canals, the distant settlements.

At the time I had been somewhat alarmed. "Do they actually mention you by name?" I had asked.

Bob had smiled. "They warn the people about the American spy in Al-Nahra, but they only identify me as Mr. Bob, so I guess we shouldn't be too worried."

The Ba'athists, when they took power in the 1970s, severely persecuted the Communists. The south always seemed to be on the losing side.

Ahmed, the driver of our Ministry of Information car, broke into my silent reminiscences.

"I am from near here," he announced. "I am from the tribe of Abu Sultan. I know about the sheikh you lived with. He was the leader of a group of tribes south of us."

"The Al-Agra confederation," said Bob.

"Yes, and they fought the British with us," Ahmed continued excitedly. "My sheikh was very famous for fighting the British."

"So was Sheikh Atiyah, the father of the sheikh we lived with," put in Bob, not to be outdone. "The British tried to break him, but couldn't until they cut off the water supply in the middle of the summer, and bombed his house. Sheikh Hamid, his son, was still living in that house when we were in Al-Nahra."

"Bad! Bad!" said Ahmed. "People still remember that bombing."

The fields stretching away in both directions to the horizon,

marked by the dark fans of date palms, looked quiet and serene, not the
site for a punishment as cruel as cutting off people's water supply in
the burning summer heat. The British referred to this as "an act of
pacification of the unruly Diwaniyah tribes, who were wreaking havoc
in the south."

"And my sheikh," went on Ahmed, "he died before the revolution. But my father told me that hundreds of tribesmen came from all
over to pay their respects. He had a big rich house, but he wanted to die
outside, in a tent."

Bob sat up. "I think I was there," he said. "I think I drove Sheikh
Hamid. Don't you remember, B.J., when I went to this great funeral of
the sheikh who wanted to die in a tent?"

"Why?" I didn't remember this story very well.

"He said the Bedouin way was the best way, and he was a
Bedouin."

Ahmed smiled broadly in the rearview mirror. Bob smiled in
return.

"Maybe we could stop and see my sheikh, I mean his son, on our
way back to Baghdad?" he asked.

Hadi said we would have to see.

We had left the banks of the Tigris River, which flows east. We
were heading south, close to the Euphrates, past Hillah and ancient
Babylon, where the Euphrates bifurcated. One branch led to the holy
city of Najaf and the ancient city of Kufah, described by Ibn Jubayr as a
"large city of ancient construction, over which ruin has secured mastery." The other branch of the Euphrates passes through Diwaniyah,
our first destination, a city that apparently did not exist in Ibn Jubayr's
time, but rose to importance as an administrative center when the Ottoman Empire ruled Iraq. Diwaniyah was still the district capital, where
the train stopped in the old days. But we did not need to go into the
city, for there was now a designated exit from the main highway for
Al-Nahra. The village had always stood along both sides of a bifurca-
tion of the Euphrates, which is now a major irrigation canal. On the
world atlas this tributary is indicated by a faint blue line which continues west from Al-Nahra to Afaq and the ancient Sumerian intellectual
city of Nippur, and ends as a small marsh.

We had gone near Afaq forty years ago with our friends from Al-
Nahra, to witness the annual passion plays. These were performed dur-

ing Muharram, the month of mourning for the Shia martyr al-Hussein, cut down in Kerbela during the struggle over leadership of the
early Islamic community. The subsequent split in Islam, between Shia
and Sunni, persists to this day. The passion plays were forbidden in
Al-Nahra. Why? Some said it was punishment left over from the
opposition to the British in the 1930s. Others cited the government's
fear of an armed uprising among the tribes. How better to express
rebellion, Bob had said, than in the metaphor of religious drama, a cry
of protest against contemporary conditions, sanctioned as a religious
ritual.

"B.J., does this look right to you?" Bob roused me from my
reveries.

We had taken the Al-Nahra exit and were continuing on an access
road across unplanted fields, toward clumps of palm trees and sand-
colored houses, the edge of a settlement—or a town.

"There's the shrine!" I pointed out. "But it's much bigger than it
was and it's all spruced up." It was covered with blue tiles and there
were several new buildings attached to it.

Bob looked at me. We remembered the shrine well, because this
was the place we had turned over into a small canal when Jamal lost
control of his Land-Rover and dumped us in the water. We had been
able to crawl out and make our way to a small cluster of houses nearby,
where we sat shivering until someone got a taxi to take us all back to
Al-Nahra, cold and wet and muddy, but thankfully alive.

"Well, B.J., there it is! Al-Nahra!"

Ibn Jubayr might have termed Al-Nahra "a large village," but to
us it looked as though it had developed into a city in our absence,
houses and streets spreading out on either side of the main street, the
street on which stood, one after the other, the one-story buildings
housing the office of the *mudir nahiya* (the mayor), the jail, the government health clinic, and the girls' school. In 1956 the entrance to the
souk opened out just before the bridge, but now the shops had prolifer-
ated and could be seen stretching away on both sides of the canal.

"Cross the bridge, please, and then turn right," Bob said authoritatively. Ahmed slowed to avoid the crowds of tribesmen in their *dish-
dashas* and brown abas, their black and white kaffiyehs, who stared
curiously at us while we maneuvered the bridge, which still seemed to
be slightly skiddy on the ramp.

"I half expect to see a familiar face," said Bob, almost to himself. "But of course that's ridiculous."

Since I saw few women in the crowds along the main street and near the entrance to the souk, I didn't expect to see anyone I knew, but I realized my stomach was lurching, and not from the motion of the car. We were almost there.

"Turn right," repeated Bob. "Oh good, the road's paved. It used to be mud, mud, and more mud."

"There's the mosque!" I leaned out and pointed. "But now it's got a minaret."

Hadi said quietly, "All mosques have minarets, *madame*."

"This one didn't used to, though," explained Bob. "They didn't have money to build a minaret. But now the whole building is painted, and the minaret even has tiles!"

"Okay, then, where's your house?" Tom asked. "I've read your book, B.J., and your house should be . . . right there, where the road turns up the hill."

We stared. There was the irrigation canal on our right, there was the mosque across the canal, and here was the turn in the road, heading up. Our house should indeed be here, its high mud wall marking the corner of the path that led into the tribal settlement and prevented passersby from peering into the sheikh's beautiful old garden.

But the wall was not there. Neither was the garden, nor the two-room mud house, where we had spent the first years of our married life. We stared at a large pool, in which a few broken date palms stood, casting wavering shadows on the still, sunlit water. Ducks were actually paddling in the pool! It looked as though our house had drowned in the water, collapsed along with the pomegranate and bitter-orange trees, the grapevines, the banana and lemon trees.

Our house was gone. The garden was gone. We knew that the sheikh had died in the 1970s. Why had we come? Whom could we expect to see? I tried to suppress tears and told myself we had made a dreadful mistake. Obviously, everything would be different; no one would remember us. And wasn't it arrogant to just march into the village again, without warning, after forty years? Even if some of our friends were there, why should they want to see us?

But in the moment it took to think these thoughts, we had reached the end of the road, and Ahmed had parked on a raised platform of packed earth in front of a long white building, with arched doors. It looked much like the old grange halls of the American Midwest.

"Can this be a new mudhif?" Bob asked, eyeing the white plastered walls, the steel front door secured with a large padlock.

He turned and said, quite sharply, to Ahmed, "This is not a parking lot! Put the car somewhere else!"

His vehemence startled me, as it must have done Ahmed, who looked at Bob in surprise, but did as he was told.

Well, we had arrived. Now what? A small boy said yes, Nour the sheikh's son was here and he went running to a house nearby to get him. Tom and I walked back and forth across the platform before the mudhif. Hadi stood at the edge of that platform, looking down on the tribal neighborhood which had expanded and now seemed to be built of cement blocks, not mud brick.

A man rushed out of the house nearby. He passed me quickly, his *dish-dasha* a bit rumpled, and raced toward Bob.

"Nour!" cried Bob. And the two old friends embraced.

I looked at Bob and at Nour, the sheikh's son, and at the small boy who was now unlocking the mudhif, and without even thinking, I turned back toward the sheikh's house, the women's quarters. Only weeks later, when we discussed this reunion, did we reflect how we had both fallen naturally into our old village routine. Forty years had fallen away. Bob was the man, who went with other men to the mudhif; I took my place with the women. I had catapulted back in time, into my earlier self who had learned, soon after marriage, to live most of the time in the village in a different world from my husband, the women's world. For Al-Nahra was then a sexually segregated society, and in my automatic reaction forty years later, I took for granted that was still the case.

And thus, at this point our text must diverge, to record both of our experiences, *Bob's tale* and *B.J.'s tale*.

Of course, the man should come first. On this point everyone in Al-Nahra would agree—in public, at least.

BOB'S TALE

"What happened to the old mudhif?" This was the first question I asked Nour after initial greetings and inquiries about our respective health were over. I expected that, in the forty years I had been gone, many people would have disappeared. Sheikh Hamid, our host, had died in the mid-1970s. But it never occurred to me that the mudhif itself, the center of the tribal settlement, the site of traditional ceremonies and the symbol of tribal glory, would have disappeared.

"It burned down," said Nour. "In 1974. We think some boys did it."

This seemed strange, but I felt it was not a subject he wanted to pursue. "And this one," he added, "is of cement bricks, a lot cheaper to build than the old one."

But the old one was so magnificent, I thought to myself. Grand, dignified, yet made out of natural vegetation. The mudhif design is said to be Sumerian, at least five thousand years old; the reeds and ropes used in its frame come from the marshes of southern Iraq, as do the specialists, the builders who direct local tribes in the process of its construction. Tall reeds are gathered into bundles to form the arches, which, in large mudhifs, may rise to a height of thirty feet or more. The ends of the bundles are set in two rows, twenty feet or so apart, and buried in the earth. These flexible columns are then brought together from each side and interwoven to form arches, thick at the base and thinner at the apex. Bound together with rope and reinforced at the base with cement these days, the bunched reeds support the layers of overlapping reed mats that roof the building. Mats of the same sort are used as flooring; they keep out the damp cold in winter. And a mudhif designed on this basic model can be made larger or smaller, depending on the wealth of the owners, and on its projected use, for domestic or public purposes.

The new cement mudhif was locked when I arrived, which was something of a surprise. The old mudhif had no doors and was always open to accommodate visitors. A young boy had opened it with a key, and inside I saw that a number of wooden benches lined the white plaster walls, though there were still some rugs and pillows on the floor. But there was no fire pit where the *gahawchi*, the maker of coffee, used to tend a bed of hot coals, roasting and pounding coffee

beans and preparing both tea and coffee. He served us coffee in a kind
of secular communion rite, passing the same two small cups along the
rows of assembled men. After a couple of sips, I, like others, learned to
shake the cup slightly, thus indicating to the *gahawchi* that the coffee
should go on to the next person. In 1996, of course, there was no coffee
on the market to buy; but it was discouraging to find that it would not
have mattered anyway. The absence of the convivial coffee ritual made
the new mudhif seem even more commonplace than its structure.

Forty years ago in the old mudhif we used to sit on rugs, leaning
against the reed pillars, cross-legged, with pillows at our backs, talking
or just resting, sometimes for hours. If the sheikh was present, there
was always an entourage with him—his brothers and sons, a few
tribesmen-bodyguards—who sat at some distance from their leader.

Today there was a buzz of conversation among some school-aged
boys, who sat with their backs to the wall, across the room from Nour
and myself. A few other men came in and sat down. But except for
Nour, I did not recognize anyone. We all seemed to be strangers.

"I don't see any animals around," I said. "No water buffalo, or
sheep or donkeys, and where are the horses?"

Nour laughed, as did the other men, whether at my naïve question or my clumsy Iraqi Arabic, I could not be certain.

"This is an agricultural area," Nour answered. "We're not allowed to raise sheep and water buffalo here."

"And the horses all died in an epidemic in the 1970s," said another man.

Some discussion followed about the exact date of the equine epidemic. I sat, looking around, and noticed a gallery of photographs at the
far end of the room. Nour got up and took me to see them. They were
black-and-white studio portraits of his father, Sheikh Hamid, and of his
uncles and great-uncles, all of whom I presumed to be deceased. The
only portrait of a living personage was displayed on an easel below the
tribal portraits; it was a color poster, at least five feet high, of Saddam
Hussein in military uniform. Saddam Hussein could also be seen in
another photo, standing in the midst of a group of local tribesmen.
Nour pointed out this picture to me specially. I didn't remember that so
many pictures had hung in the old mudhif.

Suddenly, as I turned away from the photos, I was startled to see
one of those faces from the past coming toward me. A frail old man was

carefully walking through the door at the other end of the room. It was Abdulla, second eldest and lone survivor of Sheikh Hamid's brothers. He was ninety-one years old. We embraced gently, two anachronisms in these new surroundings. Abdulla still stood erect and still spoke with the distinctive accent he had gained during his youth, living with a Bedouin tribe on the desert. He had married a woman from that tribe more than sixty years ago.

Abdulla and I sat together on one of the benches and tried to carry on a conversation. This was difficult, for neither of us had ever understood each other very well in the old days, and now his kaffiyeh was wrapped over his mouth, muffling his words. I wondered about the kaffiyeh. A protection against germs? Against a too intimate embrace? However, Abdulla was too weak to stay very long.

When Abdulla had gone, I sat down once more on the bench, near Nour, and we resumed our conversation. Tom had by then gone off with Hadi to take pictures in the village. Suddenly, six men in brown suits and white socks walked into the mudhif. Nour put his hand on my arm and murmured, "Security—but don't worry." The young boys who had been giggling at me slipped outside and the older men rose to greet the new guests. They took off their shoes, like the rest of us, but without greetings they sat down beside different men and engaged them in low-toned conversations. After a few minutes one of the gentlemen came over and took Nour's place next to me.

"Why are you here? Where do you come from? Are you a journalist?"

I answered as best I could. I really wasn't very worried, though Nour and the other men seemed to be, and I wished Hadi would come back quickly to confirm our official status. By the time Hadi and Tom finally showed up at the mudhif door, my conversation with the security official had begun to seem more like an interrogation.

But after a few words between Hadi and the gentlemen in the brown suits, smiles replaced their looks of concern. They came over to shake my hand; they said they hoped that I would have a pleasant visit in Al-Nahra. I assured them that I would and they returned to their cars outside.

It seemed proper to me that these officials had come to the mudhif rather than send someone to take me to their office. In the past, all but the highest officials came here to visit the sheikh, where he took care of tribal affairs and personal business. Men would come to complain about the irrigation engineer's decisions, or about their fear of the police, or to discuss their own personal problems. Many of the tribesmen were then tenant farmers on Sheikh Hamid's own land and they needed to check with him about the progress of the barley and wheat crops. Sheikh Hamid was often called upon to mediate disputes between members of neighboring tribes. And if the police needed information about a fugitive, or a stranger like myself, they asked the sheikh for help. Sheikh Hamid cooperated with the police, but I somehow gathered that he often resented their presence.

Sheikh Hamid, after all, had been a member of Parliament, and Nour told me that one or another of the local tribesmen had served in Saddam Hussein's Parliament. Nour's own son Kamal had recently served. Sheikh Hamid had been appointed by the king, but parliaments were no more powerful than they are now, a significant bit of continuity over the years.

As I sat there with Nour, I found I missed the ordered ways of the old mudhif, almost as much as the old arched reed building and the people who once frequented it. Then, when the sheikh was presiding, as he did for several hours a day whenever he was in residence, men sat in the mudhif according to their position in life. The more important you were, the closer you sat to the sheikh. Tribesmen helped each other in deciding where to sit. Those already seated would feign a move, gesturing for the new arrival to take a prestigious seat, but a polite person would not take the first place offered, but move down to a more modest position. For men of great importance, the sheikh might rise, but ordinarily all visitors came forward to him, after taking off their shoes and enunciating the customary greeting to those already present, "*Salaam alaikum*" (Peace be with you). Handshakes then followed. A more humble way to greet the sheikh was to attempt to kiss his hand, but the sheikh nearly always pulled his hand away before the kiss could be bestowed. Matters requiring discretion might be whispered in the sheikh's ear, but public discussion was eventually required if the matter was to have credibility. We played chess sometimes (he nearly always beat me) and asked each other questions. I sometimes drove his car (the only one in the tribal community) when his young city chauffeur ran off back to Baghdad. Though in terms of age he could have been my father, we were nevertheless quite informal in our relationship, even though I always showed him respect. I knew he enjoyed having me around, and this made accepting his hospitality for two years much easier for me.

The ordered ways of the mudhif now seemed replaced by a helter-skelter coming and going of boys and men, some of whom stood around and then finally sat down with no to-do at all. The handshaking and formal greetings were observed by some and not by others. Within the old formalities, younger boys had learned the styles and manners of tribal behavior, how one speaks and positions oneself, the obsequiousness of age-old patriarchy. But even in 1957 there were some young men, even from the sheikh's family itself, who seldom came to the mudhif, rebels who could not bear the hypocrisy of showing respect they did not feel. In forty years had the old patterns disappeared? Was the torching of the mudhif by unknown "boys" a symbolic act against traditional authority? There had been much talk before the 1958 revolution of the injustice and oppression of tribal leaders. Had the rebels won, so to speak, and the new mudhif become a casual meeting place, not much used and not of much importance? Or had I just come on a day when things were out of sorts? Perhaps on other occasions more order, more formality, prevailed. But since it was unclear just who the present sheikh was, or if there was one at all, this seemed unlikely.

I expected to have lunch in the mudhif. This was always the pattern in the past; the sheikh ate there every day. And mudhif meals, whether on ordinary days or at the time of feasts, were always ceremonial occasions. The trays of food were brought to the sheikh first, who sat in the middle of the mudhif; men of highest rank came to sit with him first, eating without any small talk and then returning to their original places on the rugs, along the wall, so the next group of men could come forward for their share. What was left on the trays was carried back to the sheikh's house, whence it had come, to be eaten by the children and the women who had done the cooking. On the great holidays, hundreds of tribesmen would gather on the beaten earth in front of the mudhif, chanting poems about the heroic acts of sheikh and tribe, firing their guns in the air and joining in the line dance of the *hosa*. Tribesmen came from settlements miles away, for neglecting such occasions was noticed and remembered by the sheikh and his retinue. Absence was not a good idea, for it was seen as a lack of loyalty.

In the new mudhif, when the tray of food was brought in, I looked around for the familiar pitcher of water and the basin with which to wash my hands before eating, but there was none in sight. In times past, bringing the washing utensils was a duty of the younger men or of the coffee-maker. Nour called for water; a pitcher and tray were finally produced.

Lunch was ample, but not extravagant, as it used to be when guests were present. Rice, vegetable stew, bread, and some meat, which I suspected was unusual in these days of food shortages. But it was clear that an animal had been slaughtered in our honor, for the sheep's head lay before me on the tray of rice. I tried to eat the eye, the traditional morsel given to the guest, as I thought I was expected to do, but the socket was too hot for my finger, and, feeling conspicuous, I gave up. No one commented. I could not help remembering the time forty years before, when the sheikh offered me my first sheep's eye. He handed it to me on his thumb and could hardly contain his amusement at my initial reaction of shock. He would have laughed this time.

I suggested to Nour that we take a walk to the market in the village, hoping we would have a chance to talk together more personally. The conversation in the mudhif was a public affair. While the exchange of personal confessions, so much the currency of American friendships, was never part of my relationship with Nour, the mudhif was too public a place for *any* personal questions, and my fractured Iraqi Arabic evoked giggles from the young boys present.

Nour and I thus took off. A few small boys followed us, then more and more joined the train as we moved into the crowded street near the bridge over the canal. Al-Nahra was no longer a village. There were hundreds of people in the market, which was, Nour confirmed, five times larger than before. Like the mudhif, the old market was gone. The long wood-roofed passage with small shops on either side, which was cool in summer and rainproof in winter, had been replaced by a structure of cement, arched to cover sidewalks on both sides of the north-south and east-west streets. Shops stood open all along this way. It was a practical arrangement and certainly less likely to catch fire, but hardly "charming." When I remarked at the size of the market, Nour did say that the old divisions between the people of the market and the people of the tribe still held. "But these days," he added, "everyone must have an identity card stating an occupation." Apparently, a farmer stays a farmer, a merchant a merchant. No movement is allowed across these boundaries, and no urban migration is permitted.

My attempt to get a few minutes alone with my old friend was again frustrated by the novelty of my presence in Al-Nahra. Nour and I were soon surrounded by curious onlookers in the market and he was at least as uncomfortable as I was, so after a brief look we returned to the mudhif. We had now spent the better part of the day with our friends in Al-Nahra and the question was where to spend the night. I could probably have slept in the mudhif, though it didn't look as if that was a common practice anymore, but B.J. and Tom as well as Hadi and Ahmed posed another problem. The people had had no advance warning about our visit (which might have prompted more expense and trouble than we wanted to cause), and already there was some argument about which family B.J. should stay with. So we went back to a Diwaniyah hotel, promising to return in the morning.

Next day many more men had gathered in the mudhif to await my arrival, and it became ever more clear that I would never have a chance to move beyond the conventional exchanges with anyone. I had become a public event; there was no way to achieve the being-taken-for-grantedness that colored my nostalgia about times past. And of course, the minder from the Ministry of Information was an almost constant presence. So when my old friend Malalla showed up in his car, insisting that the four of us must come to his house for lunch, I was happy to change the scene.

Malalla came from a family of shopkeepers as well as landowners. His father owned small cloth stores in Al-Nahra and a nearby village. Malalla was the eldest son and heir to the business, it seemed. Since we left, the family had acquired a considerable amount of agricultural land and built a small villa on the edge of town. Enclosed by a wall, the house boasted a verandah and a garage, a yard with a garden, ample rooms inside, and expensive decor; it was certainly the nicest house I had ever seen in Al-Nahra. Though he had become deaf, Malalla also seemed to have gotten quite rich.

"I was one of the first men from Al-Nahra to join the Ba'athist Party," he boasted. "That was in the mid-sixties." He pointed out a photo on the table, of himself receiving a decoration from Saddam Hussein. "That was because I contributed to the Party Museum an Iraqi newspaper from 1962 with one of the first published articles about the

Ba'ath Party. I was given an award." Party membership, he said, was also involved in the acquisition of his car, though I didn't understand just how. What did seem clear was that things had gone very well for him, and that his early political allegiance was one reason. His eldest son, a lawyer in Al-Nahra, ate lunch with us. He also seemed to be doing well, as was his curly-haired five-year-old son, who was persuaded to sing a patriotic song for us.

"So when is the embargo going to end, Bob?" asked Malalla.

"How do I know?" I answered. "I suppose when the price of oil gets too high, and Western politicians want to increase the supply of oil."

"You mean when Clinton wants to end it," said Malalla's son.

"Well, it's not just Clinton," I said.

This was what I had said a number of times, in answer to the same question. It seemed to make sense.

In this house it was hard to believe that times were or had ever been hard; we had also felt this way when visiting some Baghdadi homes. The weight of the wars and of the blockade had not fallen equally on everyone.

Though Malalla was very forward in talking about himself, we were also among strangers, and I felt it was less through words than through looks and smiles that we conveyed what we wanted to tell each other. He served a wonderful lunch, one that fully lived up to some of my best memories, and I was conscious of the fact that he would not sit down and eat with us, but insisted on serving us himself. This is a very complimentary thing to do for a guest and a way of making one feel particularly welcome.

ON MY LAST VISIT to the mudhif before departing, a number of middle-aged men came forward and identified themselves as the sons of men I had known long ago. Unfortunately, I did not recognize any of them and sometimes had to fake a memory of their now-deceased fathers. There seemed to be no formal order at all in the introductions and conversations. In this new, less hierarchical social scene, therefore, when B.J. suddenly walked through the door with Muhammad, I was less astonished than I would have been forty years ago.

For the mudhif then was an exclusively male place. In all the time

I spent in the mudhif, I saw only one woman set foot there. But she was in male dress. I thought at first she was a man, but as she leaned forward to talk in low tones with the sheikh, I noticed that she had a smooth, browned face, with no sign of a beard, and yet certainly wasn't a young boy. When she left, I asked the sheikh and he laughed. "Well," he explained, "she is all alone in the world." The woman had no kinsmen nor husband to support her, so the sheikh had given her the management of a walled enclosure he owned near the market, a kind of parking lot where men left their horses and camels while shopping or doing other business in the village. "She couldn't do such work dressed as a woman," he explained, nor, I presumed, could she have visited the mudhif. But then, this wasn't the old mudhif.

All the way back to Baghdad, B.J. talked about what had happened to our friends, for the women had been much more forthcoming in their news than the men. But of course, as B.J. herself pointed out, she had a much more private setting for her visit. Unrelated men were still not welcome in the women's quarters, and Hadi, our representative from the Ministry of Information, definitely fell into that category. This was not unlike the situation when we had lived in Al-Nahra years ago. While the men had sometimes been tight-lipped and uninformative about difficult problems, the women had often explained to B.J. what was actually going on. Men could not control what women talked about with each other, much as they might have liked to do so.

Therefore, when Hadi and Ahmed began gossiping about the current struggle over the selection of the next sheikh, B.J. had already heard about this issue, an issue about which I was totally ignorant. It seemed that Abdulla, Sheikh Hamid's only surviving brother, was still formally recognized as the sheikh and would be until he died. Perhaps his almost continual absence from the mudhif, thanks to his feebleness in old age, might have contributed to the informality I had witnessed. Who was going to replace Abdulla? The contest was between Abdulla's son Ali, and Feisal, Sheik Hamid's son by his last wife, the beautiful Selma. The two cousins had their own supporters. But Hadi and Ahmed laughed as they discussed this, which seemed to indicate that they did not think the matter to be of much importance.

"So what's a sheikh these days?" asked Ahmed.

All the same, the fragility of the reigning sheikh, Abdulla, and the unsettled question of succession could have contributed to my feeling of disorder in the new mudhif setting. But it was clearly a question I would have to leave unresolved.

I could not help but envy B.J.'s greater ability as a woman to get beyond the more formal aspects of Al-Nahra social life. It occurred to me then that I could not, even after two years in the village, have written anything other than the rather formal politico-economic analysis that was my dissertation for the University of Chicago. Nor could B.J. have written something other than her much more person-oriented book *Guests of the Sheik*. In the field, in trying to learn about another culture, we learned, as we should have known long ago, that one has very little control over the course of events, over what we learn or do not learn, over the perceptions that we carry away with us.

Since leaving Iraq, we have heard that Saddam Hussein has been paying some court to the fragmented and thoroughly disempowered tribal leadership of the Shia south, addressing the leaders as supporters of his policies. We have no way of assessing this information. My visit with the tribesmen of Al-Nahra suggested that the patterns of behavior associated with tribalism, that ancient source of identity, had perhaps not disappeared so much as fallen into disuse. As a form of identity rooted in common blood and shared histories, tribalism remains a part of the national legacy.

B.J.'S TALE

Children rushed out the door of the sheikh's house as I approached, but for a moment I was unsure that I was in the right place. In the past this street door had opened into a large, sunny courtyard enclosing a kitchen against the far wall and the separate small houses where the sheikh's wives and children lived. Another small room near the kitchen housed an ancient grandmother of the sheikh's. Now I found myself looking into a dark passage, with a room on each side, and the bright courtyard beyond.

"This is Sheikh Hamid's house?" I ventured, speaking in the Iraqi dialect, which, to both Bob's and my surprise and pleasure, had begun to return to us after our arrival in Baghdad.

"Yes, yes," chorused the children, who then turned away, giggling. "But not Sheikh Hamid," said one pertly.

How stupid of me. Of course Sheikh Hamid had been dead for

twenty years. I was led into the room on the right of the door, where a young women in flowered dress and black head scarf was down on the floor kneading bread. She leaped to her feet, her floury hands aloft, nodded at me, and indicated I should sit down near her, on a chair by the wall. I sat down. She resumed her position on the floor and continued to knead, rapidly, skillfully, the muscles in her thin arms moving as she punched the heavy bulk of dough, pulling it, pushing it, with nary a glance at me. Another woman hurried in, a bit older, also in flowered full-length dress and head scarf. She ducked her head at me and got down on the floor to help finish the kneading, pulling the dough into pieces and shaping it into round, springy loaves. I counted eight round loaves laid almost lovingly on the pans to rise again before baking.

Who were these women? What was I supposed to do? I glanced around me, at what was clearly a new modern kitchen, though the room was dim.

A four-burner gas stove in one corner, cupboards, and a refrigerator with a television set perched on top. Certainly an improvement over the old arrangements. In earlier days each wife had her own small kitchen, though the family bread was baked in the central oven *(tanour)* in the courtyard. It was Selma, the youngest wife, who was responsible for cooking the meal served in the mudhif each day. The large kitchen, dark and smoky, was only used on great occasions— preparing for the feasts, when more than a hundred tribesmen would gather to greet the sheikh and partake of the festal lunch, cooked by all the women of the sheikh's family.

"Is Selma here?" I finally got out. I knew Sheikh Hamid had died, but I had not heard anything about my friend, his beautiful fourth wife.

The two women, putting finishing pats on the bread, nodded at me and smiled. Did that mean yes or no? I had spoken in Arabic, but perhaps they didn't understand? I reminded myself that in the old days one sent a message in advance of a visit to the sheikh's house. For the women worked hard all day long, and it was inconsiderate to interrupt their daily tasks—cleaning, child care, and cooking daily meals for at least fifty people. One didn't just drop by, as I was doing now, just dropping by after forty years.

A good-looking man hurried in. "I'm Selma's brother," he announced in English. "I have heard of you. *Ahlan wusahlan!*"

Older brother or younger? I thought older brother, by the white grizzle of his hair, but he appeared still strong and healthy and he spoke to the women, now standing up with the bread trays balanced on one arm, with authority. I thought he was saying something like, "What's the matter with you? A guest! An old friend! Why haven't you made her some tea?"

The younger woman shot me a smiling glance and gestured to the stove with her free hand, where indeed a kettle was coming to the boil.

"Come into the *diwan, madame,*" Selma's brother said, speaking in Arabic now, ushering me across the passage into another new room, a proper *diwan* with coffee tables, a bookcase, and a set of sofas and overstuffed chair upholstered in brown flowered velvet. The beautiful Persian rug covering the floor was illuminated suddenly as he flicked on the electricity.

"How is Selma?" I asked. Where was she? Was she ill?

"Not too well," he answered, and shook his head sadly. "Her leg bothers her a lot. She doesn't walk much now. But she knows you're here and she'll be with us in a minute."

The second, older woman in the flowered dress set down a tiny glass of tea on the table in front of me.

"I am Feisal's wife," she said. "Amina. Welcome! So she speaks some Arabic," she added in an aside to Selma's brother. "An American who speaks Arabic? How come?"

Amina? Who could that be? And Feisal? I did remember that he was Selma's oldest son, good-looking and mischievous, spoiled by both his parents. As if in answer to a summons, a portly man entered, in the full regalia of a tribesman. He was fingering amber worry beads as he came into the room, and he shifted them to his left hand as he greeted me, laughing and smiling as he did so. I must have looked blank, for he added, "I'm Feisal. Don't you remember me?"

"Of course. But you've grown up, Feisal."

This sent him off into a fit of giggles punctuated by the click of his worry beads. "I remember you, Beeja. You took a colored picture of me when I was a little boy, feeding the baby gazelle we caught. With a bottle." He giggled again.

Yes, I nodded. I remembered very well that day of picture taking. Selma's boys, Feisal and Abbas, and their young sisters and cousins frolicked in the courtyard, feeding the gazelle, jumping around me in delight. We had come back to the village from Bahgdad at the time of the feast to say goodbye before leaving for America, not guessing that forty years would pass before we saw our friends again. Could that curly-haired little boy really have turned into this portly man, fingering his worry beads? Feisal must be nearing fifty, I calculated.

The children crowding round the door parted as a square figure, all in black, pushed them aside and limped into the room.

"Beeja!" she cried.

I rose to embrace her and stood back to get a better look at my old friend, the gorgeous sexy Selma, admired by all the women of the settlement for her position, her beauty, and her education. It was Selma who had urged the sheikh to send the tribal girls to that first elementary school in Al-Nahra; she herself was a secondary school graduate, and believed strongly that women should know how to read and write to get along in the world.

We were the same age, Selma and I, but now before me stood a very old woman, limping and in obvious discomfort until she had maneuvered the rug, holding onto the chairs and tables as she did so, and had sunk with relief into one of the brown velvet chairs.

"Oh, Beeja!" she said again.

"Selma!" It was Selma, all right. The throaty voice was the same, the beautiful milk-white complexion showed scarcely a wrinkle, though the bit of hair that peeped out beneath the tightly wrapped black head scarf was not lustrous and black, but gray with touches of white.

"I'm so happy to see you again," I said. "It has been a long time."

"Why didn't you come before? Why did you wait so long? Why didn't you write?"

War, I said. Politics, I said. She nodded, and her eyes filled with sudden tears.

"The war was terrible. Both wars."

I took her hand and squeezed it.

Feisal, standing at the door fingering his worry beads, said, "Mama, you mustn't be sad."

"Why not?" she flashed back. "It's a sad time." But she seemed to compose herself and sat up straight.

"Feisal is so grown-up," I offered. "I hardly recognized him."

Selma glanced up at him. "He thinks he's going to be the next sheikh," she said. "But what good will that do us? The sheikhs mean nothing these days." Her tone was hard and strange.

"What about Abbas?" I asked. The second son had always been lively and more intelligent than Feisal.

"Oh, Abbas!" Selma did burst into tears this time. "He's gone, disappeared. The war!"

"Mama! Now, Mama!" Feisal came forward and tried clumsily to comfort her, but she did not want to be comforted. She wept, and chose her own moment to pull herself together . . . and ask polite questions of me, her guest.

"So how many children did you finally manage to have, Beeja?"

This was a flash of her old spirit. For the women, my childlessness was the central fact of my existence in those years in the village, commented upon constantly, sometimes sympathetically, sometimes in a teasing tone, but never ignored.

"Three!"

"Only three?" Selma wiped her eyes with a handkerchief produced from an inside pocket of her black garments, looked up at me, and smiled a bit mischievously. The smile reversed those sorrowful lines into which her face had fallen, and lightened her eyes. "The charm didn't work, then."

I looked at her questioningly.

"We sent you a charm, a gold charm after your last daughter was born, to encourage you to have more. You got it, didn't you?"

"I thought it was to keep my children safe."

"That, too."

"Okay, okay, I have only three kids, but they are good ones," I said, and I produced photos of David and Laura Ann and Laila, which were passed around, to the children hovering in the doorway, to Feisal, his wife, Amina, and to the younger woman I had first seen, kneading the bread. This was Ali's wife, Samiha.

"Ali?"

"He was born after you left, Beeja. Maybe I was pregnant with him before you went away."

We figured it out, counting on our fingers, that it was not Ali she had been pregnant with, but a daughter, Maha, now married and living on the other side of the canal. "The girls all got married and moved away," said Selma. "I kept some of the boys here. There's Ali. Come and say hello."

She beckoned to a tall, grave man with a neatly trimmed black beard. No sheikhly regalia for him. He wore a white shirt and dark trousers and he nodded at me perfunctorily.

"So." Selma took command of the multitude by the door, who were pushing into the room to stare at me, as of old.

"So," she repeated, "you finally got three children, thanks be to God." She laughed. "You know, we were worried about you, we were afraid you wouldn't get any, and then where would you be when you got old—like we are now."

I felt myself bridling a bit. Come on, I said to myself. You're a mother and a grandmother and now you're letting yourself be provoked just as you were as an uncertain young bride in a strange land, far from home.

I took a deep breath, smiled, and said loudly, "I always knew I would have kids, Selma. Actually, I wanted four, but Bob said enough after three."

This information provoked a moment of absolute silence, and then a buzzing in the crowd, which parted to admit a small boy. He called out, "It's a stranger, a stranger. A man!" He brought in Tom. "And the stranger has a camera," he added.

Tom greeted Selma and grinned widely as I introduced him as "our cousin, but he's like my own son."

"Your fourth child you never had, huh?" Selma said with a laugh. She looked at Tom and to my amazement said, "Take our picture. I never had a picture taken with Beeja."

She posed as Tom cocked his camera and announced, "And I want to meet Mr. Bob after all these years. We're both old ladies now, Beeja, so what difference does it make?"

Bob was sent for, and duly brought in, trying, I noticed, not to look too hard at the legendary Selma, whom he had never seen. "A picture with the three of us," instructed Selma.

But the children pushed through the door again before the shutter clicked.

It was Muhammad, tall and smiling, who swept in as Selma announced, "See! It's that boy Muhammad who used to help you in the house and shop for you in the market. He's grown up, too!"

Muhammad! I would have recognized him anywhere. I was so happy to see him I could hardly refrain from embracing him, which would, even in this more relaxed social situation, have been absolutely the wrong thing to do. We wrung each other's hands. How could I have survived in the village without his help, his advice, as I stumbled with the etiquette of a completely unfamiliar culture?

Tom took a picture of the four of us, and then Bob was led away, back to the mudhif. Muhammad sat closer and conversed with Selma, across me, almost in whispers. A few words did filter through, even to me, words like "war" and "never to return" and "disappeared." After a decent interval, I broke in to inquire about their conversation.

"Selma told you Abbas has disappeared," said Muhammad. "My brother Abad is gone, too." And tears stood in *his* eyes. "You remember Abad, Beeja, Mr. Bob supported him through secondary school so he could go to the university."

Abad was the bright boy who studied his lessons under the streetlight outside our house, because the family was too poor to install electricity. Yes, I had a very clear memory of Abad.

"I am very sorry," I said, and tried to enunciate the formulaic phrase repeated to the family at the time of a loved one's death. Fortunately, I stopped myself in time, for I realized that neither Selma nor Muhammad had mentioned the word "death." Muhammad was talking on to Selma, earnestly.

"And I believe they are alive," I heard him say. "I know it, Selma. God will care for them and bring them back to us."

Muhammad excused himself, and I promised to come visit his wife and family.

A barrage of questions was now directed at me, questions that were not unexpected, but everyone had been too polite to ask them until the formal requirements of welcome, of inquiries after family health, had been properly fulfilled.

How had Bob and I gotten here? Who paid our airfare? The United States government? The Iraqi government? What was the name of the man who was with us, from the Ministry of Information? The ministry approved of our visit? What was the matter with that great country, the United States? Did they care more about oil than about other people? And, from Selma, what did Hillary, the president's wife, have to say about all this? Why hadn't we sent them our books? Other people had told them about the books, in Al-Nahra, in Diwaniyah, even in Baghdad, but they had not seen them.

"But we did!" I insisted. "Bob sent his book *Shaykh and Effendi*, and I sent mine, *Guests of the Sheik*. We sent them to Sheikh Hamid, because he was our host."

"Do you think we saw them?" asked Feisal. "My father kept them for himself."

"Feisal," said Selma warningly.

"Well, we're writing another book now," I said. "That's one reason the ministry let us come to see you."

Very quickly, Selma said, "Don't write about politics, Beeja, or about the war. Don't do that, please."

"We're not going to. The book's not about politics, it's about people, about everyday life. In fact, it's about the whole Arab world. Iraq is one chapter."

"One chapter?" repeated Feisal, clicking his worry beads.

"One chapter only?" repeated Selma's brother, his white grizzled head the only uncovered adult head in the room except for mine.

"A long chapter," I qualified. It did sound absurd, stated that way.

The arrival of lunch suspended discussion. The children at the door parted again to let Amina through, then pushed and pulled against each other to get a better view of us. Selma called them to order.

"Stop it!" she called to them. "Stop fighting. Calm down! it's just our old friend Beeja."

She looked up at Amina, her oldest son's wife, bearing on her shoulder a big tin tray loaded with food. And she exerted her authority in the household once more by saying crisply, "Bring a table! Don't you have enough sense to see that our guest needs a table! She's a foreigner!"

Amina set down the tray on the floor, brought a table, put the tray of lunch on the table.

I had a curious sense of déjà vu, looking at the generous repast before me—rice, soup, salad, vegetable stew, and meat, a great honor in this rural society which now had no animals but must buy meat on the market. We had seen the incredible prices in Baghdad.

"Thank you," I murmured. I surveyed the lunch and looked up to see Selma, Feisal, Amina, Selma's brother, Samiha, Ali, and at least eight children hanging on the next move of the Amerikiyah, the village curiosity, come back after all these years.

"Won't you eat with me, Selma?" I asked as I had in the past.

And Selma smiled, as though she had expected that question. "You used to ask that, Beeja, but you should know better now. You know guests are supposed to eat alone here, it's a sign of respect. Oh, but look, here's your good friend Basima. Maybe she'll eat with you. She's important now, a principal of the secondary school!"

"I'm retired now, remember, Selma?" returned Basima, with some asperity, as she came into the room, loosening her abbaya.

I rose, almost upsetting the tray, and embraced the figure before me in a black dress, the chin pointed as it had been long ago, the dark eyes full of intelligence, a few strands of gray in the black hair, which was not tied up in a head scarf at all, in contrast to the women of Selma's house, and Selma herself. This was Basima, the younger sister of my good friend Laila, nieces of Sheikh Hamid. It was Basima who read the Koran at the *krayas* held in her house, Basima who had gone on to college in Diwaniyah.

"Basima! Where is Laila?"

A slight pause. "Laila has been dead for many years," she replied.

"I am so sorry."

Selma, her sarcastic tone gone, said, "Come, come, girls! The lunch is getting cold. Basima, she's asking for somebody to eat with her, just like she used to. I thought we taught her better than that." She plucked playfully at the sleeve of my black blouse.

"Well, I will," said Basima. "Why not? But I need a spoon. And where's the bread? Amina? Samiha?"

"Bread," repeated Selma. "Bread!"

And the two young wives rushed to do her bidding. The mother-in-law was clearly in charge of this household. When Amina came back with the loaves still hot from the oven, I asked, "Is this the bread you were making when I came?"

Amina smiled and nodded.

"And you kept her waiting?" from Selma.

"How did I know who she was?" Amina returned. "If I had known, I would have brought her in here right away."

I opened out my hands apologetically. "I'm sorry we didn't tell you in advance we were coming."

"You're here now. So eat," Selma instructed. "There's a spoon, Basima; you can join her."

So the past fell away, as the two women demonstrated subtly the old rivalries between the houses of Sheikh Hamid and his brother Moussa. It was not a question of ascendancy or political power, because Moussa had no sons to compete for the sheikhship, the leadership of the community. No, it was between the women, a question of manners, etiquette, education, social behavior, and status within the community of women.

THE PAST AND PRESENT also came together briefly as I went around the tribal neighborhood, crossing through narrow lanes behind the sheikh's house to visit Muhammad, who lived with his cheerful, sturdy wife and his eight children and his two grandchildren in a much expanded version of the tiny two-room house they had occupied in the settlement. In Moussa's house, of the nine girls, only his daughter Basima still lived there, with her husband, Nour's son Kamal, and their eighteen-year-old son, Ahmed, who was bound for college in Baghdad in the fall. Laila had always said that it was she who was to remain unmarried and care for her mother in her old age, since she had a skill—dressmaking—to support them. But Laila was dead these twenty years, and the task had fallen to her younger sister. Fortunately, Basima's husband had not seemed to object, and why should he, I thought, trading the somewhat helter-skelter abode of his father and grandfather for this well-kept, orderly, quiet domain.

Two other sisters had died as well as Laila, Basima reported, one in childbirth and one, more recently, of "sickness." I hesitated to inquire too closely into the causes of the deaths in the community and their relation to the privations of war. No one wanted to discuss the war and its aftermath. Conversations were focused more on the long-ago past, when Bob and I had lived in Al-Nahra, or on the future.

"We could go and visit my sisters if you'd stay on a bit," said

Basima. "Two are in Diwaniyah, one in Kerbela, and two just on the other side of the canal, in the new neighborhood outside the market."

I explained that we had permission to come down just for two days.

Basima nodded. "Yes, my husband saw the car and said that was probably what happened. He was a member of Parliament the last two years," she said proudly. "He's a lawyer, graduated from law school in Baghdad."

Basima's mother received me cordially, as she had always done. Now ninety-two, she was erect as ever in the black garments of the older woman which Selma also wore. She wanted to know what I had been served at the sheikh's house, "and she must come to us tomorrow, Basima," she said. But then a frown creased her forehead. "What will we have to eat?" she asked, a slight quiver in her voice.

"Don't worry, Mama, there's plenty."

Basima looked at me and smiled. "Do you remember the big room where we all used to sit, Beeja, and sew and clean rice, and tell stories and say poetry? Where you used to embroider pillow-cases . . ."

"Or at least try to," I amended, remembering the general mirth that had greeted my awkward attempts to embroider Arabic sayings on our pillowcases. "Of course I remember."

"Don't you wonder what happened to it? After my sisters got married and Laila died, we took out the room. My husband and I thought it would be a great place for a kitchen garden, but we had to wait till after my father died."

"Why?"

"He was a very traditional man," said Basima. "He thought gardens should be outside, not in the house," she explained. "Come see what we've done."

I excused myself to her mother and followed Basima out into the wide courtyard, half of which had been turned into a flourishing garden, where peas and mint and onions and tomatoes grew, beneath a pair of young date palms, a fig tree, and a pomegranate tree.

"Hamid said why not put in the garden? The government took a lot of our land after the revolution, and the piece we still own is far away. This is much more convenient."

The garden was set off from the rest of the swept, paved courtyard by a neat fence of woven palm fronds, "to keep the sheep and . . ."

I raised an eyebrow, and Basima hurriedly added, "We aren't allowed to have animals anymore, but each family can have a sheep and chickens, for food and wool."

"But no flocks."

"The law is to farm and raise grain, to feed people. And when the embargo is lifted, life will be easier for everyone."

The plot of peas was already waist-high against the wall, a wall of fired brick, rather than the mud brick of old.

Basima saw my glance moving to the wall and said, "We've built everything of fired brick here. My father always wanted to, he said they'd last. And I'm happy that we were able to do it while he was still alive. Kamal hired men from the village, and with his salary and mine, we could afford to do the whole house."

I made admiring noises as I surveyed the house built around the courtyard, stout doors reinforced with alternating layers of bricks, iron-work window screens in variegated patterns, door sills and frames painted blue, against the evil eye. A well-kept house, as always, and now a strong and well-built one.

"At least it won't melt, like yours did," said Basima with a slight smile.

"Basima! Basima!" It was her mother's thin voice, and we hurried into the room. She was sitting calmly on her neatly made-up bed, wiping her eyes and her pale cheeks with a small handkerchief, a square of bright yellow, fringed, which she then tucked into a corner of her full black sleeve.

"Tell me what they gave our guest to eat at the sheikh's house," she said, pulling out the yellow square again and wiping her eyes once more.

Basima whispered to me, "Mother forgets sometimes, she's ninety-two," then patiently recounted the menu to her mother, who nodded her head and then launched into a tale of her digestive problems.

"I can't eat meat anymore," she told me. "Vegetables. Rice. Yogurt. They're fine. My daughter here says to try fish, but when I eat fish, I have a bad taste in my mouth afterward. My neighbor tells me to try Pepsi and so they get me Pepsi. It's too expensive really, but it also doesn't help."

"How about lemon juice?" I suggested.

Basima agreed. "That's what you should try, Mama. I told you."

"Yes, yes," said the old lady, wiping her mouth carefully with the yellow handkerchief, folding it again into a small square that fit in her hand. "Tell me about your children, Beeja," she said, sitting forward expectantly.

"And tell me about Laila," I added softly.

Basima did not answer. She went instead to the big polished armoire opposite her mother's bed, its top piled high with folded comforters and blankets, and produced a large, black-covered photo album. She pointed out an old picture of her dead sister Laila, my good friend, and then, among the school class photos, pictures of her wedding to Hamid, in which she is wearing white satin and looking delighted. And there was a picture of me, taken in my twenties, looking romantic and sad. Why sad? I couldn't even remember when the picture was taken, but while I was trying to place it, Basima had turned the pages of the album, to point out pictures of her son Ahmed as a baby and pictures I had sent of my own children as babies, Laura Ann at three months, David in the Cairo playground, Laila showing her first tooth.

"See, Mama." Basima took the album over to her mother. "Here are Beeja's children." To me, she added, "Did you ever get the charm we sent you when your last daughter was born, the little gold hand with turquoises?"

"I thought it was from Selma. That's what Bob told me."

Basima shook her head. "No, it was from all of us. We all paid together."

"It was beautiful," I said, not adding that it was lost. "Did you find it here?"

"No, in Diwaniyah."

"Well." It was the thin voice of Basima's mother again. "You weren't too bad-looking when you were young," she pronounced after a look at the picture. "And your children look healthy enough."

A knock at the front door was a summons from Bob, who came inside the door, as invited by Basima, to consult. "I think we should stay at the hotel in Diwaniyah, rather than in the village," he said.

"Yes." It was true that we had been invited by everyone, but Tom and Hadi and our driver, Ahmed, had to be accommodated as well. This would be awkward at Basima's; we would upset her mother. Muhammad's place was large but full and so was the sheikh's, housing not only Selma and her brother but the wives and children of Feisal, and also the wife and children of Abbas, the beloved, the disappeared. We departed, announcing that we would come back in the morning and drink a glass of farewell tea before returning to Baghdad.

THE HOTEL, the only decent hotel, Ahmed said, was barely adequate, not even as comfortable as the old irrigation rest house, where we would stay after arriving from Baghdad on the night train, to wait for the morning taxi to Al-Nahra. This was surprising for a city as large as Diwaniyah appeared to be now, row upon row and street upon street of well-built villas with walled gardens, with restaurants and government buildings and a public square.

"Maybe the hotel used to be better," said Ahmed. "Nobody is traveling these days."

The tributary from the great Euphrates River flows through the center of the city, dividing the market from the residential areas, just as in Al-Nahra. The old wooden bridges we remembered had been replaced by sturdy cement spans, better designed by far than the Al-Nahra bridge, and each side of the river was flanked by a cobbled promenade where people might walk along and go into the busy market. Perhaps, I thought, I could find a replacement for the gold charm here, where my village women friends bought it years ago for me and my children.

The sun was low, and the market was full of people, and, compared to Baghdad, full of food stuffs: open sacks of rice and lentils and dried peas, counters of produce fresh from the fields—tomatoes, zucchini, squash, onions, garlic. Agricultural tools and the old men who sharpened agricultural tools were close beside each other, with used hardware, radios and radio batteries, dresses on hangers suspended from the doors of small shops, bolts of cloth, crimson, blue, black, brown, displayed on the diagonal shelves. And, where I remembered it, the gold and silver markets, but expanded from one small street into a confusing "quarter" of many streets.

Hadi, who had joined us with Tom while Ahmed went off on his own business, remembered our efforts along Abu Nawwas Street in Baghdad. He began to ask politely, at each gold shop, for charms, charms for babies and small children, he specified. The gold merchants were helpful and sent us on to jewelers in other streets, whose purported specialty was the kind of charm I was seeking.

"How can I help you?" asked the old man at whose door we finally arrived after being referred from one small street to another, around the corner, turn to the right, look for Abbas. He surveyed the three of us calmly, but I heard him ask Hadi where we had come from.

I drew a rough outline of my treasured bit of gold. He shook his head. "An old design," he said, "haven't seen it in years. But I have Korans and crosses, if you like, and a lotus blossom."

I shook my head. I could see the old charm clearly in my mind; Selma's and Basima's mention of their long-ago gift had only increased my desire to find a replacement.

"Give it up, B.J.," said Bob. I nodded, and resolved to try once more in Baghdad.

"Have you noticed the prices here, Bob?" It was no longer "Professor Fernea," I noticed. Hadi seemed to be more at ease with us. "I should move down here. Everything costs about seventy percent less than in Baghdad."

"We're closer to the agricultural areas," pointed out Bob.

"And people grow some of their own food," I added, thinking of the flourishing kitchen garden in Basima's courtyard and the collection of tomato plants in Muhammad's house. His wife had said, yes, they were back to drying tomatoes on the roof again. "The cans were so expensive," she said. Sun-dried tomatoes had been a staple of Old World cooking long before American gourmet cooks discovered them. But they were not eaten as delicacies, separately, but dried to a thick paste and stored for use in cooking during the long winters.

In the morning I divided the border purchases into three parts— one sack for Selma, one for Basima, one for the house of Muhammad. Medicines, coffee, chocolate for the children, tea, vitamins. Back in Al-Nahra, I sat in Selma's parlor, describing the doses of ibuprofen that might ease the aching of her joints, when Tom arrived to announce that we were to go to Malalla's for lunch—a command performance, it seemed. I was not particularly pleased; I had hoped to stay longer at

Muhammad's house, talking with his three teacher daughters, and to revisit Basima and her aged mother. And I had never been particularly close to the women of Malalla's house, who lived across the canal and were termed *ahl-es-suq* by the tribal women, "people of the market."

"Come on, B.J., they've even sent a car for us. Now!" said Tom. There was no choice!

In Malalla's house the room into which I was ushered was large, light, and clean, lush in comparison to the sheikh's house. Carefully textured plaster walls, heavy pile carpets, an enormous bed with carved oaken headboard, brand-new green comforter and spread, a scattering of decorative throw pillows. I was given a seat on comfortable cushions on the floor, beside a round old lady, her head wrapped in black, her full flowery dress tucked up around her feet. She must be Malalla's wife, I thought, though I did not recognize her.

She smiled at me and held out her hand.

The smile gave her face a familiar look. What was Malalla's wife's name? Madina, it came to me, the name of one of the holy cities of Islam, and an appropriate name for her, since she, like her husband, was a descendant of the Prophet.

"How are you?" I asked.

"Not bad." She smiled again. "Aches and pains. My legs hurt. I'm just old."

Two young women, one blond, one dark, came in and sat down with us. They wore fashionable house caftans, green and pink, and introduced themselves. The blonde was the new wife of Malalla's youngest son, and we were sitting in her bedroom. She smiled in a lazy, pleased way, glancing perhaps unconsciously at that great bed as I congratulated her on her marriage. The dark woman, Malalla's daughter Laila, began to quiz me, just as Selma had earlier, but in a far less friendly manner.

Why had we come here after so many years? Were we journalists? Were we really Americans? What was the matter with the United States? Couldn't we see that it was our stubbornness and unkindness that kept people in Iraq from eating?

"Now, now, dear," Malalla's wife, Madina, broke in gently. "Remember, she is our guest."

The dark-haired Laila was silent, but I felt obliged to answer the questions, and added that their family seemed to be doing all right, despite the sanctions left over from the Gulf War.

Madina nodded her head, saying, "Yes, that is true. My husband is a good businessman . . ."

"And a good member of the Ba'athist Party, Mama, don't forget that," finished Laila. Turning to me, she said, "Of course you are right, *madame*. You can see that in this house we live well and we eat well. But many people, even in this village, are hungry. Many babies are dying, and old people, because there is no medicine, and the machines for operations don't work because there are no spare parts. And all this misery because of the American embargo. What do you have to say to that?"

She was clearly trying to draw me into a confrontation which I did not want. I tried to murmur pleasantries about how glad I was to be back. It didn't work.

"Well?" she persisted. "What is your answer to my question?"

There was no help for it. "It doesn't seem to me," I said rather slowly, "that things in Iraq are too different from the way they used to be. When we lived here, many people were poor, and hungry, and sick. There was no medicine then, either."

Her eyes, large and black, seemed to snap at me, as though I had hit her.

"Yes," she began. "Yes, you say that . . ."

But the door opened in the middle of her sentence, and a middle-aged woman, in fashionable black silk, her head also wrapped in black, entered, stepped across the space between me and her sister, bent down, and held out her hand.

"Hello," she said in English, and laughed a bit. "I don't know much English at all." I stood up to greet her, glad of the interruption, and she shook both my hands warmly.

"I remember you," she said, sitting down near me and opening a pack of cigarettes. She offered it around, but we all refused. Her mother frowned.

"I know you don't approve, Mama," she said in answer to her mother's expression. "But this is a hard time for me and cigarettes help. My husband died a month ago," she said to me. "We were very close. I miss him." She drew deeply on her cigarette and exhaled a cloud of smoke which floated upward in the glossy room.

"You are too young to remember Madame here," she said dismissively to her belligerent sister and the lazy-eyed blond bride. "She used to visit this house long ago, when her hair was even blonder than yours, my dear. Our father was a friend of her husband, and also of the engineer who lived down the street with his sister. Remember Khadija? She left after Jamal was killed. No one ever heard from her again."

I had not thought of Khadija for years, Khadija who was not quite prepared for the role her brilliant elder brother Jamal had decreed for her: as his housekeeper in the village where he, in his position as the government irrigation engineer controlling the flow of water to the crops, was almost as important as Sheikh Hamid himself.

"Poor Khadija," said Madina next to me softly, echoing my own thoughts. "She never could learn to keep house. You tried to help her, didn't you?"

"I wasn't much help," I replied, thinking of the disastrous cakes Khadija had tried to bake, following my recipe, her inability to communicate to the local servant girl how to set a table with a tablecloth, or even how to polish Jamal's new furniture with a cloth soaked in oil. And she never understood why hot water and soap were better for washing dishes than cold rinses.

"I was just a little girl then," went on the lady in black. "I'm Bahiga, you wouldn't remember me. But I used to stare at you, at those funny clothes you wore, and wonder why you came all the way here from America. My mother said you came to be with your husband. But you had no womenfolk with you, and we wondered about that, whether your people didn't care about you, or what."

You're right, I thought, I was alone, and I knew I seemed strange, and I couldn't have survived if the women of the village, Selma and Basima and even Madina in her way, had not helped and supported me. And the teachers in the girls' school. What about them? Sitt Aliyah had died, said Bahiga, and her sister Hind moved away, but their early efforts had borne fruit. There were ten schools in Al-Nahra now, including two coeducational secondary schools.

"Ten schools?" It was hard to believe. In 1956 there were only two, both primary schools, one for girls and one for boys.

"And my dear daughter Bahiga is the principal of one of the secondary schools," put in her mother proudly.

"You work with Basima, my friend, the niece of Sheikh Hamid?"

Bahiga nodded. She lit another cigarette from the end of the first.

This was too much for Madina, who burst out, "Please, my daughter, please . . . think of yourself and your health."

"I do, Mama, I do," said Bahiga calmly, inhaling deeply. "In answer to your question, *madame*, I used to work with Basima, but of course now she's retired. She was the first one from the sheikh's family to get educated. Now all the tribal girls go to school. Things have changed here for women."

These remarks were cut short as the dark-haired daughter cleared her throat loudly and returned to the prickly subject of the embargo.

"It is true," she said a bit too loudly, "what you say . . . that in the old days many people were poor. But Iraq is different now. With the money from our oil, our leader had modernized everything, and we are one of the advanced nations in the world. Everybody goes to school. Women do well. And until the embargo of the United States, things were good for everyone."

I was silent, hoping she was finished, but she was not. "So," she asked, "when will the all-powerful United States of America lift the embargo?"

Madina put her hand on my arm, as if to protect me. "How would she know, Laila?" she asked. (She didn't say "she's only a woman," but the phrase was implied.)

"Well," I began, "many people in America, including me and my husband, think the embargo is bad. But when it will be lifted? Who knows? We do not know exactly what our government will do, just like you don't know about yours. But my husband thinks the embargo will be lifted soon."

The whole room came to attention at that.

"Maybe in the early summer," I continued, "so the Americans can cut the price of gas in time for summer holidays."

Laila's black eyes looked puzzled. "For the summer holidays?" she repeated.

"Yes. In America many people travel in their cars when they go on holiday in the summertime. If Iraqi oil were available on the market, then the price of oil would go down all over the world. My husband thinks that would be good for President Clinton, so he would get elected again. And that's why he'd do it. Not for Iraq, but for himself."

The women all stared at me in amazement. No one spoke. Had they understood me?

"My Arabic is very bad," I offered. "Maybe what I say is not clear . . ."

"No, no," answered the blond bride. "We understand. Your Arabic is okay, really . . ."

"And you really think that will happen?" Bahiga asked, stubbing out her cigarette.

Laila, the dark-haired aggressive sister, shook her head. But she did not speak. She stood up and opened the bedroom door, "to let the smoke out," she said.

"I'm not sure," I said, and spread my hands, "but that's what my husband says." (Husbands are authorities in such matters.)

Madina, the mother of the household, filled the uneasy pause after my speech with an announcement. "Lunch is coming, my dear. We are happy to see you again."

I doubted that this household had a shortage of anything, but I remembered a bottle of ibuprofen in my purse. "For your aches and pains," I said, presenting it to Madina, who thanked me profusely.

The small bottle of ibuprofen was still being passed around and examined carefully by the sisters and the sister-in-law when the food was brought in by still another sister.

"Please." Madina held out her hand graciously to indicate that I should try some of the food that had been placed in front of me, kibbe, salads, rice, yogurt, and a large plate of grilled kebab, all on beautiful china plates.

As I dipped the kibbe into the homemade yogurt, Laila, who was looking at the ibuprofen bottle, said loudly, "This medicine was made in America."

"Yes, yes, my dear," returned her mother. "Where else do you think she got it? Thank you again, my dear Beeja. Now eat!"

WE LEFT THE VILLAGE late in the afternoon, after final cups of tea, and promised to send copies of our old books and our new books, to write and send pictures of this reunion. But before we left, Bob insisted that I at least visit the new mudhif, of which the tribe was very proud. So I walked in where I had never walked before, where no women of the tribe had ever sat. I took off my shoes at the door and trod gingerly down the long strip of red-patterned carpet that covered the floor, to admire the ancestral portraits on the wall. The men of the tribe sat on cushions or stood against the wall, eyeing me, as Bob, Muhammad, and Nour identified the pictures, black-and-white photographs, many of the prints yellowed with age in their frames. I recognized Sheikh Hamid, our host, full face, in a serious mood, his round steel eyeglasses caught by a reflection from the photographer's flood lamp. There was Sheikh Atiyah, father of Hamid, leader of the Al-Agra, famous in Iraqi history for his leadership of the Diwaniyah tribes against the British. And another photo of Sheikh Atiyah, which I remembered had hung in Hamid's bedroom in the old house that he and Selma had occupied. Atiyah sat in the garden of what must have been a hospital, because he was surrounded not only by his sons and brothers and bodyguards but by doctors in their whites and a nurse in an old-fashioned long cap who stood behind his wheelchair. There was Moussa, father of Basima, and Abdulla, older brother of Hamid, young and vigorous. Abdulla now was frail, at ninety-one, but still acted and was treated as sheikh. And a group picture of the men of the tribe, gathered together before the old mudhif, its impressive reed arches rising so high they were out of the range of the camera.

"Yes, I see," I said. "Oh," I said, but I was uncomfortable in this male-only setting.

The past was gone, but fragments of its socialization patterns remained in me. I still felt I did not belong here, although I told myself I was being irrational. I thanked everyone, stumbled over my own shoes at the door, and climbed into the taxi, where Ahmed held the door open for me. We were headed once more for Baghdad.

I NEVER DID FIND A gold charm to replace the one I had lost, though I searched again in Baghdad, with Hadi's help and Tom's. Even Bob came to look as we searched in one gold shop after another, hoping to find among the rows of fine gold chains a row of charms to hang upon them.

"An old design. Haven't seen it for a long time" was the general conclusion.

"No one's making it anymore," said a young goldsmith, near the end of Abu Nawwas Street.

It was time to leave. We had been fortunate to find, on our return visit to the scenes of our youth, friends who remembered us kindly, who took us back, briefly, into their homes and their hearts. What was it the women had said when I had tried to say thank you for helping me, thank you for everything, living here with you changed my life? They had said, "It was fun." They had said, "We enjoyed it" and "We'd never met an American." "At least we taught you to cook rice properly." We knew we would not come back again. But for a brief moment we had revived the memories that were pasted into the photograph albums of our friends, that had remained in the minds of those friends, as well as within ourselves. But it was over, disappeared, like Selma's son Abbas, like Muhammad's brother Abad, like my friend Laila, like our youth, gone, like the tiny gold charm set with three turquoises, disappeared forever into the past.

THE END OF PATRIARCHY?

HE MIDDLE EAST is usually described in terms of internal conflicts, religious fanaticism, and oil. We have tried to provide some sense of the ways these sources of headline news affect, or don't affect, the kinds of life that people there actually live. To do this, we have relied primarily on our experience there with friends and colleagues over the past forty years, and especially our recent visits to the area between 1990 and 1996.

If we can draw any conclusion from our experience, it is that the people we have known have proved to be much stronger than the events that have surrounded them. What is the source of this strength, this perseverance? Clearly, it must be found in the personal lives of these people, lives that persist, adapt, and adjust to new circumstances in the face of difficulties which, by comparison, make ours in America seem secure and carefree. So rather than summarize what we have already said, we would like to turn to people's lives in the Middle East and consider what is perhaps the most significant change of all, a fundamental realignment now taking place in the relationship between men and women. It is a realignment that touches all classes and communities to one degree or another as the twentieth century comes to a close.

Why this change in gender relations? The material foundations on which patriarchy was built and (for millennia) continued to flourish are deteriorating with the advance of world capitalism in the region. The resultant turmoil is unsettling to both men and women, and its outcome will reshape the social fabric of the Middle Eastern world. Yet this general decline in patriarchy has been hard to discern, if not invisible, in the storm of reports about women's oppression, in the attention paid to the *hijab*, or Islamic dress, and in the headlines of Islamic revivalist movements driving women out of public life and back to the home. And these are merely the symptoms of more basic, infrastructural changes now in progress, which are bringing with them a major shift in the relative positions of men and women. In the long run, this is far more revolutionary than anything else, for it will alter the foundations of daily life.

Changes in gender relations in the Middle East affect religion and the family, which are closely interlinked. This region, after all, gave birth to three patriarchal religions, often called Abrahamic, since they take the prophet Abraham as a common ancestor. For more than three thousand years, Abrahamic belief has been fundamental first to Jews, then Christians, and finally Muslims, and that belief long ago redefined the spiritual life of Europe and America, as well as much of Asia and Africa. One god. God the Father. Perhaps this is the most potent statement of patriarchy, one that gives religious sanction to male authority.

In the family, which is the basic social unit of the Middle East, the father has been the embodiment of that Abrahamic god, the unquestioned head of the household. Now this principle is being subverted by economic, social, and ideological forces which no one can control.

In Western academic circles, the concept of patriarchy and the idea of male domination have been out of fashion until very recently. By the 1950s social scientists had dropped use of the term, arguing that "male domination" in any society really consisted of diverse sorts of political organizations, too complex to be understood in such a simple term as "patriarchy." "Patriarchy," it was argued, might be used to refer to male rule in family organization, but even in this case families were better understood in terms of the complementary sexual division of labor, men's work and women's work. Women and men were different, yes, but mutually dependent.

How did social scientists miss the continued existence of patriarchy? Perhaps because they took male empowerment for granted. Their world was largely constructed by men; masculine ways of thinking shaped the discourses of the scientific disciplines as it did most other discourses of Western social life. But that has begun to change. As women have won equal rights to employment and have fought against sexual discrimination and harassment, female scholars have begun to find a place in the scholarly world, conducting research, and making the uncovering and describing of male hegemony in the construction of thought as well as deed a major academic enterprise. Perhaps it is now fair to say that masculine assumptions about the world are no longer universally regarded in the Western world as the "natural" bases of social life.

Today, in the Middle East, the material and conceptual bases of patriarchy can also clearly be seen to be eroding. Much of that change has occurred in the last generation and it has taken place at a much faster rate than was true in the West; thus, the adverse social and cultural response to this development is very strong indeed. As in America, a wife's work outside the home has become essential for millions of Middle Eastern families, especially those in the new middle class. Forty years ago, in Al-Nahra, the town in southern Iraq where we lived, the only women who worked outside their homes in southern Iraq were the four female teachers in the elementary girls' school. A 1973 study of countries around the world showed that those of the Middle East (exclusive of Israel) had the *lowest* number of women in the world working outside the home. But in the last forty years Arab women have been educated with men and trained for many of the same occupations. Women, like men, are working to help put bread on the table for themselves, their husbands, their children, and often their parents and parents-in-law.

Cooking, sewing, housecleaning, and child care: these have always been women's work and are still felt to be so by most men and women, at least in the Middle East (and to some extent in the West); and despite the rapidity of change in the demands made on women, this is still the way things are seen as naturally meant to be.

But as women continue to assume many of the tasks once limited to men, the gendered division of labor is disappearing in schools, factories, clinics, business offices, and the public arena in general. Women have become a vital part of the national economy, not to mention essential wage earners for their families. Of course, one could argue that this is scarcely new, as, in the past, millions of Arab women shared agricultural tasks with their men, in their homes, which allowed them to care for children at the same time. Still, this was under the supervision of husbands and fathers. With urban employment this is no longer true. Women are no longer confined to the home, which has unsettled the old patterns of socializing children into bifurcated adult roles. And today it is neither kith nor kin, but rather strange men, bosses in public settings, who are telling women—other men's wives and daughters—what to do.

Men's partial loss of control of the labor of their women certainly deviates from the traditional practices of patriarchy. But what is perhaps even more troublesome to people in the contemporary Islamic world is the subsequent departure from the Word of God (about the proper role of men and women) as expressed in the Koran. Sura IV, verse 34, states, "Men are in charge of women, because Allah hath made the one of them to excel the other, and because they spend of their property (to support women)." At the end of the twentieth century, husbands are no longer universally able to support their wives and children. And though a woman's wages earned from work outside the home do not automatically give her greater decision-making powers in the family, the conditions for negotiating the use of this resource have been established.

Even in America control over the wife's money is still one of the biggest sources of domestic conflict. But in the Middle East the situation is quite different. Though sacred texts indicate that husbands should support the family, they also suggest that husbands should share fiscal authority with their wives. Muslim women have had the right to inherit and to own property since the seventh century, the time of the Prophet, much longer than in the Christian world, where women in most of Europe and in America only gained the right to own property in this century. Thus, granting women control over what they earn as well as what they inherit may appear to be part of God's intention. And however deeply some Arab men may resent and struggle against any loss of personal control over their women, including their earnings, many of our Arab friends, men and women alike, feel that Divine precept gives Muslim women the right to some degree of control over the money they earn.

We have also become aware of the considerable pressure placed on husbands to do women's work. Working wives are not superhuman, and some help may be required to keep the household moving. Perhaps, at first, assistance from the husband is seen as a favor, an exceptional gesture on a special occasion. But particularly when children arrive, the husband's help may become imperative. And as he helps in what are traditionally seen to be women's tasks, a married man perforce loses something of his privileged status as head of the household, however much both spouses may regret or deny the fact. The sharing of a woman's work at home can be seen on some levels as a subversion of patriarchal authority.

Traditional gender stratification is also being undermined by economic necessity. Millions of Middle Eastern men have been obliged to become migrant workers, who live far from their homes, even outside their home countries. And no longer are other male family members always nearby to take their place as household authorities, as was true until recently in both urban and rural communities. Many of the urban couples in large cities like Cairo or Amman are now unable to live near their husband's natal families, as would have been preferred in the past. Often, not enough space remains near the family dwelling, or what does remain available has become too expensive.

Many families have been forced out of older urban districts into new residential areas by government urban planning and development schemes. Relocated families often live at considerable distances from their parents, and easy movement is becoming more difficult between members of the households of the older and younger generations. So, with husbands away and parental homes across town, women are increasingly finding themselves as heads of households, taking over the male's traditional position of prime authority and decision-maker, in matters of child-rearing as well as economics. This is unsettling to everyone, including the children, who now form half the original area's population and are growing up, critics note, without proper traditional male authority.

Such problems should resonate in American minds as well, for if there is a form of nostalgia common to militant believers, Jewish, Christian, and Muslim, it lies in a desire to return to a better past where the "natural," God-given relationships between men and women prevailed. If this relationship were "put to rights," it is argued, other social problems would soon be solved. The "crisis over family values," which is currently the clarion call of right-wing Christian sects like the Promise Keepers, bemoans the lack of male authority in the home and the fact that women are not at home but outside, in the workplace. This is in America, not the Middle East, but in both regions public disorder is often laid at the feet of the "disordered" family.

Many Arab intellectuals have noted the weakening of the old patriarchal system, some with dismay, some with satisfaction. In 1988 the distinguished Arab political scientist Hisham Sharabi published in both Arabic and English a book entitled *Neopatriarchy: A Theory of Distorted Change in Arab Society*. He argued that "neopatriarchy" is a contemporary development in which the patriarchal society no longer "derives its strength from its ability to satisfy basic needs." This failure occurs when "a person is cut off from the family, the clan or the religious group." The State, he suggests, cannot replace these protective primary structures. Despite this failure, says Sharabi, both conservative and reformist thought in the Middle East has continued to "reflect in their discourse the dominant ideology of neopatriarchical society: a conservative, relentless, male-oriented ideology." Males keep privilege and power "at the expense of females, keeping the latter under crippling legal and social constraints." The only way out of this bind, Sharabi feels, is "a (democratic) [parentheses his], nuclear family (usrah) where children are no longer brought up under tyrannical fathers." So whose fault is public disorder? In the Middle East is it "too much father, too much patriarchy" in the family? In America, on the other hand, is it "too little father, too little patriarchy"? In both cases, men appear to be the real culprits, even if women are frequently blamed.

Professor Sharabi believes that neopatriarchy is failed patriarchy. Only an increase in secular thinking will bring about a reformation in child-rearing and result in a more democratic society. Sharabi does not explain how more secular thinking and family reform are going to occur, but his proposal to remove traditional constraints on women does suggest some essential and profound modifications in male thinking and behavior. This behavior is conditioned by three thousand years of historical experience, of course. But more than history operates against men giving up "crippling legal and social constraints" against women in the Arab world, for such patterns of behavior have a great deal to do with the emotional relationship between men and women. That relationship is crucial to the understanding of the profound changes now in progress in the region.

Male domination over women is eroticized in the Middle East, and the Western reader should be able to appreciate this because, East or West, *all* male domination over women is to some degree eroticized. This is emphasized by feminist scholars who are following the theoretical views of most psychoanalysts. However, the ways in which the erotics of domination are acted out varies greatly, and the sadistic rituals of the Marquis de Sade are at one extreme, one distant extreme, from most male behavior anywhere in the world. In the West, patriarchal behavior, especially male domination over women and children, is sanctioned by religious admonitions, but frequently expressed through violence in private life. Such violence—spousal abuse, rape—is apparently on the increase in American homes and appears to be far more common than it is in the Middle East. When male aggression against women is discussed in America, what are cited as the underlying reasons? Male frustration, defeat, and general sense of helplessness in a rapidly changing public sphere; arbitrary loss of jobs, unfair competition, any kind of failure in a capitalist system where men are expected to succeed. These are all given as answers as to why American men may beat their wives and children and/or turn to drink or other drugs. But the deterioration of the personal relationship between spouses presumably begins before the first beating occurs and may well involve a loss of self-esteem along with a decline in sexual desire.

The situation appears different in the Middle East. Despite the fact that men's self-image has been damaged by the colonial experience, that many men today can no longer fulfill the religious and cultural ideal of supporting their households, men and women remain partners in the patriarchal system, "mates as well as inmates" in the struggle against oppressive governments, as the Arab woman critic Saddeka Arebi points out. In the Middle East most husbands still struggle to remain sultans in their own households, the last bastion of their authority in a region that still lacks any truly democratic government. Moreover, women serving their husbands continues to have an erotic dimension. It is not only an acting out of male mastery and female submission but an affirmation of both male and female sexuality. Only among a closeted minority of couples do more egalitarian attitudes prevail. For the great majority, however, the loss of a wife's deference toward her husband implies a final deterioration of patriarchy, the loss of a husband's responsibility for a wife's material and sexual needs, both of which are very explicitly expected of men according to the Word of God in the Koran.

We are told by some Muslim males that "Islamic dress," clothing all or most of women's bodies, is necessary to keep down the *fitna*, the "disorder" that can result from those rampant male desires that the sight of women's flesh must necessarily arouse in men. Men, many Middle Eastern men, most men everywhere, do feel themselves attracted by women's bodies. The question is, how greatly attracted, and by how much body, under what circumstances? In Saudi Arabia special police are detailed to make sure that women are not showing even a bit of ankle; of course, in American history ankles were once objects of male attention. Victorian gentlewomen were urged to clothe the legs of their pianos so as not to create an improper impression of the female anatomy. In Israel orthodox communities decree that women must cover their heads and dress modestly; some extremist Jewish communities require women to shave their heads after marriage, so as not to attract men with their luxuriant hair. In Algeria women who do not cover themselves in the "Islamic manner," prescribed by men, are subject to attack or even death. In Afghanistan the recent Taliban movement has taken the forceful exclusion of women from public life to new absurd, cruel extremes. Patriarchy thus does not pass away easily.

Of course, in public life, "Islamic dress" may also carry for women some right to resist male domination. Many writers, including ourselves, have pointed out that this form of dress provides women with a personal Islamic identity, an identity that commands male respect. It says, "keep your hands to yourself and your speech civil; I am not a form of public property." It reminds unrelated men of the fact that women on the street and in the factory or office are not their women even if they are proximate and ready to do their work. Perhaps this can be seen as a pragmatic response to changing conditions of street life, for the abuse of young women wearing Western dress has been a major problem in the cities of the Middle East in recent years.

Islamic dress does not just signify a Muslim identity, however. Such dress is also a sign of the authority of the woman's kinsmen and her husband: strange men are expected to respond with the deference due the honor of the unseen spouse and male relatives. Thus, it is not the authority of the husband, father, or brother that may be challenged by the woman's wearing of Islamic dress. What is being challenged is the right of strange men to treat a woman as if she had no relatives and thus no claim to personal propriety. Once more the discourses of family and religious ideology are blended. In this sense, a woman's empowerment through wearing *hijab* remains deeply embedded not just in her individual self but also in her family relationships and her religious ideology.

The effects of patriarchy's decline, then, are different in the Middle East than in the West. We have argued here that the alignment of genders in the Middle East is changing by force of material circumstances, particularly the circumstances of modern world capitalism which are making women into wage earners who are essential to the well-being of their households. But belief in male superiority remains as part of religious conviction and within the processes of family life (as Professor Sharabi says). Belief in such superiority also enhances male desire and female desire and thus the man's relation to the woman as the focus of that desire. Is there any stronger, more resistant form of discourse than that which develops around sexual desire?

FORTY YEARS AGO many Arabs believed that the Marshall Plan, which had reconstituted Western Europe after World War II, would make its way to the Middle East, not just to Israel, but to the entire region, perhaps. However unrealistic this may have been, it would have been hard to imagine what actually did happen—the United States abandoning Gamal Abdel Nasser at the time of the High Dam, three American military attacks in the region, and most of all, support for Israel perceived time after time to be at the expense of the Arab world by the Arab world. Our power, our domination, is unmistakable. Elections are dismissed (as in Algeria) and military governments helped to stay in place by our leave and often with our assistance. Indeed, the context of personal life in much of the Arab world is one in which individuals feel little control over their governments and even less over our government, which feeds some countries, like Egypt, and starves others, like Iraq.

We cannot but admire the achievements of our friends, their struggles against great obstacles in many cases, but we also cannot help but wonder at how much various forms of neocolonialism, Western neocolonialism, still prevail in parts of the Middle East. Given the resulting levels of frustration, it is not the outbreaks of violence but their general absence in the Arab world that should be admired, for daily life in Middle Eastern town and country is much less violent than in America at the present time. In this respect, Arab masculinity, male honor, male self-respect, male pride, male sexuality—all these have remained active and well, despite the humiliations that have been part of public life in this century.

Have the last forty years brought more democracy to the Middle Eastern countries, more opportunity for people to govern themselves, more independence from the overlordship of foreign countries like the United States? No is the answer in all of these cases. But despite the neocolonialism and the humiliation of military defeats, what has remained relatively stable is family life, the relationship between men and women, reinforced by religious belief and doctrine. Rather than worry too much about the fact that this may include symbolic and practiced forms of male domination, we might better admire this stability, this ongoing process of adaption with a minimum of domestic violence, and wish America could do so well.

Furthermore, before we cast blame about the conflicting ways in which men and women are struggling with the advent of middle-class capitalism in the Middle East, our own contribution to the persistence of patriarchy—or "neopatriarchy"—in the region must be acknowledged. Patriarchy and paternalism are closely related; in fact, paternalism is a form of patriarchy in which someone makes the decisions for someone else, "in their best interest," of course. And this is most often the plate on which American foreign aid to the Arab World is served. At present, for example, USAID gives $3 billion annually to Egypt and to Israel as rewards for the Camp David peace accords. But Israel receives the money without strings in the form of a single grant, whereas Egypt must justify each expenditure, large and small, by submitting proposals for projects which then must be sanctioned by American officials.

We in America say that we are champions of equality among all peoples, but we do not act that way, either at home or abroad. The American white male Establishment continues to act as patriarch in relation to our own minorities, our own women, as well as the rest of the world. Arab men and women, as it happens, are actually participating in the decline of their own patriarchy, through changed material circumstances, however enmeshed they may be in an ideology resisting that change. America does not do what it says; the Arab World does not say—or perhaps recognize—what it is doing. The end of patriarchy, in both societies, must begin with a recognition of such contradictions and be followed by a continuing effort to resolve them, in public as well as in private life.